REVOLUTION

Volume 18

NEITHER WAR NOR PEACE

NEITHER WAR NOR PEACE

The Struggle for Power in the Post-War World

HUGH SETON-WATSON

LONDON AND NEW YORK

First published in 1960 by Methuen & Co Ltd

This edition first published in 2022
by Routledge
4 Park Square, Milton Park, Abingdon, Oxon OX14 4RN

and by Routledge
605 Third Avenue, New York, NY 10158

Routledge is an imprint of the Taylor & Francis Group, an informa business

© 1960 Hugh Seton-Watson

All rights reserved. No part of this book may be reprinted or reproduced or utilised in any form or by any electronic, mechanical, or other means, now known or hereafter invented, including photocopying and recording, or in any information storage or retrieval system, without permission in writing from the publishers.

Trademark notice: Product or corporate names may be trademarks or registered trademarks, and are used only for identification and explanation without intent to infringe.

British Library Cataloguing in Publication Data
A catalogue record for this book is available from the British Library

ISBN: 978-1-032-12623-4 (Set)
ISBN: 978-1-003-26095-0 (Set) (ebk)
ISBN: 978-1-032-16431-1 (Volume 18) (hbk)
ISBN: 978-1-032-16435-9 (Volume 18) (pbk)
ISBN: 978-1-003-24852-1 (Volume 18) (ebk)

DOI: 10.4324/9781003248521

Publisher's Note
The publisher has gone to great lengths to ensure the quality of this reprint but points out that some imperfections in the original copies may be apparent.

Disclaimer
The publisher has made every effort to trace copyright holders and would welcome correspondence from those they have been unable to trace.

NEITHER WAR NOR PEACE

The Struggle for Power in the Post-War World

HUGH SETON-WATSON

METHUEN & CO LTD
36 Essex Street · Strand · London WC.2

First published 1960
© 1960 Hugh Seton-Watson
Printed in Great Britain
by the Camelot Press Ltd.,
Southampton
Cat. No. 6264/u

Contents

INTRODUCTION page 9

Part One: The Post-War World, 1945-1953

1: EUROPE 19

The End of the War (19)—The United Nations (20)—Soviet Europe (22)—The Borderlands (26)—Western Europe (31)—The German Problem (36)—The Western Alliance System (41).

2: THE ARABS AND THEIR NEIGHBOURS 48

The Arab World (48)—Between the World Wars (50)—The Second World War (55)—Palestine, Egypt and Iraq, 1945-9 (57)—Revolution in Egypt, 1949-52 (60)—Syria Between Egypt and Iraq, 1949-52 (62)—North Africa, 1945-53 (64)—Turkey and Persia (66)—Turkey and the Soviet Union, 1945-50 (69)—Persia, the Soviet Union, and the West, 1945-53 (70).

3: ASIA 73

Japan (73)—India and Pakistan (76)—South-East Asia (82)—China (91)—The Korean War (96).

Part Two: Forces of Revolution

4: LAND AND PEASANTS 103

Agrarian and Industrial Societies (104)—'Advanced' and 'Underdeveloped' Societies (107)—Types of Agriculture (108)—Types of Ownership (110)—Land Reforms (114)—Peasant Poverty (118)—Collectivization of Agriculture (121)—Peasants as a Political Factor (125).

5: WORKERS AND BOURGEOIS 131

The Bourgeoisie (131)—The Industrial Workers (136)—Western Industrial Societies (138)—Soviet Society (150)—Underdeveloped Societies (155)—Trade Unions and World Politics (162).

6: THE INTELLIGENTSIA 164

The Growth of the Intelligentsia (164)—The Examples of Russia and Japan (168)—Military Intelligentsia (175)—In Soviet Society (176)—In Western Societies (180)—Underdeveloped Societies (182).

7: THE SEIZURE OF POWER 188

Definitions (188)—Types of State Power and Types of Revolution (191)—Revolutions by Frontal Assault (193)—Revolutions from Within (200)—Revolution by Foreign Conquest (207)—Vulnerability to Revolution (208).

Part Three: Totalitarianism

8: THE TOTALITARIAN RÉGIME *page* 213
Liberty and Representation (213)—Dictatorship and Totalitarianism (216)—The Origins of Totalitarianism (218)—The Will to Total Power (222)—The Totalitarian Party (224).

9: TOTALITARIANISM AND LIBERTY 238
Forces of Freedom in Totalitarian Society (238)—Forces of Totalitarianism in Free Society (245).

10: TOTALITARIANISM AND FOREIGN POLICY 252

Part Four: Imperialism

11: NATIONALISM AND IMPERIALISM 261

12: EUROPEAN COLONIAL POLICIES IN AFRICA 267
British Imperial Policy (267)—British Africa (270)—West Africa (270)—East Africa (276)—The Central African Federation (282)—French Africa (286)—West Africa (287)—Equatorial Africa (291)—Madagascar (292)—Belgian Africa (293)—Portuguese Africa (295).

13: OTHER IMPERIALISMS 297
The Soviet Empire (297)—National Domination in Asia (303)—The American Indian (306).

14: RACIALISM 310
Racial Conflicts in South Africa (310)—The American Negro (319)—Afro-Asianism (325).

Part Five: The World since Stalin

15: EUROPE 331
The New Course (331)—The Soviet Union and the West (333)—The Year of Revolution (338)—The Debate on Disengagement (346)—Western Europe in 1959 (350)—The Balkans (354).

16: THE ARABS AND THEIR NEIGHBOURS 360
The New Egypt (360)—The Baghdad Pact (363)—North Africa (366)—Suez and Baghdad (370)—The West and the Arabs (378).

17: ASIA 384
China (384)—India (395)—Japan (403)—South-East Asia (408)—Indonesia (412).

18: LATIN AMERICA *page* 416
   The Political and Social Background (416)—Post-War Years (420)—Dependencies in America (427)—Inter-American Relations (431).

19: PROBLEMS OF WESTERN POLICY 437
   Defence (437)—Relations with the Underdeveloped (444)—Relations with the Totalitarians (452)—Future Prospects (457).

Appendix: Constitutions in British and French Africa

British Territories
   1: Gold Coast (468)—2: Nigeria (468)—3: Uganda (469)—4: Kenya (469)—5: Tanganyika (470)—6: Northern Rhodesia (471)—7: Southern Rhodesia (472)—8: Nyasaland (472).

French Africa
   1: Afrique Occidentale Française [AOF] (472)—2: Afrique Equatoriale Française [AEF] (473)—Representation in the French Assembly (473).

REFERENCE NOTES	474
BIBLIOGRAPHICAL NOTE	478
SUBJECT INDEX	487
INDEX OF PERSONS	493
INDEX OF PLACE-NAMES	499

Maps

1: THE MIDDLE EAST	*pages* 46-47
2: SOUTH-EAST ASIA	83
3: WEST AFRICA	271
4: CENTRAL AND SOUTHERN AFRICA	277
5: CENTRAL AMERICA AND THE CARIBBEAN	429

Introduction

Since the Second World War ended the world has not been at peace. There was an international war for three years in Korea, there were civil wars in China and Greece, and there have been colonial wars in Indochina, Algeria, Malaya and Kenya. But for most of the time in most of the world the guns have been silent. Yet there has been no peace.

After the First World War there was peace for at least thirteen years. Even the invasion of Manchuria and the advent of Hitler did not at first destroy the optimism that prevailed in most of the world. Only after the civil war began in Spain did it become clear that, though world war had not yet come, the world was not at peace. But when in 1945 Hitler's Reich was crushed, the Anglo-Saxon and Soviet victors were separated by a chasm of mistrust and hostility. The years have passed, but the chasm has not been bridged. The world has remained in a condition that is neither war nor peace.

The landscape of world politics since 1945 has differed fundamentally from that of 1919-39: by contrast, the differences between the 1920s and the 1890s appear almost trivial.

Between the world wars there were seven Great Powers—five in Europe (Britain, France, Germany, Italy, Russia), one in Asia (Japan) and the United States of America. Since 1945 there have been two giant Powers, the United States and the Soviet Union. Admittedly the old Great Powers of Western Europe are still factors to be reckoned with, and in Asia there are two countries of vast population, China and India, which are capable of reaching giant Power status within a few decades. But the two giants of today overshadow the rest of the world in a manner that is new in human history.

Between the world wars the threats to peace came from the rivalries of the Great Powers, which in the jargon of the period were divided into 'Haves' and 'Have-Nots'. The United States, though essentially a Have, and the Soviet Union, though essentially a Have-Not, stood on the margin rather than in the centre of the conflict. The conflict was aggravated by the general misery produced by the world economic depression, and by the trade policies of individual Have Powers, including the United States. But though the German, Italian and Japanese leaders talked much of access to raw materials and outlets for surplus population, they were more interested in national and personal power and glory than in economic gain. Totalitarianism made its first appearance in these years, as the dictatorship of Lenin evolved into the régime of Stalin, and as Hitler began to build the

Third Reich. But Stalinism was little known or understood abroad, and the international demands of Hitler seemed to fit a traditional pattern of Great Power policy. Hitler demanded territory, security or revenge. The leaders of the Have Powers might be unwilling to satisfy him, but they were reluctant to admit that they faced in him a new phenomenon, the search for total power. However, since 1945 it has become clear to all but the wilfully blind that the conflict is of a different kind. There are of course still major clashes of economic interest in inter-state relations: to name only a few, Japan's trade position is dangerously precarious, Latin American economies are dangerously dependent on the export prices of a few raw materials, and the United States tariff frustrates or seriously damages many interests all over the world. Again, territorial disputes have played their part in the history of the last fourteen years: the Saar, Trieste, Kashmir and the eastern frontier of Germany are examples. But these problems are overshadowed by the challenge of the Soviet Union to the West, whose essence is the claim to represent the scientifically predictable, ineluctable forces of history, destined to impose themselves on the whole human race. The submission to totalitarian communist dogma of 600 million Chinese has vastly increased the effectiveness of the challenge.

Between the world wars it was generally recognized that nationalism, a doctrine of unmistakably democratic origin, repudiated by the peacemakers of 1815 but favoured by those of 1919—especially by President Woodrow Wilson—was one of the main sources of international tension. But this recognition related chiefly to Europe, where the conflicts between the small states that had succeeded the Habsburg and Ottoman empires gave Hitler and Mussolini their best chances of action. Outside Europe nationalism was stirring, but with the exception of the Chinese revival under the early Kuomintang it hardly affected the relations between Great Powers. Since the Second World War the situation has radically changed. It is in Asia and Africa that nationalism is now strongest; large numbers of new independent states have come into being; the governments of these states show active sympathy for nationalist movements in colonies which have not yet attained independence; and this sympathy extends also to victims of racial discrimination within states where there is no question of forming territorial independent states, for example in South Africa and in the American South. Today almost every nationalist movement and racial conflict is an international problem. Indeed it is on this ground that the conflict between the totalitarians and the West is principally fought.

There are, then, two main themes in the story of the last fourteen years—the expansion of totalitarianism and the growth of anti-European nationalism.

The books on international relations that appeared between the world wars for the most part treated the subject as a continuation, based on admittedly insufficient and uneven material, of diplomatic history. Outstanding among the exceptions was E. H. Carr's *The Twenty Years' Crisis*. This brilliant work of analysis has enlightened generations of students.

It would be ungenerous to disparage the efforts of those who have produced invaluable chronological surveys of the relations between governments both between the world wars and since the Second World War. But it must be said that the study of international relations is not the same thing as diplomatic history. Diplomatic history is an exacting craft, something between an art and a science, and it requires access to secret diplomatic documents. A good deal of these have now been published for the period 1919-39 (though whether sufficient for sound diplomatic history must still be a matter for argument). The flood of reminiscences and documents on the Second World War itself makes a relatively scientific study of at least large parts of that period possible. But secret official documents on the years since 1945 are, for understandable reasons, not available. For these years chronological surveys, based on press reports and public statements by political figures, are possible, but diplomatic history is not.

There is another vast field, essential for the writing of serious history, which is inevitably lacking for these years—the biographical. History which leaves out the characters of the leading personalities can hardly be called history at all. Journalists' impressions of Mr. Nehru, and anecdotes about President Eisenhower, may be revealing, but they cannot be a substitute for the family papers, the correspondence and the memoirs of intimate friends, which will no doubt be available fifty years hence (perhaps sooner), and will make it possible for the historian to have, of these and other leading statesmen, a picture approximately as complete as we now have of Abraham Lincoln, Sir Robert Peel or Louis Napoleon.

Study of world politics since 1945 cannot then be diplomatic history, and it is doubtful even whether it can be called history at all. But this does not mean that it is not both possible and worth while to study both the events and the political and social forces which underlie them. One man will of course see only part of the picture, and he may well be afflicted with some form of colour-blindness. Nevertheless my own experience of literature on international affairs convinces me that this inevitable failing of any single author (inevitable because no single mind can grasp the whole world situation) can be outweighed by the advantage of a unity of approach to world problems. This is almost always lacking in the symposia, with chapters by different regional or departmental experts, which are so much in vogue on both sides of the Atlantic.

Study of the events imposes an extremely difficult task of selection. The events that most concern the diplomatic historian are the communications that take place between governments. But the events which bulk largest in the last fourteen years of world politics, and on which comparatively reliable information is available in vast volume, belong very largely to what has been traditionally regarded as 'internal politics' rather than 'foreign policy'. The distinction between these two fields can hardly be upheld any longer (outside the specialized craft of diplomatic history). I have stated my conviction that the two main themes of the last fourteen years are totalitarianism and anti-European nationalism. The subject-matter of the first are the structure of totalitarian régimes, the establishment of totalitarians in power and the activities of totalitarian parties in non-totalitarian states; of the latter, the creation and development of nationalist parties and their struggles against European colonial governments.

Study of the forces of totalitarianism and nationalism takes us still further away from the conventional field of inter-state relations. Both totalitarianism and Afro-Asian nationalism are revolutionary movements, which have their roots in the rise and the conflicts of social classes. No comparison of the relations between classes in the three main types of society of the contemporary world (the Western, the Soviet and the underdeveloped) can make any sense without frequent reference to earlier history, especially of nineteenth-century Europe, Russia and Japan, but also at times of still earlier periods. The choice of historical examples must be a matter of personal preference of the writer, and my own choice is as fallible as any other's: I hope only that my examples enlighten more than they confuse.

If the distinctions between 'internal politics' and 'foreign policy', and between the present era and the historical past must be frequently ignored, it is also necessary at times to trespass on the ground of the sociologists. The boundary between politics and economics is, however, clearer. In the following pages there is often occasion to draw attention to economic factors, but no attempt is made at economic analysis, for which I have in any case no ability. This implies no disrespect for economics, and no unwillingness to admit the importance of economic factors in world affairs. But this is a book about political conflict.

It can be argued that books on world politics should be either descriptive or analytical. It seems to me, however, that description and analysis are necessary to each other, and I have tried to combine them in this book. The problem of how to combine them is formidable. The attempt which I have made undoubtedly lacks neatness. This I believe is inevitable, because the subject itself is not neat. I would ask those who believe that a book should be neat, or should not be written at all, to put this book down unread.

The method which seemed to me the least objectionable, after a good deal of thought, was to begin with a simple narrative of the events of the immediate post-war years; then to proceed to a discussion of the main themes of revolutionary forces, totalitarianism and imperialism; and to conclude with a more detailed narrative of the last six years, in the light of the preceding analysis.

Even if this admittedly unsatisfactory order is accepted, a number of detailed points need to be explained.

The narrative of Part One is divided into three regional chapters. The first, Europe, is clearly definable. The second is entitled 'The Arabs and Their Neighbours', rather than 'The Middle East', because it includes French North Africa, which is Arab but not Middle Eastern, as well as Turkey, Persia and Israel, which are Middle Eastern but not Arab. The third is entitled 'Asia', but excludes both the Middle Eastern countries and Soviet Asia (some of whose problems are discussed in Part Four).

With regard to the chronological dividing-line between Part One (the post-war years) and Part Five (the more recent period), there are the following deviations from the landmark generally observed, which is the death in March 1953 of Stalin. In the section of the chapter in Part One on Europe, which deals with the Balkans, I have taken the story up to the Ankara Pact of 1953 and the Italo-Yugoslav settlement of the Trieste question in 1954. In the chapter on the Arabs and their neighbours, I have broken the narrative with the advent to power of the Egyptian Free Officers in July 1952, the deportation of the Sultan of Morocco in August 1953 and the overthrow of Mosaddeq in Persia in the same month. In the chapter on Asia, the section on Japan ends with ratification by the Japanese parliament of the San Francisco peace treaty in April 1952; the section on China with Chinese military intervention in the Korean War; and those on India and South-East Asia around 1950, when independence had been established in most countries, but war was still in progress in Indochina and Malaya.

These differences in dates, and these deviations from the most usual geographical definitions may cause some inconvenience to the reader. There are also inevitably some references which anticipate events described in later sections. However I have prepared a comprehensive index of persons and subjects, which I hope will help the reader, when confronted by a name or a problem that has not yet been explained, to find the passage in which the explanation is given.

Two major regions are not mentioned in Part One.

The events and problems of tropical and southern Africa are examined in Part Four, which deals with Imperialism and Nationalism. It has seemed to me more convenient and enlightening to discuss these together with other examples of Imperialism (the Soviet empire, imperialist claims by Asian states, the status of the American Indian and American negro), than to attempt a separate narrative of events in Africa. The formal distinction between the Arabs of the Middle East, Morocco and Tunis who live in independent states, and those of Algeria, who have not yet attained independence, corresponds to a real distinction of situation and problems. It has however seemed more enlightening to discuss all the Arabs of North Africa together with the other Arabs than with the tropical Africans.

Latin America must clearly be discussed as a distinct region. But the distinction between the post-war era and recent years, which seems valid in most of the world, is barely applicable in this sub-continent. If the last fourteen years are divided at all, it is into three rather than two periods (one of left-wing democratic régimes in 1945-8, of reversion to dictatorship in 1948-55, and of democratic régimes once again since 1955). It seemed best to devote a single chapter to the region. It also seemed necessary to say a few words about the British West Indies, though these, unlike Puerto Rico, the United States Caribbean dependency, cannot be described as 'Latin'.

This book is concerned with conflicts. Where political life has been peaceful, and totalitarian parties are not a significant force, as in Britain, the United States, Canada, the Pacific Dominions, the Low Countries and Scandinavia, internal politics are barely mentioned. In the chapters of Parts Two, Three and Four which deal with class conflicts in urban societies, with the appeal of totalitarianism to elements of Western society, and with racial discrimination against the negro in the United States, social problems in both Britain and America are discussed. This book also does not examine the relations between states which are consistently friendly to each other. Thus there is no systematic discussion of Anglo-American relations, though these are of course often referred to, nor of relations between Britain and the Pacific Dominions or Canada. If this were a book about international economic relations, these subjects would of course have occupied a large space.

The book thus begins with a survey of events from 1945 to about 1953.

It then considers in turn four problems which are fundamental to revolutionary movements of the twentieth century—the problem of peasants and the land in agrarian countries, the relations between industrial workers and industrial upper classes, the role of the intelligentsia as a revolutionary factor, and types and examples of revolutionary seizure of power. This is followed by a third part on totalitarianism. Part Four examines nationalism and imperialism in various parts of the world and in various forms, discussing racialism as well as colonialism and considering colonialism as far as possible according to the facts about domination by nation over nation rather than by whether the word 'colony' is officially used or not. Part Five takes up the narrative again, from the death of Stalin to the spring of 1959. In the last chapter we consider some of the problems facing the West.

In conclusion a few personal observations. I have tried honestly to understand and discuss the problems which are the subject of this book. But I am not neutral in the conflict between the totalitarians and the West. I do not subscribe to the view, widely held by Western radicals, that one cannot be a serious scholar unless one is neutral. It is of course possible to make a point of always denouncing one's own government and one's own allies: but this seems to me as 'partial' an attitude as its opposite. It is however possible to take a 'Western' attitude, and yet honestly admit Western errors and crimes and seek to be fair to the opponents of the West. This I have tried to do.

As for my sources for this work, the main one has been the fact that I have lived as an adult through the years covered here, and have followed events day by day to the best of my ability. A selected list of published sources is given at the end of the book. Reading has been complemented by a certain amount of personal experience of Europe, the Middle East, the United States and South Africa. Of all my travels I think the most enlightening were in the Balkans, whose combination of intellectual subtlety and crudity, of tortuous intrigue and honest courage revealed more truths about the political animal man than are to be found in most text-books of political science. I should like also to express my appreciation to all those whose conversation inspired me with ideas or exploded empty bubbles of my imagination. Among these I would mention my colleagues and students at the three universities in which I have studied in these years—Oxford, London and Columbia. Greatest of all has been my debt to my wife, whose patience has been miraculous. But for the final result no one is to blame but myself.

Part One

The Post-War World,
1945–1953

1: Europe

THE END OF THE WAR

In the Western hemisphere only two nations fought the Second World War through from beginning to end, Britain and Germany. But when Germany was at last defeated, her whole territory occupied by her victors, Britain was only third in strength of the Allies, being surpassed both by the United States and by the Soviet Union.

At the height of his power, Hitler had ruled, by alliance or by conquest, all Europe except the British Isles, Ireland, the Iberian Peninsula, Sweden, Switzerland and Turkish Thrace. Yugoslavia, Albania and a large part of Greece were liberated by their own people, in resistance armies led principally by communists and armed in large part by weapons sent them by the Anglo-American forces in the Mediterranean. When the war ended in Europe, Soviet armies held Poland, Hungary, Roumania, Bulgaria, a third of Austria and Germany and nearly all Czechoslovakia; Anglo-American armies were in France, Italy, the Low Countries, Denmark, Norway, Greece, most of Germany and Austria; the restored armies of France and Italy had played an honourable part in the liberation of their countries; and Finland alone among Germany's former allies, by the generosity of the Soviet government, had been spared complete occupation by the armed forces of a victorious power.

The Middle East and North Africa had also been a theatre of war. Turkey had remained neutral, and thus interposed a barrier between German-held Europe and the British-held Arab lands. Persia had been jointly occupied by British and Soviet forces. In Iraq and Syria a German occupation was narrowly averted by British action in the summer of 1941. Britain held Egypt throughout the war, and conquered Abyssinia and the Horn of Africa from Italian armies. Morocco and Algeria were occupied without resistance by American forces in November 1942, and in the next six months the German forces in Tunisia, with their increasingly reluctant Italian allies, were defeated by the British advancing from Egypt and the Americans from Algeria. When war ended French authority had been reasserted in North Africa but transferred to new independent governments in Syria and Lebanon. Small British forces remained in Egypt, Iraq, Palestine and Transjordania.

War had spread to the Far East in December 1941 when the Japanese bombed Pearl Harbor and invaded Malaya. Singapore and Java fell with little resistance. General MacArthur's forces gallantly defended Bataan in the Philippines and the British army in Burma retreated in good order.

Both returned in 1945, defeating the Japanese armies in their turn. Japan itself was grimly ravaged by bombardments, culminating with the two atomic bombs on Hiroshima and Nagasaki in August 1945. These disasters were followed by the belated entry of the Soviet Union into the Pacific War. Soon after war ended there were American troops in Japan itself, the Philippines and smaller islands of the Pacific where bitter struggles had been fought; British forces had recovered Burma; and Soviet forces were in Manchuria. Some weeks later Korea was occupied by American and Soviet forces according to previous agreement, Indochina was similarly divided between British and Chinese, and British forces arrived in Malaya and Indonesia.

War had brought to the victor nations both terrible losses and unbounded hopes. In countries liberated from German or Japanese rule the sufferings had been greater and the hopes were perhaps even higher. Foreign occupation had in many cases deepened the old divisions of class and ideology, and resistance had promoted social revolution or led to civil war. Where European colonial rule had been overthrown by Japan, plans for national independence had been made which lost none of their force when Japan was defeated. The two greatest victor Powers stood each for a different answer to the general demand for a new deal for the world. America offered liberal democracy, but insisted that this was not possible without private capitalism and the pursuit of business profit. Russia offered what it called 'socialism', but maintained that this could be achieved only through the one-party state which forcibly suppresses all critics of its policies. On the Elbe and the Rhodope, in the jungles of Tonkin and along the 38th Parallel of Korea, were already present the class conflicts, nationalist movements and ideological claims that shaped the post-war world.

THE UNITED NATIONS

The United Nations Organization, whose Charter was adopted at the San Francisco Conference, and signed by fifty nations on 26 June 1945, was the outcome of wartime hopes and high idealism. The hopes may perhaps be summarized under three headings: that the new organization would increase the amount and quality of international co-operation on practical problems requiring treatment on a world scale; that it would preserve peace and set new and better standards of international behaviour; and that it would in time bring about world government.

In the first field a great deal has been achieved. UN publications on economic and social problems, based on information collected in many parts of the world, have enriched human knowledge. Such specialized agencies as the World Health Organization and the Food and Agriculture Organization have directly benefited the lives of millions of people. In this respect UN has continued, and has on balance probably improved upon, the work of the League of Nations.

In the second and third fields the results have been disappointing. The fact that a third world war has been prevented is due not to the action of UN but to the caution of the two greatest Powers—the United States and the Soviet Union. That aggression in Korea was resisted, and that the subsequent war was held within limits, is due to the policy, perhaps at times mistaken yet as a whole marked by a quite exceptional combination of courage and patience, of President Truman. The formation of an UN force to liquidate the Suez crisis of 1956 was a much smaller achievement than was supposed at the time or has been suggested since. Its function was not to impose peace or arrange a settlement of the issues that had caused the crisis, but simply to ensure smoothly the political victory of Egypt while saving a minimum of 'face' for Britain and France.

It has become apparent that the United Nations cannot become a world government for two reasons. The first and most important is that none of the member nations, least of all the Great Powers, is willing to give up its sovereignty. The provision that decisions of the Security Council require the unanimity of the Big Five gives the governments of these countries a veto on all decisions that do not please them. Moreover, the General Assembly, in which totalitarian and liberal democratic states, Great Powers and dwarf Powers, independent nations and satellites each have one vote, is unfortunately no more representative than the British Parliament of 1831 with its rotten boroughs.

However, the United Nations is useful as a forum of opinion. The rotten boroughs did not prevent most existing political opinions from being expressed in the eighteenth-century British parliament, and practically every opinion that exists in the world on international problems finds a mouthpiece in the UN. The fact that these opinions are often expressed with fanaticism, or in grotesquely demagogic terms, only enhances the variety of the forum. The absence of communist China and of Germany is the more to be regretted from this point of view, though the political factors which cause their absence are of an altogether different degree of importance.

This is not the only value of the United Nations. A great deal of serious secret diplomacy goes on from time to time behind the scenes of UN meetings. It is a physical meeting-place at which leading statesmen of the world meet each other. The character of these meetings, even when their results are disappointing, is inevitably influenced by the symbolic moral quality which the UN possesses in the minds of millions of people all over the world.

In the following pages we shall frequently refer to various UN meetings and decisions, but we shall not at any point discuss the organization, constitution or broader functions of the UN. This interesting subject would exceed the scope of this book.

In this and the following two chapters we shall examine the main political forces which emerged in the immediate post-war years, first in Europe and then in the Arab countries and in Asia.

SOVIET EUROPE

The peoples whose territories were occupied by the Soviet Army differed greatly from each other. By religion most were either Catholic or Orthodox, but there were also Protestants and Moslems. By language they were mostly Slav, but the Roumanian language belongs to the Latin group, while Hungarian and Albanian are virtually unique languages. The Czech Lands had a developed industrial and urban society, Poland and Hungary were partly industrialized, while Roumania, Yugoslavia and Bulgaria had overwhelmingly agrarian societies. Before 1939 liberal democracy had been strongly rooted in Czechoslovakia, Hungary had an oligarchic system with some liberal elements, while Poland, Roumania, Yugoslavia and Bulgaria were ruled by various forms of dictatorship. Moderate democratic parties were of three main types—urban liberalism, strongest in Czechoslovakia and of some importance in Poland and Hungary; peasant movements, strongest in Poland and Bulgaria and of considerable though lesser importance in Roumania and Yugoslavia; and social democracy, which was in fact confined to Czechoslovakia, Poland and Hungary. The two totalitarian movements of communism and fascism also had their supporters, and gained ground as a result of the economic depression of the 1930s. Fascism was strongest in Roumania, Hungary and the Croatian provinces of Yugoslavia, but also had a lesser following in Poland. Communism existed as a legal party in Czechoslovakia until 1938, and was supported by about half the working class. Elsewhere communists could only operate illegally: their most efficient underground movements were in Yugoslavia and Bulgaria, their weakest in Poland and Roumania.

Between the world wars the peoples of Eastern Europe had been bitterly divided against each other by disputes concerning territory and by problems of treatment of national minorities. To take one example only, Hungary claimed territories that were included by the 1920 Treaty of Trianon in Slovakia. More than half a million Hungarians had thereby become subjects of Czechoslovakia, believed themselves to be persecuted by the Czechoslovak authorities, and were regarded by the Czechoslovak government as potential traitors to the state. Such divisions enabled Hitler to play off the small states against each other, to conquer some with the help of others, and to incite different national groups, in the countries he had conquered, to fight each other. The most horrible example was in Yugoslavia, where Croatian fascists exterminated tens of thousands of Serbian and Jewish men, women and children, and Serbian nationalist guerrilla forces committed mass reprisals against Croatian men, women and children. Largely as a result of the national rivalries, and of their exploitation by Hitler, Hungary and Roumania and Bulgaria became allies of the Axis Powers in the Second World War while Poland and Czechoslovakia and Yugoslavia were allies of the West.

The Soviet Union had only the most formal relations with the East European states between the wars. With the partial exception of Czechoslovakia, their governments were hostile to the Soviet Union since they feared communist subversion: they had the more reason for this as their régimes were unpopular with their own peoples, who might be expected to listen readily to revolutionary propaganda. In 1944, when the Soviet armies first penetrated into Eastern Europe, there was a general desire not only for peace, but for an end to fascist régimes and for a social revolution. There was also a widespread desire, among both the educated *élite* and the masses, for friendly relations with Russia, whose military heroism they admired and whose revolutionary and democratic slogans they heard with sympathy. The first contact with the Soviet armies was not encouraging: the 'liberators' behaved in a manner that had not been seen in Central Europe since the Thirty Years War, and which was the more terrifying as it was deliberately encouraged by the Soviet Command. But even after this shock, the people of Eastern Europe were determined to put an end to the old enmity with Russia, and to establish permanently correct relations with the great eastern neighbour. This was also the desire of the American and British governments, whose spokesmen lost no opportunity of urging the nations of this region to come to terms with the Soviet Union. But by the summer of 1945 at latest it had become clear that the Soviet rulers had their own 'interpretation' of the phrase 'friendly governments'. They were determined to have along their western frontier a series of satellite states, ruled by men who in all matters of policy took their orders from Moscow. Their trusted agents, the communist parties, were to convert their countries into Soviet bases, whether defensive to guard the approaches to Soviet territory, or offensive as starting points for the next phase of communist expansion in Europe.

The communist parties showed considerable skill in their tactics, infiltrating and subverting the democratic parties with whom at first they shared power in coalition governments, branding as 'collaborationists' or 'fascists' not only those who had served Hitler or his nominees, but the whole educated class of the pre-war society and all persons who admired Western culture or institutions or had western friends, and monopolizing the epithets 'democratic' and 'progressive' for those who (whatever their personal or political past) would show themselves subservient to Soviet and local communist wishes. The communists also showed a fine realistic understanding of the strategic points in the modern state, placing their party members or their intimidated or bought agents in the key posts in the armed forces, police, press, broadcasting, youth movements, factory managements and trade unions.

Yet it was not this skill, but the might of the Soviet Union, which gave power to the communists. Soviet force was most crudely used in the case of Poland. In September 1939 Stalin joined Hitler in the partition of that country. It is true that the majority of the population of the annexed territory was not Polish, but Ukrainian or White Russian. This does not, however, make the method used to recover them less odious, and in any case it is highly doubtful whether the majority of the Ukrainian and White Russian peoples, forcibly incorporated in the Soviet Union in 1919-20, would choose to remain there if given a chance. In 1941 the Soviet government restored diplomatic relations with the Polish government in exile, but in 1943 it broke them off, and prepared a puppet administration of its own to impose on the Polish people. When Soviet troops entered Poland in 1944, they treated the Polish Home Army, the splendidly organized resistance movement supported by all classes and all significant political groups in Poland in the national struggle against Hitler, as an enemy force. Instead they set up their puppets as the government of 'liberated' Poland. The attempts of the British and American governments to ensure real liberty for Poland were cunningly and obstinately resisted by Stalin. Nominal concessions were made, and some prominent exiles were allowed to return home and take part in the government. But all real power remained in the hands of Soviet agents, some Polish and some Russian. In the summer of 1947 the last pretences were abandoned, the last voices of opposition silenced and the last democratic Polish politicians arrested or forced to flee into exile.

In Roumania direct Soviet intervention in February 1945 caused the appointment of a communist-controlled government in place of the previous genuine coalition of democratic parties with the communists. Similar intervention in Bulgaria in the spring and summer of 1945 produced similar results. In Hungary the crisis came in the spring of 1947, when Soviet police broke the resistance of the Smallholders' Party by directly arresting its outstanding leader, Béla Kovács. In Czechoslovakia there was a greater restoration of democratic liberty after 1945 than in Hungary, and much greater than elsewhere in Eastern Europe. The overthrow of Czechoslovak democracy by the communists in 1948, in which there was no direct Soviet intervention, is discussed in greater detail in a later chapter.

The victims of communist action in Eastern Europe were not the fascists, who had been destroyed by military defeat, or the big landowners and capitalists, on the division of whose estates and nationalization of whose factories all democrats were agreed, but the workers and peasants and intelligentsia, and the peasant and socialist parties who represented their interests and aspirations. The régime set up by the communists was intended to be a close copy of its Soviet model. The system of political power, with the communist party in control of the regular organs of central and local government, the armed forces, the security police, the trade unions, the schools and the means of communication and publicity, was in fact virtually indistinguishable from the Soviet system.

Economic policies could not of course be carried through so quickly, but a good start was made. Various measures were devised to bring the peasants under state control and to appropriate to the government the fruits of their labour. Forced collectivisation of agriculture began in Yugoslavia and Bulgaria in 1949, and in Hungary and Czechoslovakia in the early 1950s. Forced industrialisation was also based on the Soviet model of the early 1930s. As in the Soviet Union, the priority was given to capital goods, and especially to mining, metallurgy and engineering: rapid output was considered more urgent than quick improvement in the workers' standard of living. The latter deteriorated especially in 1951 and 1952, after the five- or six-year plans adopted in 1949 had been 'revised upward', to achieve still higher output targets in heavy industry, as a part of the general process of militarisation which was introduced throughout the Soviet empire in connexion with the Korean War.

The most important event, after communist power had been consolidated in Eastern Europe, was the denunciation by the Soviet leaders in June 1948, through the medium of the Cominform, of the communist leaders of Yugoslavia. The essential cause of this dispute, which involved several subsidiary problems of economic, military and foreign policy, was that Marshal Tito and his colleagues, who had themselves made their own revolution, and won their own civil war and founded their own army and state machine, were for this very reason regarded in Moscow as less reliable than the other East European communist leaders, who had returned to their countries from exile in the Soviet Union as Soviet agents specially trained as Soviet provincial governors over their own people. Tito had in fact strongly supported the Soviet Union from 1945 to 1948 in all major international questions, though he had privately disagreed at times with Soviet leaders about the problems of Trieste and Macedonia.[1] But in Stalin's view he was too independent-minded to be tolerated. The Cominform statement excommunicated him and called on the faithful in Yugoslavia to overthrow him. But Tito resisted Soviet threats and economic boycotts, and the communists who controlled the army and police and bureaucracy were loyal to him. As for the people of Yugoslavia, many disliked communist rule, but virtually all preferred Tito's form to that which would be imposed by Moscow's agents. So Yugoslavia stood firm, and the area of Soviet domination in Europe was reduced.

Tito's unexpected resistance was met by a campaign in all East European satellite states against the 'nationalist deviation'. In each country leading communists who might be suspected of sympathy for Tito, or of generally placing the interests of their own country in certain circumstances above those of the Soviet Union, were disgraced and arrested. László Rajk in Hungary, Traicho Kostov in Bulgaria and Kochi Dzodze in Albania were publicly tried and executed. Wladyslaw Gomulka in Poland was more fortunate: he was denounced in 1948, removed from his political posts in 1949, and arrested in 1951, but he was neither tortured nor brought to public trial, and so survived until a milder period. The persecution of 'nationalists' in 1949-50 was followed by a further wave of purges and arrests in 1951-2. This time the victims belonged rather to the extreme 'left' wing most subservient to Moscow, and several of them were Jews. The most prominent were Rudolf Slansky in Czechoslovakia, who was executed, and Anna Pauker and Vasile Luca in Roumania, of whom the first was merely dismissed from her positions and rebuked while the second was sentenced to life imprisonment. The purges were in fact most severe in Czechoslovakia and Hungary, where between 1949 and 1954 they removed half the supreme leadership of the parties, and least in Bulgaria and Poland, where those removed amounted to about a quarter.[2]

THE BORDERLANDS

Between Soviet satellite Europe and Western Europe lay a belt of countries whose future was especially uncertain. The most important of them was Germany, which must be discussed more fully later. The others were Finland, Austria and Greece, to which after 1948 must be added Yugoslavia.

Finland was allied with Germany against the Soviet Union in 1941. The main reason for this was that in 1939, with German approval and encouragement, the Soviet Union had invaded Finland, and after initial defeats had been able to impose its demand to annex the two districts of Vyborg on the Gulf of Finland and Petsamo on the Arctic Ocean. In 1941 Finland went to war again, not from love of Hitler but to regain territory. It was defeated again, but in 1944 its army was still well disciplined, its state machine efficient and its people united. The Soviet government decided to treat Finland relatively generously. The disputed territories, recovered by the Finns in war, had to be given back to Russia, with certain further additions, but Soviet military forces were stationed on Finnish soil only in the Porkkala peninsula, 10 miles from Helsinki, which was leased to the Soviet Union for 50 years. Finland had to pay reparations to the Soviet Union. The Finnish economy was also strained by the need to provide for 400,000 Finns from the ceded territories who, though given the right to remain as Soviet citizens, chose almost to the last man and woman to leave their homes and become refugees in Finland.

Communism in Finland drew its strength from the bitter memories of the civil war of 1918, in which the victorious Whites had cruelly suppressed the revolutionary socialist workers. In the first post-war election, in 1945, the communists won 48 seats out of 200, while the socialists won 50 and the agrarians 49. A coalition government was formed, with a pro-communist as Premier, and the Ministry of Interior was given to a communist, Yrjo Leino. However, events did not follow the East European pattern. Leino was unable to make the police an instrument of his party, and in May 1948 (three months after the seizure of power by communists in Prague in a crisis which also began with a dispute about police appointments) he was forced to resign by a vote of censure in parliament. In the subsequent parliamentary election the communists lost ten seats, while socialists and agrarians gained eleven between them. The socialists also regained control of the trade unions. The Soviet Union took no action to help the communists.

The Finns were able to survive as an independent state for two reasons. Firstly, they had the civil courage to stand up against foreign threats, however powerful. The Finns also had a profound distrust of everything Russian and were extraordinarily impervious even to cultural influence from Russia. Secondly, they were helped by the fact that their country does not lie across the main road of Soviet advance into Europe. Budapest lies on the road to Vienna, Warsaw on the road to Berlin, but Helsinki only on the road to Stockholm. The Soviet government was in no hurry to conquer Sweden. Rather, it had a certain interest in encouraging Sweden to remain neutral. It knew that any Soviet action against Finland would drive Sweden into alliance with the Western Powers. It therefore contented itself with concluding in April 1948 a treaty of alliance with Finland. Thus Finland has remained an independent democratic country allied to Russia.

Austria had been part of Germany since 1938, with the consent of a great part, perhaps a majority, of its people. In 1943 the Allied Powers had announced their intention of restoring an independent Austrian state. In April 1945 Soviet troops entered Vienna. They set up an Austrian government under the socialist elder statesman Dr. Karl Renner, and based on a coalition of the socialists, communists and Catholics. The Western Powers recognized this government, and in due course took over the military administration of the zones of Austria which had been allotted to them. The Soviet zone, Lower Austria, was the richest province, but Vienna itself was divided into four occupation sectors, one for each Power. It was fortunate for Austria that a single government had at once been recognized by all four Powers, with at least a minimum of civil authority over the whole country. The absence of a central government for Germany led, as we shall see, to the creation in the Soviet zone of a separate communist state. The Soviet authorities could not do this in Austria, since they recognized a central Austrian government. If they had hoped that the Renner coalition government could be turned into a satellite régime as in Eastern Europe, they were disappointed. Renner had never been any one's tool in his long political career. At the parliamentary election of March 1946 the communists won only 4 seats out of 165, the rest being divided between the socialists and the People's Party (Catholic democrats). The communists had held the Ministry of Interior for a year, but had had small success in packing the police. After the election they had to content themselves with the Ministry of Fuel, and in the autumn of 1947 they left the government. The Austrian people showed itself remarkably impervious to communist influence. This is especially true of the working class, which was loyal to its long and honourable tradition of democratic socialism. Austria faced great economic hardship, and the inability of the occupying Powers to agree on the terms of a peace treaty meant that foreign troops remained on her soil in large numbers. But at least conditions were better than in the eastern neighbour countries, and in the 1950s American aid made possible rapid economic recovery.

In Greece, the British troops who landed in October 1944 found that, as the Germans had retreated northwards, the communist-led resistance movement had taken over the greater part of the country. An agreement had been made, after difficult negotiations, between the communist leaders and the exiled politicians who had represented Greece with the Allies during the war. There were communist ministers in the first government in liberated Athens. But it proved impossible to agree on the disarming of the resistance forces and the formation of the new army. Fighting broke out between communists and British troops in Athens in December 1944 and lasted two months.[3] The communists were defeated, and had to accept disarmament, but were promised full freedom of political action for their party. But in fact the reaction of the Greek electorate against the communists, who had ruthlessly suppressed their opponents in their months of power, led to a victory of the extreme right in the parliamentary election of March 1946. The result was that persons suspected of left-wing sympathies, and especially persons who had served in the communist-led resistance forces under German occupation, were subjected to forms of persecution which varied from acts of violence in villages to arrests and heavy sentences, often on questionable evidence, in the cities. Bitterness grew, and was expressed in a new outbreak of civil war in the autumn of 1946. Though this can be partly explained as a reaction against right-wing brutality, it can hardly be doubted that it was planned by the international communist command in Moscow. The communist rebels were systematically supplied with arms and equipment from Albania, Yugoslavia and Bulgaria. For more than three years they controlled a large part of Macedonia adjoining the frontier with the three communist states. They also had bands of terrorists operating in other parts of the country. If left to its own resources, the Greek government would probably have been defeated. The British government, which had sustained Greece from 1944 to 1946, felt no longer able to supply aid, in view of the economic troubles of Britain. However, in March 1947 President Truman made his famous announcement, subsequently known as the 'Truman doctrine', which promised American aid to both Greece and Turkey. This statement gave Greece hope of survival, but there were still two years of bitter fighting before the communist rebels were defeated. The final victory was due not only to the brave fighting of the Greek army and to American material aid but also to the decision of Marshal Tito in July 1949 to close the Yugoslav-Greek frontier, thereby cutting off the Greek rebels from their main source of supply.

Yugoslavia attempted to maintain a policy independent equally of the Soviet empire, whose leaders had cast her from their midst, and of the West. The economic boycott by the Soviet Union and the satellites, introduced in the summer of 1949, forced her to look for economic aid to the West. In the next years the Yugoslav régime underwent considerable change. The Communist Party still retained a monopoly of political power, but the administration was decentralized and made more flexible. Workers'

Councils, elected by the workers in the factories, exercised certain managerial powers. The Five Year Plan was modified, the priority on heavy industry diminished, and more attention was paid to living standards. In 1953 a new Constitution was introduced, and in the same year peasants were told that if they wished they might leave the collective farms, which at that time included about 25% of the country's arable land. The result was a mass exodus. In general in these years the Yugoslav leaders stressed the evolution of their régime away from the Soviet model, and the search for a new form of socialist democracy.

Yugoslav relations with Greece steadily improved from 1949. In February 1953 a treaty of friendship and co-operation between Yugoslavia, Greece and Turkey was signed in Ankara. Though Yugoslavia would not join NATO,* to which Greece and Turkey had belonged since 1952, she was now indirectly associated with the Western defence system.

Yugoslav relations with Italy were less satisfactory. The Yugoslav claim to the border region of Venezia Giulia, the majority of whose inhabitants were Yugoslavs, was satisfied by the peace treaty between Italy and the Allies of February 1947. But in addition the Yugoslavs claimed the port of Trieste, whose population was in great majority Italian but whose economic importance was as an outlet for the whole area that had once been Austria-Hungary, whose heir Yugoslavia in effect claimed to be. The Western Powers opposed the Yugoslav claim on Trieste, and the Soviet Union adopted an equivocal attitude, being unwilling to make things difficult for the large communist party in Italy. The peace treaty decided to create a Free Territory of Trieste, divided into two zones, of which the first ('Zone "A" ') with the city itself should be occupied by British and American forces, and the second ('Zone "B" ') by Yugoslav, until the United Nations should appoint a Governor to take over the whole territory. It proved however impossible to agree at UN on a candidate for Governor, and meanwhile the Yugoslavs in effect annexed Zone 'B' to Yugoslavia. In March 1948 the American and British governments proposed that Zone 'A' should be handed over to Italy, but this was prevented by Soviet opposition. In the autumn of 1953, when a more nationalistic government in Italy under the right-wing Christian Democrat Giuseppe Pella began a belligerent campaign for the return of Trieste to Italy, the Western Powers first stated that they would hand Zone 'A' over to Italy and then, after demonstrations had been held in Yugoslavia, stated that they would postpone this action. The deadlock lasted a year more. In October 1954 the more moderate government of Mario Scelba at last reached an agreement with Yugoslavia which saved face on both sides. Yugoslavia formally

* See below, pp. 42-3.

incorporated Zone 'B', and received a further small strip of Zone 'A', while the rest of Zone 'A' including the city of Trieste was incorporated in Italy.

WESTERN EUROPE

In Western no less than in Eastern Europe the war had aroused powerful if ill-defined hopes for a social new deal when peace should come. In all countries where free elections were held after the war there was a marked swing to the left. The first post-war years were also a period of great economic difficulty, which reached its most acute stage in the winter of 1946-7. The tide turned with the decision of the United States government to give peacetime economic aid on a large scale to Europe.* From 1948 onwards this 'Marshall Aid' stimulated the general economic recovery of Western Europe. There was also a certain movement to the right in the internal politics of most European countries. During these years came into existence the system of Western military alliances, directed against the threat from the Soviet Union, and two separate and mutually hostile German states arose. The period can conveniently be ended with the death in March 1953 of Generalissimo Joseph Stalin.

In 1945 there were six states in Western Europe whose political institutions had remained unchanged through the war: Great Britain, Ireland, Sweden and Switzerland had parliamentary régimes, Spain and Portugal had dictatorships.

Wartime economic policies had had far-reaching social effects in Britain, and the process of change was continued under the government of the Labour Party, which came to power with a large majority in the election of July 1945. The Labour Party won a second election in 1950, but it had by now lost much of its original drive and the electorate was turning against it. At the third post-war election, in 1951, the Conservative Party returned to power by a small majority. In Sweden and Switzerland a prosperous neutrality during the war made life more comfortable. In both countries democracy emerged stronger than ever, with a marked socialist influence in Sweden.

The defeat of Hitler did not bring the collapse of the fascist dictatorship of either General Franco in Spain or Dr. Salazar in Portugal. Hostility to Spain was very deep among democratic parties in the West, as well as among communists. The memory of the Spanish Civil War of 1936-9 was still fresh, and Franco had shown a benevolent attitude to Hitler from 1939 to 1945, even if he had remained neutral. It was hoped that exhortations by the United Nations, and the withdrawal from Madrid of diplomatic representatives of nations belonging to UN (required by a General

* See below, pp. 41-2.

Assembly resolution of December 1946) would bring about the downfall of the dictator. But General Franco ignored these gestures; that portion of the Spanish people which accepted his rule rallied round him in outraged national pride; and that portion which hated him remained unimpressed by the ineffective display of 'world public opinion'. In 1950 the General Assembly resolution was revoked, and most member states of UN re-established relations with Spain.

Of the democratic states which were conquered by Hitler, three—Denmark, Norway and Holland—were quickly restored to their old political systems. A fourth, Belgium, underwent a serious crisis in 1945 in connexion with the future of the monarchy. Belgian opinion was bitterly divided as to whether King Leopold III had betrayed his country in 1940 by signing an armistice with Germany, or had acted for the best to save what could still be saved. The division overlapped, though it did not exactly coincide with, that between the two ethnic groups of which Belgium is composed—French-speaking Walloons and Dutch-speaking Flemings. A compromise was made. Leopold abdicated and his son Baudouin became king. Thereafter democracy was assured, and the efforts of the communists, who had increased their support rapidly in the first year of peace, were frustrated.

The two largest continental states of Western Europe, France and Italy, developed in a manner which permits of interesting comparisons.

In two important respects they differed profoundly.

France was, for all the differences of history and tradition between her provinces, a homogeneous country, with long experience of centralized administration and with a uniform culture based on what even today is probably the best system of education in the world. Italy was a country of two nations, North and South. Each of the two could be subdivided into further categories, but the basic difference between the industrial, urbanized and educated people of the North and the agrarian, rural and largely illiterate people of the South was clear. Northern Italy was a part of Western Europe, one of the glories of western civilization, but the South was some intermediate zone between Europe and Africa. The poverty of the South, whose population has continued to increase more rapidly than that of the North, has been a drag on economic and political progress ever since the formation of the kingdom of Italy.

The second major difference between France and Italy is, of course, that from 1922 to 1943 Italy was ruled by the dictatorship of Mussolini and his Fascist Party, whereas France had a liberal democratic government until her defeat by Hitler in 1940. The political habits of mind of the people in the two countries were thus very different: four years of dictatorial government by the Vichy régime and the German invaders did not suffice to weaken the French democratic outlook. But it must be added that if the majorities in France and Italy thought differently, the political *élites* of the two nations were much closer to each other. Italian political thought ever since the French Revolution had been profoundly influenced by French models. Radicalism, anti-clericalism, socialism and conservative liberalism were almost identical in the two countries. Even fascism was in a sense an offshoot of French right-wing nationalism, as expounded by Charles Maurras, and French syndicalism, as expounded by Georges Sorel. Communism was of course derived from Marx and Lenin, but even this non-Latin doctrine acquired in France and Italy a certain distinct flavour. Finally, the Christian Democratic movement, as a branch of Catholic political thought, developed on parallel lines in the two countries. It had greater obstacles to face in Italy owing to the long opposition of the Papacy to the very existence of the Italian state, but it also had greater opportunities in Italy than in France, for the Italian people was on the whole more devout, more traditionalist and less critical than the French.

The resistance movements against the Germans were strikingly similar in the two countries. In both the communists played a leading role, and were able during the underground struggle to secure the grip over the trade union movement which proved their main source of strength after the war was over. In both countries the second most powerful political trend in the resistance was Christian Democracy, while between these two was the considerable force of a Socialist Party, inclining now to the one now to the other. In both countries there seemed for a time to be some prospect of an armed bid for power by the communists. There were in fact many acts of violent revenge, described often euphemistically as the 'punishment of collaborators', and there were minor insurrections in some areas. But the presence of large, disciplined American and British armies made seizure of power by communists on a nation-wide scale impossible, and the Soviet government did not at this time wish to antagonize its great Western Allies. The communist leaders therefore chose constitutional methods of action, and in both countries took part in the first coalition governments and in the preparation of the new Constitutions.

The strength of the three main parties—communists, socialists and Christian democrats—was similar in both countries, but the attitudes of the socialist leaders were different, and this had important results.

In France after the election of October 1945 the communists, who had won 26% of the poll, and the socialists, with 25%, could have formed a majority government. The socialist leader Léon Blum however insisted on a three-party coalition with the Christian democratic *Mouvement républicain populaire* (MRP). In the two general elections of 1946 both communists and MRP increased their vote, while the socialists lost some of theirs. The differences between socialists and communists became more marked, but the communists were unable to split a left wing off the socialist party. The three-party coalition lasted until May 1947, when major disagreements on economic issues and on colonial policy (Indochina and Madagascar) caused the communists to go into opposition.

In the election to the Constituent Assembly in Italy in June 1946 the Christian democrats won 35% of the poll, the socialists 21% and the communists 19%. The two left parties thus outnumbered the Christian democrats but did not have an absolute majority in the Assembly. The three-party coalition was therefore maintained. The Italian socialists however were much closer to the communists than were the French, and they were not able to preserve their unity. The majority of the party followed its leader, Pietro Nenni, in a 'pact of unity' with the communists, while a minority, led by Giuseppe Saragat, broke away in January 1947 and later called itself the Social Democratic Party. The three-party coalition came to an end in May 1947, the immediate cause being differences on financial and economic policy. The Christian democratic leader, Alcide de Gasperi, formed a new government based principally on his own party but with support from smaller groups further to the left. In April 1948 a second general election was held, at which the Christian democrats won 48% of the poll and the Popular Democratic Front (socialists and communists) 32%.

In both countries the communists remained a mighty force, but they had no hope of attaining power. They could not win a majority in free elections, and if they tried insurrection they would be defeated. This was shown by the failure of the violent strikes which they undertook in France in the winters of 1947-8 and 1948-9 and in Italy in July 1948. The Italian communists made good use of agrarian as well as industrial discontent. The agricultural labourers of Emilia and the Po valley were their loyal supporters, and they had a large following among both the share-cropping small farmers of Tuscany and the agricultural proletariat of the South. But their plan to organize nation-wide agrarian disturbances, based on 'committees of the land' modelled on the Russian peasant soviets of 1917, was a failure. In neither country do the communists seem to have had much success in placing their supporters in key positions in the armed forces or the civil administration. There was never any question of the state machine being so infiltrated that in the event of a communist insurrection its loyalty to the government would be in doubt.

Nevertheless in both countries communist success had most important effects on the political system as a whole. In both, the limits within which parliamentary government operates were narrowed. By voting communist or Nenni socialist, between a quarter and a third of the French and Italian nations, including the great majority of the industrial working class, placed itself outside the political life of the nation. The political centre of gravity was shifted to the right, the economic policies of governments were increasingly determined by business interests, the interests of the workers were neglected, the workers became still more alienated from the rest of society and still more loyal to communism, and so the vicious circle continued.

French governments rested on an uneasy combination of socialists, radicals and various brands of conservatives. Various permutations were tried in succession. One might provide a majority on financial policy but would disintegrate on foreign policy. Another might agree on colonial questions but would break up on the question of state aid to religious schools. No government could be formed capable of assuming responsibility for a major decision, for no government could expect to survive more than a few months. The administration, one of the best in the world at its top level of *préfets* and *inspecteurs des finances*, carried on bravely. But there were limits to what it could do. Some questions, such as the future of North Africa and the reform of the taxation system, required new decisions, one way or the other: efficient administration was not enough. Only the politicians could take these decisions, and they would or could not do so. The instability of the Fourth Republic was different in kind from that of the Third: the machinery of government was running down. French politics were no longer an agreeable intellectual exercise, but a mortal disease. The remarkable progress in certain branches of industry, due not only to generous American economic aid, but also to vigorous leadership by intelligent and enterprising French business-men, mitigated but did not compensate for the decline of France.

In Italy the shift to the right was reflected in the dominant position of the Christian democrats, who in contrast to the French groups of right and centre remained a single large party. However, there was little internal unity in this party. It gave Italian politics a minimum stability which was lacking in France. But it might have been better for Italy if the Christian democrats had split, with the majority gravitating to the left and left centre, and a right-wing minority joining up with the neo-fascist and monarchist groups on the extreme right. This would, however, only have been possible if the genuinely democratic majority of the Christian democratic movement had found a partner on its left, if there had been a strong democratic socialist party. In this case the polarization of Italian politics between extreme left and right could have been replaced by the domination of a democratic and progressive centre. But this was made impossible, not by any fault of the Christian democrats, but by the devotion of Pietro Nenni to the pact of unity with the communists. Nenni's great personal authority ensured the support of the bulk of the party in the first years, and in the following period the communists so successfully infiltrated their agents into the machine of the party that Nenni could not withdraw even if he wished. The social democrats of Saragat remained only a small faction of the once powerful Italian socialist movement. Thus the left and left centre of the Christian democratic movement received no significant outside support, and could with difficulty hold their own against their right wing. After the resignation in July 1953 of the elder statesman De Gasperi, who died in August 1954, this became still more difficult. Inevitably the influence of the old bureaucracy of the fascist era increased. Italian democratic intellectuals probably exaggerate the influence of the most reactionary elements of the Roman Catholic Church hierarchy: the clerical bugbear is something of an obsession. Nevertheless, it can hardly be argued that the Italian Church has made much effort to use its vast influence in favour of social reform. Italy, like France, has made great economic progress. The share of American aid has probably been greater, and of domestic business enterprise smaller, in Italy than in France. But in general in the 1950s Italy, perhaps just because it was a poorer country, and its people more primitive, made a more encouraging impression. It had a long way to go, but it was moving. Side by side with irresponsible luxury and corruption there were patient honest effort and energy, hope in the future rather than an atmosphere of decay.

THE GERMAN PROBLEM

The wartime agreements between the Allied Great Powers provided that Germany was to be administered by them in three territorial zones of roughly equal size. Later the British and Americans agreed each to hand over part of their zones to the French, who thus became a fourth occupying Power. It was not however intended that Germany should be partitioned. A central authority was to be set up, the four-Power Allied Control Council in Berlin. The former capital was divided into four sectors, one for each occupying Power. In due course a German government was to be formed, and the victors would sign a peace treaty with it. But the Powers were in no hurry, Germany was in ruins, no suitable German political forces were clearly visible, and the horrors of Hitler's war had left so much hatred in all Europe that the Germans could at first hope for little sympathy.

The Germany which was divided into four occupation zones was already smaller than the Germany of 1939. The union with Austria was annulled, and the Bohemian borderlands (or Sudeten German lands), taken from Czechoslovakia by Germany in 1938 according to the Munich Agreement, were restored to that country. In the north-east a still more drastic change took place. Not only did Poland recover the territories which Germany had annexed in 1939, but the Polish frontier was advanced far westward at German expense. These territorial gains were intended to compensate Poland both for a part of the sufferings she had endured at German hands and for the loss of her eastern provinces, which had been seized by the Soviet Union with Hitler's consent in 1939, and taken a second time in 1944. The Allied Powers had in principle agreed that the Polish frontier should be advanced to the river Oder, but had not committed themselves to the Soviet proposal that in the south it should follow the western Neisse river to its confluence with the Oder, thus giving Poland all Silesia, with its great industry and its ancient German capital of Breslau (renamed Wroclaw). The Western position was that the final frontier between Poland and Germany should be decided by the future peace treaty, but that meanwhile the area up to the Oder and the western Neisse should be placed under Polish administration. The Western Powers did however agree to the annexation by the Soviet Union of German territory in the north-eastern corner of East Prussia, including the city of Königsberg (renamed Kaliningrad). In 1945 the Soviet military authorities handed over to Poland the rest of the territory up to the Oder-Neisse line, and since then both the Soviet and the Polish governments have officially maintained that these lands are not merely temporarily administered by Poland, but are an integral part of the Polish state.

The transfer of the new lands to Poland, and the restoration of the Sudetenland to Czechoslovakia, were accompanied by mass expulsions of the German population. German sources estimate that in 1943 there were about 11,500,000 Germans living in the new and old territory now held by Poland, and that in 1950 there were 8 million of these within Germany's present frontiers and somewhat less than a million still living in Poland. When various necessary adjustments are calculated, they claim that 2 million Germans perished as a result of the expulsions. The German population of Czechoslovakia is estimated by German sources as having been 2,360,000 in the summer of 1945: by 1947 there were 240,000 left. Sudeten German expellee sources in Germany some years later claimed that 300,000 Germans from Czechoslovakia had perished during the expulsions. These figures cannot be accepted uncritically. The numbers of missing persons must include many killed in military operations, and the death-rate was so high, disease and undernourishment so widespread throughout these areas, that many would have died even if there had been no expulsions. But, even if the losses attributable to the expulsions were only half as large as is claimed, it was an appalling tragedy. It is relevant to mention that Polish losses at German hands amounted to about 6 million, of whom about half were Jews. The Czechs had some 200,000 dead and missing through German action. Though their sufferings had been far less than those of the Poles, they had still endured six years of oppression, fear and humiliation.[4]

The arrival of some 10 million expellees from the east, for whom food and lodging had to be provided, and ultimately jobs found, placed a major additional strain on the German economy. In later years the hard work and skill of these men and women proved a great asset to Western Germany, but at first it inevitably increased the already grievous hardships of the whole German nation. A further burden was reparations, which were understandably demanded by the victims of German aggression. It was agreed that each occupying Power should take reparations from its zone in the form of capital equipment, but should leave enough to enable the German population to keep alive without external assistance. The current production of industry should in the first instance be available to pay for imports approved by the Control Council as necessary to the German economy. The Allies also had various plans for reducing the volume of German industrial production, especially steel output, including the grotesque scheme of the United States financial expert Morgenthau for the pastoralisation of Germany. As long as policy consisted of general phrases, some sort of agreement among the Allies on reparations seemed possible. But the Soviet Union concretely demanded reparations amounting to $10,000 million, and as this could not be provided from the sole resources of the Soviet zone, it claimed a share of the resources of the Western territories, especially of the Ruhr heavy industry, which was in the British zone. It soon became clear that, if Soviet demands were to be satisfied, the Western Powers would have to subsidize their zones, in order to keep alive the Germans whose livelihood was being removed to Russia. In other words, Soviet demands amounted in effect to a claim for reparations not only from Germany but also from her Western Allies. These claims the latter rejected, and the numerous inter-Allied discussions in 1946 and 1947 failed to secure an agreed policy.

Soviet policy in Germany had two aims, which were not easy to reconcile. One was to extract all the compensation that could be got for the destruction that had taken place in Russia. The Soviet zone was ruthlessly stripped of its resources, and often in so wasteful a manner that the

German economy was damaged without the Soviet economy gaining any advantage. The second aim was to establish in Germany, as in Eastern Europe, a communist-led dictatorship. The Soviet government must soon have realized that it was hated throughout Germany. It decided, however, to impose the rule of German communism by force in its own zone. The decisive step in this direction was the forced 'fusion' of social democrats and communists into the Socialist Unity Party (SED) in April 1946. This was achieved by a few weeks of terror, blackmail and promises brought to bear on the socialist leaders, the most prominent of whom, Otto Grotewohl, surrendered. The new party was of course, like the 'united' parties which came into existence by similar forced 'fusion' in Eastern Europe in 1948,[5] completely controlled by the communists. The Soviet authorities also introduced a land reform, which put an end to the large estates that had till then played so great a part in the economic and social life of that part of Germany, and confiscated many large factories on the ground that these were 'fascist property'. The five provinces into which the Soviet zone was divided each had its government, nominally composed of a coalition of parties but actually dominated by SED. Central administrative departments were also set up in Berlin to supervise the main branches of the economy throughout the zone. They formed a skeleton zonal government, and were the channel through which the Soviet Command transmitted its orders to the provincial governments.

In the Western zones there were differences in the general policies of the three occupying Powers. In particular the British, acting on behalf of a Labour government, felt greater sympathy for a policy of nationalization of some industry, and of reforms in the interests of the working class, than the Americans, who tended to stress the virtues of private business enterprise. But in all three zones there were democratic liberties, and free political parties organized themselves. Far the most important were the Christian Democratic Union led by Dr. Konrad Adenauer, and the Social Democratic Party, led by Kurt Schumacher. Both leaders had irreproachable records of opposition to Nazism and were men of quite outstanding courage and understanding. Unfortunately these two strong personalities were incapable of co-operation with each other. Their increasingly bitter personal antipathy had a lasting and harmful effect on German politics.

In January 1947 the British and American zones were placed under a single economic control. In February 1948 a conference was held in London of the three Western occupying Powers together with Belgium, Holland and Luxemburg. It agreed on the creation of a separate single Constitution for all Western Germany and of an international authority for the control of the Ruhr industrial area. Meanwhile in the Soviet zone an allegedly representative body was set up called the People's Congress, the embryo parliament for the whole zone. The city of Berlin continued to be divided into four sectors, though entirely surrounded by the territory of the Soviet zone.

Further economic progress in Germany urgently required a reform of the currency. When Western proposals had been refused by the Soviet representatives on the Allied Control Council, the three Western authorities introduced a new currency in their zones in June 1948. This resulted in rapid increases in production. It was the starting-point of the extraordinary economic recovery which made Western Germany, by the mid-1950s, once more one of the great industrial and trading countries of the world. The Soviet reply was to blockade the supply routes between Western Germany and the Western sectors of Berlin. This blockade brought Europe to the verge of war. The Western Powers were, however, able to maintain supplies to the city by an organized airlift, with the wholehearted political support of the people of Berlin. In May 1949 the Soviet government ended the blockade. It had in no way promoted Soviet interests, but the airlift did more than anything to achieve the miracle of restoring friendship between millions of Germans and millions of Americans and British and Frenchmen.

The division of Germany into two was completed in 1949. In May the Western Powers approved the Basic Law which was to be the Constitution of the Federal Republic of Germany. The first election for the federal parliament was held in August. The Christian Democratic Union won the largest number of votes, and Adenauer became the first federal Chancellor, forming a coalition government with the Free Democratic Party. The Social Democratic Party was in opposition. In the Soviet zone the People's Congress approved a Constitution based on the East European model. In October 1949 the executive body formed under this Constitution, the People's Council, declared itself the government of the German Democratic Republic. Its Premier was the renegade socialist Grotewohl, but the dominant figure was the first deputy prime minister and first secretary of SED, the veteran communist Walter Ulbricht.

Thus the 'iron curtain', which had already cut off the East European satellites of the Soviet Union from the West, was now definitely drawn through Germany. There was now a German republic with a population of some 50 million, whose government also exercised civil authority over the Western sectors of Berlin; and there was a German satellite of the Soviet Union with 17 million inhabitants, in which German communists exercised dictatorial power on behalf of Moscow, protected by the Soviet occupation army. The division of Germany had been intended neither by the West nor by the Soviet Union, and was resented by the German people. But as the Soviet government had been unable to extend communist rule to the whole of Germany, and had been unable to extract from the whole of Germany economic wealth which would in any case have had to be largely provided by the West, it had contented itself with retaining one third of the country. As the Western Powers did not wish to rule Germany themselves, or to impose by force a particular party or ideology, they were glad to hand authority to a free German government, provided only that it pursued general policies friendly to them.

THE WESTERN ALLIANCE SYSTEM

As Soviet actions had increasingly shown that Generalissimo Stalin regarded the Western Powers not as friends but as enemies, the need for greater unity in the West became widely felt. From 1947 onwards a number of important economic and military agreements were made.

In March 1947 President Truman announced economic aid for both Greece and Turkey. On 5 June, General Marshall made his famous speech at Harvard, declaring that the United States 'should do whatever it is able to do to assist in the return of normal economic health in the world, without which there can be no political stability and no assured peace', and urging the European governments to concert a joint economic programme. On British and French initiative a conference was held in Paris at the end of June. The Soviet government also attended. The United States had not rejected in principle the idea of aiding communist countries. Indeed in the first years after the war the United Nations Relief and Rehabilitation Administration (UNRRA), mainly financed from America, had done splendid work in ravaged areas of Eastern Europe, including the Ukrainian and White Russian republics of the Soviet Union. UNRRA had ceased its operations at the end of 1946. There had been widespread and not unjustified feeling in America that the communist governments had used this aid principally to reinforce their dictatorships. Nevertheless, if the Soviet government had been prepared to adopt a more friendly political attitude, and to join a general programme of economic reconstruction, the United States would hardly have refused aid to the Soviet Union. But at Paris the Soviet Foreign Minister, Vyacheslav Molotov, bluntly rejected the plans that were put forward by the British and French governments, and refused an invitation to attend a second conference that was to work out details.

Not only did the Soviet government refuse the invitation, but it forbade its satellites to accept. This was a disappointment to the Polish and Hungarian governments, which had at first shown signs of accepting. It was a still more serious blow to the government of Czechoslovakia, which was at this time still a democratic coalition, allied to the Soviet Union since 1943, but sovereign in internal affairs. A majority of the Czechoslovak ministers were for acceptance, but at the last moment they were compelled by the direct intervention of the Soviet government to refuse. This was a landmark in the post-war history of Czechoslovakia: thereafter the Soviet and Czech communist leaders decided that they must have a more reliable government in Prague. The Soviet rejection of Marshall Aid was followed two months later by a direct blow against the West. This was the foundation in September 1947 of the Communist Information Bureau (Cominform) to co-ordinate the activities of the communist parties of the Soviet Union, six East European states, France and Italy. The Cominform also published in Belgrade a fortnightly journal, grotesquely entitled *For a Lasting Peace, for a People's Democracy!*, which reported news and laid down the 'party line' for all countries in the world. From the summer of 1947 the pretence of a 'popular front' policy for communist parties in internal affairs, and of 'Great Power unity' in foreign policy, was at last abandoned, and both non-communist parties and pro-Western governments all over the world were treated as enemies.

The West European states proceeded with their plans for economic co-operation. The Organization for European Economic Co-operation (OEEC) was set up in Paris in April 1948, with sixteen member nations.* In the same month the United States Congress passed the Economic Co-operation Act, and in the following three years Marshall Aid provided $12,500 million. It was ended in 1951, though individual states that were members of OEEC continued thereafter to receive American aid.

The first military alliance between West European countries was the Anglo-French Pact of Dunkirk, signed on 4 March 1947. It was originally conceived as directed against any revival of the German danger rather than against Soviet Russia. On 17 March 1948 the Brussels Treaty was signed between Britain, France, Belgium, Holland and Luxemburg. Concluded a few weeks after the communist seizure of power in Czechoslovakia, it provided for mutual assistance against an aggression which to its signatories seemed more likely to come from the new than from the old enemy. In April 1949 it was followed by the North Atlantic Treaty, in which the five Brussels Powers were joined by the United States, Canada, Denmark, Norway, Iceland, Italy and Portugal. The treaty provided for mutual

---

* Austria, Belgium, Denmark, France, Greece, Iceland, Ireland, Italy, Luxemburg, the Netherlands, Norway, Portugal, Sweden, Switzerland, Turkey, the United Kingdom.

assistance in case of aggression against the territories of a member in Europe, North America, French Algeria, islands in the Atlantic north of the Tropic of Cancer, and vessels at sea within this area. In October 1951 Greece and Turkey were admitted to the alliance. It also had a permanent central organization, known by its initials as NATO.

There grew up in these years a strong movement for greater European unity. This had several motives. One was a general belief that European peace required unity, indeed that the lack of unity among European nations whose culture was essentially one had been the basic cause of the two world wars which had ruined Europe. Another was a desire for greater unity in the face of the Soviet and communist threats. Another was the belief that the best way to overcome the ancient rivalry and distrust between France and Germany was to merge both nations in a greater unit. The movement had much support from the United States, both because it might strengthen resistance to Soviet pressure, and because many Americans thought, perhaps rather naïvely, that it would be good for the Europeans to adopt some version of the federalism which they believed had made the United States so great.

The British attitude was on the whole negative. One reason was that the Labour Party, still in power in Britain, was suspicious of a policy whose main champions were the leaders of non-socialist parties with a strong Catholic flavour (Robert Schuman of France, Adenauer of Germany and de Gasperi of Italy). Another was that British political leaders of both parties wished to preserve a special bilateral relationship between Britain and the United States, and did not wish to place themselves on the same level as all other European states in relation to America. It may be said that this was a selfish desire of Britain to monopolize an excessive share of American favours. But it may also be argued that Britain had in the past proved herself a more loyal and valuable friend of America than any other European nation, and that British advice and help were still of greater value to America than the relative size and wealth of Britain would suggest. A third reason given by British spokesmen was that Britain's special ties with the Commonwealth made it impossible for her to commit herself so closely to an united Europe as could purely continental Powers.

It is extremely difficult to discover how much truth there is in this last argument, whether in fact the Commonwealth would object to Britain being closely associated with Europe, whether this constant invocation of a Commonwealth *mystique* by British spokesmen was statesmanship and realism, or a dishonest alibi, or muddled emotional thinking, or all of these at once. Certainly British leaders have not been indifferent to the needs of

Europe, or unaware that Britain belongs culturally to Europe. Nor has the practical record of British foreign policy shown British governments to have been 'bad Europeans'. But there can be no doubt that British politicians and the British press have underestimated the depth of feeling for European unity, and that both by what they have said and by what they have left unsaid they have unnecessarily offended other Europeans. An irritation against the British, a renewed conviction of the meanness and perfidy of Albion, came to replace, in the minds of some of the best and most constructive democrats on the continent, the admiration and even love they had for Britain in 1940.

Two important European projects took shape in these years. The first was economic. In May 1950 the French Foreign Minister, Robert Schuman, put forward a proposal for a single authority to control the French and German coal and steel industries. After long discussions, the European Coal and Steel Community was set up in July 1952. It was to cover not only France and Germany, but also Belgium, Holland, Luxemburg and Italy. It was to have a supra-national High Authority, whose first chairman was the French economist and statesman Jean Monnet. The second project was the Pléven Plan, put forward by the French Prime Minister, René Pléven, in 1950 as a means of permitting a military contribution by Germany to the defence of the West, which, in the new and more alarming situation created by the war in Korea, was admitted to be necessary, without creating a Germany Army or a German General Staff. The plan proposed the formation of an European Army, with no national formations above the level of brigade, or even of battalion. The existing armies would have their own national commands within their own countries, but Germany would not acquire one. Though this was somewhat humiliating to German national pride, it was acceptable to the Adenauer government, because Adenauer put the unity of Western Europe above all else, and because he was particularly anxious to establish friendship between France and Germany, and because in any case there was little enthusiasm in Germany for the creation of a new national army. A series of discussions took place during 1951 and 1952, which resulted in modifications of Pléven's original scheme. In particular, it was decided that national formations would have to be at least of as large a size as divisions. The scheme on which the six Powers finally agreed, the European Defence Community Treaty, was signed in Paris on 27 May 1952. It still had to be ratified by the individual parliaments.

Thus, when Generalissimo Joseph Stalin died on 5 March 1953, Europe east of the 'iron curtain' and north of the Rhodope mountains was firmly controlled by the Soviet Union; twelve European and two American states were united in the North Atlantic Treaty; five of these were proposing to become more closely associated, together with Western Germany, in the ECSC and EDC; Yugoslavia was independent of the two main blocs but was bound by a treaty of friendship with Greece and Turkey; and Sweden, with considerable military forces, remained uncommitted, politically close to the West but holding a certain protective shield over Finland, which was allied to the Soviet Union yet internally free.

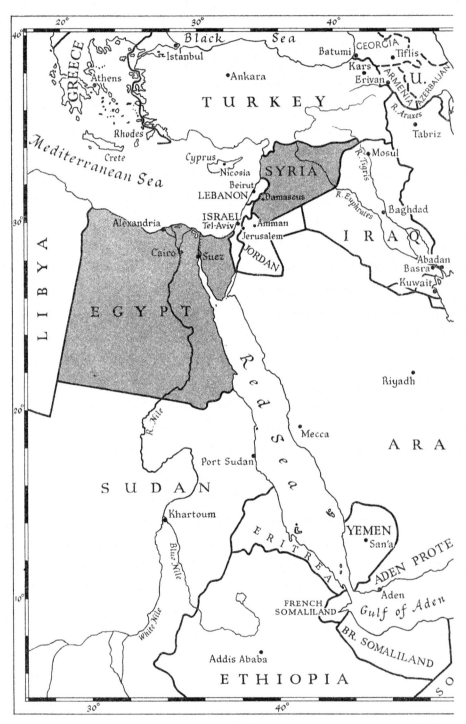

2: The Arabs and Their Neighbours

THE ARAB WORLD

The notion of Arab nationalism is modern, and is not easy to define, for in it religion, language and geography are interwoven. The original homeland of the Arabs was the Arabian Peninsula. It was from its deserts and oases and mountain valleys that Islam spread out over the world—first to Syria; thence eastward to Persia and Central Asia, westward to Egypt and North Africa and Spain; later to India and Indonesia and Africa beyond the Sahara. Arabic was the sacred language of Islam, and it became the spoken language of many of the peoples whom the Moslems conquered. It reached its limits when it came up against other languages possessing a great culture, like Persian or Greek, or a powerful military organization, like Turkish or Spanish, or which were protected by inaccessible terrain, as were the Berber dialects spoken by the Moroccan tribes.

There were great states ruled by Arabs and peopled by men and women whose language was Arabic, but these were not Arab national states. The Umayyad and Abbasid Caliphates were Moslem empires. When they fell there were for a time strong Moslem states in Egypt and Spain in which Arabic was the language of government. In the sixteenth century virtually all the Moslem lands of Arabic speech came under the empire of the Ottoman Turks, whose centre of power was not in any Arab land, but in the Balkan Peninsula, making it the heir to the Emperors of Constantinople as well as to the Caliphs of Baghdad.

As the Ottoman Empire declined in military power, it came under the influence of European Powers, first of France and then of Britain and of Russia. In the nineteenth century European Powers began to occupy Arabic-speaking provinces. The first were the French in Egypt under Napoleon. Their stay was brief, and was followed by the creation of an Egyptian state, independent of Turkey in all but name, by an Albanian soldier named Mohammed Ali. In 1830 the French conquered Algeria, formerly a fortress of Moslem pirates. In 1802 the British occupied Aden, at the south-western corner of Arabia and the mouth of the Red Sea, and in the following half-century established a series of protectorates around the south and east coasts of Arabia, to suppress the slave trade and to guard the approaches to India. In 1881 the French set up a protectorate over Tunisia, and in the following year the British occupied Egypt. In 1911 the Italians conquered Libya from the Turks, and in 1912 the French imposed a protectorate on Morocco. Thus by 1914 the western part of the Arabic-speaking world was ruled by France, the eastern part by Turkey, while Egypt, though nominally still subject to the Sultan of Turkey, was held by the British, who also controlled the coasts of Arabia. By this time also European economic influences had begun to affect social development, at least in the cities of the Arab lands, and modern education, especially in Egypt and Lebanon, had produced an intelligentsia that was impatient of Turkish rule and that was both attracted and repelled by Europe. The Turkish army was a centre of radical ideas, which were reflected in the Young Turk Revolution of 1908. Arab officers too were affected by these influences. In Egypt the emphasis was rather on the modernization of Islam and resistance to European domination than on the solidarity of Arabs as such: for the nationalist leader, Mustafa Kamil, the enemy was Britain, not Turkey. But there were at least two secret societies with Arab nationalist ideals—*al-Fatat*, an organization of civilian intelligentsia centred in Syria, and *al-Ahd*, an association of army officers based on Baghdad and Mosul.

In the First World War Turkey was the ally of Germany, and the Allies were therefore well disposed to her enemies. British military authorities in Egypt were in touch with the ruler of Mecca, the Holy City of Islam: Sheikh Hussein, head of the Hashemite family which claimed direct descent from the Prophet Mohammed. Hussein's hostility to the Turkish government was inspired rather by local patriotism and dislike of reforms that proposed to centralize the Empire than by modern nationalism. But his elder son, Emir Feisal, was in touch with the two secret societies, and had a wider vision of an united Arab Kingdom of Syria, Mesopotamia and Arabia. The Arab Revolt of 1916, which was supported by the British, and gave some help to British military operations in Palestine, was the first effective expression of Arab nationalism. When Feisal entered Damascus in 1918 the Arab Kingdom seemed a reality.

Unfortunately, the situation was more complicated. There were other factors influencing British policy in the Middle East besides the group in Cairo who had dealt with Hussein. The India Office was interested in Mesopotamia, where Indian Army units had fought against the Turks, as a strategic position which was expected to be safer if directly ruled by the British than if handed to unknown and unpredictable Arab nationalists. The French government had a traditional interest in Syria, especially in the Lebanon. A secret Anglo-French agreement of 1916 had provided for a division of the Arab lands of the Ottoman Empire into British and French spheres. Finally, the claim of the Zionists to set up a Jewish National Home in Palestine had strong support in Britain, and still more in the United States. Conditional acceptance of this claim was expressed in the Balfour

Declaration of 2 November 1917. Thus, by the time the war ended, a number of mutually incompatible hopes had been aroused by British diplomacy. From the contradictions between them much of the trouble in the Middle East has resulted.

No single Arab kingdom was created. The Peace Settlement set up Mandated Territories, to be administered by Britain and France on behalf of the League of Nations. The French territories were Syria and Lebanon. Feisal, who had established his government in Damascus in October 1918, was forcibly expelled by the French in July 1920. He became King of Iraq, as the Mesopotamian territory under British Mandate was called. Before he arrived, the British had had to suppress a serious rebellion in Iraq in the summer of 1920. Palestine was assigned to Britain. Jewish immigration was to be permitted, but there was not to be a Jewish state. This was less than the Zionists wished and more than the Arabs were willing to give. Yet another British Mandated Territory was created beyond the Jordan river, the Kingdom of Transjordan, over which the Emir Abdullah, brother of Feisal, was made king. In Arabia the power of the Hashemites was challenged by another ruler, the prince of the puritan Wahhabis, the Emir Abdul Aziz ibn Saud, who had for some years maintained good relations with the British India Office. In 1925 he drove the Hashemites out of the Hedjaz, and in the following years built up the Kingdom of Saudi Arabia, which has since controlled the greater part of the peninsula, including the Holy Places.

Thus though the Arab lands had been detached from Turkey, they had attained neither independence nor unity. This disappointing result was not due solely to the imperialist ambitions of the Great Powers: the Arabs' own divisions had played their part. In this stage of social development, national movements could not do without the leadership of the traditional rulers, and these had their own dynastic or personal ambitions. Moreover, the British had obligations to the rulers. It may indeed be argued that Britain did not do enough for them, but it can hardly be maintained, in the circumstances of the early 1920s, that it should have done nothing at all. From the Arab point of view, however, the peace settlement after the First World War was a step forward. It was at least clear that the notion of Arab nationalism was internationally recognized as a fact. The growth of new social forces, especially of the intelligentsia in Egypt, Syria, Iraq and Tunisia, was now to give it greater strength.

BETWEEN THE WORLD WARS

In Egypt the British had repudiated Turkish sovereignty in 1914. When war ended, the demand for national independence became more pressing.

Its main spokesman was the *Wafd*, led by Saad Zaghlul. This was the first modern party in Egypt, but it was both less and more than a party. It was less, in that it was loosely organized and contained quite disparate elements. In European terms, it may perhaps be compared with the Italian Liberal Party of Giolitti before 1914: it combined the support of liberal intellectuals, small shopkeepers and even proletarians in the cities with that of large landowners who could deliver blocks of peasant votes in rural constituencies. But at the same time it was a genuine national movement, representing the whole people's desire for independence. In March 1919, when Zaghlul and other nationalist leaders were arrested, there were riots all over the country on such a scale as to amount to armed rebellion. In 1922 the British government declared Egypt an independent State and its protectorate ended, though military forces would still be retained on Egyptian soil. The descendants of Mohammed Ali became Kings of Egypt. During the next years Egyptian politics, within the formal framework of a parliamentary constitution, comprised a three-cornered struggle between the King, the *Wafd* and the British. In 1936, when the *Wafd* was in power, an Anglo-Egyptian treaty was signed, which provided for a military alliance between the two countries, defined the status of British troops in the Canal Zone, readmitted Egyptians to the Sudan,* and removed the privileges which had exempted foreign subjects in Egypt from Egyptian jurisdiction.

The treaty did not remove Egyptian resentment. The basis of Egyptian resistance to the British had been first a defence of Islam against infidels, then of the land of Egypt against foreigners. There was sympathy for neighbouring people on religious grounds, but hardly at first a feeling that the people of Egypt shared with the people of Iraq and Syria a common Arab nationality. The Egyptians had played no part in the Arab Revolt. But by the 1930s this was changing. The struggle between Arabs and Jews in Palestine was a decisive factor in strengthening in Egypt, among both the devout Moslems and the growing secular intelligentsia, a feeling

---

* The Sudan had been conquered by Mohammed Ali, Pasha of Egypt, in 1820. Egyptian rule was overthrown in 1881 by a religious rebellion headed by a prophet who claimed to be the Mahdi. The Sudan was reconquered in 1899 by Kitchener, and ruled under a system described as an Anglo-Egyptian Condominium. Decisive power was in British hands, but there were also Egyptian troops and officials. When, in 1924, the British Commander-in-Chief of the Egyptian Army and Governor of the Sudan, Sir Lee Stack, was assassinated, the British government demanded the removal of all Egyptian officials from the Sudan. The British government, however, in 1929 made an agreement with Egypt on the use of the Nile waters, which reserved for Egypt twelve times as much water for irrigation as for the Sudan. Egyptian nationalists insisted that the Sudan was an integral and inseparable part of Egypt. Their slogan was 'the unity of the Nile valley'.

of solidarity with Arabs as such. An important influence in all Arab lands was the Panarab ideologist Chékib Arslan, a native of Lebanon who set up his headquarters in Geneva, maintained contacts in many European countries and published *La nation arabe*, which was read by intellectuals throughout the Arab lands.

The British Mandate in Iraq was ended by a treaty of 1930, which gave Britain the lease of air bases, but otherwise declared Iraq an independent state. In 1932 Iraq was admitted to the League of Nations. In 1936 a combination of army officers and left-wing intellectuals seized power. The officers, however, soon quarrelled with their civilian allies, and within a year the military leaders had been overthrown, and government was again in the hands of old-style conservative politicians. Throughout these years, however, anti-British nationalist feeling was growing. At the same time the development of rich oil resources in Iraq increased its strategic importance for Britain.

In Syria the French Mandate remained unpopular. In 1926 a rebellion by the Druses, and disorders in Damascus, had to be put down by force. In Lebanon, with its strong Christian element, the French enjoyed greater support, especially among the Catholics (Maronites).* In 1936 the French Popular Front government of Léon Blum signed treaties with both Syria and Lebanon. In both countries the Mandate was to be ended, and both were to form alliances with France as independent states, granting France air bases and the right to maintain troops. However, the French parliament never ratified these treaties. Meanwhile, nationalism grew, and the influence of Chékib Arslan inclined Syrian intellectuals to look with hope towards the Fascist Powers.

The three French North African territories differed considerably from each other. Algeria was considered a part of France, and its administration came under the Ministry of Interior. Morocco and Tunisia were separate states but subject to French military and civil advisers, and their foreign policy was in French hands. The population of Tunisia was almost entirely Arabic-speaking. In Algeria and Morocco were large populations in the mountains which spoke only Berber, and a still larger number who, though speaking Arabic, had the customs and way of life of Berbers: only the people of the towns and the coastal plains were for the most part Arabized. In all three territories considerable numbers of Europeans had settled. These were mostly Frenchmen, and were most numerous in Algeria. There were, however, Italians in Tunisia and Spaniards in

* All the Chrisian sects together amount to about 53% of the population. The largest single Christian group are the Maronites, who form 29% of the population. Other Christian communities include the Orthodox and the Armenian.

Morocco. In addition there was a separate Spanish Zone in northern Morocco, facing Spain, while Tangier city was an international free zone.

Of the three territories Tunisia had the best educated and most politically conscious people. The Young Tunisian movement, led by members of the French-educated intelligentsia, existed already before 1914. In 1920 the Constitutional Party (*Destour*) was formed. In 1934 a new party, known as the *Néo-Destour*, appeared, led by Habib Bourguiba. In contrast to the old *Destour*, it recruited its supporters from a much wider section of society; it stressed Tunisian independence rather than a general defence of Islam and of Arabism; and its political ideas were formed much more by those of the French left than by the older liberalism. It soon became, and has since remained, by far the strongest political force in Tunisia. In 1937 the Blum government proposed a series of reforms, but opposition by French settlers (*colons*) and a violent strike by Tunisian phosphate workers created an atmosphere in which no progress was possible. In the winter of 1937-8 the *Néo-Destour* preached civil disobedience, and in April 1938 there were riots which led to the proclamation of martial law and the arrest of Bourguiba and other nationalist leaders.

In Algeria three political trends emerged between the world wars. One was the Association of *Ouléma*, whose struggle for independence from France was based on Islam. Inspired by the Egyptian Islamic modernist Mohammed Abduh, they wished to reform and purify their religion, and incorporate the lessons of modern science within the framework of religion. The second trend was that of the younger intelligentsia, already largely secularized and strongly influenced by French culture and radical political ideas, whose outstanding spokesman was Ferhat Abbas. At this time it desired integration of Algeria with France, but on the understanding that Algerian Moslems enjoyed true equality with Frenchmen. The third trend was a combination of proletarian revolutionary doctrine and nationalism, expressed by the *Etoile nord-africaine*, whose main support was among Algerian workers in France. Its leader, Messali Hadj, had been influenced both by French communism and by Chékib Arslan. In 1937 the *Etoile* was reorganized as the *Parti populaire algérien*, and in the following year Ferhat Abbas created the *Union populaire algérienne*. In Algeria too the Blum government proposed reforms, which would have admitted a much larger number of Moslems to French citizenship, but these were prevented by the opposition of the French population of Algeria.

In Morocco in the 1920s the resistance of the Riff mountaineers, under Abd el-Krim, to the Spaniards in their zone, which also involved the French army in a fierce campaign of more than a year, gave an impetus to nationalism. In 1930 Moroccan national and religious feelings were bitterly offended by the *dahir berbère*, a decree signed by the Sultan under pressure from the French, by which the Berber population were placed under the jurisdiction of French criminal law. This unwise measure was part of a general policy pursued since the retirement in 1925 of Marshal Lyautey, the greatest of all French colonial administrators and a true friend of the Moroccans. The new policy set itself to play off Berbers against Arabs. It raised the more indignation because there had been indiscreet talk by French Catholics of the prospects of evangelizing the Berbers. It was therefore believed that the purpose of the *dahir* was to remove the Berbers not only from Arab culture but from Islam. Protest against the *dahir*, well exploited by Chékib Arslan from Geneva, led to the formation of the first Moroccan political party, the *Comité d'action marocaine*, in 1934, whose leading personality was Allal el-Fassi. In 1937 it split into two factions. The same year there were riots in the cities, parties were dissolved, and Allal el-Fassi was deported to tropical Africa.

The most dangerous situation in the whole Arab world was in Palestine. Here an uneasy relationship existed in the 1920s between the Arab population, the Jewish community represented by the official Jewish Agency, and the British Mandatory Power. British policy was irresolute, and the phrase 'National Home' for the Jews was capable of various interpretations. On the whole the British authorities tended to prefer the Arabs to the Jews, and the British government itself was increasingly reluctant to antagonize Arab, and non-Arab Moslem, opinion in other countries by giving the Jews what they asked. The situation became acute when the persecution of the Jews in Germany by Hitler, and the increasingly intolerable situation of Jews in Poland, Roumania and Hungary, provided strong humanitarian reasons for increasing Jewish immigration to Palestine. In 1935 the number admitted rose to 60,000. Arab opposition became desperate, and in 1936 began a campaign of terrorism which amounted to guerrilla warfare, engaged considerable British military forces, and lasted into 1939. The British government in 1937 proposed partition into a Jewish and an Arab State, as recommended by the Peel Commission. The Arabs refused to consider it. In 1939 the British government reversed its policy. Its White Paper of 17 May proposed to establish within ten years an independent Palestine on terms much more acceptable to the Arabs than to the Jews, whose immigration and right to buy land were to be strictly limited.

The truth was that the points of view of the Jews and Arabs, and of their respective British or European sympathizers, were virtually irreconcilable. The appalling plight of the Jews in Europe clearly called for help by the democracies, but the Arabs did not see why they should pay the bill. It was

THE ARABS AND THEIR NEIGHBOURS 55

all very well to argue that Jewish enterprise would benefit all inhabitants of Palestine, and would raise the standard of living of the Arabs. This was certainly true, but most Arabs at this time did not wish a Western way of life. The creation of modern industries, in which they would get relatively well-paid jobs, and be able to buy modern consumer-goods, did not appeal to them. They wanted to keep their land, and cultivate it their way, even if it was inefficient. They feared that their whole way of life, including their Islamic faith, was in danger. They did not believe Jewish assurances, sincere though these were, of respect for Islam. Their fears were successfully exploited by their fanatical leader, Hajj Amin el-Husseini, Grand Mufti of Jerusalem. For him Palestine was simply an Arab Moslem land, and the Jews were foreign imperialist intruders. But for the Zionists Palestine was the Promised Land to which Jewry, exiled and persecuted for centuries, must at last return. The gulf between them was impassable. Increasingly the intelligentsia of Palestine Arabs looked for salvation to Hitler, and to a lesser but important degree the same trend affected the younger generation of the intelligentsia in Syria, Iraq and Egypt. If Britain was to secure the friendship of the Arabs in the coming struggle, she could not afford to favour the Jews. Yet it may be asked whether the nationalism of the Arabs had not already made them enemies of Britain, and of her ally France: Palestine was only the first of a number of reasons for Arab hostility to the Western Powers.

THE SECOND WORLD WAR

During the Second World War Britain retained control of the eastern half of the Arab world, and from 1942 American and British forces occupied also the western half. Arab nationalism gave small trouble to the Allies and small comfort to the Germans. But this was due more to overwhelming British strength and to the failure of the Axis armies than to love for Britain on the part of the Arabs.

The only political movement in an Arab country which took a definitely pro-British attitude was the *Wafd* in Egypt. Its leader Nahas Pasha was a convinced democrat, and had no use for Mussolini. He declared his sympathy for the Allies, and with the people of Egypt the *Wafd* still counted for much more than the pro-fascist intelligentsia or the friends of the Axis in the army or in court circles. In February 1942, a dangerous moment of the war, when relations between the British and King Faruk of Egypt became critical, the British Ambassador forced the King to appoint Nahas Prime Minister by direct military threat. The *Wafd's* loyal support of the British war effort contributed to the Allied victory, but did irreparable harm to its own prestige in Egypt. It remained the strongest party in the country, but it lost its former unique status as a great national movement of the whole people.

In Iraq there was a dangerous moment in April 1941, when the pro-German Rashid Ali seized power together with a group of nationalist officers, and attacked the R.A.F. base at Habbaniya. British forces were rushed from Palestine, and quickly suppressed the rebellion. The dangerous situation in Syria, where a French High Commissioner loyal to Vichy allowed German infiltration, was ended by the British and Free French invasion of June 1941. During the following two years relations between the British and French authorities in Syria and Lebanon were far from happy. The British pressed the French to carry out the promise made by General de Gaulle to give them independence. On several critical occasions the British, who, being in command of military operations in the whole East Mediterranean area, could impose their will, supported the Syrians or Lebanese against the French. The French became convinced that the British were pursuing an imperialistic policy of pushing them out in order to take their place. Traces of this bitterness remain among the makers of French policy to this day. Syria and Lebanon became members of the United Nations in 1945, and attended the San Francisco conference. The last British and French troops were removed by the end of 1946.

In North Africa French authority was restored. Bourguiba, who had been liberated by the Italians in 1940 from his confinement in France, brought to Rome and then allowed to return to Tunis, had given no support to the Axis cause. He was, however, placed under surveillance by the French authorities, until he escaped from the country in March 1945. The *Néo-Destour* supported the Allied war effort from 1943 to 1945, but did not diminish its nationalist claims on France. In Morocco the presence of the Americans embarrassed the French authorities. The meeting between Sultan Sidi Mohammed ben-Yusef and President Roosevelt in June 1943 was greeted by nationalists as a recognition of Moroccan nationhood distinct from France. The Sultan became the idol of the nation as he increasingly identified himself with nationalist claims. In December 1943 a new nationalist party, *Istiqlal* (Independence) was created. It was not till June 1946 that Allal el-Fassi was allowed to return from Gabon, to become the leader of *Istiqlal*. In Algeria, Ferhat Abbas on 12 February 1943 published an Algerian Manifesto, which demanded autonomy for Algeria and various economic, political and educational reforms. The French Provisional Government was prepared only to offer an extension of the franchise. Its proposals of March 1944 were rejected by the nationalists. The atmosphere grew steadily worse. The climax came on 8 May 1945, when a meeting called by the authorities in Sétif to celebrate the

Allied victory, turned into a demonstration for Algerian independence, which was followed by outbreaks of violence in a large part of Constantine province. There were about 200 French casualties, and much material destruction. The French reprisals, in which the army was assisted by armed civilians, are believed to have cost more than 5,000 Moslems their lives.

PALESTINE, EGYPT AND IRAQ, 1945-9

The end of the war, the proclamation of the principles of the United Nations, and the ascendancy of the United States and the Soviet Union, the former traditionally anti-colonialist, the latter a revolutionary Power, brought a revival of nationalism in all the Arab lands, and an increasing tendency among its participants to regard themselves as engaged in a common struggle for Arab freedom. Syria and Lebanon were now entirely independent. Saudi Arabia had gained in prestige from its ruler's unhesitating support of the Allies, his meeting with President Roosevelt and the rapidly growing production of his oil-wells, worked by the Arabian-American Oil Company (Aramco). In Iraq and Egypt there were still British forces, whose departure was the immediate aim of the nationalists. In North Africa the movements were at an earlier stage. In both Britain and France the left was dominant in the first post-war years, and there was a strong desire to come to terms with the Arabs. The attempts, however, failed. Not only could the specific points at issue in each country not be solved, but the whole atmosphere was poisoned by the unresolved and insoluble problem of Palestine.

As the war receded from the Middle East, the calm which had been preserved in Palestine was broken. The Jewish organization *Irgun Zvai Leumi*, created by the extreme right-wing Revisionist party, and the still more militant Stern Gang, conducted a terrorist campaign against the British forces. Meanwhile, in the United States propaganda in favour of a Jewish state in Palestine was extremely effective, and President Truman used his influence in its favour, even formally asking the British government to admit 100,000 Jewish immigrants. The request could be supported by strong humanitarian arguments. Six million Jews had been exterminated, in the biggest single massacre of modern history, a crime committed in the name of a nation that had until recently ranked as one of the most civilized in the world. The dead could not be restored to life, but at least something could be done for the survivors. At the same time, the old argument still retained force, that it was unjust to make Palestinian Arabs pay the bill for European crimes. The Arabs of Palestine had the moral support of all Arabs from Morocco to Iraq. Moreover, the British government, faced with the problem of the future defence of the Middle East and of preserving its access to the irreplaceable oil-fields of the Arab lands, was anxious not to antagonize any Arab government, while the successive murders of British subjects by Jewish terrorists did little to commend the Jewish cause to the British public. The British government strongly encouraged the negotiations between Arab governments which resulted in the formation in March 1945 of the Arab League (Egypt, Transjordan, Iraq, Syria, Lebanon, Saudi Arabia and Yemen). It was, however, clear that seven states so different in political institutions and social structure, and ruled by men of so divergent ambitions, could agree in little but opposition to Jewish aims in Palestine. The government of the British Labour Party, traditionally a strong supporter of Zionism, continued and even intensified the pro-Arab policy of its Conservative predecessors.

Britain also had to place its relations with both Egypt and Iraq on a new footing, and in both cases was unsuccessful.

Profiting from the *Wafd's* growing unpopularity, King Faruk dismissed the government of Nahas Pasha on 8 October 1944. His successor, Ahmed Maher, was no less devoted to the Allied cause, and even performed on 24 February 1945 the formality of declaring war on Germany. This action cost him his life: he was assassinated the same day by a nationalist fanatic. His successor, Noqrashy Pasha, opened formal negotiations with the British on the two questions of evacuation of the Canal Zone and the future relations of Egypt and the Sudan. Nationalist agitation now mounted to a frenzy. Its most militant exponents were the university students, among whom now for the first time communist influence had become a serious factor.

In October 1946 an agreement was initialled in London by Ernest Bevin and Ismail Sidqy Pasha. It provided for the evacuation of Egypt in two stages, a continued alliance between the two countries, and the right of British troops to return in the event of aggression against Egypt or neighbouring countries. No decision was taken about the Sudan. Despite violent opposition by the nationalists, and pitched battles between students and police, the treaty was approved by the Egyptian parliament. Just at this moment, the British governor of the Sudan, on his return from London, made a statement of policy which emphasized the 'preparation of the people for independence'. The view universally accepted in Egypt was that Sudan was part of Egypt, and that 'independence' was not the wish of the Sudanese, but a manœuvre of the British imperialists to destroy the God-given 'unity of the Nile valley'. The statement therefore naturally provoked a new wave of nationalist protest, with which the government now associated itself. Sidqy Pasha resigned, and his successor, Noqrashy, broke off the negotiations with London. In August 1947 Egypt put her case before the United Nations. She got small satisfaction. In particular the idea of an independent Sudan, which was put forward as the aim of British policy, was well received by the United Nations.

Iraq had a much less developed political life than Egypt. Since the end of the British Mandate in 1930 it had been ruled, except for the interludes of military dictatorship in 1936-7 and 1941, by conservative politicians of the small wealthy class, backed by the landowners and tribal sheikhs. After the war new political parties were formed, at first with some encouragement from the Regent.* They were recruited from the urban intelligentsia, and were in varying degrees nationalist, some liberal and some authoritarian. A communist party was also created, and played a part in organizing in July 1946 a strike of the Kirkuk oil workers employed by the Iraq Petroleum Company. In January 1947 the police arrested all the chief communist leaders. They were sentenced to prison, but subsequently hanged in 1949. The government of Saleh Jabr opened negotiations with Britain, and in January 1948 signed a treaty in Portsmouth. This restored the air bases to Iraq but renewed the alliance of the two countries and provided for a Joint Defence Board. The treaty in fact completely assured Iraq's sovereignty. The objection to it, from the nationalist point of view, was that it associated Iraq with Britain at all. Anti-British feeling had increased as a result of the approaching crisis in the Palestine question. Saleh Jabr had also shown a lack of political tact in not consulting the leaders of the political parties before negotiating with Britain. The Iraqi parliament was dominated by the nominees of the sheikhs, but in the streets of Baghdad the parties were strong. The announcement of the terms of the treaty provoked violent riots, in the face of which the Regent decided to abandon the treaty.

Unable to devise any solution for Palestine that would satisfy both Jews and Arabs, the British government decided to bring the question before the United Nations. A special session of the General Assembly appointed a Special Committee, which visited Palestine and produced a majority report in favour of partition and a minority report in favour of a single federated state. On 29 November 1947 the General Assembly voted for partition, which was supported by both the United States and the Soviet Union. Meanwhile, both Jews and Arabs prepared for war. The British government on 1 January 1948 announced that British troops would be evacuated on 15 May, thereby simply washing its hands of responsibility.

* On the death of King Ghazi in a road accident in April 1939, Prince Abd al-Illah became Regent on behalf of the infant King Feisal II.

In May a Jewish state of Israel was proclaimed, and Arab forces from the four neighbour states and from Iraq invaded. The Jews, enormously inferior in numbers, had a considerable number of trained soldiers who had seen service in the Second World War. They were well armed, had an excellent morale, and the whole Jewish population was united in a passionate patriotism. The Arabs were militarily inexperienced, poorly equipped and politically disunited. The Jewish forces repelled all their opponents. The war was twice stopped by temporary armistices proposed by the United Nations mediator. It was not until the summer of 1949 that a series of armistices were signed in Rhodes between Israel and the several Arab states. The result was that the new Israel received substantially more territory than the United Nations decision of November 1947 had approved, and that the rest of Palestine (the east-central area on the west bank of the Jordan) was united with Transjordan, whose king Abdullah renamed his country the Hashemite Kingdom of Jordan. The other Arab states were displeased to see the aggrandizement of Abdullah's kingdom; the fact that his troops had been the only Arab forces which had fought well did not endear him to them any more. The armistices were not followed by peace treaties: none of the Arab states recognized the existence of Israel. In Israel less than 200,000 Arabs remained: the others, whose numbers were reported by the United Nations refugee organization as 940,000 in 1955, were established in miserable conditions in the Arab states.[6] Nearly 200,000 Jews were expelled from Iraq and arrived destitute in Israel. The creation of Israel was a heroic achievement by the Jewish people, but a terrible legacy of hatred remained.

REVOLUTION IN EGYPT, 1949-52

The patriotic exaltation in Egypt which had accompanied the war against Israel, brought increased support to the Moslem Brotherhood (*Ikhwan al-Muslimin*). This organization had been founded in 1929 by a schoolteacher named Hassan el-Banna, a pious believer of exemplary personal life, a fine orator and a man possessed of unusual personal magnetism, the gift of leadership and the ability to inspire unlimited devotion in others. He wished to reform and purify Islamic society. He was not primarily a politician, nor was the Brotherhood a party, but existing political parties and institutions provoked his wrath. In particular, he was against Western cultural influences, which he considered subversive of morals, and against Western political interference in the Moslem lands. His support came mainly from the cities, from the small shopkeepers and artisans as well as from the very poor. The Brotherhood also had a large following in the intelligentsia, especially among the students, not only at the traditionalist

Moslem university of Al Azhar, but still more at the modern state university of Cairo. In the countryside its slogans enjoyed general sympathy, but peasant membership was not an important part of its strength. Lust for political power, religious enthusiasm and social revolutionary feeling were combined in this movement, which in 1947 and 1948 was perhaps the strongest political force in Egypt. Its groups of volunteers in the Palestine War fought well, but alarmed the king and the government. The outbreak of the war had made possible a severe police terror. This was at first used against Jews and against left-wing groups, but at the end of 1948 it was turned against the Brotherhood as well. It replied by assassinating several high officials. On 8 December 1948 the Brotherhood was dissolved by government order. On 28 December its assassins struck down the Prime Minister, Noqrashy Pasha. On 12 February Hassan el-Banna was murdered in the street, probably on orders of the police. This was a fatal loss to the Brotherhood, but it was not yet crushed. The king himself did not wish it to be destroyed: rather, he hoped to make it an instrument of his own power. A new leader was found in a pious judge named Hassan el-Hodeibi, who was regarded in the palace as a reliable man, but who in fact exercised little control over the Brotherhood's most extreme elements.

Defeat by Israel had not deflated Egyptian nationalism: rather, it had exasperated public feeling against the British, whose forces were still in the Canal Zone. King Faruk, who now held most of what power there still was in the tottering Egyptian state, was bound to identify himself with this feeling, yet did not wish it to get out of control or completely to antagonize Britain, whose support he might need in future, either for his country or for his régime. In November 1949 he dissolved parliament, and held elections, which brought the *Wafd* once more to power. Nahas Pasha was still immensely popular in Egypt, but was compelled, if he did not wish to be reproached with his wartime association with the British, to take a strongly nationalist line. Agreement with Britain was now much more difficult than in 1946. The Sudan was definitely being prepared for independence, while Egyptian nationalists continued to demand its union with Egypt. Moreover, Britain was less willing to evacuate the Canal Zone than she had been in 1946. The Soviet threat to Turkey and the civil war in Greece made it necessary to keep a strong base somewhere in the Eastern Mediterranean, and it seemed far better to the military experts to maintain the valuable installations that already existed in the Canal Zone than to begin all over again somewhere else. One way out was to make the base an international one, if Egypt would definitely join the Western Alliance. But this Egypt would not do. When war broke out in Korea, Nahas Pasha declared that Egypt was neutral: in the existing state of Egyptian opinion, he could not have done otherwise. In October 1951 the Egyptian parliament passed two decrees, by which the Anglo-Egyptian treaty of 1936 was unilaterally abrogated, and King Faruk was proclaimed 'King of Egypt and the Sudan'. Large-scale guerrilla activity was started against the British troops in the Canal Zone, supported by the Egyptian police. The British Commander-in-Chief considered it necessary to order the storming of the police barracks in Ismailia on 25 January 1952. Next day there were large demonstrations in Cairo of policemen, students and political organizations, which were soon joined by vast crowds and by gangs of incendiaries. About 400 buildings were destroyed, 12,000 families made homeless, and several British civilian residents were burnt alive by the mob. The army took no action against the crowds.

This disaster brought the fall of the *Wafd*, but it brought no advantage to the king. Whether he had deliberately allowed the sacking of the capital in order to discredit his old enemy, Nahas, or had merely, like most people in Cairo, been too frightened to act, it certainly destroyed his authority. The next six months were a political vacuum. It was generally understood that neither the king nor the politicians were capable of governing. In such an atmosphere, things which had been passively accepted for years—the misery of the peasants and the urban masses, the ostentatious wealth of a tiny upper layer of society, the favouritism and immorality of the court, the corruption extending even to the army and depriving it of supplies in the Palestine War—became intolerable. But who was to express the general rage remained in doubt. The answer was given in the night of 22-23 July, when a group of officers, led by Lieut.-Colonel Gamal Abd el-Nasser, efficiently and bloodlessly seized control of the capital. Three days later Faruk abdicated and left the country unharmed. A new period in the history of Egypt and of the Arab world had begun.

SYRIA BETWEEN EGYPT AND IRAQ, 1949-52

In Iraq the crisis of January 1948 and the failure in Palestine were followed by a return to conservative government. The political parties were powerless in parliament or outside it. The dominant figure was the veteran statesman, Nuri es-Said Pasha, who was at times Prime Minister and at times in the background, but always powerful. His power was based on alliance with the tribal sheikhs and on police rule in the cities. He favoured rapid economic development, and the wealth derived from oil was used to this purpose by the Iraq Development Corporation. But Nuri was against any drastic social reforms, especially against a redistribution of land, which would have antagonized his allies, the sheikhs. Thus he ignored the interests of the peasants and repressed the intelligentsia: the first remained passively obedient, but the second bitterly hated the régime. Nuri Pasha's policy was based on the hope that after a period of stable authoritarian government and economic growth, social reforms and democratic rule would become possible. It may be roughly compared with the policies of Kemal Atatürk and Reza Shah. Unfortunately, there was an important difference, to the disadvantage of Nuri. In Turkey and Persia the dictators had embodied the spirit of nationalism, but in Iraq Nuri Pasha, an old friend of Britain, was identified in the minds of the nationalist intelligentsia with subservience to the foreigner.

Nuri Pasha was a firm believer in Arab unity. But his conception of unity excluded Egypt: Nuri was primarily concerned with the 'Fertile Crescent', from Palestine to the Persian Gulf. The two Hashemite states, Iraq and Jordan, formed a nucleus. To these should be added Syria and Lebanon, and if possible Palestine too—for Nuri was no more tolerant of the existence of Israel than other Arab leaders. The project of a Greater Syria under Hashemite leadership was distasteful to the old dynastic adversary, King Ibn Saud of Saudi Arabia. It was also opposed by King Faruk of Egypt, who did not wish to see the rise of an Arab state, or grouping of states, powerful and rich enough to cast doubt on Egyptian leadership in the Arab world. Egyptian public opinion was also hostile to the idea, for all Egyptian nationalists by the 1940s had convinced themselves that Egypt was an Arab state, and that there could be no Arab unity without Egypt. The Western Powers were also concerned in these rivalries. The British government favoured the Hashemite states and approved Nuri's plans. The United States inclined towards Saudi Arabia, not least because that country contained the largest single American interests in the Middle East—Aramco's oil wells and the Dhahran air base. France hoped to preserve some influence in Syria and Lebanon, and did not wish to see either absorbed by Iraq. An important element in French policy was resentment against the British for their role in the expulsion of the French from Syria and Lebanon in 1943-5. This factor would induce France, if in doubt, to oppose whatever the British proposed.

The object of these various rivalries was Syria. In 1949 three successive military *coups d'état* took place. The first would-be dictator, Colonel Husni Zaim, who seized power on 31 March, began by courting Iraq and Jordan, but soon reversed his course and inclined towards Egypt. On 14 August he was overthrown by Colonel Sami Hinnawi, who preferred a pro-Hashemite policy. On 19 December he was removed by Colonel Adib Shishakli, who moved closer to Egypt and Saudi Arabia, though the supporters of the Iraqi orientation controlled parliament. In July 1951 the Hashemite cause suffered a severe blow when King Abdullah of Jordan was murdered by a follower of the former Grand Mufti of Jerusalem. Shishakli was overthrown in February 1954. His four years of power had consolidated the young state, had given it the beginnings of a state machine, and had speeded up the growth of radical nationalism, looking rather to Egypt than to Iraq. The replacement of Faruk, a figure unattractive to the radical intelligentsia, by Nasser's military group, increased this trend.

NORTH AFRICA, 1945-53

In all three territories of French North Africa the first post-war years were marked by hesitant attempts at reform, which were rejected by the growing nationalist movements, whose clamorous and at times violent opposition led to repression by the French administration.

The Tunisian leader Habib Bourguiba escaped abroad in March 1945 and spent the next four years pleading his cause in exile. At home his party was led by Salah ben-Yussef. The movement was strengthened by the creation of a Tunisian trade union movement, distinct from the French CGT and closely linked with the nationalists—the *Union générale des travailleurs tunisiens* (UGTT). The *Néo-Destour* now asked for national independence for Tunisia. This the French government was not prepared to consider. At the end of 1949, however, Bourguiba was allowed to return to Tunisia, and in the following spring came to Paris to put his case. A new attempt was made to break the deadlock: the *Néo-Destour* leader Salah ben-Yussef entered the government of M. Chenik. The new policy was bitterly opposed by the leaders of the French population of Tunisia. During 1951 the French government proposed further concessions to the Chenik government, but these were met by counter-claims, and French *colon* opposition grew. In December 1951 the French government yielded to the pressure of the *colons* and refused the proposals of the Chenik government for 'internal autonomy' for Tunisia. A new French Resident, M. de Hauteclocque, arrested Bourguiba and other nationalists, and dismissed the Chenik government.

In Morocco the French authorities ignored the demands of the nationalists for independence, and showed special dislike of the *Istiqlal* party. The most important development of this period was that the Sultan of Morocco, Sidi Mohammed ben-Yussef, felt increasing sympathy for the ideas of the nationalist intelligentsia, and especially of the *Istiqlal*. In April 1947 the Sultan made an official visit to Tangier, and publicly expressed his sympathy for the Arab League, which had 'strengthened the links between all Arabs'. The speech made no reference to the protecting Power, France. This direct affront to the French government led to the replacement as Resident of the reformer Erik Labonne by General Juin, who carried to hitherto unprecedented proportions the policy, sometimes pursued in the past, of playing off Berbers against Arabs. He found a willing servant in the Pasha of Marrakesh, el-Glaoui. Using the threat of a march of the Berber tribes on the capital, he compelled the Sultan in February 1951 to sign a statement dissociating himself from all political parties, condemning 'the subversive ideology of violence' and rendering homage to 'the generous action of the French Republic'. The declaration had small effect, for it was generally understood by Moroccans that it had been extorted from the Sultan by threats. The nationalist parties decided to combine their efforts for independence, and their popular support increased. In December 1952 the nationalists declared a strike to express solidarity for the murder in Tunis of Ferhat Hached, the leader of the Tunisian trade unions (UGTT). This led to arrests, demonstrations and clashes with the police in Casablanca. *Istiqlal* and the Communist Party were both dissolved by government order. Meanwhile the Sultan had not changed his attitude, and the French authorities in Morocco decided, without authorization from Paris, to remove him. In the summer el-Glaoui and other notables were induced to petition the French to depose him. The Sultan was forced to sign a document transferring all his powers to a joint Franco-Moroccan Council, thus replacing the sovereignty of Morocco under French protection by a Franco-Moroccan 'co-sovereignty'. Though this humiliation satisfied the government in Paris, the French in Morocco wanted more. Sidi Mohammed was deported to Madagascar in August 1953, and his elderly relative, Mohammed ben Arafa, was given the now empty title of Sultan.

In Algeria the leader of the moderate nationalists, Ferhat Abbas, who had been arrested after the Constantine province massacre of May 1945, was released in March 1946, and formed his supporters into a new party, the *Union démocratique du manifeste algérien* (UDMA). The more radical leader, Messali Hadj, was still in prison. At the June election to the French Constituent Assembly, UDMA won 11 out of 13 seats allotted to Algerian Moslem voters. As a result of the debates in the Assembly on the Algerian problem, a new Statute was introduced in September 1947. This provided that the Algerian Assembly and the Algerian seats in the French National Assembly should be elected in two separate colleges, each of which should have half the seats. The electorate of the first college amounted to 464,000 Frenchmen and 58,000 Moslems; that of the second college to nearly 1,400,000 Moslems. Separate colleges were also created for the municipalities in Algeria. The main task of the Algerian Assembly was to be the application of French laws to the special conditions of Algeria, but it was also to have the power to issue special regulations of its own within rather narrow limits. This Statute was a step forward, but representation remained weighted heavily in favour of the French tenth of the population, and the powers of the Assembly fell far short of autonomy.

In October 1946 Messali Hadj had been allowed to return to Algeria, and his party, *Mouvement pour le triomphe des libertés démocratiques* (MTLD), put up candidates at the municipal election in the city of Algiers in October 1947. The electorate of the second college gave a large majority to MTLD, while Ferhat Abbas's moderate UDMA fell far behind. The French reaction to these disagreeable results was to deprive the Moslem voters of the liberty of choice assumed by the makers of the 1947 Statute. At the election to the Algerian Assembly, held in the autumn of 1948, the administration put direct pressure on the second college electors to give their votes to 'independents' chosen for their obedient devotion. The results were 'satisfactory': out of 60 seats MTLD won only 9 and UDMA 8.

TURKEY AND PERSIA

Turkey and Persia are two lands of ancient civilization, a land-bridge between Europe and India and a barrier separating Russia from the Arab world. Persia's history goes back more than 2,500 years, to Cyrus and beyond. The empire of the Ottoman Turks was shorter-lived, but it was the heir to the Byzantine, Roman, Greek and Hittite rulers of Asia Minor, now the reduced homeland of the Turkish people. Only Egypt and China have longer records. Both countries in the eighteenth century felt the pressure of the rising Russian Empire. Turkey had to abandon her vassals, the Crimean Tatars, and then to yield territory on the northern coast of the Black Sea, in the Caucasus and in western Transcaucasia. Persia lost most of Azerbaidjan and her portion of Armenia. In the nineteenth century other European Powers—Britain, France and Germany—also pressed heavily upon both states. Their rulers were saved by the rivalries between the Europeans, which they exploited with varying skill. Though forced to make damaging economic concessions, and to grant humiliating privileges to European subjects, both Turkey and Persia still managed to survive as independent states. Of the two, Turkey had been by far the stronger in recent centuries, but was also the more vulnerable: the religious and national variety of her subjects, including Balkan Christians, Arab Moslems and many small minorities, was a source of internal weakness. Numerous attempts to modernize the Ottoman Empire, to give it a new unity on dynastic, or pan-Islamic, or secular parliamentary principles, all failed. Defeat in the First World War brought its dissolution. Persia was more compact and more distant from Europe. Though it too contained national and religious minorities and unruly tribes, the tradition of an united Persian state, and respect for the authority of the Shah even if not for every ruler who embodied it, saved it from complete collapse. But the development of its oil, while a valuable source of wealth, increased its importance in the eyes of the Great Powers.

Between the world wars both countries were ruled by modernizing dictators.

Kemal Atatürk was a greater man than Reza Shah, and his achievement was the greater. The essence of his policy was that it was based on the Turkish nation alone: Kemal accepted the loss not only of the Balkan provinces but also of the Arab lands. The two past ideals of a multi-national secular state or of an Islamic supra-national empire were definitely abandoned. The Turkish people, till then the most forgotten of the peoples of the Ottoman Empire, was to come into its own. Even solidarity with the other Turkic peoples—the Azerbaidjanis, Crimeans and Central Asians in the Soviet Union—did not interest Atatürk. His patriotism was to be limited to Anatolia, and this was to be a Turkish national state, in which minorities (Kurds, Armenians, Greeks or minor groups) were expected to be loyal to Turkish interests. The Turkish Republic was radically secularized, and its law and schools and economic development based on Western models. It is important to note that, at the present time when the notion of 'Asianism' is so popular with half the population of the world, the Turks insist proudly that they are Europeans.

Reza Shah of Persia modelled himself on Kemal, but did not go so far. Like Kemal, he was an army officer, but unlike him he decided, once he was firmly in power, not to introduce a republic, but to proclaim himself Shah. He was not the first *parvenu* in Persian history to rise to the highest honour. He introduced a European legal system, developed European types of school, and encouraged European dress and, for the upper class in the cities at least, the emancipation of women. Like Kemal, he built railways. But he kept the Arabic alphabet, and he did not risk the brutal frontal assault on Islam that Kemal permitted himself. In his later years he became much more conservative, and he also used his power greatly to enrich himself and his family.

In the 1920s both countries enjoyed comparatively good relations with Soviet Russia, though Reza Shah had to suppress by force a communist 'republic' that was set up with Soviet help in the north-western province of Ghilan in 1920-1. But as the European Powers abandoned their earlier hostility to both régimes, their mutual relations improved, and relations with Moscow cooled.

Turkey concluded alliances with Britain and France in 1939, and rejected strong Soviet diplomatic pressure to break with these Powers. In November 1940 Molotov, during his Berlin conversations with the German leaders, asked to be given a military base in the Straits. This they would not agree to, though they were prepared to accept a regulation of the Straits Question more favourable than any Russian government in history had ever enjoyed.[7] Disagreement on the Straits was one of the causes of the ultimate breach between Nazi Germany and the Soviet Union. Before invading Russia, the Germans informed the Turkish government of the demands that Molotov had made. This knowledge contributed to the Turkish decision to sign a non-aggression treaty with Germany in June 1941. Turkey in fact remained neutral until February 1945, when she made a formal declaration of war on Germany in order to obtain admission to the United Nations conference at San Francisco. In practice the Turkish sympathies were curiously divided: they inclined to the German side in the German-Soviet half of the war but to the British side in the Anglo-German half. Turkish neutrality probably benefited the Western Allies by creating a land barrier between the German-occupied Balkans and the Middle East in 1941-2. The Soviet Union, however, was alarmed by a certain growth of 'pan-Turkish' propaganda in Turkey, demanding liberation, presumably by German arms, of the Turkic peoples of the Soviet Union, and urged the Western Allies to press for active Turkish participation in the war.

In Persia German influence was very strong. To many educated Persians the Germans commended themselves as the opponents of both the Powers which in the past had humiliated Persia—Britain and Russia, which had first drawn together in 1907 at the expense of Persia, dividing that country into spheres of influence and at times occupying parts of its territory with their troops. Fear of German activities in the rear both of Soviet Transcaucasia and of the British-held Middle East caused the two Powers in 1941 to repeat their action of 1907 on a more drastic scale. In August 1941, after the Persian government had rejected an ultimatum to expel Germans from its territory and to allow the transportation of Allied war material for Russia over its roads and railways, Soviet and British troops invaded Persia. Reza Shah abdicated in favour of his son, and the Trans-Iranian Railway, the most striking material monument of his twenty years' rule, which had been completed by 1939, became a major channel of Allied supplies to Russia. The Persian government maintained a minimum of sovereignty thanks to the conflicting policies of the Soviet and British occupiers, and later to the rather more disinterested protection of the United States. In 1943 it formally declared war on Germany, and in 1945 took part in the San Francisco conference of the United Nations.

TURKEY AND THE SOVIET UNION, 1945-50

In the summer of 1945 the Soviet government put its demands to Turkey. It asked for the cession of the regions of Kars and Ardahan, which had been Russian between 1878 and 1918. The Soviet press also gave space to the demands by prominent Georgian and Armenian citizens of the Soviet Union, asking for still larger territorial gains: these were not officially claimed by Moscow, but were used to create an atmosphere of tension. The Soviet government also asked for Soviet military bases inside both the Bosphorus and the Dardanelles. Finally, it asked that the existing international Convention on the Straits, signed at Montreux in 1936, be replaced by one which would substitute for an international control of the Straits an exclusive joint control by Turkey and the Soviet Union. It was this last demand which was most seriously pursued by Moscow. If Turkey had accepted it, and thereby separated herself from the West and become a virtual satellite of the Soviet Union, the more offensive demands for territory and for military bases could well have been dropped. But Turkey refused all three demands. Soviet pressure continued throughout 1946, and Turkey was therefore compelled to keep large numbers of troops under arms, at great cost to her economy. This burden was substantially relieved in March 1947, when President Truman announced his intention to grant large-scale aid to both Greece and Turkey.

Fortunately, the Turkish government had no fears for internal security. Strengthened by more than twenty years of modernization and nationalism under Kemal Atatürk and his successor, Ismet Inönü, the Turkish people had become united in opposition to Russian imperialism, no less objectionable in its Soviet than in its Tsarist form. The influence of communism, even in the intelligentsia, was negligible. This is not to say that there were no internal political divisions. On the contrary, the new educated class, in business and bureaucracy and intelligentsia alike, was impatient of the dictatorial methods which had been necessary under Atatürk, but now seemed to have outlived their usefulness. It was a measure of the strength of the régime created by Atatürk that its leaders in 1945 allowed the formation of an opposition group, the Democratic Party. At a general election held in 1946, in conditions that strongly favoured government candidates, the Democrats won 60 out of 465 seats. In 1950, however, a new electoral law was introduced, which was designed to ensure a genuinely free election. This was held in May, and resulted in a large majority for the Democrats, who won 408 seats while the Republican People's Party, formerly in power, won only 79. The new party stood for wider civil and political liberties, and aimed to encourage private initiative in industry, while paying less attention than its predecessor to state-run enterprise. In 1950 the prospects of Turkey seemed bright, and this first instance of a modern dictatorship being transformed into a democracy appeared to have encouraging implications for other countries too.

PERSIA, THE SOVIET UNION, AND THE WEST, 1945-53

During their occupation of Persia the Soviet authorities had encouraged the formation of a communist party, which called itself *Tudeh* ('Masses'') Party. Communism made a strong appeal to a large part of the intelligentsia, and it was not difficult, with Soviet financial and political aid, to build up a following among the urban poor, including textile workers at Isfahan and oil workers employed by the British-owned Anglo-Iranian Oil Company (AIOC). In September 1945 the communists in Tabriz, instigated by the Soviet authorities, set themselves up as a separate Democratic Party of Persian Azerbaidjan, and proclaimed that region an autonomous Republic. Persian Azerbaidjan is populated by people closely akin to those of Soviet Persian Azerbaidjan. They are not Persians. Their language is Turkish, but by religion they belong to the Shia branch of Islam, which is dominant in Persia. The Persian Azerbaidjanis certainly had grounds for discontent. In addition to the poverty and misrule which was the fate of most Persian subjects, there was an element of national and cultural discrimination against them. It was, however, obvious that the Soviet government had engineered the events with the aim either of annexing Persian Azerbaidjan or of forcing the Persian government into satellite status. They also set up a Kurdish autonomous area with its capital at Mahabad, intended as a centre of disaffection for the Kurds of Persia, Iraq and Turkey, whose total numbers may be as large as four million.*

The Persian government complained to the United Nations of the Soviet action. In March 1946 the six-month period from the end of hostilities, within which the Soviet and British troops must be withdrawn, expired without a Soviet withdrawal. About this too the Persians complained at the United Nations, with little result. The Persian Prime Minister, Qawam es-Sultaneh, therefore made concessions to the Soviet Union. He took

*The numbers of the Kurds are extremely uncertain, as the governments of the four states in which they live share an interest in making them appear as small as possible, and no reliable impartial statistics are available. In 1950 they were estimated at 1,700,000 in Turkey, 1,000,000 in Persia, 700,000 in Iraq and 200,000 in Syria. The Turkish Kurds have been to a considerable degree dispersed throughout the country, but in the other three states they live in fairly compact areas. There is also a small minority of Kurds in the Armenian SSR of the Soviet Union, estimated at 20,000 (*The Middle East: a Political and Economic Survey*, Royal Institute of International Affairs, London, 1950, p. 436).

three communists into his government, and he agreed to the formation of a Soviet-Persian joint company for the exploitation of oil in northern Persia. These seem to have been regarded in Moscow as a sufficient price for withdrawal: to have persisted in the earlier policy would have meant a serious danger of war with Britain and the United States, which were determined not to allow Soviet control of Persia. In May 1946 the Soviet forces withdrew.

In practice, however, the Soviet government got a bad bargain. A threat of revolt by southern tribes caused Qawam to dismiss the communist ministers. In December 1946, after negotiations with the Azerbaidjani separatists had failed, Qawam sent troops to occupy Tabriz. Deprived of Soviet armed help and now hated by the population, which it had ruled for months by ruthless terror, the Azerbaidjani régime collapsed. Its leading figure, Jaafer Pishevari, who had played a prominent part in the 'Ghilan republic' of 1920-1, fled for the second time to the Soviet Union. Finally, in October 1947 the Persian parliament refused to ratify the oil concession. Whether Qawam had originally intended to deceive the Russians, or had been reluctantly compelled to break his word, it is certain that the Soviet government had suffered a complete defeat.

Persians were grateful to the United States for support in the crisis. But its solution did not lead to close relations between Persia and the West. Communism remained a considerable force, although *Tudeh* was banned in 1949 after an attempt on the Shah's life by one of its members. The communists were able to make use of discontent with oppressive social conditions and poverty. These could only have been improved by years of reform, and in practice little attempt was made to begin reform. At the other extreme of Persian politics were the nationalists and traditionalists. *Fedayan Islam*, a religious organization of much the same outlook as the Moslem Brotherhood in Egypt, was led by the *mulla* Kashani. On the political level, extreme nationalism was represented by the National Front of Mohammed Mossadeq. The nationalists had supported the resistance to the Soviet Union, but now wished also to end Western influence in Persia. In particular, having refused an oil concession to the Soviet Union, Persia should, they argued, take over the existing oil concession that was held by the British-owned AIOC. Agitation against the British company of course also suited the interests of *Tudeh*: on this issue the communists supported Mossadeq and Kashani, however little they might agree on other points. In 1949 and 1950 the nationalists gained popularity as a result of the disappointingly small amount of aid granted to Persia by the United States. The visit of the Shah to Washington at the end of 1949 produced no more than a statement of sympathy. The Shah hoped that he might increase American sympathy by social and administrative reforms, which he announced soon after his return. But in October 1950 he received a mere $25 million from the Export-Import Bank.

In March 1951 a follower of Kashani assassinated General Razmara, the Prime Minister in whom the Shah had placed his hopes as a strong man and a reformer. A few days later the parliament passed a bill nationalizing the AIOC, and in May Mossadeq became Prime Minister. By the end of the year all British employees of AIOC had left Persia, most foreign buyers refused to buy oil from the Persian nationalized enterprise, and the government's revenues were greatly reduced. These economic troubles did not, however, worry Mossadeq, or diminish his popularity. Nationalist frenzy increased, and the communists, though not formally reinstated in their civil rights, came out on the streets without fear and successfully recruited support. In August 1952 Mossadeq was voted full powers, broke off diplomatic relations with Britain and dissolved the parliament. He was now dictator, but the State machine itself was tottering. In the summer of 1953 the Shah and his family left the country. On 19 August 1953, however, General Zahedi managed to seize power in the capital and arrest Mossadeq and his supporters. A military dictatorship was introduced, the communists were fiercely repressed and the Shah returned from his temporary exile. Throughout these months of chaos the Soviet government had taken no action.

3: Asia

JAPAN

When on 15 August 1945 the Emperor of Japan ordered his subjects to surrender to the United Nations, his commands were carried out with complete obedience. The defeated Japanese soon showed themselves willing to co-operate fully with the victors and eager to adopt the form of government recommended by them. For the next years the real power was in the hands of the American occupation authorities. The Emperor remained on his throne, but as in the centuries before 1868 power was exercised by a *Shogun*, so now this role fell to the imperious General Douglas MacArthur.

Political reforms began with the occupation directive of 4 October 1945, which established freedom of speech, meeting and association, release of political prisoners and a reduction in the powers of the police. Trade unions and political parties could now be organized, and a variety of opinions could be expressed in the press. A new government was then appointed under a former Foreign Minister of mildly liberal sympathies, Baron Shidehara, which held power until the first parliamentary election in May 1946.

Japan had had parliamentary government and political parties from the 1880s until 1940, though in practice their operation had been limited by powerful extra-parliamentary forces. The 1920s were the only period in which Japanese politics began to approach Western patterns, and even then the reality was different from the appearances. In these years there were two main parties, *Seiyukai* and *Minseito*. The differences between them concerned personalities and interest groups rather than principles of policy, but *Seiyukai* was the more conservative of the two and *Minseito* the more liberal. In 1946 some of the lesser former leaders of these two parties reappeared to form two new parties of the right—the Liberal Party, which was a continuation of *Seiyukai*, and the Progressive Party, a continuation of *Minseito*. A third party were the socialists, led by men who had been active before the war in the labour movement. The fourth main group were the communists, whose leaders emerged from prison or from exile, thanks to General MacArthur's decree.

At the election of May 1946 the Liberals won 139 seats out of 463, the Progressives 94 and the Socialists 93. The Liberal leader, Shigeru Yoshida, became Prime Minister. Under his first government the land reform was passed, and the new Constitution, drafted essentially by General MacArthur's staff, came into force. The Constitution reduced the status of the Emperor or from Head of the State to 'the symbol of the State and of the unity of the people'. It introduced full parliamentary government, with the cabinet responsible to a bicameral legislature. A feature for which there was no known parallel in history was its Article 9, which laid down that 'the Japanese people for ever renounce war as a sovereign right of the nation and the threat or use of force as a means of settling international disputes', and that land, sea and air forces, as well as other war potential, will never be maintained'. The Constitution was finally promulgated on 3 November.

The winter of 1946-7 was a time of great economic hardship. The newly rebuilt trade unions, some controlled by socialists and some by communists, expressed and canalized the discontent of the working class and in general of the poorer urban groups. The communists sought to create a Popular Front with the socialists. As in France and Italy at the same time, the socialists were divided in their reaction to communist blandishments. A communist-led campaign was intended to culminate in a general strike on 30 January 1947, but at the last moment MacArthur intervened to forbid it. In view of the bitter popular feeling, however, he ordered the government to hold a new general election. It took place in April, and was a success for the socialists, who became, with 143 seats, the largest single party. Their leader, Katayama, formed a government with the support of the Progressives, while the Liberals were in opposition. In February 1948 a Progressive became Premier and received socialist support, and in the autumn Yoshida returned to power, with Liberals and Progressives in alliance and socialists in opposition. Economic conditions continued to be bad, and the socialists lost ground both to the right and to the communists who outdid them in demagogy from the left. At the third general election, in January 1949, the socialists won only 48 seats, less than a third of their number in 1947, while the communists increased theirs from 4 to 35. The Liberal Party far surpassed its rivals, and Yoshida remained in power.

Though the communists had increased their following, they were still only a small party, and their strength outside parliament was neither very large nor very well organized. In January 1950 an important new directive to the Japanese communists was published in the Cominform journal, *For a Lasting Peace, for a People's Democracy*, the main point of which was that the party must now direct its main attack against 'the imperialists'— that is, the United States. In the spring there were a number of violent outbursts against American soldiers instigated by communists. MacArthur replied by instructing the Japanese government to forbid a number of communist party officials and editors, listed by him, to engage in any political activity. The result of this 'purge' was to make overt action by the communists virtually impossible. Less than three weeks later, on 25

June 1950, the Korean War began. The communist party was not formally banned in Japan, but its leaders went into hiding and it became essentially an underground organization.

The Korean War had two important effects for Japan. Firstly, it benefited the Japanese economy. The years of acute shortages and business uncertainty were replaced by a boom in trade and opportunities for industrial progress. Secondly, it caused the United States government to modify its view of the strategic importance of Japan. Instead of a danger-point to be neutralized, it now became a strategic asset to be strengthened. The intervention of China in the Korean War at the end of 1950 made it clearer still that America's enemy in the Far East was now China, and that Japan was a potential ally.

Since 1945 General MacArthur had ruled Japan on behalf of all the Allies, but in fact had paid little attention to the wishes of Allied representatives. A Far-Eastern Commission of eleven nations taking part in the war in the Pacific had been set up in Washington in 1945, and there was an Allied Council in Japan with a representative each from the United States, British Commonwealth, Soviet Union and China. But neither body exercised any notable influence. With the new situation created by the Korean War, it became more urgently desirable to make a peace treaty with Japan, and to put American relations with her on a more lasting basis. It was idle to expect that the Soviet Union, which was at least indirectly responsible for the North Korean aggression, would accept any terms that satisfied Western needs, and impossible to wait for a time when Soviet aims would be more conciliatory. The diplomatic negotiations were therefore conducted principally between the United States and Japan, with some consultation of the non-communist former allies. A formal peace conference was held in San Francisco, and the peace treaty was signed on 8 September 1951. The consent of Australia and New Zealand, whose general attitude to Japan was understandably less conciliatory than that of the United States, was obtained in return for a formal alliance between them and the United States, known as the ANZUS Pact and signed in the same year. Under the San Francisco treaty Japan renounced her sovereignty over Formosa and the Bonin and Ryukyu Islands in the Pacific: the latter were placed under American trusteeship as strategic trust territories, nominally under supervision of the United Nations Security Council. Japan made a separate agreement with the United States permitting American armed forces to be stationed in Japan, no longer as occupiers, but as allies.

The peace treaty, and especially the agreement on American troops and bases, was bitterly attacked in Japan by communists and left-wing opinion generally. It was, nevertheless, ratified by the Japanese parliament in April 1952.

INDIA AND PAKISTAN

Preparation of India for independence had long been the avowed aim of British policy. With the end of the war, the demand for the return home of the troops, and the advent to power of the Labour Party, the achievement of this aim became a matter of urgency. Yet two problems that had bedevilled Indian politics for decades past still remained for solution. One was the relationship between the Moslems, who numbered nearly a third of the sub-continent's population, and the Hindu majority. The second was the position in the future independent India of the protected States, whose subjects, amounting to over 80 million out of over 380 million, were ruled not by British officials, but by Indian princes.

The ancient civilization of India was Hindu. Another of the world's great religions, Buddhism, was born in India. From the eleventh century, however, Moslem dynasties established themselves in northern India, and in the sixteenth century the Mogul Empire was created, which ruled most of the sub-continent until the British conquest. But Hinduism, which had survived and partly absorbed Buddhism, passively but successfully resisted Islam. The Moslems were the ruling community, and made many converts, especially in Bengal, but the bulk of the population remained Hindu. Under British rule, the upper class of Hindus adjusted themselves better to the new conditions than the upper class of Moslems. Hindus were better suited to civilian secular professions and to business activity than Moslems, who excelled as soldiers. At the beginning of the twentieth century leading Moslems felt that their faith, which is not so much a set of theological doctrines as a way of life and a society, was being threatened not only by British rule, but also by rising Hindu nationalism. Indeed, the second appeared the more formidable of the two. There was antagonism between Moslems and British, but there was also mutual respect. There was a sense of comradeship between some Moslems and Hindus, a feeling that both were Indians and both opposed to foreign rule, yet there was also contempt by Moslems for Hindus as a community inferior to Islam, as people destined to be servants rather than masters. As the British authorities began to talk more seriously about self-government, the Moslem leaders began to fear that they would be dominated by Hindus.

The Indian National Congress, founded in 1885, was at first a moderate organization advocating parliamentary government for India. It included many Moslem members, and even some British. By the turn of the century, however, it began to acquire a more militant Hindu character, especially in Bengal. As a reaction against this trend, in 1906 a number of leading Moslems created the Moslem League. In the same year Moslem leaders asked the British Viceroy that when self-government institutions were set up in India there should be separate electorates for Moslems. This request was carried out in the Morley-Minto reforms of 1909. During the following thirty years Congress and the League co-operated with varying degrees of success. In 1937, under the Government of India Act passed by the British parliament in 1935, both parties contested the elections to provincial assemblies. Congress was extremely successful, but the League's following was disappointingly small. It hoped, however, that in those provinces of Hindu majority where there was a substantial Moslem minority, Congress would form coalition ministries with the League. Instead, Congress imposed unacceptable terms for League participation, and when these were refused it took into its ministries individual Moslems who were members of Congress, not of the League. From this time relations between Congress and the League rapidly deteriorated.

Congress maintained that it was making legitimate use of its constitutional majorities in seven provinces. It denied that it was a 'communal' organization representing only one religious community: on the contrary, it was a secular nationalist movement in which all Indians, whether Hindus or Moslems or believers of any other religion, could have their place. As far as its leaders were concerned, this could hardly be doubted. Mahatma Gandhi was a profoundly religious Hindu, but he was utterly devoted to the principle of religious toleration and had no intention of setting up a theocratic Hindu state. His closest collaborators were also tolerant men. The Moslem leaders, however, did not believe that the Hindu masses whom Congress represented were tolerant. Congress rule, they feared, would prove to be not secular but communal. Moreover, many Moslems did not in any case desire a secular form of government: they wished government to be based specifically on Moslem principles. From this point of view, of course, Congress rule was quite unacceptable. In any case the League leaders, whether they were themselves for secular or theocratic government, objected strongly to Congress's insistence that it too had Moslem members: they demanded that the League be recognized as the only true representative of the Indian Moslems. After the disappointment of 1937 the League's leader, Mohammed Ali Jinnah, who had previously favoured co-operation with Congress against the British, conducted a bitter campaign on the theme that Islam was in danger. It was extremely successful, and the League became, as never hitherto, a mass organization. Moslem public opinion showed itself more radically communal than the

Moslem leaders, who now put themselves clearly on its side. The climax came with the resolution of the League's Lahore meeting of February 1940, when it formally demanded an autonomous Moslem state in India. For this future state the name Pakistan, invented by a Moslem writer in 1933, was adopted.* Its territory was to include all the provinces in which Moslems were in a majority, and the whole area of each of them, even those—Punjab and Bengal—where the majority was slight. The leaders of Congress utterly opposed the claim. They insisted that there could not be two states or two nations in India, and repeated that the Moslems had nothing to fear from their movement, which was secular and nationalist and committed to religious toleration.

Congress in 1939 objected to the fact that India was considered to be at war with Germany without the Indian people having been consulted. In October the Congress provincial ministries resigned. A year later Gandhi launched a campaign of civil disobedience, which resulted in the arrest of most of the Congress leaders. The Moslem League did not formally support the war effort, but its leaders and organization in practice gave limited co-operation. The Indian Army, including both Moslem and Hindu soldiers, fought bravely on many fronts. The formation by the Japanese of an 'Indian National Army', recruited from Indian prisoners-of-war taken in Malaya, did not affect the loyalty of the army elsewhere. In April 1942 Sir Stafford Cripps visited India with constitutional proposals from Mr. Churchill's government for post-war India, which included the right of individual provinces to stay out of the Indian Union. This was too much for Congress, too little for the League, and was rejected by both. In August 1942 Congress called for 'a mass struggle on non-violent lines on the widest possible scale'. Its leaders, who had been released in 1941, were rearrested, and most of them were not again set free until the war was almost over.

When the Labour Party came to power in Britain, and the war with Japan ended, elections were held for provincial assemblies and a Central Assembly. The League won an overwhelming victory in the Moslem constituencies and the Congress elsewhere. It thus became clear that the League's claim to represent Indian Moslems was justified, and that the

* The word *Pakistan* was said by its author to be taken from the first letter of the names of five Moslem lands—Punjab, Afghania (meaning the North-West Frontier Province), Kashmir, Iran, Sind, Tukharistan (*sic*) and Afghanistan—and the last letter of a sixth—Baluchistan. The author, Choudhary Rahmat Ali, explained his conception of Pakistan in his book, *Pakistan, the Fatherland of the Pak Nation*, published 1935. In his words, it means 'the land of the Paks—the spiritually pure and clean. It symbolizes the religious beliefs and the ethnical stocks of our own people; and it stands for all the territorial constituents of our original Fatherland' (op. cit., 3rd edition, 1947, p. 225).

future of India would depend on the ability of the two great political movements to come to terms.

In March 1946 a mission of three British cabinet ministers came to India, and in May put forward its own proposals, which in effect allowed the predominantly Moslem provinces to form the nucleus of a Pakistan within an Indian Union. An Interim Government was to be formed of representatives of both parties. The League accepted the plan, but Congress refused. The League then expected that the Viceroy, Lord Wavell, would go ahead with the plan against the wish of Congress. When the Viceroy did not do this, but negotiated for the formation of an Interim Government on a basis that would give Congress a somewhat larger representation, Jinnah withdrew acceptance, and called for a campaign of 'direct action' to create Pakistan. When the League withdrew, Congress accepted, and a predominantly Hindu government was thus formed. Communal tension reached its climax, and there were massacres in Calcutta in which 4,000 people lost their lives. In the face of this horror, Jinnah decided in October to enter the Interim Government. But agreement was still far away.

The last phase was introduced by the declaration of Prime Minister Attlee, on 20 February 1947, that the British government would grant independence to India not later than June 1948, whether to a single Indian authority or to several. At the same time Lord Wavell was replaced as Viceroy by Lord Mountbatten. The new Viceroy found a bitterly divided central government, growing fanaticism in both communities, despair among civil officials and growing disintegration of the police. Only the army still maintained its discipline, and it was uncertain how long this would last. After further discussions, he decided that India must be divided, and Pakistan must be created. He did not, however, consider it just or possible that Pakistan should acquire the complete territory of all those provinces in which there were Moslem majorities: it should as far as possible be confined to districts of Moslem population. Therefore both Bengal and Punjab would have to be divided. Two Dominions of the British Commonwealth were to be created, Pakistan and the Union of India. This plan was accepted by the British government on 3 June, and the date for transfer of power was fixed as 15 August. Both Congress and the League agreed, and boundary commissions decided the frontiers in Punjab and Bengal.

The division of India was a tragedy. The accusation that the British brought it about by a machiavellian policy of 'divide and rule' is hardly supported by the facts. The British may have played off Hindus and Moslems in the nineteenth century, but in the twentieth the doctrinaire arguments of Congress and the religious fanaticism of the League were sufficient cause for the disaster. At no time after 1937 was Jinnah prepared to trust the Hindus, and Congress refused to compromise its formal right to govern the whole country as the majority party. Perhaps a secular democratic majority rule was ideally the best system, but it could not be imposed against the passionate feelings of 100 million Moslems. Even in June 1946 there might have been a Constituent Assembly for all India, acceptable to both communities, had not the Congress leader, Pandit Nehru, insisted on one more seat in the Interim Government for his party and on the overall supremacy of the central government over the provinces.

The praise so widely lavished on British evacuation, by commentators in America, Europe and Asia, is gratifying to British *amour propre*. But the immediate consequences can hardly be considered admirable. In Punjab, Moslems, Sikhs and Hindus massacred each other. Each side claimed that the other was responsible. However this may be, it is certain that about 500,000 people lost their lives and 12 million became homeless. Refugees set out in their thousands for the frontier, in carts or trains or on foot. At many places along the roads or railways they were ambushed and butchered, thousands being bestially tortured to death. The Indian and Pakistan governments tried to stop the slaughter, but in large areas they had no authority. The Congress leaders were undoubtedly horrified, above all Gandhi himself. But his appeals to his people to behave humanely did not produce quick results, and he himself was assassinated in January 1948 by a Hindu fanatic. The tragedy of India in its hour of triumph was indeed dramatically symbolized by the martyrdom of its greatest statesman and saint.

When British rule came to an end, British authority over all princely states also ended. They could theoretically become independent states, or join voluntarily with India or Pakistan. Mountbatten strongly advised them to choose the latter course. A dangerous crisis soon arose in Kashmir, in the north of the sub-continent, whose ruler was a Hindu, but the majority of whose subjects were Moslems. Moslems revolted in the Poonch district, and there were mass expulsions and slaughter of Moslems around Jammu city: in both cases reports of the Punjab horrors contributed to the outbreak of violence. In October 1947 tribesmen from the North-West Frontier poured into Kashmir, determined to defend the Moslem cause, and received at least some help from officials in Pakistan territory through which they passed. The Maharajah of Kashmir, having no adequate force of his own, then appealed to India for help. This was given on condition that he should declare the accession of the state of Kashmir to India. To this he agreed, and Indian troops then occupied most of

Kashmir, while Pakistan troops occupied a western strip. There was some local fighting between the two armies, until an armistice was arranged in January 1949 by a Commission appointed by the United Nations.

Neither then nor in the following years were the United Nations able to effect any agreed settlement. There was talk of a plebiscite, of an independent Kashmir, and of a partition between India and Pakistan. But in practice India maintained her possession by military force. The Indian government argued that the Maharajah was entitled to choose between India and Pakistan and had chosen India; that Kashmir had been invaded by aggressors from Pakistan against whom it was India's duty to defend it. The Pakistan government argued that the people of Kashmir had been given no chance to express their preference, and that the action of an unpopular autocratic prince could not be allowed to decide. Kashmir was also strategically important to Pakistan, since it contained the head-waters of three of the five great rivers that irrigate the West Punjab and Sind. The other two rivers rise in Indian territory. By annexing Kashmir, India would be able to control Pakistan's whole irrigation system and threaten her with economic ruin. These are sufficient grounds for any Pakistan government to be alarmed. But the conflict between Pakistan and India was enormously increased by the depth of popular feeling throughout Pakistan. No conceivable Pakistan government could agree to the new situation. Yet Pakistan was not strong enough to change it, and the United Nations could do nothing to help. Thus the two states have remained bitterly estranged.

The other large princely state, Hyderabad, with a population of 17 millions, had a Moslem ruler and a Hindu population, the exact opposite of the situation in Kashmir. But here too India won, using the argument of the rights of the majority which she had ignored when it was advanced by Pakistan in relation to Kashmir. In Telengana district the communists for a time set up their own state within the state, modelled on the 'liberated areas' of China or Yugoslavia during the revolutionary struggle in those countries. In September 1948 the Indian army moved in, took over Hyderabad and suppressed both the communists and the Moslem extremist guerrillas.

After the horrors and conflicts of 1947-8, however, India settled down to relatively stable government. The tragic fate of Gandhi did not weaken the young state: rather, it gave a salutary shock to leaders and people, showed them that they must curb their passions and unite for India's good. In Prime Minister Jawaharlal Nehru they had a great leader, and the machinery of government at the higher levels proved solid and efficient. The future of Pakistan looked much more uncertain. It consisted of two regions separated by more than 1,000 miles of Indian territory—the western provinces, with the capital, Karachi, and a population of 35 million, and East Bengal, with a population of 46 million. The people were united by Islam, but by little else. They could ill afford the loss of their outstanding leader, Jinnah, who died in September 1948.

SOUTH-EAST ASIA

The south-eastern peninsula of Asia consisted before the Second World War of one independent state—Siam or Thailand—and three colonial territories—Burma, Malaya and Indochina. The last three regions contained a number of different protectorates, sultanates and tribal areas. In recent years, in the current jargon of international politics, 'South-East Asia' has come to mean not only the peninsula, but also the islands stretching outwards from its coasts. The vast Indonesian Archipelago includes some British and Portuguese islands, or portions of islands, but by far the greater part of it belonged before 1941 to the Netherlands East Indies, now known as Indonesia. Beyond it lies the other great archipelago, the Philippines. Finally, the phrase is sometimes used to include Ceylon. Though adjacent to India, and separated by hundreds of miles from the south-eastern peninsula or archipelagos, Ceylon does have some of the characteristics and problems of the south-eastern countries. Its people belong to the same Buddhist civilization as those of the peninsula, and its status as a small, insecure state resembles that of the south-eastern lands rather than that of the giant India, of which it is far from being a satellite.

The peninsula and archipelago can be roughly divided into three cultural areas according to their religion. Ceylon, Burma, Siam and Indochina are Buddhist countries; Malaya and Indonesia are Moslem; and the Philippines are principally Christian and Catholic, owing their conversion to the same Spanish rule which made Catholics of the people of Central and South America. There are, however, numerous religious minorities scattered over the area. There are important foreign minorities of Chinese and Indians. The indigenous peoples themselves show an intricate variety of language and custom. Indeed in ethnical diversity the peninsula can bear comparison with the corresponding portion of Europe, the Balkan Peninsula, and the complexity of the archipelago is even greater.

During the Second World War Siam became an ally of Japan, and the remaining territories were overrun by Japanese armies. This was the second great victory of Asian over European armies in modern times, the first being Japan's defeat of Russia in 1905. Its effect on the minds of the south-eastern peoples was no less damaging to European prestige.

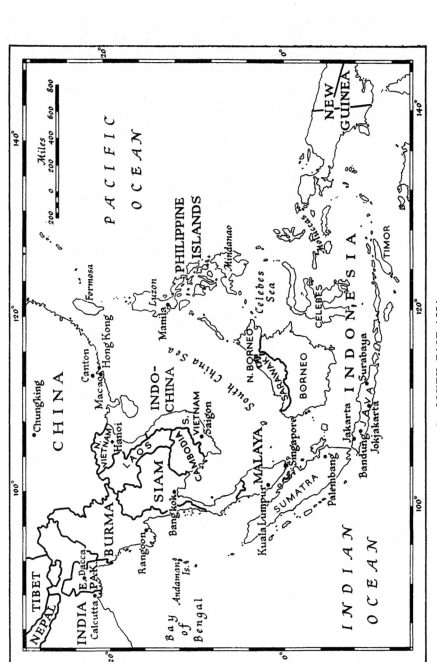

2 SOUTH-EAST ASIA

In the mood that followed victory, with the triumph of parties of the left in Britain and France and Australia, and with a strong tide of radical, anti-colonialist and internationalist idealism in the United States, it was inevitable that the governments of the returning Europeans should be well disposed to at least a wide measure of self-government for the south-eastern peoples. The strength of metropolitan idealism and colonial nationalism, the practical opportunities and obstacles, varied in the different territories, with different results.

The state of war between Siam and Britain was ended by a treaty signed in Singapore on 1 January 1946. In the first half of 1946 the chief political figure in Siam was Nai Pridi Panomyong, a man of left-wing views (in so far as such a term has meaning in the context of Siam, a country without modern political institutions or parties, and with very little popular interest in politics). Pridi had been the leader of Siamese resistance to the Japanese, and was on good terms with the Allies. His main rival, Marshal Pibul Songgram, who had ruled Siam in collaboration with the Japanese, was imprisoned for some months at the end of the war, but released in March 1946. He soon returned to politics, and in November 1947 he overthrew the government by a bloodless *coup d'état* and had himself made Commander-in-Chief. In April 1948 he made himself Premier. Pibul made efforts to atone for his pro-Japanese past by sedulously courting the Western Powers, especially the United States.

The Philippines had in 1935 adopted a constitution closely modelled on that of their protector, the United States, and were to become completely independent within ten years. When the period ended, the islands were in Japanese hands. Philippine soldiers had fought bravely beside Americans at Bataan, and Philippine guerrilla forces had resisted the Japanese rulers with some success. Once the invaders had been expelled and order restored, the American promise was kept. On 4 July 1946 the Philippine Republic became independent. At the same time the new republic concluded an alliance with the United States, and leased bases on its territory to its ally.

The British government had little difficulty in concluding an agreement with Ceylon, whose independence appeared a natural result of that of India. In February 1948 Ceylon became an independent member of the Commonwealth, without bloodshed or bitterness.

The case of Burma was more difficult. The most radical nationalists had collaborated with the Japanese, but in 1944 had made contact with the British South-East Asia Command and in the last stages of the war had resisted the Japanese. It was not clear whether they should be treated as accomplices of the defeated enemy or heroic anti-fascist liberators of their country. On the British side there was some disagreement between the former administration (both British and Burmese officials), who were, to say the least, sceptical of the Anti-Fascist People's Freedom League (AFPFL) led by Aung San, and Lord Mountbatten and his advisers, who believed that it must be accepted as the spokesman of the Burmese people. The second point of view prevailed. The British government agreed to allow a freely elected Burmese Constituent Assembly to decide between independence within or outside the Commonwealth. The Constituent Assembly was elected in April 1947, AFPFL had a large majority, and it decided to leave the Commonwealth. In July 1947 Aung San and six of his ministers were murdered by political opponents at a cabinet meeting, but neither the party nor the government broke up. The new Premier, U Nu, made the last arrangements with Britain, and Burma became an independent state on 4 January 1948.

In Malaya, Indonesia and Indochina no such precise agreements could be quickly reached. In Malaya there was no obvious authority to whom the British could hand power. In Indonesia the Dutch were unwilling to treat with those who presented themselves as nationalist leaders, and the task was complicated by the great diversity between the parts of the archipelago. In Indochina the theoretical differences between French left-wing conceptions of the future relations between France and the French Union and the Indochinese demand for independence were a serious obstacle to agreement, and the situation was further complicated by the opposition of local French officials and residents to nationalist aims. These three countries must therefore briefly be considered in turn.

We must, however, first mention one further factor which appeared in five of these countries immediately after the war—the increased strength of communism. The oldest communist party of the region was the Indonesian, which was founded in 1921 and had led an armed revolt in Java in 1926-7. During the Second World War communists played an important part in resistance to the Japanese in Malaya, the Philippines and Indochina. In Burma they were partly responsible for persuading Aung San in 1944 to abandon the Japanese cause. In the hour of victory the communists combined the demand for independence with insistence on the maintenance of the Great Power Alliance: British and Americans could not be denounced as complete enemies as long as they were the friends of the Soviet Union. The attitude changed slowly, less through Soviet pressure than from local conditions.[8] A markedly new phase, however, began all over South-East Asia in 1948, and it must be assumed that this was the result of a directive from Moscow. Everywhere insurrection was the aim. In Indochina this merely meant a continuation of the existing situation. But in Indonesia the communists rose at Madiun in September

1948, not so much against the Dutch as against the nationalist government. In Burma the communists rose in the summer. In Malaya an armed rebellion by the Chinese communists broke out in May. In the Philippines the communist-led resistance bands, the *Hukbalahap*, who still had arms, but had been fairly inactive since 1945, did their best to organize a large-scale rebellion. These actions coincided with the activities of the Indian communists in the Telengana district of Hyderabad state. The general communist line at this time was to treat the independence of India, Burma, Philippines and Ceylon as a sham, and to regard even the Indonesian nationalists with suspicion. Only the communists and those who followed their lead were recognized as true fighters for independence: only by exclusive reliance on the Soviet Union could true independence be won.

The special difficulty of a political solution in Malaya resulted from the diversity of its population. In 1947 Malaya had a population of 5,800,000, of whom 43% were Malays, 45% Chinese and 10% Indians. If the island of Singapore, with about 1 million inhabitants, almost wholly Chinese, were excluded, the Malays formed about half the population. Before the war Malaya consisted of nine protected Malay states, each under a Malay sultan, and three settlements directly ruled by Britain, one of which was Singapore. The British governor of the three settlements was at the same time high commissioner of the Malay states, in which his authority was wielded by a British resident attached to each of the sultans. The Malays, a people of farmers and fishermen, took little interest in politics, and were loyal subjects of their sultans. The Chinese were socially developed and politically conscious people, with an extremely cultured intelligentsia, rich business-men, small merchants, skilled workers and a large unskilled working class in industry and agriculture. Before the war Malaya produced more than half the world's rubber and nearly a third of its tin. Some of its mines and its plantations were among the most modern in the world.

The British Labour government of 1945 decided to simplify and centralize the Malayan political system and bring the country further along the road towards self-government. It proposed to create a single Malayan Union of the nine states and two of the settlements, leaving Singapore with its Chinese majority as a separate colony. In the new Union Chinese and Indians were to be able to acquire full citizenship. The plan was reluctantly accepted by the sultans, but strongly opposed by the politically minded Malay intelligentsia, which created the first Malay mass movement—the United Malay National Organization (UMNO). In the face of clear evidence that the Malay half of the population were utterly opposed to what it had intended as a measure of democratic progress, the

British government abandoned the Union plan. Instead, there was instituted in February 1948 a Federation of Malaya, in which the states were to have greater autonomy and it was to be much harder for Chinese to become citizens. It was estimated in 1949 that only some 375,000 Chinese out of a Chinese population in the Federation of nearly 2 million were citizens. Under the new régime UMNO was the strongest single political party, but in 1949 a Malayan Chinese Association (MCA) was formed to defend Chinese interests. It was led by spokesmen of the big Chinese business interests, and its policies were conservative. Malayan politics in fact were dominated by the 'communal' conflict between Chinese and Malays. But from the summer of 1948 all normal politics was pushed into the background by the communist insurrection.

In the Netherlands East Indies under Japanese rule several of the leading nationalist politicians of the pre-war era, mostly rather young members of the intelligentsia, had been allowed to hold subordinate political positions. The Japanese combined a certain sympathy for Indonesian aspirations with an imperialist arrogance of their own: the Indonesians admired Japanese achievements, and made use of Japanese aid, yet always aimed at independence for their own people. In August 1945 the nationalist leader, Ahmed Soekarno, with at least tacit Japanese consent, proclaimed an independent republic of Indonesia. When British troops landed in Java in September 1945 they found the Indonesian Republicans in control. Though the task of the British forces was to prepare the return of their Dutch allies, the British commander was obliged to enter into relations with the Republicans. The Dutch government considered that Soekarno and his colleagues were Japanese agents, traitors to the Netherlands and unrepresentative of the people of Indonesia. The Indonesian Republicans claimed to represent the people of the whole archipelago. Though their leaders sought to negotiate with both the British and the Dutch, extremist groups committed atrocities against Dutch civilians and British troops, and there was serious fighting in Surabaya in November 1945. The Soviet government also entered the scene by proposing to bring the action of British troops in Indonesia before the UN Security Council in February 1946. In Australia the Labour Party government showed sympathy for the Republicans, and Australian dockers refused to load Dutch ships. Early in 1946 fighting came to an end and negotiations opened between Dutch and Republican spokesmen, which led to a political agreement signed at Lingaddjati in November. This recognized the Republic as having authority over the islands of Java, Sumatra and Madura, which contained more than 80% of the population of the archipelago. The Republic was to be a unit in a larger Indonesian

Union which was in turn to be united with the Netherlands. The Indonesians had thus obtained less than independence and less than territorial unity. Their sovereignty within the area recognized as theirs was limited by the presence of large forces of well-armed Dutch troops. The last British forces left Indonesia in November 1946.

Four major political groups appeared in Republican territory. The Nationalist Party (PNI) derived its main support from the intelligentsia and minor government officials. Its real leader was Soekarno, though as President of the Republic he was supposed to be above party. His emotional oratory, very effective with the masses, was one of the party's main assets. PNI was not Marxist, but it made liberal use of left-wing slogans and rhetoric. The second important party was *Masjoemi*, whose political ideology was specifically based on Islam. It had the largest following among the peasants, who were by far the most numerous social class. Its leaders believed in modernization and democracy, but some were more conservative and some more inclined to sympathy with socialism. The third party was the socialist, which had pro-Western and pro-communist wings. The fourth was the communist party, whose exiled leaders returned to Indonesia during 1946.

From November 1945 to June 1947 the right-wing socialist leader, Sjahrir, was Premier of the Republican government. He was succeeded by the left-wing socialist, Sjarifoeddin. During the first half of 1947 it proved impossible for Dutch and Indonesians to agree on the formation of regional governments in the outer islands, or even on the definition of Republican territory. In July the Dutch army made a major attack on the Republicans (the 'first police action'). India and Australia brought a complaint before the UN Security Council, and a three-man Committee of Good Offices was sent to Indonesia. The compromise which it arranged, in January 1948, was accepted by Sjarifoeddin, but opposed by *Masjoemi* and PNI. The latter then formed a new government, but then accepted the agreement, while Sjarifoeddin now joined the communists and other smaller groups in a People's Democratic Front with an extreme anti-Western and pro-Soviet line. This phase reached its climax in the communist insurrection of September 1948 in Madiun. It was suppressed by the Republican army, and many of the communist leaders lost their lives.

The Republicans were, however, still unable to agree with the Dutch on the organization of a Federal Indonesian Government. In December 1948 the Dutch army launched another offensive (the 'second police action'). This time they captured the Republicans' capital of Jogjakarta and arrested the main Republican leaders. Again the UN Security Council intervened and appointed an UN Commission for Indonesia. As a result of its pressure, the Dutch evacuated Jogjakarta at the end of June 1949 and released the Republican leaders. In August negotiations began in The Hague between the Dutch and Republican governments. It had by now become clear that many of the leaders of the outer islands, whom the Dutch had hoped to balance against the Republicans, preferred to come to terms with the Republic. Agreement was achieved in November. The Dutch were to withdraw all troops and to transfer sovereignty to the United States of Indonesia, composed of the territory of the Republic and sixteen other states of the archipelago. The whole was to be linked with Holland in a Union whose head was to be the Queen of Holland. The transfer was made on 27 December 1949 in the capital of Java, the former Batavia, now renamed Djakarta. In practice the separate existence of the sixteen other states was short-lived. In August 1950 the trappings of federalism were abolished, and Indonesia was proclaimed a unitary state. The association with Holland was also a pure formality. Indonesia became a member of UN in September 1950, pursued policies quite distinct from those of Holland, and finally signed an agreement in The Hague in August 1954 formally dissolving the Union.

The Republicans had certainly showed themselves the strongest force in the archipelago. It is, however, doubtful whether, without the repeated intervention of the United Nations and the support received from the Asian countries, Australia and the United States, they could have prevailed against the Dutch.

In Indochina the Japanese had occupied strategic positions in July 1941 by agreement with the French government in Vichy. The liberation of metropolitan France in 1944 at first made no difference. It was not till March 1945 that the Japanese decided that they could no longer trust any French authority, and took over all power. They then proclaimed an independent state of Vietnam (the three provinces of Tonkin, Annam and Cochin China, inhabited mainly by Annamites or Vietnamese) under the Emperor of Annam, Bao Dai. During 1945 resistance to the Japanese was conducted partly by Frenchmen, some of whom already earlier had been in contact with General de Gaulle's Free French movement, and partly by Vietnamese. The most important Vietnamese group was the Vietminh, founded on Chinese territory in 1941 by the veteran communist, Ho Chi-minh. Vietminh was itself dominated by communists, but co-operated with non-communist nationalist groups which had Chinese Kuomintang support. When the Japanese surrendered in August 1945, Vietminh forces seized the capital of Tonkin, Hanoi, and soon became a force also in the southern province of Cochin China.

The Allied Powers had agreed that after the Japanese surrender, and until French forces could be brought in sufficient numbers, Indochina should be temporarily occupied by British and Chinese troops, the dividing line being the 16th Parallel. When the British forces landed at Saigon, capital of Cochin China, in September, they found the city controlled by Vietminh. In October substantial French forces arrived. By January 1946 the French, after some serious fighting, had established themselves firmly in Cochin China and southern Annam, and in March 1945, the last British troops were withdrawn. In the north the Chinese troops cooperated with the Vietnamese nationalists, but in fact favoured the non-communist groups at the expense of Vietminh.

The French were now masters of the south, but could clearly not impose their will in the north against the combined opposition of Vietminh and the Chinese. It was therefore to their interest to reach some agreement with Vietminh in order to get the Chinese out of Indochina. For his part, Ho Chi-minh feared Chinese aims, disliked the politics of the Kuomintang, had a certain personal love of France and French culture, and placed his hopes in the strength of the left in metropolitan French politics. Both sides therefore wished to agree, and on 6 March 1946 a settlement was reached. French troops were to be allowed to return to the north, and the Chinese therefore had no further grounds for remaining. At the same time the French recognized the Republic of Vietnam that had been created by the Vietminh, as a part of the Indochinese Federation and of the French Union. Political negotiations were to follow in France and in Indochina.

The crux of the negotiations, which filled the greater part of 1946, was the definition of Vietnam and of the Indochinese Federation. Both sides were agreed that Cambodia and Laos, whose people are not Vietnamese, should be separate members of the Federation.* But whereas the Vietminh negotiators maintained that the French by recognizing their republic in March had recognized its authority over all three of the Vietnamese provinces, the French argued that the republic did not extend to Cochin China, which should be a separate member of the Federation. In the south the French set up a Cochin Chinese administration opposed to Vietminh. Its claim to representative qualities was highly doubtful. More important was that there were substantial French business interests in Saigon and

---

* Cambodia in 1950 had a population of 4 million of whom 86·7% were Cambodians (Khmers). After a period of splendid civilization, based on the great city of Angkor, from the beginning of the ninth to the middle of the fifteenth century A.D., the Khmer kingdom disintegrated. The Khmers were originally Hindus, but later became Buddhists, and remain so today. The historical cultural links of Cambodia are with India, while those of Vietnam are with China. The kingdom of Laos had a population of 1,300,000 in 1950. Its people are closely related to the Siamese, and are also Buddhists.

in plantations in the area. The discussions in France failed to secure agreement. In November there was a serious clash between French and Vietminh forces at Haiphong in Tonkin, and on 19 December the Vietminh decided on a general insurrection, which began with a massacre of French civilians in Hanoi.

The subsequent war imposed an increasing burden on French economic and military resources. Unable to crush Vietminh, the French government made in May 1949 an agreement with the former Emperor and instrument of Japanese rule, Bao Dai. They recognized his authority over Cochin China as well as Tonkin and Annam, thus granting him the unity of the three Vietnamese provinces, the refusal of which had been the main cause of the breach with Vietminh. But measures to entrench French economic interests, and to ensure French control of Vietnamese foreign policy, meant that Bao Dai's state was to have very much less independence than a pre-1939 British dominion. There was little sign that Bao Dai could compete in popularity with Vietminh. At the end of 1949 Chinese communist forces reached the Tonkin border. From then onwards Vietminh received material aid, as the Greek communist rebels had received aid from the communist Balkan states. Within the Vietminh areas the supremacy of the communists became more marked. In January 1950 the Chinese and Soviet governments recognized Ho Chi-minh's régime as the government of Vietnam. The 'liberated areas' of Tonkin were ruled by a totalitarian régime, which liberally used terror and certainly aroused the hatred of many of its subjects. But it was also true that the Vietnamese communists, like the Yugoslav and Chinese communists in their heroic period, aroused much genuine enthusiasm, and enlisted in their struggle great reserves of natural ability and human effort which no previous leadership had tapped.

CHINA

China is second only to Egypt in the length of its existence as a state, and over the centuries Chinese cultural and political achievements have been more impressive than Egyptian. Like Turkey and Persia, China in the nineteenth century escaped the European conquest which subdued India and South-East Asia, but was unable to escape humiliation by Europeans through the policy of modernization so successfully adopted by Japan. Early revolutionary and reform movements failed, and the traditional autocracy survived at the expense of general political decay. The monarchy came to an end in 1911. It was succeeded not by democracy, but by a period of struggle between territorial military potentates ('war-lords'). The fact that China was ruled by generals rather than by civilian officials chosen through an examination system, as in the centuries of her greatness, was in itself a sign of degeneration. It might have been mitigated if any of them had been able or patriotic, but they were not.

The first revival came in the 1920s with the triumph of the Kuomintang. This movement, founded by Sun Yat-sen, stood at first for nationalism, modernization and democracy. There were, however, three reasons why it failed to do for China what Kemal Atatürk did for Turkey. Firstly, it had a dynamic rival on the left in the Communist party.[9] The Chinese communists at first co-operated closely with the Kuomintang, and were even admitted individually as members of it. There was, however, always some mutual mistrust, and after General Chiang Kai-shek became effective leader of the Kuomintang in 1926 this increased. Complete and violent breach between the two parties came in 1927. The communists retreated into the interior of China, and for the following ten years fought a civil war of varying intensity against the Kuomintang, who controlled most of China. The second reason for the Kuomintang's failure was that its victory of 1926-7, when its forces marched northward from Canton, was not as complete as it seemed. Having finally broken with the communists, and still uncertain of the attitude of foreign Powers to his régime, Chiang Kai-shek could not afford to pursue to the bitter end his conflict with the northern war-lords. In fact, a compromise was made. The war-lords recognized the Kuomintang government as the government of China, but a great deal of local administration remained in their hands. Thus the Kuomintang revolution stopped half-way, with many of the abuses of the past preserved. The third reason for Kuomintang failure was that in 1931 the Japanese attacked China in Manchuria, following this major invasion by a series of minor aggressions in the next years and resorting to large-scale war in 1937. The strain on material resources and skilled leadership for defence purposes prevented effective internal reforms. The Kuomintang lost most of its initial reforming fervour, and became little more than a coalition of vested interests, often intriguing against each other. At the highest level it had some able leaders, but lower down it was an inert and corrupt bureaucracy.

In 1937 the Chinese communists, following the 'popular front' adopted by the international communist movement in the face of fascism and of German-Japanese aggression, made its peace with Chiang Kai-shek. In the war against Japan which began in July, communist forces at first fought loyally in co-operation with Chiang's regular armies against the Japanese. But when the Soviet Union made treaties with Germany in 1939 and with Japan in 1941, the communists' anti-fascist fervour diminished. At the same time, Chiang began to fear the communists more than the Japanese, who now left him alone as long as his forces were confined to the internal provinces. Chiang was convinced that the United States and her allies would defeat Japan in the end: his preoccupation was to deal with his internal enemy. Thus both sides tended to concentrate their main forces against each other rather than against the enemy, and at times there was open fighting between communists and nationalists. The communists, however, were far more successful than their opponents in building up underground organizations in Japanese-held territory. By 1944 they controlled vast regions, organized as 'liberated areas' with a communist military and civil administration.

When the Second World War ended, there were thus two armed forces in China, looking for protection respectively to the United States and the Soviet Union. Chiang Kai-shek maintained that his was the legal Chinese government, but declared that when the communists had made it clear that they recognized his authority, and had placed their forces under his command, he would be glad to discuss political and social reforms. The communists demanded that the political system should be made more democratic before they gave up their separate power. Each side rightly distrusted the intentions of the other. The United States recognized Chiang's government as the spokesman of China, her military ally, but was strongly in favour of democratic reforms to satisfy the long-repressed wish for freedom and social justice of the whole Chinese people, which included communists. The Soviet government had its own connexions with the communists, and helped them substantially by allowing them to acquire a large part of the military equipment surrendered by the Japanese to the Soviet army in Manchuria. But the Soviet government also recognized Chiang as the head of the legitimate government of China, and was sceptical of the ability of the communists to attain power. This was clearly shown by the treaty which the Soviet government signed with Chiang Kai-shek in August 1945. China was thereby obliged to give the Soviet Union a half-share in the ownership of the Chinese Eastern and South Manchurian railways, now renamed 'Chinese Changchun Railway', and to lease to the Soviet Union the naval base of Port Arthur and the commercial port of Dairen. Essentially this amounted to a restoration of the privileges that Imperial Russia had had in Manchuria before its defeat by Japan in 1905. It was obvious that if the Soviet government found it necessary to make such unpleasant demands, suggesting an imperialistic outlook hardly in keeping with the international opinion of 1945, it expected the Chiang government, which it had long distrusted, to remain in power in China for some time. The Soviet authorities also robbed the Japanese-built factories in Manchuria of their machinery on a vast scale, thus denying them to a Chinese government which was expected to be no friend of the Soviet Union.

In August and September there were negotiations between the communists and Chiang in Chungking, but without precise results. The Soviet government agreed in November to allow Kuomintang troops to land at ports in the Gulf of Liaotung giving access to Manchuria. When they arrived, they found Chinese communist troops strongly entrenched and ready to prevent their disembarkment by force. The government forces had to be landed further south, and forced their way into Manchuria after hard fighting.

On 15 December 1945 President Truman announced that General Marshall was about to leave for China as his ambassador of goodwill, to try and bring the two warring factions to peace. His mission began with some successes. An armistice was concluded on 13 January 1946, a National Assembly was to be convoked in May, and an agreement was made on the proportion of communist to nationalist units to be included in the new national army. But the promise was not fulfilled by events. Both sides broke faith, and both tried to exploit Marshall for their own ends. Fighting broke out again in Manchuria. The National Assembly was not summoned until November 1946, and then met without communist representatives. Chiang's government ignored Marshall's advice. The communists bitterly denounced Marshall, and chose to interpret the fact that government troops were transported in American ships—under existing arrangements between wartime allies—as proof of American intervention in a Chinese civil war. In face of communist distrust and Kuomintang obstruction, Marshall was powerless. In January 1947 he gave up his mission.

By the end of 1946 government troops had occupied the main centres of Manchuria, and appeared to be in control of the rest of China too. But the countryside between the cities and the main lines of communication was mostly in communist hands. The communists made good use of guerrilla tactics and of propaganda, and by now they also had large stocks of modern weapons—Japanese, which the Russians had given them, and American, which they had acquired from nationalist prisoners and deserters. Throughout China discontent with the Kuomintang was growing, and the loyalty of the Kuomintang generals began to waver. At the end of 1948 the largest city of Manchuria, Mukden, surrendered after little resistance. In January 1949 the commanders of Peking and Tientsin handed their cities over to the communists without a fight. The communist armies then moved south to the Yangtse, and by the end of the year were in Canton. The last stages of the communist advance were a triumphal parade, not a military campaign. The people welcomed the communists, because they were utterly sick of the old régime and hoped that the new rulers would be better. The intelligentsia, which by tradition had greater prestige and influence in Chinese than in most other societies, was for the most part attracted by the democratic and revolutionary slogans of communist propaganda. Many students and former graduates had served in the communist armies, and some had entered the cadres of the communist party and state machines. As for the Kuomintang bureaucrats, corruption, fear and consciousness of their own unpopularity utterly demoralized them. They had lost the ability to give orders, no less than their subjects had lost the will to obey.

The victory of communism in China was the most important event in world history after the defeat of Hitler and Japan. The whole balance of power in the world, and especially in Asia, was transformed. The victory was also a tremendous defeat for the United States.

It is, of course, not true that America had been engaged in the Chinese civil war. The American government had drifted into a certain material support for one of the belligerent parties because it had been America's ally for years and was believed to be entitled to some help. The situation was very similar to that of France and Britain in regard to the Russian civil war of 1918-20. In neither case did these governments pursue an ideological war against communism. If the resources of France and Britain in 1918, or of America in 1945, had been thrown into support of the enemies of communism on a massive scale, there could have been no communist victory. But in both cases the main concern of the Western nations was to demobilize their armies and get back to peacetime life. Moreover, public opinion in the West on both occasions was hardly less hostile to the White military dictators (Denikin or Chiang) than to the communists. On both occasions it would have been wiser for the Western Powers either to do nothing or to do much more.

But if it is untrue that America had fought the Chinese communists, and therefore untrue that the communists had beaten the United States, this is undoubtedly what the communists themselves felt. They launched a mass campaign of hatred against America, interpreting the history of China in the nineteenth and twentieth centuries in such a way as to make America the principal aggressor and oppressor of China. This grotesque distortion was especially painful to those many Americans who as missionaries or educators had given many of their best years to serving the people of China. In the anti-American campaign of the new Chinese régime American public opinion first experienced something to which the British and French have long been accustomed—hatred, lies and insults from those whom they had benefited. This was America's first lesson in the unpleasant truth that powerful nations are often hated not so much for their crimes as for their virtues.

It was not surprising that the United States government could not in 1949 bring itself to recognize Mao Tse-tung's régime as the government of China, and that it was far from pleased when the British government did so. The British decision was influenced partly by fear for the island of Hong Kong and partly by a desire to please the Indian government, but was also based on the general principles that one must recognize facts of international power even if one does not approve of them, and that China was too great a country ever to be a mere satellite of Russia. There was much to be said for the British arguments, and the British hope of slowly creating tolerable relations with the new China might perhaps have achieved results if peace had been preserved. But on 25 June 1950 war broke out in Korea.

THE KOREAN WAR

Korea, which at the end of the nineteenth century was the object of a three-cornered struggle between Japan, China and Russia, had been annexed by Japan in 1910. It was agreed in 1945 that it should become independent again, and that it should be temporarily occupied by Soviet forces in the north and by American in the south, the boundary being the 38th Parallel. Neither negotiations between the American and Soviet occupation authorities nor discussions by the UN General Assembly had been able to bring about a unified Korean government. As in Germany, the two zones developed on mutually incompatible principles. In the North a communist-controlled 'popular democratic' régime was created, while in the South was a government responsible to an elected parliament, led by the veteran Korean nationalist, Syngman Rhee. At the end of 1948 Soviet troops were withdrawn, leaving a well-equipped and politically indoctrinated Korean communist army and police. In the summer of 1949 American troops were withdrawn from the South.

The extent of Soviet responsibility for the North Korean aggression of June 1950, and the aims of Soviet policy, cannot be known until official documents are available. The action was, however, well prepared, and the greatly superior North Korean army swept its South Korean opponents before it. On 27 June President Truman decided to oppose the aggression with American armed force, and the Security Council of UN, freed from the Soviet veto by the absence of the Soviet delegate, passed a resolution that members of UN should furnish assistance to South Korea. The UN military effort in Korea was primarily American, though the British

Commonwealth and Turkey also contributed substantial forces. The retreat of the South Koreans was halted, and in October UN forces moved north of the 38th Parallel. The aim was now not only to save South Korea from aggression, but to unify Korea under a democratic government.

The Chinese communist government had issued, through the Indian Ambassador in Peking, Sardar Panikkar, a guarded warning to the United States that China could not remain neutral if the 38th Parallel were crossed.[10] In November large-scale Chinese intervention began, in the form of so-called 'volunteers'. At the beginning of 1951 the UN forces were driven back, but eventually a more or less static front was established close to the 38th Parallel. The communist forces were able to build up supplies safely behind the Yalu river, on Chinese territory. General MacArthur rightly pointed out that he could not win the war with his 'hands tied', and argued that if he were authorized to bomb Manchurian cities and supply lines he could obtain a complete victory. President Truman was not prepared to assume the consequent risk of an extension of the war, should China then invoke the treaty of alliance which she had signed with the Soviet Union in February 1950. He therefore relieved General MacArthur of his command of the UN forces and of the United States occupation forces in Japan. The stalemate continued, while truce talks, opened in July 1951, were protracted without result.

The Korean War had far-reaching effects. It created a general fear of world war, and accelerated the process of alliance-making in Europe. It created an economic boom, greatly helping the economic recovery of Japan, Germany and the Western industrial nations but at the cost of increasing the trend to inflation almost everywhere. In the United States it intensified the mounting dismay at communist foreign policy and created an almost hysterical fear of communist subversion, which was exploited by the sinister Senator Joseph McCarthy, and in turn created in the rest of the world the image of an America moving towards fascism. America's West European allies were alarmed by her Far-Eastern policies, and a large part of American public opinion felt that the European allies were ungrateful and disloyal. Relations between the United States and the independent non-communist countries of Asia, especially India, also deteriorated. India had at first approved UN action against North Korea, but Chinese intervention had raised fears for Indian security and also created the impression that the war was now no longer between law and aggression, but between Europeans and Asians. When the issue was put in this light, Indian and South-East Asian sympathies switched. Whereas until 1951 the leaders of these nations had considered the Soviet Union a greater menace to peace than the Western Powers, they now professed to see the main danger in American militarism. There was also much talk of American preference for 'reactionary' régimes in Asia, of which Chiang Kai-shek and Syngman Rhee were considered examples. The decision of President Truman to guard with American naval forces the island of Formosa, on which Chiang had set up his government, with the remnants of his army, when he had left continental China in 1949, was regarded as an unjustifiable intervention by the United States in an internal Chinese conflict.

In China itself the Korean War led to an increase of totalitarian pressures. At various times in their history the communist leaders had practised various forms of terror. In 1946 in Manchuria their land reform had been accompanied by mass public executions and public torture of opponents denounced as 'landlords'. But in 1949, though they had introduced a form of government based on the Soviet model and assuring a complete monopoly of power to the communist party, they had treated the non-communist population mildly, even with courtesy. They had emphasized that there was an honourable place in the new China for the old intelligentsia, and even for business-men (except for those who had had close connexions with the Chiang régime and were dubbed 'bureaucratic capitalists'). But the Korean War brought an end to such liberal policies. Xenophobia and spy-mania reached a hysterical pitch. All business-men, Chinese and foreign, were treated as potentially disloyal. Foreigners suffered little more than obstruction and insults, but Chinese were robbed of most of their possessions, many were arrested, driven to suicide or executed. Two mass campaigns of denunciation, known as the 'Three Anti' and the 'Five Anti', set in motion a wave of denunciations and a vast hunt for scapegoats among business-people and non-communist government officials.[11] The honeymoon between communists and intelligentsia also came to an end, and the latter were subjected to a painful process of brain-washing,[12] with long public meetings of criticism and self-criticism, confession and self-abasement, designed to kill all inclination to independent thought and to re-educate the intellectuals in the Thought of Mao Tse-tung. China was moving to full totalitarianism at a faster pace than the Russia of the 1930s.

The essential trends, which emerge from the events which we have briefly surveyed in the previous chapters, are the conflict between the Soviet Union and the Western Powers in Europe; the growth of nationalist movements in the Arab lands and Asia, some though not all of which had won power by 1953; and the victory of totalitarianism in China.

We must now examine totalitarianism and nationalism more closely before we take up again the story of international conflict, in the years since the death of Stalin.

Both totalitarianism and nationalism are revolutionary forces, and derive their strength from revolutionary conflicts, between class and class and between nation and nation. We shall therefore begin by discussing the two main forms of class conflict which are to be found, whether clearly evident or only latent, in most parts of the world. The first of these is the conflict between peasants and other classes, for control of the land and the wealth derived from it. This is characteristic of agrarian or 'underdeveloped' rather than of advanced industrial and urban societies. In this conflict the opponent of the peasant may be a landowning upper class or a government bureaucracy, and the latter may be of a traditionalist or a revolutionary type (for example, Imperial Russia or Soviet Russia). The second conflict is between industrial workers and the upper classes of urban society. This conflict takes different forms in three types of society, which we must examine separately—the advanced industrial, the underdeveloped and the Soviet. In each case it is necessary to discuss not only the opportunities of political struggle available to the working class, but also the nature of the urban upper classes, which are very different in the three types of society. We next must examine a distinct social group, which in the present century has provided the leadership for most revolutionary movements—the intelligentsia. Though the importance of men of ideas in such movements has long been recognized, the significance of the intelligentsia as a social group has not been sufficiently studied, except by historians of Russia. But the phenomenon is in no way specifically Russian: it is of the greatest importance for all underdeveloped societies. Finally, we examine the problem of revolutionary seizure of power, in the light of the most important revolutions of this century. Throughout this second part of the book, we have not hesitated to take examples from nineteenth-century history of Western Europe, Russia, Japan or other countries where we felt that they threw light on contemporary problems; and in introducing the main social groups and classes in each chapter we have found it necessary to make occasional references to still earlier historical periods.

From the discussion of revolutionary forces we proceed to an examination of the nature of totalitarian power, with special reference to the Soviet Union and Nazi Germany. Here too we have to consider to some extent the historical record of the two régimes in the period before the Second World War. We must also consider certain historical factors, from a much more distant past, which appear to favour the rise of totalitarianism. It is also necessary to devote some space to the definition of totalitarianism, to the features which distinguish it not only from liberal democracy, but also from dictatorships of the classical type. This part of the book ends with a discussion of the weaknesses of totalitarianism, of its attractions for free societies, and of its relationship to foreign policy.

In the fourth part we examine nationalism and imperialism. Under this heading we include all forms of domination by one nation over another, and of struggle by one nation to free itself from the rule of another. Thus, in the contemporary world, we must consider not only the surviving European colonies, most of which are in Africa, but also the Soviet colonial empire in Europe and Asia; various examples of national domination, or attempts to impose domination, by Asians over other Asians; the situation of the American Indians in North and South America; and the two main examples of racial discrimination at the expense of Africans—*apartheid* in South Africa and the negro problem in the United States. After this we resume the narrative in Europe, the Arab lands and Asia, and also add a chapter on Latin America. The last chapter of the book is concerned in general terms with problems facing Western policy at the end of the 1950s.

Part Two
Forces of Revolution

4: Land and Peasants

Agriculture—including livestock farming, forestry and fishing—is the basic human activity, on which all others depend. Until the nineteenth century the overwhelming majority of the human race were farmers. The Industrial Revolution, with its concentration of people in huge cities, beginning in England and spreading over the earth, has changed this. Yet even to-day three-fifths of the human race are in agriculture. An estimate of 1949 showed 1,285 million persons, out of a world total of 2,177 millions, as agricultural population.[13] The proportion varied widely according to regions. In North America it was only one-fifth, in Europe and Oceania one-third, in Central and South America two-thirds, in Asia 70% and in Africa 74%.

Though both agricultural and industrial labour involve toil and sweat, and both produce things that support or enrich human life, they differ fundamentally from each other. To work in open fields, to tend flocks among the mountains, or to spread the nets for fish at sea is not the same as to work under discipline in a factory. It may or may not be physically or morally better, more or less exhausting, better or worse paid: it is in any case different. It also produces different attitudes of mind. The farmer is both more individualist than the worker and more conscious of group loyalties and traditions. He has to make his own decisions, where the worker is given a precise job to do. But while the worker is looked after by a vast impersonal organization, by the factory management while he is at work and by municipal and commercial services when he is at home, the farmer is dependent on his neighbours, requires their help and goodwill, and gives them his. These factors, of course, vary according to the material position of the farmer and the degree of organization of the city: New York has more varied services to offer its citizens than Djakarta. However, the general difference is valid.

Political and social ideas have almost always originated in cities. Until very recent times the great majority of farm workers lived in poverty and discomfort, even in Western Europe and North America. But economic hardships alone did not usually create a sense of injustice. The existing order, with its recognized obligations and social relationships, was accepted as a part of the human condition. Injustice was felt, and discontent expressed, often in violent form, when the recognized obligations were broken, when, for example, a nobleman or a monarch demanded more than the customary services, or failed to give the protection that was due to his subjects or his serfs. Peasant risings in medieval Europe, in nineteenth-century Russia, or in Asia, if they were not caused by religious movements, or patriotic reactions against foreign rule, were normally protests against social injustices committed within an accepted framework. The idea that the framework itself was wrong, that the social and economic system was antiquated and unjust, and must be replaced by something new, did not originate with the farmers. It came from the cities, where it was thought out by the men of learning or semi-learning. The spread of radical ideas from the city to the scattered villages of the countryside has encountered great physical obstacles, but these have been diminished by the cinema, wireless and television. The process has been much quicker in the twentieth century in Asia and Africa than it was in earlier centuries in Europe, where the growth and diffusion of political ideas preceded modern technical inventions, and required hundreds of years.

AGRARIAN AND INDUSTRIAL SOCIETIES

It will be useful at this stage to divide present-day human societies into three general categories.

The first is the predominantly urban and industrial. Here the majority of the population is not engaged in agriculture, and those who remain on the land are profoundly influenced by urban civilization. The proportion engaged in agriculture may vary considerably. Approximately comparable figures for the four main countries of this type in the 1950s show the percentage of the labour force engaged in agriculture as 29% in France, 23% in Western Germany, 12% in the United States and 7% in Great Britain.[14] Nevertheless, all four countries, and all others that belong to this category, are alike in that there is one single culture, essentially urban, which prevails throughout the whole society. Its main features are mass industrial production, standardized consumer tastes and universal elementary education, with a large and growing proportion of children (including many country children) going on to secondary schools. Of course the differences between urban and rural ways of life remain, and town and country people feel different from and in some ways superior to each other. Yet the differences are less important than the similarities. To this category of societies belong, apart from the four countries mentioned above, all those of northern Europe, together with Canada, Australia and New Zealand. To these may be added the Czech provinces of Czechoslovakia, northern Italy, north and north-eastern Spain, Argentine and Uruguay.* Japan should also be included in this category. The fact that

* The following percentages of the population living in urban areas are of interest. It should be noted that the non-urban portion includes persons whose occupation is not agriculture: Australia (1946), 69% urban; New Zealand (1950), 61%; Canada (1950), 57%; Argentine (1946), 63%; Spain (1950), 61%.

the cultural values of the Japanese village are very different from those of Western urban society should not obscure the fact that they are becoming ever less different from those of Japanese urban society, which, of course, are also very different from those of Western urban society. We are here concerned not with general differences between cultures, but solely with the degree of urbanization.

The second category of societies is the overwhelmingly rural. Here not only is a large majority engaged in agriculture, but the rural way of life is dominant in the society as a whole. There are cities, some of which may be extremely old: Cairo and Kyoto are nearly as old as London and Paris, and Damascus is older than Athens or Rome. But the cities have been administrative and cultural rather than industrial centres. In the twentieth century modern industry has spread to virtually every land on earth. But in the overwhelmingly rural societies, industry still plays only a relatively minor role, and the spread of urban influences to the villages is prevented by poor means of transportation, illiteracy and the paucity of schools. It is only when most rural children go for at least several years to elementary school that the single urban culture penetrates to the village, and only when the first generation of these children has reached middle age that its triumph is complete. Admittedly the process can be, and is being, shortened by the use of cinema and television. To this category belong the whole of Asia except Japan, all Africa except the Union of South Africa, and most of the republics of Central and South America.

The third category consists of societies in which there is a certain balance between urban and rural culture, with the former gaining ground, but not definitely predominant. Industry is well developed. The urban population, which is about half the whole, has modern urban habits of consumption and is served by modern means of communication. Urban children go to school, and schools have begun to spread on a considerable scale to the countryside. But the rural way of life still exists, separate from the urban. There are two societies, almost two nations, side by side. This category is transitional, between the second and the first categories, but it is distinct from either, and deserves study on its own. It is in this category of society, in the present-day world, that social and political conflicts are particularly acute. To it belong most of southern and eastern Europe—both the non-communist regions (southern Italy, southern Spain and Greece) and the communist-ruled 'popular democracies' from Poland to Bulgaria. To this category also belongs the Soviet Union. Here a highly developed industrial and urban civilization, capable of the highest scientific and technical achievements, coexists with a backward agriculture in which many million peasants live in material conditions little if at all better than those of peasants under the last Tsar. Yet another example is the Union of South Africa, where the division between the urban and rural societies cuts across, but does not exactly coincide with, that between the races. The white population enjoys a standard of living comparable to that of the United States—if city-dwellers be compared with American city-dwellers and white farmers with American farmers—but the black majority lives in insecurity and squalor. The white community is not a mere tiny ruling caste: it amounts to nearly a quarter of the total population, and it has no other country but South Africa. There are two separate societies, the European and the Bantu, with large minority groups—Cape Coloured and Indian—placed somewhere between the two, and both suffering from their own forms of insecurity. Possibly Brazil should also be placed in this category. This vast country, with more than 60 million inhabitants, is a complex mixture of urban and rural, European and Indian and negro communities, which no simple formula will describe.

If these three categories, which we shall call 'predominantly urban', 'predominantly rural' and 'mixed industrial-agrarian', exist and can be reasonably easily distinguished, it is also sometimes the case that more than one category is found within one state's frontiers. An obvious example in Europe is Italy. The North belongs without doubt to the first category, the South and the islands to the third, the two merging imperceptibly into each other in the area from Rome north-eastwards. In different provinces of Spain any of the three categories may be found. In Czechoslovakia, the western provinces belong to the first, Slovakia to the third. In Yugoslavia between the wars Croatia and Serbia were mixed industrial-agrarian societies, while Bosnia, Montenegro and Macedonia were predominantly agrarian and Slovenia predominantly urban. Since the Second World War there have been far-reaching changes in both these countries, but the differences have not entirely disappeared. Even the United States has enclaves in its territory. If the greater part of the country is the outstanding example in the world of a predominantly urban society, it is still true that a large part of the population of the former Confederate States—perhaps a third or more of their 40 million inhabitants—live in a mixed industrial-agrarian society of a rather backward type. It is misleading to think of the agricultural population of the United States in terms of the prosperous Iowa farmer, and to forget the negro share-cropper of Mississippi. And the Indians of the South-West live in a still more backward society, that should probably be placed in the predominantly rural category.

'ADVANCED' AND 'UNDERDEVELOPED' SOCIETIES

The phrases 'underdeveloped society', or 'underdeveloped country', have become widely used since the Second World War. All too often 'underdeveloped' is merely an euphemism for 'backward', a word whose use is avoided in the rather naïf desire not to offend Asians or Africans. But the phrase can be a valuable one, as it describes a real phenomenon. In order to avoid confusion, it will be well at this point to explain in what sense it will be used in the rest of the present work.

The word 'underdeveloped' implies that development is taking place. Applied to a country in the physical sense, it means that there are resources which have not yet been fully exploited. In this sense, Australia is an underdeveloped country, though its society is certainly of the predominantly urban type. Applied to a society, 'underdeveloped' means that it is developing in a direction, but that it has still a long way to go. The whole trend of human society throughout the world in the last 100 years has been in the direction of industrialization, urbanization and the creation of a mass secular culture. This trend one may applaud or regret, but it cannot be denied that it exists. In this context, the most meaningful use of the phrase 'underdeveloped society' is to denote a society that is becoming industrialized, urbanized and secularized, but in these respects still lags behind the most advanced. Such societies are not 'backward', a word which implies a static condition. They are, indeed, anything but static: their movement is in many cases much faster than was that of European societies in the industrial revolution of the eighteenth and nineteenth centuries. The condition of 'underdevelopment' is in no way shameful, though it is usually uncomfortable. Nor does the distinction between 'advanced' and 'underdeveloped' societies imply any notion of spiritual, ethical or cultural inferiority. For a believer, a religious society, whether Christian or Mohammedan or Buddhist, is superior to a secular society, even if the latter pays higher wages and manufactures more refrigerators. The ethical practices of employers in nineteenth-century Manchester or twentieth-century Sverdlovsk or Calcutta are not markedly superior to those of feudal lords in the reign of Saint Louis. Neither Houston (Texas) nor Novosibirsk can rival the artistic achievement of Luxor or Angkor.

In the rest of the present work the two phrases 'advanced industrial society' and 'underdeveloped society' will be often used. The first corresponds to the first of the three categories discussed earlier—the predominantly industrial. The second corresponds to the second category—the predominantly rural—in so far as the impact of modern economic forces has been felt and change is taking place. There may still be remote regions in Africa and South America where there are static rural societies untouched by modern forces. If so, they are perhaps lucky, but they are certainly few and dwindling. To some extent 'underdeveloped society' covers societies of the third category—the mixed industrial-agrarian—at least those which are on the margin between the second and third. Brazil, Greece and Bulgaria, for example, may be considered 'underdeveloped', but hardly Poland or the Soviet Union. In any case, it should be clear that these are not precisely defined divisions: rather, they are rough groupings intended to assist analysis, to reduce the area of error and obscurity, but hardly completely to eliminate it. It should also be clear that 'underdevelopment' is here treated as a characteristic not of countries (a geographical notion), nor of states (a political notion), but of societies; and that it refers only to the limited field of economic and social development, to the processes of industrialization and urbanization, without moral or aesthetic judgement.

TYPES OF AGRICULTURE

The advanced industrial societies are rich, the underdeveloped societies poor. This is true of the output and consumption not only of industrial goods, but also of agricultural produce. Of a world output of wheat, excluding the Soviet Union, of 157 million metric tons in 1955, nearly half (70 million) was produced by six advanced countries—the United States, Canada, France, Australia, Argentine and Italy.[15] Of a total output of maize for the same area and year of 146 million metric tons, 82 million (56%) was produced by the United States alone.

Another indication of agricultural poverty and low output is consumption of artificial fertilizers. The total consumption, in millions of metric tons, of three types of fertilizers in six countries is given below, for the year 1955-6:[16]

	U.S.A.	Western Germany	Japan	France	Egypt	Turkey
Phosphates	2,214	467	324	628	15	8
Nitrogen	2,093	470	562	381	112	6
Potash	1,994	839	383	581	0·5	0·6

Consumption of foodstuffs is another indication. Information from many of the poorest countries is extremely inadequate: lack of reliable statistics is, of course, an important feature of 'underdevelopment'. It is, however, a matter of observation that the diet of peasants in Asia, Africa and Latin America consists almost solely of cereals of some sort—rice, maize, millet or beans. Little meat or milk is consumed. The following figures from the 1950s are revealing:[17]

Consumption, in kilograms per head per year

	Sugar	Meat	Milk
U.S.A.	40	81	236
Sweden	41	51	295
Britain	46	66	202
France	24	75	167
Japan	11	3	11
Greece	11	16	90
Brazil	33	27	—
India	14	1	44
Egypt	13	11	55
Turkey	9	16	30
South Africa	37	43	88

Not too much should be deduced from these figures. The South African totals are comparatively high because the high standard of living of the Europeans counterbalances the low average of the Bantu. The Japanese diet of rice and fish, though unattractive to Europeans and Americans, has enabled them to achieve high standards both of physical fitness and of industrial and agricultural skill. Nevertheless, the contrasts are eloquent, especially with regard to the poor European country, Greece, and the East Mediterranean countries, Turkey and Egypt.

Low consumption is due to low output per head, but this is not necessarily a result of inefficiency. The peasants of Egypt, China and India have been for centuries extremely industrious and skilful. One should distinguish not only between intensive and extensive methods of cultivation, but between labour-intensive and capital-intensive methods. In the first case, land and machinery are scarce, but human labour is abundant: such is the case in the great river valleys of Asia, and to a somewhat lesser degree in the Balkans or Italy. In the second case there are relatively few cultivators, and each is well supplied with machinery and has a large area to cultivate: such is the farmland of the American Middle West. Higher incomes are earned by capital-intensive methods, but labour-intensive agriculture can be prosperous, provided that the level of skill is high and the pressure of population on resources is not too heavy. Eastern Europe between the world wars provided examples of the misery of labour-intensive agriculture with low levels of skill and heavy population pressure. One figure will illustrate it. In Denmark in the 1930s there were 36 persons engaged in agriculture per square kilometre of arable land, in Yugoslavia 157, while the output of wheat in quintals per hectare was 23 in Denmark and 11 in Yugoslavia. Thus in Denmark on a given unit of land four times fewer persons produced twice as much wheat as in Yugoslavia. Here at least it was possible to argue that there was room for progress, since the introduction of better methods could yield higher outputs even with existing population pressure: the situation was worse in some Asian rice-growing countries, or in Egypt, where extremely high output had already been attained, no further improvement could be hoped for, and population pressure continued.

TYPES OF OWNERSHIP

The economic problems of agriculture form one group of causes of social unrest in agrarian societies. Another group of causes arise from problems of ownership of land. Some general remarks are necessary here on the main types of land tenure.

Among primitive peoples some form of tribal organization is frequently found, especially among nomadic pastoral communities, but also among sedentary cultivators. The herds, or the arable land, are not the absolute property of any individual, but belong to the tribe. Individual families have the use of them for a time, and in return perform obligations, of service or material tribute or both, to the head of the tribe or to his subordinates. There has been an enormous variety of tribal or clan organizations in human history, including the history of Europe. Tribal societies are still strongly established in parts of Arabia, Persia, tropical Africa and elsewhere. They are weakened, and in time dissolved, by the impact of a money economy from outside—for example, if the tribal chiefs discover that they will gain by claiming tribal lands as their own property and selling their produce in a wider market, or if great numbers of tribesmen are driven to earn a living as migratory labourers in distant regions with a different social organization. This process of disintegration of tribal society is proceeding at present in Central and Southern Africa, bringing with it many social strains and political unrest.

Another type of organization is that of large landed estates, belonging to individual rich landowners, partly leased to small tenants and partly worked by agricultural labourers. Large estates exist in many forms in many parts of the world, and have played an important part at some stage in the history of almost every nation. In most of Europe until the nineteenth century there was a landed aristocracy, including great magnates and materially more modest gentry, ancient families and descendants of upstart favourites of monarchs or of merchants who had sought respectability in land. In Poland and Hungary until the Second World War, and in Spain and some parts of Italy to the present day, there were or are aristocratic landowners enjoying both great wealth and great power.

In England and Scotland some aristocratic families are still rich and still have social prestige, but they can hardly be said to have much power, and their riches are inexorably mopped up by the tax-collector. In Asia frequent changes of dynasty and the jealousy of emperors and sultans prevented hereditary aristocracies from keeping the same lands for many centuries. Laws and customs of inheritance also operated against it. However, there have been and are great landed properties in Asia. In some cases they result from arbitrary application by European rulers of European principles. In India, for example, the tax-farmers, who bought from the Mogul emperors the right to levy taxes in a region for a sum in cash, and recouped themselves at the expense of the population, were recognized by the British authorities as owners of the lands from which they collected. This is the origin of the *zamindar* estates. In Iraq, as late as the 1930s, tribal *sheikhs*, profiting from the legal system introduced under the British Mandate, were appropriating to themselves the lands of their tribes. In Spanish America *conquistadores* and their descendants carved for themselves great territories. After the colonies became independent states, many of these properties changed hands. But in Peru, Chile and other countries of the sub-continent enormous landed estates still exist, even if most of their owners are no longer persons of impeccable aristocratic or military origin. In the southern states of the United States a landowning class grew up, based on slave labour until the Civil War. Even if, with a few exceptions in Virginia, their owners were of less noble blood than they would have liked to be thought, they did their best to adopt the manners of an European aristocracy, and though land has often changed hands and successive waves of *nouveaux riches* have replaced each other, something of this tradition, with some of the real virtues of its European prototype, still survives. Yet another type of large estate is ecclesiastical property. The Catholic and Orthodox Churches once possessed great fortunes in land in Europe, but little now remains, even in Spain. In Moslem countries *wakfs* still exist, and in the Far East there are rich Buddhist monasteries, though neither of these very closely correspond to Church lands in Christian countries.

Some great estates have been and are economically efficient, and have made or make contributions to the development of agricultural technique. Improving landlords in nineteenth-century Northern Europe, including even Russia, thus performed a useful social function. This has seldom been the case in Asia. Persian and Iraqi landowners in recent years have mostly been content to live luxuriously on their rents, spending them largely in the cities or abroad, little concerned with the quality of the land, provided that its revenues satisfy their expensive tastes. A contrast is provided by certain newly rich Syrian landowners who since the Second World War have shown remarkable gifts for private enterprise, creating new wealth in almost unused land, making fortunes for themselves, but benefiting the whole economy too.[18] But on the whole in Asia and Latin America the nearest approach to efficient capitalist enterprise in large landed property is the plantation, usually though not always owned by foreign business, employing a large labour force for wages and developing by modern methods some specialized local resource—fruit or rubber or tea or the like. The improving landlord and the plantation are economically progressive, where the absentee landlord is a 'fetter on production'. But it does not necessarily follow that the persons employed by or dependent on the former enjoy better material conditions than those of the latter. Conditions will depend on the state of the local labour market, the level of skill and education, and political circumstances. Certainly the million and a half wage-labourers and estate servants employed by Hungarian great estates up to 1945 and the workers employed on many plantations in Ceylon or Java or Peru were or still are a fairly wretched proletariat.

Most large landed properties other than plantations are leased to tenants. Human history can show a great variety of forms of tenancy, many of which are still in force in some part of the world. The most satisfactory for the tenant is a fixed sum in money or a fixed quantity of produce. The amounts may, of course, be slight or extortionate, but in either case the tenant has an incentive to work hard, for he knows that everything he produces above the agreed amount is his, to consume or to exchange. It cannot be said categorically that money rents are preferable to rents in kind. Prices of products fluctuate, but so also, in the twentieth century if not in the nineteenth, does the value of money. Certainly less satisfactory is the system known as share-cropping, by which whatever crop is harvested is shared between landowner and tenant in a previously agreed proportion. Admittedly, if the landowner's share is not high, the burden on the tenant may be less than in the case of a fixed rent, but there will always be a disincentive to produce more, for however well the tenant works his landlord will always have claims on him. In fact, the shares are often most inequitable. In Persia they vary between a fifth and three-quarters, depending on whether the landlord provides livestock, irrigation or other services.[19] In Iraq before 1958 the share on irrigated land was usually half in the northern provinces and between two-thirds and three-quarters in the south.[20] In the 'black belt' of the American South the negro share-cropper for long suffered from the lack of legal protection in dealing with a white landowner. As a court would always take a white man's word against a negro's, the landowner could interpret or reinterpret his agreement with his tenant according to his interest.[21] Such injustices have become fewer in the post-war years, but they have not altogether disappeared. In South America there is great variety. In Argentina a law of 1948 reduced the share to one-fifth of the gross crop, but in the Andean republics the share is usually much higher, approaching the Asian level of half or more. In some parts of Peru a particularly onerous form of tenancy exists, whereby the tenant pays in part by a share of the crop and in part by labour services performed for the landlord. In fact, his status is essentially that of a serf in medieval Europe. In 1947 the Peruvian government passed a law relating to this form of tenancy, known as *yanaconaje*. The law limited the amount of rent and the rate of interest to be paid to the landowner on agricultural equipment lent to the tenant (*habilitación*). It prohibited labour services, and forbade the insertion into contracts of clauses obliging the tenant to sell to the landowner any excess crop he might have after satisfying his family's needs, or to make improvements on his farm without compensation, or to trade only with shops belonging to the landowner. This law was, however, never enforced, and with the overthrow of the reforming President Bustamante in 1948 it became a dead letter.[22] In Peru also the wage-labourers (estimated at 26% of the agricultural population in 1940) are paid only partly in money, the bulk of their remuneration consisting of the free use for their families of a small plot of land. Similar conditions are to be found in the other Andean republics and in parts of Venezuela. Labour services as a form of rent are rather uncommon in Persia, and are being abolished in India.

In many countries at the present time large estates are few, and the predominant unit consists of small farms. The word 'small' is apt to be confusing, for much depends on the quality of the land and the methods of cultivation. A farm which would be called 'small' in the American Middle West, or even in England, would be considered large in Eastern Europe or Asia. Farms of 10 to 20 acres in France or Denmark may provide their owners with a very decent standard of living. Output per unit of land is high, and high-quality crops are produced for the market. A farmer who owns his own holding may rent additional land in order to increase his total marketable output. In Eastern Europe farms are very small, and both methods of cultivation and output per unit are low. Between the world wars subsistence farming prevailed, and only a minority of the more prosperous produced mainly for the market. Subsistence farming is the rule among smallholders and tenants in a large part of Asia.

Communal forms of tenure, other than the tribal, are also to be found. One example was the Russian commune (*obshchina*), which existed before 1917 in most of central European Russia. Land was liable to be redistributed from time to time in accordance with the needs of households—more for a family with more children, less for one with fewer mouths to feed. The rotation of crops, binding on all households in the village, was decided by a majority in an assembly of heads of households. This system had the merit of providing a minimum livelihood for everyone, but formed a powerful disincentive to economic enterprise and technical progress.[23] In the Andean republics of South America, village *comunidades* persist among some Indian peoples, a modified survival of forms of ownership which preceded the Spanish conquest. In Mexico the *ejido*, a form of ownership derived from pre-Spanish Mexico, but stabilized in a new form by President Cárdenas (1934-40), somewhat resembles the Russian commune. The members have the use of their land for their own families, but the ultimate ownership of all the land is with the State, which can assert its rights over it in case of public necessity. The member families can retain their allotment as long as they keep it under cultivation by their own labour. They may not sell or mortgage it, and lose it if they stop cultivating it. During his presidential term, Cárdenas redistributed 37 million acres of land, far more than had been done in the quarter-century since the revolution began in 1910. In 1940 *ejidos* comprised 57% of all the holdings in Mexico, and possessed 47% of the arable land. A minority of 15% of the *ejidos* were organized on collective principles, without individual holdings, and with payment to members according to the amount and quality of the labour performed.[24]

In Israel co-operative farm settlements have been established since the period of the British Mandate in Palestine, between the world wars, and have developed further since Israel became a state. According to a statement by the government of Israel, there were at the end of 1952, 218 such settlements with a total population of 70,000 persons. 'No money payments are made and all economic relationships between the settlement and its members are based upon the principle of "everybody will work according to his ability and will receive benefits according to his needs".'[25]

Finally, there is the Soviet type of collective farm, the *kolkhoz*, introduced between 1928 and 1933, of which more will be said later. Here there are no individual holdings, and payments to members are made by 'labour days' (*trudoden*), a unit calculated according to the amount and quality of labour performed. Collective farms of the Soviet type have been introduced in varying degrees in Eastern Europe and in China.

LAND REFORMS

The situation which is most likely to produce a revolutionary class feeling among small farmers or peasants is one in which large estates exist side by side with dwarf holdings, in which the peasants desperately need to acquire more land, or to be relieved of the burden of rents. When to economic misery is added resentment at some infringement of customary rights by the landowners, or ideas of political reform become familiar to the peasants, or the system of government becomes shaken by rebellions or by foreign war, the discontent of the peasants is liable to flare up into a mighty flame. An example is Russia, where the peasants believed themselves cheated of land by the Emancipation Act of 1861. Another is Hungary, where, as education spread in the nineteenth century, the peasants became familiar with liberal and socialist ideas, yet the ruling class forcibly prevented the formation of parties or unions to defend peasant rights, and redistribution of the land was refused. Another is Mexico, where the revolution which began in 1910 shook the whole established order and led to peasant risings, of which the most important was that led by Emiliano Zapata from 1913 to 1919. In other countries peasant risings and civil wars have been forestalled, or at least postponed, by redistribution of landed property, or land reforms. In others again land reform has been a result of violent revolution.

Eastern Europe has been the scene of numerous land reforms in the twentieth century. The years after the First World War saw very radical reform in Roumania, less drastic reforms in Czechoslovakia and Yugoslavia, and some redistribution of land in Poland. The great estates remained almost untouched in the small Hungarian state created by the 1920 peace treaty of Trianon, though in formerly Hungarian provinces annexed by Czechoslovakia, Roumania and Yugoslavia, landowners of Hungarian nationality lost their estates. Indeed, one important feature, and defect, of the land reforms of the 1920s was that often social justice took second place to nationalist revenge: large landowners belonging to the dominant nation in each state suffered less than those who belonged to a national minority. The second wave of East European land reforms came after the Second World War, and were the work of the communist parties. In Hungary the long-awaited distribution of land took place. Its immediate author was a communist Minister of Agriculture, Imre Nagy. Though the Hungarian peasants had their doubts about the communist party, they were genuinely delighted by the reform. In Poland the large estates had mostly been in the eastern provinces, which were annexed by the Soviet Union. In the new Poland, however, as also in Czechoslovakia, huge expropriations of land took place. The beneficiaries were Polish or Czech peasants, but the victims were the German communities, about 12 million in all, the rural element in which consisted overwhelmingly not of large landowners, but of peasants. In Roumania and Yugoslavia much smaller quantities of land changed owners: here too German peasants formed a large proportion of the expropriated.[26]

The largest number of persons affected by a land reform in recent years has been in China, where the communist régime swept away the landed gentry class, and also seized the holdings of many persons arbitrarily labelled *kulaks* (rich peasants), first and most savagely in Manchuria and later and more slowly in the rest of the country. This reform, like the Russian redistribution after 1917 and the post-Second World War reforms in Eastern Europe, was followed within a few years by massive collectivization of agriculture, which will be discussed later.

Three countries in which non-communist governments have carried out land reforms of considerable importance are Japan, Italy and Egypt.

The Japanese reform was largely the work of American experts in the Occupation forces. Under the law of December 1946, the government was to purchase all land belonging to absentee owners; all land belonging to non-cultivating owners resident in the same village in excess of $2\frac{1}{2}$ acres (10 acres in the island of Hokkaido); and all land cultivated by its owner in excess of 7·5 acres (25 in Hokkaido). Various provisions were made for dealing with exceptional cases or hardships requiring special treatment. The land thus purchased was to be made available to those who needed it, in practice usually to the persons cultivating it as tenants. Compensation to the landowners was negligible, as the inflation deprived the agreed prices, based on wartime rents, of their value. The allocation of the land was entrusted to local commissions composed of landlords, owner-farmers and tenants elected by the population. By the end of 1949 4·5 million acres, one-third of Japan's cultivated land, had been transferred to new owners, and 3 million cultivators, half the total number of farm households, had acquired some land. The proportion of all cultivators who owned all the land they cultivated had increased from 29% to 70%; that of tenants not owning any land had fallen from 20% to less than 6%; and that of persons who owned some land and rented some more as tenants had decreased from 51% to 24%. Among this last group of part-owners part-tenants, the proportion of their holding which was owned was proportionately greater than before the reform.[27]

In Italy a draft bill for land reform was presented to the Senate in May 1950, but was not passed. However, laws affecting certain regions in the South were enacted during 1950. Together they affected about 20 million acres out of a total agricultural area of nearly 70 million acres in the country. The amount to be expropriated under these laws was about 1·75 million acres, whereas the original land reform bill had proposed to take over about 3·25 million. Expropriation was primarily of uncultivated or extensively cultivated land, and the government's policy has been to improve the quality of this land, by deep ploughing, drainage and irrigation, before settling it with new owners. The result has been that the process of redistribution has been slow, and the number of peasant families benefited has not been very large, certainly not sufficient to make much impact on the problem of rural overpopulation that plagues Southern Italy. On the other hand, the Italian reformers have argued that a solid economic achievement for a considerable number of people is better than demagogic legislation for the masses that does not bring tangible benefit. The most impressive single achievement was in the Sila district of Calabria, where by March 1953 more than 130,000 acres of reclaimed land had been distributed to nearly 14,000 families. Other schemes were carried out in Maremma, Apulia and Lucania, and beginnings were made in the islands.[2]

In Egypt a land reform law was introduced by the revolutionary military régime in September 1952. It declared that 'no person may own more than 200 acres of land', but a further 100 acres was to be allowed if 50 acres were given to each of two children of the owner. The amount of land affected by the law was about 1·17 million acres out of 6 million acres of agricultural land in Egypt. The amount liable for expropriation—the excess over 200 or 300 acres—was officially estimated at 656,736 acres, but was probably less than half a million. Nearly 200,000 more acres were available from the estates of the royal family. These were seized without compensation, whereas other landowners were offered compensation in government bonds at a rate based on land tax assessments, which was in practice much lower than the real value of the land. By the end of 1955 an area of 250,000 acres had been distributed to 69,000 families, comprising 415,000 persons, in holdings averaging 3½ acres.[29] The reform law also set a maximum level for all rents, and in practice by January 1955 rents had fallen by about 40%. The law also provided that the wages of agricultural labourers should be fixed annually by an official committee. Agricultural labourers were for the first time allowed to form trade unions. A later decree prescribed minimum wages for agricultural labour, but it is doubtful how effective this has been.

In India land reform laws have been passed in a number of the federal states. Their general characteristic is to abolish *zamindari* ownership. The land is purchased by the state against compensation, the value of which varies considerably from one state to another. In some cases the purchased land has been sold to the tenants, in others the tenants have become tenants of the state, which retains the property. In Bolivia the revolutionary régime of President Paz Estenssoro decreed a sweeping land reform on 3 August 1953. Large estates were to be abolished, and land given partly to private peasant holdings, partly to Indian *comunidades* and partly to the state.

Countries in which large estates still exist side by side with impoverished peasant holdings, and where no significant land reform has taken place, include in Europe, Spain and Portugal; in Asia, Pakistan and Persia; and most of the states of South America. In the latter case the problem is often aggravated by the fact that the tenants or labourers are of different ethnic origin from the landowners: social conflict is exacerbated by racial hatred.

PEASANT POVERTY

Land reforms remove the sense of bitter injustice and class conflict, but they do not in themselves solve the economic problems of the peasants or end their poverty. The peasants' subsequent fate depends on economic conditions, which are largely determined by the action or inaction of governments.

Governments of predominantly agrarian societies in modern times have usually been preoccupied with industrial development. Their spokesmen have often expressed a certain sentimental affection for the peasants, but they have not been thereby deterred from taxing them heavily in order to pay for industrialization and for armed forces, and they have seldom been eager to put back a large share of the tax revenue into the countryside in the form of material improvements. There have, however, been variations. In Russia from 1861 to 1905 the government mercilessly squeezed the peasants and almost completely ignored the development of agriculture. After 1906 Prime Minister Stolypin reversed the trend. He introduced legislation which favoured enterprising peasant farmers, and enabled them to escape from the shackles of the village commune, with its depressing influence on farming methods. These reforms only benefited a minority of the peasants, and they had only been in force for a few years when Russia was plunged into war and then revolution. In modern Japan too the peasants were squeezed by heavy taxation, but at least a part of the revenue found its way back to agriculture. Material improvements were encouraged, including small innovations in equipment and methods which could be easily adopted by small farmers. Artificial fertilizers were introduced. Village schools were rapidly set up, and the Japanese, including farm boys and girls, soon became a literate nation. Within fifty years of the Meiji Restoration—the introduction of Japan's modern era in 1868— the output per unit of land had doubled. No comparable improvement took place in Russia.

The East European countries between the world wars provide an example of the inadequacy of land reform unsupported by government economic policy. The Roumanian and Yugoslav peasants in the 1920s had land. For a few years farm prices were good, and they did fairly well. Then came the world economic depression of the 1930s, and they were faced with disaster. The governments had not used the brief period of prosperity to improve agricultural methods, or to encourage the peasants to help themselves. In some provinces there were efficient co-operatives, for marketing or for credit—for example, in Bulgaria, in parts of Serbia and Vojvodina and in some districts of southern Roumania. But the co-operative networks were never extended over whole countries, and the governments gave them little help. Indirect taxation was a heavy burden on the poorest families. Roads and transport services remained primitive. Elementary education was still backward, though progress was certainly made. The instruction given by the existing schools was seldom devised to meet the needs or improve the skills of farmers. The poverty grew worse as family holdings became divided, on the death of a farmer, between his numerous children. If his holding included land of different qualities, then each heir must, for fairness sake, have a piece of each quality. The villages were often a patchwork of tiny plots, and owners of quite small holdings might have to walk miles to visit all the strips of which they were composed. Efficient farming was impossible in these conditions. Inefficiency meant poverty, and poverty made inefficiency worse.

The authors of some of the post-1945 land reforms have tried to avoid these pitfalls. The Italian government has laid stress on the improvement of land before redistribution. In India several states have passed acts in favour of consolidation of holdings, of bringing the scattered strips together into viable units. In the state of Madhya Pradesh the number of holdings was reduced by 1952 from about 5 million to less than 1 million, and over the greater part of this area the average size of holdings was raised from 0·48 acres to 2·5 acres.[30] In Japan the government has paid great attention to consolidation, and from 1950 to 1952 an area of about 1,600,000 acres was in process of regroupment. The target for consolidation for the period 1950-7 was to be about 4,200,000 acres—approximately 30% of the total area of farmland. The Japanese government has also developed a comprehensive system of general purpose co-operatives, to which the great majority of farmers belong, and which are in effect an official agency for agricultural improvement policies.[31] In Egypt government control over farmers is still more extensive. All farmers who have received land under the 1952 reform are obliged to be members of a co-operative, and these are essentially instruments of the Ministry of Agriculture, directed by managers appointed by the Higher Committee for

Agrarian Reform. The co-operatives are to provide loans to their members and to organize the supply of seed, fertilizers, livestock and agricultural machinery, and the storage and transport of crops. Their functions also include 'organizing the cultivation and exploitation of the land in the most efficient manner, including seed selection, varieties of crops, pest control and digging of canals and drains'.[32] How this paternalist system will work has yet to be seen.

One of the basic causes of peasant poverty is rural overpopulation. By this is meant that there is a very large number of persons engaged in agriculture per unit of agricultural land, not that there is a very high density of total population in the country as a whole. There are many more persons per square mile in Great Britain or Belgium than in India, but in large parts of India there is acute rural overpopulation, which is not a problem in Britain or Belgium. The United States is certainly not as a whole agriculturally overpopulated, but this condition probably does exist in some rural areas of the 'black belt' in the Southern states. Where the output per unit of land is low, the problem is made worse. The comparison between Denmark and Yugoslavia in the 1930s, quoted above, illustrates the point. Improvement of output per unit of land would, of course, reduce poverty, and raise the standard of living of the peasant population. But in so far as improvement were brought about by mechanization of agriculture (which is not an universal panacea for all types of farming), this might even increase the disproportion between the number needed to perform the job and the number actually engaged in farming. One aspect of rural overpopulation is peasant poverty: another is mass underemployment, wastage of manpower. In a rural community few people are completely unemployed, but most are inadequately employed. Too little work is spread out over too many people. Estimates of the surplus manpower available in overpopulated rural areas can never be very accurate, but they may vary between one-third and one-half of the population, or even more. This condition of rural overpopulation and underemployment, with its effects of misery, hopelessness, human despair and loss to the national economy, was characteristic of Imperial Russia at the beginning of the century, and of Roumania, Poland or Yugoslavia between the wars. It is characteristic of Southern Italy, India, Egypt, Algeria and many other 'underdeveloped societies' at the present time.

Emigration has at times provided an outlet for surplus population—for example, from European Russia to Siberia in the early twentieth century, or from Austria-Hungary to the United States. In recent decades the restrictions imposed by the more empty overseas countries, in the American continents and the southern Pacific, have combined with growing

LAND AND PEASANTS 121

nationalism in the parent countries to cut down the flow of emigration to a mere trickle.

Industrial development is, of course, the obvious answer. Industry can provide jobs for the rural surplus and produce goods that can increase the general standard of living. It can also increase the material and military power of the state, and the self-esteem of its rulers. But industrial development has to be paid by the peasants. It is, of course, in their long-term interest. But meanwhile they toil and sweat, and no one pays much attention to their wishes. Such at least has been the usual practice in the past. Here we would stress the vast difference between a programme of industrialization which treats the peasants as partners and one which regards them merely as raw material to be exploited.

COLLECTIVIZATION OF AGRICULTURE

There is another policy for dealing with rural poverty and backwardness. It is that which has been adopted in communist-ruled countries—the collectivization of agriculture.

The Russian communists, following their master, Marx, had small use for peasant small holdings or for the peasantry as a whole. The future lay, they believed, in agriculture as in industry, in large units, which alone were capable of efficient modern production. From an economic point of view, large private estates were at least capable of being efficient, but from a social and political view they were unacceptable to communists. The solution was to preserve large units, but to dispossess the landlords. This could be done by setting up collective farms. In 1917, however, needing the peasants' support for his revolution, Lenin postponed collectivization, and gave the peasants what they themselves most desired—the redistribution among them of the landlords' estates. During the civil war the communists were obliged to use force to extract from the peasants the foodstuffs needed to feed their armies and the town population. But when the war was won the peasants were confirmed in the private ownership of their holdings.

A new phase came at the end of the 1920s. Stalin had decided to speed up the industrialization of Russia, with special emphasis on heavy industry. Supplies of foodstuffs to the towns were, however, not satisfactory, and as the urban population grew with industrialization the shortage was certain to become acute. The peasants were producing mainly for their family needs, and indeed were living better than they had ever lived under the Tsars, but they were not much interested in increasing their output for the market. They could be induced to do so either by incentives or by coercion. A policy of incentives meant that consumer goods must be produced and imported on a large scale, and this must retard the growth of heavy industry. Moreover, the consequent rise of the standard of living of the peasantry would, it was believed, redound mainly to the advantage of the rich minority, the *kulaks* or rural *bourgeoisie*, whom the communists considered a dangerous class enemy, capable, if thus economically strengthened, of challenging the communist party's political power. Thus, for economic and doctrinaire reasons alike, a policy of incentives had to be rejected. More foodstuffs must be obtained from the countryside without giving better real prices to farmers. A policy of coercion was chosen. Between 1929 and 1933 the peasants were forced into collective farms, at the cost of several million human lives and of the destruction of half the livestock population of the Soviet Union.

During Stalin's lifetime the essential purpose of the collective farm was to ensure supplies to the State of foodstuffs and of recruits for industrial labour. The collective farms were in fact a more efficient system of centralized control over the peasantry than had ever been imposed on any agrarian population.

Most discussions of the collective farm system concentrate on two points —the merits of farming in large units and the willingness or unwillingness of peasants to give up their private holdings in favour of membership in a collective. Communist dogma insists that large units are always more efficient than small. This is highly questionable for some kinds of crops, but for large-scale production of cereals it is probably true. The highly mechanized, capital-intensive large farms of Iowa are clearly more efficient than were small cereal-producing holdings in Russia in the 1920s. But in fact the achievements of the Soviet collective farms (*kolkhoz*) in grain-production since the mid-1930s have not been impressive. Output per acre has only very slightly increased.

There is little doubt that peasants normally prefer private farming to collective farming. Unwillingness to be deprived of their holdings was the main motive in their resistance to Stalin's policy. Even the victory of Stalin involved some measure of compromise, for members of collective farms have been allowed to retain small family plots on which they can keep livestock, and they have shown much more interest in cultivating these plots than in working on the collective lands, despite constant exhortations and threats. It should not, however, be thought that cooperative cultivation need necessarily be against the interests of the peasants, or even necessarily unpopular with them.

The essence of the Soviet collective farm, in Stalin's lifetime, lay neither in its potentialities as a large economic unit, nor in its co-operative character, but in its function as a government instrument for getting foodstuffs cheap, for making the peasants pay the bill of industrialization. It was above all a device for the economic exploitation of the peasants. Though the output of crops per unit of land only slightly increased, the proportion of the crop which was marketed enormously increased. The compulsory deliveries to the State at very low prices were the first charge on the collective farms. These cheap grain supplies, which the government then sold to the consuming public at a huge profit, were one of the foundations of industrial progress in the Soviet Union from the 1930s onwards. Far more ruthlessly and far more effectively than Imperial Russia or Imperial Japan, Soviet Russia squeezed the farm population.

Since Stalin's death there have been important changes. In 1953 the First Secretary of the Communist Party, N. S. Khrushchov, admitted that Soviet agriculture was still extremely backward. He decided on a policy of limited but considerable incentives. Farm prices were increased, taxes and compulsory deliveries reduced. The results of these reforms cannot yet be assessed. Two general comments can, however, be made.

The first is that the Soviet government remains faced with a dilemma which it has not yet escaped. It can have either a docile peasantry or an efficient peasantry. The collectivization of agriculture under Stalin achieved the first, but not the second. Since the 1930s the peasants have been cowed, incapable of any overt opposition, but they have shown their passive resistance by inefficient farming. They will only become efficient farmers, working eagerly and skilfully, if the government gives them material incentives far greater than those of 1953-8, and in general treats them as equals of the urban population, not as mere second-class citizens.

The second comment is that the communist leaders have not abandoned their dogmatic attitude to the peasants. They do not recognize the peasantry as a social class that has a permanent place of its own in society. Peasants to them are petty *bourgeois*, destined to be converted into a section of the working class. This will be achieved only when they live in urban settlements, have an urban way of life and outlook, and work according to factory discipline. They will have become crop-producing industrial workers, and their places of work large rural factories. This conception not only does violence to physical and psychological facts about farming, but can only be carried out at great cost even if the peasants willingly co-operate. Khrushchov himself in 1951 proposed the creation of agrarian cities (*agrogoroda*) with urban amenities, but the plan was abandoned. Since 1953, in his settlements in the 'virgin lands' of Kazakhstan, which are worked not by local people, but by colonists brought from European Russia, largely from the towns, he has been experimenting with a new organization of rural labour which may later be applied in some form to the old settled parts of rural Russia. But to create for the whole rural population the amenities, social security and standard of living of the urban workers—modest though these still are by Western standards—would be a heavy burden on the economic resources of the Soviet Union. Whether the solution will be to recognize that farmers are different from urban workers, that they must be allowed to live their own way, that even highly industrialized countries still have substantial farming populations (France 29% and West Germany 23%), and that the collective farm system itself must be fundamentally modified, as it has not yet been; or whether the alternative will be pursued of imposing on the farmers an urban way of life, together with urban amenities, urban hours of work and urban social services—it is too soon even to hazard a guess.

Meanwhile, collectivization on Soviet lines has been introduced in other communist-ruled countries. In Eastern Europe the biggest results have been attained in Bulgaria, where at the end of 1958 more than 90% of the arable land was in collective farms. In Czechoslovakia at the same time, about 70% of the arable was in collective or state farms. In Eastern Germany and Roumania collectivization was much less advanced. In all these countries coercive measures had been used against the peasants (differential taxation and compulsory grain deliveries, and sometimes physical violence), but there was no famine or mass slaughter of livestock, as in Russia in the 1930s.

Three other East European countries made progress towards collectivization and then retreated from it. In Yugoslavia between 1949 and 1951 rather more than a quarter of the arable was collectivized, but in 1953 the government decided to allow those peasant families who wished, to leave the collectives. The result was a mass exodus, which in a few months reduced collective farming to a tiny share of Yugoslav agriculture. In Hungary in the summer 1953 the right of secession was allowed, but in practice was hedged about with restrictions. About one-tenth of the collectives were dissolved. During the 1956 Revolution there was a mass exodus. In 1959, however, the communists introduced a new collectivization drive. In Poland about 10% of the arable was in collectives before October 1956. There followed a mass exodus, reducing the number of collectives from about 10,000 to 2,000.

In China the communists had barely completed the redistribution when they embarked on large-scale collectivization. This was to take place in three stages, each marked by its own type of organization. The first was the 'mutual aid team', in which peasants pooled their tools and worked together during the harvest season, but retained full ownership of their holdings. The second was the 'producers' co-operative', in which the land was pooled, but individual families still retained nominal ownership of the holdings which they had brought into the co-operative, and were paid partly according to their labour and partly in the form of rent for their holdings. The third was the 'fully socialist' collective farm, in which payment was only according to labour.

Mutual aid teams were rapidly developed in 1952-3. A poor harvest in 1954 induced the party leaders (as the poor harvest of 1927 had induced the Soviet leaders) to accelerate the process. In a speech of 31 July 1955, Mao Tse-tung announced that by the end of 1956, half the peasant households of China were to be in producers' co-operatives, and the transformation to collective farms was to be completed by 1957. However, the pace was still further quickened. At the end of 1955 it was stated that more than 60% of households were already in producers' co-operatives. In January 1956 the date for complete transformation into collective farms was advanced to the end of 1958. In the summer of 1958 a still further stage was introduced with the creation of 'People's Communes', a form of organization which ensures a stricter regimentation of the peasants than Soviet collective farms have ever achieved.

The policies of 1955-8 appear to have been carried through without such peasant resistance, famine or mass slaughter of cattle as took place in Russia in the 1930s.

PEASANTS AS A POLITICAL FACTOR

In the democratic politics of Western Europe and North America in the modern era, farmers' votes have been important, but it cannot be said that either the farmers as a whole or any economically defined section of them ('rich', 'poor' or 'medium') has shown a consistent political attitude, as a class or a social group. In France a large part of the peasantry supported the Great Revolution, but another part formed the core of resistance in the Vendée. Many peasants voted for Louis Napoleon in his plebiscites, others made a habit of voting for left-wing slogans. The traditional 'leftness' of peasants in the southern provinces of France has led many in recent years to vote communist. In the United States the farmers at one time voted for Jefferson's agrarian democracy, and later for Populism in the South and the West. But the Republican Party, not only in its heroic early days, but also in its respectable middle age, from Taft through Hoover to Eisenhower, has received massive farmer support.

In Western countries there have not been class parties of the peasantry. Various parties have at different times depended mainly on peasant support, and for brief periods this has become so dominant that these parties have in fact become the expression of farming interests. But these periods have been short. Leadership has been in the hands of urban elements—lawyers or business-men or persons closely linked with the bureaucracy. The Italian Christian Democratic Party and the Austrian People's Party are examples. In both cases the influence of the Catholic hierarchy on the one hand, and of business on the other, has been powerful at all times, and in the Italian case the State machine, with its strong element of continuity from late nineteenth-century Piedmont through fascism to the post-war years, has been strongly felt. The farmers in Great Britain, the United States, France and West Germany today are essentially a pressure group, which any government—conservative or socialist alike— would ignore at its peril. The farmers' lobbies represent the rich and powerful farmers rather than the poor. Iowa hog and corn business entrepreneurs are more influential than Mississippi negro share-croppers, successful Lincolnshire farmers than Scottish West Highland crofters, big French *betteraviers* than smallholders of Auvergne. But even the poorer farmers get a substantial part of the largesse handed out by munificent and vote-hungry governments.

The region in which specific class parties of the peasantry were for a time important is Eastern Europe. The doctrines of agrarian socialism, a mixture of watered-down Marxism and romantic worship of the simple folk, received their fullest development in Russia, from the 1860s onwards. But the Socialist Revolutionary Party which expressed these doctrines never achieved power. From its foundation about 1902 until the collapse of Tsardom it was persecuted, or at least inhibited, by the Imperial régime. At the Constituent Assembly election of November 1917 it won half the total votes cast in Russia. But in January 1918 Lenin suppressed the Assembly, and in the civil war the Socialist Revolutionaries, persecuted by both Reds and Whites, torn between their enthusiasm for revolutionary slogans and their distrust of the Bolsheviks, were reduced to impotence and disappeared from history.

The Russian agrarian socialists, however, had disciples in Eastern Europe.[33] The most successful was the Bulgarian Agrarian Union, which, under a popular and gifted leader, Alexander Stamboliiski, held power from 1919 to 1923. Some organization remained after its violent overthrow in 1923, and the Bulgarian peasants stayed loyal to its tradition. In Poland the peasant movement was a mixture of agrarian socialism from the part of Poland which had been under Russia, and moderate democracy from the part which had been under Austria. In the resistance movement to the German invaders from 1939 to 1945 both the leaders and the members of the peasant movement played an active part. In Roumania a Peasant Party came into existence after the First World War, with an agrarian socialist ideology definitely influenced by Russian Populism. In 1938 it was suppressed by the dictatorship of King Carol II. Nevertheless, the party, and its leader, the veteran nationalist statesman Iuliu Maniu, retained much goodwill among the peasants. In Croatia a strong radical Peasant Party was founded before the First World War. But in the Yugoslav state, founded in 1918 by union of Croatia with Serbia, most of the energies of the Croatian Peasant Party were diverted into the national struggle against the Serbs, and the specific fight for peasant interests took second place. In Hungary after 1919 there was a small Farmers' Party, but the oligarchic dictatorship under Admiral Horthy used the open ballot in village elections and repressive measures by the gendarmerie to prevent the party from achieving great mass support. The Czechoslovak Agrarian Party began as an organization of small farmers, with a democratic and nationalist programme. But by the 1930s it had become dominated by urban business and professional elements, and was in fact the main representative of the Czech *bourgeoisie*.

A special case is the Finnish Agrarian Party, which has remained powerful to the present day. Its founders were influenced by agrarian socialism in Russia, with which Finland was linked before 1918 in a personal union. But after the land reform in independent Finland, which gave the land to the peasants, they became much less radical in outlook. Since the Second World War the Agrarian Party has been one of the two great parties in Finland, almost exactly equal in voting strength to the Social Democratic Party. It has remained primarily a farmers' party, with comparatively little influence by business-men or other urban elements. Finnish politics since 1945 has been an uneasy balance between farming and industrial working-class interests, reflected in the two main parties, sometimes in coalition and sometimes opposed to each other.

After the Second World War the East European peasant parties, repressed by pre-war dictatorships or by Nazi German occupation or by both, had a brief resurgence before being again suppressed, this time by communists. In 1945 the Polish People's Party, as the peasant party was called, enjoyed wider support than any other party in Poland. The same was true of the revived Bulgarian Agrarian Union and Roumanian National Peasant Party. In Hungary the Small Farmers' Party for a short time achieved the mass support that the old régime had denied it. The land reform carried out by the communist Imre Nagy worked to its advantage. The Hungarian peasants, having received the land they had desired for so many generations, were now a moderately conservative rather than a radical element. The party even won, at the freely held parliamentary election of October 1945, an absolute majority (57%) of all votes. This poll undoubtedly included urban middle-class elements, but it is equally beyond doubt that it also included the overwhelming majority of votes of the peasants, who formed approximately half the Hungarian electorate. It looked for a time as if Hungary would at last become a small property-owning democratic society.

The successes of the peasant movement in Poland, Bulgaria, Roumania and Hungary were short-lived. The communists, by terror and intrigue, and with powerful help from the Soviet army of occupation, ousted them from the government coalitions, engineered artificial splits in their ranks, recognized puppets of their own as leaders of the 'real' peasant movement, and arrested or killed the real leaders. The Bulgarian leader, G. M. Dimitrov, was removed from the leadership of his party as a result of intervention by the Soviet General Biryuzov. His successor, Nikola Petkov, was executed on trumped-up treason charges in 1947. In the same year the Polish leader Mikolajczyk escaped arrest by fleeing the country, and the Roumanian leaders, Maniu and Mihalache, were sentenced to long terms of prison on trumped-up charges. Maniu, the leading Roumanian statesman of the twentieth century, died in prison at the age of eighty in 1956. In Hungary the death-blow to the Small Farmers' Party was the arrest by Soviet security police of its leader Béla Kovács in the spring of 1947. Many of its parliamentary deputies were arrested in connexion with 'treason conspiracies' staged by the communist-controlled security police.

The story of the East European agrarian parties is thus one of failure. They were not strong enough to repel attack by the old ruling classes—whether landowners in Hungary between the world wars or a combination of bureaucrats and business-men in the other countries—or by totalitarian fascist or communist movements backed by German or Soviet armies. Their failure is primarily due to the strength of the forces arrayed against them. It was aggravated by their own weaknesses—lack of internal discipline, conflicts of economic interest between peasants of different regions or different degrees of material wealth, a tendency to take their leaders from urban lawyers rather than farmers, and to become side-tracked from their social demands by nationalist demagogy. Perhaps the basic weakness was the inescapable physical fact that peasants live in small communities, scattered in villages or even isolated farms over great areas, and cannot therefore be so easily mobilized for any sort of political action as town-dwellers.

Peasants are today a conservative force in political life in Western Europe. The same is true of Japan, where after receiving ownership of their farms without any burden of compensating the former landowners, under the 1946 land reform, they have given their support to the conservative parties. It is also true of Turkey, where the nationalism of the Kemalist régime has for forty years rallied the people behind its leaders. The Turkish peasants may be more attached to Islam, and less keen on cultural modernization, than the urban politicians and bureaucrats; they may vary in the distribution of their votes between the parties which compete for their support in the periodical half-free or free elections; but their claims, and their opposition, are put forward within the framework of the Turkish Republic as it now is: they do not seek the forcible overthrow of the régime.

In the rest of Asia, Africa and Latin America the situation is uncertain and fluid. Here there is great misery, great economic backwardness, and in many cases grievous oppression by a ruling class. Even where the political system is not oppressive, it may be felt intolerable by the peasants because it is foreign: this is liable to be the case in any colonial territories. In southern Europe similar conditions exist in Spain, in Greece and in Italy, despite the notable achievements of the Italian land reform. It is interesting to note that in the first post-war parliamentary elections the communist party gained votes more rapidly in the South than elsewhere, though this trend was arrested in 1958. Finally in the communist world, collectivization of agriculture has nowhere been willingly accepted by the peasants, and a great volume of suppressed discontent remains below the political surface.

As we have already noted, economic misery does not necessarily cause peasants to be politically restive. Peasants, being physically scattered and isolated, are less accessible to modern ideas than townspeople, though modern communications have been breaking this isolation down in recent decades, even in remote areas of India or Bolivia or tropical Africa. Other obstacles are the devotion of peasants to traditional beliefs, to their religion and to patriotism, their respect for established institutions and their habits of obedience to well-known hierarchies. It is only when the hierarchies and institutions break down, when the beliefs are forsaken by the ruling class itself, and especially when the machinery of State is crippled by defeat in war, that peasants in large numbers follow revolutionary leadership.

The three victorious communist revolutions of the twentieth century—the Russian, Yugoslav and Chinese—depended in crucial stages of their struggle on peasant support. Yet in all three the communists became a force capable of seizing and maintaining power only when the old régime had been smashed by external force. It was only after defeat in war, and disintegration of the State machine, that the communists were able to mobilize the peasants for their purposes. Peasant support for revolution, in fact, was not a cause, but a consequence of the fall of the old régime.

Revolutionaries have their best opportunity of mobilizing peasant support when the old machinery of government has broken down, but the religious beliefs and patriotism of the peasants do not appear to be in conflict with the revolutionaries' aims. This was the case in both China and Yugoslavia, where the communists appeared as leaders of resistance against the German or Japanese invaders, and made no attacks on religious beliefs or organizations as such. A similar situation existed in Indochina in the early days of the Vietminh movement.

Today agrarian backwardness and peasant misery form the background to revolutionary movements in a large part of the world. This is not to say that they are the main cause of revolutionary movements, and still less that the peasantry is an initiating force of revolution. Rather the peasants are an inert force, which may be used to great effect by revolutionaries when once political or military events have given them their chance of bidding for power. Indeed, it may be that the relevance of peasant misery to revolution is not so much that misery causes peasants to wish to start a revolution as that knowledge of peasant misery creates indignation among that section of the educated class which is most accessible to revolutionary ideas. This is certainly what happened in Russia, Yugoslavia and China. In the Arab countries, nationalist intellectuals speak with indignation of peasant misery, and the Egyptian officers' group led by Nasser introduced a land reform once they had obtained power. But the role of the peasants in the Arab world has been essentially passive. They have followed religious or nationalist leaders—the Moslem Brotherhood or Nasser or the Algerian National Liberation Front—they have not themselves initiated the action. Today the peasants are potential material to be used by revolutionaries in most of Asia and Africa, as well as in Spain, Italy and Latin America. Whether they will be so used must depend on what leadership is offered to them by the urban classes. To these we must now turn.

5: Workers and Bourgeois

All civilized societies have had their cities—ancient Egypt and Mesopotamia as well as ancient Greece and Rome, medieval China and India as well as medieval Europe. Cities were centres of government, fortified places that contained the court of a monarch or a great nobleman, the palace of a bishop, or some great temple or mosque or monastery that exercised power over the surrounding country. They were also marketing centres, serving at first only a small region, then extending their influence as their produce reached more distant provinces or foreign kingdoms. They were also centres of crafts or small industries, of sculpture and painting, and if they were the seat of some rich or powerful court, of literature and learning too.

As Europe recovered from the effects of Arab, Norman and Magyar invasions, and a stable civilization took shape, these three functions of cities—the political, the commercial and the cultural—became important. In the Hanse towns of the Baltic, in Flanders and Venice, and then more widely throughout Europe, from Scotland to Sicily and from Bohemia to Castile, urban society unfolded its rich variety. In its growth the Catholic Church played a leading part. It provided a large custom for merchants and craftsmen, and the main demand for artists in colour and in stone. It was also a training ground for administrators and scholars, whom it not only employed in its own complex organization, but also supplied to secular rulers. Bureaucrats and intellectuals, civilian experts as opposed to men of arms, came chiefly from the Church, and it was within its ranks that opportunities existed for men of humble rank to rise to influence, bypassing the more rigid hierarchy of birth in the secular world.

THE BOURGEOISIE

The secularization of European society, which came with the Reformation in the sixteenth century, and which affected not only the countries whose rulers and subjects became Protestant, but also those such as France and Spain where Catholicism retained its hold, marked a further stage in the growth of urban social groups.

The connexion between the Reformation and the rise of capitalism has often been pointed out, by Max Weber and R. H. Tawney and their many disciples. Rather than dogmatically assert that the one was cause, the other effect, it is wiser to say only that both processes developed together. The common factor was the stress on individual judgement: men accustomed to think for themselves about their religious beliefs were more likely to be able to think for themselves about business, and conversely.

During the following three centuries three social groups gained notably in numbers and influence. The first were the capitalists—the merchants, bankers and manufacturers. These had, of course, existed in the Middle Ages. But the growth of sea-borne commerce, the discovery of the great ocean routes, enormously extended their opportunities. It was the seafaring Atlantic nations that were the most successful. The Portuguese and Spaniards were the pioneers, but though they produced great explorers and sailors, they were surpassed in commercial enterprise by the English, Dutch and French. The second group were the civilian government officials. Government became more complicated, more centralized and above all more secularized. Rulers sought their administrators outside the Church as well as within it, and used both noblemen and persons of humbler birth. Skills other than military began to be prized. The civil state machine makes it appearance with Louis XI of France and Henry VII of England, was more formidable in the Spain of Philip II, and reached unprecedented efficiency with Louis XIV. The third group was the secular intellectual *élite*, increasingly freed from ecclesiastical control, from which came the great political thinkers and natural scientists of seventeenth-century England and eighteenth-century France.

These three groups formed a middle layer between the aristocracy and the labouring classes. The relative importance of each group differed in different countries, and at least among government officials and intellectuals there were individuals of aristocratic birth. The relationships between *noblesse d'épée, noblesse de robe* and *grande bourgeoisie* in the France of Louis XV were more complicated, the barriers more formidable, than between the equivalent groups in contemporary England. Nevertheless, by the end of the eighteenth century in north-western Europe at least these middle classes had become fairly clearly distinguished both from the old ruling class and from the mass of subjects. More than this, these middle classes were coming to resemble each other, to form in fact one middle class, or *bourgeoisie*. Their way of life, their habits of thought, their cultural and moral values were coming closer to each other, and were growing more different from those of aristocrats or peasants. Something was being formed which can best be called the *bourgeois* ethos. It is beyond the scope of the present work, or the abilities of the writer, to define this mentality. It is, however, worth while to note two essential features of it, which represent perhaps its irreducible core—the sanctity of individual opinion and judgement, and the precedence of civilian over military standards.

The *bourgeoisie* was and is essentially a social and cultural, not an economic category. It is not simply identical with business entrepreneurs, or owners of capital. Confused use of the word *bourgeoisie*, both by Marxists and by non-Marxists influenced by Marxist phrases, derives from confusion in the works of Marx himself, who used the word in different senses in different contexts. The confusions in Marx can to some extent be explained by the fact that Marx believed the capitalists to be the dominant element, and other middle-class elements not directly concerned with business (civil servants, professional people) to be conscious or unconscious tools, agents or hangers-on of the capitalists. Marx based his view mainly on his observations of Victorian England. Even in that society, the assertion that the capitalists dominated the other middle classes is highly disputable, but at least it had a certain plausibility. It is, however, curious that later generations of Marxists should have insisted that the example of Victorian England was universally applicable. This backhanded compliment may cause some British breasts to swell with pride, but it is a doubtful guide for other societies. This is especially clear when one looks at societies outside western and northern Europe. In Russia, for example, in the century and a half that followed the death of Peter the Great (1725) there were government officials and there were merchants, and in the last part of the period there was a secular intellectual *élite*. But the three groups existed apart, they were not united by any common ethos, and there was no question of any primacy of individualist or civilian values in any of the three groups. In short, there was no *bourgeoisie*. The same may be said of the Turkish Empire, China or India.

In Western Europe the Industrial Revolution of the eighteenth and nineteenth centuries greatly increased both the strength and the homogeneity of the *bourgeoisie*. The great technical inventions led both to a vast increase of industrial output and to its concentration in vast new urban agglomerations. The capitalist element in the *bourgeoisie* was increased by adding to the bankers and merchants the new industrial employers. At the same time the greater complexity of the economy led to greater complexity of the machinery of government and much greater numbers of state officials. Finally, the demand for modern skills—in medicine, engineering, the sciences, teaching and journalism—caused the expansion of the originally very small secular intellectual *élite* into the 'free professions' of modern urban society. The three main components of the *bourgeoisie*—business-men, bureaucrats and professional classes—were cemented more closely together by the common *bourgeois* ethos. Certainly the process was not a smooth one. There were painful social frictions, conflicts of moral and aesthetic values, and a distressing outburst of hideous taste in architecture. There were also great differences between Western countries in regard to the relative esteem in which different groups were held. The professional officer and the bureaucrat enjoyed greater prestige in Prussia, the business-man in the northern states of the United States, the landowner in the southern states or in rural England, the intellectual in France, the Presbyterian minister in Scotland. Yet throughout North America and Western Europe the *bourgeoisie* was growing more powerful and more homogeneous. Its most influential and richest members could no longer be said to belong to a *middle* class except by their historical origin. The term has none the less persisted to the present day, but it is an anachronism. The highest levels of the *bourgeoisie* were absorbed in, and in the end absorbed, the upper class. In England the process was hastened by the so-called public schools, as developed by Arnold, Ridding and their disciples, where children of landed gentry, business and the professions were educated together and acquired a similar outlook. The public school mentality was not pure *bourgeois* ethos, but the *bourgeois* virtues were the dominant ones. In the United States the process was made easier by the absence, at any rate after the victory of the North in the Civil War, of the traditions of a pre-capitalist upper class. In France the victory of the *bourgeoisie* required three revolutions and two Napoleons, and its consequence was a certain secession from French public life (except to some extent from the army and the colonial administration) of the aristocracy and smaller nobility, which harmfully limited the sources from which French political leadership could be supplied. In the German Empire of Bismarck it seemed that the Prussian gentry or *Junkertum* was supreme, yet in fact a steady process of *embourgeoisement* took place in the reign of William II. Sons of Prussian Junkers who became bureaucrats or professional men differed less in outlook from their colleagues of middle-class extraction than might have been expected. No doubt a fusion of Junker values and *bourgeois* ethos took place, but the share of the former has probably been overrated. Far more both of the virtues and of the sins of Imperial Germany were due to non-Prussian *bourgeois* than popular historians have recognized.

As industrialization and modernization spread to countries outside North America and Western Europe, the three main social groups from which the European *bourgeoisie* had arisen—business-men, government officials and free professions—made their appearance, but they did not constitute a *bourgeoisie*. Imperial Russia and Imperial Japan are the two most striking cases. In both countries the bureaucrats, while eagerly adopting modern technical inventions, retained a traditionalist outlook, military rather than civilian, strongly nationalist and authoritarian, contemptuous of *bourgeois* values. In both countries capitalists flourished, but as instruments of government policy, not as makers of policy. Both governments wished to make their countries into powerful military empires, and for this reason needed modern industries. Both governments believed that the people who knew best how to do this job for them were capitalists, and knew that what capitalists expected in return for their efforts were steady high profits. They therefore did all they could to help them do their job, and ensured them extremely fat profits. The Japanese showed more business talent than the Russians, but in both countries the relationship of business to government was similar. The general direction of industrial development was decided by the government rather than the capitalists. As for politics, that was no concern of business-men, and in practice the business-men took no interest in it. Their individualism was strictly confined to matters of economic enterprise: it did not extend to political opinion. The facts that the Mitsui, Mitsubishi and lesser Japanese business magnates were given, or were sold at ridiculously low prices, enormously valuable business properties and opportunities; that Russian capitalists thrived on absurdly high protective tariffs and fat government contracts at prices above the economic level; and that foreign capitalists investing in Russia, and foreign holders of Russian bonds received their profits and their dividends with unfailing punctuality, though Russian peasants and workers might be little above starvation level—these well-known facts have caused many, Marxists and non-Marxists alike, to conclude that Japan was ruled by the *zaibatsu* and Russia by French or English capitalists. But the facts prove nothing of the sort. The capitalists grew rich, but power remained with the government. In the partnership between business and bureaucracy, the second was the senior partner. Japanese and Russian business-men did not impose a *bourgeois* ethos on the bureaucrats, if only because they did not have one themselves. It is true that in Russia between 1906 and 1914, and in Japan in the 1920s, there were the beginnings of such a development, but the period was too short. In post-Second World War Japan, however, the prospects of *embourgeoisement*, for better or for worse, seem more promising.

As for the professional classes, their problems will be more fully discussed in the following chapter. Here it may suffice to say that there was hardly a trace of *bourgeois* ethos in the Russian intelligentsia before 1905, and not much after that, while in Japan the initial enthusiasm of modernizing intellectuals for all things Western (including the works of Herbert Spencer and Samuel Smiles) soon met with strong resistance both from traditionalist and from revolutionary quarters.[34]

In Eastern Europe, the borderlands that separated the West from Russia and from the Moslem world, the *bourgeois* ethos struck deeper roots, and the middle classes were tending to cohere into a *bourgeoisie*. This was more the case in Greece, where seafaring and commerce had a long history, and in Serbia and Bulgaria, where the end of Turkish rule left societies composed almost exclusively of peasants, village shopkeepers, pig-traders and the like, than in Hungary and Poland, where a landowning nobility retained great political power and a dominant cultural role.

In the Moslem world, and in Asia beyond, nothing approaching a *bourgeoisie* or a *bourgeois* ethos was to be found. Government servants and merchants existed, but the intellectual *élite* was provided by the established religions, except in China, where scholars and bureaucrats were one in origin and outlook. Conquest, or indirect economic domination, by Europeans brought economic advantage to some merchants and ruin to others, but did not much increase their influence as a social class. Government servants continued to be needed, and to some extent acquired the system of values of the foreigners—the Indian Civil Service of British rule being the most striking example. Western domination, however, created for the first time, by its schools and its economic impact, a modern secular intellectual *élite*. It was this group, rather than the business-men or the bureaucrats, which played the leading role in the political awakening of Asia and the Arab world in the twentieth century, as had been the case in Russia in the nineteenth. But of *bourgeoisie* or *bourgeois* ethos hardly a trace can be found.

THE INDUSTRIAL WORKERS

With the modern factory and the modern urban agglomeration came the industrial working class. The workers were recruited both from the artisans already living in towns and from peasant labourers from the countryside. As industry expanded, the rural influx became by far the more important source. In England population and industry grew together. In other countries population growth preceded industrial growth—for example, in Russia, where even before the abolition of serfdom in 1861 there were areas in which, in relation to existing output, there was pressure of population on resources, at a time when industry was still very little developed. But whatever the chronological connexion between growth of population and of industry, the early stages of industrialization have usually been marked by competition for factory jobs by large numbers of boys and girls from crowded villages. Both because competition for jobs favours the employer, and because the peasant labourers have no skill to offer, only strong arms, their wages are low. There is a great reserve in the countryside they came from, to force wages down if required. The workers will also be content at first with very low wages, for their families still live in the village, where they have some means of livelihood and food. Therefore a wage too small to support a whole family is still acceptable. At this stage of industrialization the employer makes his profit by low labour costs at a low level of productivity. At this stage too the worker is ruthlessly exploited.

But the worker suffers not only from material hardships. He is socially uprooted as well. In the village he may have been poor, and life may have been brutal and unjust. But he belonged to a community with a system of values. In the urban agglomeration, strange and hideous as well as unhealthy and uncomfortable, he has no place. He has been torn up from one society, and has not found a new one. Material misery and emotional bewilderment combine to create a state of mind to which a revolutionary creed, promising justice instead of oppression, and a way out of isolation into new certainties and a new solidarity, must strongly appeal. In this condition, the workers have indeed 'nothing to lose but their chains'. They await only revolutionary leaders.

Such was the working class which Marx saw in his younger, and intellectually formative, years. Others before him had propounded socialist doctrines, but he was the first to insist on the messianic role of the industrial 'proletariat'. He also foretold that there would be a continuous concentration of wealth in the hands of a few great capitalists, that the proletariat would grow more numerous and poorer, and that the middle classes would be whittled away. Though, by the end of his life, industrial development in England was already taking a different course, he stuck to his view, and among his Leninist successors it remains a dogma.

The prophecy as a whole has not been fulfilled, but bits of it have. The concentration of wealth did take place, until the advent of the very high income taxes of recent times. But the workers became not more miserable, but more prosperous, and the proportionate size of the middle classes increased. Curiously, also, the impoverishment and proletarization of the masses did take place, not in industrial, but in agrarian societies, such as nineteenth-century Russia and much of twentieth-century Asia. Its main cause, as we have seen, was the disproportion between the growth of rural population and the slow advance of agricultural technique, and the slow growth of new jobs outside agriculture. But this rural impoverishment was not, despite the doctrines of Lenin and Stalin about *kulaks*, accompanied by any marked and systematic concentration of wealth in the hands of a wealthy rural upper class.

At present the relationship between industrial workers and the urban upper class is different in each of three types of society—the underdeveloped societies now in early stages of industrialization and urbanization; the advanced industrial and urban 'capitalist' societies; and the

Soviet Union, which is not only far advanced in industrialization and urbanization, but also claims to be a 'socialist' society. These must each be considered in turn.

WESTERN INDUSTRIAL SOCIETIES

In Western Europe and North America the industrial workers are no longer a socially uprooted, bewildered, exploited proletariat: on the contrary, they are an extremely powerful force in society and in politics. The workers, in the century that has passed since Marx wrote *The Communist Manifesto*, have improved their material conditions directly through trade unions and indirectly through democratic political parties. In Britain, for example, the Liberal and Conservative parties competed for working-class votes by offering social legislation in their interests, until a sufficient body of working-class opinion became convinced that a separate Labour Party should be founded. In the United States, the Republicans and Democrats still compete for workers' votes, and no Labour Party has arisen as a major force. In France, Germany and Italy strong socialist parties developed before the First World War. The establishment after the Bolshevik Revolution of communist parties, owing allegiance to the Third International in Moscow, split the labour movement in Western Europe. The split certainly damaged the interests of the German workers under the Weimar Republic, and of the French and Italian workers after 1945. Nevertheless, in all industrial countries where free political institutions exist the workers remain a potential political factor.

This road to progress—by trade unions and democratic political parties —is, of course, open to the workers of underdeveloped countries. But two features of Western experience should be mentioned. The main advances of the Western workers took place during a period of economic expansion, interrupted but not reversed by periodical depressions; and the West European nations had long traditions, admittedly of varying strength, yet in all cases substantial, of individualism, civil liberties and political freedom. In many underdeveloped countries today neither of these conditions exists, and in none is either condition firmly based.

The industrial working class in the West is more complex and contains more subdivisions, than the proletariat of Marx's day. Western statistical surveys distinguish between skilled and unskilled workers, but their definitions of skill are not easily comparable. Nevertheless, it may be of interest to give estimates from three Western countries.

In the United States the official category of skilled workers increased from 11·7% of the working population in 1910 to 13·8% in 1950, that of semi-skilled in the same period from 14·7% to 19·8%, while that of unskilled diminished from 21·5% to 16·5%.[35] In Great Britain, Professor G. D. H. Cole estimated, on the basis of the 1951 census figures for actively employed heads of households only, that 38·7% were skilled manual workers, 15·4% were semi-skilled and 11·6% were unskilled.[36] In Italy in 1956, of the total of manual workers employed in manufacturing industry only, 16% (352,514) were skilled (*specializzati*), 43% (926,131) were semi-skilled (*qualificati*) and 41% (898,902) belonged to various unskilled occupations.[37]

Another important trend in recent decades in Western countries is that the proportion of workers engaged directly in production has declined relatively to that engaged in distribution and services, and that in all branches of industry and commerce the proportion of clerks and office-workers—'white-collar' employees—has grown. Whether these latter should be considered a part of the working class, or a middle-class group, is by no means clear. Neither they themselves, nor the social scientists who study their problems, are in agreement on this question.

The situation of the working class, taking it in a broad sense, improved in the first three decades of the present century, but there was a disastrous reversal in the slump of the 1930s, with its mass unemployment, especially severe in the United States, Britain and Germany. The memories of these terrible years, and the fear of a new period of unemployment, are still very vivid, at any rate among workers in their middle years. Since the Second World War, however, workers in the West have on the whole enjoyed full employment and prosperity. Labour has been in demand, and this has strengthened the trade unions. Western unions, however, still face grave economic and social problems. One which is common to all is the problem of inflation. There is controversy as to whether inflation should be allowed to diminish the differences of income between different social groups or whether the differentials should be protected. This is not a simple matter of conflicting interests between the middle classes and the working class: it equally concerns the differentials between the wages of skilled, semi-skilled and unskilled workers. Everywhere the tendency has been to reduce the differentials, which may be regarded as a healthy development in the direction of social justice for the poor, or as a dangerous disincentive to skill and to productivity of labour, harmful to the economy as a whole. Another problem is that of automation, already widely introduced in the United States and spreading in Western Europe. It raises in a new form the argument, familiar from the earlier history of labour, between those who fear inventions because they will at least temporarily displace labour, and those who defend them on the ground that they will in time increase the general wealth, and so also the workers' standard of living.

These problems may and do cause serious friction between employers and labour, industrial unrest and strikes. But as long as general economic conditions are favourable they do not cause widespread deep fear or bitter hatred. There is little sign in the West of revolutionary class struggle. Should a major depression occur, with new mass unemployment, poverty and hunger, the whole picture could, of course, quickly change. This is, however, only a possibility of the future. It is more useful at this point briefly to consider the different fortunes of the trade union movements in the main industrial countries in recent years.

In the United States trade unions have greatly increased since 1935. The Wagner Act of that year guaranteed the right of workers to organize themselves, forbade action by employers that might interfere with this right, and set up the National Labour Relations Board. This body is responsible for elections, with secret ballot, by the workers of a plant or department or craft, to decide which union shall represent them. The union that wins a majority of votes is recognized as their only representative in negotiations with the employer. In the last twenty years practices known as 'union security' have grown up. The most extreme is the 'closed shop', under which no one may be employed by a business unless he is already a member of the appropriate union. Other variations include the 'union shop' (under which a new employee is given a specified period within which he must join the union if he is to keep his job) and the 'check-off system' (under which the employer collects the union's membership dues for it by deducting them from workers' wages at source). In 1947 Congress passed the Taft-Hartley Act, which forbade the closed shop, and authorized state governments to enact measures ('right-to-work laws') forbidding any union security practices within their respective states. Some states made use of this provision. Nevertheless, United States Labour Department statistics showed that in 1954 more than 80% of the workers affected by collective agreements in that year were covered by union security provisions, of which 65% were some variation of the union shop. The Taft-Hartley Act also introduced a number of restrictions on certain types of strike, and laid down procedures intended to make all strikes more difficult to launch.

The American trade union movement was for twenty years divided into two main organizations. The American Federation of Labour dated from 1886. By 1935 it was still mainly a craft union organization, but it did also include a few large industrial unions. In that year was formed the Congress of Industrial Unions, based avowedly on the principle of organizing in one union the workers employed in each industry. In 1938 AFL had 3·6 million members and CIO 4 million. For the following ten years the two organizations were of approximately equal size, AFL winning with a slight lead, but both increasing their membership. In the 1950s, however, AFL shot far ahead of CIO: in 1953 their respective membership was 10,778,000 and 5,252,000. It was widely recognized that unity would strengthen the movement, and after a period of negotiations this was at last achieved in December 1955. The new organization, with more than 15 million members, called itself simply AFL-CIO.

Impressive though the growth of American unions has been, they still include only a minority of the industrial workers. In 1933 only 11·5% of American workers were in unions, in 1953 34·2%. The proportion varied between different states. It was highest in the extreme north-west (Washington, 53%) and the industrial Middle West (Michigan, 43%), and lowest in the South. The weakness of unions in the South was largely due to racial conflict between white and negro workers. Yet there were striking differences within the region: in Alabama 25% of the workers were in unions, and even in Georgia and Mississippi 15% each, but in South Carolina only 9·3% and in North Carolina 8·3%.[38]

There is no doubt of the great increase in the standard of living of American workers in the last thirty years. It is estimated that average real wages increased from $0.77 per hour in 1929 (on the eve of the great depression) to $1·63 in 1953—in fact, that they doubled.[39] Average hours per week fell from forty-seven in 1920 to forty-one in 1953. In 1955 it was estimated that seven out of ten families in the United States had a private motor-car, and this would cover about half the industrial workers. During the first half of this century productivity per worker increased on the average by 3% per year, but since 1945 the average has been 3·5%. Against this must, however, be set the fact that a considerable minority of the working class, consisting of negroes, Mexicans, Puerto Ricans and to some extent persons of East or South European immigrant extraction, live at a level far below the average. When there is a business recession, it is the negroes who are the first to lose their jobs, and this is usually due to the pressure of the white workers rather than to prejudice by the employers. In the words of a recent work of social analysis, 'there are two working classes in the United States today: a white one with relatively ample opportunities for upward mobility; and a Negro-Mexican-Puerto-Rican working class which is socially insulated and forms a kind of a lower-caste working base which facilitates the upward careers of whites'.[40]

In Great Britain the number of trade unionists is about 9½ million, representing approximately half the country's employed population, a far higher proportion than in the United States. There is, however, probably a greater multiplicity of unions than in America, and there is no law corresponding to that portion of the Wagner Act which provides for the recognition of one single union as a partner in negotiations for the employer. In some cases the difficulties of employers are greatly increased by rivalries between different unions, particularly in cases where one represents a more skilled group of workers within the same industry and wishes to preserve a wage differential in favour of its members, which the other is determined to level out. In such a case the employer cannot grant the claims of one union without causing a breach with the other. A situation of this sort arose, for example, in British Railways.

British unions appear more preoccupied with the fear of a return of unemployment than are American, though the sufferings of American workers in the great depression of the 1930s were not less than those of the British. There is in Britain a general unwillingness to distinguish between large-scale lasting unemployment—which is clearly a catastrophe for any society—and temporary displacement of labour caused by the rise of some industries and decline of others, or by the introduction of automation. Full employment in Britain is thought by some economists to threaten the economy with a freezing of the labour force in its existing occupations. Expanding industries suffer from labour shortage, and industries which are losing ground are compelled to maintain an excessive labour force: the railways are an example. Restrictive practices cause a great deal of general frustration and at times substantial economic loss: cases such as that of the London meat market porters ('bummarees'), are grotesque. It is arguable that to some extent unemployment has been replaced by underemployment at the expense of employers, and that a slightly greater mobility of labour would benefit not only the national economy, but the majority of the working class.

Inflation, a general characteristic of Western Europe and North America, has been especially alarming in Britain, whose future depends so largely on maintaining competitive prices in international trade. The British trade unions are unwilling to tie wages to productivity, as has been widely done in the United States, to the advantage of both workers and employers, as in the agreements between General Motors and the United Automobile Workers' Union. Rather, they have preferred to make demands for wage increases when the official price index rises. Inevitably this increases inflation. For years past there have been endless speeches in Britain, from politicians, employers and unionists alike, on the need to stop inflation, but inflation continues. Instead of taking strong measures to halt it, the protagonists argue as to whether higher prices are caused by higher wages or by other causes, and in the arguments less attention is paid to economic factors than to sectional interests or political needs. One factor that has aggravated the problem is that governments since 1950 have had small majorities, and politicians have consequently been more afraid than normally in a democracy to antagonize any large group of voters. Another is that there are important differences of interest between groups of employers as regards wage increases. In industries with a high ratio of capital per worker, a wage increase may not be a serious burden. Industries working only for the home market need not fear a rise in price of their product, resulting from higher wages, so much as those which depend on export markets.

Another important feature of British labour conditions since 1945 has been the occurrence of 'unofficial strikes', not approved by the leaders of the union concerned, but carried out by local shop stewards. It is often pointed out that this situation arises because the unions become bureaucratized, and their officials are out of touch with the men. This may be true, and it may be that the quality of the new generation of union officials is inferior to that of the older men, though it is only fair to note that the unattractive pay of union full-time officials is hardly likely to recruit the ablest people. But the blame cannot all be put on the union leaders. The other main cause of this situation is apathy by union members. If they will not attend union meetings, or vote in elections of shop stewards or of trade-union committees, it becomes much easier for small well-disciplined groups to take over a union, and use it for their purposes. The most important group of this sort is, of course, the British Communist Party. Though the communists are a negligible force in national, and even in municipal, politics in Britain, there are unions in which they are extremely strong. A communist will decide on a strike or any other action according to instructions received from his party, not according to the wishes of his union's members. His party's decisions depend on the wishes of the Soviet Government, whose main purpose in regard to British industry is to damage the British economy. There are, of course, limiting factors. Moscow will be reluctant to order some action that is demonstrably against the British workers' interests, for it would thereby risk losing any influence. Moreover, there is no reason to doubt the sincere conviction of most communist labour organizers that they are the best defender of the workers' interests. The fact remains, however, that the first priority is political, not economic, and the service of Soviet, not British aims.

In Western Germany the trade-union movement, destroyed by Hitler, was reconstructed after the war. In October 1949 a convention of about 500 delegates set up the *Deutscher Gewerkschaftsbund* (DGB). In 1954 it had a membership of more than 6 million, the largest single industrial union being the metal-workers', with 1·66 million members. During the nine years of its operation the standard of living of the German workers has rapidly risen, and there have been rather few strikes. The rate of unemployment has been substantially higher than in the north-west European countries, being somewhat over a million in the winter months in the 1950s (1,112,331 in February 1957) as compared with about 300,000 in Britain, whose total population is about equal to that of Western Germany and whose industrial labour force is substantially bigger. In general, however, the German workers enjoy better conditions than they have ever had before.

An important aim of the German trade-union movement has been the demand for representation of workers on management (*Mitbestimmungsrecht*). In the Ruhr steel industry the British occupation authorities had granted this in 1946. In the independent Federal Republic a law was enacted in December 1951 for the coal and steel industries only. It provided for supervisory boards of eleven persons in enterprises in these industries, of which five were to be elected by the shareholders, five by the workers and the eleventh by the other ten. Of the five workers' representatives, two were to be chosen by the enterprise's own elected works council, one by the national leadership of the trade union, one by the DGB national leadership and one by the last two jointly. The supervisory board has the power to appoint and dismiss the managing board of the enterprise, and it is understood that the labour manager shall in practice be chosen only by the worker-elected members of the supervisory board. The DGB wished to extend *Mitbestimmungsrecht* to other industries. The law which was eventually passed in November 1952 did not satisfy them, as it established conditions markedly less favourable to the workers than in the coal and steel industries. Only one-third of the members of the supervisory board were to be elected by the workers, and the first two persons chosen by the workers must be employees of the enterprise. Thus only when the board has at least nine members can there be a member chosen by the trade-union organization from outside the firm.

In France and Italy trade-union affairs have been distorted by political issues. In both countries the unions emerged from the war under dominant communist leadership. As long as the communists were members of the government coalitions, their influence in the trade unions was used to urge labour discipline and a mighty reconstruction effort. But after the communists left the government in both countries in 1947, the trade union movements were split. In France since 1945 there had been two organizations, the majority *Confédération générale du travail* (CGT) and the Catholic movement, *Confédération française de travailleurs chrétiens* (CFTC). In 1947 the veteran trade-union leader Léon Jouhaux led a group of non-communists who broke away from CGT and set up a dissident movement called *CGT-Force ouvrière*. In Italy all unions had been combined after 1945 in the *Confederazione generale italiana del lavoro* (CGIL). In 1948 the Catholic unions seceded, and in 1949 a group associated with the Social Democratic and the Republican parties broke off. In 1950 most members of these two groups combined to form the *Confederazione italiana di sindicati del lavoro* (CISL), but a social democratic rump preserved its separate existence as *Unione italiana del lavoro* (UIL).

In both countries these splits led to a general loss of trade-union membership in the working class. In France after the war there were about seven million trade unionists (6 million in CGT and 1 million in CFTC). By 1955 the total had fallen to something over 2 million, of which there were over 1 million in CGT and less than half a million each in *Force ouvrière* and CFTC. In Italy the post-war peak membership was 7,200,000. By 1955 it had fallen to about 5 million, of which it was estimated that there were 3,500,000 in CGIL, 1,200,000 in CISL and 250,000 in UIL.

In both countries the preoccupation of the communist trade union leaders with serving the aims of a foreign state, the Soviet Union, has diminished their ability to defend working-class interests. But the communists' grip over the key positions in the trade-union machine has proved too firm to dislodge. In the political field the workers' interests have suffered, as the communists have cut themselves off from the bulk of the nation, while in the industrial field the employers have been strengthened in relation to the workers. Much less has been accomplished in the workers' interests than would have been the case had there been strong united unions concerned with social rather than political aims.

In France there was some progressive social legislation, including generous family allowances, after the war. But inflation has swallowed up wage increases to a much greater extent than in Britain. Housing conditions remain among the worst in Europe, and the disincentive to house-construction resulting from government economic policies since 1945 promises to make this problem more acute as the population, in reversal of a trend of many decades, began once more to increase. There has been impressive expansion in some branches of French industry, and unemployment has remained low. But working conditions, especially in the small businesses which remain so important a part of the French economy, are often extremely bad.

In Italy the general standard of living of the workers is lower than in France, but the trends are more encouraging. The workers in the North enjoy better conditions than ever before. Unemployment, however, is more serious than anywhere in Western Europe, remaining somewhat over 2 million in the 1950s (2,111,000 in March 1957) in a country of similar total population but much smaller industrial labour force than Great Britain, where total unemployment was one-sixth the size. And if the workers of Milan or Turin enjoy a good life by Italian standards, those of the South—of Naples or Palermo or the smaller towns of the region— live in hideous squalor. The pressure of population from the southern countryside will continue to have a depressing effect on living standards even if future governments pursue a much more progressive policy.

The only Asian country with an advanced industrial economy is Japan. Here trade unions had existed between the world wars, but had been weak. This was partly the result of police repression of all left-wing activities. It was also due to the important place in the Japanese industrial economy of small enterprises conducted on paternalist lines, in which the owner assumed responsibility for the welfare of his employees, many of whom might be relatives, or persons who had some special relationship to his family. In such firms the employees had no thought for trade unions, and the owner would not have tolerated them if they had. This feature of Japanese industry survived after 1945, and is still a strong obstacle to trade-union organization. But in those industries where large factories exist, and in mining, transportation and government service, trade unions were organized after 1945 with the encouragement of the American occupation.

Two major federations of trade unions emerged—the All-Japan Council of Industrial Unions (*Sanbetsu*), which was dominated by the communists, and the Japanese General Federation of Labour Unions (*Sodomei*) under socialist leadership. In 1950 a strong attempt was made to create a single major federation—the General Council of Trade Unions of Japan (*Sohyo*), composed of most of the *Sodomei* unions, some groups which had broken away from *Sanbetsu* and some others which had belonged to neither. But *Sohyo* was soon split by political differences, in regard to Japan's relations with the United States and the San Francisco peace treaty, corresponding to the differences which in 1951 split the socialists into two parties, left and right.* The majority opposed the proposal that *Sohyo* should join the pro-Western international federation ICFTU, while a minority broke away and in 1954 formed yet another federation— All-Japan Trade Union Council (*Zenro*), which joined ICFTU. In 1957 *Sohyo* had about 3 million members and *Zenro* about 700,000. In 1956 there were 6,300,000 trade unionists in Japan, which means that nearly half did not belong to one of the nation-wide federations. Moreover, many unions which nominally belonged to federations paid little attention to the national leaders. In 1956 all unions together covered about 37%

* See below, p. 403.

of industrial workers. In 1954 it was estimated that over 13 million wage-earners were employed in establishments of less than 100 workers, and more than half of these in workshops of less than 10, while only 3 million persons worked in enterprises employing more than 500. The trade-union movement is thus far from controlling the industrial working class of Japan. Many of the most militant unions are in white-collar professions, such as government clerks and school-teachers. The federations are very politically-minded, but union members in small enterprises are mainly concerned with immediate material problems.[41]

In Latin America the most developed trade-union movement is in Argentina. The General Confederation of Labour was a powerful weapon of Perón's dictatorship,* and at the time of his fall had some 2,500,000 members. The attempts of the new government after 1955 to remove Peronist leaders from the unions were largely interpreted as signs of its preference of capitalist to working-class interests. Its attempts to combat inflation, and to repair the economic chaos left by Perón, forced it to resist claims for wage increases. It thus had to face prolonged labour unrest. President Frondizi, elected in 1958 in part through Peronist support, soon found himself compelled to follow his predecessor in opposing working-class pressure. There was a further wave of strikes in the winter of 1958-9. At this time it was estimated that about 600,000 workers belonged to 62 unions led by Peronists, and about 1,400,000 to 32 unions with democratic leaders. The Peronists were strongest in the metallurgical, meat-packing, textile and light and power industries.

The middle classes of North America and Western Europe also have their problems. Their numbers, contrary to Marxist prediction, have been maintained or increased. Their composition is, however, different from fifty years ago. Between 1910 and 1950 in the United States the proportion of 'professional persons' in the total working population rose from 4·4% to 8·5%, of 'proprietors, managers and officials' from 6·5% to 8·6%, and of 'clerks and kindred workers' from 10·2% to 18·9%. These gains were mainly at the expense of independent farmers, whose share of the working population fell in the same period from 16·5% to 7·3%. There was also an important change within the group of 'proprietors, managers and officials', which these figures do not reveal. This was from small independent business-men to managers of various sorts. Within the 'professional' group too there has been a relative decline of independent persons and a growth of salaried—for example, in hospitals, law firms and

* See below, pp. 206, 422-3.

engineering businesses. In short, the old middle classes of propertied individuals have been largely replaced by new middle classes of property-less salaried employees, whose salaries, of course, vary enormously, from a managing director to a shop-girl who receives less than many semi-skilled workers. The change should not be exaggerated: not only do the old middle classes still exist, but the more prosperous of the salaried managers and professionals acquire property. Yet the general trend of change is unmistakable.[42]

In Britain in 1951 the equivalent groups were 'higher administrative, professional and managerial workers, including large employers', who formed 3·3% of actively employed heads of households; 'intermediate administrative, professional and managerial workers, including teachers', who formed 11·2%; shopkeepers and small employers, who formed 4·9%; clerical workers, who formed 5·1%; and shop assistants, who formed 3·1%. These add up to 27·6% of heads of households, as compared with 36% of the working population in the American estimate.[43]

French statistics for February 1956 give the following approximately equivalent categories. Large and small employers together (*patrons de l'industrie et du commerce*) formed 13·5% of the active population; senior professional and administrative people (*professions libérales et cadres supérieurs*), 3·1%; medium professional and managerial ranks (*cadres moyens*), 6·3%; and white-collar employees (*employés*), 10·5%. This gives a total of 33·4% of the population.[44]

The study of social mobility, of movement upwards or downwards between social classes, is still too little developed to allow precise conclusions about Western urban industrial societies. It is, of course, clear that the rich are better placed to get the best medical care, legal advice, education and access to well-paid and interesting jobs than are the poor. The highest posts in the political and economic hierarchy very largely go to persons whose parents belonged to the top stratum in society, and the most brilliant scientists and intellectuals tend to be children of similar people. It is equally true that no conceivable social system could enable all children of workers to become business tycoons or generals or ministers of state. The significant questions are whether social institutions form so formidable a barrier to talent as to prevent many persons of unusual ability from rising; whether the consequent losses are depriving society of abilities to a dangerous extent; whether resentment of the barriers is creating dangerous political tension; and whether the trend is towards a lowering or a restoration of barriers. All societies have, of course, had some element of social mobility—for instance, the Catholic Church hierarchy in feudal Europe—and no society has ever convinced all its citizens that equal opportunity for all exists. It may be justifiable here to risk the view that in the United States there is less opportunity than in the days of the 'open frontier', but still more than in most European countries; that in France the education system has since the mid-nineteenth century offered excellent opportunities to all, whatever their social origin, who passed the very severe tests required for the intellectual *élite*; and that in Britain the great expansion of social welfare and education in the present century, and especially since 1945, has widened and is widening opportunities. Improvements sometimes create more discontent than pleasure, and from any point of view it must be admitted that much remains to be done, but the facts admit of no doubt that enormous changes have occurred.

In the nineteenth century the political attitude of the urban middle classes was traditionally liberal. It is, however, an exaggeration to speak of the triumph of liberalism in Europe at that time: strong military and authoritarian elements were preserved in the outlook of the old ruling classes and were taken over by the *bourgeoisies* as their highest levels became fused with the previous top strata. This was true even in England, and much more so in Germany. The 1930s saw the spread of fascism over Europe. It must not be forgotten that German National Socialism had very strong working-class support before Hitler became Chancellor in January 1933. But middle-class support for fascism in Germany and Italy was relatively still stronger, and it was considerable in France and not unknown in England in the 1930s. In Germany it was in large part a reaction against defeat in war and inflation. Fear of finally losing their social respectability, and a passionate desire to be revenged on Germany's victors, were perhaps the most powerful motives of middle-class Nazis. Some of the same emotions were found in Mussolini's Italy: Italy had not lost the war, but Italian nationalists had got much less from the peace settlement than they had demanded.

After 1945 liberal democracy had a revival in Western Europe. It always remained strong in the United States, Britain, the Low Countries and Scandinavia. In France, Germany and Italy it was restored. At present it appears to be much healthier in Germany than in Italy, and the failure of the Fourth Republic in France, and the return of General de Gaulle to power, cast some doubt on the political attitude of the French *bourgeoisie*. In Britain too there are danger points. The futility of a great deal of party politics and parliamentary proceedings, the continuance of inflation and the unending series of insults to British interests all over the world are producing an exasperation which sometimes alarmingly recalls the climate of Weimar Germany. But though the devotion to liberal democracy of the urban classes in Western industrial society has its limits, it is safe to conclude that on neither the *bourgeois* nor the proletarian side is there much sign today of a revolutionary class struggle in Western Europe or North America.

SOVIET SOCIETY

In the last ten years before 1917 the Russian working class was becoming modernized, and a considerable skilled element had been trained. It was from this *élite* of the working class that the cadres of the Soviet régime were formed. The skilled workers became communist party organizers, key government officials and officers of the Red Army, and most of them never returned to the factory bench. The working class that emerged after 1920 was, like the Russian working class of the 1890s, a mass of unskilled peasant children.

In 1917 trade unions greatly extended their membership. But in the chaos and exaltation of revolution their functions could have little in common with those of trade unions in a normal industrial society. During the civil war they had been completely subjected to the communist party, and had indeed served principally as a means of mobilizing manpower for the armed forces, transportation and necessary public works.

When the civil war was over some of the trade-union leaders had put forward political demands. A group known as the Workers' Opposition had a plan for reorganizing the new state on syndicalist lines, with the unions managing the economy. At the 10th Congress of the communist party in 1921 they were defeated, and the supremacy of the highly centralized party over political, social and economic institutions was reasserted. At the same time the new régime was threatened with serious labour unrest in Petrograd, in which the socialist opponents of the communists were involved, and with the armed rising in the nearby naval base of Kronstadt. All these threats were, however, mastered by force. The trade unions remained instruments of the party, and were able to do little to defend the workers' interests.

What little freedom the unions had, they lost with the adoption of the final draft of the First Five Year Plan in 1929. Stalin's determination rapidly to create a heavy industrial base in the Soviet Union caused him to prefer, in the treatment of the workers as of the peasants, a policy of coercion to one of incentives. Industrialization requires raw materials, a labour force and skill. Russia had great natural resources, and the overpopulated villages had great reserves of manpower. What was lacking was skill in both its forms—living technicians and skilled workers, and machinery produced by past labour. If the Plan had to be fulfilled at breakneck speed, the only way was to compensate for lack of skill by the use of much larger quantities of labour. The output that could be produced by one skilled worker with the appropriate machine, could be produced by three or five or ten pairs of bare hands. During the First Five Year Plan period the industrial labour force swelled far above the numbers intended by the planners. Swamped by an influx of millions of unskilled peasant boys and girls, the trade unions could not hope to insist on even minimum living conditions. They could only provide a certain number of harassed and overworked drill-sergeants desperately trying to weld these raw recruits into an industrial army.

The plight of the Russian workers in these years was that of any unskilled working class in the early stage of industrialization, but it was aggravated by the fact that the speed was artificially forced beyond anything that any private capitalists had ever attempted, and that the orders were given by a dictator who was unmoved by economic considerations of profit or loss. The fact that an enterprise might be completely uneconomic, which would have deterred even the most ruthless private business-man, would not and did not deter Stalin.

Unable to strike, and too backward to organize themselves into any sort of pressure group, the workers reacted to these terrible conditions by constantly changing their jobs. The government refused to slacken the pace of construction, to pay better real wages, or to divert to building houses resources which were destined for factory plants. Disciplinary offences were punished by expulsion of families from their dwelling-place, or by terms of imprisonment. Penalties were imposed on managers who accepted workers who had left a previous job without permission, or had been dismissed by another employer for some offence. It was also possible for the police to decide that a labour offence came under the category of 'counter-revolutionary crimes' listed in Article 58 of the Criminal Code. Wastage of materials could be treated as 'sabotage', grumbling as 'anti-Soviet propaganda', which could be punished by long terms of forced labour in 'correctional labour camps', or even by death. During the Second Five Year Plan period (1933-7) conditions improved, but the Great Purge of 1937-8 had the important effect of enormously increasing the population of the forced labour camps, whose numbers reached perhaps 8 millions, perhaps much more. From 1939 to 1941 conditions again improved. But the war with Hitler inevitably brought renewed economic hardships to the whole people. It was only from 1948 that a real recovery set in. Twenty years after the First Five Year Plan had been launched, the standard of living of the workers was still miserably low, but their level of skill had enormously grown. They were still poor, but they were no longer a mass of unskilled peasant labourers. Russia now had something like a modern industrial labour force, with skilled and semi-skilled workers many millions strong.

The situation of the workers was also affected by the appalling losses of population caused by collectivization of agriculture, the Great Purge, the battle losses and starvation of the war, and the fall in births due to the absence for many years of so many males both in the armed forces and in the forced labour camps. The population of the Soviet Union—including the territories annexed with the help of Hitler in 1939 and 1940—was about 195 million in 1940. With a normal annual increase of about 3 million, it should by 1955 have risen to 240 million. In fact in 1955 it was just over 200,000,000. Even a very powerful nation cannot afford to lose 40 million people. If surplus manpower had been an asset to Stalin in 1929, in 1955 labour was no longer expendable, but something precious, to be carefully preserved. This fact, together with their new skill, strengthened the position of the Soviet working class. For the last ten years the government has felt the need to conciliate the workers, to some extent at least to replace coercion by incentives. The severe penalties for offences against labour discipline have been abolished. Real wages have improved, pensions and social services have got better, and there have even been unmistakable signs of the same trend that is so visible in Western countries for an evening-out of wage differentials between levels of skill.

Stalin's forced industrial revolution of 1929-37 had another important effect which he had doubtless not intended: it created a new upper stratum of society. In the West industrialization had been the work of the capitalists, who had existed before the technical inventions that made modern factories possible; but its effect was both to increase the social power of capitalists and to strengthen the numbers and influence of the other sections of the *bourgeoisie*. In Soviet Russia industrialization was decreed by the leader of the communist party, but it created the demand for hundreds of thousands of managers and skilled professional people. Whatever these people might be, they were not workers, even if their parents had been. During the 1930s Soviet schools, technical colleges and universities trained hundreds of thousands of young people—sons of workers or peasants or pre-1917 professional people or officials of the Imperial bureaucracy —to be engineers, technologists, doctors, scientists, teachers and administrators of all kinds. The Great Purge of 1937-8 swept away a large part of the surviving pre-1917 experts. Their places were taken by the new Soviet-trained educated stratum.

These people were described by Stalin in the late 1930s as the 'toiling intelligentsia'. In 1939 it was stated that there were 9,700,000 of them. The corresponding groups in 1955 numbered about 15 million—with family dependents perhaps two and a half times as many. This very large number is, of course, composed of a great variety of occupations, which have in common only that they do not involve manual labour. Soviet official statistics show two main professional categories which cover these occupations, and amount to 25% of the employed population.* They include government officials, managers in industry, the higher ranks of the professions and also large numbers of miscellaneous clerks and white-collar workers. Separate figures are available for certain professions, and show a remarkable growth in twenty years.

School-teachers in 1937 numbered 969,000 and in 1955 1,733,000. Between 1940 and 1955 fully trained doctors (including dentists, but excluding military medical officers) increased from 155,000 to 334,000. From 1941 to 1955 engineers with a higher education increased from 290,000 to 586,000.[45]

The higher levels of the 'toiling intelligentsia' enjoy great material privileges. Those luxuries that are available in the Soviet Union—food, drink, clothes, jewellery, expensive household equipment, the use of holiday villas and rest-houses, motor-cars—are at their disposal. In the 1940s official policy seemed designed to make these privileges hereditary. In 1940 fees were introduced for tuition at universities and in the top classes of secondary schools. At the same time a system of Labour Reserves was introduced, by which a large proportion of children aged between fourteen and seventeen—especially of rural children—were sent to special industrial training schools, and effectively deprived of the chance of higher education. Children of parents in the higher income brackets, however, who lived in great cities and had social contact with families of influential officials or managers, were correspondingly favoured. After the war this policy was gradually abandoned. The tuition fees were not increased though prices and wages rose, and in 1956 they were abolished. The Labour Reserves system fell into disuse. Secondary education was much more widely extended. Nevertheless, it is clear that children of richer and

* These two categories are: (1) 'engineering-technical workers, officials, junior supervisory personnel, commercial employees' (*inzhenerno-tekhnicheskie rabotniki, sluzhashchie, mladshii obsluzhivayushchii personal, rabotniki torgovli*), who formed 10·2% of the employed population; (2) 'those employed in unproductive branches (education, health services, housing and communal economy, passenger transport and communications, the state administration and the administration of public and cooperative organizations)', who formed 14·8%. The last category may include some manual workers, at least in transport. These figures are given in *Narodnoe khozyaistvo SSSR*, published by the state statistical publishing house, Moscow, 1956 p. 188.

better-placed families enjoy great advantages. More roomy living quarters, a more cultured home and influential acquaintances and friends are as much an advantage in the 'socialist' Soviet Union as in 'capitalist' America or Britain. Moreover, certain universities and certain secondary schools giving best access to those universities are known to offer far better chances of careers, and places in them are keenly competed for. Here the child of genius from a humble home may get in, but the merely competent child of an influential father will certainly do better than the child of equal ability who has no such advantage.* In all this, of course, the Soviet Union is neither worse nor better than 'capitalist' countries. In general it seems that social mobility is still very high in the Soviet Union. The chances for an able child to better himself, to get into *some* sort of a university or college and to get some sort of professional or managerial job, are fairly good. But access to the really influential jobs, to the careers that bring great prestige or power, is not easy. And, of course, in so vast a country, still containing very remote provinces and a great number of languages, there are difficulties of access to careers that do not exist in homogeneous West European countries. The chances of a Yakut collective farmer's son can no more compare with those of a Moscow boy than a South Carolina negro's with a Philadelphia business-man's.

The Soviet upper stratum, with its material privileges and the favourable chances in life for its children, is hard to define. There is an interesting difference between it and the upper strata of Imperial Russia. In the latter, as we have seen, the three middle-class elements of business, bureaucracy and professions were separated from each other, as it were by vertical compartments. They lacked the common ethos which, in the historical evolution of the same social groups in Western Europe had drawn them together into an increasingly homogeneous class—the *bourgeoisie*. By contrast, the upper stratum of Soviet society has something approaching a common ethos—a mixture of more or less digested Marxist theory, sense of obligation to serve the state, and a narrow but deeply felt nationalist pride in the Soviet state. There are some curious resemblances to the outlook of the nineteenth-century business class. There is the same dreary puritanism in private morals—at least as publicly professed. There is the same tendency to equate outward and visible prosperity with inward and invisible grace, the same condescension or even contempt of the self-made man for the people of coarser clay who have failed to rise. There is the same aggressive bad taste in arts and literature, the hatred of

* The narrowing of opportunities of entry into universities, which results from Khrushchov's educational reforms of 1959, must inevitably increase the relative advantages of children of well-placed families.

artistic originality, the preference for nice catchy tunes, the love of a pompous architecture to symbolize the achievements of the self-made. The Soviet upper stratum differs from the nineteenth-century Western *bourgeoisie* in that it does not own the means of production, but administers and has the use of them on behalf of the state. There is also no trace in its outlook of the individualism that was the essence of the *bourgeois* ethos in the West. But this Soviet upper stratum *has* a common ethos, and the points mentioned above in which it resembles that of the Victorians are striking. The Victorians were the product of an Industrial Revolution brought about by private initiative, the Soviet upper stratum of one initiated by the State. One is tempted, for lack of a better name, to call this Soviet stratum a State *bourgeoisie*, distinguishing it thereby from the historical Western private *bourgeoisie*, with its outlook of individualism. Though this name is not entirely satisfactory, it seems to the writer the most useful yet available.

The problem of the relations between the state *bourgeoisie* and the working class, and between both and the Soviet state, cannot be discussed without reference to the nature of the Soviet political system, and so must be left to a later chapter. At this point we must consider the problem of urban classes in the third type of society—the 'underdeveloped'.

UNDERDEVELOPED SOCIETIES

In these countries the condition of the urban working class most closely resembles that observed by Marx 100 years ago. There are the same influx of unskilled labour from the villages, the same competition of surplus manpower for jobs, the same factors forcing down the level of wages, the same social uprootedness. The last factor is indeed more acute in Asia and Africa today than it was in Europe in Marx's time, for the contrast between the background of the Asian or African worker and life in the big city is greater than it was then. Skill and education at all levels of society are rarer than they were in a Europe which had centuries of feudal and *bourgeois* culture behind it. Entrepreneurial skill is especially scarce, and is often provided by foreign elements (European big business or immigrant Chinese or Syrian or Greek small business), which adds a strong element of nationalist resentment to social discontent. An especially difficult situation arises when European and local working classes exist side by side, as in Northern Rhodesia or the Union of South Africa. On the other hand, in some cases the Asian and African workers of today are more favourably placed than their European predecessors. The English workers had to fight hard for their trade-union rights. But British and French colonial governments, on recommendations from the government in London and

Paris, have quickly granted recognition to labour organizations, and have even helped in their formation. This is, of course, above all a result of public opinion and trade-union influence in the metropolitan country. In independent Asian and African countries the new rulers have nearly always encouraged working-class organizations, partly because they are themselves largely influenced by left-wing ideologies and partly because they hope to find in the unions valuable instruments to support their own political power.

Some of these problems can be better understood by taking as illustrations the present state of trade unions in some Asian and African countries.

In India in 1951 the census showed 9·2 million persons employed in processing or manufacturing, of whom 5·4 million were independent producers and 3·5 million worked for wages or salaries. Of the latter number, only 1,632,000 were employed in enterprises that had at least twenty employees and used mechanical power. Cotton and jute textile factories together employed nearly two-thirds of these.

The Indian workers have been organized in three separate trade-union movements. The largest membership is claimed by the Indian National Trade Union Congress (1,400,000 in 1957), which is closely linked to the Congress Party. The communist-controlled unions of the All-India Trade Union Congress in 1956 claimed to have 750,000 members. The Hind Mazdoor Sabha, linked to the Socialist Party, claimed 485,000 members. These numbers show that many persons are enrolled in trade unions who are not factory workers. The Indian authorities do not look with favour on strikes. But the past record of the use of the strike as a political weapon in the struggle for independence gives it a certain traditional respectability. Thus the authorities are more tolerant of strikes whose motives are political than of strikes for economic reasons. Strikes caused by the desire for better living conditions may therefore be camouflaged by their leaders as 'political', a curious reversal of the pattern familiar in European labour history. The division of the labour movement into three political groups may appear unfortunate at first sight, but it has the compensating advantage that the Congress unions, faced with the competition of their rivals, are compelled to pay more attention to the workers' interests. The non-Congress unions are 'the gadfly that prevents the INTUC from becoming a passive labour-front type of organization, and the check to possible excessive government and party control'.[46]

In Indonesia the Central Organization of Indonesian Labour (SOBSI) was formed in 1946, and since then has been controlled by the communists, being indeed their strongest political weapon. In 1957 it claimed 2,600,000 members, mostly agricultural and plantation workers. A non-party organization, the All-Indonesian Trade Union Council (KBSI) was formed in May 1953, but its membership is much smaller than that of SOBSI.

In the Middle East there has been an increase in trade-union membership since the war, but it can hardly be said that any strong labour movement, primarily defending the workers' interests and independent of political control, exists. In Turkey membership increased between 1949 and 1952 from 75,000 to 173,000, the latter number amounting to about one-quarter of Turkey's industrial workers. The largest single union were the coal-miners of Zonguldak, with 17,000 members. In 1958 strikes were still illegal, under an Act of 1936, which provided for compulsory conciliation and arbitration by bodies which included workers' elected delegates. In Egypt the number of trade unionists doubled between 1953 and 1955, in which year there were nearly 500,000. In the same year was founded a central body, the All-Egyptian Trade Union Congress, which changed its name in March 1957 to General Confederation of Egyptian Workers. In 1956 the AETUC had played the leading part in founding an International Confederation of Arab Trade Unions. Though there was no doubt of the Egyptian revolutionary government's desire to improve the workers' conditions, it was also clear that it regarded both the Egyptian and the wider Arab trade-union movement as instruments of its internal political power and its international ambitions. In Persia trade unions quickly developed after 1945, with a strong communist element in their leadership. The suppression in 1949 of the *Tudeh* (communist) party led to the collapse of the Central Council of Unified Trade Unions of Iran, which its members had controlled. In 1954 there were 80,000 workers in Persian trade unions, about one-fifth of the industrial and commercial labour force.[47]

In the Sudan a trade-union movement grew up very quickly in the post-war years. Its founders were politically conscious railway employees, who had learned their ideas in Workers' Clubs in Atbara and Khartoum from the mid-1930s. In 1946 they set up a Workers' Affairs Association of workers in the mechanical department of the Sudan Railways. In July 1947 it organized a successful railway strike, and obtained official recognition from the British authorities. This success was, of course, due not only to the efficiency and militancy of WAA, but to the fact that the British Labour government in London was anxious to go very far in concessions to a working-class movement. In the following years the Sudanese trade-union movement was involved in political agitation for independence, and some of its leaders were active communists. In November 1950 a central body was set up, the Sudan Workers' Trade Union Federation. A year later there were 41 registered unions with 38,000 members of whom nearly half (17,000) were in the Sudan Railways Workers' Union. When Sudan became independent the SWTUF lost ground, as its leaders, following communist international policy, denounced the Anglo-Egyptian agreement of 1953.

In tropical Africa a particularly important problem is that of migrant labour. The comparatively few centres of industry—for the most part mines—attract workers from a considerable distance. These come from different tribes, with different languages and customs, and in certain cases from territories ruled by different European administrations. These are factors aggravating their social uprootedness, for which there is no parallel in European early industrial history. There is a rapid turnover of seasonal labourers, who go back to their homes as soon as they have earned the sum needed by their families, for which they came. But a growing proportion remain in the cities and become more or less urbanized. At least the African workers have certain advantages over their European nineteenth-century predecessors in that the governments, both colonial and independent, are more aware of the nature of the problems, and are more convinced of their duty to do something about them, than were European governments in the heyday of *laisser-faire*. On the other hand, when governments have to deal with colour bars, as in Northern Rhodesia, or are themselves inspired by a racial ideology, as in South Africa, passions and conflicts are generated which Europe never knew.

In British West Africa some progress was made in dealing with migrant labour problems. In the post-war years Departments of Labour established Labour Codes, which were increasingly observed, and unscrupulous intermediaries were less able to deceive and coerce ignorant persons than was the case in the past, when they were recruited in remote villages by false promises, transported to the place of employment in frightful conditions and forced to work with barely enough to eat or a place to sleep. Turnover of labour remains very high—in the Gold Coast in 1952 it was estimated that the average underground mining worker remains in his job for six months. The lack of a stable labour force clearly made it very hard to organize trade unions. Lack of work discipline and of a sense of solidarity as workers (as opposed to a sense of community with others who were members of one's tribe or ethnic group) were further obstacles. It was generally recognized that African supervisory workers were much needed, but not much was done to train them. In spite of these huge difficulties, trade unions rapidly grew. In Nigeria there were 27,000 paid-up members of registered trade unions in 1945 and 151,000 in 1954: this was said to be 47% of all employed workers in the country, but as the number of workers had probably been underestimated the percentage was almost certainly a good deal lower. In Ghana there were 6,000 paid-up trade-union members in 1945, and 46,000 in 1953, the latter figure representing 26% of all workers. The trade unions were less effective than these numbers would suggest, for many of them were very small and purely local, and in neither country was there a united central leadership. Trade-union division was bound up with political divisions. In the case of independent Ghana, the relationship of the trade unions to the dominant party of Dr. Nkrumah raised difficult problems for the future.[48]

In Northern Rhodesia the main industrial area, the Copper Belt, had in the mid-1950s a labour force of some 6,000 European and 35,000 African miners. The European workers expect to live at an European standard of living (in fact, higher than most workers in Europe can aspire to). The wages they receive are enormously higher than those of the Africans, who, however, are accustomed to very much lower living standards. In the early period of the mining industry, skilled jobs could in fact only be done by white workers. But as Africans became more skilled, the question of advancement of Africans to jobs of a higher grade arose. The European workers, however, feared that if this were done their own wage levels would be undermined, and their special standard of living collapse. In 1937 they had formed their North Rhodesia Mine-workers' Union (a purely white body), and in 1940, when the government in its wartime need for copper pressed the employers to be conciliatory to labour, they were able to extract a closed shop for the union and an assurance that none of the jobs recognized as 'European jobs' at that time would be given to Africans. In 1949 the African workers, whose discipline and sense of solidarity had notably improved, created their own African Mine-workers' Union, having received some help and advice from trade unionists in Britain. The white union did not at first oppose it. In 1950 the two unions made an agreement, by which the white union promised not to oppose African advancement and the African promised that its members would not accept jobs hitherto reserved to Europeans unless they were given European pay. The employers, however, had no interest in paying Africans the artificially high rates received by Europeans: if they had got to pay these rates, they might just as well employ Europeans. Thus the Africans had been tricked into depriving themselves of their only practical prospect of improvement—namely, to accept wages substantially lower than the European rates. Meanwhile, the employers continued to occupy an unenviable situation, unable to satisfy one group of workers without dangerously antagonizing the other: they could not go on ignoring the Africans, as in the past, for they were becoming an organized force to be reckoned with. In 1955 one of the two mining companies, the Rhodesian Selection Trust, after long negotiations made an agreement with the white union, by which 24 categories of jobs could be transferred to Africans at rates below the European. By mid-1956 it was estimated that 230 Africans were doing jobs in the 24 categories and that a further 250 were under training —a total of 500 out of 35,000 African miners.[49] This modest beginning was, however, of some importance as a breach in the structure of European privilege.

Industry is more developed in the Union of South Africa than in any part of the continent south of the Sahara. It is also in this country that racial conflict between European and Africans is most acute. The Rand goldmines employed in 1956 an average for the year of 51,000 white workers and 336,000 Bantu. Of the latter, 62% were from outside the territory of the Union.[50] By African standards, their wages are good, and they are given some medical care while they work for the mines. But the social tensions, inevitable in so large an urban area as Johannesburg and the Rand, with so many immigrants from African rural society, are enormously aggravated by the determination of the South African government for doctrinal reasons to regard the Africans as merely temporary dwellers, belonging essentially to native areas to which they must in time return. The government is deliberately opposed to settling Africans with their families, or creating urban amenities for Africans. The results are the miserable housing conditions, the overcrowded encampments of squatters, the growth of African prostitution and violent crime, the oppressive system of pass laws brutally enforced, the treatment of Africans by the police as if they were conquered enemies, and the steadily mounting volume of race hatred.

In industries other than mining, conditions are rather more hopeful. In 1953 nearly 260,000 Europeans and nearly 560,000 Africans were employed in manufacturing.[51] Both European and African trade unions exist, but only the former may be officially registered. Under the Industrial Conciliation Acts of 1937 and 1954, only registered unions may be represented on the Industrial Councils or Conciliation Boards which handle industrial disputes. Moreover, under a wartime Emergency Regulation of 1942, African workers are prohibited from striking under any circumstances. Thus the ability of African trade unions to defend their members' interests is very limited. In fact, African workers are at the mercy of their employers and of the government, who may or may not choose to take measures for their welfare.

In 1956 there were three main groups of unions. The South African Federation of Trade Unions, representing 13 unions with 60,000 members, was registered. So was the Co-ordinating Council of South African Trade Unions, representing 14 unions with a membership of 20,000. The Co-ordinating Council was closely linked to the Nationalist Party, and consisted overwhelmingly of Afrikaans-speaking workers, and strongly upheld *apartheid* doctrines. The third group, the South African Trade Union Council, representing 47 unions with 148,000 members, was not registered, as some of its member unions included non-European branches, and no union possessing a non-European branch could be registered under the Industrial Conciliation Bill of 1954.[52] The division of the trade-union movement would be more harmful to the interests of the European workers, were it not that these, in comparison with the Africans, represent a privileged class. As long ago as 1922 the European miners were a discontented element. In the Rand strike of that year violence was used, and four European workers' leaders were hanged. But in recent years the European workers have on the whole made common cause with employers and governments against the African workers, any improvement in whose situation they fear. Their attitude resembles that of 'poor whites' in the South in the United States, but it is more uncompromising.

In the urban sector of underdeveloped societies the three social groups mentioned earlier—bureaucrats, business-men and the intellectual *élite* —exist, but do not form a single middle class, whether a 'private *bourgeoisie*' or a 'State *bourgeoisie*'.

In those societies which remained independent states, the bureaucrats were local people, but the business-men were largely foreigners or members of local minorities with special commercial abilities (Jews, Armenians, Greeks, Lebanese or Chinese). In those societies which became colonies of European Powers, the prevalence of foreigners and of ethnic minorities in the business class was still more marked, while the upper ranks of the bureaucracy and of the armed forces were predominantly filled by foreigners.

In both cases, the element in the urban upper stratum which played the leading political role was the third social group—the intellectual *élite*. It was this group which provided the leadership and organization for the democratic and nationalist movements which set themselves, by peaceful or revolutionary means, to overthrow the colonial régime or the local traditional ruling classes or both. It is the intellectual *élite* which, in those countries where national independence has been achieved, has provided the governing cadres of the new states. The social predicament and political significance of this intelligentsia is the subject of the next chapter. It is, however, first necessary to say something of the world-wide trade-union organizations as a factor in international politics.

TRADE UNIONS AND WORLD POLITICS

The Second World War was felt by trade unionists to be very much a war for the working class against fascism, which had smashed trade unions and destroyed all genuine working-class organization in all the lands which it ruled. There was also a widespread feeling, not shared by experienced Western union leaders, yet no less powerful for that, that the Soviet Union, one of the great Allies, stood for the rights of the workers. It was therefore natural that at the end of the war there should have been a desire for a single world-wide trade-union organization, to include former members of the Amsterdam International of free unions, and the former communist unions of the so-called Profintern,[53] and new trade-union movements which might come into existence in future. The result was the foundation of the World Federation of Trade Unions (WFTU) in 1945.

It soon, however, became clear that the Soviet trade unions were concerned not so much with the interests of the working classes of the world as with the promotion of Soviet foreign policy. As the conflict between the Western Powers and the Soviet Union became acute, and communist parties left the government coalitions in Western Europe, a breach in WFTU became inevitable. The non-communist trade unions decided to form a new international organization of their own, and this came into existence as the International Confederation of Free Trade Unions (ICFTU), founded at a congress in London in December 1949.

In 1956 WFTU consisted primarily of the monolithic monster trade unions of the Soviet Union (claiming 40 million members), China (12 million) and the East European countries. These are not independent workers' organizations at all, but government institutions designed to mobilize the workers for the governments' purposes, to tighten their discipline and to extract a greater output from them. WFTU members outside the orbit have the task of furthering the interests of the Soviet state by disrupting the economy of their own countries, defending workers' claims in so far as they need workers' support, but using it essentially for political aims. The most important of these are the French CGT, the Italian CGIL and the Indonesian SOBSI. In India the communist-controlled All-India TUC is a considerable force. In Latin America the most impressive figure of membership is shown by the Ecuadorian CTE (*Confederación de trabajadores de Ecuador*, claiming 115,000 in 1956). Communist influence is strong in the Sudanese movement, but a proposal that it should join WFTU was not accepted.

The important members of ICFTU are the great trade unions of Western Europe, North America and Australasia. The leaders of ICFTU have, however, made great efforts to extend their influence in other continents. The majority of Indian trade unionists are members, through the Indian National TUC and the *Hind Mazdoor Sabha*. A large number of Japanese trade unionists (about 1,700,000 members in 1956) are affiliated to ICFTU individually, with a co-ordinating committee in which decisions must be taken unanimously. The Israel trade unions of *Histadrut*, with 550,000 members, also belong. So do the trade-union confederations of Brazil, Cuba and Mexico, though their right to be regarded as the independent representatives of the working class is questionable. The Tunisian organization (*Union générale tunisienne du travail*) became a member, and received help and advice from ICFTU, when Tunisia was still a French protectorate, and has continued to be since Tunisia won independence.

Certain important trade-union movements belong to neither camp. Among these it is worth mentioning the Japanese *Sohyo*, in which there is some communist influence, and which is dominated by the left-wing socialists; the Arab federation, controlled by the Nasser régime; and the Argentine unions, in which *Peronista* influence is still strong after the Perón régime has ceased to exist.

The activities of the ICFTU in the underdeveloped countries are based on the genuine conviction that it is its duty to help weak young workers' movements and to prevent them from being led astray by communist propaganda. In these objectives they have had some success. Their critics argue that, by forcing the growth of trade unions in countries where social and educational conditions are not ripe for them, they have created difficult problems which might have been postponed, and thus have been of use to the communists even when opposing them. This argument can be neither proved nor refuted in abstract terms, but only considered according to the facts of each case. It is probably more usually true than not that delay in these matters is more dangerous than haste.

This brief survey has shown that the materially depressed and socially uprooted working class of underdeveloped societies is a potentially explosive revolutionary force, and that in both Western industrial societies and Soviet society working-class pressure is a factor which governments have to take into account. It is now necessary to consider the role of intellectual leadership in revolutionary movements, and the special importance of the intelligentsia as a social group and as a political factor in underdeveloped societies.

6: The Intelligentsia

It is a commonplace that revolutionary movements have their origin not only in economic conditions and social conflicts, but also in the growth of political ideas. Less recognized is the need to study the social group that specializes in the formulation of political ideas.

In medieval Europe the Catholic clergy provided not only theological doctrine, but also such worldly intellectual leadership as society required. It was after the Reformation, itself closely linked with the rise of urban classes and the expansion of ocean-borne commerce, that a secular intellectual *élite* became an important social factor. In the Islamic and Buddhist countries traditional religious thought set limits to learning and culture, and there was no significant secular intellectual *élite* until the advent of European military and economic power forced these countries to modernize themselves. In China learning was subject not so much to ecclesiastical control as to the traditional wisdom of secular Confucian thought, which was hardly more suited than Islamic or Buddhist theology to equip its adherents to face the new tasks inflicted on them by the intrusion of the West. In China too the modern secular intellectual *élite* was created under European influence.

The intelligentsia, the social group that produces modern political ideas and provides the leadership of revolutionary movements, thus has two distinct stages in its history, the first in Europe from the Reformation to modern times, the second in the underdeveloped countries which came under Western influence at different times between the eighteenth century (Russia) and the twentieth (Africa).

THE GROWTH OF THE INTELLIGENTSIA

The development of the intellectual *élite* differed very substantially between Catholic and Protestant countries. Both had secular *élites*, for modern skills and knowledge were needed by both. In both also a powerful priesthood was backed by the lay power, by Kings of England and Lutheran princes in Germany as well as by Catholic monarchs in France and Austria and Spain. But in Protestant countries the limits set to thought expanded. The Churches confined themselves fairly narrowly to matters of faith, and the growing belief in the importance of individual judgement in religion and in business gradually created a climate favourable to individual judgement in matters of science and of politics. Protestantism and capitalism led to constitutional government and toleration. Admittedly, the process was long and painful, and included such epic conflicts as the

English Civil War. But in Catholic countries the process did not take place. Ecclesiastical censorship was more far-reaching and more severe, the secular arm unequivocally supported the Church, the monarchs remained absolute, and political dissent was not permitted in principle even if it was often possible in practice under the protection of a powerful patron.

It was in France that the conflict of the secular intellectual *élite* with the authorities of State and Church had the most fateful consequences. Under Louis XIV flourished a most brilliant civilization, which expressed the thought and wit and taste of the most intelligent nation in Europe. Yet the same monarch who gloried in these achievements, impossible without a free exchange of sceptical and at times irreverent opinion, gave his backing to an intolerant Church. In 1685 he repealed the Edict of Nantes, which had assured the freedom of France's large Protestant minority. Many talented Frenchmen went into exile, and in France itself the intellectual *élite* were bitterly hostile to the alliance of throne and altar. Under the successor of the *roi soleil*, the alliance was too weak and irresolute to command respect, yet strong and bigoted enough to commit isolated acts of persecution.

The result was that in the minds of French intellectuals of the eighteenth century, which included many of the most humane and penetrating of the age, political tyranny and religion were indissolubly connected. The revolt of the humane conscience against the King was also a revolt against God. Disillusioned with the worldly Church, they lost their religious belief itself. The gap was filled by the new doctrines of the Enlightenment. It is important to understand that the new ideas were more than a political programme: they were a substitute for religion. This helps to explain the passionate utopianism which found expression during the Great Revolution which began in 1789, and also appeared in other Catholic countries to which the ideas of the Revolution spread, especially in Spain, where the search for a total political doctrine, which would embrace all man's social and emotional needs, remained a factor right through the nineteenth century and well into the twentieth. In Protestant countries, on the other hand, religion and politics have on the whole been kept in separate compartments in the last two centuries. Anti-clericalism is not unknown, especially in Germany, where the alliance of the Lutheran Church with the princes had brought on it some of the odium which attached to the Catholic Church in France. But there has been in Britain, Holland and Scandinavia no necessary connexion between radical politics and anti-clericalism, and certainly none between left-wing ideas and rejection of religion. On the contrary, the British labour movement was closely connected with the chapels of Nonconformity. In Protestant countries in the twentieth century it is perhaps true that deeply religious people have more often been conservative than radical in their politics, but this is not an argument that should be worked too hard. In general it is true that citizens of Protestant countries go to the polls or to political meetings if they want politics, to church or chapel if they want religion, and to neither if they are indifferent.

In nineteenth- and twentieth-century Western Europe and North America the secular intellectual *élite* grew into the much more numerous free professions, and these were increasingly merged in the *bourgeoisie*, increasingly united by the *bourgeois* ethos with the business and official classes. Nevertheless, intellectuals, in the narrow sense, have played an important part in political movements in the West. It was, of course, intellectuals who first elaborated both liberal and socialist doctrines. The labour movements which arose at the end of the nineteenth century were in fact the joint creation of workers seeking organizations to defend their material interests, and of radical intellectuals seeking to realize their socialist doctrines. The relative influence of the two elements varied between different countries. In Britain the trade unions were strong before there was a working-class party at all. When the Labour Party was founded, it did not for some time commit itself definitely to socialism. In Germany the intellectuals were more influential. Though the founders of the Social Democratic Party had serious disagreements with Karl Marx, the party eventually committed itself to his ideas, and among its leaders there were both working men and intellectuals. The trade unions were large and important by 1914, but were less important as a spokesman for the workers than was the party, which largely controlled them. In France the influence of intellectuals and workers was more evenly balanced. The trade unions were independent of the socialist party, and had relatively more prestige among the workers than in Germany, though less than in England. These differences in the origins of the three movements have had effects that have not entirely disappeared, but the later trend in all three was similar. All three became mass parties based mainly on the workers, but attracting also a considerable number of middle-class people, including intellectuals, and all three loudly proclaimed socialist principles while they were in opposition.

Modern radical political doctrines grew up in Western Europe, and were derived from the social realities and cultural past of the countries in which they were born. Russia, the Balkan countries, Asia and Africa received them ready-made. There the cultural past was different, and the social realities which had given birth to the ideas in Europe, existed hardly or not at all. The ideas, however, quickly appealed to the small number of young people in underdeveloped countries who had access to them through a modern secular Western education, either in a Western school or university or in a Western-type educational institution in their own country. Against the exciting new ideas the old orthodoxies, propounded by the old intellectual *élite* of Russian priests, Moslem *mullas*, Buddhist monks or Confucian *literati*, were increasingly helpless. Attempts at some synthesis of the new and the old were seldom successful, whether made by Russian Slavophiles or Moslem conservative modernists. Japan is the only notable exception. The general trend has been a repudiation of traditional values, secularization, worship of Western material success and acceptance in turn of the series of ideas fashionable at different stages in the West. Yet the ready acceptance was deceptive. Not only did the application of the ideas tend to create anti-Western nationalism, stronger and more dangerous than the earlier anti-Westernism of the old orthodoxies in decline; but also, under the surface of conformity to Western models, the old ways of thoughts, and remnants of the old moral and cultural values, remained, difficult to identify and analyse, not only for outside Western observers, but for the non-Western intellectuals themselves.

There are certain features of the predicament of the modern-educated intellectual in an underdeveloped country which are common to them all. Its essence is the frustration caused by their awareness of the contrasts between their own cultural level and standards of life and those of their people; between the backwardness of their country's economy and the needs of the modern world; and between the political ideas they have learned in their Western-type education and the tyrannical régime that rules their country.

These contrasts are most striking in cases where economic backwardness, by Western standards, is combined with political oppression. Here the intellectuals are not only appalled by the backwardness—of which they are aware through their Western knowledge at a time when the peasant masses, lacking such knowledge, have not yet found it intolerable—but are quite helpless in the face of a political system which will not admit them to its service unless they abandon their principles, and refuses them freedom to express their opinions if they remain outside it. Such, for example, was the situation of Western-educated intellectuals in Russia under Alexander III, in the Ottoman Empire under Abdul Hamid, and in China under the Empress Dowager. A rather different situation prevailed in the British and French colonial empires. Here the economic and cultural contrasts were no less appalling, but political opinions could be expressed freely, and at least a measure of organization for political action was permitted. But a further factor of frustration existed in the form of the arrogance of the foreign masters, who reserved to themselves the positions of decisive power, and showed various forms of contempt towards the 'natives'. Some of the differences that resulted from different forms of European colonialism will be discussed in a later chapter. It suffices here to say that European colonial rule added a special bitterness to the opposition of the Asian and African intellectuals, and counterbalanced in their minds the advantages of political liberalism, which were lacking in such sovereign states as the old China and the old Turkey.

A further distinction is also necessary with regard to the cultural contrast between the modern intelligentsias and the primitive masses. In some cases it was a matter of a great disparity within one culture, in others of a gap between different cultures. Clearly Voltaire had not much in common with an illiterate French labourer of his time. Yet both belonged to the same French civilization. Voltaire's ideas were derived from the cultural heritage of France, which had been created by the ancestors of the labourer as well as by the intellectual precursors of Voltaire. The relationship between the mid-nineteenth-century Russian socialist Chernyshevski and a Russian peasant is different. The ideas of Chernyshevski were derived from study of Western models, the product of a society and a cultural heritage quite different from those of Russia. Chernyshevski and the *muzhik* were not opposite extremes of one culture, but belonged to two quite distinct cultures. In China or India or tropical Africa the gap was still wider. It is not easy to draw a clear line between societies in which the gap is within one culture, and those in which it is between different cultures. But though the borderlines are blurred, the two types of situation are distinct. Russia in the 1860s was of the second type, but Russia in 1913 was a borderline case. Hungary or Southern Italy at the end of the nineteenth century were of the first type. In both these countries the economic contrasts—between the Hungarian peasant and the Hungarian aristocrat, between the economies of Sicily and Piedmont— were hardly less glaring than in Russia or China. But the intellectual *élite* had not just acquired its ideas ready-made from the West: it had been uninterruptedly in touch with the ideas and culture of the Catholic West for centuries.

THE EXAMPLES OF RUSSIA AND JAPAN

When an underdeveloped society first feels the economic and cultural impact of the West, when a small intellectual *élite*, reared on modern secular Western ideas, comes into being, the gap between it and the bulk of the people is bound to be vast, and this cannot fail to be a social and political danger. It is one of the inevitable strains of the processes of industrialization, urbanization and secularization that since the nineteenth century have affected the greater part of the world. The subsequent course of events, however, largely depends on what measures the government of such a society takes to narrow the gap, and how quickly it can be narrowed, by bringing the masses up to a level not intolerably far below that of the *élite*. At the beginning they must be intolerably far below, for no progress at all can be made unless the first nucleus of an *élite* is created. But the narrowing of the gap is the vital question.

The experience of two great countries which underwent this process in the nineteenth century is extremely revealing. This experience was sufficiently long-drawn-out, and is sufficiently well-documented, to provide valuable lessons for nations engaged in the process in our time. The two countries are Russia and Japan.

The period of accelerated modernization coincided very closely for both countries. Admittedly, European influences were much older in Russia. Peter the Great introduced his great and brutal reforms at the beginning of the eighteenth century, and even in pre-Petrine Russia there were influences from the West. In Japan the Tokugawa *shoguns* excluded foreign influences from the early seventeenth century, and it was not until the mid-nineteenth that the combination of internal social changes and external pressure became irresistible. But rapid movement of industrialization and urbanization can be best dated in Russia from the emancipation of the serfs in 1861 and in Japan from the Meiji Restoration in 1868.

The governments of both countries, in the second half of the nineteenth century, were convinced that if they were to create powerful military empires, strong enough to hold their own with the Great Powers, they must modernize and industrialize them. Commodore Perry's naval expedition in 1853 and the Russian defeat in the Crimean War of 1854-6 had similar effects. If they were to modernize, they must develop Western skills, which meant develop Western-type education. The main motive for both education and industrial growth was the same in both countries: to strengthen the power of the State. As we have seen, the two governments pursued rather similar policies with regard to industry, though the Japanese paid more attention than the Russian to the improvement of agriculture. The greatest difference between the two, however, concerned their education policy.

Russian education made very little progress in the eighteenth century, between Peter the Great and Alexander I. In 1802 a Ministry of Education was established, and in 1804 a Statute was accepted by the Tsar, which set up a consistent system of four levels of schools, from the parish to the university. It was the Tsar's intention that able children of humble origin should be helped to mount the ladder of education, that no one should be excluded by birth or poverty. But to put such a policy into practice in an extremely poor country with hardly any persons competent to teach, required enormous and sustained effort. Unfortunately, the government's energy became mainly concentrated on war, on resisting the aggressions of Napoleon. After 1815 the Tsar's reforming zeal was spent, his mind was on foreign policy; Russia was economically exhausted, and government was in the hands of reactionaries. The following reign began with an unsuccessful revolution, which strengthened the arguments of the reactionaries that education, which puts dangerous ideas into young people's heads, must be carefully controlled, and as far as possible confined to the upper class. Under Count Uvarov, Minister of Education from 1833 to 1849, and his still more reactionary successors, a definite class bias was introduced into Russian education. The aim was to restrict higher education to children of the nobility, with those of medium-rank public officials and richer business-men reluctantly admitted as well. This policy was maintained, with the exception only of a few short intervals, right up to the end of the century. It was not in fact possible altogether to exclude talented children of lowly origin, but comparatively few managed to overcome the barriers. At the Census of 1897 it was found that of a total of 104,000 persons who then possessed a higher education, 70% were of noble origin. As late as 1887 the Minister of Education, Delyanov, had issued a circular in which he urged his subordinates to try to prevent children of 'cooks, coachmen, washerwomen and similar occupations' from getting an education above their station. The result of this policy was that the gap between the *élite* and the masses was not quickly narrowed, but on the contrary was kept wide needlessly long. In the first decade of the twentieth century the trend was reversed, and, thanks especially to the work of provincial, county and municipal authorities, often despite the obstruction of the central ministry, much progress was made. Even so, on the eve of the First World War less than half the school-age children of Russia went to elementary school.

The word 'intelligentsia' is of Russian origin, and was first used to describe the intellectual *élite* of the mid-nineteenth century. It meant at first the intellectuals in the narrowest sense—writers and teachers—but was soon extended to the wider category of the professional classes. The Russian intelligentsia suffered from a threefold isolation. It was isolated from the Russian people by its utterly different material way of life and mental outlook. It was isolated from the government by its opposition to the autocratic system: men of intellectual ability could enter and rise in government service only if they repudiated their principles and became willing tools of what they considered an outmoded and repulsive régime.

It was isolated from the other middle-class groups—business-men and officials—by its completely different set of values and its rejection of the social and political orthodoxies which these groups still accepted: in Russia, as we have seen, there was no homogeneous *bourgeoisie* and no *bourgeois* ethos. Only in the decade 1906-16 were the trends of the previous century reversed. Then the cultural level and standard of living of the masses were rising, autocratic government was replaced by a kind of constitutional monarchy with considerable freedom of opinion, and the three middle classes were drawing nearer to each other and were acquiring a *bourgeois* outlook. But it was then too late.

The Russian intelligentsia of the nineteenth century learned the political ideas of contemporary Western Europe and sought to adapt them to Russian conditions. In the first half of the century two main groups can be distinguished, which would best be described as radicals and conservatives, but have in fact become known by the misleading names that were then given to them, of Westernizers and Slavophiles. It is commonly supposed that one group uncritically admired the West and sought to follow Western models, while the other glorified the Russian past and believed romantically in a mission of Russia to save humanity in general, and the small Slav nations of Eastern Europe in particular. This distinction is, of course, partly true. But the essence of the division between the groups was different. The most eminent of the Slavophiles admired many aspects of European culture and even of Western forms of government, while most Westernizers believed in some form of messianic mission for Russia. There were two basic differences between them. The Slavophiles were Orthodox Christians, while the Westernizers were mostly atheists. The Slavophiles were conservatives in the sense that they believed that the existing structure of Russia could be modernized if a number of reforms were carried out (including such drastic measures as emancipation of the serfs), while the Westernizers believed that the structure should be swept away, and replaced by something created by human reason according to deliberately formulated principles.

The Slavophiles were defeated not so much by the superior wisdom of the Westernizers, which in the conditions of the 1840s or even 1860s is questionable, but by the obscurantism of the government. If Alexander II had been willing in the 1860s to create some sort of central assembly with consultative powers, elected by a restricted suffrage, there could have been a public battle of opinion between radicals and conservatives which would had been valuable for both and for the government, would have hastened the formation of an intelligent public opinion in Russia, and would have laid the foundations for democratic growth. Only the most cocksure dogmatist will assert that Russia was incapable of such development. It did not, however, occur, because the dogma of autocracy, maintained in the Tsars by their close advisers as an article of religious faith, would permit no major political, as opposed to merely economic or social, reform. When circumstances forced the reform, in 1905, it was too late.

The result was that the conservative reformers, repeatedly ignored or insulted by the government, were themselves discouraged, and were discredited in the eyes of later generations of the intelligentsia. Radicalism, on the contrary, gained prestige. Not only were completely radical solutions alone acceptable, but revolutionary violence was considered the only way to achieve them. Not only must revolution be the aim, but all intellectual activity must be judged by its relevance to revolution. Thus a philosophical doctrine was judged not by its intrinsic merit, but by whether it could be used to advocate revolution, a novel, not by its literary distinction but by whether it would inspire in its readers a sympathy for revolution.

The majority of educated persons in Russia were not, of course, active revolutionaries, but the majority were certainly completely alienated from the existing régime, had no loyalty to it, would not defend it, and would prefer revolutionaries to the legitimate rulers. To have made the whole educated class into its enemies was a notable achievement for a government which for more than 100 years had set itself the task of modernizing and strengthening its country. It was this general climate of educated opinion which made possible the growth of a minority of active revolutionaries. Certain weeds grow only in certain soils. If opinion in general had not been alienated, the revolutionaries would not have been so numerous, so devoted or so effective.

The 'Great Reforms' of 1861-4 in Russia had not involved any violent change: they had been carried out by the same Imperial bureaucracy at the Tsar's orders, with only a fairly small number of new appointments in the highest ranks. In Japan the Meiji Restoration of 1868 had been carried through by violence, and had resulted in a sweeping change in the persons exercising power. This difference partly accounts for the differences in policies.

The Japanese reformers of the 1870s and 1880s, unlike the Russian statesmen from Uvarov to Delyanov, were not afraid of educating the people. They did not believe that the introduction of elementary schools for peasant boys and girls would lead to the spread of dangerous ideas and subvert the State. On the contrary, they believed that an educated people would be a people of more efficient farmers, housewives, workers and soldiers. The Japanese observers who travelled in Europe after 1870 no doubt took note of the *cliché* that 'the battle of Sedan was won by the Prussian village schoolmaster'. In the first decades of the new era, higher education and village schools were developed side by side. Japanese universities may not have achieved such high standards as those of Russia, which by the end of the century were equal to all but the very best in the Western world and in some cases perhaps unsurpassed anywhere, but whereas Russia neglected the education of the masses, Japan quickly established universal elementary education. This was introduced for a period of sixteen months when the Department of Education was founded in 1871, and the decree was made effective during the 1870s. In 1880 the period of instruction was increased to three years, in 1886 to four and by the end of the century to six years. In 1903 no less than 93% of all boys and girls of school age were attending school.[54] The Japanese had achieved in thirty years twice as much as the Russians in more than a century. The achievement is the more remarkable when it is recalled that the Japanese language is ideographic, and simply to learn to read and write is thus immensely harder than for a Russian child.

The result of this policy was that the gap between the *élite* and the masses was rapidly narrowed to the dimensions that exist within any modern society. The Japanese culture of the age of mass literacy was a mixture of the old and new, full of imperfections. But, such as it was, it was shared by the whole nation. The difference between a Japanese professor of mathematics and a Japanese factory worker was similar to the difference between members of the same professions in a Western country. It was unlike the difference between Chernyshevski and the Russian *muzhik*, who belonged to different cultures. The Japanese *élite* were also not excluded from government service, and were not prevented from expressing their opinions. There could, of course, no more be a mass democracy in the Japan of the 1870s and 1880s than in nineteenth-century Russia: the mass of the people had no political opinions. But within the educated class there could be and were bitter political arguments. The Constitution of 1889 was not a parliamentary democracy. The parliament was elected on a restricted franchise, and the government was responsible not to parliament, but to the Emperor. But it was an important step in the direction of a parliamentary régime, a step which various European nations had taken at various moments of their history. The Japanese intellectual *élite* were also not sharply cut off from the other middle-class groups. Civil servants and professional people had indeed a very similar outlook, which was derived from Japanese traditional values, and can certainly not be equated with the *bourgeois* ethos of Western Europe. Western individualist values were, however, penetrating, and by the 1920s the traditional *samurai* contempt for money-makers was weakening, as the business-men became not only richer, but also more self-confident and more influential in politics. This change in the social standing of business-men, from disreputable types with whom well-bred persons would have nothing to do to highly respected pillars of society, has its parallels in the modern history of Europe, including Britain and even the early United States.

Thus the Japanese intellectual *élite* did not experience the threefold isolation which afflicted the Russian intelligentsia. Japan thereby escaped one of the greatest strains from which underdeveloped societies are liable to suffer. This is not to say that Japanese development after 1868 was wholly admirable, from the point of view either of the Japanese themselves or of the rest of the world. But it is foolish if either Japanese or foreigners allow their feelings about the events of December 1941 or the collapse of 1945 to blind them to the remarkable achievement of Japan in the field of education. Admittedly there were strains which Japan did not escape. The conflicts between traditional Japanese moral and religious values and the new ideas from the West tormented and probably continue to torment Japanese minds. Western democrats can hardly approve in principle of the purposes to which the Japanese rulers put the schools which they so successfully founded. After a period of American influence, when Dr. David Murray of Rutgers University was adviser to the Department of Education (1873-9), the government preferred more authoritarian German models. Under Minister of Education Mori, from 1886, greater emphasis was laid on discipline, nationalism and traditional virtues. The Imperial Rescript of 1890 became the basis for patriotic indoctrination. The schools were consciously regarded as an instrument for building up the formidable military power which wrought so much havoc a half-century later. It may thus be argued that the integration of the Japanese intellectual *élite* into society was too successful, that the intellectuals failed in their duty by not protesting more effectively against the policies which in the 1930s were clearly leading to disaster. In this, as in other fields, the parallel between Japan and Germany is suggestive.

In most underdeveloped countries the pattern has been closer to the Imperial Russian than to the Japanese. Admittedly, the extreme social bias of the Russian Ministry of Education has no parallel, not even in nineteenth-century Hungary, where the aristocracy was very powerful and the peasant masses poor and neglected, but certainly there was no absolute determination of the government to deny education to the masses. However, everywhere the emphasis was on higher education rather than on elementary. In the Balkan states between the wars more was done for village schools than in Imperial Russia, but relatively more still was done for universities and for secondary schools in the big towns. The same priority was also found in colonial territories under European rule, and in the old China or the old Turkey. In recent decades colonial administrations have devoted more attention to the lower levels. Both Kemalist Turkey and independent India have made and are making great efforts, but both have still a long way to go before they can bear comparison with the Japanese achievement. It is only in underdeveloped societies ruled by communists that mass education has equalled, and perhaps even surpassed this model. The educational record of Soviet Russia is the antithesis of that of Imperial Russia, and Communist China too is resolved to abolish illiteracy. Both régimes, of course, treat the school as an instrument of indoctrination to an even greater extent than did the Japanese rulers of the Meiji era.

MILITARY INTELLIGENTSIA

In certain circumstances the intelligentsia may include army officers. In countries of underdeveloped society which preserved their independent sovereignty, the first modern skill which governments felt an urgent need to acquire was military skill. Army officers were the first social group which became familiar with Western democratic ideas. The outstanding examples are Russia and the Ottoman Empire. The Russian Decembrists of 1825, the Young Turk leaders of 1908, and Mustafa Kemal himself were professional officers, but they were also intelligentsia. The same is true of the Arab officers serving in the Ottoman army at the beginning of the twentieth century, who founded the first Arab nationalist organization. In China, where the social status of the military profession was low under the old régime, soldiers were less conspicuous among the radical intelligentsia, though the Kuomintang, which started as a civilian movement, soon produced its military element. In countries under foreign colonial rule national defence was in the hands of foreigners, and the rising intelligentsia found opportunities only in civilian professions. British India and Burma are examples. It is worth noting that in British India Moslems showed less inclination to civilian professions, and more aptitude for military careers, than the Hindus, and this contrast has been reflected in the different development of Pakistan and India since independence.

In the West the military conspirator is traditionally thought of as a reactionary, a restorer of order and very often of class privilege. One thinks of General Cavaignac or General Franco. But though military conspirators may play this role in some underdeveloped countries (Latin America can provide many examples, and perhaps Ayub Khan of Pakistan is one), they may also play the opposite role of social revolutionaries, allied with, or even indistinguishable from, the civilian radical intelligentsia. Egypt and Iraq are examples. The frequent use by Western commentators of the portmanteau phrase 'military dictatorship' is misleading: one must distinguish between the order-restorers and the intelligentsia-in-uniform.

We shall now briefly consider the role of the intelligentsia in the three main types of society at the present time—the Soviet, the Western and the underdeveloped.

IN SOVIET SOCIETY

The leaders of the Bolshevik Party were largely members of the intelligentsia, none more than Lenin himself. Like the other socialist parties in Imperial Russia, the Bolsheviks benefited from the general hostility of the educated class to the régime, from the prevalence of revolutionary utilitarianism in attitudes to thought and learning and the arts, and from the widespread belief of intellectuals that it was their duty to use their talents to serve not so much themselves as the People. This last belief was first strikingly expressed in the 1870s by the students who 'went to the people', naïvely propagating socialist ideas among illiterate peasants. From this unsuccessful venture developed the first socialist movement, usually known by the general term of Populism (*narodnichestvo*). The Russian Marxist intellectuals, who became a serious force about ten years after the suppression of the first effective Populist group, Peoples' Will (which assassinated Tsar Alexander II in 1881), disagreed with the political doctrines of the Populists: Lenin as a young man polemized bitterly against them. But Lenin and the Bolsheviks inherited from them the belief in the duty of the intellectuals to serve the people by organizing revolution. It is useful to distinguish between Populist doctrines, which the Bolsheviks rejected, and the Populist mentality, in which they shared.

In the last years before the First World War revolutionary utilitarianism was in decline, and the generation in the universities was less obsessed with the revolutionary struggle than any since the 1820s. But neither the young nor the old had any love for the régime of the Tsar, and when this collapsed in March 1917 there was general rejoicing. The intelligentsia for the most part supported the left-wing parties on which the successive Provisional Governments were based between March and November. When Lenin seized power on 7 November, overthrowing a government of Socialist Revolutionaries (Populists) and Mensheviks (moderate Marxists), the intelligentsia was against him. This hostility he repaid with interest. But as the original confused struggle between the Bolsheviks and their varied opponents changed at the end of 1918 into a fight between Lenin's dictatorship and a military dictatorship of the extreme right, a very large part of the intelligentsia came to look on Bolshevism as the lesser evil. At the same time the communists needed as many men of special skills as they could get, professional army officers or doctors or civil servants or even university professors. When the communists had won the war, by the end of 1920, a large number of important posts were held by members of the old intelligentsia who were not communists, or not even socialists.

For the following fifteen years these men and women were used and contemptuously tolerated. They were comparatively well paid, worked in decent material conditions, but were openly distrusted and often insulted, cumbrously supervised by party men of orthodox ideological quality but small technical knowledge, and spied on by a host of police informers. If something went wrong with their enterprise, they were liable to be made scapegoats, accused of sabotage or espionage in the service of British or French imperialists, and sent to a labour camp or even shot. The second communist revolution, Stalin's drive for industrialization in 1929, increased both the general discontent and the need for experts, made the members of the intelligentsia more valuable than ever both as specialists and as scapegoats. Stalin at first preferred them in the second role, but in a famous speech in 1931 he stressed the first role, and urged party members to show more consideration for them. At the same time the schools and colleges were turning out new generations of post-revolutionary politically indoctrinated specialists who had never known any society other than that of the Soviet Union. These were serving under the pre-1917 experts, waiting to take over their jobs when the time came.

It came with the Great Purge of 1937-8. This fell with special severity on those intellectuals who had been genuine Bolsheviks before 1917, or had joined the party from genuine conversion to its ideas. But by sweeping away the pre-revolutionary experts, the purge opened dazzling opportunities to the young, even the very young.

We have seen that Stalin used the phrase 'toiling intelligentsia' to describe the upper stratum of Soviet society. It is easy to see why this name was chosen. The word 'bureaucracy' had unpleasant associations with Tsardom, and had been one of Lenin's favourite terms of abuse. But the intelligentsia had existed in the old Russia, and though not identified with Bolshevism and often sorely berated by Lenin, had a certain revolutionary respectability. The epithet 'toiling' marked it off from the earlier intelligentsia, references to which could be preceded by the epithet *bourgeois* or 'feudal'. The old Russia of landlords and capitalists, it could be argued, had produced its intelligentsia, which none the less, owing to the inherent artistic and scientific gifts of the Russian people, had shown positive qualities transcending the evil régime in which it had arisen. The new

Russia of 'socialism', as established by 'the Party of Lenin and Stalin', was now producing its own intelligentsia, of sons and daughters of workers and peasants, immeasurably superior to the old.

We have suggested that this upper stratum should more properly be called a state *bourgeoisie*, the epithet 'state' to mark it off from the traditional *bourgeoisie* of Europe, which should be preceded when necessary by the epithet 'private'. But whether this terminology be accepted or not, there can be no doubt at all that the stratum is misnamed if it is called an intelligentsia. It is a far wider category, including bureaucrats and managers, the equivalents in their function of the civil servants and businessmen of Western society. The intellectual professions, however, which formed the nucleus of the intelligentsia of Imperial Russia, still exist in Soviet Russia.

One of the most interesting questions about the Soviet Union is whether the intelligentsia, in the older and proper sense, has been absorbed with the other elements into the upper stratum as a whole, or has preserved a separate existence as a social group. Certainly the trend may be expected to be towards absorption. The gap between the *élite* and the masses has long since been narrowed. Soviet culture, such as it is, includes all Soviet citizens. The intelligentsia are not cut off from the government service: on the contrary, one can rise high in an intellectual profession only as part of the government service, which embraces all activities. And the ethos of the upper stratum, as far as can be seen from the rather scrappy evidence, a curious mixture of Victorianism, Marxism and chauvinism, with remnants of Russian Messianism and Populism, appears to extend to the intelligentsia component no less than to the managerial and the bureaucratic.

There are splendid social and material prizes for intellectual or artistic eminence. Nowhere does a ballerina, a physicist or a surgeon enjoy such prestige as in the Soviet Union, and if their material rewards may be less than those of some Westerners at the top of these professions, they are still far above those of the Soviet working class. On the other hand, it may be argued that freedom of thought is as indispensable to an intellectual as his tools to a workman, and that its absence is resented by intellectuals with an intensity that is not found among other social groups. Some evidence for this view can be found in the reactions of Soviet writers since Stalin's death, in such works as Dudintsev's *Not by Bread Alone*, and still more Pasternak's *Doctor Zhivago*. In their revolt against established society, they are to some extent consciously maintaining the tradition of classical Russian literature, more devoted to liberty perhaps than any other in the world. It is a curious irony that revolutionary utilitarianism as a doctrine for literature and the arts, which arose as a protest of the radicals against the censorship of Imperial Russia, was mummified under Stalin into the doctrine of 'socialist realism'. The prophets of this doctrine, while ceremonially intoning the radical words of nineteenth-century critics, use them to compel abject conformity to the established order willed by Stalin or Khrushchov. The spirit of Pobedonostsev has proved strong in Russia, even when it is wrapped in the language of Belinski. But the universal genius of the great Russian writers escapes these artificial frames. There are those in the Soviet Union who understand and honour it.

In other communist-ruled countries the intelligentsia is a force to be reckoned with. In China the attitude of intellectuals to the communists before their triumph was similar to that of the Russian intelligentsia to the revolutionary movement before 1917. The old régime was utterly discredited, and its successor, the Kuomintang, became discredited in the 1940s. The communists were believed to be Chinese patriots and social reformers: they had staunchly fought the Japanese for many years, and in their 'liberated areas' they were believed to have avoided extremism and to have improved the peasants' lot. They were also believed to be enemies of corruption, and to have a finely disciplined army which did not plunder. The intelligentsia of the great cities welcomed them in 1949. Then came the rude reawakening. The war in Korea led to a general tightening of dictatorship, and the intellectuals were subjected to the torture and humiliation of 'brain-washing'. Then once more pressure was relaxed. Like the Bolsheviks in the 1920s, the Chinese Communists needed 'specialists'. In 1956 Mao Tse-tung went further still. His propagandists launched the slogan, 'Let a hundred flowers bloom, let a hundred schools of thought contend'. He himself urged the intellectuals to voice their criticisms, to speak frankly, to have no fear. After some hesitation, they began to respond. For a time they were given a free hearing. Then the régime clamped down on them. The freedom had been intended only for 'constructive' criticism, not for 'rightist' and counter-revolutionary views. These must be punished. It is the party that decides what criticism is constructive, what is counter-revolutionary. Whether the whole episode was a deliberate trap for the unwary, or whether Mao was genuinely surprised by the extent of the criticism—as seems to have been the case with Stalin when he deliberately encouraged some freedom of speech in Russia in 1936, only to react to it by the holocaust of the Great Purge—the evidence is too scanty to show.

In Eastern Europe the discontent of intellectuals is unmistakable. In 1944 the intelligentsia in Eastern Europe was less distinct from the other middle classes, more a part of a *bourgeoisie*, than in Russia before 1917, but there were differences between different countries. In the Czech Lands the situation was as in any Western country; in Bulgaria and Roumania it was nearer to the old Russian pattern. To all Eastern Europe except Yugoslavia, communism was brought by foreign conquest, and was for that reason odious. Intellectuals were treated by the new communist régime with the same mixture of material rewards and distrust as in Russia in the 1920s, but on the whole rather better, unless they were active members of anti-communist political parties. But the régimes set to work to train their successors, to create a new intelligentsia of children of workers and peasants. In this they were outwardly very successful. Hundreds of thousands of children of poor parents, who before the war would have found it difficult or impossible to get a higher education, now found places in the rapidly expanded colleges and universities. In them the communists placed their hopes. They knew that they were hated by the older generations. But the new proletarian-peasant intelligentsia would, they hoped, be the brains of their régime, the hard core of loyal support. But they were disappointed. In Hungary and Poland it was the young intellectuals, who owed their careers to the communists, who led the movement against the Stalinist régimes. In Czechoslovakia and Roumania the university youth clearly expressed their opposition to the régimes, though with less sensational results.

IN WESTERN SOCIETIES

In Western societies the intelligentsia is not a separate category, with an ethos and a political role of its own. Nevertheless, intellectuals sometimes express more clearly the discontents of the middle classes as a whole, and there are some specific frustrations of intellectuals which may acquire political significance.

The desire for a complete answer to all problems, for some magical secular creed that will give total solutions, is fairly widespread in Western society, and applies perhaps most to those of intellectual pretensions rather than to those of intellectual distinction, to the semi-intelligentsia rather than to the *élite*. In so far as it affects the *élite*, it is often those who combine great knowledge, and great ability to test evidence, in their own special field, with great ignorance and *naïveté* concerning politics. Such people are especially addicted to a conspiratorial view of politics, to a belief that 'we are ruled by crooks'. If they can concentrate their wrath on the convenient scapegoat of politicians, they can absolve both themselves and the general public—with which they are inclined, in a sort of Populist sentimentality, to identify themselves—from any moral responsibility for the mess into which the world has got. One example of this mentality is the admiration of some scientists for the Soviet Union. Not only are such men impressed by the fact that in the Soviet Union scientists have relatively greater material privileges and absolutely higher social standing than in Western societies, but they take seriously the claim of Soviet spokesmen that their whole society is based on scientific foundations. This general attitude is, however, by no means confined to natural scientists, and it by no means necessarily leads its victims to support of communism—some other totalitarian oversimplification may well attract them more.

There are political habits of mind in Western societies, chiefly professed and popularized by intellectuals, which must be regarded as significant, if marginal, political factors in their own right. An example is the traditional slogan of many French intellectuals, *pas d'ennemis à gauche*. There can hardly ever have been a more conservative attitude in history than this, conservative in the basic sense of unimaginative mental inertia. Ritual incantation of the magic words 'left' and 'right' can induce in the faithful the appropriate reflex actions, regardless of the facts of a particular political situation. Another example are the guilt complexes that have been so widespread among Western intellectuals, especially since the First World War. In the first years of Hitlerism, it was a common opinion among intellectuals in Britain that, since the victors of 1919 had imposed harsh terms on Germany, the victor nations had no moral right to oppose Hitler, who was but expressing the German people's rejection of those terms. The argument that only he whose conscience is as pure as snow may resist evil, is, of course, the best guarantee that evil will triumph. Yet this doctrine played its part in justifying the 'appeasement' policy in the 1930s, in opposing resistance to North Korea and Communist China in 1951, and has reappeared in great strength in the form that no Middle Eastern country in which there are rich landowners and wretched peasants should be defended from aggression. A third example is nationalist exasperation—the opposite of a national guilt complex, yet no less dangerous. This is strong and probably growing in both France and Britain. As the volume of hatred, insults and murder, directed against their compatriots, grows in all parts of the world, it is not surprising that the French, and even the more complacent British, should react with rage. The Suez enterprise of 1956 aroused storms of approval from such persons. The Algerian *coup d'état* was inspired in large part by such feelings. The record of the Weimar Republic in Germany shows that exasperated nationalism in a highly civilized country can lead to militant insanity.

Probably the most that can be said is that intellectuals in Western societies contribute to the formulation of extremist political views, of whatever variety, but that whether extremist groups remain freakish sects or become powerful political movements depends less on the influence of intellectuals than on economic conditions. In Western societies the intelligentsia is not a separate social group, and though intellectuals can contribute to revolutionary movements they cannot create them. In underdeveloped societies, however, their role is more far-reaching.

UNDERDEVELOPED SOCIETIES

In the underdeveloped societies it is the intelligentsia that is leading the nationalist, modernist and revolutionary movements. It is the intelligentsia that clamours most loudly for short-cuts to utopia, to complete social justice, vast industrial progress and national greatness. It is also the intelligentsia that feels with the greatest passion the need for these things. The poverty and squalor of the labourer in field or factory is more keenly resented by the intelligentsia than by the labourer himself. It is not that the labourer enjoys poverty and squalor, but that he is less aware, even in the age of radio and television, of the practical possibility of a better life. The intellectuals wish a better life for the labourer partly from sincere compassion, and partly from the feeling that the existence of poverty and squalor casts shame on the whole nation, and on themselves as the *élite* of the nation.

Like their predecessors in eighteenth-century France, the Asian and African intellectuals are readily inclined to reject the traditions of their countries, including their religious beliefs, because they identify these with a social order and a political hierarchy that are incompatible with modernization, and in many cases are further discredited by association with foreign rule or protectorate. They are enthusiastic Westernizers in the sense that they wish to see immediately established in their countries the material amenities of Western civilization. At the same time, however, they hate the West as a conquering and oppressing force, not only blaming it for its real sins, which they inevitably magnify, but making it the scapegoat for their own failures. When well-intentioned Westerners speak to them of slow, steady progress and reform, they are furious. They are unshakably convinced that such talk is but a hypocritical excuse of the oppressor to deny them their rights. In this it may often be that there is truth. But it is also true that the material achievements of the West were the result of centuries of toil, and that the intelligentsia of the underdeveloped countries fanatically refuse to admit that this historical truth has any relevance to their problems. It is seldom that they have any appreciation of the relevance of law to social progress. Observance of the law involves delay, and can be used by conservative groups to postpone change, therefore let the law be ignored. The need to have clearly defined standards, binding on all, against which actions can be measured, and in the light of which choices can be made, is lost on them. It is equally seldom that they understand what is meant by free institutions. The word 'democracy' has their enthusiastic approval, but this normally means the triumph of the people, which by definition is the triumph of themselves. The notion that different opinions should be expressed, that freedom is valid for one's opponent as well as for oneself, is usually incomprehensible. There are, of course, numerous distinguished exceptions, but they are not typical.

There have been many examples of what we have called the Populist mentality, the belief that the intellectual should devote himself to the service of the people, to raising it up out of squalor and to freeing it from oppression by others. This mentality, which has inspired and inspires much unselfish toil and even heroism, can be found among disciples of ideologies of both 'left' and 'right': in this context the distinction is of dubious validity. The present writer had some personal experience of two examples in Eastern Europe before the Second World War.

In Serbia at that time an active minority of the university students and recent graduates (perhaps a majority of all those who were politically minded) were strongly influenced by communism, accepted a potted form of Marxism, looked for leadership to the Soviet Union, and believed that they could best serve their own people by working for a socialist revolution. Many were themselves children of poor peasants or ill-paid minor officials, who well knew the misery in which the people lived. Others were children of the rich, stricken with conscience like the 'repentant noblemen' of mid-nineteenth-century Russia. It was this generation that provided the cadres of the People's Liberation Army of Marshal Tito—those who were or became members of the communist party provided the inner core, and those who merely sympathized formed the secondary cadres. They were a brave and honest lot, even if also narrow-minded and cruel, and they fought and toiled hard for their victory.

In the neighbour country Roumania, the same generation in the universities were strongly influenced by Hitlerism, accepted anti-Semitic and fascist slogans, looked for inspiration to the Third Reich and believed it was their mission to free their people from exploitation by the Jews. In their social origins, their emotional attitudes to politics and their desire to serve the people, they closely resembled their Serbian counterparts. They too suffered for their beliefs, though less severely and for a shorter period, but unlike the Serbian students they were defeated. It is, of course, true that the ideologies of Marxism and Iron Guard fascism were implacably opposed, but the two social phenomena, and the human virtues and defects of those involved in them, appeared to the present writer's personal observation strikingly alike. Emotive reactions to symbolic words such as 'left' and 'right', dubious assertions about the inborn heroic qualities of Serbs and lack of these among Roumanians, and the historical fact that Serb communists were allies of the West in the last war while Roumanian fascists were enemies, should not be allowed to confuse judgement of the nature of social movements.

The Populist outlook in various forms can be found in other countries within the last decades. To take three diverse examples quite arbitrarily, something of this mentality is visible among the Peruvian and other South American students from whose political agitation in the 1920s emerged the APRA movement; among young intellectuals in the Indian independence movement of the 1930s; and in the Egyptian Moslem Brotherhood in its great days.

If the Populist outlook is one aspect of the mentality of the revolutionary intelligentsia in underdeveloped countries, the other is the desire for power, prestige and brilliant careers, both for individuals and for the educated group as a whole. If the Populist outlook implies struggle for freedom for the people, this second motive implies the claim to power over the people. Both motives can exist with great sincerity within the same mind, and indeed there is not felt to be any contradiction between them. The intelligentsia cannot doubt that its rule will be more beneficial to the people than that of the existing reactionaries or 'Uncle Toms' or 'imperialist stooges'. And the heroic intellectuals who are giving their lives to the people's service will naturally deserve a reward from the grateful masses.

The attraction of communism is that it appeals to both attitudes. The Bolsheviks were, as we have seen, in a sense heirs to the Populist tradition. Communists claim that the people have been freed by their revolution and their socialist construction, and that 'exploitation of man by man' has ceased to exist. At the same time the Soviet Union offers shining examples of the heights of power and influence to which intellectuals can attain. Not only do writers, engineers and scientists enjoy wealth and prestige, but, so communists believe, the whole society is organized on scientific lines—rationally, intelligently and progressively, in contrast to the inefficiency, wastefulness and injustice of all pre-'socialist' régimes. Fascism exercised something of the same double appeal in the 1930s. It stood, its spokesmen claimed, for liberation of the people from oppressive rulers (especially if these were Jews, Englishmen or Frenchmen, or persons friendly to any of these), and in Germany or Italy great careers stood open for nationally-minded, virtuous young people of ability. It is no accident that it is in the Arab lands, where fascism won so many keen (if ineffective) adherents in the 1930s, that admiration for the Soviet Union, Soviet social ideals and methods of action (which need not necessarily also include acceptance of Marxism *in toto*) is especially strong today.

The intelligentsia is a specific social group of the greatest political importance in a transitional period of social development, in the 'underdeveloped' stage which leads from a purely agrarian and static society to a modern industrial and urban society. The intelligentsia loses much of its importance when the general material and cultural level of the people has risen, when a large skilled working class exists, when other middle-class groups have become more numerous and influential, and the intelligentsia has been merged with them in a new urban upper class with a unifying ethos of its own. This urban upper class may be a *bourgeoisie* of the Western type, a 'private *bourgeoisie*' as we have called it earlier; or a non-Western variation of this such as grew up in different circumstances in Japan; or a 'state *bourgeoisie*'; or a mixture of private and state elements, as, for instance, in modern Turkey. It is certain that in the future industrial development of Asian and African countries domestic private capital (which is very scarce and has few resources, as well as being politically suspect in the eyes of the rising political movements) will play a far smaller part than in the corresponding historical period in the West, that foreign private capital will suffer from political suspicion, and that the State will therefore have a large gap to fill. It is therefore likely that in the Asian and African countries, if and when they become industrialized and urbanized, the upper stratum will be some sort of State *bourgeoisie*.

The general trend and the general social result are clear. It is not, however, clear whether this result will be achieved by peaceful development or by violent revolution, whether from within or by foreign conquest. The difference between these different political procedures may be decisive for world peace or war, for the survival of the human race. In each case the procedure adopted will depend on the extent to which the intelligentsia in the transitional period is captured by external totalitarian ideologies, communist or other, and on whether the machinery of government is strong enough to resist revolutionary conspiracies, whose leaders and upper cadres inevitably will be drawn from the disaffected intelligentsia.

This is the problem of the narrowing of the gap between *élite* and people, which we discussed earlier in connexion with the Imperial Russian and Japanese examples. It is a problem of educational priorities and of political stability.

Higher education is essential, but should not be allowed too far to outpace elementary education, while secondary education is of course essential, apart from all else, to train teachers for elementary schools.

But there is no infallible proportion between the three levels, applicable to all cases: each government, whether of an independent state or of a colonial power, has to make its own decisions. There should also be a balance between more practical and theoretical types of education; between the training of lawyers or journalists (so necessary to political parties) and doctors or engineers; between the production of city physicians and theoretical engineers who sit in city offices, and of men and women willing to work in public health services in the villages or to go and talk to farmers about practical methods of cultivation. Yet this too is no simple problem. Any attempt to make education less theoretical is liable to be interpreted by nationalist journalists as an imperialist trick to deprive the people of the means of acquiring the magic elixir of political knowledge and power. If a government pays more attention to agricultural training it will be accused of neglecting industry, if it concentrates on industrial skills it will be denounced for ignoring farmers. The policies chosen in these problems will have a decisive effect on the speed and success in narrowing the gap. Faced as they are by the same difficulties, governments of newly independent and colonial territories would do well to consult and help each other. But in the age of Afro-Asianism and of the oratory of the United Nations General Assembly, it is perhaps idle to expect anything of the sort.

Political stability is even more difficult to achieve. Japan was fortunate in this respect. Independent India has been fortunate for ten years. It has benefited from the great gifts and recognized authority of Pandit Nehru, and from the working of the political structure left by British rule. In Indonesia this has not been the case. It has become fashionable to blame the previous Dutch administration and to extol British rule in India by comparison. Even if this were justifiable—which is dubious—it would still remain obvious that the Indonesians have not the aptitude for administration of the Indians, and that they have not yet produced leaders who can compare (unless in rhetorical talent) with Nehru or with scores of his assistants. In Iraq a political structure was left by the British Mandate which appeared more solid than others in the Arab world. It was manned by Iraqis who proved themselves efficient administrators. In Nuri es-Said the country had a leader of great experience and courage. Nuri kept order and stability for many years. But he ignored the injustices of the land system and repressed the intelligentsia without giving it a constructive outlet. In the end pressures from within and without Iraq proved too strong. Though he has fallen, it is arguable that Iraq greatly benefited from his rule. It cannot be expected that those who incited the mob to mutilate and spit on his corpse will refrain from spitting on his memory. But if historical records survive, another generation may honour his name.

There is no more a precise formula for political stability than for educational priorities. But it is a factor in itself no less important than the social conflicts on which we have so far laid the main emphasis. If the social conflicts create the conditions for revolution, the issue whether there shall or shall not be a revolution depends on considerations of political leadership and power. To these we shall now turn.

7: The Seizure of Power

DEFINITIONS

The word 'revolution' is so often used in so many different senses that it is necessary to begin with a provisional definition. It is not claimed that the following is the only justifiable use of the word, only that it is the one relevant in the present context.

A revolution must involve two things—the use of violence to deprive opponents of power, and the radical transformation of social and political institutions. The presence of only one of these things does not constitute a revolution.

Seizure of power by violence may not radically transform institutions. It may merely lead to the replacement of one group of rulers by another group, which will rule in much the same manner as its predecessors. The best name for this type of action is the French phrase *coup d'état*. There are countless examples in history, and in the twentieth century they have been particularly frequent in the Balkans, Latin America and the Middle East. It should, however, be noted that a revolution may begin by a *coup d'état*. Conspirators who have seized power for themselves may use it to transform social and political institutions. In this case the *coup d'état* broadens into a revolution.

Radical transformation of social and political institutions may take place without the use of violence. The obvious historical example of this is the process known as the Industrial Revolution, which took place in England from the end of the eighteenth until well into the nineteenth century. Its effects were profound and far-reaching, but it was not accompanied by violence. Governments changed many times during the Industrial Revolution, but by legally recognized means. The institutional framework was modified but not rebuilt, repaired but not smashed. In more recent times the word 'revolution' has been used to describe the social changes in England during and immediately after the Second World War, and in the United States in the administrations of President Franklin D. Roosevelt. These changes too were profound, and have provoked passionate approval or rejection. But in both countries the institutional framework remained intact, and in neither was violence used to destroy political opponents.

A familiar distinction is that between 'social' revolutions and 'merely political' revolutions. If by the latter is meant a *coup d'état* which has no radical changes as its result, and if by the former a period of peaceful transformation, then neither are revolutions in our sense. On the other hand all revolutions in our sense are almost inevitably social as well as political. Radical transformation of institutions by violence must have social as well as political consequences, and must affect the relations of social classes with each other. There is no clear dividing line between political and social institutions; and even between political parties and social groups the border line is often blurred. It is an oft-repeated cliché that the Bolshevik Revolution was social and the Nazi Revolution was not (some would deny that the latter was a revolution at all). But on even superficial examination the distinction is seen to be of small value. Lenin's government expropriated the not very large number of landowners and capitalists in Russia. Hitler's government expropriated the proportionately rather similar number of Jews in Germany. Both governments placed rigid restrictions on the use of property by those who were not expropriated. But treatment of property is not the most important thing about either revolution. More important is that both turned upside down existing notions of law and morality, deprived every citizen (including members of the ruling party) of guarantees of security, and set up totalitarian régimes of a new type.

A distinction which is of importance, because it is taught as scientific doctrine to nearly 1,000 million people, is the Leninist distinction between *bourgeois* and 'socialist' revolutions. *Bourgeois* revolutions are said to perform the historical function (regardless of the conscious aims of their leaders) of replacing 'feudalism', or rule by a landowning aristocracy, by the rule of the capitalists. The most illustrious example is said to be the French Revolution of 1789. Socialist revolutions overthrow the capitalists and give power to the working class. The most illustrious example is said to be the 'Great October Socialist Revolution' of 1917 in Russia, which, it is claimed, set up a dictatorship of the proletariat and provided a model for all socialist revolutions of the future. That revolutions have taken place, and may in future take place, which strengthen capitalists relatively to landowners, or workers relatively to capitalists, may readily be admitted. But to fit all modern revolutions (other than those rejected as *coups d'état* or as 'counter-revolutions') into this pattern, is an exercise not in historical, but in the quasi-theological method. In particular, one must question the assertion that the main significance of the French Revolution of 1789 was to transfer power from 'feudal' rulers to capitalists, and still more the assertion that Lenin's action in November 1917 gave power to the workers. Lenin set up a dictatorship not of the proletariat, but of the communist party, or, rather, of its autocratic rulers.

Another important distinction is that between a revolution and a counter-revolution. This should be a fairly simple matter. 'Counter-revolution' must clearly mean the violent overthrow of a régime established by revolution, with the purpose of restoring the régime that had existed before the revolution. In practice there have been very few examples of counter-revolutions in modern history. Counter-*coups d'état* have, of course, been abundant: conspirators who seize power from one clique in order to rule in the same way in its place are violently overthrown by the survivors or avengers of those whom they dispossessed. But if a *coup d'état* is not a revolution, a counter-*coup d'état* is not a counter-revolution. The fascist revolution in Italy in 1922-6, and the Nazi revolution in Germany in 1933-4, were not counter-revolutions: they did not restore the old, but created something new. Even General Franco did not restore the past. France in 1815 was very different from France under Louis XVI. The restoration of Louis XVIII was in any case the result of foreign invasion. So were the two clearest examples of a counter-revolution in the twentieth century, both of which took place in Hungary. The first was in the summer of 1919. A revolution had placed communists in power, and they had been defeated, despite some initial victories, by the armed forces of the neighbouring states. The Roumanian army occupied Budapest, and under its protection was formed the government of Admiral Horthy, which proceeded to establish an almost complete replica of the oligarchical rule of landowners and big business which had existed in Hungary until the revolution. The second example occurred on 4 November 1956. A revolution had overthrown the totalitarian régime of the communist party. The revolutionary régime existed for a week, at the end of which large Soviet armies invaded Hungary and reimposed an almost exact replica of the previous totalitarian régime.

The distinction, however, is commonly blurred in Western minds owing to understandable historical prejudice. The political systems of Britain, the United States and France are each derived from a Glorious Revolution—of 1689, 1776 and 1789. The word 'revolution' thus has for these three nations, and for others whose political thinking has been influenced by them, a positive and progressive sound. Revolutions are regarded as movements for liberty. They may be temporarily disfigured by abuses or crimes, but their movement is forward and upward. After a revolution men are freer. Therefore a violent movement which does not increase liberty or vindicate justice cannot be a revolution. Some other name must be found for it, and 'counter-revolution' is the most convenient. But twentieth-century experience unfortunately shows that revolutions may be made for liberty or against liberty, to give justice to one group but to deny it to all others. Leaders of great revolutions usually believe that they are fighting for great ideals, but historians and social scientists are concerned with the real nature and consequences of the movement, of which the emotions of the actors are an important part, but only a part. It is of course possible to divide all violent movements of radical social and political transformation into those one approves and those one dislikes, and to call the first category 'revolutions' and the second 'counter-revolutions'. But this is an emotional, not a scientific distinction, and it makes it more difficult to understand the events of our time. One may admire Lenin's revolution and dislike Hitler's, or admire Hitler's and dislike Lenin's, or dislike both. But both must be admitted to have been revolutions.

The social scientist is in principle neither for nor against revolutions: he is concerned to describe or analyse or compare them in the light of historical facts, as far as these can be known. The individual citizen of liberal or totalitarian convictions (whether he be a social scientist or not) is neither for nor against revolution as such: he is for revolutions which can help his friends and damage his enemies, and against revolutions which damage his friends and help his enemies. This basic fact is concealed from both the public and its leaders—in communist countries by the dogma that every violent change which furthers the interests of the Soviet Union is a revolution, to be labelled *bourgeois* or 'socialist' as the lay priesthood decides, and that every such change which harms Soviet interests (such as the overthrow of the Gerö régime in Hungary) is counter-revolutionary; in the West by the belief that revolutions are praiseworthy enterprises.

TYPES OF STATE POWER AND TYPES OF REVOLUTION

In the field of economic and social structure we have distinguished between advanced industrial societies and underdeveloped societies. In the field of political structure we must now distinguish two types, which we will call the pre-modern State and the modern State.

The modern State arose in societies in which urban civilization was already well developed. Its growth was marked by the development of a complex bureaucratic mechanism. It was strengthened by industrialization, the rise of the large factory and the post-industrial urban agglomeration. It reached its full development with universal compulsory education. Its development in Europe may be said to stretch approximately from the France of Louis XIV to the German Empire of Bismarck.

The pre-modern State is one in which these forces have made themselves felt but are still weak, in which urban civilization and industry are not yet dominant, in which modern bureaucracy is only beginning to replace a traditional hierarchy of government, and in which educational development is uneven and elementary education especially inadequate—in fact, the type of State machine characteristic of an 'underdeveloped society'.

One might also put the difference between the two types of State figuratively in the following terms. The pre-modern State is imposed on its subjects vertically from above, the modern State is linked horizontally with all levels of society. The functions of the pre-modern State are essentially coercive, the modern State exercises positive as well as coercive powers. The modern State has access to its subjects precisely because they are literate, because it can get at them through the printed word, can not only give them orders, but also permanently influence and persuade and mobilize them for its purposes. The pre-modern State gives orders, but it can mobilize its subjects only occasionally, for exceptional purposes, such as war or common action against pestilence or famine. The modern State has greater power over its subjects than the pre-modern. It is a commonplace that democracy is a sham without popular education, and that education increases the subject's liberty, opens to him a wider range of choices. If education is understood as training to think for oneself, this is true. But if it means no more than instruction, the inculcation of knowledge, then it need not be true. Mere literacy and factual knowledge may simply make the citizen more vulnerable, more amenable to persuasion. If modern mass democracy requires mass education, so also does modern totalitarianism.

Our distinction is concerned with the structure of the State, not with the form of political institutions. The latter will be discussed in the following chapter. A pre-modern State may be a liberal oligarchy, or a dictatorship, or may have definite elements of democracy. A modern State may be a liberal democracy, or some sort of oligarchy or dictatorship, or it may be totalitarian. At present there are modern States in North America, the Pacific Dominions, almost the whole of Europe, the Soviet Union, China and Japan; pre-modern States in most of Asia, Africa and Latin America; and marginal cases in such countries as Turkey, Spain, Greece, South Africa, Argentine and Brazil.

Revolutions are attacks on the State power. Twentieth-century revolutions can be conveniently divided into two types—frontal assault and seizure of power from within. In the first case the revolutionaries lead their massed armies in direct attack on the citadel of power and overwhelm the defenders. In the second case, though the leaders have a mass following outside the citadel, they enter it without a battle: either they are invited by a section of the garrison or they are themselves the commanders of the garrison. In both types of revolution violence is ruthlessly used *after* seizure of power. But violence *before* victory, which is bound to be considerable in frontal assault revolutions, is small, or may even be completely avoided, in revolutions from within.

In the twentieth century there have been successful frontal assault revolutions only against pre-modern States, in underdeveloped societies. The most striking examples are Russia, Yugoslavia, China and Turkey. Successful revolutions from within have taken place in States of both types. The most important have been those of Mussolini in Italy, of Hitler in Germany and of the communists in Czechoslovakia in 1948. The victories of Perón in the Argentine (and his overthrow ten years later) and of the Egyptian colonels in 1952 belong to this category.

We shall examine in turn these examples of each type.

REVOLUTIONS BY FRONTAL ASSAULT

The background to the three communist revolutions—Russia, Yugoslavia and China—is remarkably similar. All three revolutionary movements passed through three stages.

The first stage was the formation of discussion circles of intellectuals, with no mass following at all, which discussed social theories and began to think of conspiracies to overthrow the government. In Russia this stage, known as *kruzhkovshchina* (from *kruzhok*—a little circle), covered the 1860s and the first half of the 1870s, the age of the Populist revolutionaries: the first Marxist groups of this sort appeared in the mid-1880s. In Serbia there were Populist groups in the 1870s and Marxist towards the end of the century, but as political conditions were freer than in Russia, less strictly conspiratorial methods were necessary. In China there were groups of revolutionary conspirators, professing a mixture of Western radical ideas, at the end of the century, but Marxist groups became important only from 1918, with the example of Lenin's revolution to inspire them.

The second stage came when the groups of intellectual revolutionaries acquired their first mass support, which they found in the place where it was most accessible and most susceptible to organization—in the cities. In Russia the Populist conspiratorial party, Land and Liberty, which was for theoretical reasons more interested in peasants than in city workers, nevertheless recruited its mass following in the working class of St. Petersburg. Twenty years later the Russian Marxists, who on theoretical grounds in any case preferred industrial workers, won a mass following in several large cities of the Russian Empire, and in 1905 the socialist-led working-class movement became for a time a serious political force. In Serbia and Croatia there were small but active socialist workers' parties on the eve of the First World War, and in the first years of the new state of Yugoslavia (1919 and 1920) the communist party, which was formed from them, for a time won a considerable mass support. In China the Marxist intellectuals who founded the communist party won a following among the railwaymen and the factory workers in the big cities, and extended it during the years up to 1927.

A combination of revolutionary intellectuals and the urban poor may suffice to seize power if the intellectuals have won over key officers in the army. In this case power can be seized in what is essentially a revolution from within the citadel. Iraq in 1958 is an obvious example. But if the officers remain loyal to the government, then revolution cannot be achieved at this stage. A further stage is required. In overwhelmingly agrarian societies, revolutionaries must win over a large part of the peasantry. But, as we have seen, peasants are not easily accessible to revolutionary propaganda and are inclined to respect existing hierarchies as long as these work. It is only when the machinery of government begins to totter, under the impact of an external blow, that their loyalties are shaken, that they are both able to hear, and are inclined to receive with hope, the ideas of revolutionaries. This happened in 1905 in Russia, in the 1920s in China, and in the chaotic circumstances in which the Habsburg Monarchy collapsed and the Yugoslav state was created in 1918. But the Tsar's régime was saved from collapse in 1906, the new Yugoslav state was consolidated in 1919, and the communists were defeated by the Kuomintang in 1927. Disastrous military reverses for Imperial Russia and Kuomintang China, and complete destruction of the Yugoslav state, were necessary for the victory of the three communist movements. These three revolutions have in fact one basic common feature: they were made possible by defeat in war.

We will not repeat here the well-known stories of the three revolutions, but will briefly consider some of the main points of similarity and difference between them.

The Russian Revolution began in the classical manner of the eighteenth and nineteenth centuries, in the capital city. The mass demonstrations, and the fraternization of the troops with the masses, in February 1917, and the insurrection of the Bolsheviks against the demoralized government forces in October, both recall 1789 and 1848. In Yugoslavia and China, by contrast, the communist revolution built its machinery of power, and gathered its popular support, not in the capital, but in the provinces. In the nineteenth century, revolutions began at the centre and sought to extend their power to the rest of the country: in twentieth-century Yugoslavia and China they began at the periphery and ended at the centre.

The Russian Revolution may also be compared with the French in that it passed from the 'moderate' to the 'extremist' stages. The Bolsheviks themselves were much aware of this parallel, and saw themselves as Jacobins to the Girondins of the Mensheviks and Socialist Revolutionaries. The comparison has been made by non-communist writers, such as Crane Brinton.[55] The analogy is not in fact so close as it seems, but there is something in it. In the case of Yugoslavia and China there is nothing of the sort. It would be a fantastic distortion to compare the whole decade of Kuomintang rule (1927-37) with the Girondin period in France. In both Yugoslavia and China, the movement which finally triumphed was a disciplined communist movement, whose political aims, ideology and form of organization remained essentially the same throughout the struggle. The communists were 'extremists' from the beginning, though they often used 'moderate' tactics to win popular support.

The Yugoslav and Chinese movements became powerful in a war of liberation from a foreign conqueror: they made their social revolution in the name of patriotism. This patriotic element was not important in the Russian case. The Bolsheviks made some use of the argument that their White opponents were agents of foreign Powers, and Soviet historians have retrospectively exaggerated the role of Anglo-French 'Intervention'. But in the case of Yugoslavia and China, the struggle against the German and Japanese invaders was a fact which no one had to invent. A special feature of the Yugoslav revolution was the success with which the communists united Serbs and Croats against the invaders and their fascist satellites. The slaughter of Serbs by Croatian fascists, and counter-slaughter of Croats by Serbian nationalist bands, had been deliberately encouraged by the Germans and Italians. It had brought the people of Yugoslavia nothing but suffering, and had benefited the invaders. The communists consistently argued that fratricidal nationalism was harmful to both peoples alike, and that salvation lay only in unity against the conquerors, and after a time their arguments found hearers. In the end nothing did so much to win Tito's army popular support as this 'nationality policy'. Its potential application to Asian or African countries of multi-lingual or multi-religious population is obvious.

In other respects, however, all three revolutions were very similar to each other.

In all three the decisive period was one of civil war. In Russia it was the civil war, which lasted nearly three years, which caused the greatest loss of human life and material devastation, and which laid up the treasure of hatred on which the Soviet Union has so richly drawn. In China there was civil war in the early 1930s and again in the last phase, from 1946 to 1949.

In Yugoslavia the war of liberation was as much a civil as a national war. In all three countries the decisive struggle consisted not of street-fighting and barricades, but of military operations between great armies. This similarity between the three is more important than the difference noted above, that Russia did have its street-fighting period and the other two did not.

Another common feature is that in all three countries the struggle was not between two forces, but between many. In Russia in 1917 there were three political forces—the conservatives symbolized by Kornilov, the socialists symbolized by Kerenski, and the Bolsheviks led by Lenin. The first two hated each other as bitterly as they hated Lenin, and he profited from their conflict. In 1918 there was again a three-cornered struggle. Resistance to the Bolsheviks was organized in the name of the Constituent Assembly, which Lenin had dissolved in 1918 and which was dominated by socialists. But these socialists could not come to terms with the conservative elements, which were especially strong in the army commanded by Admiral Kolchak. When Kolchak overthrew the Directory of left-wing politicians, the anti-Bolshevik movement came under increasingly right-wing leaders, and people of socialist opinions found themselves reluctantly forced to regard the Bolsheviks as the lesser of two evils. The scene was still further complicated by the existence of non-Russian political movements, which wanted neither White nor Red Russian rule, and vacillated between the two camps. By 1920, however, Lenin had to a considerable extent persuaded the people of Russia that it was now a struggle between two forces—revolutionaries and supporters of the reactionary past régime. That people did become convinced of this, was not the least success of the Bolsheviks. In Yugoslavia the conflicts were even more complicated. The communists were fighting the German and Italian invaders and the Croatian and Serbian fascists, but they were also fighting the Croatian and Serbian democrats, and the last four groups were fighting each other. The communists in the end convinced a large part of the people that they were the only effective force fighting the invaders, and that anyone who wished to fight for his country's independence must accept their leadership. Thus by 1944 it had become a struggle between two forces, though even then there were regions and groups that did not fit so simple a pattern. In China the struggle, at least after 1931, was three-cornered, between communists, Kuomintang and Japanese. The success of the communists in organizing guerrilla warfare against the Japanese, and in persuading millions in China and abroad that they were the only effective fighters against the Japanese, was decisive for their final victory in the last stage, the straight civil war of 1946-9.

Another important common feature of the three revolutions was the ability of the communists to draw on reserves of human energy and ability that had never been touched. The vast majority of Russian, Yugoslav and Chinese peasants had been inert objects in politics. No one had been interested in their aspirations. The communists showed interest. Peasants or workers who had no formal schooling, but an ability to lead men in action, or to organize a community for simple needs in an emergency, could rise quickly in the new apparatus of the communist-ruled state. Thousands of careers were made, and hundreds of thousands more seemed possible. Young people and women were especially attracted. Side by side with the horror and injustice and cruelty the communists also brought hope and enthusiasm not only to their indoctrinated and disciplined party members, but also to the masses. Without understanding this, one cannot understand the revolutions.

It is often argued that the Yugoslav and Chinese cases differ from the Russian in that the communists recruited their main support from the peasants. This is a difference in degree, not in kind, and it has been exaggerated, largely because the glamour attaching to the events in Petrograd in 1917 has caused historians and commentators to underrate the civil war period. In the Petrograd events the workers played a leading role (though even then the soldiers—peasants in uniform—were important). But the Red armies of 1918-20 were mainly composed of peasants, and many of those who made careers as officers or civil administrators or party officials were of peasant origin. In Yugoslavia and China the peasant element was more obvious because the struggle was mainly fought in remote rural areas, where the only manpower available for recruitment was peasant. In order to win peasant support, the Yugoslav and Chinese communist leaders proclaimed studiously 'moderate' policies. In particular, they took care (after a certain number of 'excesses' by 'sectarian' extremists at the beginning of the movement) not to attack religious beliefs or to question the right of peasant families to own their own holdings. But neither the Yugoslav nor the Chinese communists were ever 'agrarian socialists'. Peasants were to them valuable manpower, not equal comrades. Those peasants whose ability and devotion raised them in the hierarchy of power ceased in effect to be peasants: they were merged in the classless cadres of the communist movement. This truth is in no way altered by the fact that Tito and Mao may feel a certain genuine paternal affection for their peasant subjects, and be loved by them.

Finally, the three revolutions resembled each other in that the international situation, despite great dangers, was basically favourable to them. The Bolsheviks were fortunate that the Allies won the First World War.

If the Germans had won, they would certainly not have tolerated so uncomfortable a neighbour. But France and Britain were far more remote from Russia than Germany was, and French and British politicians had to win parliamentary elections, which they would certainly not have done if they had kept the men in the army, to fight another war against Russians. The 'intervention' by Allied troops in Russia was of negligible military importance, and arose not from any determination to destroy communism, but from obligations to those Russians who were believed to be still fighting, or trying to fight, against the Germans after Lenin had made peace with Germany. A very similar situation arose in regard to American 'intervention' in China in 1946-9. American troops did not fight, and if President Truman had tried to keep the men in the army to fight a new war in China, his party would have lost the congressional and presidential elections. Such material aid as America gave to Chiang was a consequence of wartime obligations to an ally. In the case of Yugoslavia, the favourable international factor consisted of the fact that the German army was held down on its major war fronts, and that there was therefore a limit to the number of German and other Axis forces that could be used against the communists. Large forces were used, and the communists fought them heroically: still larger forces might have crushed them, but they could not be spared.

In Greece and Albania in 1943 and 1944 the communists organized strong resistance movements, and used these to build up an effective apparatus of military and civil power. The history and structure of the two movements were both very similar to the Yugoslav. International factors were, however, decisive. These favoured the Albanian communists, who had contact through Yugoslavia with the Soviet armies that held Eastern Europe at the end of the war, but were fatal to the Greek communists, who were defeated by the British forces which landed in Greece in the autumn of 1944. The Greek communists' second attempt to seize power, in the civil war of 1947-50, was also unsuccessful, both because they could not enlist so much mass support for an internal rebellion as they had won for a patriotic war, and because the foreign aid which they received from the Balkan communist states was matched by American aid to the Greek government, and fell off after Yugoslavia was expelled from the Cominform in 1948. Another example of successful communist seizure of power through a resistance movement and guerrilla war is Indochina, where the Vietminh began by fighting the Japanese and continued against the French. Its military and civil machines were built in this period, by methods similar to those of the Yugoslav and the Chinese movements, but its final victory was facilitated by material aid from Communist China.

THE SEIZURE OF POWER

A successful revolution by frontal assault, which has features in common with these cases, but was not led by communists, is Kemal Atatürk's revolution in Turkey. The active force in this movement were young officers, who had learned not only military technique but political ideas from the West. The prologue to Kemal Atatürk's revolution was the Young Turk revolution of 1908-9, which overthrew the autocracy of Sultan Abdul Hamid. The consequent régime was unable seriously to reform Turkey, and defeat in the war brought the country into danger of extinction. It was in these dark days that Atatürk rallied the Turkish nation behind him. Atatürk was a brilliant commander, and repelled the Greek invasion of the Aegean provinces. He also set up a new political and social régime, secularizing the State, introducing a Latin alphabet in place of Arabic, imposing Western forms and habits, giving a new urgency to education and to economic development. His achievement was far more than military victory: it was a deliberate remoulding of social and political institutions, with violent suppression of such internal conservative opponents as objected to his policies. Like the Yugoslav and Chinese communist leaders, the nationalist revolutionary Kemal Atatürk owed his success to his ability to draw on reserves of unused human ability and energy. From the formally uneducated, long-ignored and exploited Turkish peasants he recruited brave military leaders and efficient administrators, and inspired them with his own vision of a regenerated Turkey, territorially smaller, but now homogeneous, united and strong.

There is one more frontal assault revolution which should be mentioned, though it is difficult to fit into any category. This is the Mexican. It began in 1910 with the armed revolt of a liberal-minded landowner, Francisco Madero, against the decaying régime of the octogenarian dictator, Porfirio Diaz, who had ruled the country for more than thirty years. The victory of Madero was followed by a series of wars between individual rebel commanders. Madero himself was killed, and civil war continued for ten years. During this time there were peasant risings, of which at least that led by Emiliano Zapata can reasonably be called a movement of social revolution. Zapata was murdered in 1919, and the country settled down into a régime of military dictatorship combined with intermittent social reform. Persecution of the Catholic Church under President Calles (1924-8) led to armed rebellion, and the following years were marked by assassinations, executions and the gradual emergence of a new conservatism based on the vested interests of the surviving leaders of the revolutionary period, now a clique little interested in wider social reform. This trend was however reversed by President Lázaro Cárdenas (1934-40), who, as we have seen, carried out a far-reaching land reform. Thus the Mexican Revolution lasted some thirty years, during which violence was frequently used on all sides, revolutionary rhetoric was a national pastime, and great changes took place not only in governing personnel, but in public institutions. There was also created the reputation of Mexico as the country of a great and unique revolution, different from communist or fascist actions, related to the real needs of the Mexican people without regard to foreign-imported doctrinaire formulae. Whether this reputation is deserved or not, it has certainly been an inspiration to reformers and revolutionaries throughout Latin America, and even further afield. As such it is a political factor in its own right.

REVOLUTIONS FROM WITHIN

In Germany in 1932 the National Socialist Party of Adolf Hitler was the strongest single party in the country. It had its own military formations, not strong enough to resist the regular army, but certainly capable of fighting the armed forces of other political groups in street-brawls and of intimidating unarmed citizens. The Nazi party had considerable support among all classes of the population—among the workers who believed Hitler's promises that he would end unemployment; among peasants who were impressed by Nazi propaganda about 'blood and soil' and the need to create a new Germanic *élite* of peasant stock; among the middle classes who hoped that Hitler would restore their social status and standards of respectability and save them from the supreme disaster of *déclassement*; among big business-men who hoped that Hitler would suppress the trade unions and put the working class 'in its place'. Hitler also appealed to the nationalism that was strong in all classes, the desire for revenge against Germany's military victors of 1918 and for restoration of Germany's former military power.

At this time the working class was politically both weak and divided. It was weak because unemployment had broken the discipline of the trade unions, and divided because two parties, both claiming the mantle of Karl Marx, fought each other for its allegiance. Since 1928 the German communists, loyally carrying out the orders of the Comintern in Moscow, had made the social democrats their chief enemy among all German parties, and had endlessly denounced them as 'social fascists'. This policy had led the communists in 1931 and 1932 into parallel action with the Nazis, and in general had been of great help to Hitler. It had been designed in Moscow to serve the interests of Soviet foreign policy, but it proved fatal to the German workers, German democracy and the Soviet Union. However, the despair caused by unemployment in 1932 caused the communists somewhat to increase their following at the expense of the social democrats.

As the working class became more evenly divided it became inevitably still more ineffective as a political force.

The forces of the right were represented by political parties, army leaders, big industrialists and President Hindenburg and his circle of friends. Though re-elected President by the votes of democrats, Hindenburg had no sympathy for democracy, and wished to create an authoritarian, conservative régime with a militarist bias. Unfortunately, the candidates for leadership of such a government, especially the civilian Fritz von Papen and the general Kurt von Schleicher, were bitter rivals. Hitler was able to exploit their intrigues against each other. The army command was of decisive help to Hitler. German officers understood very little about politics, for which they professed a lordly contempt. Had they taken the trouble to learn more about the nature of Hitler's party, they might have seen how deadly a menace it was to their country and to the best values of the Prussian military tradition. But in fact all that most of them knew was that they despised the Republican régime, feared the working class and approved of the nationalistic slogans that Hitler's Nazis proclaimed. When General Groener, one of the few senior officers who was loyal to the Republic, wished as Minister of Interior to ban Hitler's military formation, *Sturm-Abteilungen* (SA), he was forced by General von Schleicher, speaking on behalf of the army command, to resign his post as Minister. In January 1933 too, intrigues in the army command proved of decisive help to Hitler.[56]

A most important factor was the bogy of a communist danger, which paralysed the minds of conservative politicians and middle-class people generally. There had never been the slightest chance that the communists would ever get power in Germany. The episodes of 1919 in Berlin and in Bavaria were doomed to failure from the beginning. In 1932, though the communist party had gained some electoral votes, it had no prospect of making a bid for political power by force. Nevertheless, the events of 1919, the economic hardships of the early 1920s, and the continuing revolutionary rhetoric, combined with ponderous insults against traditional German moral values and patriotism, which poured from the orators of the left, had created on the right an obsessive fear of communist revolution which the Nazis most skilfully exploited. In the face of this non-existent danger, individuals and groups of the right were willing to give their support to Hitler. They did not much like him, his friends or his manners, but they believed that with the help of the army and the President they would be able to control him—indeed, to make him a sort of obedient gendarme to defend their interests. These fellow-travellers of the right, both anti-communist idealists and naïvely machiavellian politicians, played their part in Hitler's victory.

The government of Hindenburg's friend, von Papen, was brought down by the intrigues of von Schleicher, whereupon von Papen intrigued with Hitler and was able to persuade the President to appoint Hitler as Chancellor. The right-wing big business-man and politician, Hugenberg, brought his party into the new coalition, and von Papen became Vice-Chancellor, believing that through his links with the President he would be the strong man of the government. But Hitler's henchman, Göring, now Prime Minister of Prussia, purged the civil service and police, created an auxiliary police force of 50,000, of whom half were Nazi storm-troopers, and organized the Reichstag fire of 27 February. Hitler used this to create a state of panic, and persuaded Hindenburg to approve a decree that enabled him to abolish all civil liberties and guarantees of individual freedom under the Constitution. The parliamentary election, in which Nazi terror still did not succeed in preventing millions of voters from voting against Hitler, gave him and his right-wing fellow-travellers a bare majority. It was increased by the arrest or flight of the communist members. On 23 March the parliament voted for an Enabling Law which gave Hitler absolute power and put an end to the remnants of political freedom in Germany. Only the social democrats voted against the Enabling Law. During the next months all parties other than the Nazi were dissolved or dissolved themselves. The fellow-travellers of the right saw all their hopes of power disappointed. A year later, in the massacre of 30 June 1934, Hitler destroyed the leaders of oppositional factions within his own party and a number of prominent politicians of the right, including von Schleicher: von Papen was lucky to escape with his life, to serve Hitler in several secondary posts, and to escape any penalties from the Denazification tribunals after 1945. Already in March 1933 Hitler was supreme, and proceeded to remould Germany according to his desires.

The seizure of power by the communists in Czechoslovakia in 1948 has interesting points of similarity. Here too there were an ailing President with illusions, a widespread fear of a mythical danger (a fascist bogy in place of a communist bogy), and fellow-travelling groups (of 'left' not 'right'), led by ambitious intriguing politicians.

In 1945 Czechoslovakia was liberated from the last fighting armies of Hitler by the Soviet Army, after General Eisenhower at the request of the Soviet High Command had forbidden General Patton to advance to Prague. For six months Soviet troops occupied all Czechoslovak territory except a strip from Plzen westwards, where there were American forces. Their presence enabled the communists to seize key positions in the local administration, and their military glory combined with the general initial enthusiasm of the Czech people for their liberators to increase the communists' popularity. Ambitious careerists, and persons vulnerable to charges of collaboration with the Germans in the past, hastened to jump on the communist band-wagon. However, at this time the Soviet government, and hence the Czechoslovak communist party, adopted the position that there must be a coalition of all democratic anti-fascist parties, in which the communists were to share power with others and not attempt a dictatorship of their own.

The resultant régime was a liberal democracy with certain reservations. The Czech Republican (Agrarian) Party was banned on the grounds that some of its leaders had collaborated with the Germans in 1939: its former supporters among the peasants and the middle classes had to choose between the other parties. Each of these had hoped to gain votes by this dubious transaction, but in practice it was probably the communists who did best out of the affair. Their ability to win Czech peasant votes was increased by the fact that it was they who held real power in the northern and western border regions. Empty farms and good jobs in the management of ownerless factories were distributed by favour of the local communist bosses. The communists also made sure that when ministries were distributed in the coalition government they should get key power positions. They got the Ministry of Interior, with control over the police, and the Ministry of Information, with control over radio and over censorship of the press. They were also well entrenched in the counter-intelligence department of the Ministry of Defence. They had a generous share of the directorships of nationalized industrial plants, and they saw to it that the factory guards, which had charge of stocks of arms in the factories, should be in the hands of their party. Finally, the revived trade unions were controlled from the beginning by communists, with a sprinkling of alleged social democrats, most of whom were completely obedient to communist orders.

A free parliamentary election was held in 1946, in which the communists were the strongest party, with more than a third of the poll. For the next year they behaved as constitutional democrats. A change came in the summer of 1947, when the refusal of the Marshall Plan on orders from Moscow and the foundation of the Cominform marked the end of the Soviet policies of democratic coalition and Great Power Alliance. A new election was due in the summer of 1948, and it was clear that the communists would not win so much support as in 1946. To anticipate this, they began more systematically than ever to pack the police of the capital with their men. The other parties' representatives in the cabinet objected to this, and when the communist Prime Minister, Klement Gottwald persisted in his policy, the ministers of three parties resigned, on 21 February 1948.

The democratic leaders hoped that the social democrats, who had supported them in their protests about the police, would also resign, and that President Eduard Beneš would back them against Gottwald. Beneš was not only constitutional Head of State, but enjoyed immense prestige in the country and had great authority in the army. But both hopes were disappointed. The social democrats hesitated to resign, and their party was divided between at least three groups. The leader of the so-called left wing, Zdenek Fierlinger, was completely devoted to the Soviet cause. His followers, with the help of toughs supplied by the communists, seized the social democrat party headquarters and proclaimed the party's support for Gottwald. Fierlinger also had the benefit of the advice of the Soviet Deputy Foreign Minister, Zorin, who was in Prague during the crisis. With social democratic support, the communists had a bare parliamentary majority, and thus had a strong constitutional claim to be entrusted by the President with the formation of the new cabinet. Beneš was a younger man than Hindenburg had been in 1933, but he was in poor health and badly advised. Just as Hindenburg was unable to believe that a former corporal in his army would not do as he wished, or that a man who ranted of the military glories of the German fatherland would destroy Germany, so Beneš could not believe that the communists, who claimed to be the most progressive democrats of all, would destroy democracy, or that the leaders of Soviet Russia, who had freed the Czech people by their victory over Germany, would impose on the Czechs an alien yoke no less grievous than Hitler's. He was cut off from the army and the wider public, as all broadcasting and the press were controlled by the communists through the Ministry of Information and the communist-led printing workers' union. He felt bound to reappoint Gottwald Prime Minister, but tried to persuade him to base his new government on the same coalition as before. This, however, Gottwald refused to do.

Meanwhile, the communists had brought their factory guards out on the streets, mobilized their police machine, and set up in most provinces so-called Action Committees. These were groups headed by the local communists, but including prominent local members of the other parties who threw in their lot with the communists. In order to preserve an appearance of coalition government, Gottwald appointed to his new cabinet several individuals who nominally represented the three democratic parties whose ministers had resigned. These men were in fact fellow-travellers or agents of the communists who had been selected for their jobs not by their own parties, but by the leader of the communist party.

THE SEIZURE OF POWER

They were the minor Hugenbergs of Gottwald's revolution. Its von Papen was Fierlinger, who had fared well in the following decade. In the summer of 1948 he took the rump of his party, now thoroughly purged, into fusion with the communist party. The fellow-travelling social democrats who followed him did not do so well, for many of them fell victims to the purge which devastated the party's ranks between 1950 and 1952. But Fierlinger himself, like von Papen, survived his dupes.

The communist success cannot be understood without reference to the anti-German myth which is the equivalent of the anti-Bolshevik myth in Germany in 1932. In one sense the myth was no myth at all. The German Nazis had ruled and exploited the Czech lands for six years. The hatred thereby created in Czech hearts expressed itself in the mass expulsion of the German population of the Bohemian borderlands (who had lived there since the Middle Ages), which was accompanied by much brutality and led to tens of thousands of deaths. Thereby hatred of Czechs could be assumed to have been created in German hearts. It was thus understandable that Czechs should both hate Germans and fear future German revenge. But just as in Germany in 1932 there was no practical prospect of communists attaining power, so in Europe in 1948 there was no practical prospect of Germans revenging themselves on Czechs. The widespread Czech argument was that, as Germany would one day seek revenge, Czechoslovakia must maintain its alliance with Russia, and as the Russians wanted the communists in power in Czechoslovakia this must be accepted. But this meant that in order to avoid a hypothetical revenge in the future the Czech people must accept communist tyranny in the present; and in order to ensure their independence from a non-existent German menace, they must hand their country over to the agents of Soviet imperialism. It was this that was decisive rather than the absence of Western military aid against the Soviet Union. A few months later, a potential crisis arose in Finland through the same cause which had started the crisis in Czechoslovakia—packing of the police by a communist Minister of Interior. Finland was militarily no less at the mercy of Russia than Czechoslovakia had been, and no Western aid was conceivable. But the Finns refused to be intimidated. They voted in parliament against the Minister, he resigned, there was no crisis and no Soviet intervention. The Finns suffered from none of the illusions about Russia that afflicted the Czechs.

Once in power, the communist dictatorship of Gottwald proceeded to remould Czechoslovakia according to the formulae of 'Popular Democracy' as elaborated from Moscow. A totalitarian régime was set up which claimed its victims first from the opponents of the communists and then from the ranks of the communist party itself.

Another example of a revolution from within is that of Colonel Juan Perón in Argentina. He built up his power as Secretary of Labour and Social Welfare in the military dictatorship that was introduced by a *coup d'état* in June 1943. Perón created a genuine system of social security, increased wages and helped some of the more backward workers to organize trade unions. He canalized collective bargaining through his office and favoured the workers against the employers in negotiations. But in return for these benefits, he insisted on placing his own men in control of the workers' organizations. Labour leaders who opposed him, and unions led by his opponents, suffered from various forms of discrimination. In 1944 Perón rose to be Vice-President and Minister of War.

The victory of the democratic nations over Hitler, however, threatened the position of Perón and his friends, who had shown themselves keen admirers of Hitler and Mussolini. In 1945 the dictatorship was relaxed, there were demonstrations by democratic parties and university students, and in October a *coup d'état* by officers of democratic sympathies set up a new government and placed Perón under arrest. He was saved by the workers of the meat-packing houses, led by bosses loyal to Perón and exhorted to action by the actress, Evita Duarte, who later became Perón's wife. On 16 October 1945 they invaded the capital, and by the next day they were masters of the streets of Buenos Aires. The army would not fire on them, and Perón was released. From now on he was dictator. He did not completely suppress opposition parties, but reduced them to helplessness. He muzzled the independent press. He created his own mass party and firmly controlled the trade unions. He used his power to introduce social reforms which were of real advantage to the workers in industry and the labourers in agriculture. The whole régime was based on his supreme political power, but the changes were so radical as to constitute a revolution.

After ten years, however, he was overthrown by the same force to which he owed his first rise to power, a military *coup d'état*. The officers who decided to overthrow him were largely motivated by dislike of his increasing interference with the Catholic Church, the only organized force left in the country that was independent of his control. The combination of Church and army was too strong for Perón: the loyalty of the workers, in particular of the *descamisados*, or 'shirtless' unskilled workers, was not enough to save him. In October 1955 he had to go into exile.

Another revolution which began as a military *coup d'état* is the Egyptian revolution of July 1952.* Here, as in Turkey in 1919, it was in the officer corps that the men of radical ideas were to be found. Once in power, the new leaders proceeded to carry out social reforms and to abolish political

* This is discussed below, pp. 360-1.

parties. The result was a one-party régime with a radical social programme, not unlike that of Perón. Like Perón, Colonel Nasser was a passionate nationalist and imperialist, aiming at the domination of neighbouring countries, whose people were united with his by language, religion and past history. The opportunities of an active foreign policy were more favourable for Nasser than for Perón, and in consequence internal reform has been relatively more overshadowed by international ambitions in the Egyptian than in the Argentine case. But Nasser's achievements and aspirations entitle him to be considered not merely as the maker of a *coup d'état*, but as the leader of a revolution. The Iraqi action of July 1958 may also qualify as a revolution. As in Egypt, the action was initiated by army officers. But whereas Nasser and his friends kept power in their hands and set up a régime of their own choice, General Kassem soon showed himself to be a weaker version of Kerensky, allowing power to pass to the communists. Iraq seems likely to follow the example of Czechoslovakia rather than of Egypt.

REVOLUTION BY FOREIGN CONQUEST

In Eastern Europe after 1944 communist revolutions were carried out in five countries (Poland, Hungary, Roumania, Bulgaria and Eastern Germany) by the agents of the Soviet government, relying on the presence and support of the Soviet army. There were differences between each case. Soviet intervention was most obvious and most lasting in Germany, somewhat less so in Poland and Roumania and least in Bulgaria and Hungary. But in all five cases it was a decisive factor. These five cases differ from those of Yugoslavia (where a communist revolutionary movement fought its own war), Albania (where the same was true, but foreign —Yugoslav—aid played a significant part) and Czechoslovakia (where the communists were undoubtedly helped by the presence of the Soviet army for six months in 1945, yet mainly owed their victory to their own strength and skill, to the weak resistance of their opponents and to the prevalence of useful illusions among the people). It was not the skill of the communist leaders or the ingenuity of their parliamentary or non-parliamentary manœuvres—real though these at times were—but the presence of the foreign invaders that gave them their victory. The results were a revolution, but the seizure of power was an act of foreign conquest.

A certain parallel can be drawn with the transformation of the political and social structure of Japan by American conquest. The establishment of a Constitution of a liberal democratic type and the distribution of land to the peasants has the work of the occupying Power. This revolutionary change would not have come unless Japan had been conquered. It is true that the régime thus imposed is one of political freedom, which allows the people of Japan to choose its rulers, and to elect persons who can if they wish undo previous legislation. This is, of course, not the case in the communist régimes of 'popular democracy' imposed by the Soviet army in Eastern Europe. Whether one holds that the MacArthur revolution was a blessing to Japan, or that the abrupt rejection of Japanese traditional ways has demoralized the Japanese people, it cannot be denied both that the change was drastic and that it was the work of foreign conquest.

These considerations do not apply to Western Germany, where a political system was established which had roots in the German past. The defeat of Hitler enabled German democratic forces, which had been numerically strong before 1933, and indeed before 1914, to assert themselves again. The presence of Allied forces both helped and hindered these forces, but they did not create them, and they did not impose basic social transformation on them.

VULNERABILITY TO REVOLUTION

Revolutions by frontal assault in the twentieth century have been successful only in countries with a pre-modern state. Even in these cases they have almost always been the result of a defeat in war. The only case of the disintegration of the State machine without any external blow to it is the Mexican Revolution, and its opening phase—Madero's insurrection—is perhaps less a popular revolution than a local military rising, which was fatal to the régime of Diaz only because it was already, like its leader, decaying from old age. One should not dogmatically conclude from this that only defeat in war can bring about the degree of collapse of the State machine that can make possible a successful revolution by frontal assault. But the connexion between the two in most past cases is significant.

In countries with a modern State, even defeat in war does not seem sufficient to cause a collapse of the state machine, and a consequent opportunity of revolution by frontal assault, unless the whole territory is occupied by the victorious enemy and he then imposes a revolution. There are two interesting examples that illustrate this point.

The first is Germany in 1918. Military defeat was definite. But the army retreated and demobilized in good order, the machinery of civil government and justice continued to work smoothly, and there was no collapse of the state machine. The mutiny in the fleet and various disorders in the big cities caused first the abdication of the Emperor and then the formation of a provisional government of the two workers' parties (Social Democratic Party and Independent Social Democratic Party). But the workers themselves desired no violent upheaval. There was no question of the Workers'

Councils, which superficially resembled Russian Soviets, seizing power. When the Congress of deputies of the Workers' Councils met in Berlin in December 1918, they voted by a large majority (of Social Democratic persuasion) for their own abolition and for the election of a Constituent Assembly to decide the future form of the German Republic. These were important events, but they amount to much less than a revolution.

The second case is the Soviet Union in 1941. The military defeats and loss of territory suffered in the first months of the war by the Soviet Union were far greater than those endured by Imperial Russia, which brought about the collapse of the Tsar and his régime. But on their own side of the front, the Soviet rulers maintained military discipline and their civil government machine, and their industry went on working. Something may, of course, be explained by the difference in quality of leadership between Stalin and Nicholas II, and still more by the fact that Soviet Russia was industrially far more developed, and thus better able to meet the needs of war economy, than Imperial Russia. But the essential difference is that between a modern State and a pre-modern State.

Revolutions from within have occurred in the twentieth century in countries with both modern and pre-modern states. They may be begun by a military *coup d'état* (as in Egypt) or by the seizure of a monopoly of power by a totalitarian power from within a coalition (as in Czechoslovakia in 1948 and in Germany in 1933). The opportunity for action may be given, in an advanced industrial country, by an economic slump with mass unemployment. It is worth noting again in this connexion that, as mass unemployment weakens all working-class organizations, a slump is not a favourable situation for action by a party whose main mass support comes from the working class (for example, a communist party), but rather favours one which recruits mass support from several social classes (as the German National Socialist Party). Revolution from within is a type of action which can be tried by any political faction in any type of state and society, and there seems no point in further generalizations about it.

It is worth noting that all the major revolutions which we have discussed in this chapter (Russian, Yugoslav, Chinese, Turkish, Mexican, German, Czechoslovak, Argentine, Egyptian) have led to the establishment not of liberal democratic régimes but of dictatorship, and most of them to a totalitarian régime. They have been revolutions not for liberty, but against liberty.

Part Three
Totalitarianism

8: The Totalitarian Régime

The use of political terms has been subject in recent times to an appalling degree of confusion and inflation. The confusion is perhaps inherent in the subject itself, but the inflation—the incessant use and abuse of certain words in different contexts until they have as much lost meaning as paper money printed in excessive quantities has lost value—is man-made, and has gone so far that it cannot now be reversed. Thus if we are now to discuss forms of government, we must try to define our meaning. It should be understood that we are not claiming that the use we shall give here to various well-known words is the only possible use, or that it is in any sense the 'correct' use: there can in fact be no correct use after so much confusion and inflation. We are merely seeking to use words in a consistent manner, and one which will make intelligible our examination of political systems, and especially of totalitarian régimes.

LIBERTY AND REPRESENTATION

We shall consider forms of government from two points of view which are closely connected yet distinct—the extent to which they permit freedom to their subjects, and the extent to which their subjects participate in the process of governing. We thus distinguish on the one hand between free and dictatorial government, and on the other hand between institutions which are in varying degrees or in no degree representative.

The nature of liberty has been and will continue to be the subject of endless, inconclusive discussions. Unlimited liberty is impossible in any human society, in which the desires of individuals must conflict with each other, and there has never been a government in history of which it was not possible to show that it denied some liberties to some individuals and groups. Nevertheless, there is a perfectly valid common-sense distinction between governments which allow a great many liberties (including the expression of a large variety of religious convictions and political opinions) to all their subjects, and governments which do not. We may call the first governments of free institutions, the second dictatorships. Free institutions may vary considerably, but there are two features which they must include. They must ensure free expression to many opinions, including opinions held only by minorities of their subjects, and they must allow their subjects from time to time by some regular procedure to choose and to replace those who wield power over them.

The degree of participation by subjects in the process of government has varied greatly through history, and still varies greatly in different parts of the world. But it is possible to divide most examples into one of three categories—autocracy, oligarchy and democracy.

In an autocracy all power is concentrated in the hands of one man. He is succeeded either by his legally-defined heir or by a person chosen by himself. There is no mechanism for the appointment or replacement of high officers of state other than his personal choice. No independent institutions exist which have a legal right to share his power. In practice, of course, the nature of an autocracy will vary according to the ability and strength of character of the individual ruler, the qualities of the advisers whom he selects, and the extent to which any of these advisers obtain a personal ascendancy over him. Two other words that may be used to describe this form of government are 'tyranny' and 'despotism'. But as both these words, in common usage, have an unmistakable undertone of moral disapproval, the morally more neutral word 'autocracy' is preferable.

In an oligarchy power is held by a privileged minority, whom the ruler is obliged to consult according to some legally accepted procedure. Appointments, dismissals and major decisions of policy require their approval. The dividing line between autocracy and oligarchy is not sharp. There have been various compromises in history between rulers and privileged upper classes. In some eighteenth-century monarchies the balance was so even as to make it difficult to label them autocracy or oligarchy. Such powerful rulers as Frederick II of Prussia and Joseph II of Austria had to respect established institutions and procedures, and could not make a habit of directly antagonizing the privileged classes. In Russia under Catherine II, however, there was no significant legal limitation on the power of the sovereign, whose will was carried out by a subordinate official hierarchy. The name 'absolute monarch', which was applied to all three rulers, and to others in Europe at the time, did not have the same meaning in each case. In eighteenth-century England, however, the régime was definitely oligarchic. Another word which once had a meaning similar to that of 'oligarchy' is 'aristocracy'. This word has, however, come to be used rather for a social class than for a form of government. The phrase 'government by aristocracy' usually means specifically government by a hereditary landowning class. This is only one form of oligarchy: another is 'plutocracy', or government by the rich, who may be landowners or capitalists or a combination of the two.

In a democracy power is exercised by the whole people. The nearest approach to this in practice has been found in very small communities, such as Swiss cantons (and even there children do not have a vote). In the Greek city-states that were said to be democracies, a large part of the population was excluded because they were slaves. In modern times 'democracy' has meant government by persons elected by a majority of the votes of the adult population. There have been three main varieties—the parliamentary (as in Britain and France), the presidential (as in the United States) and the plebiscitary (as in the France of Louis Napoleon).

In theory, degrees of freedom and degrees of representation in government may be variously combined.

It is difficult to combine much political liberty with autocracy. At most there may be some freedom of public discussion. The comparatively free press of the first years of the reign of the Russian Emperor Alexander II is perhaps an example. But as there can be no appointments or replacements to high office except by the ruler himself, the element of choice by the subject, which is one of the essential conditions of freedom, is inevitably absent.

Oligarchy, however, may be combined with considerable freedom. Strongly opposed opinions may be expressed. There may be bitter controversy on fundamental political or moral issues. Governing ministers and officials may be replaced by others taken from within a fairly numerous privileged class. The majority of the people may benefit from the struggle between the factions in the upper class. Such was the situation in England before 1832, or in Poland in parts of the sixteenth, seventeenth and eighteenth centuries. On the other hand, an oligarchy may suppress important groups of opinion, and prevent widely desired social change by force. Such was the case in Hungary between the world wars, and in Spain for a large part of the last century and a half.

Democracy, as the word is commonly used in Western countries—especially in Britain and the United States—assumes liberty. The assumption is correct in parliamentary countries and under the American Constitution. But it is not necessarily always correct. It may happen that a majority wishes to subject itself to the will of a dictator. This happened when the French elected Napoleon III and the Germans elected Hitler. In the last case it may be pointed out that Hitler's Nazi Party did not ever receive an absolute majority of votes in a real election, but in 1933 it received a relative majority for itself and an absolute majority with its minor allies. It is, of course, true that in the long run there cannot be democracy without liberty. Once the majority has given power legitimately to a dictator, it cannot take it back again. No government which does not at regular intervals submit itself to elections, at which there is a real choice before the voters, can be called democratic. After a time, a dictatorship which permits no opposition can no longer be considered to possess majority support. Nevertheless, it is not in principle impossible that a majority should prefer slavery to liberty.

We therefore prefer to use the phrase 'liberal democracy' for what in the West is normally called 'democracy', thus recognizing that there could be such a thing as 'totalitarian democracy'. We deliberately reject the phrase *'bourgeois* democracy', used by Marxists to describe the Western forms of liberal democracy. This is not because we deny that there may be forms of democracy in which the *bourgeoisie* is powerful, but because we deny that it is the extent of *bourgeois* influence or power that gives its distinctive character to liberal democracy. There have been illiberal forms of government in which the *bourgeoisie* has been powerful, and there are forms of liberal democracy in which the working class has about as much power and influence as the *bourgeoisie*. For example, one may argue as to the respective power in contemporary Britain of trade unions, employers' and professional organizations, but the truth is not so clear that any fair-minded person can be sure whether Britain is ruled by 'the *bourgeoisie*', 'the workers' or any other category. All that one can say with certainty is that the exploited class, the submerged layer of the social pyramid, consists of old age pensioners—particularly of the widows of those who gave a lifetime of service to the state.

DICTATORSHIP AND TOTALITARIANISM

The word 'totalitarianism' came into use in the 1920s. It was accepted with pride by Mussolini, who liked to describe his fascist régime as a *stato totalitario*—though it must be doubted whether he ever attained the goal he set himself. Other practitioners have rejected the title. Communists in particular deny that the Soviet, Chinese or East European régimes are totalitarian. The word has acquired an unmistakably pejorative quality. Indeed, in the West it has suffered from the general inflation of political language. It is commonly used in journalistic polemics to describe such figures as General Franco or Colonel Nasser, and it is even applied to traditional absolutisms in the European past.

This misuse of the word is unfortunate, for it is a useful one, fitted to describe a twentieth-century form of government that differs significantly from past forms, not only from liberal democracy, but also from dictatorship as usually known in history. We shall use the word, since there is no other that describes the phenomenon, in the hope that in this case it is not too late for verbal inflation to be checked.

The essence of totalitarianism is that its claims are total.

The power of classical dictatorships was essentially negative. They forbade their subjects to do and say certain things. Totalitarian régimes exercise positive as well as negative power. They too forbid certain things, but they also unceasingly tell their subjects what they must do and say and think. They keep them permanently mobilized.

THE TOTALITARIAN RÉGIME

Dictatorships confine their claims on their subjects to the public aspects of their lives. Totalitarian régimes recognize no distinction between public and private life. Everything is political. It is not only that if the subject is torn between loyalty to his family and loyalty to the government, he must put the second first: other régimes in the past have made this claim. It is that even in his home the subject must think of his duty to the government and perfect his grasp of the official ideology. No family affections or private interests must divert him from these sacred obligations as long as he is alive and awake. Whether this claim is in practice effective, one may doubt. But the claim is made.

Dictatorships will not tolerate institutions or associations whose aims conflict with their policies. Totalitarian régimes will not permit any institutions or associations that are not directly controlled by them. Society must be atomized: the individual must face alone the immense power of the all-controlling party. Persons who regularly meet for the purpose of chasing butterflies, without an official of the party or of the security police being present, may develop an independence of thought which may ultimately lead to specifically oppositional thought. This risk cannot be taken.

Dictatorships confine themselves to matters of political power, which admittedly may be widely interpreted. They will not hesitate to act in a manner which contradicts prevalent standards of morality if the defence of their power requires it. But they do not claim themselves to be the source of morality. Totalitarian rulers deny all absolute standards external to themselves. Everything is relative except the power of the boss. Unlike eighteenth-century monarchs, whose power was limited by laws and institutions, totalitarian rulers are truly 'absolute', for they alone decide what is law and what is morality. It may be argued that their ideologies provide a standard external to themselves. Even Hitler asserted: *Recht ist, was dem Volke nutzt*. But it was he alone who decided what was of advantage to the *Volk*. The Russian Bolsheviks believed that their party embodied the immanent interests of the proletariat of the whole world, and that it was merely accelerating by its policies the ineluctable processes of history, as they had been scientifically explained by Marx. But the only authority for attributing any such quality to the party was the assertion of its leader, Lenin. Later, under the personal autocracy of Stalin, the party's policies were decided, the immanent interests of the world proletariat interpreted, and the ineluctable processes of history revealed, by one man, the 'teacher of genius of progressive humanity'. Since Stalin's death the 'cult of personality' has been disowned. But the doctrine that morality is determined by the class struggle of the proletariat, whose immanent interests are embodied in the communist party, whose decisions on all matters are taken by its highly centralized leadership, remains valid.

THE ORIGINS OF TOTALITARIANISM

This phenomenon cannot be sufficiently explained by an account of the immediate circumstances which made possible the victory of the Russian Bolsheviks, German Nazis, Chinese Communists or other lesser totalitarians. Nor is it enough to say that totalitarianism is simply the form of dictatorship suited to a society that possesses modern means of communication—especially radio and television. Certainly the special circumstances of the Bolshevik and Nazi victories are important. Certainly total control over a nation requires such instruments as radio and television. It may well be argued that certain rulers of the past—Peter the Great, perhaps Philip II of Spain—might have set up totalitarian régimes had they possessed these instruments. But the existence of the instruments is not the only condition needed. Much must depend on the national traditions, institutions and habits of mind, which may favour or impede totalitarianism. There must also be a will to total power in the rulers, and this depends on the climate of opinion in which they grew up. These factors can thus only be estimated by reference to the social and intellectual history of the countries concerned.

A basic distinction must be made between communities in which political and social power have been, through most of their history, controlled by a single hierarchy, and those in which there have long been organizations, recognized by the supreme political authority, which exercise power autonomously over their members and dependents.

In a recent work of great brilliance, the Orientalist and social scientist, Dr. Karl Wittfogel, distinguishes between what he calls 'Oriental despotism' and feudalism, as the latter existed in medieval Europe and to some extent in Japan. The great ancient despotic civilizations arose, he argues, in areas where the most important task of human communities was to control great rivers by irrigation and flood-prevention. This could be done only by large numbers of centrally directed people. Hence the rise of great bureaucracies headed by a despot. Wittfogel describes such communities as 'hydraulic societies'. The most striking examples are China, based on the Yellow River, and Egypt, based on the Nile. Mesopotamia, Persia, northern India and Turkestan are other cases. The Inca kingdom of Peru was founded on a bureaucracy concerned with irrigation, and some parallels can be found in Mexico, in the Indian tribes of the south-western part of the United States, and in parts of South-East Asia. At different stages in the history of these societies there were rich landowners and merchants, but their property did not suffice to give them any independence in regard to the despotic power. 'Control over the State apparatus rather than the manipulation of private property created supreme power, prestige and wealth.'[57] In China the laws of inheritance caused property to be split among heirs, so that bureaucrats who were endowed with land did not found landed dynasties that could become independent centres of power. Still more important, neither landowners nor merchants, in China or the other hydraulic societies, possessed any corporate organization that could negotiate on equal terms with, and obtain legally established rights from, the ruler.

The situation was very different in feudal Europe. Leninists (though not all Marxists) use the word 'feudalism' loosely to denote any pre-industrial social system in which the main wealth is in land, and this is held by large landowners on whom depend the rest of the agricultural population, whether as formal serfs or formally free tenants and labourers. But feudalism in Europe was more than a system of land tenure. It was also a system of contractual relationships between landowner and monarch and between landowner and peasant. Moreover, the political order in feudal states was based on a division of power between monarch and nobility, between central government and regional magnates and smaller gentry.

European feudalism, which arose out of the disintegration of the Roman Empire, was composed essentially of three factors. One was the tradition of Roman Law, which embodied elements of Greek thought and civilization as well as of Roman, and which was preserved essentially by the Catholic Church. The second factor was the social organization derived from the Germanic tribes which created the European states (the Franks in France, Angles in England, Visigoths in Spain and Lombards in northern Italy no less than those tribes which remained in Germany proper), in which the members of the tribal aristocracy were essentially equals, with their king *primus inter pares* rather than a supreme autocrat. Germanic notions of honour, very different from Greek or Roman values, were superimposed on the latter and produced a new spirit compounded of the two. The third factor is the trading city, which never quite disappeared in the Mediterranean regions of Western Europe, and later developed in Flanders, the Baltic, the Rhine valley and northern Italy. The city formed, even in the greatest age of feudalism, a counterweight to the power of the rural landowners and a centre of autonomous institutions and even of independent ideas.

In feudal Europe the monarch had to negotiate both with the landed nobility and with the cities, both of which had their own organized power, their own corporate estates and corporate consciousness. The history of

Europe in the Middle Ages is largely the history of the conflict between the monarchical power and organized social *élites*. The long struggle inclined sometimes in favour of the one, sometimes of the other, and it continued into the post-feudal era, into the age of the Reformation and the age of the Industrial Revolution. One may perhaps say that in England and Holland on balance it was the *élites* that triumphed, in France and Prussia the monarchs. But the struggle gives their essential character to the histories of all four nations. Of this struggle there is hardly a trace in the history of the hydraulic societies.

There are other great historical States of a despotic character, which cannot literally be described as hydraulic, for massive organization of irrigation and flood control played no part in them. But in so far as these States were strongly influenced by hydraulic societies, whether by conquest or otherwise, it can be argued that the despotic régimes which they operated owed their origin to this source. The two main cases are Russia and the Ottoman Empire. In early Russia a loose aristocratic régime existed, which was overthrown by the Mongol invasion of the thirteenth century. The régime established by the Tatar successors of the Mongol conquerors certainly owed much to the system of government that had existed in Turkestan, an area of fairly advanced civilization of a hydraulic type. The Ottoman Turks were certainly greatly influenced by Persian traditions of government, as these had developed from ancient Mesopotamia through the Achaemenid, Sassanid and Moslem periods. It is also certain that both Russian and Turkish governments owed a great deal to Byzantine traditions, but it may also be argued that the Byzantine and Roman Empires had been influenced by the hydraulic societies with which they had so long been in contact in Mesopotamia or Egypt.*

Whatever one's view of the distant origins of Russian forms of government, it is certain that the Russian State, as it emerged from the Tatar yoke in the fifteenth century, was utterly unlike feudal European States. The difference remained in later centuries. There was no long struggle, as in Europe, between monarchical power and social *élites*. There was in fact no social *élite*, and there were no autonomous corporate organizations. The ambitions and plots of certain great *boyar* families in periods of

* Wittfogel's discussion of the nature of the impact of hydraulic societies on the Roman and Byzantine Empires and on the Russian state is not entirely satisfactory, and his terminology is not quite free from ambiguity. He himself recognizes these defects. But his work as a whole is a pioneering study of major importance, and certainly one of the most illuminating books that it has ever been the good fortune of the present writer to read. It may be hoped that historians will not be content with pointing out individual inaccuracies or uncertainties in it, or engaging in angry polemics, but rather will be inspired by it to explore new approaches to the comparative study of the origin of human societies.

disputed succession or minority rule add up to much less than an attempt to change the system of government or defend the interests of a class. There were, especially in the eighteenth century, *coups d'état* to replace one weak ruler by another, but there was no attempt to replace autocratic government by limited monarchy (even of the European 'absolutist' variety). Great innovations in Russian history came from the initiative of the Tsar, not of a social *élite*. The nobility was not an independent social or political force, but an instrument of government. In the century between the accession of Catherine II (1762) and the emancipation of the serfs (1861) there was some talk of greater political freedom for the nobility, and there were even some acts of government designed to this end. But little came of it all, and mainly because the nobility themselves were not interested in it. The traditional Russian view of rights and privileges for limited groups has been the antithesis of the European. In Europe, and perhaps especially in England, the granting of privileges to a few has been a step towards freedom for all. The original privileges are extended to greater numbers, new privileges are conferred on a new *élite*, and these in turn extended to greater numbers. This is a continuous process in English history, from King John's barons to the Trades Union Congress. But in Russia, long before Lenin was born, the typical view was to regard all privileges as wicked. Oligarchy was the supreme evil, autocracy the natural order of things. The people should receive benefits from the ruler, are indeed entitled to be angry if they do not. But the benefits come from the goodness of the ruler, not from any action either by the people or by any intermediate *élite*, and to single out one particular group for exclusive benefits is wrong. Here too, in the traditional view if not perhaps always in the practice, there is continuity from Ivan the Terrible to Stalin.

It is a commonplace that liberal democracy has flourished in societies where there has been a strong *bourgeoisie* (not just a capitalist class, but a *bourgeoisie* in the wider sense, with a *bourgeois* ethos, as discussed above), and has proved fatally weak where the *bourgeoisie* is weak or does not exist. It is less generally recognized that there has been a strong *bourgeoisie* only in those societies which had passed through a feudal period. This is clearly true of Europe, and can be said also of the United States in the sense that the ancestors of the first American colonists had lived in feudal Europe.

It seems likely that the great successes of Japan in modernizing herself, unique outside Europe, are in large part due to the moral values and social organization formed in her feudal period, also unique outside Europe, much of which survived in the period of the Tokugawa shogunate. Admittedly these values and organization are very different from those of Europe. But the parallels between Japan and Europe, and the differences between Japan and hydraulic Asian societies, are sufficiently striking at first sight to deserve greater attention from those who are equipped for a comparative study.

It is interesting to note that the two great countries which have communist totalitarian régimes both have a history without a period of feudal order, and that totalitarian ideas make so strong an appeal to the intelligentsia of at least two lands with a long hydraulic past—Egypt and Mesopotamia. One is inclined to suggest that the combination of an absence of feudalism, a tradition of despotic bureaucratic government (whether of direct hydraulic origin or only indirectly affected by hydraulic societies), and the possession of modern means of mass communication provide the most favourable setting for totalitarianism. It should, however, be noted that this formula does not fit the case of Germany, whose Hitler was undoubtedly a totalitarian, but whose history was undoubtedly European, with a long feudal period. In any case, the historical setting is only part of the problem: even in the most favourable setting, totalitarianism will not arise unless it is willed. We have discussed some of the historical factors that favour totalitarianism, we have not yet considered why men should wish to have total power.

THE WILL TO TOTAL POWER

Total power is not compatible with traditional moral or religious inhibitions. The man who seeks it must clear himself of them completely.

Historically the main obstacle in the minds of men to the desire for total power has been the influence of other-worldly religions. If there is another life after death, then the struggle between good and evil cannot be settled in this world: paradise will not be created by man on earth. Equally, great power over the people and riches of this world can little profit a ruler whose soul will survive death and will be judged, like the souls of his subjects, according to his behaviour in this world. In medieval Europe the priesthood represented a Power over which the secular ruler could have no authority, even if he could treat individual priests with scant courtesy. These considerations apply in varying degrees to all the major religions. Christianity has emphasized the equality of human souls in the sight of God. Its essential unit is the individual soul, not society or the nation, though these too it holds in respect. Islam lays greater stress on society, on the community of all Moslems. But the teaching of Islam, as of Buddhism and Hinduism, limits the field of authority of the secular ruler.

But other-worldly religions are not opposed to secular power as such: all have come to terms with it in some way. Jesus said: 'Render unto Caesar the things that are Caesar's.' This has been variously interpreted.

On the whole the Catholic and Protestant Churches have taught that if a ruler does violence to Christian principles, it is the Christian subject's duty to resist. But certainly there have been times when the leaders of the Churches have shown very great tolerance of the sins of rulers from whose generosity they benefited. In the Orthodox Church, especially in Russia, obedience to the secular ruler was more strictly enjoined on the faithful. Among Russian religious dissenters there was a strong belief that the State had got into the hands of Antichrist, but that it was nevertheless the duty of the faithful to allow Antichrist to dispose of their bodies as he wished, provided that they preserved the inner purity of their faith. In the next world the Antichrist-Tsar would be punished and the faithful rewarded. Marx's sneering comment that religion is the opium of the people, because it compensates them for the miseries of this world by promising felicity in the next, meanwhile ensuring that they dutifully serve their exploiters, has had an element of truth in it at many periods in many countries, but perhaps nowhere so continuously as in Imperial Russia.

It would also be wrong to suggest that aspirations towards total power cannot appear in religious societies, or even within a Church itself. The danger may be acute either if the Church is completely subordinated to the will of the monarch, as it came close to being under Peter the Great in Russia, or if the monarch submits himself to the will of the priests in all things, or even takes it upon himself to impose by force the dictates of the priests, as tended to be the case in Spain in the reign of Philip II. The attempts of medieval Popes to subordinate the Holy Roman Emperors to their will were, however, not successful: neither Gregory VII nor Innocent III achieved his aim. Theocratic régimes have been installed for brief periods in various small communities. An example was the Anabaptist régime in Münster in 1534, marked by physical and spiritual terror of a most intense kind, and suppressed with appalling cruelty. Geneva in the time of Calvin was a theocracy which interfered more intimately and ruthlessly in its people's lives than most secular rulers of the time. The history of Islamic and Buddhist sects may offer comparable examples.

Yet though a religious fanaticism which controls secular power can be terrible, and though Churches have betrayed and betray their faith, that faith is a challenge to total tyranny. The assertion of total claims by the State—over public and private life, politics and morals alike—is incompatible with Christianity, and no doubt with the other great religions. The totalitarians are bound to reject God, because if there is a God their power is not total. The Churches are bound to clash with the totalitarian régimes, however sincere be their desire to avoid interference in politics. Totalitarians cannot limit their authority to politics, or perhaps it would be better to say that by 'politics' the totalitarians understand all sides of human life. The history of the relations of the German Nazi, Soviet, Chinese and East European communist régimes with Christianity and Islam proves this.

There is a connexion between the decline of religious belief and the rise of totalitarian ideologies. As we have seen, the intellectuals of the eighteenth century, especially in France, were in revolt against both State and Church, both King and God. Emancipation from religious belief brought the same exhilarating sense of freedom as the overthrow of a secular tyranny. Free from superstition, man, it was believed, could at last build a just society. Paradise could be built on this earth, human nature was perfectible and virtue could triumph over vice. It was necessary only to identify virtue and vice, and to elaborate the secular ideology that would take the place of the rejected religion. To the disciples of the ideology, truth was known and the road to the achievement of the reign of virtue was clear. Those who opposed the onward march were benighted reactionaries or active apostles of vice: they must be exterminated. There was no need any more to worry about the next world: not God but the party leader knew the way to paradise. The Valhalla of Germanic man, purified by the annihilation of the Jewish race, and the classless society, built on the corpses of landowners, capitalists, *kulaks*, enemies of the people and conscious or unconscious agents of the world *bourgeoisie*, were glorious visions to fill the hearts of the true believers.

It does not follow that all who have lost religious faith will fall victims to totalitarian secular ideologies. On the contrary, in most Western countries religion has been replaced by a sceptical tolerance that seems to be compatible with liberal democratic institutions. We have already noted that believers in an other-worldly religion are capable of the most cruel tyranny. But it is difficult to resist the conclusion that the fanaticism which exists to some extent in most men's minds, and the fanatical groups that exist in varying strength in all societies, are more deadly when the belief in a Power higher than man and a life after death decays.

THE TOTALITARIAN PARTY

In all secular non-totalitarian societies, political and religious organizations—State machines and Churches—are separate. In totalitarian societies, political and spiritual power are wielded by the same institution. The totalitarian party monopolizes government and is the guardian of the one true faith.

The two totalitarian parties that have achieved power in the twentieth century—the National Socialist Party in Germany and the Communist

Party in Russia, China and Eastern Europe—professed very different ideologies. Marxism-Leninism, the official faith in all communist-ruled countries, is a complex structure of secular theology, which embraces economics, history, philosophy, ethics and the natural sciences. The Nazi ideology was little more than a number of unsupported assertions about blood and soil and the superior virtues of the Nordic race. The whole was given a certain respectability, in the writings of such prophets as Alfred Rosenberg, by the use of language so obscure as to be unintelligible. Whereas communism had an universal quality, appealing to the poor and oppressed of all nations and invoking the brotherhood of man, the Nazis confined their Germanic paradise on earth to persons of Nordic racial extraction. Communists also insist more severely on active profession of the faith by their subjects. Regular indoctrination is carried on in all social groups and professions. The Nazis insisted on the observance of their doctrines in matters of 'race'—marriages between 'Aryans' and Jews were forbidden, and Jews were deprived even of such legal rights as were available to Germans, and were progressively excluded from economic life. But they did not insist on regular recitation by German subjects of the doctrines of Hitler and Rosenberg.

Both ideologies were, however, much more than a mere political programme. Both were secular religions, planning to transform social relationships and private morals. The future communist society, and the future Nordic earthly Valhalla, were to be peopled by a remoulded man.

The control by the party ideologists of the means of information was much more than the censorship of publications that had long been an instrument of traditional dictatorships. Past knowledge was obliterated by the purging of public libraries or public bonfires of books. Exhortation was unceasing. This is especially a feature of communist régimes, with their public loud-speakers continually braying forth to the people in the streets the official radio programmes; the official agitators in the factories explaining why the workers must work harder for the same pay in order to increase the output needed by the State of which they are the masters; and the wall-newspapers in the workshops pillorying some individual employee guilty of some disciplinary or moral offence. The schools were used by both Nazis and communists as an instrument of power. The violent seizure of the minds of the young was regarded by both as a legitimate means of furthering its own aims: how successful it has been is less certain.

The relationship between the State and the party in Hitler's Third Reich was only vaguely defined by a Statute of 1 December 1933. The party, it stated, was 'the bearer of the Germanic idea of the State and is indissolubly mixed with the State'. Decrees were made by the government, which was unchecked by any elected assemblies. The members of the government were members of the National Socialist Party. The Head of the government was the Chancellor, Adolf Hitler, who was also Leader (*Führer*) of the party, and on the death of President Hindenburg in 1934 replaced him as Head of State with the title of Leader of the German nation. In all three capacities Hitler was an autocrat, his will being in practice limited only, as in the case of other autocrats of the past, by the influences exercised by his closest lieutenants. Beneath the government, the bureaucracy worked much as it had before 1933, though its personnel had been purged, new institutions had been added to it, and many of the decisions it had to carry out were of a quite new kind. At the same time the party had its own bureaucracy, some sections of which overlapped in their functions with regular ministries. A decision by the party might not have the same formal validity as a decree of the government, but in practice it too was law. Conflicting orders and conflicting jurisdictions caused a certain amount of confusion and inefficiency. Hitler could himself take a final decision, but in practice he was not always able to clear up the mess, and indeed one may doubt whether even one greater and wiser than he could have done so.

In the Soviet Union also the relationship between party and State is formally vague. Article 126 of the Constitution states that the Communist Party is 'the directing nucleus' of public organizations and government. The structure of government was formally remoulded in 1917, to a far greater extent than in Nazi Germany. It was based on a hierarchy of soviets, elected at each of the main levels of administration (village, county, province, constituent republic, all-union or national parliament). These soviets were to be essentially deliberative bodies, the business of government being conducted by their executive committees which they themselves elected. At the all-union level the equivalent of the executive committee was, of course, the Council of People's Commissars, renamed in 1946 Council of Ministers. In practice it was inevitable that each of the central government Commissars should have charge of a department of State, and that this should have its subordinates at the lower levels of administration. In fact, though the bureaucracy of Imperial Russia was formally abolished and replaced by soviets, a bureaucratic structure came into being which was in many respects similar to the old, and to some extent at least in the first decade was staffed by the same people. This, of course, shows not that the Bolsheviks 'betrayed' their promises, but simply that they had to take account of the necessities of modern government.

The communist party had its own machinery, from the 'basic'

organizations or cells in places of work upwards through county, provincial and republican committees to the All-Union Central Committee. Nominally the supreme authority of the party is the All-Union Congress, elected by the party membership as a whole at intervals of time which in practice have varied since 1917. This national parliament of the party elects the Central Committee. Since 1919 the Central Committee has elected smaller bodies from its own ranks, especially the Politburo, which was to deal with all current political business between meetings of the Central Committee, and the Secretariat, which was to deal with appointments in the party and State machines, and with various matters of personnel, organization and discipline as well as with the supervision of the propaganda apparatus of the whole régime. In practice the powers of the Congress were soon assumed by the Central Committee, and these in turn by the Politburo and Secretariat. In 1952 the Politburo was renamed Presidium. The extent of its powers has been in some doubt since the end of the Second World War, and since 1957 it has appeared to have lost importance in favour of the Secretariat, now probably the supreme focus of power in the Soviet Union.

From the 1920s there was close integration between party and government. All People's Commissars and probably all influential subordinate bureaucrats were members of the party: by the mid-1930s this was certainly the case. The People's Commissars were normally members of the Central Committee, and the more important ones were members of the Politburo. When the Council of People's Commissars became greatly increased in membership with the establishment of a large number of industrial ministries as the Five Year Plans progressed, there came into being an unofficial inner cabinet consisting of Deputy Prime Ministers: these were usually though not always members of the Politburo. The link between party machine and government was above all in the person of Stalin, who was General Secretary of the party from 1922 and always a member of the Politburo. The formal link was strengthened in 1941 when Stalin took over the Premiership. After Stalin's death the two offices were separated after Malenkov had held them for a few days only. In 1958, however, N. S. Khrushchov decided to combine them again in his own person.

The Communist Party's organization does not at first sight appear so autocratic as that of the National Socialist Party in Germany. It is based on the principle of 'democratic centralism', by which discussion of issues of policy is freely permitted until the party leaders have taken their decision, whereafter all must obey. In 1921, however, at the party's 10th Congress, before and during which there had been criticism of Lenin's policy by groups of party members, who had put forward alternative 'platforms' of their own, a decision was taken to abolish 'fractionalism'. It was henceforth laid down that any individual party member who had criticisms or proposals to make was entitled to lay them before the party as a whole, forwarding them upwards to the Central Committee, but must not combine with even one other member in support of his views. Presentation of views jointly by more than one member was 'fractionalism'. Persons guilty of this sin could be expelled from the party by a joint vote of the Central Committee and the party's Central Commission of Control, the body charged with the maintenance of discipline. These decisions in fact put an end to any possibility of free discussion within the party. All initiative lay with the leaders, who controlled all the means of communication available to the party.

Moreover, the Central Committee and Politburo and Secretariat were autocratically controlled by one man. It is true that in Lenin's lifetime there was some freedom of argument at this highest level, though Lenin was a man of harsh dictatorial temper whose toleration of disagreement had fairly narrow limits. Under Stalin the autocratic principle was pushed much further. There was a period of transition (1923-7) before Stalin had silenced (though not yet exterminated) those of his rivals who had an organized following. Three years later he had humbled the remaining leaders, who, though lacking any organization, still possessed great authority in the party and thus might at some time have become rivals. From about 1930 until his death Stalin was supreme autocrat. The adulation which was lavished on him was in no way inferior to that conferred on Hitler. He resembled Hitler in his fear of plots and his contempt for those closest to him. In 1936 he launched the Great Purge, which lasted more than two years and claimed millions of victims. He stopped it early in 1939 only just in time to prevent a collapse of the State, for the mechanism of arrest, torture, false confession, deportation and execution had acquired a momentum of its own which must have exceeded the original intentions of the autocrat.[58] After the Second World War there was a minor purge in 1949 known as the 'Leningrad affair', when a number of leading party officials who had held office in Leningrad and had been personally connected with the still more eminent A. A. Zhdanov (who died, probably, though not certainly, from natural causes in August 1948) were shot, and many others sent to prison or labour camp. In 1952 the announcement of a plot of Jewish 'poisoner-doctors' was made to the accompaniment of a campaign of vituperation whose style very closely recalled the atmosphere of 1937. Whether a new Great Purge was intended cannot at present be known, as Stalin very conveniently died in March 1953. His death was followed by denunciation of the 'personality cult' (autocracy) in the party and the proclamation of the principles of 'collective leadership'. But less than four months later one of the inner circle had been arrested, and by successive stages in the next four years the possible candidates for power were removed from their posts until only Khrushchov was left supreme, with a cautious Mikoyan as the only other first-class leader from before 1953 who still held a place near the top. Whether the new chief would follow the defeat of his rivals by their extermination it was still too early to say. But the inherent tendency towards autocracy in a totalitarian party had been strikingly reaffirmed.

The Nazi and communist régimes share an utter contempt for law. Both have denounced legal formalism, meaning thereby that they objected to the establishment of any objective standards, according to which problems of law had to be settled, regardless of the subjective wishes of the ruler or of his representatives at a lower level. Both on the other hand insist on the execution of the law when they mean the execution of their own will. Thus both hastened to distort and mutilate the existing system of law and to substitute their own system, equipped with loopholes allowing the administration to act as it wished. In Germany the Secret State Police (*Gestapo*) was assigned its own jurisdiction, within which the regular courts of law had no authority whatever. It could remove persons it disliked to concentration camp without trial. In the Soviet Union the authorities had the right to remove persons regarded as 'socially dangerous'. Article 58 of the Criminal Code listed a number of 'counter-revolutionary crimes' for which the penalty was a very long term of confinement to a forced labour camp or death. These crimes (such as sabotage, propaganda and espionage) were so vaguely worded that they could be interpreted as the authorities wished. Under a decree of 1934 special tribunals were set up to judge such cases secretly. The defendant was not necessarily even present at his own trial. This decree was recently repealed, but as far as is known Article 58 is still in force.

The phrase 'police state' is an old one, used, for example, for the régime of Metternich in Austria after 1815. Arbitrary arrest, secret trials, censorship of both publications and private mail are no modern invention. But in Nazi Germany and the Soviet Union the police exercised greater powers, primarily for the reason that the leaders whom the police served claimed to control private as well as public life, to keep the people permanently mobilized for their aims as well as to forbid them undesirable liberties, and to lay down and enforce moral as well as political standards. The name 'police state' is a misnomer for the Nazi and communist régimes. The police is only an instrument—however cruel or terrifying—of the totalitarians. The essential point about the Nazi and Soviet régimes is not that they used police terror, but that they were totalitarian.

Two features of the police systems of both countries which arise out of their totalitarian nature deserve mention. One is the outlawing of whole categories of persons, membership of which is not a matter of choice. Past régimes had suppressed groups holding proscribed beliefs or allegiances, including women and children. But at least the acceptance of these beliefs or allegiances was a matter of choice by the individual or the head of the family: it was possible to recant from the belief or to abjure the allegiance. To be born of Jewish parents was in Hitler's Third Reich sufficient reason to be deprived of one's possessions, denied the chance to earn a living, sent to a concentration camp and exterminated in a gas chamber. In the Soviet Union in the 1920s children of former landowning or *bourgeois* parents were subjected to various forms of social and economic discrimination, though not to imprisonment, because of their parenthood. In the Great Purge various actions or associations in the past, which had not then been criminal and indeed had been undertaken in the service of the régime, were made sufficient cause to deprive people of liberty or even life. Such were service abroad, visits abroad and association with foreigners in the Soviet Union, even if these foreigners were communists. In the Second World War whole nations (Crimean Tatars, Volga Germans, Chechens, Ingush, Karachays, Balkars, Kalmyks) were deported from their homelands in circumstances which meant the death of a very large proportion of them. In all these cases the cause of the punishment was no conscious action or belief of the victim, but the fact that he or she possessed 'objective characteristics' which brought their fate upon them.

The second special feature is the construction of states within the State in which the totalitarian power was wielded by the police independently of the regular administration or machinery of justice. The members of Hitler's *Schutz-Staffel* (SS) lived in a world of their own, with their own moral rules and their own system of training and indoctrination, designed to produce of them the German *élite*, the master caste of the master race of 200 million pure Nordic Germans that were to rule the earth.[59] They had their own military formations, the *Waffen SS*, a political army with all the best modern equipment the war industry could supply, essentially independent of the regular military command except during operations on the front. They also had their army of slaves, concentration camp inmates and deported forced labourers from the conquered countries. In the 1930s and 1940s most of this was also true of the Soviet security police. Their morality was not supposed to differ from that preached by the Agitation and Propaganda Department of the Central Committee of the communist party to all Soviet citizens. But their great material privileges, social prestige and sense of power produced in many of them a brutal and cynical contempt for all outside their ranks which differed substantially from the spirit of the Soviet bureaucracy as a whole and approached the mentality of the Nazi SS. In other respects the two cases were extremely similar. The Soviet police had its private army—the Interior Troops of the NKVD—with its own modern military equipment, tanks and air force. Its slave empire was more numerous and more extensive than that of the SS. Millions of square miles were occupied by the industrial, mining and forestry establishments worked by forced labourers under the police, who even managed to make financial profits out of the enterprise: the loss of human life from undernourishment and climatic conditions was not regarded as a loss, for the lives of counter-revolutionaries were expendable. Apart from its own territorial empire, the Soviet security police had its apparatus inside the rest of Soviet society. This was institutionalized in the form of the 'special sections' or 'secret sections' which existed in the armed forces and in industrial plants, to spy on the members, set them against each other, blackmail individuals into acting as secret informers and, when necessary, to manufacture and then triumphantly 'unmask' counter-revolutionary plots. After the death of Stalin and the fall of Beria, large portions of the police empire were dismantled. The numbers of forced labourers were greatly reduced (though the camps were not entirely abolished), and the enterprises formerly controlled by the police were transferred to the appropriate industrial ministries. The Ministry of State Security was renamed Committee of State Security and placed under the Council of Ministers. It still remains a powerful weapon, which can quickly be expanded if required.

The control of the party over society outside the machinery of government and police was more effective in the communist than the Nazi case. In Germany the army preserved a certain independence in professional matters, and after the massacre of 30 June 1934, which was to some extent a concession by Hitler to his generals, little attempt was made to propagate the Nazi ideology in the officer corps or to replace traditional conceptions of military honour (which in any case proved, from Hitler's point of view, satisfactorily elastic where the enemies of Germany were concerned) by the ethics of the future Germanic racial *élite*, whose guardian was the SS. It was only in the last months of the régime, after the 1944 attempt on Hitler's life, that a major attempt was made to Nazify the army. In the Soviet Union the institution of political commissars was created in the civil war. These were members of the communist party, charged both with the supervision of the regular officers, whose political orthodoxy was uncertain, and with the indoctrination of all ranks. The division of command between regular officers and party commissars was never completely solved. The tendency, however, was towards greater authority for the regular officers, who themselves belonged more and more to an age-group that had not known a non-indoctrinated society, and thus largely accepted the party's doctrines. By the end of the Second World War the political commissars were less formidable than they had been in the 1920s. They were largely concerned with problems of welfare and education, which have to be handled by some authority in any modern army. The relations between political commissars and officers were often reasonably good. Both had reason to be afraid of the third hierarchy in the armed forces —that of the police 'special sections'. These continued to exist even in the period of greatest political power of the army, when Marshal Zhukov was Minister of Defence (1955-7). Zhukov's fall was followed by an attempt to revive the influence of the commissars in the armed forces.

In Nazi Germany private ownership of industry was not abolished except in the case of Jewish owners. Under Hitler the big business-men, especially in heavy industry, made huge profits. Those who had financed the Nazis in the early 1930s in order to protect themselves from 'Bolshevism' could feel they had made a good investment as far as their money was concerned. But their right to dispose of their enterprises, to decide what to produce and how, was much less sure. They were subordinated to a bureaucratic machine, culminating in the Ministry of Economics and the Four Year Plan Office controlled by Marshal Göring. The Nazi party also had its own economic enterprises, the most important of which was the *Reichswerke Hermann Göring* in the metallurgical industry. These facts can be variously interpreted. The fact that business-men did well materially can be taken to prove that private profit was the motivating power behind the whole Nazi régime, its internal terror and its foreign aggression. An alternative view is that the motivating power was the will to total power of the Nazi leaders, that a greatly expanded German industry was a necessary means to achieve their totalitarian aims, and that the high profits of business-men were the price that they were willing to pay for the result, not the driving force behind the régime. The latter is at least the present writer's view. In the Soviet Union the situation is clearer, for the government took over what was left of Russian industry in the revolution and civil war, and created the immensely larger industry that was built up under the Five Year Plans from 1929 onwards. Soviet industry is directed by managers who are government officials. The purpose of industry is to increase the power of the State and of its totalitarian masters. This does not mean that there are not difficult problems of relations between managers and party: of these more will be said later.

Both régimes established a rigorous control over industrial labour. The Nazis abolished the trade unions and substituted their own Labour Front (*Arbeitsfront*). It would be wrong to say that the Nazis completely ignored the interests of the workers, for Hitler's rearmament policy did abolish unemployment, and there were social security laws in force, some decreed by the Nazis, that protected the workers. It is, however, certain that the main interest of the Nazi leaders in the workers was to ensure that they worked efficiently to produce the large industrial output that was needed for the German war economy. There could be no question of allowing the workers to constitute an independent force, capable of bargaining on equal terms with the employers or the State. In the Soviet Union, as we have seen, trade unions had little power even at the beginning of the régime, lost most of that after the defeat of the Workers' Opposition and banning of 'fractionalism' at the 10th Congress in 1921, and with the introduction of the First Five Year Plan became little more than instruments of the government to channel millions of unskilled peasant labourers into the new industries. The trade unions were not run by the workers, but imposed on them; they defended the interests not of the working class, but of the employer-State. Speed-up devices like Stakhanovism and 'socialist competition' were used to extract more labour for the same real wage. Savage penalties punished even trivial breaches of labour discipline. The main differences between the position of the workers under Hitler and under Stalin seemed to be that the factories belonged in the one case to private business-men and in the other to the State, and that sacrifices were demanded of them in the one case in the name of the *Volk* (of which they were reckoned a part) and in the other in their own name—the Soviet State being 'the workers' State'. In the 1950s, as we have seen, the conditions of the workers improved, but it is still true that the workers are at the mercy of the authorities, that they receive benefits by the bounty of the leaders, not by exacting them through their own organizations.

Nazi control over the peasants consisted of a combination of heavy demands on their crops, in order to feed the military and industrial populations, with turgid rhetoric about the virtues of the Germanic ploughman, to whom the conquered soil would be given as a heritage. In practice, though peasants may have liked the rhetoric, and certainly disliked the requisitions, their habitual life was less radically affected than that of other classes. In the Soviet Union the forced collectivization of agriculture had, as we have seen, the effect of subjecting the peasants more fully to the will of the central government than ever before. The main instrument of the party's policy in the countryside were the Machine Tractor Stations (MTS). These provided the machinery for the cultivation of the collective farm lands, and were paid for their services by a share of the crop, additional to the compulsory deliveries of grain at low fixed prices which the farms were obliged to make to the government. The MTS were also the main centres of party authority in the rural areas. In the early 1950s the party leadership decided to start a campaign for the amalgamation of existing collective farms into larger units. By the end of 1958 the number had been reduced from more than 250,000 to 78,000. The amalgamation may have been economically beneficial, in creating larger units for production. It also had political consequences. Before the campaign started, the majority of collective farms had no party group among their members: leadership by the party had to be ensured from outside and above, through the MTS and the county party committee. But the great majority of the enlarged collective farms now have party groups: when a farm with a group was amalgamated with two others that lacked one, the party group of the first farm expanded its membership in the new amalgamated farm. It thus became possible in 1958 to do away with the MTS as an intermediate stage in the chain of command of the party over the peasantry.

Treatment of the family by the Nazi and Soviet régimes has been less different than is generally supposed. The Nazis proclaimed their respect for the family as the repository of Germanic virtues, while the communists in their first years of power denounced the family as a bulwark of *bourgeois* influence. But in practice the Nazis treated the family with less respect than they had promised, while the Soviet régime by the 1930s began to take a more positive view of it as an institution. The true explanation is simple and obvious. At the time of seizure of power by totalitarians, the family is a centre of values and loyalties older than the régime, different from it and often incompatible with it. Therefore the totalitarians, whether they are in theory for it (as the Nazis) or against it (as at least some communist theorists), must in practice suspect and dislike it, and seek to undermine its loyalties. In this stage they will urge the young to disobey and even to denounce their parents on behalf of the greater loyalty to the *Führer* or to the glorious party of Lenin and Stalin. Soviet encouragement of such behaviour is well known, and is symbolized in the figure of the peasant boy, Pavlik Morozov, who denounced his parents to the police, was murdered by the indignant peasants and had monuments built and dithyrambs written to him all over the Soviet Union. Yet the fact that so much fuss was made of one boy suggests that communist attempts to disrupt the family were not generally very successful. In the Third Reich the same tendency existed, and the authorities would intervene to remove children from the care of parents thought to have an undesirable influence over them, whether communist or even Catholic. But both régimes, once firmly established, preferred to try to use the family as an instrument of their own power. As long as it escaped their influence, it was a potential threat, but in so far as it could be penetrated and indoctrinated, it could be the best guardian of the régime. In the 1930s Soviet legislation and public statements tended to extol the family. The contradiction between the positive and negative aspects of the family from the régime's point of view have never been resolved, nor were they resolved in the Nazi case.

A last aspect of both régimes which deserves brief mention here is their obsession with enemies to be fought. In both cases it was doubtless true that the leaders believed themselves to be constantly threatened by enemies. Hitler believed in a world Jewish plot to destroy Germany, that his country was encircled by merciless enemies, and that this hostile ring had to be broken by force. It was assumed by Lenin and his lieutenants that, as they themselves were resolved to destroy 'capitalism' throughout the world, therefore 'the capitalist Powers' must be permanently considering ways to destroy their régime. But it is equally true that both régimes sought deliberately to maintain hysterical hatred of the foreigner and of 'conscious and unconscious agents' of the enemy in their midst. The existence of encirclement and of enemy agents was the main reason advanced for the necessity of maintaining the police terror which the citizens of both Germany and the Soviet Union would much rather have dispensed with. This hysteria reached unusual heights in the pogroms of German Jews in the autumn of 1938, and still more in the Great Purge in the Soviet Union in 1937 and 1938, but artificial inducement of xenophobia is a constant feature of totalitarian régimes.

The Nazi régime was to some extent modelled on the fascist régime in Italy, but far exceeded it. Mussolini never had a secular religion or ideology comparable to that of Hitler and Rosenberg, and in general his régime was both milder and more inefficient. If one were to judge his régime by the more violent of his speeches, made *pour épater les bourgeois*, one would consider him a prince of totalitarians, but the practice, though extremely unpleasant for freedom-loving Italians, fell far short of the rhetoric. The same can be said, *mutatis mutandis*, of General Franco's régime in Spain, Dr. Salazar's in Portugal and even Perón's in Argentina, though the latter was moving in an increasingly totalitarian direction when the Catholic Church and the army joined to overthrow it in 1955.

The communist régimes of China and of the East European and East Asian satellites are faithful copies of the Soviet model in varying degrees of development. The Chinese régime differs from the others in that it is not directed from outside. In the People's Communes it has original institutions of its own, which make it rather more than less totalitarian in comparison with that of the Soviet Union.*

There are, however, two communist régimes in Eastern Europe which can hardly be described as totalitarian—in Yugoslavia and in Poland. Yugoslavia is a one-party State with a Marxist-Leninist ideology, close control by the party over the State machine, a very powerful security police and State control over industry. But there is much less interference with intellectual life outside the purely political field than in the Soviet Union or its satellites, the peasants are no longer forced into collective farms, and a genuine, though muddled and not very efficient, attempt has been made to democratize industry through elected Workers' Councils. This régime is less than totalitarian. In Poland too there is a one-party State, a Marxist-Leninist ideology, party control over State and industry and a security police. But there is very considerable intellectual freedom outside political matters, probably more than in Yugoslavia. The Catholic Church was given, at least for two years after the crisis of October 1956, much greater freedom than anywhere in Eastern Europe, including Yugoslavia. The peasants were allowed to leave collective farms, and were indeed economically favoured at the expense of the urban population. Workers' Councils were introduced in industry, but their powers were progressively whittled away during 1958, until they had less power even than in Yugoslavia. Though the Polish security police, which had almost ceased to exist in 1956, regained ground in 1958, it exercised self-restraint, arrested few people and treated those arrested with humanity. Though in 1959 the prospects of Gomulka's régime in Poland were uncertain, it was at that time less than totalitarian.

The name 'totalitarianism' is, of course, quite unsuited for such revolutionary one-party dictatorships as those of Turkey and Mexico. In both countries there were trends that might at one time have turned into totalitarianism, but this did not happen. Both countries enjoy considerable freedom of speech and press, and in both there are legally functioning opposition parties. In Turkey the opposition even won an election in 1950. It must be admitted that its behaviour in power has disappointed those who had predicted that Turkey was changing from dictatorship into

* See below, pp. 387–9.

a liberal democracy. Nevertheless, the trend was in that direction. In Mexico the official party, which has changed its name and its leader many times, has not yet lost an election. In contrast to the German National Socialist Party or the 'democratically centralist' communist parties, however, there is open discussion and struggle between different groups within its ranks.

9: Totalitarianism and Liberty

FORCES OF FREEDOM IN TOTALITARIAN SOCIETY

The Nazi régime did not last long enough, and most of its history was too much dominated by the tasks of war, for it to provide any significant indications of the internal strains and stresses that may weaken a totalitarian régime. There was certainly very little effective resistance to the Nazi leaders. The working class was made powerless by the suppression of the left-wing parties and trade unions: underground communist and socialist groups existed, but achieved little. The business-men were content with their position. The legal profession and the army managed to some extent to preserve an esoteric existence of their own, privileged islands in a totalitarian sea, offering no comfort to those struggling in the flood around their shores. The only organizations which, in their own sphere, unhesitatingly resisted some of the claims of totalitarianism were the Roman Catholic and Confessional Protestant Churches. The Churches had so large a following in all classes of the population (and even inside the Nazi party), and were so much a part of German history and national character, that the Nazi bosses did not dare (though some of them would certainly have liked) to treat them simply as enemies to be smashed.

In the first years of the régime there was an impressive economic recovery, and Hitler's foreign policy won an unbroken series of successes, first without having to use force and then by the military victories of 1940 and 1941. A large part of the nation positively admired him, and most of the rest gladly acquiesced in his policies, glowing with patriotic pride and conveniently ignoring the unpleasant features of the régime. The minority who rejected Nazism on principle were bitterly discouraged. Only when the tide of war had definitely turned against Hitler did it begin to appear an urgent task to overthrow him and to save what could be saved for Germany. The unsuccessful attempt of 20 July 1944 was the work of a small number of noble individuals—army officers, conservative civil servants and democratic politicians. It may be said on the whole to have been an enterprise by members of the pre-1933, even of the pre-1914, ruling class, of men inspired not by political programmes so much as by traditional morality and patriotism. Had Hitler won the war, he would have carried his revolution further, would have sought finally to crush the Churches, to abolish the remaining islands of pre-Nazi society, and to impose on the whole nation the values of his nihilistic Germanic SS *élite*. Fortunately, the human race was spared the opportunity of seeing whether the attempt would have provoked resistance, and how fully it could have been achieved.

The Soviet régime has existed for more than forty years. Though far too little is known of the internal stresses and strains it has endured, still some observations are possible. Organized opposition by anti-communist political groups has long been impossible. There may or may not be groups of people who hold, and discuss with each other, such opinions, but if so they can only survive by keeping their secret so well that their existence is known only to their members. They are even less a political force than the *kruzhki* of the early 1860s: whether, like the latter, they will in time give birth to something more deadly, remains to be seen.

Passive resistance by the collectivized peasantry, refusal to do more work than the necessary minimum for a régime that denies them the fruits of their labour, is the only possible explanation for the continued low productivity of Soviet agriculture which so alarmed the party leaders in 1953 and has led to the series of reforms of the last years. The government has notably increased the incentives to the peasantry, but it will probably have to go a good deal further still before it obtains whole-hearted co-operation. It cannot bypass the peasantry by special developments in Kazakhstan and Siberia. These are certainly important, but the Soviet Union cannot obtain so much output from them that it can afford to let the bulk of European Russia go on producing at the low level of recent decades. It needs the output of the collective farm peasants, and it will have to pay a higher price for it yet.

Another vast category of people who have varying degrees of grounds for discontent are the non-Russian nationalities, forming nearly half the population of the Union. Their situation will be discussed later.* It suffices here to note that their opposition, like that of the peasants (many of whom, of course, are non-Russian) is passive. It can act as a serious drag on the freedom of action of the government, but it can never threaten to overthrow it.

Potentially more dangerous, but far more difficult to judge, is the attitude of the working class. As we have seen, its material standard of living has substantially increased in the last decade. The experience of other nations suggests that it is when men and women are free from the fear of hunger that they begin to discover wider needs, and to resent restrictions on their freedom. But the experience of the Soviet working class has been different from that of other working classes. In Europe the workers had political freedom—the right to profess their own opinions and to form their own associations—and used this to obtain economic improvements. In the Soviet Union they had and have no such freedom, but their economic situation has improved, through their increased skill and the régime's

* See below, pp. 296-303.

greater need to treat its manpower more carefully. The interesting question for the future is, whether the Soviet workers will use their economic strength to obtain political freedom. It is unlikely that this will happen suddenly, but it would be foolish to deny that such a trend is possible. Here the example of Eastern Europe is suggestive. In both Poland and Hungary it was the workers who provided the mass support and driving force in the movements of October 1956. It is, of course, true that patriotic revolt against rule by foreigners or their agents played a decisive role, and that this factor is absent for the Russian worker. But the workers of Warsaw who brought Gomulka to power can look back on a long tradition of political struggle in the Polish socialist movement, going back to the days when they fought against the same enemy as did the Russian workers under Lenin or his Menshevik rivals. In Warsaw in 1956 they were fighting not only for national independence, but also for political rights for the working class. The same was true in Budapest. If the Zeran motor works in Warsaw in 1956 played the part of the Putilov works in St. Petersburg in 1905, the Hungarian fighting workers' councils unmistakably recall the St. Petersburg soviets. It would be unwise to assume that these parallels were lost on the Russian workers, or on Russian soldiers from working-class families.

Another extremely interesting question is the relationship between the Soviet State *bourgeoisie* and the party. The State *bourgeoisie* has wealth, prestige and executive power, but it does not hold political power, or have more than an indirect effect on decisions of policy. Most leading members of the State *bourgeoisie* are, of course, members of the communist party, and it is probable that half or more of the party's total membership is recruited from the middle and lower ranks of this non-manual working stratum. But membership of the party may be no more than a formality. The party's strength depends not on its membership but on its permanent officials—the *apparatchiki*. To speak of a conflict of interest between the higher managerial levels of the State *bourgeoisie* and the party shows confused thinking; but a conflict between these people and the party bureaucracy is a more convincing hypothesis. Their functions are essentially different. The industrial managers and government officials are administrators and experts: for them the first priority is professional efficiency. The party bureaucrats are mainly concerned with political indoctrination and propaganda: for them the first priority is ideological orthodoxy. This is, of course, an oversimplification. Party bureaucrats are largely concerned with administration inside the party machine, and the responsible party bosses—secretaries of county and provincial committees—are supposed to be good all-round men, with a knowledge of many different professions and human types. But the distinction between those for whom the decisive criteria are professional and those for whom they are ideological is valid, even if it means that some *apparatchiki* are from this point of view split personalities.

The Soviet managers are impressive people, who have come through a hard school.[60] They have had to achieve their output targets under the plan with inadequate resources. They could only do this by ignoring the regular channels and breaking the law. They have hoarded precious materials and conducted barter deals with other managers; overspent their wages fund in order to have a reserve of labour for emergencies or even for barter; understated their capacity and overstated their achievements; and employed professional lobbyists to intercede for them with central ministries or other important government agencies. If a manager failed to achieve his target despite such violations of the law, he would be punished both for his failure and for his illegal actions; but if he achieved or exceeded his target, he would earn praise, rewards and promotion, and no one would look closely into the means he had used. At the same time managers must know their Marxism-Leninism well enough at least to recite the correct phrases for each occasion, and they must keep on good terms with the communist secular priesthood—the agitators in their factory, the propagandists from the county or city committees and the powerful secretaries themselves. Times have been less difficult since Stalin died, but managers still require great resourcefulness, energy, tact and staying power. One might say that they thrive on a combination of the qualities required for success in a boom town of the American West in the late nineteenth century and in the Spain of Philip II and the Inquisition. They have reason to be proud of themselves, and they are proud. The greatness of their country, its rise to be the second industrial power in the world, are due, they feel, to them. Yet they are at the mercy of the party *apparatchiki*, masters of verbiage whose role in society seems to them essentially parasitic. What they would like is less ideology, a more normal and business-like society, in which they would have more social recognition and a direct political influence. Their situation may be compared roughly with that of the French *bourgeoisie* at the end of the eighteenth century. They too had much of the reality of social power, but they lacked the trappings of social authority and the means of deciding policy. They were denied these by what seemed to them the parasitic popinjays of the nobility.

If the State *bourgeoisie* dislike the *apparatchiki*, the latter have grounds to reciprocate from their own point of view. *Apparatchiki* are not parasites in the sense that they do not work: on the contrary, they are extemely busy men living under great strain. The most earnest of them (and there is no convincing ground to doubt the prevalence among them of earnestness) feel themselves to be the protectors of the people against abuse of power by the managers. Though it would be unthinkably impious to admit that there could, in a 'socialist' society, be a new upper class or State *bourgeoisie*, it is generally admitted that high office has its temptations and that 'remnants of capitalism in the consciousness of people' still exist. This poison is especially strong in high places in the state and industrial bureaucracy. The frequent appeals of Khrushchov and subordinate party officials to revitalize the spirit of the party, to reassert its moral and political leadership in the country, are not just the cries of a ruling clique concerned to preserve its hold. It would be foolish to underrate the moral fervour of the party *apparatchiki*, their conviction that the abuses of Stalin's reign were due to moral decline in the party, and that it is their task to restore the pristine purity. If the managers' remedy for present discontents is to play down ideology and normalize society, theirs is, on the contrary, to have ever more ideology and enthusiasm.

One may indeed argue that the communist party is an instrument for the maintenance of a permanent condition of revolution. The question is often asked why the Soviet Union, unlike revolutionary France, has never 'settled down'. Trotski's labelling of Stalin's rise to power as a 'Soviet Thermidor' is not convincing, for Stalin introduced none of the respectable conservatism that marked Napoleon's succession to the Revolution. On the contrary, Stalin first carried out a new revolution against the peasants and forced Russia at unprecedented speed along the path of industrialization, and then turned the party and army and State machine upside down in the Great Purge. The effect of these measures was to prevent society from stabilizing, to prevent the crystallization of new social classes. Whether this was Stalin's deliberate aim, or whether as a doctrinaire Marxist he denied to himself that once the 'socialist revolution' had been made there could ever be a new class arising to replace the old, we do not and probably shall not know. In his later years Stalin had certainly down-graded the party to some extent: it was only one of several mechanisms of power controlled by him (the others being police, army, government bureaucracy and industrial hierarchy). He continued, however, to the end to keep society in flux, and it is probable though not certain that he was preparing a new major purge when he died. Khrushchov has reasserted the primacy of the party over the other instruments of power. Like Stalin in the 1920s, he has risen to the top by his control of the party machine, by the use of appointments to pack the Central Committee with his own men. But it is reasonable to assume that his renewed emphasis on the party is due not solely to a desire to strengthen the source of his power, but also to a belief, shared by many of his subordinates in the party machine, that it is the party's duty to give new leadership, energy and ideological enthusiasm to the whole régime. Whether this constant pressure for social instability and moral fervour will be defeated by the pressures of the State *bourgeoisie* for normality and for merely professional criteria of efficiency is one of the great questions for the future of Soviet totalitarian society.

Another serious problem is that of the generations. The Great Purge, by sweeping away the old leadership of the party and the experts trained before 1917, offered dazzling opportunities to the generations trained in Soviet schools and colleges in the early 1930s. At the 18th Congress of the communist party in 1939, which met as the Purge was coming to an end, the age composition of the delegates (who may be regarded as the top *élite* of the party machine, 1,570 persons) was revealing. No less than 80% were aged under forty and 49·5% under thirty-five. At the 20th Congress, held in 1956, the proportion of delegates (numbering 1,356) aged under forty had fallen to 23%. Men in their late twenties had a chance of rising to the highest positions in 1939, but their children, now in their twenties, will have many years to wait, while the age-groups between have been increasingly frustrated. The men of 1939 have been sitting in the same places of power for twenty years, and may well count on sitting for another twenty. This disparity in career chances cannot fail to aggravate the conflict between generations which exists to some extent in all societies at all times, and is particularly a Russian tradition, of which every reader of classical Russian literature (Turgenev's *Fathers and Sons* and many other works) is well aware. As in Imperial Russia, frustrated ambition and frustrated ideals reinforce each other, especially among the intellectual *élite* of the younger generation (or younger generation of the intelligentsia, in the classical Russian sense of that term).

The experience of Poland and Hungary in 1956 is here especially revealing. All the East European communist régimes had taken great trouble to open schools and colleges to children of workers and peasants, hoping thereby to create a new intelligentsia of persons wholly devoted to Marxism-Leninism. But in fact it was this younger generation, both in colleges and in secondary schools, that provided the leadership and the fighting vanguard of the Hungarian Revolution. That the lesson was not lost in the Soviet Union is shown by the evidence of astonishingly uninhibited public discussions at Moscow University in the autumn of 1956, at which searching questions were asked about Hungary and attacks were made on the nature of the Soviet régime as such—something unthinkable in Stalin's lifetime.

The Hungarian Revolution showed not only that intellectual youth, even of pure proletarian social origin, is unreliable as a bulwark of totalitarianism, but that a modern totalitarian régime can be overthrown by frontal assault. Within a few days the whole régime had collapsed.* It was defended only by some thousands of security policemen and some Soviet army divisions, and these were not strong enough to save it. Only a new invasion of far greater Soviet armed forces could reimpose the old régime by force. It would be rash to generalize too widely from the Hungarian case. The Hungarian communist party depended more than any other on the personal authority of one man, the autocrat, Mátyás Rákosi: when he was removed in July 1956 the party leaders lost their self-confidence. The fact that the régime had been imposed, and was maintained, by an odious foreign army made it particularly detestable to Hungarians. Neither of these factors apply to the Soviet régime. Its leaders have never lost their self-confidence since 1917, and the régime is autochthonous. Nevertheless, it is likely that the Hungarian Revolution made a deep impression on the Soviet young generation.

Of course, a few hundreds or thousands of university students and graduates who question the essence of the Soviet régime itself are not in themselves a threat to it. But it was from a few hundred young intellectuals that the great revolutionary movements of nineteenth-century Russia grew: of this no one is better aware than N. S. Khrushchov. The history of nineteenth-century Russia also has another interesting parallel. Under the most masterful Tsars (Nicholas I and Alexander III) opposition existed, but was cowed. When the Tsar died, however, people ceased to be afraid. This is especially true of the years after the death of Alexander III in 1894. His death changed not the balance of political power, but the climate of opinion. People were no longer cowed: they began to talk of the coming Revolution. Something of the same sort happened with the death of Stalin. Of course, many years passed, and great events took place in and outside Russia, between 1894 and 1917. But the process could not begin until the climate of opinion changed.

This discussion may be summed up by the comment that in Soviet society there exist both pressures for reform and pressures for revolution, the former coming mainly from the State *bourgeoisie* and the latter mainly from the intellectual youth. At present the former are the stronger of the two. The communist party is far stronger than either. It is thus possible that the party will resist both types of pressure for a long time. But Russia no more than any other country can remain impervious to change. One may perhaps suggest that the more the present leaders of the Soviet Union

* See below, pp. 341-4.

succeed in thwarting the pressures for reform, the better will be the chances of revolutionary pressure against their successors.

FORCES OF TOTALITARIANISM IN FREE SOCIETY

Totalitarianism may appear to liberal democrats a disagreeable form of government, but there is no doubt of its ability to make converts. In underdeveloped societies the revolutionary appeal of communism and of various shades of fascism is primarily to the intelligentsia. This has already been discussed. But it is worth while here to consider some of the factors within the liberal democratic Western societies which may be favourable to totalitarians.

The most obvious, of course, are the totalitarian fifth columns. Fascist parties in Western countries, especially in France, were of considerable help to the foreign policy of Nazi Germany in the 1930s. Since 1945 they have been a negligible factor in Western Europe and North America. They might reappear in the event of a major economic depression. The same may be said for Japan, where fascist revival has hitherto not been marked. The only comparatively advanced industrial society in which a strong fascist trend was visible in 1959 was Argentina, where the defeated Perón still had a mass following, especially in the working class. Fears of fascist revival in France, expressed by the opponents of General de Gaulle, hardly seemed to be supported by the facts.

Communist parties are large mass movements in both France and Italy. The cadres of the French Communist Party can indeed hardly be regarded as Frenchmen at all: rather they are French-speaking *homines sovietici* living in a closed society of their own, geographically located in France, but virtually impervious to the influences of French life. Maurice Thorez well described their situation in his famous phrase: '*La France est mon pays, mais l'Union Soviétique est ma patrie.*' The events in Hungary in 1956 made no impression on the loyalty of these cadres, placed outside class and owning no allegiance except to 'the fatherland of the toilers'. For thirteen years they were able to mobilize a much larger volume of support, the majority of the working class of France and about a quarter of the French electorate. They suffered a serious loss for the first time at the referendum of September 1958, when the prestige of General de Gaulle, as the saviour of the French nation, won 1 million votes, presumably of workers, away from them. Whether this loss will be lasting cannot yet be said. The situation of the communist cadres in Italy is comparable, though the Hungarian Revolution aroused more serious and widespread doubts than in France. The Italian communists too have long been able to mobilize a majority of the working class, but in 1958 they began to lose part of their following to the socialists, led by Pietro Nenni.

In other advanced industrial countries communist strength is much smaller. Iceland and Finland have strong communist parties. In Britain the communist party is small and weak, but communist influence in the trade unions is considerable. This is largely due to the apathy of trade-union members, who cannot be bothered to vote in elections to union offices, and thus enable a small but disciplined caucus of communists to get their men elected. When the communists get control of a union, it is difficult to dislodge them, as the case of the Electrical Trades Union in 1958 clearly showed. In Japan the situation is somewhat similar. The communist party has been small since 1949, but communist influence within the trade unions has been considerable. The campaign of violence conducted by the Teachers' Union in 1958 was a striking example.

Communist parties in advanced industrial countries are able to damage the national economy, and to exploit for their political ends moods of public opinion that are favourable to Soviet policy. But even in France and Italy it may be doubted whether the communist parties seriously threaten the democratic system. They will not win a clear majority in an election; they will find no democratic party of importance willing to form a coalition government with them, for the lesson of the treatment by communists of their coalition partners in Eastern Europe from 1944 to 1948 will not be quickly forgotten; and if they attempted to seize power by force, they would soon find that their opponents' armed strength was far greater than theirs.

But if the positive forces available to them can give only limited encouragement to the totalitarians, and need not dismay the democrats, the prospects are less clear when we consider the negative assets of the totalitarians, the weaknesses of democratic societies. Indeed, a sceptic might observe that the race between totalitarianism and democracy, of which so much is said today, is a race to see which competitor will first collapse from his own ill health. We have already discussed the weaknesses of Soviet society. Discussion of the weaknesses of democratic society is more difficult. It is easier from outside to see through the cant and the slogans of the totalitarians, than from inside to escape the influence of democratic slogans and cant.

One of the great merits of democracies is that they are plural societies, that their citizens may belong to a number of distinct circles and organizations, each claiming different loyalties. This is a source of strength in comparison with totalitarian societies, where all corporate activity must be subordinated to a single State machine, controlled by a single all-powerful party, led by a single all-wise leader. But one must not confuse pluralism with sectionalism. The existence of many different associations and loyalties is a source of strength, provided that there is a basic general loyalty to the nation and the State. Passionate loyalty to a sectional group, combined with contempt for all other groups and for the community as a whole, can be dangerous. This argument, of course, needs to be carefully watched. The pretensions of every interest group appear outrageous to those who are most directly affected, who expect to be praised as defenders of the common weal when they put forward different pretensions on behalf of their own group. But it is hard to escape the conclusion that in Western democratic countries as a whole, during the last thirty years or so, there has been a powerful growth of sectionalism, particularism and indifference to the common national interest. If this is so, it is alarming. The fact that fascist demagogues misused the appeal to the common good, that coins in Nazi Germany were engraved with the words *Gemeinnutz vor Eigennutz*, is irrelevant. A society in which loyalties are excessively diverted towards sectional interests becomes very vulnerable.

Indifference to the national interest is often combined with contempt for parliamentary government. Here too the trend of recent years is alarming. The collapse of the Weimar Republic is, of course, the classical example. The events of France in 1958 showed widespread hostility to the existing form of parliamentary government: whether their effect will be to regenerate and strengthen democracy or to destroy it, it is too early to predict. But in neither Britain nor the United States can it be said that parliamentary politicians enjoy very high prestige. Among the middle classes in Britain there is a widespread feeling that there is no basic difference between the two dominant parties, that both are concerned merely to win votes, to surrender to any powerful interest group (whether business or labour) and to trample on those who cannot defend themselves, especially the government's own most loyal servants, in the armed forces and the Civil Service. The speeches that are made in Parliament often seem to have little relevance to anything that happens, or fails to happen, in real life. Exasperation is greatly increased by the constant inflation, which provokes ritual lamentations, but no effective action on the part of the politicians. The angry and cynical mood that is growing in the middle classes is no doubt only partly justified. It is important that it exists. The existence of such a mood in Weimar Germany was one of the main reasons for the fall of that democratic republic. Weimar Germany was more vulnerable than contemporary Britain, because there was no long-standing devotion to parliamentary institutions, and the prevailing tradition was authoritarian. But if it is reasonable to hope that British society can resist these forces better than did Germany, it is still alarming to note that the forces are there, and are growing. Of any willingness by the politicians to remove the causes of this type of discontent, there is small sign.

Contempt for parliamentary government as it has worked in recent decades is perhaps part of a wider attitude of contempt for all authority and all *élites* as such. This attitude is very widespread in both Britain and the United States, and is fostered by the popular press, cinema and to a large extent the schools. If a whole generation is brought up to believe that persons in authority are normally selfish, unjust or cruel, that the conception of an *élite* is 'anti-democratic', and that authority as such is ridiculous, the society is in danger. Authority is, of course, often abused, whole *élites* are sometimes unworthy and individuals in high positions often betray their trust. This has always been true of all societies. Yet no society can do without authority or *élites*. Authority is not the antithesis of liberty, but its complement. An army officer must enforce regulations which may seem to his men absurd. But he is there to lead and to protect his men. When the men lose confidence in their officers they have no protection left. The terrible contrast between the experience of American and Turkish prisoners of war in Korea is revealing.[61] The Chinese captors succeeded in many cases in undermining the relationship between American officers and men, and the solidarity between the men. Abandoned to themselves, they collapsed in morale and even in physical health. An extremely high proportion died in captivity. But the Turks maintained their discipline and solidarity, and survived.

Civil *élites* are no less necessary than military. If a society does not produce leaders, and does not give rewards to the leaders it has, in government or the economy or science or the liberal professions, it is in danger. The tendency in the Western democracies is for both governments and popular press to deride the notion of *élites*, and to grudge them rewards. In regard to government service the trend is similar in Britain and the United States. In both countries the salaries, and still more the retirement pensions, of both civil servants and officers lag behind the pace of inflation. In terms of public esteem, government servants in Britain probably enjoy a better status than in America. In private enterprise (including independent professional practice) the situation is more favourable in America than in Britain. The elevation of envy into a civic virtue has not progressed so far in the United States as in Britain, where so much apparently high-minded equalitarianism resolves itself into the principle 'If I can't have that, you shan't!'

The discussion of this problem is, of course, beset by pitfalls. The defence of the principle of encouragement to an *élite* should not be, but almost always is, confused with the defence of vested interests. No principle has ever had worse defenders. One need only recall the grotesque figures who occupied the higher levels of the *gerarchia* of which Mussolini so proudly boasted, or Pilsudski's colonels who never tired of claiming that their Poland was based on an *élite*. Clearly everything depends on how the *élite* is formed. This is not a simple problem. Social mobility is not an absolute imperative. A closed *élite* will decay, but the degree to which it can or should be opened is a matter for argument. The contrast between the narrower basis of university education in Britain and Western Europe and the much wider basis in the United States is often emphasized. But university education is not the same thing in Western Europe and the United States, or at Harvard and at every minor college. British university honours degrees may be designed to produce a relatively small intellectual *élite*, but so are the graduate schools of the great eastern universities of the United States. Opportunities of education have widened in Britain in the last twenty years, but they could well be widened still more. Yet absolute equality of opportunity cannot be achieved. It is clear that an able boy from a cultured home, able to converse with his parents and their friends, to read their books and to travel with them, will have a better chance to rise than an equally able boy whose parents have no cultural interests and live in poverty. Complete equality could only be attained by imitating the janissary system of the Turkish sultans, by removing all children from their parents at birth and bringing them up in public institutions. Even then it would be necessary to change each child's nurses and teachers every week or so in order to ensure that no personal affection should lead to favouritism, or the suspicion of favouritism. No theoretically ideal balance between the desirable and the possible can be exactly calculated. It is possible to aim at a degree of mobility which will as nearly as possible ensure that no exceptionally gifted child misses its chance, and that most children of moderate ability get theirs. From this point of view, the United States and Britain are no doubt very imperfect, but they have made much progress. It would be dangerous to be complacent about the remaining defects, but it is also dangerous to become obsessed with the suppression of all existing privileges. In Britain, for example, the means test on public grants for university education now operates in such a way as to discriminate against third or fourth children of parents in the upper ranks of the professional class. Enthusiasm to suppress the so-called 'public schools', at a time when the existing State school network lacks sufficient teachers and classrooms, seems misplaced zeal.

Social mobility also has other dangers. It has often been pointed out that the Nazi movement was largely based on *déclassés* who feared that they were being forced from the *bourgeoisie* down into the proletariat. But *déclassés* upwards can be dangerous as well as *déclassés* downwards. The British Welfare State has produced the interesting phenomenon (whose importance has been exaggerated) of the 'angry young men', whom the State raised out of their social class and who could not find acceptance in the class into which they were raised. The slights, real or imagined, which they experienced, created in them a more violent hatred of the 'establishment' than their parents' generation, which had endured poverty and fear in the slump of the 1930s, had ever expressed. More serious was the phenomenon of McCarthyism in the United States, which, as American sociologists have convincingly shown, was largely based on the hatred of the newly risen social groups, created by wartime prosperity and post-war inflation, and coming largely from the South and Middle West, for the older *élites* of the East, exemplified by civil servants and diplomats in Washington and intellectuals in New York or New England.[62]

If sectionalism tends to dissolve society, and hatred of *élites* to deprive it of leadership, the pressures of mass life, mass means of communication and mechanization tend to deprive the individual of the means or desire to think for himself. Much has been written of the 'fear of freedom', of the desire to unload personal responsibility on to some all-wise authority. In the totalitarian society this is the Party or the *Führer*. In free societies the role is often assumed by a less sinister, yet potentially dangerous figure, the Expert. Though accepting the homage of the uninitiated, the Expert usually takes care to admit responsibility only within his own rigidly circumscribed field, leaving wider responsibility either to higher authority or to no one at all.

Modern civilization was made possible by specialization. In industrial organization, and in the natural sciences, still further subdivision of special functions may do more good than harm. But in the social sciences and in the art of government it can be overdone. The tendency of experts to build little empires, to entrench themselves in their own ruts, and to raise barricades against the neighbouring ruts, is indeed comic, but its consequences may be tragic. The enthusiasm with which academic experts draw arbitrary lines between history and economics and sociology, or between subdivisions of each of these branches of learning, and the rage with which they turn on those who trespass in the borderlands, reflect a morbid condition of Western intellectual life. If the atomization of society is a characteristic of totalitarianism, the atomization of knowledge contributes to it.

Much has also been written of the dehumanizing effects of labour in highly mechanized factories, of the endlessly repeated identical motions of the worker, so different from the work of craftsmen in pre-industrial cities or of peasants in the fields. Much has also been written of the effect of mass-circulation newspapers, films, television and horror comics. These things have now been denounced for decades. More recent is the brilliant analysis of the values of the 'other-directed man' who has replaced the 'inner-directed man', and whose criterion is not his own judgement (however much influenced by its environment), but simply what is popular with the neighbours.[63]

Lamentation on these themes is often overdone. Denunciation by intellectuals of 'mass culture' sometimes has a ludicrous tone of outraged innocence, which recalls the tone in which authors of academic textbooks on American government in the 1920s wrote of the misdeeds of party bosses. The remedy is the same: the high-minded citizens should enter the field—politics or mass media—and raise the level. In fact they have done and are doing it. The assumption that 'the masses' will always fall for trash, and that good literature or music can never find a wide public, has been many times proved wrong. On the other hand, in the pre-industrial age which some intellectuals extol in contrast to the present, there was no less vulgarity or bad taste or sadism than now.[64]

Nevertheless, the conception of the 'other-directed man' is alarming, and mass communications increase the pressures to conformity and towards narrow-minded specialization which are to some extent inherent in any society. Sectionalism, denigration of *élites*, departmentalization of knowledge, refusal to think of wider problems, rejection of responsibility, elevation of popularity with the neighbours to the highest social virtue—all these are unhealthy trends. They do not themselves create totalitarianism, but they weaken the resistance of society to it. There will not be totalitarianism in the free advanced industrial societies until totalitarian leaders and movements appear in force. But if some external crisis should produce these, then a society that has been accustomed to comfort and conformity, which has hated all excellence and asked its leaders to sell policies to it as a manufacturer sells soap, could quickly fall into their power.

10: Totalitarianism and Foreign Policy

The totalitarians' claim for total power is not limited by state frontiers. Hitler aimed to unite under his rule first all Germans and then all Europe. If he had achieved both objects it can hardly be expected that he would have stopped there. The Japanese extremists hoped to bring first all East Asia and then the whole world under the 'Imperial Way' as they interpreted it. To the Soviet communists the aim has always been world revolution. This, they believe, is not a matter of their preferences but of the scientifically predictable ineluctable process of history. All mankind is bound to advance through socialism to communism, passing in most but not all cases through capitalism. The process is inevitable, but its speed depends in part on human will and action. It is the task of communists to accelerate it, and as far as possible to reduce the wastage and suffering that it need involve. Men equipped with a firm grasp of Marxist-Leninist science can guide history. If they make the right analysis, and apply their Marxist-Leninist knowledge rightly to each specific situation, they can discover 'the correct' policy.

The totalitarians not only have claims for power which must extend to the bounds of the earth (and perhaps, in a future age of inter-planetary travel, still further), but they have a total conception of the nature of foreign policy which is unfamiliar to the Western public and even to many Western statesmen.

There are two traditional means of foreign policy—diplomacy and war. War may be a continuation of policy by other means, but until modern times it was easy to distinguish it from diplomacy. In war people are killed, in diplomacy they are not. Diplomacy is by definition secret: exchanges of views between governments that are not secret, are not diplomacy. Relations between states have always been marked from time to time by conflicts of interests, and these have from time to time led to war. Some wars have finally settled conflicts to the advantage of one party. Some conflicts have remained unsolved after a series of wars, and some of these have with the passage of time lost their sharpness and their importance. Relations between some pairs or groups of states have been marked by conflicts so frequently recurring that the parties to the conflicts regarded themselves as traditional enemies. But such lasting enmity has been the result of unresolved conflict rather than of a deep-seated hatred. For example, France and England were traditional enemies for centuries, but this was because England was determined to prevent France from controlling the Low Countries, or because France challenged

British power in North America and India, not because Englishmen and Frenchmen hated one another and wished to destroy one another.

At the present time these conditions are only partly valid. The distinction between peace and war has become blurred. Civil wars and guerrilla wars and various forms of subversion are used by governments, both directly against each other and in the territories of other governments which are of strategic or economic importance to either party. It is still true that diplomacy is secret, or is not diplomacy. But side by side with diplomacy has arisen another form of contact between hostile governments which can perhaps best be called propaganda. This covers a wider field than press and broadcast campaigns. One of its more important forms is propaganda-by-conference. It is often pointed out that 'summit meetings' or conferences of foreign ministers are an unsatisfactory form of diplomatic negotiation. But this argument misses the point. Such conferences are not diplomacy or negotiation at all. They are propaganda tournaments in which the protagonists are aiming not at those with whom they talk, but at their rivals' public opinion. This is well understood by the totalitarians, but only partly by democratic politicians, and not at all by the democratic public. Most meetings of the United Nations also fall into this category. That Western professional diplomats should dislike these activities is understandable, but it is a mistake to misunderstand their nature or underrate their importance.

The nature of conflicts between States has also largely changed. There are, of course, still conflicts of the traditional type, about territories and the rights of national or religious minorities and access to economic resources and strategic positions on land and sea. But the basic conflict between the totalitarians and their opponents is of a different order. Totalitarians aim to destroy all organized power that is not controlled by them, and to impose their power and their principles on all who do not yet own them. They are in a state of permanent warfare with the rest of the world. This was true of Hitler's Germany and Tojo's Japan, and it is true of the Soviet Union and the Chinese People's Republic. Some brief observations must here be made on the foreign policy of the most powerful existing totalitarian State, the Soviet Union.

The aim of Soviet foreign policy ever since 1917 has been world socialist revolution. This has remained its aim, though the motives for revolution, the urgency with which revolution was pursued and the meaning of the words 'socialist revolution' have been modified in the course of time.

In the first years, approximately corresponding to those of Lenin's leadership, world revolution was pursued as an end in itself. Communism was a world-wide movement, and world-wide revolution was its *raison d'être*, something that could not be questioned.

In the second period, corresponding approximately to the establishment of Stalin in supreme power, world revolution did not cease to be an end in itself, but greater stress was laid on its value as a means of strengthening the Soviet Union. Stalin argued, in his famous theory of 'socialism in one country', that the Soviet Union possessed the necessary economic resources to build socialism alone (which the 'Left Opposition' denied), provided only that it was left in peace by foreign Powers. But as long as 'capitalist encirclement' existed, the Soviet Union would be insecure. Only when socialism had triumphed in the main industrial countries of the world would the Soviet Union be safe, and the 'complete victory' of socialism there be assured. Thus world revolution was still of great importance to the Soviet State, and remained the aim of Soviet foreign policy. In the 1920s, however, there was not much that the Soviet Union could do about it. The hopes of communist victory in Germany in 1923 and in China in 1927 were disappointed, and the Soviet government, isolated and weak, could do no more than defend its State interests in a traditional manner.

The third stage begins with the completion of the forcible collectivization of agriculture and the First Five Year Plan. These successes, in Stalin's view, established socialism in the Soviet Union. In November 1917 a party of revolutionary Marxists had seized political power, but the task of creating a socialist society still lay before them. In 1936 the new Constitution, prepared under Stalin's personal supervision, declared the Soviet Union to be 'a socialist state of workers and peasants'. It followed from this that socialism was what existed in the Soviet Union, and that nothing else was; that socialists were persons struggling, under Soviet direction, to create in their countries a régime copied from the Soviet model, and that no one else was; that socialist revolutions were revolutions carried out under the leadership of such persons; and that the world-wide victory of socialism must mean the establishment throughout the world of régimes of the Soviet type. Thus the only true socialists were persons who accepted a direct or indirect communist leadership (whether as members of communist parties, non-party followers of communist parties or members of parties allied with communist parties). Social democrats were not and are not socialists. Their leaders were and are traitors to the working class, paid agents of monopoly capitalists, hired to deceive the workers. Individual members of social democratic parties may, however, be sincerely deluded workers, who wish to struggle for socialism, and do not understand that their treacherous leaders are leading them not towards socialism, but away from it.

The change in the meaning of socialist revolution, from a workers' revolution carried out by the working class of a country in accordance with that country's needs and conditions, to the imposition of a régime taken from a Soviet blueprint, was a gradual and perhaps not even a fully conscious process. The case of Outer Mongolia was little known in the outside world, and the annexation of the three Baltic states in 1940 appeared to be 'just' a case of old-fashioned territorial aggression. The significance of the new Soviet view of socialist revolution fully revealed itself only in the years 1944-8, when Soviet military power imposed Soviet-type régimes on five East European countries, one-third of Germany and half of Korea. It would be an exaggeration to say that, in the Soviet view, such régimes must always be imposed directly by Soviet military power, for the Soviet government at first welcomed the establishment of a Soviet-type régime in Yugoslavia by the Yugoslavs' own efforts in 1944-5 and in China in 1949. But the subsequent breach with Yugoslavia, the evolution of the Yugoslav régime away from the Soviet model, and the uncertainties about Chinese internal developments in the 1950s make it clear that direct Soviet supervision is what is preferred in Moscow.

Pursuing world socialist revolution, as interpreted according to its doctrine, the Soviet government is in a permanent state of war with all countries not subordinated or (as in the case of China) closely allied to it. Soviet spokesmen and publications usually describe all parts of this non-controlled world as 'capitalist', though the more sophisticated theorists will admit that the extent to which a capitalist economy prevails in different countries does vary considerably. 'Capitalist' is in fact normally a geographical or pejorative adjective, not an economic category.

But if the Soviet Union is thus in a permanent state of war, this does not mean that it has any preference for the use of armed force. Here Soviet totalitarianism differs significantly from fascist or national-socialist. Hitler and Mussolini were romantics who loved war for war's sake. To the Soviet leaders the choice of means is a matter of expediency. Secret diplomacy, propaganda by mass media, propaganda by international conference, espionage, subversion, economic aid, the granting or withholding of foreign trade, guerrilla war, the threat of war, war with conventional forces and war with atomic weapons, are all potential instruments of policy, to be used in accordance with the needs of the moment, the chances and the cost of success.

The Soviet leaders are neither for nor against 'shooting war' in principle. They have, it is true, a theory about shooting war, the theory of just and unjust wars. A just war is a war undertaken in defence of the working class against capitalist oppression, or in defence of a national-liberation movement against colonialism and imperialism. It is important to understand what this means. The interests of the working class throughout the world are expressed solely by communist parties. The struggle of the workers of Budapest in October 1956 was not a struggle for the interests of the working class: it was a counter-revolutionary rebellion organized by fascists. The struggle of Ukrainian partisans against the Soviet army in 1945-7, of Georgian nationalist demonstrators against the Soviet police in 1956, or of Tibetan guerrilla forces against the Chinese communist invaders in 1959 were not national-liberation movements against imperialism, but imperialist adventures directed against the power of the proletariat. A just war, in short, is any war undertaken by the Soviet government, a government allied to it, a communist party or a nationalist movement which has the Soviet blessing. All other wars are unjust wars.

The phrase 'cold war' came into use in the West to describe the condition intermediate between peace and war in the traditional senses, which has marked relations between the Soviet Union and the West since 1947. It is a useful phrase, but it can be misleading if it is regarded as a policy of the West, which the West can adopt or relinquish at will. Cold war is not a Western policy, but a state of affairs, and results from the basic Soviet attitude. The Soviet Union is in a permanent state of war, which may or may not become violent, with the West. To 'stop the cold war' is possible only in one of two ways. One is that the Soviet leaders should finally abjure their aims of world socialist revolution—that is, of world-wide Soviet imperial domination. This they have never done, and it is unlikely that the present generation of leaders will, though it is possible to be more optimistic about those men and women who are now in their twenties. The other possibility is that the Western governments should give up all resistance to Soviet policies. This is what the Soviet leaders are asking for when they ask that 'the West should stop the cold war'.

It is as certain as anything can be in the fundamentally uncertain field of international politics, that the Soviet government will persist in its basic aims, and will use whatever means are best suited to attain them. As long as the West is militarily strong, and Western policy is reasonably clear and resolute, they are unlikely to resort to a major war, though this danger cannot be absolutely excluded. But the fact that they do not resort to a major shooting war does not in any way alter the fact that they remain in a state of permanent warfare with the West. There is not necessarily any harm in using their phrase, 'peaceful coexistence', provided that it is understood that peaceful coexistence and cold war are exactly the same thing. To refrain from direct military action, and to make maximum use of friction within the Western camp (which they call 'the internal contradictions of capitalism'), is no new policy for the Soviet government. It is precisely what the Soviet government tried to do from 1921 to 1941. Stalin himself recommended a return to this policy in his last published work, *Economic Problems of Socialism*. It was adopted not as a result of his death, but on his advice. It is only when it is believed in the West that 'peaceful coexistence' is something new, denotes a change of heart in the Soviet leaders and a desire for true friendship with non-controlled governments and nations, that harm is done. Provided that this error is avoided, there is no reason why the West should not successfully endure the condition of permanent warfare without shooting war, and survive until, whether through evolution or revolution, men come to power in the Soviet Union who genuinely renounce totalitarian imperialism.

Part Four
Imperialism

11: Nationalism and Imperialism

Loyalty to a common physical homeland and its ruler, and a sense of solidarity between those who share a religious faith or a language, are as old as recorded human history. Nationalism is more recent. It derives from the word *nation*, which was made familiar throughout the world by the French Revolution. In place of hereditary monarchs, radical doctrine attributed sovereignty to the nation. It followed from this that nations had a right to independence, and that fractions of a nation, separated by frontiers based merely on the whims of dynasties or the facts of geography, had a right to unite with each other. Nationalism in fact is inescapably derived from the democratic principle, and a world order based on the unit of the nation-state is the logical application of democratic doctrine to international relations.

During most of the nineteenth century in Europe the struggle for national independence and national unity went together with the struggle for liberty. Examples are Germany and Hungary up to 1848, and Italy and the small Balkan states until a good deal later. But towards the end of the century nationalism in Europe acquired a new illiberal flavour. The emphasis was now not on the struggle for freedom against an alien ruler, but on imposing the nation's will against its neighbours and rivals. Both sides invoked national rights in the struggle for Alsace-Lorraine. Italian patriots, in claiming the completion of unity by incorporating Trento and Trieste in Italy, paid little attention to the rights of Tyrolese or Slovenes who lived in these provinces. The *nationalisme intégral* of Charles Maurras had only contempt for the rights of minorities.

In the older nations of Western Europe this new aggressive nationalism took the form of imperialism, adding new territories to old colonial empires or creating new empires, especially in Africa. But aggressive nationalism was by no means confined to old or large nations. In Central and Eastern Europe the national revivals of Slavs, Hungarians, Roumanians and Greeks soon passed through the liberal into the aggressive stage. This was partly because there were large areas, such as Transylvania, Macedonia, Voivodina and the Polish-Russian borderlands, where populations were so mixed that no clear 'ethnical' frontier could be drawn. In such areas each nation was determined to seize the whole, reducing the other national groups to an inferior status. Each supported its claim, not only with distorted statistics of population, but with economic, strategical and historical arguments.[65]

The creation of small states, by a series of agreements between the Great

Powers from the 1820s onwards, and especially in the Paris peace treaties of 1919-20, did not and could not solve the problems. The conflict between the states that had gained territories—Czechoslovakia, Yugoslavia and Roumania—and those which had lost—Hungary and Bulgaria—was exploited first by Mussolini and then by Hitler to keep Central Europe in a state of perpetual unrest and fear. The large Polish state created in 1918-21 could only survive as long as Germany and Russia were weak, or at least opposed to each other. When Hitler and Stalin made a robber's bargain in August 1939, Poland was doomed and Europe plunged into war. In 1945 the problems were still not solved. In the Danubian countries the frontiers of 1920 were restored with but a few exceptions, while Poland was deprived of her eastern provinces, but compensated in the West at the expense of Germany. But as all these countries except Greece fell under communist rule, the national conflicts were frozen. A single Soviet totalitarian rule prevails throughout the region. Nationalist fanaticism and small-power imperialisms were thus the ruin of all the small nations alike, and doomed them to conquest in turn by the Third Reich and the Soviet Union. Whether, when the Soviet grip at last loosens, the old conflicts will break out once more, it is impossible to predict.

The same trends can be clearly discerned already in the newer nationalisms of Asia and Africa. Some states, as China, Persia or Ethiopia, have a certain geographical unity and ancient historical and cultural traditions. Only Japan and Turkey have in addition to these an almost complete ethnical and linguistic unity. Many are creations only of their European conquerors. It is perhaps sophistical to place India in this category, for there were certainly great and powerful Indian kingdoms that ruled most of the sub-continent before Europeans arrived. There is a much stronger case for saying that Indonesia was created by the Dutch. Such great or populous territories as French West Africa, Nigeria, Belgian Congo and the Union of South Africa are European creations.

The mixture of languages that marks southern Asia and trans-Saharan Africa has been aggravated but not created by European-made frontiers. Language groups are not necessarily endowed with national consciousness, though European experience suggests that they are likely to acquire it. The problem becomes more serious where differences of language coincide with differences of religion. Examples are the Burmese and Karens in Burma, and the northern and southern peoples in Nigeria. That religion can be the basis for the creation of a new state is shown by the case of Pakistan: whether a Pakistani nation has been created, is still an open question. Conflicts over border regions of mixed allegiance occur between independent Asian states no less than between European. The desire of a newly independent state to impose its will on another territory, of utterly different ethnic population, is illustrated by the claim of Indonesia to West New Guinea. On the other hand, the predicament of the Ewe people, divided quite arbitrarily between British and French Togoland and north-eastern Ghana, is the result of forces quite beyond their control.

European and Asian attitudes to nationalism are today very different. No liberal European can in principle deny the right of a nation to independence and unity. But European experience has shown how easily nationalism can turn to imperialism. Nationalism indeed seems to thoughtful Europeans with a sense of human history a disagreeable adolescent phase, to be passed through as quickly as possible. But Asians and Africans quote the earlier history and doctrines of the Europeans against them. They are resolved to savour the delights of nationalism. They argue that the Europeans' present disapproval of nationalism is inspired rather by selfish interests than by genuine conviction. They passionately deny that they themselves are, or could ever conceivably become, imperialists.

The nature of imperialism is the subject of a vast literature of description, analysis and dogma. We are not here concerned to propound a definition that is more 'correct' or 'scientific' than preceding definitions. Our subject is the fact of domination of nation over nation, which may take many forms, but is always a source of conflict, and in the age of modern communications can more easily than in the past provoke an international crisis.

The essence of imperialism is domination of one nation over one or several others, and the essence of a colony is that it is established by persons coming from another land and imposing their will on its original inhabitants. Colonization from Europe has in most cases been by sea, but expansion overseas is not inherently more imperialistic than expansion overland. The Russian Empire in Siberia (the Kazakh steppes and Turkestan) was won by the same methods as the British Empire in India or Africa, or the European conquest of the Red Indians in North America. The great empires of the Chinese and Indian past were built in the same way. The view that expansion on land is not imperialism is not any the less ridiculous because it is today widely held in Asia.

The notion of the fight of colonial peoples for independence is also surrounded with confusion. Two things should be clearly distinguished: the struggle of an autochthonous people against foreign domination, and the struggle of foreign colonists to uphold at the same time their independence from a metropolitan government and their domination over an autochthonous people. The twentieth-century struggles of Asian and African peoples belong to the first category, the struggle of the North and

South American colonists against Britain and Spain to the second. The Algerian *colons* who revolt against Paris, and the Kenya or Rhodesia settlers who clamour for emancipation from the British Colonial Office, are much closer to the predicament of eighteenth-century Americans than are the nationalists of Ghana, Indonesia or the Arab lands. This is not, of course, to say that M. de Sérigny or Sir Roy Welensky should be regarded as the spiritual or intellectual heirs of Thomas Jefferson or Simon Bolivar.

Dominant nations have used their power for economic ends. There have been many examples of economic exploitation of the vanquished, in the Roman and Chinese Empires, in European overseas colonies from the sixteenth to the eighteenth centuries, and in the modern empires of the age of industrial capitalism and totalitarianism. European capitalists have at times made outrageously high profits in Asia and Africa. Economic exploitation has also not necessarily required direct rule over the lands where the profits have been made: the Chinese and Ottoman Empires were politically independent but economically subject. It does not, however, follow from this that the search for profit has always been the main cause for the creation of empires, even in the late nineteenth century; or that foreign capital is always rapacious and exploiting; or that on balance the subject nations have economically lost more than they have gained from investments by foreigners in their lands. The elaborate theories about economic imperialism, propounded by Hobson, Hilferding and Rosa Luxemburg, and popularized by Lenin, threw much light on the subject. But they do not fit all the facts and situations of imperialism, and if they are treated as a sacred dogma they mislead more than they inform. In particular, there could be no conclusion more false than that there can be no imperialism, no subjection or exploitation of one nation by another, where there is no private ownership of the means of production.

Modern colonial empires have arisen through a number of different processes. The great explorers of the sixteenth and seventeenth centuries sought adventure, knowledge, glory for their monarchs, riches for themselves and their friends and the propagation of the true faith among the heathen. In each individual case the ingredients were differently mixed. With the growth of capitalism and the expansion of world commerce, traders penetrated ever more remote regions, needed orderly government to pursue their business, and invoked the protection of their home governments. Warships sailed up Chinese rivers to assert the claims of British merchants on reluctant mandarins. Armies moved to avenge the wrongs of Tatar merchants from Kazan, subjects of the Tsar, against the Emir of Bokhara.

Another cause of empire-building was the rivalry between European

Powers, concerned to seize strategic points that guarded their own supply routes or threatened those of an enemy. This was an important consideration in the creation of the earlier British and French empires in North America and India, in the contest for Manchuria and Korea between Russia and Japan in the 1890s and in the expansion of France and Britain in Western and Central Africa around the turn of the nineteenth and twentieth centuries. It is hardly possible to disentangle the strategic and economic factors. The arguments used at the time cannot be taken at their face value. In the nineteenth century, when military enterprise was contrary to the liberal and *bourgeois* spirit of the age, even the militarists had to use arguments of economic gain to make their projects respectable. In the twentieth, when capitalist greed is the popular bogy, it is more respectable to speak of national interests and strategic needs.

In the last decades of the nineteenth century imperialism became a matter of public enthusiasm. The traditional British concern to suppress the slave trade provided a motive, without doubt sincere in its champions, for penetrating East Africa to end Arab slave raids. In earlier centuries the British had been less concerned to spread Christianity than the Catholic nations, especially the Spaniards. But in the late nineteenth century British Protestant missionaries made great efforts in Africa. Imperialism also developed a secular ideology, of which Rudyard Kipling and Theodore Roosevelt were spokesmen. President McKinley combined the secular and religious notes: 'There was nothing left for us to do but take them all, and to educate the Filipinos and uplift and Christianize them.'[66] It is commonly believed that democratic societies are more pacific than oligarchic or autocratic, and that when public opinion becomes a factor in foreign policy its influence is against aggression. This is not borne out by the facts. Democracies can be at least as belligerent as other forms of government. In Italy, a newcomer to the imperialist race, the conquest of Tripoli in 1911 was represented as an enterprise to benefit the poor peasants of the South, who would receive new land. Italy was a proletarian nation, entitled to its share of colonial spoils. A famous speech in defence of the war, by the poet Pascoli, was entitled *La grande proletaria si è mossa*.[67] Mussolini later used the argument of a 'proletarian Italy' to defend his conquests. Hitler carried the argument further with his aim of turning Poland and Russia into vast colonies to be peopled by German farmers, who would be served by the slave labour of the half of the original population that was not exterminated. This plan too appeared to enjoy not inconsiderable support from his compatriots.

A special form of domination, present in some but not all colonial empires, is the imposition of a doctrine of racial superiority. Economic, cultural and psychological factors are here intricately mixed. The contrast between physical types, and the disparity between cultural standards, are more obvious between Europeans and Africans than between Europeans and Asians or between Asians and Africans. The physical contrast explains the sexual fears that play so large a part in the discrimination against negroes, institutionalized in the practices known as the 'colour bar', in areas where white men and negroes live side by side in large numbers, especially in South Africa, Southern Rhodesia, Kenya and the American South. It should be noted that racial discrimination against negroes has come more naturally to Europeans of Protestant religion and Germanic language (Dutch and Anglo-Saxons) than to Catholic and Latin nations (French and Portuguese). In Asia the colour bar has never been so severe as in Africa, but it has been most practised by the British: the Dutch in Indonesia did not show the same horror at interracial marriage as the Dutch in South Africa. Asians in Africa have also shown a considerable reluctance to mix socially with Africans. Of all forms of domination the colour bar has perhaps created the most bitter resentment. An important reason for this is that it has most affected precisely that social group which has succeeded in overcoming the cultural barrier, and thus claims to lead its people—the intelligentsia.

Imperialism then has various origins and aspects, and is supported by diverse forces. The search for a comprehensive and 'scientific' definition that would do justice to them all seems hopeless: in any case it is one in which the present author has neither the ability nor the inclination to engage. Instead, we will examine in turn different types of imperialism, in the form of domination by one nation or race over others, that exist today.

The next chapter is concerned with European policies in Africa, the main area in which European colonial rule still exists. In the case of British and French policies some general introductory remarks are needed, which apply also to some extent to areas other than Africa. (The relations of Britain and France with the Arab and Asian peoples, including those which have not yet attained independence, are discussed in the last part of this book.) The third chapter of the third part is concerned with other imperialisms—in the Soviet Union, independent Asia and the Americas. In the fourth chapter we discuss racialism in the Union of South Africa and the United States, and the development of the Afro-Asian movement.

12: European Colonial Policies in Africa

BRITISH IMPERIAL POLICY

British political thinking about empire was decisively influenced by the loss of the American colonies in the eighteenth century. In the following period there was little enthusiasm for colonies in Whitehall. It was felt that they cost money and brought little advantage, that they were bound to become independent in the course of time, and that when the demand for independence became strong it should be granted.

But it was not and is not always easy to put these principles into practice. It was comparatively simple to deal with populations of British origin and language. Australia and New Zealand obtained their independence without much difficulty. British colonists in New Zealand had first to fight a bitter struggle against the autochthonous Maoris, but this ended comparatively happily, with the Maoris definitely forming part of the New Zealand nation. The much more primitive aborigines of Australia had a sadder fate, resembling that of the North American Indians. But both Australia and New Zealand are English-speaking countries, and agreement between them and Britain was not hard to reach.

The task was more complicated when dealing with a population of European origin which was only partly of British stock. This was the situation in Canada, where two-fifths are French, and in South Africa, where two-thirds of the Europeans are descendants of Dutch settlers and speak Afrikaans, a language derived from Dutch. The creation of the Dominion of Canada, and its growth to its present complete independence, were achieved in an atmosphere of friendship between Britain and Canada, despite the profound differences of social and political outlook that separate at least a large part of the French Canadians from their English-speaking fellow-citizens. In South Africa the process has been much less happy. The Union was created only after British military force had crushed the two Afrikaner republics in the Boer War, which was itself the culmination of a conflict between British and Boers that went back over several generations. The South Africa Act of 1909 was intended to heal the wounds, and has been acclaimed as a triumph of Liberal statesmanship. As long as the South African scene was dominated by Botha and Smuts, both convinced that friendship between English and Afrikaner and between South Africa and Britain was necessary and possible, the Liberal policy seemed to have justified itself. But forty years after the Act was passed, it was clear that the bitterness had not passed. Moreover, in contrast to Canada, the majority of the population of South Africa was not of European stock.

In the last decades the relations between Europeans and Africans have entered a phase of acute conflict and growing fear and hatred.

The tasks of British policy were and are still more difficult when dealing with non-European nations, whose history, religion and culture are utterly different from those of Europe. Here two especially difficult sets of problems arise.

The first is what criterion should be used to judge the political maturity of a nation and the effectiveness of its demand for independence. The claim is, of course, first advanced by the intelligentsia, that most active social group of underdeveloped societies, whose predicament we have discussed in an earlier chapter. What right has an intelligentsia to speak for the nation? What evidence is needed to prove that the intelligentsia has the support of the nation? There are no universally applicable answers to these questions.

The second set of problems arises when within a territory there are profound divergences of outlook, or even bitter political conflict, between major ethnic or religious groups. Where these exist, can or should the unity of the territory be preserved, or should there be partition, and if so where should the boundary be drawn? The most obvious example of such a problem is the division between Hindus and Moslems in India, which led to the partition of the sub-continent and the creation of Pakistan. Hardly less formidable was the division between Chinese and Malays in Malaya, which, however, appeared to be sufficiently overcome to make possible Malayan independence in 1957. Whether Malaya will long survive as an independent state, and whether Pakistan will survive in both or either of its parts remains uncertain. Similar problems exist in Nigeria, where the divisions between the three regions, and especially between the Moslem North and the rest, delayed the achievement of independence. The relationship of Buganda to the other parts of Uganda is another example. In all such cases the imperial government is inevitably accused by the nationalists of a machiavellian policy of *divide et impera*. The accusation may sometimes have been justified in the case of Great Britain, but it is also true that no 'imperialist intrigues' were needed to create the conflicts.

Nationalism is part of the intellectual heritage of British rule to the Asian and African peoples. Patriotic devotion to the faith, the ruler or the tribe existed before the British came, but nationalist doctrine is essentially an European product. Moreover, in Africa at least the national territory itself is a bequest of foreign rule. It is interesting to note that the Ibo or Yoruba or Fulani intelligentsia claims independence on behalf not of an Ibo or Yoruba or Fulani territory, but of an united Nigeria of 36 million inhabitants, a purely British creation. In this the nationalists' aspirations coincide with the natural preference of the British rulers, who do not wish to see their creation disintegrate.

British colonial policy has been greatly influenced by public opinion in Britain. British liberals have long insisted that when a colonial people proves its desire for independence it must be allowed to have it. The Colonial Service has taken pride in its mission of training and leading inexperienced peoples towards independence. Though the tone in which this claim is advanced is often marred by pomposity and self-complacency, the historical record shows that it is no empty boast. There is also a tradition in Britain of muck-raking by radical writers, who have busily smelt out and exposed scandals and injustices in colonial administration. This too is an honourable tradition, even if it has at times appeared, both to officials in Whitehall and to administrators on the spot, to make peaceful progress more difficult. The Labour Party took over both the liberal and the radical traditions. In particular, it was committed to independence for India, and when Mr. Attlee formed the first majority Labour government he fulfilled his pledge.

There was, however, another tradition in British public opinion, which may be called the paternalist. Its essence is the belief that Britain has obligations towards the colonial peoples which it is cowardice and treachery to abandon. Peoples that are still far from political adulthood should not be given a fictitious independence which merely hands them over to the mercy of ambitious demagogues and an inexperienced intelligentsia. Good government is more important than self-government. The fact that the nationalist intelligentsias assert the exact opposite does not prove that they are right. Naturally, the paternalists reply, the intelligentsias are for 'self-government', for this means power for themselves. They will not suffer from bad government; they will profit from it. It is the peoples who will suffer, and it is to the peoples that the imperial government has obligations. Such arguments can, of course, be used to camouflage a desire to retain power and wealth. But it is an unpardonable injustice to dismiss the paternalists as hypocrites, to ignore the many generations who honourably served the people of India and Africa, with very little material gain to themselves.[68]

Liberals, radicals and paternalists had this in common: that they knew and cared about the issues. But British public opinion was not always well-informed or serious. There was a third current, of crude chauvinism, combining material greed with brutal arrogance, nourished by sections of the popular press whose wisdom went no further than slogans about 'keeping the map red'. And a fourth current, in no way more admirable, was the contemptuous indifference of those who 'could not care less' what happened to wogs or niggers.

All four played their part in shaping British policy. The first two groups, *frères ennemis*, were seldom fair to each other, but both were friends of India, as their successors are friends of the Africans. India's independence was a triumph for the radicals, who deserve to share the credit with the Indian nationalists themselves, who had fought a long and tiring, if not particularly painful, struggle. But there was nothing ignoble in the belief of the paternalists that the decision of 1947 was a betrayal. The corpses of 500,000 men, women and children slaughtered in the Punjab are testimony to their case. The paternalists have received scant justice from their compatriots, and virtually no understanding in the United States, but curiously and rather movingly they have received more generous recognition of their services in independent India itself. It would be pleasant to think that independence was the work only of Indian patriots and British radicals. The British have indeed been happily congratulating themselves ever since 1947 for their realism and magnanimity, and have basked in the warmth of lavish Indian praise. But it would be a historical error to forget the influence of the fourth group, the couldn't-care-less. The truth is that indifference and scuttle also played their part, and that these are things of which Britain cannot be proud.

BRITISH AFRICA

It is convenient to divide British Africa into West, East and Central. There is a basic similarity in the problems of the West (Nigeria, Gold Coast, Sierra Leone and Gambia), and the establishment of the Central African Federation has created a certain unity of political issues there even if its three constituent territories (Southern and Northern Rhodesia and Nyasaland) are very heterogeneous; but the political conditions in the three territories of the East (Kenya, Uganda and Tanganyika) are widely different.

WEST AFRICA

The comparatively quick and painless political development in West Africa has been assisted by two features of this region which distinguish it clearly from the eastern and central territories.

The first is that there are no substantial non-African communities. It is true that there are European officials, business representatives and experts of various grades, and that recent economic progress has inevitably increased their numbers, leading at times to incidents of racial tension. There are also Lebanese Arab merchants whose business practices often

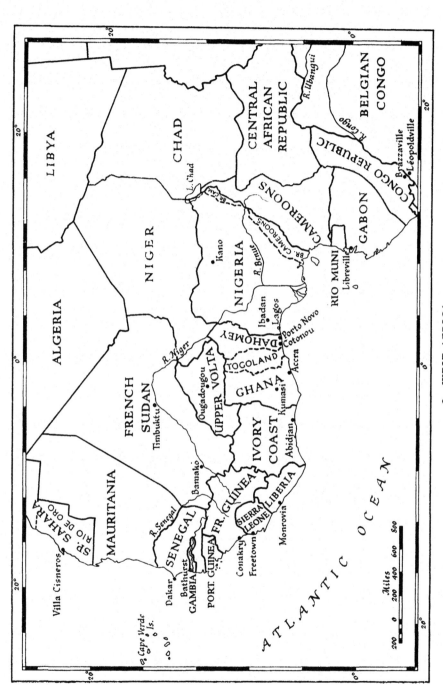

3 WEST AFRICA

arouse jealousy or resentment: their situation among Africans can be roughly compared with that of Chinese among Siamese, Jews among East Europeans, Greeks among Egyptians, or Indians among Burmese. But the difficulties do not add up to a major problem. There can be no comparison with the colour bar in Nairobi, the problem of the *colons* in Algeria or the relations between Indians and Bantu in Durban. West Africa in fact is not a multi-racial society.

The second factor is the relatively advanced social development of West African peoples. Well-established trade routes, trading cities and merchant communities existed before the British came, and expanded further under British rule. The West Africans also showed themselves eager for education, and capable of profiting from it. In 1953 the Gold Coast, with a population of nearly 5 million, had 494,000 children at primary and middle schools, and the Western and Eastern regions of Nigeria, with a population of about 14 million, had 942,000 children at primary schools.* Secondary education was beginning (8,602 pupils in Gold Coast and 22,400 for the whole of Nigeria).[69] A small but growing number received a higher education. Universities were established at Achimota in the Gold Coast and at Ibadan in Nigeria in 1948. By the 1940s already there were many African lawyers, journalists and administrative or clerical employees in government or business offices. The intelligentsia had become a significant social force.

Government in British West Africa was based on the principle of 'indirect rule'. Local administration was largely left to native chiefs. British officials were supposed to strengthen their authority, though their presence of course also limited the chiefs' power. The highest political institutions in the territories, under the Governors, were the Executive and Legislative Councils, in which elected African representatives received a larger share in the first post-war reorganizations.†

In both Gold Coast and Nigeria the growth of militant nationalist movements after the war was due to the increased influence and ambitions of the intelligentsia. To them the chiefs seemed reactionary survivals of the past, due to make way for young progressive forces: they denounced them as 'stooges' of the 'imperialists', destined to be swept away by the awakening national consciousness of the masses. The post-war history of

* The census of 1952-3 showed the population of the North as 16,840,000, of the Western Region as 6,087,000, and of the East as 7,218,000. In addition, Southern Cameroons (adjacent Trusteeship Territory) had 753,000 and the city of Lagos (the federal capital) 272,000.

† The development of Executive and Legislative Councils in the main British African colonies, and their equivalents in the main French territories, is briefly summarized in the Appendix, pp. 467-73.

Gold Coast and Nigeria is one of victory for the intelligentsia and of retreat for the chiefs as well as for the British rulers.

In the Gold Coast the first post-war years saw serious price rises and shortages of goods. Popular discontent was directed by the politicians against both Lebanese traders and British business. In these years too the cocoa trees, the country's main source of wealth, were afflicted by a disease called swollen shoot. In order to check the spread of the disease it was necessary to cut down infected trees. Though this measure was in the farmers' own long-term interest, it was understandably unpopular, and was well exploited by party propaganda. A further factor of political discontent were returned African soldiers, who in the war had seen other lands and other ways of life. To a general intellectual ferment in their minds was added the particular grievance that their civilian resettlement grants were smaller than those received by European soldiers.

In February 1948 there were serious riots in the capital, Accra, set off by discontent with food prices. A Commission was set up to investigate, and an all-African committee under Mr. Justice Coussey was instructed to study constitutional reforms and make proposals. Meanwhile, the political agitation continued. Since 1947 the Secretary of the chief political party—the United Gold Coast Convention (UGCC)—had been a young man named Kwame Nkrumah, who had studied in the United States and in Britain, and possessed in addition to his intellectual attainments an unusual organizing ability and a gift for the leadership of men. Impatient of the limited aims and mild methods of the UGCC's leader, Dr. Danquah, Nkrumah in 1949 broke with the UGCC and created his own Convention Peoples' Party, which was joined by the politically-minded youth. His slogan was 'Self-government now!' and he threatened to use a mass campaign of civil disobedience or 'positive action'. During 1949 he and his colleagues set up an efficient organization in most parts of the country, with a centralized discipline never before achieved by any African party. In January 1950 Nkrumah proclaimed his 'positive action', there were more disorders, and he was arrested. Later in the year, however, the British Government decided to accept the recommendations of the Coussey Committee of 1949, and to institute a popularly elected assembly and a Council of Ministers largely responsible to it. An election was held under the new Constitution in 1951, the Convention People's Party won a sweeping victory, and Nkrumah was released from prison to become the Gold Coast's first Prime Minister.

The new régime derived its main support from the people of the coastal region. In the Ashanti interior opposition grew. The Ashanti produced more than half the country's cocoa output, but received a rather low price from the government, which then did well out of exporting the crop. The Ashanti felt that they were being exploited in the interests of economic policies which mainly benefited others. In Ashanti territory too the chiefly power enjoyed much stronger support than on the coast. But it was not only the cocoa farmers and the chiefs that opposed Nkrumah: among the intelligentsia too there was dislike of the Premier's dictatorial methods and encouragement of a 'Nkrumah cult', and it was alleged that there was corruption among party leaders. These various grounds of discontent were expressed in the National Liberation Movement, founded in 1954 in Kumasi, which also formed an alliance with the Northern People's Party, representing the socially more backward Moslem peoples and their chiefs. The two parties demanded that the Gold Coast should have a federal rather than an unitary constitution. At the general election held in July 1956 Nkrumah won seventy-one seats out of 106. The two regional parties, however, pressed the British Government to grant separate independence to Ashanti and the Northern Territories. Mr. Lennox-Boyd visited the Gold Coast in January 1957, and was able to persuade all to accept a compromise, which created regional assemblies to which considerable powers were to be devolved from the central government.[70]

With this difficulty apparently overcome, it was possible to proclaim the independence of the Gold Coast in March 1957. The new state took the name of Ghana, derived from a medieval African kingdom on whose exact geographical location the experts disagree. It chose to remain within the British Commonwealth. Premier Nkrumah, however, did not hesitate to use dictatorial methods against opponents and critics, abolished the regional assemblies, and deprived the chiefs of all real power. Nkrumah's régime in fact has more in common with the nationalist revolutionary dictatorship of Kemal Atatürk in Turkey in the 1920s than with any parliamentary democracy. It has made enemies, but it seems to be well on the way to creating a nation.

Nigeria is a much bigger country than Ghana, with more than 30 million inhabitants. The differences between its component territories are also greater. If, like Ghana, it is not a multi-racial society, it is, still more than Ghana, a multi-lingual state. The greatest difference is between North and South. The Northern Region, with more than half the total population, is Moslem and has a long history of trade, culture and warfare as an outlying part of the Moslem world. The rulers of the North are hereditary Emirs, their policies and methods of government traditional. Among the dominant Fulani people modern education is little developed, the intelligentsia less numerous or influential than in the South. In the South there are two main peoples, the Yoruba and the Ibo, each numbering about 5 million people in 1953, and predominant respectively in the Western and Eastern Regions into which Nigeria is divided. The Yoruba have long been a people of traders, and their prosperous merchants still enjoy great social power, even though they are being challenged by the intelligentsia. The Ibo have not so long-established a social structure. During the period of British rule, starting from a lower level, they have progressed more rapidly. They have been quick to learn both at school and in business, and, as their homeland is the most densely populated part of the South, they have spread out into the rest of Nigeria.

The first militant political party of post-war Nigeria was based principally on the Ibo. It was the National Council of Nigeria and Cameroons (NCNC), founded by Dr. Namdi Azikiwe, a successful business-man and newspaper proprietor, who had travelled and studied abroad, and who organized support among the intelligentsia, especially young students. Founded in 1944, the NCNC aimed at extending beyond the Ibo territory or the Eastern Region, and being an all-Nigerian party. It provoked a reaction among the Yoruba leaders, who in 1948 formed a cultural society called after Oduduwa, the legendary ancestor of the Yoruba people. In 1951 this society was changed into a political party, entitled Action Group and led by a Yoruba chief, Obafemi Awolowo. In the North the Moslem cultural society *Jamia* was in 1951 renamed Northern People's Congress and adapted into a political party under the leadership of the Sardauna of Sokoto, the hereditary Prime Minister of the Sultan of Sokoto. An opposition group of more radical outlook also appeared in the North, which represented the still weak but growing intelligentsia, and took the name Northern Elements' Progressive Union.[71]

In response to the demands of the nationalist parties, which though suspicious of each other all desired independence for Nigeria, the British Government introduced a Constitution in 1951 which granted a wide measure of self-government. Each of the three regions was to have its Executive Council, in which elected African Ministers had a majority over the official British members. There was a Central Council of Ministers in which elected African Ministers also formed a majority.* In the following years the conflict of aims between the three regions and the three main parties did not diminish. A conference of party leaders was held in London in 1953 and continued in Lagos early in 1954, and a revision of the Constitution was introduced in August 1954. In the subsequent election the NCNC made inroads on the Action Group's territory, winning control of

* For details, see Appendix, pp. 468-9.

the city councils of Lagos and Ibadan, the two great cities of the West, and actually receiving more votes than the Action Group in the Western Region as a whole in the election for the central legislature, though not for the regional assembly.

In October 1958 a constitutional conference was held in London. Chief Awolowo emphasized the rights of minorities, and wished to create new federal units in order to counterbalance the NCNC. Dr. Azikiwe, who hoped to increase his following throughout the South, and the Sardauna of Sokoto, who was confident of his hold over the North, were less interested in principles that could obstruct their aims. A compromise was reached, at least on paper, and it was agreed by the British Government that Nigeria should become independent at the end of 1960.

EAST AFRICA

Of the three East African territories the most clearly 'African' in population is Uganda. Of its 5 million inhabitants only some 3,500 are European, and these are not landowners. The Asian minority amounts to 40,000. The country is composed of a number of tribal units, each of which has a different protectorate relationship to Britain. The largest single unit is the kingdom of Buganda, with a population of about 1,500,000. The post-war development of Uganda has two main features—the rise of nationalism, expressed by a growing intelligentsia, and the conflict of the traditional leadership of Buganda both with the British Government and with the other regions of Uganda.

In 1950 the Governor of Uganda announced a reform of the Legislative Council, which was to include African representatives from the four regions. The kingdom of Buganda was to provide two of these, one to be appointed by its king, or Kabaka, and one by its tribal assembly, or Lukiko. The Lukiko, however, argued that Buganda's status, under the 1900 protectorate treaty with Britain, could be regulated only through the relationship of the Kabaka with the Governor, representing the British Crown: there was no place for an intermediate body in the form of an all-Uganda Legislative Council. The Lukiko therefore refused to send its representatives. The Kabaka, who had previously been under pressure from his own subjects, some of whom had rioted outside his palace in 1949, was determined not to antagonize public feeling in Buganda, and therefore rejected the Governor's request that he should defend the new British policy before the Lukiko. Two further factors played their part in the conflict which now developed between the Governor and the Kabaka. One was hostility to the Asian minority, largely consisting of traders, which was to be represented in the new Council. The other was alarm

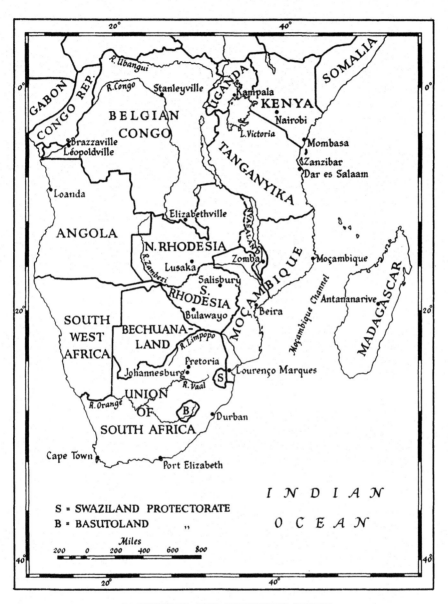

4 CENTRAL AND SOUTHERN AFRICA

caused by a speech in London on 30 June 1953 by the Secretary of State for the Colonies, Mr. Oliver Lyttelton, which had referred to the possibility of a Federation of the three East African territories. This was interpreted by the Baganda as a plan to place their country at the mercy of the White settlers of Kenya. The fact that Federation was at this time being pushed through in the three Central African territories, despite the strong opposition of the African population, increased the fears of the Baganda. When the Kabaka continued to refuse the Governor's requests, he was deported to England, by an order of 30 November 1953. The British Government then appointed Sir Keith Hancock to examine the situation in Buganda and make constitutional proposals. His recommendations formed the basis of a compromise by which the Lukiko agreed to nominate its representatives to the Legislative Council, but its own authority as a regional assembly in Buganda was strengthened. In October 1955 the Kabaka was allowed to return.

Meanwhile, the usual new social forces were beginning to make themselves felt. Though education was less advanced than in West Africa, it was going ahead fast, and an Uganda intelligentsia was growing up. Makerere College, raised to the status of an university for the three East African territories, became a centre of political ideas. The successful development of cotton and coffee farming, the growth of co-operatives and the first beginnings of a textile industry increased the numbers and influence of an African middle class. In 1952 the Uganda National Congress, a nationalist political party, was founded. Its support came at first from the other provinces of Uganda, but after the deportation of the Kabaka it was able to increase its following in Buganda too.

In October 1958 the first direct elections were held, for 10 seats in the Uganda Legislative Council*—excluding Buganda. Registered electors, from an area comprising some three-fifths of Uganda's population, were 626,000, and 85% of them voted. The result was that the Uganda National Congress won five out of ten seats. Its declared aim is independence for Uganda, and it was not slow to look for support abroad, maintaining a 'foreign delegation' in Cairo. For Colonel Abd el-Nasser, who has proclaimed his support for all African independence movements, and has serious conflicts of interest with Sudan, Uganda, the nearest negro territory to Egypt and the southern neighbour of Sudan, is obviously a country of interest.

The problems of Kenya are more difficult still. This country of about 6 million inhabitants has an European population of about 40,000 and

* See Appendix, p. 469.

an Asian of 100,000. The best farm land in the country is owned by about 4,000 persons, to whom are reserved the 'White Highlands' covering some 12,000 square miles. The greater part of the Europeans, however, live in the cities, especially in the capital, Nairobi, where there are prosperous businesses and excellent residential districts, almost entirely monopolized by Europeans. In hotels, restaurants and most public places a rigid colour bar is enforced against Africans, including the educated and prosperous minority.

The most numerous African people of Kenya are the Kikuyu, who number about 1,250,000. In the last thirty years their numbers have greatly increased, and the land which they now possess is inadequate to support them. It is also very badly farmed. The soil is exhausted by not leaving it fallow, and it is made to feed excessive quantities of livestock of very poor quality. These harmful agricultural practices are due in part to tribal customs, but their ill-effects are aggravated by the general land shortage. The Kikuyu bitterly resented the fact that when the White Highlands were set up, a part of their tribal lands (equivalent to about one-tenth of the total White Highlands area) was allotted to them. This error was made in good faith, due to the Government's insufficient understanding of Kikuyu traditional rights and customs, but it has come to be regarded by the Kikuyu as a sinister act of wilful robbery. The land-hungry Kikuyu have come to believe that they are entitled not only to recover this land, but to acquire the whole of the White Highlands, which was never theirs.

Many Kikuyu left the overpopulated land for the cities, where they live in great squalor. Nairobi has for some time had a depressed proletariat of unskilled and semi-employed Kikuyu, neglected by the authorities. In the first post-war years high prices of food and filthy slums caused great hardship, and there was an alarming growth of crime.

Education was less developed even than in Uganda, let alone West Africa. However, a small number of Kikuyu went to mission schools, and a few even to a higher education, at Makerere or abroad. Outstanding among them was Jomo Kenyatta, who studied sociology with Malinowski in London, and wrote a book, *Facing Mount Kenya*, which was a remarkable combination of social observation and tribal nationalism.

Christian missionaries at first made many converts in Kenya. But friction between individual priests and their African followers, and wider divergences between the meaning of Christian doctrine and ritual to African and to European minds, led to the secession of groups of Africans, who set up their own churches. The same thing happened with the mission schools: separate independent schools were founded, and became instruments of Kikuyu nationalism. The first political organization was the

Kikuyu Central Association, founded in 1922 mainly to protest about land policy. It was dissolved in 1939, but in 1944 it obtained a successor in the establishment of the Kenya African Union. Kenyatta, who had been abroad since 1931, mostly in England, but also for a time in Moscow, returned to Kenya in 1946 and became the leader of the KAU. In the first post-war years there was also increased activity by militant religious sects, which preached hatred of the white man. One such sect, *Watu wa Mungu* ('People of God'), had existed already in the 1920s. Its successors in the 1940s showed greater inclination to use violence.

From the comparatively sophisticated nationalism of Kenyatta and the KAU, and the savagery of the sects, emerged the movement known as Mau Mau. It both reflected and exploited the misery of the peasants and the urban proletariat. Its leaders, however, came from the intelligentsia.*
They were men with considerable knowledge of the outside world, familiar with political ideas and possessed of great talent as political organizers. The secrecy of their preparations and the discipline of their chain of command are most impressive. Though considered an 'unwarlike race' (in contrast to the warrior tribe of the Masai), the Kikuyu followers of Mau Mau showed themselves capable of fighting a guerrilla war which called for courage, endurance and resourcefulness. Among their military leaders were men who had served in the British Army during the war. The rebellion held down considerable numbers of British troops from the autumn of 1952 for more than four years. This achievement must be recognized as a fact. It is also necessary to mention the bestial savagery of the movement—the obscene oath-taking ceremonies, the torture and massacre of defenceless Kikuyu who would not join Mau Mau, and the many murders of Europeans. It is also true that these crimes provoked brutality on the European side, summary killings and maltreatment of suspects, such as the Hola Camp outrages revealed in 1959.

Inevitably the rebellion created profound distrust of the Kikuyu by British residents and officials, and though the other tribes of Kenya did not join the Kikuyu, the war was bound to some extent to increase tension between the races as a whole. At the same time it showed clearly that both social reform and political change were urgently needed. A new Constitution was introduced in 1954, but replaced by another in 1957.† The Africans elected to the Legislative Council were predominantly nationalist, and found an effective leader in Mr. Tom Mboya. They would not accept

* Whether Kenyatta himself was the leader of Mau Mau is a subject of controversy. The evidence produced at his trial was not very impressive, and one of the witnesses has since declared that he committed perjury. There is, however, no doubt that the Mau Mau fighters themselves regarded Kenyatta as their chief.

† See Appendix, pp. 469-70.

the 1957 Constitution, and demanded that African elected members should have half the seats in the Legislature and half the 'unofficial' seats in the Council of Ministers.

The prospects of political progress in Kenya remain obscure. The African nationalists aim at a democratic majority system of government, in which the vast African majority will swamp the two smaller communities. They reject the conception of a 'multi-racial society', in which smaller but more skilled and educated communities should enjoy special guarantees. At present no all-Kenya nationalist party is recognized by the government, but it seems inevitable that Mboya's Kenya African Congress will have the support of the small but growing intelligentsia, and through it will obtain wider popular support. On the other hand, the Europeans at present have the power, and even the most liberal among them will certainly not consider handing complete supremacy to an African majority. Even pressure from London for moderate concessions is resented, and there is much talk of 'independence' for an European-ruled Kenya.

The social problems are no less acute, and no less difficult to solve, than the political. The White Highlands are agriculturally far more efficient than the native lands. European enterprise both in agriculture and in industry has enormously enriched Kenya. But the demands of the Africans in general, and Kikuyu in particular, for at least part of the Highlands, will grow. Even without any transfer of land from Europeans to Africans, there remains the urgent and costly task of improving farming in the African-held land. The proposals of the Royal Commission on Land and Population in East Africa of 1955, which emphasize the development of private farms in preference to tribal tenure (and may perhaps be compared with the policy of Prime Minister Stolypin in Russia in 1906-10), are supported by strong economic arguments, but involve great social risks. It is not surprising that the government has hesitated about them. Yet inaction settles nothing. The other great social problem is the colour bar. The case of the brilliant Kenyatta, who was driven to his career of conspiracy by resentment at the humiliating treatment he received from Europeans who were often his intellectual inferiors, is a dramatic warning. As the numbers of the intelligentsia in Kenya grow, the problem will become more acute. Yet there is little sign that the Europeans will or can change their attitude, and consent to meet Africans as social equals. And the insistence on the colour bar cannot be attributed to a few rich settlers. The stereotype, popular in Britain and America, of the reactionary rich settler, a mixture of English earl and Virginian planter, is misleading. The poorer Europeans are even more fanatically opposed to equality for Africans, whether social or political, than the rich.

Tanganyika has had a less troubled post-war history than Kenya, but it has some of the same problems. There are about 5,000 European farmers, owning about a fifth of the cultivated land. The main cash crop, sisal, is farmed entirely by non-Africans. African agriculture is, however, more prosperous than in Kenya, co-operatives have made progress and there is no such overpopulation problem as in the Kikuyu region of Kenya. Tanganyika, as a former Mandated Territory, is subject to the United Nations Trusteeship Council, whose visiting missions have visited it. A nationalist party, the Tanganyika African National Union, was founded by an African school-teacher, Julius Nyerere. In 1955 the Governor, Sir Edward Twining, encouraged the formation of a multi-racial organization, the United Tanganyika Party, in the hope of creating a loyalty to the country as a whole, transcending narrowly racial nationalism. Partly to meet the criticisms and exhortations to democratic reform by the United Nations, the government decided to hold direct elections in 1958. The total registered electorate was only 29,000. There were twenty constituencies, in each of which three persons were to be elected—one European, one Asian and one African. Every voter had to vote for one candidate of each race. Elections were held in two stages, in September 1958 and February 1959. Not one candidate of the United Tanganyika Party was elected. All the successful candidates were either members of Nyerere's TANU or persons approved by it. The future policies of TANU were far from clear. Nyerere had recently stated that he was not an exclusive African nationalist, but believed in a multi-racial Tanganyika. But at a conference of African political leaders from the three East African territories, held shortly after the first election, he had urged the formation of a 'Pan-African freedom movement for East and Central Africa'. The conference adopted a 'Freedom Charter' which asserted: 'So-called trusteeship, so-called partnership, multi-racialism and white settlerism are enemies of freedom and can be eradicated only by African nationalism, virile and unrelenting.'

THE CENTRAL AFRICAN FEDERATION

The Central African Federation was formed in 1953 of three territories. Southern Rhodesia had in 1955 a population of 2,200,000 Africans, 170,000 Europeans and 13,000 Asian and Coloured. The Europeans included a substantial number of farmers in addition to business-men, professionals, officials and skilled workers. Many of the European farmers were Afrikaans-speaking recent immigrants from South Africa. Northern Rhodesia had in 1956 a population of 2,140,000 Africans, 71,000 Europeans and 7,000 Asians and Coloureds. The Europeans included a small number of farmers, but mainly consisted of persons directly or indirectly connected with the mining industry. Nyasaland had at the end of 1957 a population of 2,700,000 Africans, 8,000 Europeans and 11,000 Asians and Coloureds.

The initiative for Federation came from Southern Rhodesia, in particular from Sir Godfrey Huggins, for many years Prime Minister of that territory. Southern Rhodesia had had a form of parliamentary government, with a ministry responsible to the assembly, since 1923. In its relationship to Britain, it thus occupied a status intermediate between a colony and a Dominion. There was a growing demand from its English-speaking European population for independence of the last controls exercised by the British government. As the Nationalists entrenched themselves in South Africa after 1948, and Afrikaner immigration into Southern Rhodesia increased, the attraction of South African racialist policies could be expected to grow. This prospect was alarming both to persons of even moderately liberal outlook in Southern Rhodesia and to the government in London. Southern Rhodesia, however, was too small to stand on its own. The solution seemed to be to create a larger unit in which Southern Rhodesian political leaders would have the main say. There were also economic grounds for a closer union of the three countries, to make use of the plentiful labour supply of Nyasaland and the copper of Northern Rhodesia, and to co-ordinate plans for hydro-electric and other development.

Opposition to Federation came from two sides. On the one hand the African majority was deeply suspicious of Southern Rhodesian policies. Although Sir Godfrey Huggins rejected the *apartheid* doctrine of the South African Nationalists, there was a rigid colour bar in force. Especially in Nyasaland there was widespread fear that Federation would mean aggressive white domination and exploitation of the Africans. On the other hand, a minority of white opinion in Southern Rhodesia opposed the plan on the grounds that it would unnecessarily increase the numerical African majority: they preferred the creation of a smaller territory comprising all Southern Rhodesia and those portions of Northern Rhodesia with large European population (the main industrial areas), and proposed that Barotseland in Northern Rhodesia and the whole of Nyasaland should be protectorates jointly administered by Britain and Rhodesia. However, the scheme was accepted by the European-dominated legislatures of the three countries, and, despite African protests and opposition by the British Labour Party, it was approved by the British Parliament in July 1953.

The Federation's declared policy is Partnership. Its leaders claim to accept the aim once proclaimed by Cecil Rhodes, of equal rights for civilized men, regardless of race. For a long time yet, they argue, Europeans are bound to play the leading role, for they are far better endowed with knowledge, skill and wealth than the vast majority of Africans. They intend, however, to enable the Africans to learn practical skills, to acquire modern knowledge and to earn a higher standard of living. Ultimately there will be a mixed society. On the future of the social colour bar, however, the theorists of Partnership are vague, and they definitely oppose inter-marriage, even in the distant future.

The theory thus differs from the South African doctrine of *apartheid*. The degree of difference in practical policy will depend on the nature of social reforms and the opportunities of advancement offered to the Africans. Some improvements have been secured. The industrial colour bar on the copper-belt has been weakened, as we have seen. The government has built some permanent housing for Africans in Southern Rhodesian towns (in the copper-belt this has existed for many years). A new multiracial University College of Rhodesia and Nyasaland was opened at Salisbury in March 1957.

These are hopeful signs, but they are small. The political scene is less encouraging. In 1957 the Prime Minister of Southern Rhodesia, Mr. Garfield Todd, introduced a new franchise for that territory which gave a vote to Africans who had passed a certain educational standard. The eligible Africans were thereby increased to 10,000 in contrast to 54,000 European voters. Todd also raised the minimum industrial wage for African workers by about half, and increased government grants to African schools and hospitals. These not very startling acts of liberalism raised bitter opposition to him in his United Federal Party, which in February 1958 forced him to give up both his leadership and the Premiership. A general election was held in June 1958, in which the United Federal Party was opposed by the still more conservative Dominion Party. The UFP won a majority of the seats, but the DP a slight majority of all votes cast. Todd, who put up candidates in opposition to both, did not win a single seat.

In January 1958 the federal franchise was changed in such a way as to increase the number of African voters and African seats, but to increase the number of European seats still more. The African Affairs Board, a special standing committee set up under the 1953 settlement to safeguard the interests of the Africans, used its right to protest against this francise law to the British Colonial Secretary. Mr. Lennox-Boyd, however, overruled the protest. These events cast grave doubt on the value of the African Affairs Board. The defeat of Todd had also made it clear that European opinion in Southern Rhodesia interpreted extremely narrowly the principle of Partnership. In the federal election campaign of November 1958 Sir Roy Welensky, the UFP leader, showed himself determined not to lag behind the DP in his devotion to white supremacy. He was rewarded for his intransigence by a large majority.

It seems not unfair to sum up predominant European opinion in the Federation as an abstract willingness to give rights to civilized Africans, combined with a practical conviction that very few will ever become civilized and a determination to see to it that very few get the chance. Those white Rhodesians who take a more liberal view are not supported by most of their compatriots. From the Africans' point of view, this attitude does not differ much from South African *apartheid*. Meanwhile, inevitably an African intelligentsia is growing, and African political opinion is becoming more radical.

The leader of the Northern Rhodesian African National Congress, Harry Nkumbula, has demanded that the number of elected Africans in the territory's Legislative Council should be equal to all other elected members, and that the Africans be elected by universal adult franchise. Nkumbula was, however, unable to satisfy extremists in his party, who at the end of 1958 formed a splinter party, the Zambia Congress, whose immediate aim was a completely African state. In Nyasaland the determination to secede from the Federation became more articulate with the return in 1958 of Dr. Hastings Banda, the leading Nyasa nationalist, who had lived abroad for many years. Violent outbreaks occurred in February 1959, when for some days whole districts were under insurgent African control. The Federal government decided to dissolve the Southern Rhodesian African National Congress, which had not been involved in the Nyasaland disorders, and to arrest its leaders. Dr. Banda and his colleagues were also arrested in Nyasaland. Drastic public security laws were passed by the Federal parliament. The Nyasaland government stated that it had forestalled a plot to massacre Europeans and loyal Africans, and Sir Roy Welensky professed to believe that this was part of a sinister design jointly planned by Dr. Banda and the Soviet observers at the Pan-African Congress in Accra in December 1958.*

It is possible to feel keen sympathy for the Europeans threatened by African violence, and to understand their exasperation with doctrinaire politicians or journalists in Britain who apply to Central Africa ready-made democratic formulae which have little relevance. Such sympathy need not, however, imply approval of Sir Roy Welensky's security laws. And it is difficult to see why the overwhelmingly African population of Nyasaland should be held by force in the Federation against their will, or indeed how this can be done.

* See Appendix, pp. 470-2 for the constitutions in the territories of the Federation, and p. 327 below for the Pan-African Congress.

FRENCH AFRICA

The French lost their Empire in America in the eighteenth century not because their colonists revolted against them, but because their British enemies conquered it from them. They did not therefore suffer the shock of being defeated by their own kinsmen, or come to think of colonies as bound in the course of time to separate from the homeland. The new Empire which France created in the nineteenth century, in Africa and Indochina, has not been governed in the belief that the development of the colonies must lead to their ultimate independence. On the contrary, the aim of policy has been to bring the colonial peoples up to the French level and incorporate them in French civilization. Disaster in Indochina did not destroy the faith in the *mission civilisatrice*.

It is often pointed out that there is no colour bar in French colonies. The only important distinction is between the cultured and the uncultured: the cultured African is treated as an equal. The British, it is argued, may be kinder than the French to the primitive African, but are uncomfortable in the company of an African intellectual. The fact that an African has made the effort to educate himself, and has mastered the culture of the ruling race, seems to the Englishman an affront, the challenge of an upstart to his superiority; to the Frenchman a compliment, a proof that the African has had the good taste to accept French values.

The truth is less simple. The cultured African may receive the homage of the cultured Frenchman, but there are plenty of uncultured Frenchmen in the French colonies, *petits blancs* whose courtesy and understanding hardly exceed those of the 'poor whites' of Anglo-Saxon territories. In Paris the African intellectual enjoys the respect and friendship of his equals, but in London too African intellectuals are well received. It may be argued that Paris as an intellectual centre is immeasurably superior to London, but that is a matter of opinion, and barely relevant to the present argument. There is also the question of how an African becomes cultured, and how many have the opportunity. The quality of French education is beyond all doubt, but its quantity in French Africa still leaves something to be desired. In January 1953 there were about 230,000 children enrolled in all schools in French West Africa, with its population of about 17 million, while the Gold Coast had 500,000 at school in a population of 5 million.[7a] This contrast may be in part explained by the fact that in all French schools the French language is the medium of instruction from the beginning, while in British West Africa the medium is the vernacular until the fifth school year, when it is replaced by English.

Metropolitan public opinion has been a factor in French colonial history, as in British. The liberal, radical and paternalist schools of thought existed also in France. At first sight one might think that the radicals were stronger in France and the paternalists weaker, than in Britain. It would probably be truer to say that the radicals were dominant in France itself and the paternalists among Frenchmen in the colonies. As the rest of the world is usually well informed of Parisian opinion and ignorant of French opinion in the colonies, the radicalism was better known abroad than the paternalism. The colonies were largely founded and developed by those political and social elements of the French nation which since the triumph of the *Dreyfusard* left had been excluded, or had themselves seceded, from French political life. Even in France itself in the twentieth century the power of the so-called left has been smaller than the debates in the Chamber, the public meetings and the press seemed to show: the country was governed by the administrative cadres that owed their origin to Napoleon, or even to Louis XIV. In the colonies the superiority of the administration over parliamentary politicians was still greater. Nevertheless, critical opinion in Paris played, as in London, an important part in exposing abuses and preparing the atmosphere for reforms, and Africans who acquired the French culture which their administrators held up to them as a model, found that it contained a rich heritage of radical and revolutionary ideas. At the same time, the paternalist French administrators, though their own vision of France may have been highly traditionalist, even 'reactionary', were no less conscious of their obligations to the people they ruled than their British equivalents. The greatest of them all was Marshal Lyautey in Morocco. There were hundreds more who lacked his genius, but gave long years of honourable service to the people of Africa.

WEST AFRICA

French West Africa (*Afrique Occidentale Française*—AOF) consists of eight territories. Mauritania, Sudan and Niger are largely desert; Senegal, Guinea, Ivory Coast and Dahomey are strips of varying width stretching from a coastal base back into the interior; and Upper Volta is a land-bound territory stretching from the Ivory Coast behind Ghana to Dahomey. As in British West Africa, there is great variety of languages and customs. The people of the interior are mostly Moslems, while those of the coast have their own religions but include a certain number of Christian converts. The total population is about 20 million in 1959.

Before 1946 French West Africans were divided into citizens, who came under French law, and subjects, who were under native custom. Citizenship was obtained by evidence, in the form of education or the nature of employment, that the candidate had adopted an European way of life. A law of May 1946 conferred French citizenship on all French subjects.

The electoral laws adopted for AOF territories under the Constitution of 1946 greatly increased the number of those qualified to vote, and by 1951 the situation was such that virtually anyone who presented himself with documentary proof of his identity could vote. The people of AOF elected deputies to the French National Assembly in Paris (though not in the same proportion to their population as the people of metropolitan France), and to eight territorial assemblies (*conseils généraux*), each of which elected five representatives to a regional assembly for all AOF (*Grand Conseil de l'AOF*). In 1956 the electoral system was made more democratic, and territorial executive councils (*conseils de gouvernement*) were set up, in which persons elected by the assemblies formed a majority, and which were thus embryonic councils of ministers of their territories.*

The French Constitution of 1958, introduced by General de Gaulle, allowed the territories to choose between complete independence and membership of the French Community, either as individual states or grouped together with other states. The division of powers between the member states of the Community and the central government in Paris was defined by Article 78. The authority of the central government would include 'foreign policy, defence, currency, common economic and financial policy and policy concerning strategic raw materials'. Unless there were special agreement to the contrary, it would also include 'control of justice, higher education, the general organization of foreign-bound transport and transport of common concern and telecommunications'.

Political parties of Africans became important after the war. As in British Africa, they were led by the intelligentsia, and inspired by the political ideas current in the metropolitan country. They were more directly influenced by metropolitan politics than was the case in British Africa, thanks to the membership of leading African politicians in the National Assembly in Paris.[73]

The first metropolitan party to win a following in AOF were the socialists, who became powerful in Senegal and Sudan. In 1948 a faction broke away, under Léopold Sédan Senghor, the most eminent of all French African intellectuals and a distinguished poet, and founded a new party, *Bloc démocratique sénégalais* (BDS), which from 1951 was the strongest party in Senegal. In 1952 the socialists also lost control of Sudan, but in 1956 they were enabled by the splits in their opponents' ranks to become the leading party in Niger.

The main rival to both BDS and the socialists was a new party which, though its fortunes fluctuated, remained for the next twelve years the strongest single political organization in AOF. This was *Rassemblement*

* See Appendix, pp. 472-3.

démocratique africain (RDA), founded at a conference in Bamako, Sudan, in October 1946. Led by a Christian member of a chiefly family, Félix Houphouet-Boigny, it won an overwhelming majority in Ivory Coast and a substantial following elsewhere. At first it co-operated in the French parliament with the communist party, and supported the communists' efforts to build their own trade-union movement in AOF through the French CGT. The French administration in Ivory Coast at first encouraged both RDA and CGT, but after the break between the communists and their coalition partners in France in 1947 benevolence was replaced by repression. It also gradually became clear to Houphouet that the communists regarded RDA as an instrument designed to mobilize African nationalism for the purposes of Soviet foreign policy: its role was to be the classic one of 'mass organizations' in the communist bid for power. In 1950 Houphouet broke with the communists, and in metropolitan politics he thereafter aligned himself with the moderate left. One of his chief lieutenants, Gabriel d'Arboussier, who had been active in trade-union affairs, remained loyal to the communist orientation, and was expelled from the party. RDA's branch in the French Trusteeship Territory of Caméroun (which was administratively separate from AOF) —*Union des populations du Caméroun* (UPC)—broke away, and came under closer communist control. In May 1955 it organized violent riots, and was banned by the French authorities: some of its leaders went into exile in Egypt, Eastern Europe and China.

Houphouet's new moderation brought rewards both in popular support and in tolerance by the administration. At the first elections to *conseils généraux* under the 1956 electoral law, in March 1957, RDA won overwhelming majorities in Ivory Coast, Sudan and Guinea, a slight majority in Upper Volta and a large minority in Niger. Senegal was dominated by Senghor's party, now renamed *Convention africaine*; Niger by the socialists. In Dahomey the strongest party was the *Parti républicain du Dahomey*, led by Sourou Migan Apithy and supported by the strong Catholic element in that territory. In Mauritania, a purely Moslem territory in which Moorish and negro elements balance each other, the conservative *Union progressiste de Mauritanie*, based on the chiefly families, was in complete control. There was, however, opposition among Moorish chiefs and intelligentsia, expressed by the *Entente mauritanienne*, whose leader in 1956 emigrated to Morocco, where he publicly identified himself with Moroccan claims for the annexation of Mauritania.

During 1957 unsuccessful attempts were made to unite the African parties on a common programme. In March 1958 the socialists, the *Convention africaine* and the *Parti républicain du Dahomey* united to form the *Parti du regroupement africain* (PRA), while RDA remained separate. RDA itself was, however, far from united. Houphouet, who spent much of his time in France as a metropolitan Minister, had inevitably lost some degree of his contact with the party, and was out of sympathy with its radical elements. In 1957 he had readmitted d'Arboussier to the party. The leader of RDA in Guinea, Sékou Touré, was politically unpredictable. An active trade-union leader, he had been one of the founders, at a conference in Cotonou, Dahomey, in January 1957, of a new trade-union organization that uneasily united nationalists and communists—*Union générale des travailleurs de l'Afrique noire* (UGTAN), which did not join the communist WFTU.

In July 1958 a congress of PRA, held at Cotonou, called for independence for the people of all French Black Africa. The official policy of RDA was acceptance of the Franco-African community. A new extremist party was the *Parti africain de l'indépendance*, founded by African students in France. Strongly influenced by communists, it was supported by a part of the intellectual youth of AOF.

In the referendum of 28 September 1958 neither PRA nor RDA adopted an unanimous attitude. Houphouet was for acceptance of the Constitution, but Sékou Touré persuaded his followers in Guinea to vote against it. Thus by a large minority Guinea voted for complete independence: no other territory followed its example. On the other hand, despite its Cotonou demand for independence, PRA decided to vote for the Constitution and for membership of the Franco-African Community. In Niger however the PRA leaders urged their followers to choose independence, but a majority of the electors voted for membership.

In the winter of 1958-9 there was a regrouping of political opinion on the issue of whether the states should join the Community individually or as a federated unit. Mauretania, with its special position between Morocco and Black Africa, preferred individual membership. Ivory Coast made the same choice because, as the richest territory, it did not wish to hand over a share of its wealth to its poorer neighbours. Niger acted likewise for the opposite reason: as the poorest territory, it hoped to get more help by direct association with France than by submersion in a federation. Guinea had chosen to leave the Community altogether. The remaining four territories negotiated with each other for the formation of a federal union. On 17 January 1959 they announced their decision to form a federal republic, to be called Mali (after an African state that had covered part of this area in the thirteenth century). But the decision was short-lived. In Dahomey, Sourou Migan Apithy opposed the Mali plan, and obtained a majority in the territorial assembly for his views in mid-February. In

Upper Volta the opponents of Mali prevailed at the beginning of March, and a popular referendum of 17 March gave them an 80% majority. Thus the Mali project was reduced to an union of Senegal and Sudan. Both RDA and PRA had disintegrated: the RDA of Sudan and a large part of the RDA of Upper Volta had supported Mali, while the PRA in Dahomey had opposed it. The federalists in March 1959 regrouped, under Senghor, and took the name *Parti de la fédération africaine* (PFA). Houphouet remained a powerful figure in Ivory Coast, Dahomey and Upper Volta.

The reorganization of AOF also raised international problems. In November 1958 Kwame Nkrumah and Sékou Touré announced their intention to form an union of Ghana and Guinea as a nucleus for a future union of West Africa. It seemed possible that the British colony of Gambia, which is surrounded by Senegal, might be absorbed in the Mali state. Another possibility was that Niger might unite with Nigeria when the latter became independent in 1960. The British Trusteeship Territory of Cameroons was likely to be divided when it attained independence in 1960: the northern part was expected to join Nigeria, but the rest might either remain independent or join with French Caméroun when it too became independent in 1960.

The French West African intelligentsia was divided between those favouring a long future association with France (whose main spokesman was Houphouet) and those aiming at some Pan-African solution. Supporters of the second orientation had two rival models before them—the Ghana-Guinea and the Senegal-Sudan unions. Another possible centre of attraction was a future independent Caméroun, which might well be controlled by communists. The independence of Nigeria, whose population is almost double that of all AOF, was certain to change the whole situation. It was in any case clear that African nationalists would grow increasingly impatient with artificial state boundaries drawn by European Powers. It also seemed likely that the basic differences between British and French approaches to African nationalism, the different outlooks inherited from their respective rulers by the African intelligentsias of the two empires, and the readiness of French administrators to suspect anti-French intrigues by the British would provide the statesmen of both countries with plenty of delicate problems.

EQUATORIAL AFRICA

French Equatorial Africa (AEF) has a population of nearly 5 million, divided into four territories—Chad, Gabon, the Congo Republic (formerly Middle Congo) and the Central African Republic (formerly Ubangui-Shari). Its constitutional development since 1945 has been very similar to that of AOF. Both RDA and the socialists have obtained a following in AEF territories, but in general the people are less politically advanced and the intelligentsia is less numerous and influential than in AOF.

In September 1958 all four territories had majorities for membership of the Franco-African Community. In January 1959 they announced the formation of a Customs union, but there was to be no political federation. The richest territory, Gabon, like Ivory Coast in AOF, was unwilling to share its wealth. The most important event in AEF since the new French Constitution came into force was the outbreak in February 1959 of violent tribal riots in Brazzaville, the capital both of the Congo Republic and of all AEF.

MADAGASCAR

Though situated not far from the African coast, the great island of Madagascar is inhabited mainly by peoples of Asian stock, distantly related to the Malays. The most important of these are the Merina, whose ruling caste, known as Hova, held power before the French conquest at the end of the nineteenth century. The French rulers have at times sought to use the lesser peoples as a counterweight to the Merina, but without much success. Even under French rule the Merina extended their language and culture until by the 1950s they had spread to some two-thirds of a population of about 4,500,000. The level of education is higher in Madagascar than in neighbouring African territories. At the end of 1954, of a school age population of 674,000 nearly 275,000 were attending primary school and nearly 20,000 more, schools of higher levels.[74]

After the war a strongly nationalist political party was formed, *Mouvement démocratique de rénovation malgache* (MDRM), which in 1946 had three members in the National Assembly in Paris. In March 1947 there was an armed rebellion against the French. Several hundred French settlers were massacred, and by the time the rebellion had been suppressed more than 80,000 persons had been killed. The three Madagascar deputies in Paris were implicated, and were sentenced to long terms of imprisonment.

In 1956 six elected provincial assemblies were set up, each of which elected nine members to a central assembly. A central *conseil de gouvernement* was also created, as in AOF and AEF. At the provincial election held in March 1957 two strongly nationalist groups, *Comité d'entente et d'action politique*, in which communist influence was dominant, and *Union des indépendants*, which was supported by a large part of the Catholic Church, won about half the seats, and caused many of the moderates in the assemblies to take a more nationalist attitude. In March 1958 the French Parliament passed an amnesty for persons serving prison sentences in connection with the 1947 rebellion, but would not yet allow the three deputies of the former MDRM to return to Madagascar.

In the referendum of 28 September Madagascar voted by a large majority for the new French Constitution. In accordance with its Article 76, the Madagascar central assembly on 14 October declared itself in favour of a single state of Madagascar within the French Community, and proclaimed the island an autonomous republic.

BELGIAN AFRICA

The association of Belgium with the Congo was at first indirect, as this vast region became at the end of the nineteenth century the personal domain of King Leopold II. International protests at the treatment of the native population under his régime caused the Belgian parliament to intervene, and a more humane system of government was established by the *Charte coloniale* of 1908. The territory, now named Belgian Congo, was placed under the Ministry of the Colonies, advised by a *Conseil colonial* of fourteen (eight appointed and six elected by the two Houses of Parliament). There was also established a Commission for the protection of the natives, of eighteen appointed persons, resident in the colony and qualified as experts on native problems. Its powers were purely advisory. In addition to the Congo, Belgium became in 1918 the Mandatory Power for the territory of Ruanda-Urundi, which since 1945 has been subject to the United Nations Trusteeship Council.

Government in the Congo was essentially bureaucratic. No elected persons, whether European or African, had any share in executive power. The Belgian government has been anxious to prevent the rise of political movements, either of European settlers who might, as in Kenya or Rhodesia, demand independence from the metropolitan country, or of African nationalists. There is an advisory *Conseil de gouvernement* attached to the Governor-General in the capital, Léopoldville, and there are *conseils de province* in the six provinces. Their members are partly appointed and partly elected by organizations which represent only restricted groups of Europeans or Africans. They have no power to make the Governor-General or provincial governors listen to their advice. In 1958 Africans were for the first time elected to the office of mayor in several districts of Léopoldville.

While government has been consciously paternalist and conservative, great progress has been made in industry and education. The rich deposits of uranium and copper in the province of Katanga, which adjoins the North Rhodesian copper-belt, have given rise to a flourishing mining industry. Africans are employed at any level of skill that they can attain: there is absolutely no industrial colour-bar on employment, though

African wage rates are below European. Africans may for example be locomotive-drivers or captains of river steamers. On the other hand, African trade unions have less freedom than in the Rhodesias. In 1956, in a total African population of 12,800,000 in Belgian Congo there were nearly 3,500,000 adult males, and of these nearly 1,200,000 were employed workers. Growth of wage-paid employment has meant urbanization. In 1956 the number of Africans living outside the traditional villages (*hors du milieu coutumier*) was 2,900,000, nearly a quarter of the total population. The government recognizes this process, and seeks to provide housing for African families in the cities. Its record in this respect compares favourably with that of the Rhodesias, and is in striking contrast to that of South Africa.

Education is largely in the hands of state-aided schools operated by religious missions, mainly but not solely Catholic. In 1956 there were 1,280,000 children at school, one-tenth of the population and just about the same proportion as in Ghana. Of these 870,000 were in state-aided, 376,000 in independent and only 37,000 in government schools.[75] The government has recently opened two universities in the Congo—the State-aided Catholic free university of Lovanium (named after Louvain in Belgium) at Léopoldville, and the official university at Elisabethville. At the end of 1956 the first had seventy-three African students out of 170, the second, eight Africans out of seventy-nine. The government is definitely opposed to study by African students in Belgium. The emphasis of education in the Congo is on practical professional skills rather than theoretical learning. The government consciously aims to prevent the rise of an African intelligentsia, which, judging by British and French colonial experience, would be accessible to dangerous thoughts about independence.

Despite the great economic and educational achievement, political discontent has not been avoided. Its first expression took a religious form, in sects which proclaimed anti-European slogans. Such were the movement of Kibangu in the 1920s and the rebellion of Kitiwala in 1940-1. The growth of skilled and prosperous African *élites* has created unsatisfied aspirations. Even the most 'practical' education sharpens the intelligence, and in urban agglomerations ideas spread quickly. Those who have improved their status are often more impatient for still further improvement than are the backward for any change. The Congo has been affected by the development of AEF: Léopoldville lies across the Congo River from Brazzaville. A nationalist movement called *Abako* grew up in the capital. Its president was Kasavubu, one of the district mayors. On 5 January 1959 there was a violent outbreak in Léopoldville, led by *Abako*. Troops had to be brought in, and many Africans lost their lives. Kasavubu

and two other African mayors were arrested and brought to Belgium.
The riots were followed by a restatement of Belgian policy. On 14 January the Prime Minister, Gaston Eyskens, declared that elections would be held, with universal suffrage, for town and rural councils before the end of 1959, and that the councils would elect provincial councils in March 1960. The next stage would be the formation of a General Council of the Congo, which would be a 'skeleton' parliament. King Baudouin announced that the aim of policy was an independent Congo, to be freely associated with Belgium. The statement raised as many questions as it answered. The Belgian settlers in the Congo, who had consented to do without political representation as long as the country was directly ruled from Brussels, became alarmed at the prospect of an independent state in which they would be at the mercy of an African majority. The future development of politics in both Belgium and the Congo thus remained uncertain. It was, however, clear that the myth that Belgium had discovered a formula for ensuring progress, without the political troubles that beset other colonial Powers, had been shattered.

PORTUGUESE AFRICA

The Portuguese have been longer in tropical Africa than any other European nation. In 1950 their two main colonies of Moçambique and Angola had populations respectively of 5,780,000 and 4,145,000.

Portugal itself has had for more than thirty years a dictatorial régime. Inevitably therefore the régime in Portuguese Africa is also dictatorial. The Governors-General of the two main colonies have advisory councils, whose members are elected, but whose powers are small. In the elections there is a choice of persons, but no choice of political programmes. The councils are entitled to give advice on purely local problems, and this may be overruled.

The electors are Portuguese citizens. Great stress is laid on the fact that every civilized person has equal rights, that there is no colour bar. The colonies are an integral part of Portugal. This admirable principle depends for its practical value on the degree of opportunity available to African subjects of Portugal to make themselves civilized. In Moçambique in 1952 there were 150,000 African pupils in schools run by the Catholic missions and 258 Africans in state schools. In 1950-1 there were 13,500 pupils of all races at school in Angola. With such meagre chances of education, it is not surprising that the number of 'civilized' Africans eligible for Portuguese citizenship is small. In 1950 there were 4,353 in Moçambique and 30,039 in Angola.[76]

Portugal is a poor country, and has not been able to make much of the mineral resources of the colonies: the diamond mines of Angola are a notable exception. Attempts are being made to settle Portuguese peasants in suitable parts of the highlands of Angola. Coffee and sugar plantations have attained some measure of prosperity. One of their problems is shortage of labour. They are assisted by the authorities, who mobilize Africans who have not paid their poll-tax, and deliver them to employers. This system of recruitment is stated not to be 'forced labour', since the workers receive a contract, settling their wages and conditions of work. In practice the system lends itself to abuses, and the distinction between forced and contracted labour is by no means always clear. The government has laid down conditions for the treatment of labour, and it is possible that these will in time be effectively enforced.

Political opposition is not tolerated in Portugal, and there are therefore no political parties in the colonies. There are no signs of any African nationalist movement, and little sign even of an African intelligentsia capable of providing nationalist leadership. Unless there is a change of political régime in Portugal, and until economic development substantially affects the social structure, complete political calm is likely to prevail.

13: Other Imperialisms

THE SOVIET EMPIRE

The Soviet Union, heir to the Russia of the Tsars, is a multi-national empire. Nearly half its population are not Russians. The non-Russian peoples fall into a number of main groups.

The Ukrainians in the south and south-west, numbering more than 30 million, and the White Russians in the north-west, of whom there are some 6 million, are Slavs, belonging to the same language group as the Russians, but distinct in national consciousness. Bessarabia, in the southwest, has about 3 million Roumanians. The Lithuanians and Latvians of the Baltic region belong to the special Baltic group of languages. The third Baltic people, the Esthonians, speak a language closely related to Finnish. Esthonians and Latvians are Protestants, and belong by their history and culture to the Germanic or Scandinavian world, while Lithuanians are Catholics, and have historical and cultural associations with Poland. In Transcaucasia are two Christian peoples of ancient civilization, much older than the Russian—Georgians and Armenians.

The Soviet Union also has a large Moslem population. The most advanced of these are the Tatars of the Volga Valley, who already before 1917 had developed a strong democratic movement and had created from their own resources an excellent network of modern schools. These Tatars, whose intellectual capital was Kazan on the Volga, were pioneers of modernism in the whole Islamic world, and founders of the Turkish nationalism which later found successful expression in the Turkish Republic of Kemal Atatürk. Rather less advanced, though influenced by modern trends, were the Tatars of the Crimea, Azerbaidjan and the Bashkir steppes. Much more primitive were the Kazakh nomads of the northern steppes of Central Asia. To the south of the steppes, in Turkestan, were ancient Islamic civilizations, which had become petrified in their ancient ways at the time of the Russian conquest in the nineteenth century. In the Caucasus Mountains were a number of small nationalities, speaking a great variety of languages, mostly Moslems. Scattered across Siberia were various small tribes. In the Far East the Soviet Union includes some hundreds of thousands of Buddhist Mongols, and in the Arctic northeast some Eskimoes.

The process by which these lands came under Russian rule closely resembles the experience of other empires. The Principality of Moscow, the hard core to which the Mongol invasions of the thirteenth century had reduced Russia, expanded in much the same way as the Ile de France of the Capets or the original nucleus of Castile. By the end of the eighteenth century it had acquired the whole Ukraine and the Baltic coast, and had destroyed its once-powerful Western rival, Poland. In wars against Turks and Persians the Russian frontier was expanded across the Caucasus. In Siberia Russian colonists drove back the tribes, much as the American colonists drove back the Red Indians. In Central Asia the suppression of raids on Russian settlements, and the punishment of acts of violence against Russian subjects, led to the annexation of Turkestan and Turkmenia in much the same way as the frontiers of British India or French North Africa were expanded. Russian expansion thus was a combination of dynastic aggression in Europe and colonial expansion in Asia, neither more nor less justifiable than that of other European nations.

The Revolution of March 1917 gave the non-Russians a chance to regain their independence. The Poles and the Baltic peoples were successful. The others were reconquered by the Bolsheviks. Lenin considered himself a firm opponent of oppression by one nation of another, denounced Tsarist imperialism, and proclaimed the right of self-determination, including secession from Russia, for all its peoples. But this right had to be interpreted. In practice the Bolsheviks declared all nationalist movements not led by themselves to be *'bourgeois'* and 'reactionary'; declared that the 'toiling masses' of each nation wished to remain united with the toiling masses of Russia; and imposed their rule on them by force, using when necessary a team of puppets chosen by themselves as representatives of the true will of the masses, but often not bothering even to do this. Thus Azerbaidjan, with its rich oil, which Zinoviev cynically declared to be necessary to the Russian proletariat, social-democratic Georgia and the small nucleus of an Armenian state were reconquered in 1920 and 1921; the Ukraine was three times invaded and finally occupied by 1920; and the independence movements of the Tatars and Turkestanis were brutally suppressed.

Twenty years later, by agreement with Hitler, the Soviet forces occupied eastern Poland in September 1939, the three Baltic republics in June 1940 and Bessarabia and northern Bukovina a few weeks later. At the end of the Second World War they kept these conquests and added others. Transcarpathia was annexed from Czechoslovakia, half of East Prussia from Germany, and South Sakhalin and the Kurile Islands from Japan. The Soviet Union is the only great empire which since 1945 has seized new territory and refused to give up old conquests. And in addition to the direct annexations, the Soviet government extended its indirect rule over nearly 100 million people in Central and Eastern Europe.

Today the Soviet Union is by far the greatest imperial power in the world.*

The Soviet Union is sometimes described as a federal state. This is an error. Whereas in federal states, the regional authorities are co-ordinate with the central government, in the Soviet Union they are subordinate.[77] The states in the United States are supreme in certain defined fields. In the Soviet Union, the fifteen constituent republics have no significant powers of their own. The most that can be said is that there is a measure of devolution of authority from the central to the republican governments. The constitution gives the republics the right to secede. But if any citizen were to advocate secession, he would be guilty of counter-revolutionary activity, which is punished with special severity under Article 58 of the Criminal Code. Moreover, even the element of decentralization of government organs is of small importance, for government is entirely in the hands of members of the communist party, and the party is highly centralized.

In the first years of the régime the communist leaders equally denounced Russian nationalism (or 'Great Power chauvinism') and non-Russian 'bourgeois' nationalism. But by the 1930s it was only non-Russian nationalism that was attacked in practice. This was not because the communists had become Russian nationalists, but because Russian national feeling did not threaten the State, whose governing cadres were composed of Russians, but non-Russian nationalism might. From the 1930s a definite trend of Russification is to be observed. The only exceptions are Georgia and Armenia, where the key posts have remained in the hands of local nationals, and the local languages have had definite priority.

An interesting example is the use of Russian officials in the party and state machines of the four Central Asian republics. Here the first secretaries of the republican central committees, and of the provincial committees within the republics, are usually Asians, but the second secretaries are normally Russians, as are also the heads of department in the central committee offices. Prime Ministers are Asians, but at least one Deputy Prime Minister is a Russian. Most Ministers are Asians (the Minister of State Security being usually an exception), but many Deputy Ministers and heads of ministerial departments are Russians.

Cultural Russification is also important. It is, of course, only reasonable

* The population of all British colonial and protected territories in 1959 amounted to around 80 million. When Nigeria becomes independent in 1960, this will be reduced to less than 45 million. French colonies have a population of around 30 million: if Algeria is added to them, this brings it up to nearly 40 million. The non-Russian subjects of the Soviet Union can hardly be much less than 90 million. The Soviet colonial empire in Europe has another 95 million subjects. All these figures are approximate, but the comparative picture is correct.

that Russian should be the language of State, and that holders of responsible official posts should be required to know it. More dubious is the use of Russian as the language of instruction in non-Russian universities. Soviet encouragement of minor languages is also less liberal than it appears at first sight. Dialects have been elevated into separate languages, in order to destroy the sense of cultural unity which existed among the people of Turkestan, and to make each group more dependent on the Russians. There has been a massive introduction of Russian words into Asian languages, which surpasses the admitted necessity of creating modern technical and scientific vocabularies, and has an unmistakable political purpose. The introduction of the Cyrillic alphabet for the Turkic and Iranian languages of the Soviet Union cuts them off from the literature of their own past, which was written in the Arabic alphabet still used by their kinsmen in neighbouring Persia and Afghanistan, and from all that is published in modern Turkey, where the Latin alphabet is in use. In the post-war years several of the national epic poems of the Turkic peoples were suppressed on the ground that they expressed a reactionary nationalistic spirit. There was also a systematic falsification of the history of the non-Russian peoples. Polish influences in Ukrainian history were minimized, Poland represented as the constant enemy of the Ukrainians, and Muscovy as their generous friend. The leaders of the Caucasian and Kazakh peoples in their resistance to Russian conquest in the nineteenth century were said to be agents of British and Turkish imperialism. The conquest itself, which Lenin and the early Bolsheviks had always denounced as a crime of Tsarist imperialism, was now interpreted as an objectively progressive event, as it expedited the social development of these peoples from feudalism towards the *bourgeois* stage, and because it brought them into contact with the superior culture of 'the great Russian nation'. This is nothing but a quasi-Marxist version of Kipling's doctrine of the White Man's Burden, or of President McKinley's decision to uplift the Filipinos. It may indeed be regarded as yet another aspect of the Victorian outlook of the rising State *bourgeoisie* of Soviet society to which we have already referred in another connexion.

There is also an economic aspect to the question. The Soviet régime has exploited the vast natural resources of its huge land to create a gigantic industrial power. Among these resources are those which are derived from the homelands of the non-Russian peoples—the oil of Azerbaidjan and Bashkiria, the cotton of Central Asia. The Asian peasants and workers have toiled to produce these resources, but they have had no say in their disposal. When the British urged the Egyptians to concentrate on cotton crops, at the cost of grain, and imported food supplies, this was widely denounced as an example of colonialist specialization, in the interest of the ruling race. But this is exactly what the Soviet government has done in Central Asia, with varying intensity in different periods. There is, however, this difference, that the owners of the Egyptian cotton fields got good prices, and that the British, unlike the Soviet authorities, never forced their subjects to obey by threatening to withhold their food supplies. The Soviet government has encouraged colonization by Russian and Ukrainian peasants in the Kazakh steppes. The first wave was in the late 1930s, after the artificial famine created by collectivization had wiped out a third of the Kazakh nation.[78] The second was in the late 1950s, in connexion with Khrushchov's campaign for the development of the 'virgin lands'. The Kazakhs are now a minority within their own republic.

The most brutal acts of dispossession were, however, the mass deportations of the 1940s. Hundreds of thousands, including especially the teachers and Protestant clergy, were deported from the three Baltic States in 1940-1. Soon after the German invasion the whole population of the Volga German republic, 400,000 persons, were removed: no attempt was made to separate loyal citizens from those who might have sympathy for Hitler. In 1944 the Crimean Tatars, the Buddhist Kalmyks and four Caucasian peoples—Chechens, Ingush, Balkars and Karachays—were torn from their homes, on the ground that some of their number had given aid to the German invaders and that the others had not resisted. At least in the case of the Chechens enough is known of the circumstances of their removal to make it certain that thousands perished either by shooting or by exposure to cold and hunger.[79] It would be a parallel if the British, on returning to Burma, many of whose inhabitants had co-operated with the invading Japanese, had deported the whole Burmese nation to Arctic Canada. In 1955 Chechens were allowed to return to their homes: it seems that only a small number were able to make use of this permission.

The nationality policy of the Soviet government can be described as Russification. But it would be wrong to over-emphasize the continuity with Imperial Russian policies. Tsarist politicians were genuine Russian nationalists, keen to force their culture on more backward peoples. But the Soviet communists are not Russian nationalists. Russification is for them a means, not an end. They are equally hostile to all forms of nationalism. National consciousness, like religion, is to them a superstition which will wither away as the new socialist consciousness moulds the minds of the people. Until this has come to pass, national prejudices may be manipulated to the advantage of the Soviet régime, encouraged or damped down as circumstances dictate. One may put it a different way. Totalitarianism is implacably opposed to all associations between its subjects which are not controlled by it and do not owe their origin to it. Membership of a nation or of a religious community are such associations. They are the result of birth, geographical location and family tradition. It is thus understandable that the Soviet rulers should wage incessant war against nationalism and religion—against Islam no less than against Christianity. But the war is conducted on behalf not of the Russian nation, but of the totalitarian State and of the concept of the new Soviet man and the new Soviet patriotism. This policy is imperialist, but it is a totalitarian not a national form of imperialism.

It is difficult to decide how successful the policy has been. It is often argued that as the Soviet Union becomes ever more industrialized and urbanized, all previous nationalism will disappear. A comparison is made with the United States. Just as persons of many different ethnic origins became absorbed in a new American nation, so, it is argued, will Russians and Ukrainians, Balts and Kirgiz, be merged in a new Soviet nation. What happened in Pittsburgh will happen in Baku and Sverdlovsk; what happened on the farms of Minnesota will repeat itself in the virgin lands of Kazakhstan. But the history of America is quite different from that of Russia. From the beginning the legal and social institutions of America, as well as the language, derived from one historical tradition. All non-British elements which entered the United States were small minorities at the time of their arrival: they were many small streams flowing into an Anglo-Saxon lake. In time they modified the contents of the lake, but the lake was always far greater than any of the streams. America today is very different from England, and it owes much to the late-comers. But the late-comers had to merge themselves with what they found on arrival, and what they found had not been created by them. After they had merged themselves, they had no separate existence of their own. The only large exception are the negroes, and they are a very special problem. The non-Russian peoples of the Soviet Union have never been in this situation. It is true that some small tribes of Siberia and the Arctic north-east have been destroyed, or are disappearing, undergoing essentially the same fate as the North American Indians. But the main nations remain, each possessing not only its language and history, but its own national territory, in which it remains in the majority: the Kazakhs are the only major exception. The task of creating a new synthetic patriotism must be infinitely more difficult in the Soviet Union than in the United States.

Another unanswerable question concerns the attitude of the non-Russian, especially of the Asian, intelligentsias to the régime. There can be no doubt of the material progress of Central Asia in comparison with Tsarist times. Young Uzbeks can now obtain a higher education and rise to responsible positions in bureaucracy, industrial management and scientific work. In 1957 an Uzbek, Muhitdinov, was even appointed to the Presidium of the communist party. The new Central Asian intelligentsia, which numbers hundreds of thousands, owes its status and opportunities to the Soviet régime. But does it follow that it is grateful? The Roumanian and Slovak national movements against Hungary before 1914 were led by men who had passed through the Hungarian educational system, and many of whom had achieved material success for themselves. Indians and Indochinese in the late nineteenth and early twentieth centuries were able to get a modern education only thanks to the British and French imperial systems. But neither Nehru nor Ho Chi Minh, each in his way a fine flower of European culture, became an apologist for colonial rule. In Soviet Central Asia no political movements like the Indian National Congress can be organized. But this proves only that the Soviet security police is efficient, not that the desire for independence does not exist. There is no direct evidence either way, and the indirect evidence is inconclusive. But in the light of the historical experience of every colonial Empire to date, it would be astonishing if the intelligentsia of the non-Russian peoples did not have such a desire, and if further economic and cultural development did not strengthen it.

NATIONAL DOMINATION IN ASIA

The great historical empires of Asia, and the newly independent states, have problems of national minorities and national domination.

The most obvious case is China. The Chinese Empire included millions of subjects belonging to Turkic peoples. China also exercised at various times sovereignty over Tibet, Korea, Tonkin and parts of Central Asia. The Chinese communists took over their Imperial predecessors' claims to Sinkiang, and invaded Tibet. In general they have based their nationality policy on the Soviet model. In May 1947 an Inner Mongolian Autonomous Region was created with its capital at Ulanhot, its leading figure a Mongol communist named Ulanfu. In 1952 Suiyuan Province, and in 1956 part of Ninghsia Province, were added. In this whole region the Mongols amounted to 1 million out of a population of 6 million. Sinkiang, populated by Turkic peoples of whom the most numerous are the Uigurs, was an object of contention between Russia and China already in the nineteenth century. From 1934 to 1943 it was under Soviet influence, but for the following five years enjoyed an autonomy without precedent in modern times, free from Soviet Russian, Chinese Kuomintang or Chinese communist control. This ended with the communist reconquest in 1949-50. The following period of reorganization culminated with the proclamation in September 1955 of the Sinkiang-Uigur Autonomous Area, the leading figure in which was the Soviet-trained Uigur Saifuddin. Periodical complaints in the Chinese press in subsequent years about *bourgeois* nationalism' show that there is still opposition to Peking's authority. In the southwest of China there are numerous autonomous areas designed for various minorities related by language and culture to the Thai people of Siam. Finally, in Tibet, which the Chinese conquered in 1950, they were at first more cautious. Finding the Tibetans devoted to their ancient theocratic form of society, and unwilling to be 'liberated' from the 'reactionary priesthood' by brash young Chinese party agitators, the Peking government respected the outward forms of Tibetan institutions, while steadily seeking to deprive them of their content by pressure from without and undermining from within. In March 1959, however, an open conflict developed, Chinese troops seized the capital, Lhasa, by force, and the Dalai Lama, spiritual and secular head of his people, fled into exile in India.

Chinese nationality policy theoretically disapproves of both 'Great Han chauvinism' and 'local nationalism', just as Soviet policy denounces 'Great Russian chauvinism' and 'local nationalism'. The smaller nationalities are supposed to use their languages freely, to be ruled by compatriots, and to have a culture 'national in form but socialist in content'. In practice they are subjected to the totalitarian State machine whose centre is Peking and whose agents are Chinese. Their children will grow up as Tibetan- or Uigur- or Miao-speaking *homines totalitarienses*, bound on all possible occasions to extol the superior culture of the Han elder brother. To this effective subjection, which closely parallels the situation of non-Russians in the Soviet Union, and progressively deprives them of any real national identity, must be added in the case of China the steady colonization of their lands by Chinese immigrants, which will in a few decades make them minorities even within their own narrower homelands. In the Soviet Union this fate has overtaken the Kazakhs and Bashkirs and some of the smaller Siberian peoples, but has hitherto spared the peoples of European Russia, the Caucasus and Central Asia.

An important instrument of Chinese policy are the overseas Chinese, who amount to some 12 million, of whom Siam, Indochina and Malaya have about 3 million each. The Chinese minorities play a very large part in commerce: their role in South-East Asia is similar to the role of the Jews in Eastern Europe before the Second World War. They were largely controlled by Kuomintang agents before the war. Since 1949, communism has won great influence, especially among the youth. The Chinese communities have long maintained schools of their own, and these are well penetrated by communists. The overseas Chinese, whether communist or not, are divided in loyalty between China and their land of residence. In Indonesia an agreement was signed with the Peking government in April 1955, by which individuals were to be allowed to choose their citizenship freely. But as it contained provisions unsatisfactory to Indonesian nationalist opinion, it was never ratified.

India too has its emigrants, scattered over a wider portion of the earth than the Chinese. The overseas Indians are descendants of labourers brought by the British to work in Africa or in various island possessions. Many of them have since done well as merchants and small business-men, possessing in somewhat lesser degree the commercial qualities of the Chinese. The largest Indian community is in Ceylon, but those in Burma and Malaya are also substantial. In Africa the largest is in the Union of South Africa, the second largest in the island of Mauritius, while the three British East African territories have considerable Indian minorities. In the Caribbean, Indians form more than a third of the population in British Guiana and Trinidad. In the Pacific just under half the population of the Fiji islands is Indian.* It cannot be argued that the government of independent India has tried to use the overseas Indians as an instrument of an imperialist foreign policy. The Indian government has objected to the treatment of Indians by the South African government, but it has asked only that they should be given rights as citizens of South Africa—a request which the disciples of *apartheid* can, of course, not grant. In Africa the Indian government has urged Indians to give their support to African political movements. This advice may be objectionable to colonial administrations, but it can hardly be called imperialist. It must be added that the Africans have shown little affection for their Indian would-be friends. The attacks by Nyasaland Africans or Durban Zulus on Indian shops recall the pogroms of Jewish shops in Russia or Roumania.

Whether the Indian occupation of Kashmir is an example of imperialism is a matter of opinion. The primitive Naga peoples of the north-eastern provinces have been forced against their will to submit to Indian authority

* In Ceylon in 1953 about 2 million out of 8 million population were of Indian origin, of whom about 1 million were immigrants from India within recent times. In Burma the Indian population was about a million in 1931, but was greatly reduced by evacuation, in the face of Japanese invasion, in 1942. Post-war Burmese official figures show 323,000 Indians and Pakistanis, but unofficial estimates are as high as 800,000. Malaya in 1954 had 795,000 Indians (including Singapore). In South Africa there were 367,000 Asiatics in 1951; in Kenya 90,000 in 1948; in Tanganyika 44,000 in 1952; in Uganda 34,000 in 1948. The majority of the population of Mauritius, estimated as 579,000 in 1956, was Indian. In Trinidad Indians were 196,000 out of 560,000 in 1946; in British Guiana 163,000 out of 376,000 in the same year. In Fiji the Indians were estimated at 177,000 (49% of the total population) at the end of 1957.

and methods of government. In both cases the issues are complicated. It can only be said that the outside observer would be more inclined to give India the benefit of the doubt if Mr. Nehru were a little less lavish with his condemnation of imperialism in other parts of the world.

Another disputable case is the claim of Indonesia to West New Guinea, still ruled by the Netherlands. The island of New Guinea, with a population of about 3,500,000, is divided into a Dutch colony, an Australian colony and an United Nations Trust Territory administered by Australia. The people consist mainly of extremely primitive nomadic or mountain tribes, whose languages differ greatly from each other, but whose way of life is approximately the same in the three administrative sections of the great island. There are some thousands of Javanese and other Indonesians in Dutch New Guinea, among whom the political ideas prevalent in Indonesia are effective, and who would like the territory to be united with Indonesia, in which case they themselves would occupy more profitable and dignified situations. The indigenous New Guinea people, however, have absolutely nothing in common with the Indonesians. Their language, civilization, religion and customs are utterly different. There is no reason whatever to believe that they wish to join Indonesia.

The Indonesian claim is a curious mixture of legalism and imperialism. West New Guinea formed part of the Netherlands East Indies; therefore, they argue, it should form part of Indonesia. The Dutch are Europeans ruling a colony; therefore they should go. On the grounds of nationality, Indonesia has a far stronger case to annex British Borneo, Portuguese Timor, or even Malaya, but it has made no official claim for these. Union of West New Guinea with Indonesia would arbitrarily cut off its people from their kinsmen in the Australian territories, to which also Indonesia lays no claim. Dutch rule is foreign rule, but so would be Indonesian rule. That the quality of Dutch rule is superior to that of Javanese, which has failed so far to hold the existing Indonesian Republic together, can hardly be doubted. The Dutch gain small advantage from keeping New Guinea, but their obligations to their primitive subjects prevent them from handing them over to ruthless exploitation by Javanese politicians. The Dutch attitude is supported by Australia, which does not wish to see the unruly Indonesian state brought closer to its own borders. But anti-European racialists all over the world make the Indonesian case their own and denounce the Dutch.

THE AMERICAN INDIAN

The name 'American Indians' has been given to the great variety of peoples, differing in racial origin, language and customs, which inhabited the Americas before the advent of the Europeans. Their fate has been more tragic than that of the African negroes. Both in Anglo-Saxon and in Latin America great numbers were exterminated. Of the survivors, those in the north were soon far outnumbered by the European immigrants who built a new civilization that ignored them, while those in the south were partly reduced to various forms of slavery and partly absorbed by intermarriage in new nations founded on the religious and social values of the conquerors.

In Canada in 1954 there were 150,000 Indians, mostly living in reserves, acquiring civil rights only when they finally sever their relations with their separate community. In the United States in 1951 there were more than 400,000. It is estimated that the original Indian population in the United States was rather less than 1 million and fell to less than 300,000 in the mid-nineteenth century. Some Indian tribes, however, are today much more numerous than in the past, especially the Navajos of Arizona and New Mexico, who numbered about 10,000 in 1865 and today exceed 80,000. In the colonial period the Indian tribes enjoyed some protection from the British Crown for their lands and customs, and this was maintained by the federal government for the first forty years of independence. It was Andrew Jackson who ceased to use federal powers to prevent the expulsion of the Indians from their lands by European settlers. In the second half of the nineteenth century there was a melancholy series of broken promises and massacres. In the twentieth century conditions improved, and a landmark was the Indian Reorganization Act of 1934, a result of the New Deal. Under this Act Indian forms of self-government and land tenure were recognized, and the Indians were allowed and encouraged to create their own organizations.

In the 1950s there has been a reaction against this policy. The trend has been towards the 'termination' of the federal tutelage over the Indians. This change of policy has aroused much controversy. Its defenders undoubtedly have excellent motives. They argue that it is time that the Indians were raised from an inferior status to one of full equality, that they were treated not as children, but as full American citizens. It is also clear that the overpopulated Navajo areas cannot support their people, that jobs must be found for them in the American economy. Admirable efforts are being made to train Indians for modern urban life. That Indians can do well in modern cities is shown by the example of the Canadian Mohawks, whose home is west of Montreal, and who earn high wages as workers at high altitude on the skyscrapers of Montreal, New York and Detroit. But no simple formula will deal with the Indian problem. Assimilation into modern American civilization may be a good solution for some, but to force others to abandon their cultural identity is unjust and cruel. Dubious motives can be found behind some of the advocacy of 'termination', such as a desire merely to save public money by cutting down welfare services for Indians in depressed areas, or the desire of American business to get control of valuable resources in Indian areas.* The special conditions of each of the many Indian tribes need to be taken into account, and no single overall policy is valid. In the last decades the United States record in the Indian problem has been comparatively good, but it cannot be said that justice has yet been done.

The Indians of Latin America are far more numerous, and their situation is both worse and less documented. The definition of 'Indian' is not easy. The customary distinction between pure European, pure Indian and *mestizo* (or racially mixed) is not satisfactory. Statistics of Latin American states also throw little light on the problem. It is estimated that in Guatemala, Ecuador, Peru and Bolivia half or more of the population are Indians, speaking Indian languages, of which the most important are Quechua in Peru and Bolivia, and Aymará in Bolivia. Paraguay is considered a predominantly *mestizo* country, but for a large part of these *mestizos* the first language is not Spanish but Guaraní, and the *mestizo* of Paraguay has a much greater proportion of Indian blood than the *mestizo* of Colombia or Chile. In Mexico the census of 1940 showed 7·6% of the population speaking only an Indian language, 6·6% speaking both an Indian language and Spanish, and 37% speaking only Spanish, but living in an Indian manner (dress, food, dwelling and way of life). Thus 52% of the population could be described as 'living at the Indian-colonial level'.[80] In all the Andean republics the borderline between Indian and *mestizo* is blurred.

The Indians live for the most part in misery and squalor, and in fact sullenly withdraw into a life of their own which has little contact with the 'national' life of their country. It is not easy to draw the line between social injustice and national oppression. Certainly the fate of the Indians is bound up with land reform and the development of education. The proportion of illiterates among the population aged ten or more in 1950 was 44% in Ecuador, 69% in Bolivia and 70% in Guatemala. The land reforms planned in Guatemala and carried out in Bolivia were certainly designed

*In connexion with the 'termination' of the status of the Klamath Indians in Oregon in 1954, and the sale of their valuable timber resources to business interests, the comment was made that this seemed likely to lead to 'a brief wild spending spree by the Indians, followed by the dumping on the state of a mass of paupers' (Oliver La Farge, 'Termination of Federal Supervision: Disintegration and the American Indians', in *Annals* of the American Academy of Political and Social Sciences, May 1957, p. 45).

to benefit the Indians, and they gained greatly from the land reforms of Lázaro Cárdenas in Mexico. But for the poorest and most remote Indians the language barrier forms a formidable additional obstacle to progress. Where schools exist in the Andean republics, the instruction is in Spanish. Scarcity and inaccessibility of reliable information makes it hard to judge how much racial prejudice exists. But American missionary students in the 1930s in southern Peru found that Indian schoolchildren were made to walk behind white children and to carry their books and knapsacks for them, and that there were separate church services for the two races, as whites refused to sit with Indians.[81]

The only Latin American country whose government for many years has publicly identified itself with the Indian cause, and has praised its own past Indian civilization, is Mexico. In Peru the APRA movement put forward the ideal of Indoamerica in place of Latin America. The Peruvian Marxist José Mariátegui wrote some original and interesting work on the Indian question and its connexion with the land question.[82] The APRA leader Haya de la Torre, who was at first influenced by Marxism as well as by the ideology of the Mexican Revolution, has always laid great stress on the specific characteristics of Latin American revolutionary forces, which he believes to be quite different from those of nineteenth-century Europe, from which modern socialist theory is mainly derived.[83] But when APRA shared power in Peru from 1945 to 1947 it was unable to achieve anything on behalf of the Indians, nor has its new freedom since 1956 produced any marked result. The Guatemalan revolutionary régime of 1944-54 was diverted in the direction of subservience to international communism, and when it was overthrown reforms were shelved. In Bolivia the MNR since 1952 has strongly appealed for Indian support, but how much practical good it has done for the Indians is a matter of dispute.

The whole subject is obscured by inadequate information and strong partisan feelings. But enough is known to make it clear that great misery and oppression exist, that millions of Indians are at best second-class citizens, and that many Latin American governments which generously display their 'anti-imperialist' idealism in international gatherings would do well to pay more attention to remedying the sufferings of their own subjects.

14: Racialism

RACIAL CONFLICTS IN SOUTH AFRICA

South Africa, like the United States, owes its origin as a state to colonization by Europeans on extra-European soil, but has become fully independent. The problems of racial domination that beset South African society have nothing to do with control by a distant metropolitan Power, but arise from conflicts between national or racial groups whose only home is South Africa, who have no allegiance across the ocean. In particular, the Afrikaners have been as long in the Cape as have the Bantu. Though they are descended from Dutch colonists, they have long since diverged in national character and outlook from the Dutch in Holland, and their Afrikaans language is quite distinct from Dutch. They no more consider themselves Dutchmen than the Americans consider themselves Englishmen. In the United States the original inhabitants were exterminated or numerically overwhelmed by the immigrants, and these were absorbed into an increasingly homogeneous new nation: even the negroes unquesntioably belong to the American nation. In South Africa, with the exception of the Bushmen, the African population was neither destroyed nor outnumbered, and the different races were neither physically nor culturally welded together. English and Afrikaners remain divided against each other, both face the Africans in unresolved antagonism, and the Indian immigrants are separated from all three. The fourth group are the Cape Coloureds, descended from unions of Europeans with Africans or Malays. In short, though South Africa is a sovereign and potentially great country, there is no South African nation.

One of the main sources of conflict between English and Boers in the past was the difference in political attitudes to the Africans. Emancipation of slaves by the British Parliament in 1833 was one of the main reasons for the Great Trek which began in 1837. Whereas in America the Southern States fought for the right to secede from the Union, the Voortrekkers left their homes and moved into the interior, to found new states at the expense of the Bantu. But this heroic migration did not in the end avoid the necessity for wars with the English. There was another aspect to the relationship between the two nations. This was the conflict between the primitive and pious farming society of the Boers and the secular expansive capitalism of the British. Here too there is some parallel with the relations between North and South in the United States. The discovery of gold in the Transvaal, however, made the conflict mortally dangerous. Whatever the verdict of the specialist historian on the particular actions of Rhodes

IMPERIALISM 311

or Chamberlain, Milner or Kruger, it can hardly be denied that the Boer War of 1899-1902 shares with the Russo-Japanese War of 1904-5 the unenviable distinction of coming closest to the simple Marxist pattern of imperialist war. The Boer War caused a smaller volume of human suffering than the American Civil War, but its effects on the minds of the defeated have hardly been less bitter or less persistent.

The Act of 1909, by which the British Liberal government sought to reconcile victors and vanquished, has usually been regarded as an example of generous statesmanship. Indeed, for the next three decades it seemed that reconciliation was becoming reality. The South African Party of General Smuts had both Afrikaner and English support, and the Nationalist Party of Hertzog, though its political rival, was not a bitter enemy. In 1934 the two parties fused to form the United Party. This appeared to strengthen national unity and to promote peaceful democratic development. But it had two consequences which can hardly be described in these terms.

The price of Hertzog's fusion with Smuts was the abolition of the Cape native franchise. Since 1852 all citizens of Cape Province, regardless of race, had been entitled to the vote if they satisfied a specified property qualification. The Act of 1909 provided that this could not be changed except by a two-thirds vote of both Houses of the Union Parliament sitting together, but it did not extend the right to vote to non-Europeans outside Cape Province. In 1936 the necessary two-thirds vote was found, with Smuts' agreement, to abolish the direct African vote. Instead of having a vote on the common roll in whatever constituency they were registered, the Africans now voted on a separate roll, in three constituencies for the whole province, to elect three Europeans to represent specifically their interests in the Union Parliament. At the same time a Natives' Representative Council was set up, with some elected and some appointed members, to advise on legislation affecting Africans. In practice this body was ignored by the authorities. As for the Cape Coloureds, they remained on the common roll.

The second effect of the fusion of 1934 was that the more radical Afrikaner nationalists split from Hertzog and, led by Dr. Malan, formed a new Nationalist Party. This nucleus of bitter men, determined to break the connexion with Britain, to set up an Afrikaner republic, and to apply far more radical solutions to racial problems, soon gained ground among the Afrikaner people. Its success was largely due to the industrialization of the country, which brought thousands of young Afrikaners from the farms into the cities, where they faced the danger that their low standard of living would be forced yet lower by competition of cheap African labour. Even more than in the Southern States in America, the poor white became the driving force behind anti-African racialism. The radicalism and bitterness of the Nationalists were also increased by the growth of fascism in Europe and by Hitler's early victories in the Second World War. A considerable element in the Nationalist Party looked to Hitler to save South Africa from the triple menace of the English, the Jews and the Africans.

The defeat of Hitler did not discredit the Nationalist leaders among the Afrikaner masses, though it caused them somewhat to moderate their hostility to their English-speaking compatriots. When the war ended, General Smuts, whose United Party had won the election of 1943 in an atmosphere in which patriotic enthusiasm was the dominant though not the universal mood, was at the height of his prestige. But the tide soon turned, and at the election of May 1948 the Nationalists won a small absolute majority. This was increased and sustained at the elections of 1953 and 1958. No political forces are visible which seem likely to break their supremacy in the foreseeable future.

The policies of the Nationalists towards the non-European majority of the population are based on the principle of *apartheid*. This principle is extremely difficult to discuss, as it operates on two quite different levels, of reasoned intellectual argument and of irrational emotional prejudice.

At the first level it is maintained simply that white and black have quite different civilizations, which must be kept rigidly apart. Europeans can and must respect the Bantu, and help them to build up their own separate society. The Bantu must have their own territory, within which they may develop their own agricultural and industrial economy and possess their own self-governing institutions. Much-needed improvements in agricultural methods, and the creation of new industries, will require large investments, and the Europeans must accept serious economic sacrifices to help the Bantu. Apart from this, the Bantu will, as previously, be allowed to earn their living by labour in the European areas, but they will be discouraged, even though they cannot be entirely prevented, from settling permanently there, and in any case they will possess no political rights or institutions in the European area. Such approximately is the intellectual theory of *apartheid*, which is sincerely believed by many honest Afrikaners who believe themselves to be good friends of the Bantu, concerned to save them from a false Europeanization which can only deprive them of their own true character and put nothing in its place.

At the lower and irrational level, however, *apartheid* is simply a doctrine of race superiority. The Natives are an inferior race, whose inferiority, according to Dutch Reformed Church doctrine, is confirmed in the Bible.

It is their function to be servants of the Europeans. In all respects their interests must be subordinated to European interests. Under no circumstances must they be given any opportunity of acquiring European skills or responsibilities, of showing whether they are capable of competing with Europeans on their own ground: the doctrine of permanent and inborn inferiority must not be put to the test. This point of view, extremely popular among Afrikaner Nationalists, especially perhaps among the poor whites, is the principle of European 'boss-ship', *baasskap*.

Even if *apartheid* doctrine is taken in its most enlightened theoretical form, two points should at once be noted which are not compatible with equal status between two civilizations. First, it is clear that though in their own areas the Bantu will have their own self-government, yet these institutions are subordinated to the central government of the country, in which the Bantu are to have no share. The Bantu areas are not to have the degree of independence possessed by the states under the American Constitution. Secondly, though the Bantu form two-thirds of the population of South Africa, the Native Reserves, which are to be the homeland of the Bantu, and which consist of rather less than the original area in which the various tribes were living at the time when they were conquered by the Europeans, supplemented by land purchased for the Africans under the Native Trust and Land Act of 1936, amount to less than 10% of the area of the Union. If the full amount of land whose purchase is authorized by the 1936 Act is eventually acquired, they will amount to 13%.

In 1951 South Africa had a population of 12,646,000. Of these, 8,535,000 (67·5%) were Bantu; 2,643,000 (20·9%) were Europeans, of whom roughly two-thirds were Afrikaners and one-third English-speaking; 1,103,000 (8·7%) were Coloureds, in Cape Province only; and 367,000 (2·9%) were Asians, principally Indians in Natal.

Of the Bantu population, 42·6% were living in the Reserves, 30·3% on European farms and 27·1% in towns. The total number of Bantu living in towns was 2,312,000. When allowance is made for migrant labourers from outside the Union (mainly from Portuguese Africa and from Nyasaland) and for South African Bantu whose families are still resident in the Reserves, it is estimated that the number of Bantu permanently settled in the towns can hardly be less than 1,500,000. The rapid growth of industry in the Union has caused a very rapid increase in urban population of all races in the last decades. In the interests of the Union as a whole, this growth must continue. Economic trends, in fact, push towards ever closer integration of Europeans and Bantu in a modern economy, while Nationalist doctrine insists on their separation. The essence of the difference between United Party and Nationalist policy is that the former recognize the economic trend and the latter insist on the primacy of dogma. It should not be thought that the United Party leaders are more humanitarian than the Nationalists: it may even be argued that they are less so. They are concerned with the necessity of a labour force, not with the rights of the Africans as individual human beings. They are equally determined to ensure the permanent political subjection of the Africans, and are equally haunted by the sexual fear of miscegenation, which in South Africa as much as in the South of the United States lies at the root of racial feeling. But they are at least more realistic about economic prospects. To develop industry on a basis of temporary migrant labour from the Reserves, while making it even more difficult for Africans to settle with their families in the towns where they work, would not only increase the costs and difficulties of the industrialists but also perpetuate the mass prostitution and violent crime which have made Johannesburg one of the most unhappy cities of the world. To improve agricultural methods in the already overcrowded Reserves will require coercion and interference with African customs on a vast scale. Such interference can be successful only if the Africans have confidence in those responsible for it, and are convinced that it is in their interest: in present political conditions this is out of the question. To create new industries in the Reserves will be very expensive, and the economic prospects of such industries are dubious. The Commission for the socio-economic development of the Bantu areas, appointed by the Government under the chairmanship of Professor F. R. Tomlinson, which reported on 1 October 1954, estimated that the cost of the comparatively modest improvements which it proposed would be £104 million for the first ten years, and this is a rather optimistic estimate. It is not unfair to conclude that the Report, which is of great interest and is the work of learned and conscientious men, showed that the contradictions between *apartheid* doctrine and economic needs are irreconcilable—though it was certainly not the purpose of the Commission to show this.[84]

In practice the Nationalist governments since 1948 have ignored the declared long-term economic policies and constructive social purposes of their doctrine, and have contented themselves with negative and repressive measures, which have contributed not so much to the separation of European and Bantu civilization as to emphasizing the inferior status of the Bantu within existing South African society. Previous legislation that discriminated in various ways against Africans was reinforced, and was applied more inflexibly and more brutally by the police than in the past. The Coloured group suffered several new blows. Both marriages and extra-marital relationships between Coloureds and Europeans were made a criminal offence. The Group Areas Act of 1950, designed to ensure complete residential segregation between the races, had little effect on Africans, who were already separated from the others, but threatened the more prosperous families of Coloureds or Asians who lived in districts to be reserved for Europeans. The Nationalists also decided to deprive the Coloureds of their vote on the common roll in Cape Province, which, like the previous similar right of the Cape Africans, had been 'entrenched' in the Constitution by the Act of Union of 1909. When the Nationalists in 1951 introduced a bill to this effect, the United Party opposed it, and the necessary two-thirds majority could not be obtained. The bill was declared null and void by the Supreme Court in March 1952. This opened a constitutional crisis which lasted four years. The Nationalists finally achieved their aim in 1958 by changing the numbers and composition of the Upper House of Parliament—the Senate. The number of Senators was increased from forty-eight to eighty-nine, and the composition was so changed that the number of seats going to Nationalists increased from thirty to seventy-seven. The Nationalists thus obtained their two-thirds majority in joint session of both Houses, and passed their Separate Representation of Voters Act. The constitutionality of the Senate bill was itself challenged, but on 10 November 1956 the Supreme Court upheld it.

Perhaps the most serious blow struck by the Nationalists against the Bantu has been in the field of education. African education certainly left much to be desired in quality. The average government expenditure per school child in 1953 was £44 for Europeans and £7 for Africans. Nevertheless, the South African achievement in educating Africans could compare well with many other African or Asian states. In 1953 there were 883,896 African children at school, about 41% of those of school age. The great majority were in State-aided mission schools. In 1953 the Nationalists introduced a bill by which the Union Government would take over control of African education. It proposed to give local Bantu authorities in the Reserves a greater share in their finance and administration, but it was to supervise more directly the content of education, and to see that it was more closely related to the traditions and distinctive characteristics of the population. The meaning of this was revealed in a speech by Dr. Verwoerd, Minister of Native Affairs, in the parliamentary debate on the bill. He argued that it was undesirable to give Africans an education that creates expectations which cannot be fulfilled, or which trains them for professions that are not open to them. The Minister was in fact adopting the principles of the Imperial Russian Minister of Education of the late nineteenth century, who was concerned to prevent children of 'coachmen, washerwomen, cooks and people of that sort' from getting ideas above their station.* The reactions of the religious communities that had been responsible for African education varied. The Dutch Reformed Churches welcomed the decision. The Methodists, Church of Scotland and American Board of Missions accepted under protest. The Anglican Bishop of Johannesburg closed all Anglican African schools in his diocese. The Roman Catholic Church decided to do without State aid and to maintain its independent schools from its own funds. The government also decided to decree complete segregation in all South African universities, while creating separate colleges for Africans, with markedly inferior resources.† Despite bitter opposition from the two universities which had hitherto admitted African students to their lecture-rooms on equal terms with white students (Capetown and Witwatersrand), and protests from academic organizations in many parts of the world, the government passed its bill to this effect on 30 April 1959.

The Nationalists also struck a blow against civil liberties by the Suppression of Communism Bill of June 1950. Communism did not in fact represent a serious threat. The fact that one of the three special seats in Cape Province elected by Africans was held by a communist reflected the desperate state of mind to which discrimination and oppression had driven the Africans rather than any threat to the state. But in any case the Nationalists were concerned less to suppress what little communist activity there was than to create a political weapon to be used against other opponents. It is capable of wide interpretation, and has already been used against persons who are certainly not communists.‡

Non-Europeans have only small indirect representation in Parliament, and cannot be said to have any influence on government policy at all. There are, however, extra-parliamentary political organizations—the African National Congress, the South African Indian Congress and

---

* See above, pp. 170, 172.

† In 1954 there were 214 non-European students at Witwatersrand and 271 at Capetown. There were also 327 non-Europeans admitted to separate class-rooms in the University of Natal, 370 Africans at the all-African college of Fort Hare, and 1,145 non-Europeans taking correspondence courses at the University of South Africa in Pretoria.

‡The Bill defined four purposes of communist activity, by which it could be identified. One of these was 'bringing about any political, industrial, social or economic change within the Union by the promotion of disturbances or disorder, by unlawful acts or omissions or by the threat of such acts or omissions or by means which include the promotion of disturbance or disorder, or such acts or omissions or threat'. Organizations promoting such purposes may be dissolved, and their assets taken over by a liquidator appointed by the government, who may also compose lists of office-bearers, members and active supporters of such organizations. The Minister of Justice may then forbid persons so 'named' to take part in any specified activity, to enter or to remain in any specified area.

the National Organization of Coloured People. The most important is the first. It was founded in 1912 by four African lawyers, one of whom was a graduate of Columbia University, New York. For the first twenty years it was led by moderate men, and stressed the duty of Africans to look to their traditional chiefs. At the end of the 1920s the communists gained influence in it, but lost ground again after 1930. The Congress began to change its character after 1936. It was the abolition of the Cape common roll franchise for Africans that convinced the African intelligentsia, which till then had stood aloof both from the chiefs and from the masses, that mass political organization was necessary. The Constitution adopted by the Congress in 1943 stated its aims to be the advancement of the interests of African people, the attainment of freedom of African people from all discriminatory laws whatever, and the unity and co-operation of all African peoples within and outside the Union. In 1946 it began to co-operate closely with the South African Indian Congress, which was led by a communist, Dr. Dadoo. In 1952 the two organizations wrote to the Nationalist Premier, Dr. Malan, asking him to repeal the pass laws, the regulations about limiting livestock in African agricultural areas, the Suppression of Communism Act, the Group Areas Act, the Bantu Authorities Act and the Separate Representation Act. When, as expected, the Premier refused, they declared a mass civil disobedience campaign, burning passes and ignoring 'Europeans only' signs in public vehicles and buildings. A small number of European sympathizers joined the campaign. Demonstrators were told under no circumstances to retaliate with violence when the police attacked them, and these Gandhian tactics were usually carried out. In June 1955 a joint meeting was held at Kliptown by the African and Indian Congresses, the Coloured organization and an European body calling itself the South African Congress of Democrats. The latter was clearly a communist-inspired organization, and the meeting adopted a Freedom Charter, the slogans and style of which unmistakably conformed to world communist propaganda. In December 1956 the government arrested 156 persons on charges of treason. Among them were communists, but there were also such distinguished moderates as ex-chief Luthuli and Professor Z. K. Matthews of Fort Hare College. After two years of legal intricacies, releases of some of the accused, changes of the accusations and postponement of proceedings, it was not clear in 1959 what the government wished or could achieve.

It can be argued that the Africans in South Africa are in many ways better off than in neighbouring countries. They can earn more, get better education and better health services. South Africa is by far the most advanced and prosperous country south of the Sahara, and its African subjects get some advantage from this. But the advantages probably only make the restrictions more intolerable. Because there are enough Africans who know how good life can be for Europeans, what fine careers they themselves could make if not artificially debarred, and what striking improvements in the welfare of all Africans could be achieved if the country's economic resources and manpower were used in the interests of all and not just of one-fifth, they are filled with bitter rage. Moreover, the practical application of the unjust laws is worse than the laws themselves. It is not enough for the ruling party to impose restrictions on Africans: these are enforced with a display of contempt and brutality which is intended to wound and which certainly achieves its object.

The influence of communism in the Congress is not surprising. The communists are almost the only Europeans who have shown sympathy for the Africans, and have been prepared to suffer persecution at their side. The prestige of Russia and China is inevitably great. These two powerful countries are enemies of South Africa, therefore the Africans, especially their embittered intelligentsia, consider them friends. But communism is only one of the radical trends in the Congress. The other is black nationalism, anti-European racialism. Tactically the two can be combined. The racialists can delight in Soviet or Chinese triumphs, and the communists can exploit hatred of the white man. But the two are distinct, and have different aims. The communists aim at a multi-racial 'people's democracy' under communist leadership. They would need European experts to develop the South African economy on Soviet lines, and if ever they attained power there would be many European communists at the higher levels of government. The racialists aim to drive all Europeans out of Africa or exterminate them. It is hard to say which tendency is likely to prove the stronger, or which would be the more deadly for South Africa.

White South Africans, and especially Afrikaners, like to insist that the situation of their country is unique, and that outsiders 'cannot understand'. That it is unique, and that many foreigners condemn without understanding, one may concede. But South Africans are too inclined to confuse understanding with approval. It is possible to understand a good deal about South Africa (no one can understand *everything*, whether he be foreign or native-born), to sympathize with the Europeans' tragic predicament, and yet not to approve their policies. It is all too easy to understand the fear of being swamped by the African flood, the fear that the European civilization which has been built in South Africa will be overwhelmed by an African majority that has learned to hate Europeans. South Africa is the only home of its Europeans. They are not intruders, but the native people, and they fear that their children or grandchildren will be robbed of their home. One should not forget that the Afrikaners, who to Africans in and outside the Union and to millions throughout Asia appear a cruel master race of oppressors, seem to themselves a small, brave, freedom-loving people, sinned against, not sinners, who through many generations of toil and danger have built a homeland and a way of life of which they can be proud. Yet however much one remembers these things, and tries to feel as they feel, the conclusion remains that they are working for their own destruction, and that it will be a miracle if they escape it. For many years yet the Europeans will have so great a superiority of material power that they will be able to suppress any physical threat from the Africans and Asians. But the world is changing, and the overall balance of power will not always remain the same, in Africa or beyond. The best service that their friends can render the South Africans is constantly to warn them of the disaster that they are creating for themselves, constantly to press them to change their policies before it is finally too late.

THE AMERICAN NEGRO

In comparison with the sufferings and prospects of the South African Bantu, the lot of the negro in the United States is happy and his future bright. But if his status is judged by the proclaimed ideals of American democracy, and the real opportunities available to most American citizens, the picture is sombre. The negro problem is that of one-tenth of the population of the United States, in contrast to two-thirds in South Africa. So large a population, so prosperous an economy and so highly civilized a people as the Americans can perhaps put up with a problem of these dimensions. Nevertheless, the negro problem is a running sore in the body of American society, and for the negroes themselves a personal and a collective tragedy.

The negroes are in America as the result of one of the great crimes of human history—the mass importation of slaves by British, French, Spanish and Portuguese colonists. The American Republic inherited slavery from its former rulers, and slavery nearly broke the Republic. The Civil War was a more complicated process than a simple crusade for liberty, but it did bring the end of slavery. Unfortunately, this was not enough. Though the years of Reconstruction (1865-77) may not have been an age of such unmitigated villainy as Southerners are inclined to believe, they did little to uplift the negro. Few negroes became owners of farms, negro education was inadequate, and the negro masses were not brought into American political life. Among the Northerners responsible for Reconstruction too many were vindictive, ignorant and pettily ambitious, and the great majority of negroes were too backward to make themselves felt politically. When Northern support was withdrawn by President Hayes, white supremacy and the rule of the Democratic Party in the South were quickly restored, and have been virtually unchallenged since then. For a brief moment, at the time of the Populist movement in the 1890s, there seemed some chance that white and black workers and poor farmers might make common cause. But very soon it became clear that the contrary would be the case, that fear of being degraded to the negro level would make the poor whites the bitterest defenders of white supremacy.

In the first years of the twentieth century there were two trends among politically conscious negroes, whose numbers inevitably increased with the general progress of American society. One was represented by Booker T. Washington, the Principal of Tuskegee College, who believed that negroes could better themselves by hard work, accepting social separation as a fact and not making trouble for the white man. He hoped, by winning the whites' confidence, to improve the real conditions of the negroes. He was a brave and generous man, and the fact that he himself enjoyed material prosperity never blunted his awareness of the sufferings of his people. Without doubt he served them well. But inevitably his cautious methods, and his identification with the values of the respectable businessman, angered radical spirits eager for quicker results. The most eminent spokesman of negro radicalism was W. E. B. Du Bois, the principal founder in 1909 of the National Association for the Advancement of Coloured People (NAACP), an organization which for fifty years has played a leading part in the defence of the social and political rights of the American negro. In the next fifty years the condition of the negro improved, as the general standard of living of the American people improved. It had its setbacks too. In the 1920s persecution of negroes, including horrible cases of lynching, continued or even increased, and the negroes in both town and country suffered especially hard from the Depression. The New Deal improved their lot, even if it fell short of their hopes, and they benefited from the atmosphere of public democratic idealism that flourished in the Second World War. But if there has been a certain steady improvement, none of the essential problems of the negro's place in American society has been solved.

One important trend of the present century has been the steady movement of negroes from the South to the North. In 1950, of a total negro population in the United States of 15,042,286 there were almost exactly 9 million in the eleven southern states and 6 million in the rest of the country. This was a drastic change in comparison with 1930, when there had been 8·4 million in the South and 3·4 million outside it. No doubt the Census of 1960 will show substantial further movement in this direction. The situation of the negroes in South and North is substantially different, and it will be convenient to examine each briefly before making some general observations on the negro problem in the country as a whole.

The total population of the eleven southern states in 1950 was 36,552,000. Thus the negroes formed almost exactly one-quarter of the southern population. In five states the proportion was higher than the average, the highest being Mississippi (45%) and South Carolina (37·5%). There is, however, a broad strip of territory, stretching along both sides of the lower Mississippi through the states of Louisiana, Mississippi and Arkansas, and another stretching through the centre of Alabama and Georgia to the eastern half of South Carolina, in which negroes form more than half the population. Within these 'black belts' there are counties where the negroes may amount even to 80%, and the whites are a minority ruling race, as in colonial countries.

It is in the black belts that the negro farm tenant, usually a sharecropper, is at the mercy of his white landlord, and perhaps still more, of the white merchant. The negro farming population, however, is steadily declining. The number of non-white farmers in the South fell between 1940 and 1954 from 680,000 to 463,000. By far the greater part of this decline was in tenants paying otherwise than in cash, who fell from 442,000 to 254,000.[85] Negroes have gone in large numbers to work in the southern cities. Here their standard of living is better than on the farms, though the pressure of white workers to keep them out of skilled jobs has not ceased, and they are still far from being represented in the trade unions in proportion to their numbers.

Since Reconstruction ended, the southern negro has in effect been deprived of a vote. Among the devices used to ensure this result without formally violating the Fifteenth Amendment to the Constitution, were literacy tests and poll taxes. Various forms of intimidation and chicanery by electoral officials also played their part. Most important of all are the backwardness of the rural negroes, their lack of interest in politics, and the absence of leadership or organization to give them such interest. In the South the decisive political choice is made not at the elections, but at the Primary of the Democratic Party, where the party's candidates for state and federal office are adopted. For many years the Primary in the South was reserved for white voters. But in 1944, in the case of *Smith* v. *Allwright*, the United States Supreme Court decided that the exclusion of negroes from the Democratic Primary in Texas was unconstitutional. In 1948 and 1949 several states attempted to evade this decision by changing their Primary regulations or their state constitutions, but these efforts were frustrated by the courts. During the last ten years negro participation in elections has substantially increased, but still remains low.[86]

Education in the South has been based in theory on the principle proclaimed by the Supreme Court in 1896 in the case of *Plessy* v. *Ferguson* —that facilities must be 'separate but equal'. In practice they were separate, but not equal. The southern states were among the poorest in the Union, and thus education for all was less well endowed than in the North. The negroes, who were the poorest part of the population, could not provide much revenue for schools, and the white population, hard put to it to provide for white children, had little desire to spend their money on educating negroes as well. Southern state funds, supplemented by northern philanthropic enterprises, achieved some progress in the first forty years of the century. But what was available to negroes fell far short of 'equal' facilities. In 1940 current expenditures per pupil, and salaries of teachers, were about twice as high for whites as for negroes, and the number of books in school libraries was four times as large for white schools as for negro.[87] After the war, however, great progress was made, both in developing southern education in general and especially in narrowing the gap between white and negro Schools. The difference in teachers' salaries had been reduced to 15%, in current expenditure per pupil, to 30%, but negro school libraries still had less than half as many books as white. This better record of southern education authorities was the result of pressure of public opinion, not only in the nation as a whole, but also among white southerners. But it was not enough. There was a growing demand that education not only should be made equal, but that it should cease to be separate. The campaign was led by the NAACP, with increased support from negroes in North and South and from liberal opinion in general. A number of appeal cases involving segregation in education came before the Supreme Court at the end of 1952. After long investigations, the Court gave an unanimous judgement on 17 May 1954, that segregation in the public schools deprives American citizens of the equal protection of the laws, and so is unconstitutional. In the Court's view 'separate educational facilities are inherently unequal'.

Integration of schools now became the duty of all education authorities in the United States. Time was to be allowed for the changes to take place. Three years later very little had been done. In the city of Louisville, Kentucky, in a border state with southern traditions, integration was successfully carried out by the able and enlightened Superintendent of Schools, Omer Carmichael, himself a native of Alabama.[88] But in the greater part of the South there was bitter opposition to integration. In September 1957 Governor Faubus of Arkansas attained world fame by preventing negro children from entering Central High School in Little Rock. Photographs of a crowd of white teenagers insulting negro children were flashed round the world, a splendid windfall for those whose task it is to present the United States as a land of violence and oppression. In the state of Virginia, Senator Byrd prepared for 'massive resistance'. President Eisenhower's decision to send federal troops to Little Rock showed that he did not intend to let the law be flouted. But it also kindled into flame the smouldering resentment against the North which had not yet been extinguished in the ninety years since Appomattox. As the White Citizens' Councils increased their campaign of denunciation, it seemed that the progress achieved in ten years was to be lost.

For the root of the negro problem is not so much in institutions as in the climate of opinion. The traditional southern attitude to the negro, from which a growing minority of white southerners have more or less emancipated themselves, but which is still valid for the majority, and especially for the poorer classes, is a mixture of contempt and fear. The average white southerner seems to regard the negro as something between a man and a beast. He notes his poverty, his squalor, his uncouth habits, and claims that these prove not mere historical misfortune and economic disadvantage, but innate inferiority. Yet if a negro rises by his own efforts to wealth and cultural distinction, he will not like him the more for it. By achieving success by the white man's criteria, the negro is not acquiring merit, is not paying a compliment to the white man's culture: rather, he is showing himself impudent by trying to rise above his station. The humble negro may be less than a human, but he is entitled to kindly treatment as a good, loyal and rather comic beast. The uppity nigger must be humiliated on every possible occasion—not only be subjected to the complicated colour bar in all public places, but be compelled to observe the customary ritual of deference in personal dealings with white men. At the same time the white southerner fears the negro, is haunted by the fear that his whole way of life will be swamped by him. In South Africa such fears are all too real. But in the United States, where negroes are a minority everywhere but in the 'black belt', they hardly seem reasonable. Fear, however, is stronger than reason, especially sexual fear, which is its foundation. It is useless to point out that very few negroes wish for sexual relations with white women, and that there is little reason to suppose that many white women find negroes irresistibly attractive. The fear is there. It was responsible for the bestial lynchings, by hanging or burning alive, which now mercifully are a thing of the past. It is still responsible for the taboo on eating in the company of a negro, and the passionate conviction that white and negro children must not share their classrooms.

In the North the negro's status is better. He has the vote, he has in effect a better choice of profession, and he is not in theory debarred from facilities available to white men. Some states, such as New York and New Jersey, have set up organizations to prevent racial discrimination. In practice his economic position is precarious. He is more likely to lose his job in a depression than his white fellow-workers. Residential segregation exists in practice, though not in theory. When negroes begin to move into a district, the whites start moving out. At the same time as the Little Rock crisis of 1957, there was an unpleasant incident in Levittown, Pennsylvania. A highly educated negro couple bought a house in this district, which is inhabited mainly by professional people, medium-level business-men and 'organization men'. These respectable, well-educated northerners, doubtless firm believers in democracy, loudly objected to the presence of one negro couple in their midst, and resorted to the methods of the crudest southern poor whites. In industrial Chicago and Detroit there have been savage race riots in recent years.

Residential segregation leads in practice to segregation in the schools. In parts of Manhattan where the negro or Puerto Rican population is spreading, white parents move into the suburbs or send their children to private schools. Their motives are, of course, not racialist. The public schools,* swamped with negro or Puerto Rican children from squalid slums, in classes too large and undisciplined for the teachers to control, can provide little education. It is all very well for the progressive intellectual to point out that the standard of public schools will only rise when children from decent homes attend them: he may preach social heroism to the intellectual *élite*, but he does not wish his own children to be the first guinea-pigs in a social laboratory where they will learn little and may be a target for juvenile razor-gangs. Not racial prejudice, he insists, inspired his choice of school, but his duty to protect his children from the appalling conditions produced by economic causes. However, it is only fair to point out that comparable economic causes operate in rural Mississippi, and that sudden integration of schools in the 'black belt' would have comparable effects on white children there. Practical segregation in Manhattan and dogmatic segregation in Tuscaloosa have different motives, but from the negro point of view the difference in result does not look so large.

The negroes of the United States, taken as a group, enjoy greater material wealth, wider choice of profession, better schools and fuller political rights than any other community of African origin in the world (including independent Ghana). This must be said,to put the problem in

* 'State schools' in British terminology.

perspective. Nevertheless, it is foolish to be complacent. The negro benefits from the splendid material progress of American society. Yet within this society he is confined to a ghetto of his own. There are negro doctors, lawyers, business-men, but their skills are exercised only within the ghetto. Some are content with this. There is even a hierarchy of social snobbery within the negro community, a black *bourgeoisie* and a sort of Black Social Register.[89] To some extent negro writers escape the ghetto: the printed word is of the same colour, whatever the colour of its author's skin. Artists and sportsmen become national and world figures. But the fact that white Americans admire Joe Louis is small consolation to the educated negro who has to submit to discrimination and insult most days of his life. It is the upper stratum of the negroes, especially their intelligentsia, who suffer most, whose pent-up hatred can do most harm to America. It will not be removed by economic prosperity or gradual social reforms, but only by the formal and final repudiation, in South and North alike, of the dogma of negro inferiority. When this has been done, it will be possible to settle practical problems such as the location of schools and swimming-pools. But as long as the dogma prevails, every practical injustice will be doubly resented. And in 1959 the dogma shows little sign of withering away.

AFRO-ASIANISM

It is not surprising that the growth of nationalist movements in European colonies during the twentieth century should have created among the intelligentsias of all these lands a feeling of solidarity in a common struggle against European imperialism. Various ideologies of Asian unity, pan-Africanism and Afro-Asian co-operation have arisen.

It may indeed be argued that Asia is no more than a geographical expression; that the great historic civilizations of Asia differ as much from each other as any of them differs from the historic civilization of Christian Europe; and that Asians have treated Asians with no less cruelty and greed than have Europeans. Yet if a significant number of Asian intellectuals believe that there is a basic Asian unity, then their belief becomes a political factor. Pan-Asian feeling was exploited with some success by the Japanese aggressors in the period from 1905, when Japan defeated the European Great Power, Russia, to 1945, when the Japanese Empire collapsed. Since 1945 both Nehru's India and Mao's China have tried, in very different ways and with varying success, to claim leadership over Asia.

Africa is also a geographical expression, and little more. Vast differences separate not only the Arabs and Berbers living north of the Sahara from the negroes, but also the negro races and societies from each other. But the Pan-African idea, which originated among American negroes, has won support from the Western-educated intelligentsia of African colonies. Most of the romanticism of the original American negro pioneers has been shed in favour of political realism, but there is a historical link between Dr. Nkrumah and the 'provisional president of Africa' of 1921, the West Indian Marcus Garvey. The veteran W. E. B. Du Bois has given his blessing to the pan-African policies of the Ghana leader, and the West Indian George Padmore, a leading figure in pan-African activities between the world wars, is Nkrumah's trusted adviser.

The concept of Afro-Asian unity is even less related to historical and cultural realities than pan-Asian or pan-African unity. The main direct contact between Asia and Africa in recent centuries has been between Arab slave-traders and Sudanese or East African slaves. The relations of Lebanese and Indian merchants with Africans in West Africa and Natal have not been happy. Yet it is also true that among the nationalist intelligentsias of both continents the belief in a common destiny has become strong. The 'Afro-Asian bloc' at the United Nations General Assembly is a fact of international politics. It might be supposed that the common experience of being ruled or humiliated by Europeans for a century or more, and the common possession of a 'coloured skin', would become less important as one nation after another obtains independence. But the continuing colour bar in East and Central Africa and the brutal application of *apartheid* policies in South Africa are a constant reminder that humiliation and oppression are not yet things of the past. Indeed, such humiliations are more intolerable to nations that are independent, and are beginning to feel their strength, than they were to cowed or backward colonial subjects. The fact that the humiliations affect principally a small social group, the intelligentsia, does not diminish their impact. Perhaps the main argument of the whole of this book has been that the intelligentsia, however small in numbers, are the decisive political factor in underdeveloped societies. Their ability to mobilize the uneducated masses, and the preference of these masses for their own intelligentsia rather than for the European administrators, whether humane and benevolent or not, has been proved so often in the last decades that it is truly astonishing how far European governments and ruling groups still fail to recognize it as a fact of international life.

The first striking demonstration of the Afro-Asian idea was the conference held at Bandung, in Indonesia, in April 1955. Here three forces were at work. The first, which was most emphasized in the official statements, was the protest against imperialism in the name of liberty and equality, an appeal to the West's own values. The other two factors, less publicized yet clearly present, were anti-white racialism, and communism. At Bandung the communists did not have everything their way. Chou En-lai made a good impression by his good manners and studious moderation. But representatives of Ceylon, Turkey and Pakistan mentioned the Soviet Union as an imperialist Power. At the second Afro-Asian conference, held in Cairo from 26 December 1957 to 4 January 1958, at which the Soviet Union was represented by persons claiming to represent the peoples of Central Asia, communist influence was far stronger. In the interval the British and French had made their abortive invasion of Egypt.

Two African conferences held in Accra, Ghana, in 1958, were comparatively free from communist influence. The first, in April, was confined to representatives of independent African states. The Egyptian delegates did not impose their views, and the governments of Ethiopia and Liberia showed no sympathy for the Soviet bloc. The second conference, which met in December, was more ambitious, as it included delegates of African nations still under colonial rule. There was much denunciation of European imperialism, but neither the Egyptian nor the communist policies prevailed. The conference was clearly intended to encourage all African nationalist movements, and it is therefore not inherently absurd (as some Western left-wing commentators have suggested) to suppose that it had some influence on events in Belgian Congo and Nyasaland in January and February. But the black picture of co-ordinated activity by the Soviet Union, Egypt and Ghana, that was painted by the apologists of Dr. Verwoerd and Sir Roy Welensky, is hardly convincing. The Accra conference certainly presaged growing difficulties for European governments in Africa, but this does not mean that it was organized by communists: available evidence suggests the contrary.

The West has no choice but to regard both anti-white racialism and communism as enemies, and fight them. But these forces have not triumphed in Asia or Africa. Western governments and citizens still enjoy on a vast scale the friendship of governments and citizens of Asia and Africa. These friendships can be strengthened and extended.

Western governments should surely use their influence against colour bars and against repression of African nationalism. But moralizing rhetoric from New Delhi, or in British or American newspapers of radical opinion, are not necessarily helpful. The British people, for example, will not in the long term forget that white Rhodesians and many white South Africans are their kinsmen, and fought for Britain in two world wars. Britain is involved in these conflicts, whether British journalists realize it or not. Every liberal-minded citizen of Britain must condemn many actions of the South African government and many of the demands of Kenya settlers. But it is unlikely that the British people would passively accept the butchery of its kinsmen by black racialists, should that time ever come. It is as well that this should be understood beforehand.

For Asian or African intelligentsias the temptation is obviously very strong to shriek for all or nothing, to condemn as 'liberal hypocrisy' all proposed reforms that give them less than their maximum demands, and to accuse of cowardice all white men who, while expressing sympathy for their cause, do not agree to support all their claims. It is arguable that among the cowards should also be numbered those Asian or African leaders who will not face unpopularity by admitting that Utopia cannot be built tomorrow, and who prefer to let themselves be dragged or goaded forward by those who use demagogy only in order to establish something very different—the Sino-Soviet empire.

Asian and African nationalists have the right to expect understanding from the West. Western democrats have the right to ask Asians and Africans to abandon the double standard, to look as carefully at Soviet and Chinese practices as at British or French, to refrain from wholesale condemnations of all things British and French because they are indignant at events in Nyasaland or Algeria, and perhaps even to examine critically their own treatment of Asian and African religious or ethnical minorities in their midst. Perhaps the events of 1959 in Iraq and Tibet will help them to do this.

Part Five
The World Since Stalin

15: Europe

THE NEW COURSE

In the Soviet Union and Eastern Europe the year 1952 brought increased police terror and economic hardship. In October was held the long-overdue 19th Congress of the Soviet Communist Party. In January 1953 the Soviet press announced the discovery of a plot by Kremlin doctors to poison several military and civil leaders of the Soviet régime. It was noted that the doctors were of Jewish origin. The purges of 1951-2 in Eastern Europe had had a marked anti-Semitic character, and now in Russia itself Jews were publicly represented as enemies. The tone of the Soviet press closely recalled that of 1937, the year of the Great Purge. Then Stalin died, so conveniently for his immediate subordinates that it was widely believed (though there can be no proof) that this was no natural death.

For a few days both the offices which Stalin had held—the Premiership and the First Secretaryship of the Party—were assumed by G. M. Malenkov. Then they were divided, the Party office being given to N. S. Khrushchov. The third most powerful man in the country was L. P. Beria, who reassumed direct control of the security forces, which he had given up some years before. It was also noted that the outstanding hero of the Second World War, Marshal G. K. Zhukov, who had been relegated to obscure posts by Stalin after 1946, returned to the centre as First Deputy Minister of Defence. In their first pronouncements the new leaders stressed the principle of 'collective leadership'. Whether they were in principle opposed to government by personal autocracy, as in Stalin's time, or merely could not trust any one of their number with supreme power, was not yet clear.

In Eastern Europe there was at first no change. In Czechoslovakia, the most industrialized state, a currency reform was introduced on 30 May, depriving the workers of the savings which they had accumulated in the previous years, when money wages for skilled work had been high but there had been few goods in the shops on which to spend them. The communist régime had also suffered a serious loss in the death of its outstanding leader, Klement Gottwald, who had perished immediately after his return from Stalin's funeral. Infuriated by the currency reform, and encouraged by the apparent weakness of the régime, the workers of Plzen, the second largest industrial centre, organized a mass demonstration, occupied the Town Hall and publicly demanded the removal of the government. The rising was, however, confined to this one area, and was soon put down by troops.

At the beginning of June the East German government introduced a number of economic concessions for the peasants and professional classes, but at the same time somewhat increased the output quotas ('production norms') on which workers' wages were based. There followed a dispute between building workers and management in East Berlin, which led to a strike and a public demonstration. Within hours a wave of strikes and demonstrations swept through the city, and soon extended to all the major industrial centres of the Soviet zone. This national rising of 17 June 1953, led by the workers in whose name the communists ruled, and supported by all other classes, reduced the régime to complete impotence. Its police force would not obey orders, and the demonstrators, no longer concerned only with wage claims, loudly demanded an end to the whole régime. It was saved only by the Soviet army, whose tanks occupied the centres of the main cities.

This complete collapse of communist authority, including the police, in Germany, was probably the occasion for the fall in Moscow of Beria who had the ultimate responsibility for security affairs in the Soviet empire. His many enemies, including the army leaders, were able to use this disaster to overthrow him. His arrest was announced at the end of June, and his execution later in the year. The first breach had been made in the 'collective leadership'.

The events in Plzen and Berlin called not only for repression, but also for positive policies. In the summer of 1953 a series of reforms, which came to be widely known as the 'new course', were introduced in all the satellite states except Bulgaria and Albania.

They were most far-reaching in Hungary. On 4 July Mátyás Rákosi, who for six years had exercised autocratic power, gave up the Premiership to another communist, Imre Nagy, but kept the First Secretaryship of the Communist Party in his hands. Nagy announced drastic changes. He admitted that the previous policy of excessive attention to heavy industry had placed too heavy a burden on workers and resources. Light industry and consumers' goods production were now to receive higher priority. The government would give material assistance to agriculture, including individual peasant holdings as well as collective farms. Individual households were to be allowed to leave collective farms, and where a majority of the members of a collective desired it they might dissolve it altogether. Internment camps were to be dissolved, and considerable numbers of persons sentenced to prison for political offences were released. In the following months there was no such mass exodus from collective farms as during the same period in Yugoslavia, for whereas the Yugoslav authorities allowed the law to be carried out, in Hungary the local party officials did their best to obstruct the Premier's policy and to intimidate the peasants. Even so, by the end of the year about 10% of the collectives had been dissolved. In general a far freer atmosphere was created in Hungary. Nagy was carrying out a policy recommended by Moscow, which had chosen him for the job. But the policy represented not a mere tactical manœuvre, but Nagy's honest convictions. He was in fact the leader of those persons in the communist party who were disgusted by the horrors of the preceding period, and wished genuinely to improve the people's conditions.

In Czechoslovakia there was but little increase in freedom (the terror had been less cruel than under Rákosi in Hungary), but economic changes were substantial. In the following years there was a marked increase in output of consumers' goods, and real wages rose substantially. Since 1953 Czechoslovakia has been by far the most prosperous of the satellites. The government was in fact allowed to use the industrial equipment and skilled labour of its people to a larger extent for their benefit, and the claims of the Soviet economy and Soviet military plans were diminished. In Poland there was much less economic progress but more freedom. Police terror was reduced, and at least in non-political matters there was a new liberty of expression. The stifling insistence of the censors on adulation of Soviet models in literature and the arts was relaxed, and by 1955 it even became possible to criticize social conditions in the Polish press. In Roumania too the emphasis was on economic change, but not much was in fact achieved, perhaps mainly because the country was so poor and its administration so inefficient.

THE SOVIET UNION AND THE WEST

The new Soviet leaders showed an apparently more conciliatory attitude in foreign policy. The change was not, however, due to the death of Stalin. In the autumn of 1952 Stalin had published some articles in pamphlet form under the title *Economic Problems of Socialism*, in which he had argued that the conflicts most likely in the near future to lead to war were not the conflict between the Soviet bloc and the Western group of alliances, but conflicts within the 'capitalist world'. He mentioned specifically conflicts between Germany and the West European Powers, between Britain and the United States, and between Japan and her victors. The pamphlet, which received enormous publicity in the Soviet Union, was a clear directive to Soviet diplomacy and to communist parties to make the most of any disunity within the Western camp. The Soviet policy of 'peaceful coexistence', now loudly proclaimed, was in no way new: it was a revival of the policy of exploiting the 'internal contradictions of capitalism' practised by Lenin in the early 1920s and by Stalin himself from 1935 to 1939. But the impact in the West of the change in tactics was increased by the disappearance of the old autocrat. Western politicians and newspaper editors, longing to persuade themselves and their readers that a new and brighter age was at hand, did not hesitate to suggest that there had been a 'change of heart' in Moscow. By 1954 a mood of utopian optimism was widespread in the West. In the 'uncommitted' countries of Asia, whose leaders had always wished to remain outside the struggle between the communist and Western camps, the new Western optimism was taken as evidence of a Soviet pacific attitude, and it began to be assumed by Asians that if there were still obstacles to peace-making, they must be the fault of the West.

The most concrete achievements of this period were the conclusion of the wars in Korea and Indochina. In Europe the main effort of Soviet foreign policy was devoted to splitting the Atlantic Alliance. It cannot be said that it had much success. The French distrust of Germany, and the widespread irritation of Europeans against the United States, were not created by Soviet action or communist propaganda, though they were exploited by them. These situations resulted in the French refusal to ratify the European Defence Community treaty, but this did not in the end prove a serious blow to the Atlantic Alliance.

In June 1953 Italy had a parliamentary general election. The Christian Democrats were the largest party, but did not win the absolute majority of the poll which would have enabled them, under a new and much criticized electoral law, to secure a very large majority of seats in the Assembly. In the South the communists and their allies made substantial gains. Within the Christian Democratic Party De Gasperi lost some support, and on 28 July resigned the Premiership. In Western Germany the general election of September 1953 brought Adenauer a great victory. He won 45% of the poll, and had a slight absolute majority in the new parliament.

The American strategic position in Europe was strengthened by an agreement signed with General Franco's government in Madrid on 26 September 1953. Spain was to lease air bases to the United States in return for economic aid and the supply of material to the Spanish armed forces. Spain was thus brought indirectly into the Atlantic defence system, without the West European governments being obliged to make an alliance with her. The agreement was not popular in Western Europe. Not only did resentment against the Franco régime remain strong, but it was felt that American strategy might be based on a plan of retiring behind the Pyrenees in the event of an European war. American spokesmen did their best to reassure their allies on this point, and to stress that their aim was the defence of Western Europe, not its 'liberation' after an interval of Soviet occupation.

A conference of the United States, Britain, France and the Soviet Union, held in Berlin from 25 January to 18 February 1954, failed to settle the problem of German reunification. The Western Powers proposed that free elections should be held throughout Germany, and that the all-German government formed as a result should sign a peace treaty with the victor Powers, and should then be entirely free to decide whether it wished to make any alliances with foreign states. The Soviet Union proposed that there should first be formed a provisional government of all Germany, composed of representatives of the existing German states, that it should agree on an electoral law, that an election should then be held, and that the resultant government should sign a peace treaty and should also commit itself not to conclude an alliance with any foreign Power.

There were thus two essential points of difference. Firstly, the Soviet government was determined to uphold the communist régime which it had established in its zone. If the process of reunification began with free elections, there could be no doubt, in view of the June 1953 rising and the continuous exodus of refugees to the West, that the régime of SED and Walther Ulbricht would be repudiated by the electors. The Soviet government wished to make sure that the communists would have built-in guarantees in the new unified Germany. Secondly, the Western Powers wished united Germany to join the Western system of alliances, which it almost certainly would do if it were free to choose. The Soviet Union understandably opposed this, and wished to ensure a permanent neutralization of Germany.

What the conference did not consider was an exchange of neutralization for freedom: that the Soviet desire for a neutral Germany should be granted in return for Soviet consent to a political freedom which would have swept away the communist régime. It was most unlikely that the Soviet government would have consented to such a bargain, which would have amounted to a victory for the rebels of June 1953 and would have been a severe blow to the cause of world communism. But by their unwillingness to risk proposing it, the Western Powers placed themselves in an unpopular position with regard to a large section of German public opinion, and allowed the Soviet government to claim, not without effect, in its propaganda of the following years, that it was Western rejection of neutralization, rather than Soviet maintenance of the Ulbricht régime, that had prevented reunification.

The Berlin conference also had before it the problem of an Austrian peace treaty. The Western Powers were willing to accept all the remaining claims put forward by the Soviet Union, so that there was no longer any outstanding difference on Austria. But the Soviet government refused to sign a treaty with Austria as long as the German problem was unsolved.

In August 1954 the French Assembly rejected the European Defence Community treaty. Right and left were united against the elements of the Centre that favoured EDC. Communist devotion to Soviet interests, anti-American emotions of the non-communist left, concern by the right for the position of the French army, and the still powerful fear of Germany that was to be found in all classes, all combined in this vote. Many Frenchmen claimed that the failure was really a result of British policy. If Britain had been willing to join EDC, they would have voted for it: to be left alone in partnership with Germany was more than they could risk. Whatever view be taken of the habitual British arguments against joining European organizations, mentioned in an earlier chapter, it cannot be doubted that British abstention had a real effect on the French decision.

By refusing an European army with German units, the French government made it inevitable that Germany should have an army of her own, and should in some way be associated with the Atlantic Alliance. This was achieved by a conference held in London at the end of September 1954. On the proposal of Anthony Eden, the Brussels Treaty Organization was reorganized under the name of West European Union, and admitted, in addition to the original five signatory Powers, West Germany and Italy. WEU was to form part of the NATO defence system, and all military forces of the signatory Powers located in the NATO command area, other than those intended for overseas territories or police forces, were to be under the Supreme Command of NATO.

The agreement creating WEU was signed in Paris in October. At the same time the German Federal Republic was recognized as a fully sovereign state. The occupation came to an end, and the foreign troops remaining in Germany became purely allied forces, with no authority over German affairs. Germany gave an unilateral undertaking not to produce various categories of weapons. The Allies recognized the German Federal Republic as the only legitimately constituted German state, and promised to pursue a policy of peaceful reunification of Germany and to exercise their responsibilities for the security and welfare of their sectors of Berlin, in which military government continued to exist. The German government promised that it would never resort to force in order to reunify Germany or in order to change the existing frontiers of Germany.

The Paris treaties were followed by an agreement between France and Germany concerning the Saar territory, an industrial border area to which they had conflicting claims. It was proposed to introduce a special

Statute to 'europeanize' the Saar. But when the Statute was submitted to a plebiscite of the Saar population in October 1955, it was rejected. The victorious Saar parties favoured reunification with Germany. In 1956 a new agreement was made, by which France agreed to the political incorporation of the Saar in the Federal Republic, while full economic union was to be achieved within three years. In return, the German government gave France a number of economic rights in regard to Saar territory.

In the spring of 1955 the Soviet government reversed its attitude to Austria. The Austrian Chancellor visited Moscow in April, and the Soviet government announced that it would sign the peace treaty without waiting for a German settlement. Signature took place on 15 May, and all occupying troops were quickly withdrawn. Austria was committed to neutrality. This was a certain gain for Soviet, and a loss for Atlantic, strategy, as Switzerland and Austria together formed a long barrier separating Atlantic forces in Germany from those in Italy. The Soviet decision was also probably influenced by the desire to come to terms with Yugoslavia. A neutral Austria was considered in Belgrade to be important for Yugoslavia's security. Whatever its underlying motives, the Soviet government won some international goodwill by the Austrian settlement.

The peace treaties of 1947 with Hungary and Roumania had provided that the Soviet Union should have the right to maintain troops in both countries in order to secure communications with her forces of occupation in Austria. Once the occupation of Austria ceased, it might be expected that Soviet troops would be withdrawn from Hungary and Roumania. This was not to happen. The Soviet government declared that the WEU treaties of October 1954 were incompatible with the alliances that both Britain and France had concluded during or after the war with the Soviet Union, and formally denounced them. On 13 May 1955, two days before the Austrian treaty was signed, an alliance was signed in Warsaw between the Soviet Union, Poland, Czechoslovakia, Hungary, Roumania and Bulgaria. Under this alliance Soviet troops could be stationed in the member countries. Hungary and Roumania therefore retained their Soviet garrisons, now rather small in numbers.

In June 1955 Khrushchov visited Belgrade, and publicly admitted that the previous policy of the Soviet Union towards Yugoslavia had been mistaken: he blamed it on the executed Beria. The official Yugoslav comment on the visit was that Yugoslavia wished to remain uncommitted in foreign policy, was glad to have better relations with the Soviet Union, but did not for that reason intend to have less good relations with the West. It was emphasized that the rapprochement was between the Soviet and Yugoslav states, not between the two communist parties. The

Yugoslav party would remain, as before, entirely free from Soviet control.

Another conciliatory gesture by the Soviet government was the renunciation of the military base of Porkkala, near Helsinki, which was announced after the Finnish President and Prime Minister had paid a visit to Moscow in September 1955. In return Finland agreed to prolong the Finnish-Soviet treaty of alliance of 1948 until 1975.

The 'Summit Conference' at Geneva, attended by President Eisenhower and Mr. Khrushchov as well as by the British and French Prime Ministers, produced no agreement. The meeting of Foreign Ministers in Geneva in October-November 1955 was also fruitless. The German problem remained intractable.

THE YEAR OF REVOLUTION

The principle of Soviet 'collective leadership', shaken by the execution of Beria, suffered a further blow in February 1955, when Malenkov resigned from the Premiership. During the preceding months a series of appointments to provincial posts in the organization of the Communist Party had shown demotion of persons associated in their careers with Malenkov, and promotion of protégés of Khrushchov. During 1955 the process continued.[90] Khrushchov was now clearly the most powerful single member of the Soviet leadership, but he had not yet attained a position of domination over all the others.

The most important immediate effect of Malenkov's fall was the fall of Imre Nagy in Hungary, and the resumption of power by Rákosi, who placed one of his own favourites in the Premiership. It was not so much that Nagy was personally connected with Malenkov as that the policies for which Malenkov was blamed—especially the neglect of heavy industry—could easily be imputed to Nagy. But Rákosi found that he could not rule so autocratically as before. Khrushchov did not wish to restore Stalin's policies, and he did wish to please Marshal Tito. This last aim could not be achieved as long as Rákosi, who of all the satellite leaders had most savagely denounced Yugoslavia in the past, remained supreme. The greater freedom of discussion in intellectual circles, and especially within the Communist Party, which Nagy had encouraged, was not in fact abolished by Rákosi.

In February 1956 the 20th Congress of the Communist Party of the Soviet Union met in Moscow. There was a fresh breath of criticism of the past. Of the published speeches the frankest was made by A. I. Mikoyan, who, like Khrushchov, Malenkov and Molotov, had been a member of the inner circle of power throughout the last period of Stalin's reign. But the fiercest speech was made at a secret session by Khrushchov himself.

Its text became known in the West in July 1956. It savagely exposed the crimes of Stalin during the Great Purge and the war, confirming many of the arguments of opponents of communism in the West, which till then had been most loudly denied by Western communists.[91]

After the 20th Congress the tempo of change in Eastern Europe quickened. The Polish communist leader Bierut died in Moscow while attending the Congress. The press exposed with astonishing freedom the inefficiencies in the economy and the harsh living conditions of the population. Similar trends appeared in Hungary. Discussions took place at the Petöffi Club in Budapest, in which communist intellectuals, both older people and young students, denounced the injustices of the régime and openly demanded the removal of Rákosi. At the end of June there was a mass rising of the workers in the Polish industrial city of Poznan. It was suppressed by the army, but with little bloodshed. The Soviet leaders denounced it as a provocation by Western imperialists, but the Polish communist leaders publicly stated that it was due to the discontent of the workers with miserable living conditions, and that though they could not approve of insurrection they intended to remedy the abuses. In Hungary Rákosi was removed from the First Secretaryship of the party on 18 July.

The position of Yugoslavia in these developments was obscure. Marshal Tito welcomed the demotion of his old enemies in Hungary, Poland and Bulgaria. He wished to see the East European states more independent of Moscow, and insisted that the Soviet leaders should approve the principle of each nation choosing its 'own way to socialism'. This principle was in fact declared in a joint statement signed during Tito's visit to the Soviet Union in June 1956, when he made a triumphal procession through Russia. But at the same time he had no wish to see a challenge to communist party dictatorship. Already in 1954 there had been a crisis in the Yugoslav party which had made the issues clear. In the years after 1948 Yugoslav communist intellectuals had developed a theory about the nature of the Soviet State, which they claimed had degenerated into a form of bureaucratic State capitalism. The Yugoslav State, they insisted, could and would avoid such degeneration, by its new policies of decentralization and by the constructive role to be played by workers' councils and other associations of producers. The chief exponent of this theory was Milovan Djilas, a member of the inner circle of power ever since the war of liberation of 1941-5. But Djilas was an independent and fearless thinker, and at the end of 1953 he began to doubt the need for a monopoly of power in the hands of the Communist Party. He reached this conclusion solely from intellectual conviction. His own position was unchallenged. He was not, like Trotski in the Russia of 1922-5, under attack from personal rivals. His material interests were bound up with the existing régime. But his convictions made him challenge the régime, and advocate political liberty. In January 1954 he made a direct and scurrilous attack on the bureaucratic caste as such.[92] This was his undoing. Tito had till then tolerated his friend's heresies. But the clamour from the party machine for his removal could no longer be resisted. A special meeting of the Central Committee was summoned on 16-17 January, and Djilas was expelled from the Committee and obliged to give up his public offices.

With the memory of Djilas's heretical views, and the popularity which they had undoubtedly enjoyed within and outside the party, especially among the younger generation, Tito was most unwilling to see any such tendencies expressed in neighbouring countries. The Petöffi Club meetings were acceptable, because they seemed to assume the supremacy of the party, and in any case were directed against Rákosi. But the Poznan rising, the armed opposition of the workers to the rule of the party, was quite unacceptable. Yugoslav official comment on Poznan was much closer to the Soviet than to the Polish communist view.

Even so, Tito's point of view, combining national independence with communist dictatorship—or, as it was called by Western but not by Yugoslav or Soviet commentators, 'national communism'—was hardly acceptable in Moscow. In September a letter was circulated to East European communist parties warning them against Tito's errors. Khrushchov paid a sudden visit to Belgrade, and Tito returned with him to the Crimea, where he met Ernö Gerö, Rákosi's former close collaborator, who had been appointed his successor in July. Tito had good reason to dislike Gerö, but he accepted him as leader of the Hungarian régime, and invited him to visit Belgrade in October.[93]

It was clear to careful observers in the summer of 1956 that discontent was widespread throughout Eastern Europe. Everywhere the peasants were opposed to collectivization and to the various devices used to exploit them for the economic purposes of the régime. Everywhere the workers were hostile, and they were more dangerous to the régimes because they were concentrated in the main cities and because the whole communist ideology required that the working class should be the mainstay of communism. Most dangerous of all was the disaffection of the intelligentsia, particularly of its youth. This was most obvious in Poland and Hungary, but it was true also of Czechoslovakia, where students of both Prague and Bratislava in May 1956 put forward a series of demands, including one for political freedom. There were also some signs of student opposition in Roumania and Bulgaria. In Soviet Germany opposition was virtually universal.

The condition of unrest was common to the whole region, but two special conditions for a violent outbreak existed only in Poland and Hungary. The first special condition was that discontent within the Communist Party could polarize around two outstanding personalities, known to be opposed to current policies and leaders—Gomulka in Poland and Nagy in Hungary. These two men were alive and at liberty, whereas the leading opponents (or potential opponents) within the leadership of the Communist Parties of Czechoslovakia, Bulgaria and Roumania were dead. The second factor was that in both Poland and Hungary there were among the elder generation of intellectuals (especially of economists in Poland and of imaginative writers in Hungary) men who were Marxists, but had become disillusioned with the régime, and who had the experience and the ability to give a lead to the intellectual youth, which was also against the régime, but inexperienced and inarticulate. This was not the case in the other three countries, where the elder generation of intellectuals were not Marxists at all, and had either been suppressed or had chosen a subservience to the party which deprived them of any moral authority among the young.

It was the demand within the two parties for the return of Gomulka and Nagy, and the criticism by the writers and the students, in print and by word of mouth, which led to the crises in October in Poland and Hungary. Once the crisis had come, wider circles of society were involved, and events took different courses in the two countries.

In Poland the demand for the return of Gomulka, who had been released from prison in 1955, became effective in the late summer of 1956. It was taken up especially by the workers of the Warsaw factories. The party leaders decided to accede to it. It is important to note that Edward Ochab, the man chosen by Khrushchov to lead the party after Bierut's death, identified himself with the wishes of the party membership and of the Polish working class. The central committee of the party was convoked in mid-October, and decided to appoint Gomulka First Secretary, and not to re-elect to the Politburo the Soviet Marshal Konstantin Rokossovski, who had been appointed by Stalin to command the Polish armed forces in 1949. While the central committee was in session, Khrushchov arrived in Warsaw with his closest colleagues, but the Polish leaders stood up to his threats. The Warsaw workers were being armed, and the Polish security forces, commanded by General Wladyslaw Komar, were loyal to Gomulka. As for the army, which was well equipped, it was expected that in the last resort it would obey a Polish government rather than a Soviet Marshal. If the Soviet forces in Poland and Eastern Germany were ordered to attack, there would be heavy fighting, which might spread into German territory, with unpredictable consequences. Khrushchov was not prepared to take the risk, and he agreed to recognize the return of Gomulka.

In Hungary the crisis started with student demonstrations on 23 October. The demands put forward for social and political liberties were compatible with the maintenance of a Communist Party government. But Gerö, just returned from a visit to Belgrade, his confidence swollen by the fact that Tito now recognized his position, refused concessions. Whereas Ochab took the side of his own people, and the Polish security forces were commanded by a patriot, Gerö used his security forces to fire on the people, his orders were obeyed by his police commanders, and when this was insufficient, he called on the Soviet army to help him. It is this difference between the attitudes of the communist leaders in power and of the security forces, and not, as some Western commentators have suggested, any complicated calculations of foreign policy or difference in national character, which explains the different course of events in Poland and Hungary. The Poles were not thinking in October 1956 of the need for an alliance with the Soviet Union to protect their frontier against Germany. If Ochab had behaved as Gerö behaved, there would have been a bloodbath in Warsaw as well as in Budapest. Nor did the Hungarians, in contrast to the wise Poles, show themselves reckless romantics. The Hungarians were not given the chance which Ochab gave the Poles. They were given only a choice between surrender and resistance in a war against the Soviet army which was not of their choosing.

The first shots by Hungarian police on the crowds did not disperse them. Soon the students and chance bystanders were joined by groups of armed workers from the factories in the Budapest suburbs, and then by individual soldiers and units of the Hungarian army. Soon no one was fighting for the régime except a few thousand security policemen and Soviet troops. These available forces were too small, and on 28 October the Soviet command made an armistice. The Hungarian Revolution seemed to have won. Meanwhile, new political authorities were being formed in all the provinces and main cities. In Budapest already on 24 October it had been announced that Imre Nagy had been appointed Prime Minister, but in fact he had been held captive by Gerö's men in the party headquarters. It was not until 28 October that he was able to exercise power. He then had to choose between agreement with the new political forces, which demanded much more than the first demonstrators had asked, or continued reliance on Soviet armed help. Nagy preferred the demands of the Hungarian people to the maintenance of Communist Party dictatorship. He formed a new government, in which the old socialist and peasant parties were represented by their real leaders. Knowing that this would rouse the fury of the Soviet leaders, he sought some international solution that could preserve Hungarian independence, and so proposed that Hungary should be given the same neutral status as Austria. He hoped no doubt that the Western Powers would support this plan.

But the Western Powers were paying little attention to Hungary. The United States was preoccupied with a presidential election, and Britain and France launched their Suez ultimatum on 30 October. Whether, if they had not been so preoccupied, they could have saved Hungary, cannot be proved or disproved. The only hope was to preserve the existing situation, by delay and negotiation. It is always more dangerous to upset a *status quo* than to maintain one: between 28 October and 3 November the *status quo* was favourable to the West, not to the Soviet Union. The task of Western diplomacy should have been to alarm the Soviet government while offering inducements, in the form of a wider settlement in Europe, for negotiation, meanwhile insisting that the legal government of Hungary (Nagy had been appointed Premier by the old régime with Soviet approval) must be left undisturbed. It is, of course, true that the Western Powers did not wish a world war for the sake of Hungary, but the Soviet government was also afraid of world war. The element of uncertainty could have been made to work in favour of the West as long as Nagy maintained himself: once Nagy was overthrown by Soviet force, it operated against the West. But political pressure by the West in Moscow, exploiting Soviet fears of war and designed to postpone a decision by Soviet force until the Nagy régime was established and a compromise could be made, involving concessions to Moscow by both Nagy and the West, would have required extreme concentration of thought and of diplomatic action on this one problem. Once the Suez action had started this was impossible. And once the Soviet government had been treated to the edifying spectacle of the United States violently denouncing its European allies, any last hesitation that may have remained in Khrushchov's mind about crushing Hungary must have evaporated.

On 4 November large forces of the Soviet army, which had been entering the country for some days past, attacked Budapest. The Soviet action was justified in Moscow on the ground that a new 'workers' and peasants' government' had been formed under János Kádár, and had appealed for Soviet help against the 'counter-revolutionary' forces to which Imre Nagy had surrendered. Kádár, who had been made First Secretary of the party in succession to Gerö on 24 October, had suffered imprisonment and torture under Rákosi, and had joined the multi-party government of Nagy, had deserted on 1 November, probably because the Soviet Ambassador had persuaded him that the Suez action and the creation of a multi-party régime under Nagy were both part of a systematic onslaught by 'the imperialists' against 'the socialist world'.* The Soviet army met with bitter resistance, especially from the workers. The last important fortresses of the Revolution were the metallurgical works of Csepel, a suburb of Budapest, and Dunapentele in the South. After armed resistance had been crushed, a general strike continued for more than a month in the capital. By the end of the year cold and hunger completed the task of 'liberation' begun by the 'disinterested comradely help' of the Soviet army. For some weeks the frontier with Austria was open, and 200,000 Hungarians, mostly workers and their families, escaped to an uncertain life in exile.

In Eastern Europe the suppression of the Hungarian Revolution had a more depressing effect than anything that had happened since 1948, when the communist dictatorships had been perfected. The East German, Czech and Bulgarian leaders were triumphant, none more than Ulbricht, the outstanding survivor of the purest Stalinist breed. Relations between the Soviet Union and Yugoslavia again deteriorated. Nagy was given refuge in the Yugoslav Embassy, which he left on receipt of a safe-conduct from Kádár, only to be arrested within a few yards of the Embassy building and deported to Roumania. Marshal Tito in a speech at Pola in December justified the second Soviet intervention as necessary to crush counterrevolution, but blamed the first intervention for having prevented acceptable reforms. The dilemma of the Yugoslav leaders, eager for independence from Moscow, yet opposed to any challenge to communist one-party rule, was clearer than ever. But even this measure of criticism of Moscow's policy was resented, and the Soviet-Yugoslav honeymoon was over.

In Poland the changes of October were real. Gomulka allowed the dissolution of collective farms, and there followed a mass exodus. He decided to end the policy of exploitation of the peasants by the state: they paid lower taxes and received better prices and material aid. The peasants were in fact the class which most benefited from the new régime. Gomulka also made an agreement with the Catholic Church, of which the most important results were that religious instruction was reintroduced into the schools and that the priests urged their flock to support the government. Gomulka would have liked to improve the material conditions

* In a statement broadcast by Budapest on 1 November, Kádár, who at that time, as First Secretary of the party, was still outwardly supporting Nagy, spoke of the dangers of counter-revolution both within Hungary and from abroad. He stated: 'A grave and alarming danger exists that foreign armed intervention may reduce our country to the tragic fate of Korea.' In communist terminology 'foreign' armed action always means Western armed action, and the only action which was taking place at that time was the Anglo-French action against Egypt. Kádár must have deserted a few hours after this broadcast. The text of the broadcast is given in *The Hungarian Revolution*, ed. Melvin J. Lasky, London, 1957, p. 179.

of the working class, but the wretched state of the economy made this impossible. The best he could do was to institute elected workers' councils in the factories, which for a time gave the workers the impression that they were having some say in their own affairs. The intellectual youth, which had led the movement for Gomulka's return, fared less well. For a time there was an extraordinary freedom of speech and press, but by the summer of 1957 the censorship was interfering. The most critical paper, *Po Prostu*, was suppressed in August 1957. The government press began to denounce 'Revisionism' (criticism from within the party of Marxist-Leninist doctrine, and especially of the principle of the 'dictatorship of the proletariat', as communist one-party rule is euphemistically described) as the main danger. Nevertheless, there was still far greater freedom than before October. Non-political literature and art were almost completely free, and political argument was tolerated provided that it was confined to non-official meetings of small groups of people. Only the alliance with the Soviet Union, and the subordination of Polish foreign policy to Soviet dictates, were beyond discussion.

In the Soviet Union it might have been expected that the position of Khrushchov, who had started the campaign against Stalin's memory, had sought Tito's friendship, and had allowed the freer atmosphere in Eastern Europe which had led to the crisis of the autumn, would now have deteriorated. Molotov, who had been removed from his long tenure of the Foreign Ministry to please Tito in the summer of 1956, but was still a leading member of the party's Presidium, was the obvious leader of the attack. On the other hand, Marshal Zhukov, who had become Minister of Defence in February 1955 when Malenkov had resigned the Premiership, seemed more likely to throw the increased weight of the army behind Khrushchov. In the spring of 1957 Khrushchov had regained confidence, for he then introduced a far-reaching administrative reform of the system of economic planning. In June 1957 the existence of a crisis at the top was publicly revealed. Khrushchov announced that an 'anti-party group' had been formed in the Presidium, of Molotov, Kaganovich and Malenkov. These veteran comrades of Stalin were deprived of their public offices. At the same time Marshal Zhukov was promoted to membership of the Presidium, the first time that a professional soldier had belonged to the inner circle of political power in the Soviet Union. It was assumed that Khrushchov had obtained the support of the army against his rivals at this price. However, the army's gains were short-lived. In November 1957 it was announced that Marshal Zhukov had been deprived of his public posts. The decision was taken while he was on a visit to Yugoslavia and Albania, and so was not in touch with the army hierarchy. His dismissal caused no unrest, and Marshal Malinovski, a distinguished if less outstanding figure, became Minister of Defence. It was now clear that Khrushchov had established himself as Stalin's successor, though he had not yet claimed the adulation enjoyed by Stalin in the era of the 'cult of personality'.

THE DEBATE ON DISENGAGEMENT

The tragedy of Hungary and the precarious status of Poland, the desire for unity in Germany and the feeling of helplessness in the face of Soviet power combined to make thoughtful people in Europe and in America wish to re-examine any chances there might be of an European settlement. It was felt that some much more serious effort must be made to free the East Europeans and East Germans from totalitarian rule and to remove the whole continent from the shadow of war. Yet it was clear that the Soviet leaders would not consent to this unless they received tangible advantages in return. The best hope seemed to lie in the direction of removing armed forces from the centre of Europe. The word 'disengagement' came to be used for policies of this sort. In fact no disengagement took place in 1957 or 1958, and none of the leading governments proposed it. But the argument about disengagements deserves serious consideration, for it involves all the basic issues of European policy since 1945.[94]

The possibilities of an agreed solution can only be seen if we first consider the maximum aims of the two opposed groups.

The maximum Western aim was that all Soviet forces should be removed from Eastern Europe and that Germany should be reunified in freedom, with a central government freely elected by the whole nation, free to choose whether it should join the Atlantic Alliance. It was generally believed in the West that a free, reunified Germany would voluntarily join NATO, and that if all Soviet troops were withdrawn from Eastern Europe, it would not be long before the régimes of most of these countries would drastically change, whether by violent revolution or peaceful pressures, and cease to be totalitarian or subservient to Moscow. The maximum aim of Western policy, then, was the removal of Soviet influence from all Europe. This was obviously not acceptable to the Soviet leaders.

The maximum Soviet aim was to retain Soviet control over Eastern Europe, to retain the communist régime in East Germany, to separate West Germany from NATO, to get all American forces out of Europe, and to set up some sort of confederal government of Germany which would enable the communists to entrench themselves in key positions and prepare for the seizure of power at a later date. Clearly this was not acceptable to the West.

If progress were to be made, there would have to be compromise, each side making sacrifices in return for gains. The essence of the various schemes of disengagement discussed in the West has been to exchange the freedom of the East Europeans and Germans for the neutralization of Germany.

There are three essential conditions which would have to be secured under any scheme of this sort. Firstly, the continuance of the Atlantic Alliance among the Western nations other than Germany, and the presence of some American troops on the Continent, must be accepted by the Soviet government. Secondly, the frontier between Germany and Poland must be finally determined, and accepted formally by all parties to the settlement and it is improbable that the Soviet government would accept any frontier substantially different from the present line. Thirdly, there must be a security pact, signed by all the parties, that would bind all at once to go to war with any state whose forces should re-enter any part of the region which is declared free from foreign troops and neutralized. This proviso would have to be extended so as to cover any case where foreign troops have allegedly been invited to enter—for example, by a puppet 'government' such as the Soviet government set up under Kádár in Hungary in 1956, or in Terijoki in Finland in 1939, or in Bialystok in Poland in 1920. It would, of course, preclude re-entry by all Powers equally. For example, French forces could no more re-enter Holland by invitation to help a democratic government against a rising by communists, than Soviet troops could re-enter Roumania by invitation of communists overthrown by democrats. To make a security treaty that would cover these points would not be easy, but unless they were covered the settlement would be worthless.

Assuming that these three conditions were satisfied, the settlement would provide for a neutral area consisting of Eastern Europe and all Germany. All foreign troops would be withdrawn from Germany, Poland and Hungary; West Germany would leave NATO; Poland, Czechoslovakia, Hungary, Roumania and Bulgaria would cease to be bound by their alliances with the Soviet Union, and the Warsaw Pact of May 1955 would cease to exist.

Several variations may be considered within this framework. The reunification of Germany in freedom might be made a previous condition for the settlement, or it might be assumed that the removal of Soviet troops from Germany, and the prohibition of their re-entry, would inevitably lead to the collapse of the communist régime, either by violence or by the peaceful acceptance of free elections. Secondly, the neutralized countries might have no armed forces of their own other than police, or armed forces with restrictions on certain types of weapons, or unlimited sovereignty over defence. The first and third of these hypotheses suggest obvious dangers; the second seems the most realistic. Thirdly, the portion of Eastern Europe to be neutralized might be confined to Poland, Czechoslovakia and Hungary. This seems hardly justifiable, for if only the first three have borders with West Germany today, Bulgaria has borders with Greece and Turkey; and if the Poles and Hungarians have shown their feelings towards Russia, there is every reason to believe that the Roumanians in no way yield to the Czechs in their dislike of Soviet influence or totalitarian government.

Let us now consider what would be the effect of some such settlement on the interests of each of the two Power groups.

The Soviet Union would risk losing its control over the whole of Eastern Europe and over Eastern Germany. In return it would receive a guarantee against attack by any Western Power, including reunified Germany, and the United States would be a party to the guarantee. If the Soviet government's main concern were security against attack, this solution might have much to commend itself. But if the Soviet government's main aim is to maintain communist régimes where they have been imposed, and in due course to extend communism further, to impose it also on individual West European countries as soon as this ceases to be prohibitively dangerous, then this settlement would be a very poor bargain. All the evidence to date has been that the Soviet government's main aim is the second of these. At no time has it shown itself willing even to abandon the Ulbricht régime in East Germany, the weakest and most unpopular of all the satellites.

For the West it would be an immense gain to assure to the peoples of Germany and Eastern Europe the chance to choose their own form of government, and to overthrow totalitarianism if they are capable of it, without fear of Soviet military intervention. But there are also grave objections to disengagement from the Western point of view.

The least of these is the unwillingness of West Germany to accept the Oder-Neisse frontier with Poland as permanent. Those Germans who feel strongly on this point are only a minority, but they are a vocal and energetic pressure-group. In all West European countries other than Germany the bulk of public opinion is on the Polish side in this matter, and to a lesser extent this is probably true of the United States. Poland was the ally of the West against Hitler, suffered more than any other of Hitler's victims and also suffered heavily from Soviet aggression. Western opinion probably inclines to the view that the acquisition of these territories is a reasonable compensation to Poland for her sufferings (though it cannot bring the

6 million dead to life). There are Germans who take this view, just as there are Germans who passionately desire to recover the whole territory, or even the frontier of 1914. Most Germans are, however, comparatively indifferent. They would not admit the justice of the Polish claim, but they do not regard the matter as of decisive importance. Among the expellees, the generation that has grown up since 1945 has struck roots in the Federal Republic, and has little interest in the old homelands. Every year the numbers of the irreconcilable diminish, of the indifferent increase. As long as the West German economy remains healthy—and this is a matter for the German government and its American and European allies— there is room for the expellees in the Federal Republic. Indeed, the impressive economic recovery of West Germany is in large measure due to the hard work and skill of the expellees. But to Poland these territories are of vital importance. Poland's whole industrial development depends on them. Meanwhile the high birth-rate of the Polish nation is steadily filling up the empty places in the lands from which the Germans were expelled, while the birth-rate in West Germany remains low. In short, if the Oder-Neisse line were the only objection to disengagement, it is by no means inconceivable (though it might be difficult) that the Western governments should persuade the West German government to accept the Oder-Neisse frontier, perhaps with some minor changes in Germany's favour, in return for the reunification of Germany in freedom. The liberty of 17 million Germans now under communist rule is worth more to most Germans than territories in which very few Germans are left.

More serious is the unwillingness of the Federal German government to accept a status of neutrality. It is often forgotten by those Western spokesmen who speak in favour of disengagement, not only that Chancellor Adenauer does not wish Germany to be neutral, but that the German electorate has three times voted him to power. The clear evidence is that the majority of free German opinion is against neutrality. The Western Powers cannot force their German allies to accept neutrality, or to accept permanent limitations of their sovereignty. And there is more to it than this. It is not just that Adenauer does not wish to be neutral: he is strongly in favour of the closer integration of his country with France, the Low Countries and Italy, of which the European Coal and Steel Community and the European Common Market are examples. If Germany were to be neutralized, all these organizations would have to be dismantled. This would be strongly resisted by the other West European nations and, as the same electoral evidence shows, by a majority of West German opinion.

Thirdly, there are strong military objections. Many military experts claim that it would not in fact be possible to establish on French, Dutch or

Belgian soil the American, Canadian and British forces whose presence on Continental soil is required under NATO. If they were withdrawn from Germany, it is argued, they would have to be withdrawn from Europe altogether. To this it can be replied that the security of all European states would have been formally guaranteed by the security pact, which would oblige all signatories to go to war with any aggressor. (We have already emphasized that unless there is such a security pact, with a clause forbidding 're-entry', whether 'invited' or not, no project of disengagement can be taken seriously.) However, the paucity of conventional forces available to the NATO Powers in Europe, and the limited strength of the forces permitted to a neutral reunited Germany (in the most likely of the hypotheses discussed above) would make it impossible for the Western Powers to react to a Soviet aggression against one of the East European states unless they were to use the full panoply of total atomic war. But would any United States government be willing to subject New York and Chicago to attack by missiles with thermo-nuclear warheads in order to defend the Roumanians against a Soviet re-entry justified by an 'invitation' from a puppet 'government'? Unless this question can be answered with a confident 'Yes', the whole scheme breaks down.

To sum up, the obstacles to even the most carefully planned disengagement—the unwillingness of Moscow to allow communist régimes in East Germany or Eastern Europe to be overthrown, the unwillingness of Bonn to be neutral or to abandon West European integration, and the military dangers resulting for the whole of the Western Alliance—appear overwhelming.

WESTERN EUROPE IN 1959

The most important event of 1958 in Western Europe was the return to power of General de Gaulle in France. On 13 May a *coup d'état* took place in Algiers. The French population of Algeria demanded more energetic action against the FLN and a positive policy of 'integration' of French and Moslems in an *Algérie française*. The civilian leaders of the *coup* blamed the failures of the last years not on their own intransigence towards the Moslems, but on the weakness and indecision of the metropolitan governments and parliament. Their views were clearly shared by the majority of the resident French population. They were also shared to a large extent by the officers of the army. Many years of humiliation, first in Indochina then in North Africa, and lack of sympathy for their predicament from civilian politicians, had alienated them from the whole régime. They placed their hopes in General de Gaulle, the man who represented the indomitable spirit of French patriotism, whom they could trust to place the interests of France above those of party or class. The civilian politicians in Algiers for their part hoped that de Gaulle would be the instrument of their policies. Once the cry of *De Gaulle au pouvoir!* had been launched from Algiers, it became clear that it had strong support in France and that opposition to it was weak. The only combination of resistance that might have been effective would have been one based on a Popular Front of socialists, communists and other smaller groups, in which the communists would certainly have had the main influence. To French socialists and democrats this was unacceptable, both because they rejected communist leadership and because a Popular Front government would have been faced with a civil war, in which the parachutist *élite* formations would have been backed by the bulk of the French army in metropolitan France as well as in Algeria. General de Gaulle himself had not been in any way involved in the Algiers *coup*, but at once issued a statement that he would be willing to assume power. After days of anxious negotiations, in which President Coty set himself the task of reconciling the democratic leaders to de Gaulle's solution, the Assembly on 1 June voted by a majority of 329 to 224 for a government in which de Gaulle was Premier. A new Constitution was then prepared which diminished the role of parliament and gave the decisive powers to the President of the Republic. By a referendum held on 28 September the French electorate voted for de Gaulle's Constitution by a majority of almost 80%. In January 1959 it came into force, and the General assumed the office of President.

The reception of these events by the Western press was surprisingly hostile, considering the past record of the General. It was understandable that Western politicians and journalists should be distressed at the revelation of the rottenness and unpopularity of parliamentary government in France, even though the evidence of this had been accumulating for a long time past. It was also undeniably true that in Algiers fascist influences were strong, and that the danger of a growth of fascism in France itself was real. Finally, it was understandable that in the United States and France, and still more in Western Germany, there were fears that de Gaulle, whose conception of his country's greatness had made him a difficult partner for Roosevelt and Churchill in the Second World War, and who had been a symbol of French resistance to the German danger, would prove an awkward ally in NATO. But against these dangers could surely be set the enormous advantage that France, whose weakness and absence from Western councils as a major factor since 1946 had left an unfilled gap in the West, would now be represented by a stable government and a great statesman. This advantage was pointed out by some lonely voices in the West, but the prevalent opinion ranged from cold politeness at the official level, to strident hostility on the left. Frenchmen might indeed be pardoned for thinking that the objections of the Anglo-Saxon press were not so much to the real or imagined dangers of the new régime as to the prospect of a restored France. And indeed, though it was and is reasonable to remain sceptical as to the extent to which France can be restored as a major Power, the Western reactions often went beyond scepticism. Rather they took pleasure in making fun of the very idea of French greatness. Yet French greatness is a necessary condition for a healthy Europe; though admittedly difficult to achieve, it is hardly a ridiculous aim.

In the winter of 1958-9 a serious government crisis occurred also in Italy. The divisions within the Christian Democratic Party could no longer be bridged. At the end of January 1959 the party's General Secretary, Amintore Fanfani, who was also Prime Minister, resigned both offices. Fanfani's government was based on a coalition with the Social Democratic Party. It too had become split, as a result of disagreement on the attitude to be taken to the Socialist Party. The socialists' congress in January 1959 brought victory to Nenni, who was able to free the party from its previous dependence on the communists, though he did not adopt a clear anti-communist line. This change in the Socialist Party exercised an obvious attraction on the left wing of the social democrats, who opposed their party's support for the government coalition. The loss of part of his social democratic support in turn weakened Fanfani's left wing in the Christian Democratic Party. The government crisis ended with the formation on 15 February of a government under Antonio Segni, in which the right wing of the Christian Democrats prevailed, and which relied for support in parliament on the parties of the right. In foreign policy the new government was more devoted to NATO than its predecessor. In fact, under de Gaulle, Adenauer and Segni the governments of the three main countries of continental Western Europe were closer to each other than they had been for some years.

This was reflected in the negotiations at the end of 1958 about the European Common Market or Free Trade Area, in which the three countries found themselves united against British proposals, and the relations of Britain with her European allies became seriously strained. It was admittedly difficult to reconcile British membership of the Common Market with existing economic arrangements between Britain and Commonwealth countries. To the British negotiators it seemed that France was demanding privileged treatment of her products and refusing reasonable concessions to Britain in regard to Commonwealth trade, while the European negotiators considered the British Free Trade Area a plan to give Britain the advantages of membership while exempting her from any of the sacrifices. But behind these serious economic conflicts were political issues. British membership of the Common Market would be a long step towards the integration of Britain in Western Europe. The Common Market is intended by its champions to be more than an economic organization: it is intended to bring nearer a comprehensive union of Western Europe. British political leaders of both parties are still opposed to British participation in such a union. They do not wish to give up any of Britain's sovereignty. They wish to preserve Britain's distinct relationship both to the United States and to the Asian and African nations within and without the Commonwealth. Membership of a closer West European union would, for example, commit Britain to a support of French policy in Algeria, which would embarrass her relations with Arab and African nations. For their part, many Frenchmen suspect British policy of intriguing against France in Africa. The memory of Anglo-French conflict in the Middle East in 1943-5 is still fresh, and the announcement by Dr. Nkrumah of his Ghana-Guinea Union aroused frantic mistrust of Britain in Paris.

Closer co-operation between the Commonwealth and Western Europe is most desirable, and perhaps not so difficult as the more emotional spokesmen on either side at times suggest. Much will depend on the attractiveness of the European Common Market to the Commonwealth countries, and on the damage to British interests that British exclusion from it may cause. In the last resort it is difficult to accept the view that the British have more important interests in common with the Indians and Nigerians than with the French and Belgians. The world-wide influence of Britain may depend on relations with the Arab and African nationalists, but the security of the British Isles is inseparable from that of France and Germany. Yet it is not clear that Britain has to make a clear choice between Europe and the Commonwealth. To maintain close relations with both is a worthy aim of British policy, but this requires Britain to bring them together, not to play them off against each other.

The recriminations between Britain and her European allies provided a good opportunity for Soviet diplomacy, and it is not surprising that Khrushchov should have chosen this moment to bring up the most delicate problem in Europe, the status of Berlin. The proposed transfer by the Soviet government of all authority over the territory surrounding Berlin to the East German satellite, which the Western Powers did not recognize, coupled with the threat that any armed conflict between Western troops and East German forces would be a *casus belli* for the Soviet Union, created an extremely dangerous situation. Khrushchov proposed that West Berlin be made an international free city, but did not suggest that

East Berlin should have a similar status, and offered no guarantee that the East German communists would not interfere with the liberties of the free city. Neither the West German government nor its NATO allies could accept this proposal.

Two other Soviet demands, which arose from the new proposals, but which had been made many times before, were also unacceptable.

The first of these was that the Western Powers should recognize the East German government. To agree to this would be a brutal blow to the government of Dr. Adenauer, which ever since 1949 had shown itself a loyal partner of the West. Yet the fact remained that the East German régime existed. As a power system it worked, and unless Soviet support were withdrawn, it remained a fact of the European situation.

The second demand was that reunification of Germany should be brought about by a 'confederation' of the 'two German states' on a basis of parity of representation. This would be even more unacceptable to the West and to the West German government than mere recognition of the East German régime. In a confederation there would have to be a supreme central government with at least some powers, and the East German communists would share these on an equal basis with the West German government. The example of the Czechoslovak coalition government of 1945-8 showed to what results this could lead. Confederation on a basis of population (that is, with three-quarters of the central power held by West Germany) might make possible democratic pressures against the communist régime in the East, but this was unlikely to be acceptable to the Soviet government.

The visits of Mr. Macmillan and Mr. Nixon to Moscow, of President Eisenhower to Europe, and of Deputy-Premiers Mikoyan and Kozlov and then of Mr. Krushchov himself to the United States, which took place during 1959, served to postpone the crisis created by Krushchov's original proposals. The "summit conference" and the visit of Eisenhower to the Soviet Union, both planned for 1960, were expected to continue this process. But a solution to the German problem, acceptable to all parties concerned, seemed as far away as ever.

THE BALKANS

Between 1955 and 1958 the Western position in the Balkans was undermined by the Cyprus dispute, which coincided alarmingly with the long series of reverses to Western policy in the Arab world. Thereby the security of Turkey, the only firm position in the whole Eastern Mediterranean, was undermined. On the other hand the growth of tension between the Soviet Union and Yugoslavia to some extent benefited Western influence in the latter country.

Cyprus is of obvious strategic importance to Turkey, near whose coast it lies, but its population is more than 80% Greek and less than 20% Turkish. It has not been part of Greece since the time of the Byzantine Empire, but was ruled by Crusaders, Venetians and Turks up to 1878, when it was leased to Britain by the Ottoman Sultan. In 1914, when the Ottoman Empire went to war with Britain, the British government annexed it. Between the world wars a movement developed on the island for union (*enosis*) with Greece, and there were serious riots in 1931.

The common struggle of Britain and Greece during the Second World War aroused hopes in Greece that Britain would reward her loyal ally by ceding the island. The Labour Party was known to favour more rapid self-determination for colonial peoples than the Conservative Party. In 1945 no opposition by Turkey need have been feared, for as a wartime neutral she enjoyed far less sympathy in the Allied countries than Greece, and was in any case preoccupied with the Soviet threat to her eastern frontiers and to the Straits. Unfortunately, the situation in Greece made cession impossible. The fighting of 1944 was followed by a year of weak government, and then by a second civil war. It was not to be expected that Britain would relinquish an island of strategic importance to a country whose future was so uncertain. Moreover, as Turkey recovered from the immediate post-war dangers, its leaders too became worried by the instability in Greece, by the danger of a communist victory. Turkey was no less unwilling to see Cyprus in Greek hands than were the British, and Turkey now had influence in the Western camp.

In 1950 the civil war in Greece was ended, and two years later there came to power what looked like a strong and stable government, the first Greece had had since the war, led by a war hero, Marshal Papagos. The new government was strongly pro-Western, but it was also strongly nationalist. Inevitably it raised with the British government, through diplomatic channels, the question of union of Cyprus with Greece. It seems that Marshal Papagos' overtures received a less than courteous reception from the British government. In July 1954 the British government publicly announced the introduction of a new Constitution for Cyprus, which allowed greater self-government, but stressed that British sovereignty would not be abandoned. In fact, Britain was treating Cyprus as a colonial problem, to be dealt with by the normal procedure of Colonial Office constitutional reform, not as an international question between two friendly European Powers. Moreover, the Greek Cypriots were being offered fewer rights than the Africans of the Gold Coast had already received, or than were being busily prepared for the Nigerians. Greek public opinion was bitterly offended, and the Greek government brought the question of Cyprus before the UN General Assembly in December 1954. Diplomatic negotiation had been replaced by a public quarrel between allies.

If the British government had been tactless and unimaginative, the Greek government was guilty of the same faults. The moment was particularly ill-chosen for asking territorial concessions from Britain. The Conservative Party, in office since 1951, still resented the humiliation of Abadan and the necessity of ceding the Canal Base to Egypt. Churchill and Eden had with great difficulty persuaded their party that they must come to terms with Egypt: they could not now ask for even more retreats. Moreover, the Greek government had taken no pains to sound Turkish opinion before making a public issue of Cyprus. In 1953, the year of the signature of the Ankara Pact, relations between Greece and Turkey were probably nearer to genuine friendship than they had ever been in the history of either nation. This friendship would be in danger should Greece take an action that Turkey would feel as a threat to her. But Greek spokesmen, officially or privately, dismissed the suggestion that Turkey might be opposed to a Greek Cyprus as a mere British intrigue. In any case, they claimed, it was unreasonable that the views of 20% of the population of the island should be allowed to thwart the will of 80%. An impartial observer must admit the strength of the second argument, and there may even be historically some truth in the first. But whatever the truth about past British manœuvres, it became clear by 1955 that the Turkish government itself had the strongest objections to a Greek Cyprus, not so much because of its interest in the fate of the Turkish minority on the island as because it feared to see so strategic a position in the hands of a small, weak state. If the Greek government had inquired of the Turkish attitude before raising the issue publicly, it could have spared itself a lot of humiliation.

The General Assembly of UN could not and did not take any action in Cyprus. But Greek-Turkish relations deteriorated to the point where the Ankara Pact ceased to have any meaning, and Greek membership of NATO was a dubious asset. In Cyprus a terrorist organization called EOKA, led by a Greek army officer of fascist past named Grivas, began to murder first Greeks, then British and Turks. A conference in London in 1955 between Britain, Greece and Turkey only made relations worse. In the autumn Turkish rioters smashed the property of Greek citizens in Istanbul. In March 1956 the Orthodox archbishop of Cyprus, Makarios, whose office made him the political leader of the Greek Cypriot community, was exiled to the Seychelle Islands. Throughout 1957 and 1958 the murders in Cyprus continued. But in February 1959 the governments of Greece and Turkey, convinced that co-operation between their countries was of greater importance to each than the possession or partition of Cyprus, reached agreement on the basis of independence for the island. This was accepted by the British government, which had long since lost its original determination to maintain British sovereignty, and by the leaders of both the Greek and Turkish Cypriots, Archbishop Makarios and Dr. Küçük. British rights over the military base on the island were guaranteed. An uncertain factor for the future was the influence of the Cypriot communists, who could be expected to do their best to interfere with the operation of the base. The communists in Greece could be expected to do likewise, and they had recovered a good deal of support since 1954. In Cyprus anti-British feeling remained strong among Greek Cypriots of extreme right and extreme left. On the British side were memories of individuals murdered at random, usually by shooting in the back, and of Athens Radio broadcasts which for years extolled these actions as heroic deeds and compared British troops in Cyprus to Hitler's SS in wartime Greece.

At the other end of the Balkan Peninsula, the position of Yugoslavia changed during 1957 and 1958.

In August 1957 Tito met Khrushchov in Bucharest, and it seemed that the quarrel of the winter had been ended. In October Yugoslavia recognised the Ulbricht government in East Germany. This obliged the Federal German government to break diplomatic relations with Yugoslavia. This in turn let loose a campaign in the East European press and radio, representing Adenauer's government as an aggressive gang planning to revive Hitler's plans in the Danube valley and the Balkans. This campaign was especially bitter in the Polish press. This was the climax of Yugoslavia's reconciliation with Moscow. In the following month a conference was held in Moscow of delegates of communist parties, who had come to celebrate the 40th anniversary of the Bolshevik Revolution, and at which Yugoslavia was represented. The Yugoslavs, however, refused to sign the manifesto published after the conference by 12 parties,* for it would have obliged them to abandon their uncommitted foreign policy and definitely to join the Soviet camp. This refusal led to a new deterioration in Yugoslav-Soviet relations.

In April 1958 the League of Communists of Yugoslavia (as the Communist

* Of the Soviet Union, China, Poland, Czechoslovakia, Hungary, Roumania, Bulgaria, East Germany, North Korea, North Vietnam, France and Italy.

Party had been called since 1948) held its 7th Congress. It previously issued a Draft Programme which was a statement of theoretical principles as well as of practical policy. It contained three points which were utterly unacceptable to the Soviet leaders.

The first was that it was possible to achieve socialism without revolution. The most that Soviet spokesmen had ever admitted was that it was possible to have a 'peaceful revolution', to advance to socialism 'by a parliamentary road'. Mikoyan had said this at the 20th Congress in Moscow in February 1956, but had made his meaning clear by giving as his examples the seizure of power by the communists in Czechoslovakia and in East Germany. Stripped of its verbiage, the Soviet thesis meant that if the communists' opponents surrendered without a fight, it would be possible to seize power without force, and then set up a dictatorship which would forcibly suppress opposition. The difference between a 'violent' and a 'peaceful' revolution was that in the first violence was used both before and after attaining power, in the second only after. The result of both processes was the same: communist one-party dictatorship. But the Yugoslavs maintained in their draft programme that it was possible to achieve socialism without using violence at all.

This led to the second point, that communist parties do not possess a monopoly of the ability to lead a nation towards socialism. Socialism can be built under the leadership of parties that are not communist—that is, are not Marxist-Leninist and do not recognize the supreme authority of the Soviet Union.

The third controversial Yugoslav point was the assertion that the principal cause of the danger of war in the world was the *existence* of two Power blocs, the Western and the Soviet. In the Soviet view, of course, the danger of war was solely due to the imperialistic policies of one of these blocs, the bloc of Western monopoly capitalism, led by the United States.

All three points were equally inadmissible in Moscow. In all three the Yugoslav leaders were thinking primarily of the uncommitted states of Asia and Africa, with which they had, or hoped to establish, good relations. It was precisely in such countries as India and Egypt that the Yugoslav ideologists could conceive of socialism being built without violence by parties whose outlook was socialist, but which did not submit to the hierarchy of Moscow. As for the view of international tension which placed the two blocs on an equal level, each in principle responsible for the danger of war, though at particular moments the one might be more to blame than the other, this was indistinguishable from the view of Pandit Nehru. In short, Yugoslavia was refusing to support the Soviet bloc, and was making a bid for influence in the uncommitted countries that would weaken Soviet influence. There could be no forgiveness for such attitudes.

During the summer of 1958 there were bitter polemics between the Soviet Union and Yugoslavia, echoed in the satellite states, especially in Bulgaria and Albania, both of which claimed Yugoslav territory. The rivalry between Serbs and Bulgars for Macedonia dated from the 1880s. In 1913, 1918 and 1944 most of Macedonia had gone to Serbia and her successor, Yugoslavia. In 1948 the Bulgarian communist government had come out in favour of an independent Macedonia that would have been dominated by Bulgaria. In 1955 Bulgaria had stopped this propaganda, but in the summer of 1958 it revived it. Ever since 1948 the Albanian communist government had conducted anti-Yugoslav propaganda: even during the Tito-Khrushchov honeymoon of 1955-6 it had only slightly modified it. This propaganda had a certain genuine popular support, in so far as 700,000 Albanians—about one-third of the whole Albanian nation—lived under Yugoslav rule in the Kosovo-Metohija region.

The Macedonian problem also affected Greece. A large part of the geographical area known as Macedonia had been Greek since 1913, and in that territory there was a Slav-speaking minority of uncertain numbers. During the Greek civil war, Yugoslav Macedonian spokesmen often talked of union of 'Aegean Macedonia' with Yugoslavia. When Yugoslavia and Greece became reconciled after 1950, such talk was discouraged, though not entirely silenced, by the Belgrade government. The Bulgarian spokesmen also claimed 'Aegean Macedonia', but on behalf of an independent or Bulgarian-dominated Macedonia.

In 1958 the Bulgarian government showed less interest in Greek than in Yugoslav Macedonia. As long as Greece was engaged in bitter conflict with Britain and Turkey, it was better not to cause alarm about her northern frontier. Nevertheless, the revival of the Macedonian problem in Yugoslav-Bulgarian relations indirectly affected Greek interests, while the settlement of the Cyprus conflict gave a new incentive to the Soviet government to put pressure on Greece through Bulgaria. On his return from a journey in Asia in March 1959, President Tito declared that Yugoslavia had no intention of reviving the Balkan Pact. But while Soviet intentions in the Balkans were uncertain, the basic community of interests between Yugoslavia, Greece and Turkey remained a fact.

16: The Arabs and Their Neighbours

THE NEW EGYPT

The group of 'Free Officers' who seized power in July 1952 had no definite political programme. Some of them had had connexions with the Moslem Brotherhood, and one at least with communists. All were passionate nationalists, determined to regenerate the nation, to free Egypt from all foreign domination and to make it great. They had felt the British ultimatum to Faruk of February 1942 as a national humiliation. The defeat in Palestine had embittered them still more. They hated the dynasty as the embodiment of corruption and of subservience to the foreigner. The nation was to them more than an abstraction. They were concerned with the miserable condition of the flesh-and-blood Egyptians who composed it. They therefore passed the Land Reform Act of September 1952. But though this was an act of social reform, the Free Officers were not committed to a general left-wing attitude. On 12-13 August there were disorders in the spinning mill at Kafr el-Dawar. When the police proved unable to deal with the workers, army units were sent, eight workers were killed, 200 arrested, and two workers' leaders were tried by court-martial and hanged. The Free Officers at first made Ali Maher, the elder statesman, Premier but in September replaced him by the man whom they had adopted as the titular leader of their group, General Mohammed Neguib. The leaders of the political parties, especially of the *Wafd*, had greeted the July *coup d'état*, both because they were glad to be rid of Faruk and because they hoped that by offering the benefit of their 'experienced counsel' to the young heroes they would return to power. But Abd el-Nasser and his friends had little use for the old gang. They showed great skill in splitting the *Wafd*, and in January 1953 they finally dissolved all political parties and confiscated their property. A new official mass movement, the 'National Liberation Rally', was created in their place. In June 1953 Egypt was proclaimed a Republic. General Neguib became President of the Republic and Prime Minister, while Abd el-Nasser came for the first time into the political limelight as Vice-Premier.

The most serious crisis of the new régime came in 1954, when acute conflict arose between Neguib and Nasser. Neguib, an officer with a fine military record and a keen nationalist, had been in contact with the Free Officers in their conspiratorial period, had approved of their aims, but had taken no active part in the events of 23 July 1952. Within the inner circle, his influence could not compare with that of Abd el-Nasser. But in the eyes of the Egyptian people he was the national hero, while Nasser was hardly known. Thus Neguib's mass popularity made him a powerful political factor. Neguib believed in milder and more cautious methods. He disliked the repression of the old parties, the contemptuous or even brutal treatment of senior army officers and prominent civilians of the old upper class, among whom he had many friends. He was also well disposed to the Moslem Brotherhood. During 1953 the Brotherhood became definitely hostile to Nasser. Like the political parties, the Brotherhood had hoped to recover influence under the new régime, and was resentful when the Free Officers kept power in their hands. It denounced, both for tactical reasons and from genuine conviction, the conciliatory attitude of Nasser in his negotiations with the British. When in January 1954 Nasser decided to forbid the Brotherhood, Neguib resigned his offices. During March 1954 strong support for Neguib was expressed in the army, and the Brotherhood mobilized crowds in the streets. Nasser made a show of yielding and Neguib remained President while Nasser became Premier. But Nasser was biding his time. The real power was in his hands. Neguib had no organization at his command. The only force outside the ruling group which could have made him a power, the Moslem Brotherhood, was crushed after one of its members had made an attempt on Nasser's life on 26 October 1954. There were many arrests, and six of its leaders were hanged. In November Neguib gave up the Presidency and was placed under house arrest.

The military régime reopened negotiations with Britain on the two intractable problems of evacuation of the Canal Zone and the future of the Sudan.

Egyptians considered the Sudan a part of Egypt. The majority of its people were Moslems and spoke Arabic: less than 3 million out of 10 million were members of Nilotic negro tribes living in the southern provinces. It controlled the upper waters of the Nile, on which the very life of Egypt depends. But whereas the Egyptians demanded 'unity of the Nile valley', the British were determined that the Sudanese should themselves decide their future, and were convinced that the Sudanese would choose independence from Egypt.

During the first decades of British rule in the Sudan, the main political factors had been two Moslem religious sects—the *Ansar*, led by Sayid Abd el-Rahman el-Mahdi, the posthumous son of the Mahdi of 1881, and the *Khatmiya*, led by Sayid Ali el-Mirgani. The first secular political organization was the Graduates' Congress, formed in 1937 and consisting of members of the newly arising Sudanese intelligentsia. From the

Graduates' Congress there grew in the 1940s two political groupings—the Independence Front, which enjoyed the support of Sayid Abd el-Rahman and aimed at an independent Sudanese state, and the National Front, which was backed by Sayid Ali el-Mirgani and preferred union with Egypt. In 1948 the British authorities held the first elections to a Sudanese Legislative Council. As the Egyptian government was utterly opposed to independence for the Sudan, the National Front boycotted the election. It was therefore won by the Independence Front and the followers of Sayid Abd el-Rahman, which dominated the Council for the next years.

Whereas earlier Egyptian governments had simply opposed Sudanese independence as a British trick, Abd el-Nasser accepted the principle of self-determination, and made great efforts to win over the Sudanese to choose union with Egypt. Neguib, who had served in the Sudan and was well liked there, played an important part. Propaganda and bribery were lavishly used. The Egyptians courted not only their known friends, but also Sayid Abd el-Rahman and his followers.

In February 1953 the British and Egyptian governments reached agreement. There was to be an interim period of three years during which the Sudan would have self-government and an elected parliament, and the civil service should be rapidly 'Sudanized'. At the end of three years it should decide between independence and union with Egypt. At the first Sudanese parliamentary election, held during November and December 1953, the pro-Egyptian group, now named National Unionist Party, won fifty-two out of ninety-seven seats, and the chief advocate of union with Egypt, Ismail el-Azhari, became Premier. During the next years, however, there was a reaction against Egypt. Neguib's fall produced an unpleasant impression in the Sudan. A mutiny of Sudanese troops in the south emphasized the dangers of ignoring the wishes of the non-Arab third of the population. The old problem of the division of the Nile waters between Egypt and Sudan aroused fears. Would the Egyptians show so much respect for the needs of Sudanese agriculture once they had the Sudan in their power? Finally, the Sudanese politicians, not least el-Azhari himself, found the dignity of office agreeable, and were less attracted by the prospect of reduced status in a much more populous country. When the interim period came to an end, it was el-Azhari himself who proclaimed Sudanese independence on 1 January 1956. In the following November the Sudan became a member of the United Nations. For the time being at any rate the Egyptian cause had been defeated.

The second issue, evacuation of the Canal Zone, was simpler, but it proved more difficult to obtain an Anglo-Egyptian settlement than in the case of the Sudan. A large part of the negotiation concerned technical questions—the handling of the military equipment that was to be left in the Base, and the number and status of the British experts who would remain there when the Egyptians had taken over. The truth was, however, that the Base was of doubtful value to Britain, for if guerrilla war should break out again on the scale of 1951, the cost to Britain in troops tied down to guard the Canal Zone would be far greater than any military benefit that Britain could get from the Base. In the end the British government met most of the Egyptian demands. More serious was the question of the right of Britain to reoccupy the Base in time of war. The Egyptians agreed that this right should be granted for the event of an aggression against Egypt or a state member of the Arab League, but was unwilling to agree for the event of an attack on Turkey. On this point the British stood firm, and in the end the Egyptians yielded. The agreement was signed in July 1954. Both sides had made concessions, and had shown courage in risking unpopularity. After the disaster in Persia, British conservatives were extremely unwilling to accept any further retreat, but Eden nevertheless had his way. For his part, Nasser acted against the opposition of the extreme nationalists, Moslem Brotherhood and communists. This display of moderation and statesmanship by both parties raised the hope that a new and happier chapter was opening in the relations between Egypt and the West.

THE BAGHDAD PACT

It was clear by 1952 that it was a hopeless task to seek to incorporate the Arab Middle East in the Western system of alliances. The United States government therefore devoted greater attention to the conception of a 'northern tier' of alliances among the non-Arab states lying immediately south of the Soviet Union. Of these the most endangered, and at the same time the strongest—both in military power and in internal political morale —was Turkey. During 1953 Turkey's western flank had been strengthened by the conclusion of the Ankara Pact. Turkey's eastern neighbour, Persia, was at this time a prey to the convulsions of the Mossadeq régime. Afghanistan, which had been allied to Turkey by the 1937 Treaty of Saadabad, was now determined to preserve her neutrality, accepting economic assistance from both the Soviet Union and the United States, but aligning herself with neither, and relying also on the moral support of neighbouring neutral India. Pakistan was, however, willing to make a treaty with Turkey, not so much because this would protect her security (or even that of Turkey) as because it would enable her to receive American military aid, which she desired in view of her bad relations with India. With American blessing, the Turkish-Pakistani pact was signed in April 1954.

Turkey's south-eastern neighbour, Iraq, was ruled by Nuri es-Said Pasha, who took seriously the Soviet threat to the Middle East, wished to align his country with the West, and had long favoured a pro-Turkish orientation. During 1954 Nuri made further efforts to persuade the Egyptians to join him in aligning the Arab League (whose members had signed a Security Pact with each other in June 1950) with the West. When he was finally convinced that this was impossible, he decided to limit himself to an Iraqi-Turkish alliance, which was signed on 24 February 1955. Meanwhile, the problem of British forces in Iraq, which had been unsolved since the rejection by Iraq of the treaty of January 1948, continued to preoccupy the governments of London and Baghdad. A way out of the difficulty was found by the accession of Britain to the Iraqi-Turkish alliance on 5 April 1955. Under the new arrangement, the air bases of Habbaniya and Shaiba were transferred from British to Iraqi control, and only small numbers of British air force advisers remained in the country. Thus the old Iraqi-British alliance was placed on a new and more equal foundation. In July 1955 Pakistan, already linked to Turkey by a bilateral treaty, decided to join the group. In October 1955 Persia, which had by now recovered from the Mossadeq era, and had attained under the rule of the Shah and General Zahedi at least a minimum of internal stability, also became a member.

The Baghdad Pact, as the five-Power alliance of Britain, Turkey, Persia, Pakistan and Iraq became known, was impressive on paper, but less satisfactory in practice. The trouble was that its net was spread too far, that it raised more problems than it could solve. The conception of a northern tier alliance was sound. But this required no more than an alliance between Turkey, Persia, Britain and the United States. In fact, however, the United States decided not to join the Pact. The traditional reluctance of Congress to accept formal alliances was increased by opposition of the Jewish lobby in the United States to any association with Nuri es-Said, who, though a friend of the West, was a bitter enemy of Israel. On the other hand, the Pact did not confine itself to the two countries lying between the Soviet Union and the Persian Gulf or Mediterranean, but was extended to include Pakistan and Iraq.

It was doubtful whether Pakistan was, or even whether its leaders sincerely believed it to be, threatened by the Soviet Union, and it was doubtful whether Pakistan could give much help to Persia, let alone to Turkey, if they were attacked. Pakistan, however, wished for American military aid, and to join an 'anti-communist' alliance was an infallible way of getting this. But the Power against which Pakistan needed military aid was India. It was certainly not in the Western interest to antagonize India, to push her into a form of 'neutrality' more benevolent to the Soviet than to the Western camp. But this was the effect of the inclusion of Pakistan in the Pact.

Still more unfortunate was the decision to include Iraq. It was, of course, a convenient way of solving the Anglo-Iraqi problem. It is also true both that Nuri Pasha strongly desired to join, and indeed to play a leading part in, the alliance, and that the Turks wished to have Iraq as a member. Yet in practice the Baghdad Pact probably did more harm than good, both to Nuri and to the West. It would have been possible for the West to make a formal alliance only with Turkey and Persia, and at the same time to continue all sorts of material assistance and advice to Nuri, even strengthening his position by unilaterally withdrawing the remaining British armed forces, handing over the bases unconditionally, and urging the Iraq Petroleum Company to offer the Iraq government more favourable terms. Instead, the Western Powers preferred, by accepting Nuri's offer of membership in the alliance, to brand him in the eyes of Arab nationalists, both in Iraq and abroad, as a subservient tool of 'the imperialists'.

The Egyptians were especially angry. The old project of a Hashemite-controlled Greater Syria, of an Iraqi bid for the leadership of the Fertile Crescent in opposition to Egypt, was now revived, and this at a time when Abd el-Nasser had shown himself exceptionally conciliatory to the West. If Nasser and his colleagues were angry, Egyptian nationalists in general were still angrier. The Saudi Arabian reaction was also hostile. In Syria radical nationalism had been steadily gaining ground, and the overthrow of Faruk by the Free Officers had increased the attraction of Egypt. The strongest nationalist group was the Baath Socialist Party, which had been formed in 1953 by the fusion of several small groups, and whose outstanding leader was Akram Hourani.

Even in Jordan anti-Western feeling was becoming formidable. The annexation of eastern Palestine had transformed the nature of this small state. Its population had doubled, and the traditionalist Bedouin, loyal to the Hashemite dynasty, were now outnumbered by Palestinians, socially more advanced and diverse, better educated, more politically minded and passionately nationalist. The British government hoped that Jordan would join the Baghdad Pact, and that the Anglo-Jordan treaty of 1948, which gave Britain air bases in Jordan, could be replaced by the new Pact in the same way as the previous British bases in Iraq had been replaced. Jordan at first appeared willing to join, after the British Chief of Imperial General Staff, Sir Gerald Templer, had visited Amman. But four ministers thereupon resigned from the Jordan government, and when a new government was formed there were strikes and riots which brought its fall. King Hussein therefore decided not to join the Pact.

Deprived of American membership and complicated by involvement in the Indian-Pakistani conflict and in the internal rivalries of the Arab world, the Baghdad Pact was not effective as a 'northern tier' alliance, and contributed to hatred of the West among Arabs. Its value depended on the survival of Nuri's régime in Iraq, and with growing unrest among the intelligentsia and city population the régime depended on its police and armed forces. These were comparatively well-armed and disciplined, but neither soldiers nor policemen are more immune to the bacillus of radical nationalism than civilians.

NORTH AFRICA

The policy of repression applied by the French authorities in Tunisia, Morocco and Algeria alike during 1952 and 1953 could no longer be maintained when France suffered disaster in Indochina. The government of M. Mendès-France, which had decided to accept defeat in the Far East, was also determined to try a new approach in North Africa. It began in Tunisia.

In July 1954 Bourguiba was brought from his island confinement to France, and allowed to receive visitors freely. On 31 July Mendès-France flew to Tunis and announced in a public speech that Tunisia would be given complete internal autonomy. A new Tunisian ministry was formed, in which the *Néo-Destour* was represented. Though Mendès-France was overthrown by the Assembly in February 1955, the negotiations with Tunisia continued, and the new Premier, Edgar Faure, entered into personal discussions with Bourguiba. At the end of May 1955 Bourguiba returned to Tunisia, and the Franco-Tunisian agreement on internal autonomy was signed.

The extremists among both the French *colons* and the Tunisian nationalists still hoped, however, to upset the settlement. The latter found a leader in Salah ben-Yussef, who had spent the last years in Cairo, and opposed the 1955 agreement because it gave Tunisia less than complete independence. He returned to Tunis in September and began to agitate within the *Néo-Destour*. But Bourguiba's authority could not be shaken: on 8 October ben-Yussef was expelled from the party, and this was confirmed at the Congress of the *Néo-Destour* in the following month. Salah ben-Yussef then fled to Cairo, whence he maintained for the next years a campaign of propaganda and subversion against Bourguiba.

The phase of internal autonomy proved only transitional. The French government decided that it had in Bourguiba a friend, devoted in principle to the Western cause: this view was also strongly urged by France's allies, above all by the United States. At the same time, having decided at the beginning of 1956 to grant independence to Morocco, France could hardly refuse it to Tunisia. An agreement was signed in Paris on 20 March 1956 which recognized Tunisia's right to have its own army and fully to control its own foreign policy. For an interim period France was to have the right to station troops in Tunisia, and especially to control the naval base of Bizerta.

The removal of the Sultan of Morocco was bitterly resented by the people. It was felt to be an insult to the nation and to its religion. It affected the peasants no less than the townsmen, who hitherto had provided the main support for nationalism. It also infuriated the women, who had felt great sympathy for the Sultan because of his interest in feminine emancipation. Thus the French had united every section of the people against them as never before. After two years of terrorism by nationalist gangs, and of counter-terrorism by French extremists, the French government opened negotiations with Moroccan spokesmen at the end of August 1955 in France. It soon became clear that it would not be possible to separate the moderate nationalists from the *Istiqlal*, and that no solution would be acceptable which did not include the return of the Sultan. Even the Pasha of Marrakesh, el-Glaoui, the chief tool of the French authorities in the deposition of August 1953, decided in October 1955 to associate himself with the demand for his return. On 5 November the French government publicly recognized Sidi Mohammed ben-Yussef as the rightful ruler of Morocco, declared the Protectorate treaty of 1912 invalid, and announced its intention of negotiating an entirely new Franco-Moroccan relationship. The negotiations began in Paris on 15 February and on 2 March agreement was reached on the transfer of internal sovereignty from the French to the Moroccan government. A second agreement followed at the end of May, by which Morocco became completely sovereign in foreign policy. A Spanish-Moroccan agreement in June transferred authority over the northern zone, previously under Spanish protectorate. Finally, on 29 October 1958 Moroccan sovereignty was extended to the city of Tangier, whose special international status came to an end.

In Algeria no comparable progress was made in these years, for several reasons. Firstly, the legal status of the territory was different. Tunisia and Morocco were only states under French protection: to terminate the protectorate and restore the sovereignty was not in principle objectionable. But Algeria was regarded as an integral part of France. Secondly, the French population was much larger in Algeria than in Morocco or Tunisia, over 1 million in a total population of about 9 million. Thirdly, the economy of Algeria was far more closely interlocked with that of France than was the case in the two neighbouring territories. Algeria had fewer natural resources and suffered more severely from pressure of population. Some 400,000 Algerian workers employed in France supported nearly 2 million Algerians in Algeria from their wages. Separation from France would be economic catastrophe for Algeria. The French population of Algeria was strongly represented, both directly and indirectly, in all French governments and most political parties. It is wrong to think of French Algerians as a small caste of feudal landowners fattening on the natives—even more wrong than in the case of the British settlers in Kenya. The great majority of French land-holdings in Algeria are small, and the great majority of Frenchmen in Algeria are not farmers, but townspeople, including all the normal groups of an urban society—workers, clerks, small traders and professional people. To the pressure of the French Algerian lobby in Paris must be added the innate unwillingness of virtually all Frenchmen to believe that people who are offered the chance of becoming Frenchmen (as, in theory if not in practice, the Algerian Moslems were) could ever prefer independence. Finally, one must mention what was perhaps the decisive obstacle to any solution for Algeria—the inability of the political régime of the Fourth Republic to take any decision on any basic problem of national policy.

A new chapter in the Algerian tragedy opened on 1 November 1954 when an armed insurrection broke out. Its authors were a group which had split off from Messali Hadj's MTLD in the late 1940s, and set up a terrorist *Organisation spéciale*. In 1952 its leader, Ahmed ben-Bella, escaped to Cairo, where he was helped by the Egyptian authorities to enlist a number of Algerians who had undergone military training in Iraq. Ben-Bella established contact with Algeria, and under his directives a *Comité révolutionnaire d'unité d'action* was created. In July 1954 plans were prepared by its leaders for a rising throughout the territory. On advice from Cairo they decided to adopt the name *Front de libération nationale* (FLN). The rebels distinguished themselves by their savagery. French civilians were massacred when the chance offered. But the most numerous victims of FLN were other Algerian Moslems, both persons accused of helping the French authorities in any way and members of other nationalist groups, especially followers of Messali Hadj, with whom FLN conducted a war of its own both in Algeria and in France. Fear of massacre or torture by FLN frightened many Algerian Moslems into supporting it. But there was also growing positive support. The rising might not have started without Egyptian help, and might not have survived the first months without terrorizing the people. But once it had established itself, it attained a reputation which attracted Algerian Moslem patriots to its ranks. They were cruel, but they were also brave fighters. Treated with increasing cruelty by the French when captured alive, they acquired the prestige of martyrdom. By 1955 FLN had become the main political factor among Algerian Moslems. As such, it attracted a growing number of well-known civilian politicians, including even the former moderate leader of UDMA, Ferhat Abbas, who made his way to Cairo in 1955 and thereafter became the chief spokesman of FLN on the international political level.

Within the movement various contrasting trends appeared. There was first the conflict, inevitable in 'resistance movements', between the fighters in the field and the political leaders in exile. There was also a conflict between the Egyptian and the North African orientation: some saw Algeria's future as part of a vast Arab union whose centre would be Cairo, others as part of a smaller, and internationally more 'uncommitted', union with Tunisia and Morocco. In June 1957 the headquarters of the movement, the *Comité de coordination et d'exécution* (CCE), was moved to Tunis. In April 1958 FLN held a congress in Tangier, which was attended by Moroccan and Tunisian leaders. This was followed within two weeks by the Algiers rising which precipitated the political crisis in France itself. The great prestige of General de Gaulle affected even Algerian Moslems, and it was widely hoped that he would be able to find a way out. FLN was, of course, determined to stop this, and in the autumn announced the formation of an 'Algerian government in exile', headed by Ferhat Abbas. The announcement was made in Cairo, but the 'government' was recognized also by Tunisia and Morocco. The conflicts between Egypt and the two North African states were, however, not resolved, as was made clear in November 1958, when Tunisia left the Arab League and Bourguiba accused Egypt of helping his exiled rival, Salah ben-Yussef, to plot his assassination.

The Algerian war not only ties down French troops and swallows up economic resources which France needs to apply elsewhere, but also maintains tension between France and the independent states of Tunisia and Morocco, with which she might otherwise hope to co-operate to their mutual advantage. It also weakens the moderate elements in both countries. In independent Morocco an uneasy balance was preserved between the Sultan and *Istiqlal*. The monarch is a national hero, especially popular in the countryside and among the women. The party was the most efficient political machine in the country, but it was internally divided. In January 1959 it split. A left wing, led by ben-Barka and relying on the increasingly active trade unions (*Union Marocaine du Travail*), broke with Allal el-Fassi and set up a rival party—*Confédération nationale du parti de l'Istiqlal*. There was a further source of friction between France and Morocco, in the Moroccan claim to annex Mauritania, which had been a territory of AOF and in 1959 became one of the member states of the Franco-African Community. The potential mineral resources of this mainly desert territory added importance to the dispute. In Tunisia Bourguiba took grave risks by stressing his solidarity with the West. This did not prevent Franco-Tunisian tension, and a large part of the French population of Tunisia was virtually forced to leave the country in the first years of independence. If a pro-Western (and especially pro-American) policy should not bring results to Tunisia in the form of an Algerian settlement, Bourguiba's ability to withstand the nationalist demagogy of his exiled rival, Salah ben-Yussef, must remain doubtful.

But a year after the Algiers *coup* there was still no solution in sight. General de Gaulle had refused to commit himself to the slogan of Integration, and thereby won the hatred of a powerful section of French Algerian opinion. But his hopes of finding Moslem *interlocuteurs valables*, willing to defy FLN and to accept a compromise that would bring great benefits to all Moslems while still maintaining the link with France, were also disappointed. The Moslems elected at the 1958 parliamentary election were unrepresentative persons, committed to Integration, yes-men (*Béni Oui-oui*) of the French right. The only hope for Frenchmen and Moslems alike remained the statesmanship, firmness and patience of the French President.

SUEZ AND BAGHDAD

During 1955 Egypt's relations with the West deteriorated. The Turkish-Iraqi alliance was the first blow. At the end of February Israeli forces carried out a large-scale raid on Gaza, in which forty-three Egyptians were killed. Further major incidents followed, of which the Egyptians usually had the worst, whether they had been the aggressors or not. Thus the hatred of Israel, which had been dormant for some time, was revived, and on the generally accepted theory that Israel operated as the agent of the Western imperialists, it made for still more anti-Western feeling. The Free Officers were by now bitterly disappointed by the failure of repeated attempts to get military equipment from the United States. American public opinion and political circles were unwilling to give arms that seemed likely to be used against Israel, and the American military experts were willing only if Egypt were committed to membership of a Western defence scheme.

In April 1955 Abd el-Nasser attended the Bandung Conference. Though this was not a definite commitment to the Soviet-Chinese camp, it was a move in that direction. In September 1955 it was announced that the

Egyptian government had agreed to buy large quantities of arms and aircraft from Czechoslovakia. This action caused real alarm in the West. Yet for a time there was no open breach with Egypt. Abd el-Nasser's main interest was the construction of the High Dam at Asswan. This gigantic project was expected to make possible the irrigation of an area sufficient to provide a living for millions of peasants, and at least to give a respite of a good many years from the terrible pressure of population on resources which is Egypt's basic economic problem. It would also make possible a vast increase of electricity, a necessary base for the industrialization needed to make Egypt strong and to give employment to her people. The project would be enormously expensive—an authoritative estimate was £1,300 million. It could not be achieved without massive foreign aid. In the winter of 1955-6, well after the announcement of the arms deal with Czechoslovakia, there was agreement in principle in the West to consider helping. But in July 1956 Mr. Dulles made a public statement (without first informing the Egyptian government privately) that no American aid would be forthcoming. Though the reasons given were financial, it is not surprising that Nasser regarded the decision as a political attack. His reply was to announce, in a public speech full of mockery and denunciation of the West, that he would nationalize the Suez Canal Company.

In the face of this provocation, there were three possible courses of action for Britain and France, whose interests were most directly affected. First, they could have accepted Nasser's actions and got the best terms he was willing to give in compensation. This they were urged to do by the 'neutralist' Powers headed by India. If they had done so, they would have won some Afro-Asian goodwill, but they would have given notice to nationalists everywhere to confiscate British and French assets, and they would have infuriated conservative opinion in Britain and France. Secondly they could have retaliated by force. No doubt this would have raised indignation in Asia, but it could have been argued that the Western Powers were defending themselves against an act of aggression. The most practical argument against retaliation was that no adequate military forces were at that time available within reach of Egypt. Thirdly, they could have boycotted the Suez Canal completely, using the long route round the Cape and speeding up the production of giant oil tankers. This would, however, only have been effective if other major shipping Powers and importers of oil had joined in the boycott. It was doubtful whether Germany, Italy and Greece would have done so, and certain that the United States would not. In fact therefore the Western Powers adopted none of these three courses, but drifted for three months, until the atmosphere was unfavourable for any of them.

Meanwhile, anti-Western nationalism was making rapid progress in both Syria and Jordan. In June 1956 the Baath Socialists entered the Syrian government. In Jordan the rejection of the Baghdad Pact was followed in March 1956 by the dismissal of General Glubb, the commander-in-chief of the Arab Legion. In October a general election was held which resulted in a victory of the nationalists and the left. The strongest party were the National Socialists, led by Suleiman Nabulsi, who became Prime Minister on 29 October. The Baath and the Moslem Brotherhood also made gains.

The growth of militant nationalism in three neighbouring countries, and the prospect of Soviet assistance to Egypt, were obviously alarming to the government of Israel. The interests of Israel appeared now to coincide more closely than ever with those of the Western Powers. This was especially true of France, which, regarding Egypt as the base from which the Algerian rebellion was directed, was eager to humiliate and if possible to destroy Nasser. It seems likely that the Israeli government was encouraged to act by the belief that the Soviet Union, preoccupied with events in Hungary and Poland, would be unable to pay much attention to the Middle East. Whatever the Israeli calculations, and whatever the previous plans of the British and French governments, the subsequent events are well known. The Israeli army attacked Egypt on 29 October, and obtained brilliant successes. Then came the Anglo-French ultimatum, addressed nominally to both parties, but in fact only to Egypt, followed by the bombardments of Egyptian airfields, the landings at Port Said, the world-wide denunciation of Britain and France, the Soviet threats, the stormy scenes at the United Nations, the face-saving device of an United Nations force replacing the British and French troops, the complete political defeat of the Western Powers and the triumph of Egypt and the Soviet Union.

The Suez affair was a catastrophe for Western policy. It is possible to argue that the Western Powers should have sought the friendship of Abd el-Nasser on his terms, or that they should have destroyed him. In fact, they did neither: they made an enemy of him and they made him a popular hero in his own country and in most of Asia and Africa. It is thus necessary briefly to mention the errors involved in Western policy in these events.

The first error was to believe that preoccupations in Eastern Europe would keep the Soviet government out of Middle Eastern affairs. On the contrary, it made it easy for the Soviet leaders to convince communists, and it may have convinced them themselves, that there was a double-pronged attack by the Western imperialists on the Soviet camp, and that it must be resisted at both points. If there was any hope that Hungary might have been saved by Western political action, Suez killed it. The Soviet Union, however, scored a double triumph. By crushing Hungary, it taught a cruel lesson to future rebels. By leading the campaign of denunciation of the Western Powers for starting the Suez action, it successfully imposed the 'double standard' at the United Nations, the standard according to which aggression is aggression only when committed by a Western Power.

The second error was the failure of the Western Powers to let the Israelis complete the job they started. In a week or two more the Israelis would probably have smashed the Egyptian army and destroyed Nasser's prestige in the Arab world. The failure of his troops in the first few days of the war was in no way less shameful than that of Faruk's army in 1948. But when the Anglo-French forces intervened, Nasser could claim that he was facing the overwhelming power of Britain and France: his defeat at the hands of the Israelis was forgotten.

The third error was the unrealistic and pedantic nature of the military operations. The Anglo-French action could only have achieved its object if it had been quick and ruthless. But five days were allowed to elapse between the ultimatum and the landings. It is hardly an answer that it takes five days to transport an invasion fleet from Malta to Port Said, or that if high casualties were to be avoided it was necessary to bomb Egyptian airfields for several days to make sure that Egypt's modern Soviet aircraft were not available. The Anglo-French enterprise was a desperate aggression, justifiable (if at all) only on grounds of vital interest. Desperate aggression has to be carried out by desperate means. The risk of heavy Anglo-French casualties had to be accepted, and the fleet should have been brought up to the Egyptian coast before the ultimatum was given. In fact, however, the five days' interval were sufficient to let loose the world-wide campaign of denunciation in the face of which the British and French governments surrendered. The fact that Egyptian forces in Port Said defended themselves bravely enabled Abd el-Nasser to claim that he had driven the Western imperialists from Egyptian soil. For this disaster it is unfair to blame the Anglo-French service chiefs. They had given the best professional advice, and carried out their orders efficiently. The error was political. The two governments had failed to predict the political effects of the five days' delay.

The fourth error was the failure to inform the United States government beforehand. The British and French leaders had perhaps reason to be resentful of Mr. Dulles' lukewarm support of their cause since the confiscation of the Suez Canal Company. But it is amazing that they can have thought that they would succeed if the United States were against them, or that the American government would not bitterly resent their deceit. President Eisenhower's annoyance might be expected to be all the greater because the action came at the climax of his election campaign. It may be admitted that the sharpness of the American reaction was surprising. It may perhaps even be argued that the bitterness of the American verbal attacks on Britain and France was increased by their knowledge of their own failure to help Hungary: it is much more agreeable to denounce someone who is dependent on you, and is certain to surrender to you, than someone who will treat you with arrogant contempt.

These errors are enough to condemn the British and French leaders. They were professional politicians, and they cannot be excused for their failure to understand simple political facts. But there is also another aspect to the failure. As a result of the Suez affair Britain and France were publicly arraigned as aggressors, in the same category as Mussolini and Hitler, Tojo and Stalin. In Britain especially this humiliation was bitterly felt by a large part of public opinion. There was little consolation in the argument that a comparison with Hungary was unfair, that where the Soviet Union had reconquered a colony the British and French were aiming only to impose a tolerable settlement on a country whose independence they did not question, or that Britain and France accepted the will of the United Nations while the Soviet Union rejected it. The Western conscience was wounded, and it has not yet recovered. On the other hand, the Afro-Asians by their 'double standard' showed, in effect if not expressly, that they did not care if Hungarians were massacred, because their skins were white. The Soviet Union appeared to the Afro-Asians, and especially to the Arab nationalists, as their glorious protector, whose threats of rocket attacks had forced the West to capitulate.

It was, of course, not only the British and French who suffered a catastrophe. It enveloped also the United States. Passionately though the President and public opinion of the United States might feel that they were not 'colonialists', no Arab nationalist would agree. However unjustly, the United States has come to be regarded as the chief imperialist, capitalist, aggressive Power. The victory over Britain and France was felt to be a victory over America too. By attacking Britain and France, the United States gained no credit in the Arab world.

In Syria extreme nationalism made further progress. In December 1956 a conspiracy trial was staged against members of the People's Party, which in the past had favoured a pro-Hashemite foreign policy. In the following months the Communist Party, led by Khalid Bikdash, the most able communist in the Arab world, gained in influence. During the summer of 1957 pro-Soviet officers obtained key positions in the army. In the autumn the Soviet Union accused Turkey of preparing armed aggression against Syria. After a month of fierce propaganda, in the Soviet press and radio and at the United Nations, this artificial Soviet war scare, which does not seem to have had any foundation in reality, was allowed to drop. It had, however, served its purpose of representing the Soviet Union to the Syrians as their best friend and saviour. But now the Baath leaders, who looked to Cairo rather than to Moscow, decided to act. On their initiative negotiations were undertaken with Egypt, and on 1 February 1958 a joint announcement was made from Cairo by the two Presidents, Abd el-Nasser and Shukri Kuwaitli, that Egypt and Syria had decided to merge in an United Arab Republic. The decision was formally implemented after a plebiscite, held on 21 February, had shown a virtually unanimous vote in favour. Political parties were then dissolved, including the Communist Party. The Soviet Union was quick to recognize the new state, but it was clear that Soviet and communist aims had had a reverse.

In Jordan Nabulsi's government had been on bad terms with King Hussein from the beginning. The conflict came to a head in April 1957 in connexion with Nabulsi's intention to establish diplomatic relations with the Soviet Union and to replace several high officials especially trusted by the king. The cabinet resigned, and no new parliamentary majority could be found to support the king's policy. There were strikes and demonstrations and a mutiny at Army HQ. After an unsuccessful attempt at compromise, and the flight of the Army Chief of Staff and several politicians to Syria, the king dissolved parliament and political parties and ruled through a government of his own choice. During the crisis ships of the United States 6th Fleet were moved into the Eastern Mediterranean. The situation remained calm for the rest of the year. In February 1958, when the United Arab Republic was proclaimed, the Hashemite states decided to form a counter-union. King Feisal II of Iraq came to Amman, and the Arab Union was proclaimed by the two kings on 14 February.

Even the two states of the Arabian Peninsula, patriarchal societies in which slavery was still an established institution, were affected by the new trends. Saudi Arabia was regarded by the United States as its most reliable support in the Middle East. Aramco and the Dhahran air base still seemed fairly secure, and on 1 March 1958 King Saud (who had succeeded his father, the great Abdul Aziz Ibn Saud, in 1953) announced that he would join neither the Union nor the Republic. But at the end of the same month the king decided to transfer most of his powers over internal and foreign policy to the Prime Minister, his younger brother, the Emir Feisal, who was believed to be much more favourably disposed to Egypt. As for Yemen, a still more backward society, its ruler, who had claims against the British Protectorate of Aden, decided to unite his country in a federal union with the United Arab Republic. It was far from clear how this would work out in practice. Two things, however, were certain—that Egypt would give support to any territorial claims that Yemen might put forward to British protected or British colonial territory,* and that in both Yemen and Saudi Arabia the old social order was in rapid decline as a new, ambitious and politically-minded intelligentsia came into being. It was of no small importance that in all the Arabian territories a large proportion of the school-teachers were Egyptians.

The Lebanon, with its precarious balance between Christians and Moslems and its busy commercial capital of Beirut, had long enjoyed comparative quiet. But in May 1958 a rebellion broke out. The immediate cause was fear of the opposition parties that the pro-Western President, Camille Chamoun, whose term of office was to expire in the autumn, would seek to maintain himself in power after that date. The deeper cause was increased hostility between Moslems and Christians. The Moslems were on the whole poorer, and had a smaller share of real power, than the Christians. Inevitably they had been influenced by the increasingly militant nationalism of neighbouring Syria. Chamoun claimed that the rebellion was instigated and supplied with arms by the United Arab Republic, and made a formal complaint to the United Nations Security Council. A team of UN observers was appointed to investigate. At the beginning of July they reported that they could find no evidence of 'massive infiltration' from Syria. The Lebanese government accused them of partiality.

While the controversy about Lebanon was unsettled, a far more important event occurred in Iraq. On 14 July units of the Iraqi army led by nationalists, who happened to be passing through Baghdad at the same time, carried out a previously concerted plan to seize power. Unlike Abd el-Nasser's action of July 1952, the Iraqi *coup d'état* was neither bloodless

* The British colony of Aden, with an area of only eighty square miles, has a population of around 140,000. The claims of the Yemen are on the Aden Protectorate, which extends along the greater part of the southern coast of the peninsula, and whose population is estimated at around 800,000. In addition, the following territories in the Arabian Peninsula are in varying relationships of protectorate to Britain, proceeding from south-east to north-west: the Sultanate of Muscat and Oman (estimated population, 550,000); the trucial sheikhdoms of the Oman coast of the Persian Gulf (90,000); Bahrain (population, 1955, 120,000); and Kuwait (population, 1957, 200,000). Of these Kuwait is a major oil-producing region (its crude oil output in 1950 was nearly 55 million metric tons), while Bahrain is a considerable producer (9 million metric tons in 1952).

nor orderly. The members of the Royal family were butchered in the palace, Nuri Pasha was done to death by a mob, his corpse mutilated and spat on and paraded in the streets, and the British Embassy was sacked. King Hussein of Jordan was clearly in grave danger. The Western reaction was immediate. American forces were landed in Lebanon, and British troops flown to Jordan. The Afro-Asian reaction at the United Nations was less violent than at the time of the Suez crisis, and the Arab states even agreed on a resolution which promised that they would not interfere with each other's affairs, and did not denounce the Anglo-American action as imperialist. In September a successor was found to Chamoun as President of Lebanon in General Chehab, who was fairly generally accepted as standing above party. In the autumn American and British forces were withdrawn from both Lebanon and Jordan.

The Anglo-American action probably did more good than harm. The hatred of the Arab nationalists was hardly increased, for it had already reached a point beyond which there was little room for increase. For the time being Lebanon and Jordan had been saved. Their further prospects, however, remained dim. It was hard to see how Jordan could escape engulfment by its neighbours, or Lebanon the loss at least of the most predominantly Moslem regions, unless both came to terms with Israel and formed a compact band cutting off Egypt from Syria. Yet reconciliation with Israel was quite unthinkable even for the most moderate leaders in either country.

In Iraq the new régime was greeted with undoubted popular enthusiasm. Nuri Pasha's régime had been based on police terror, and had refused land reform. Now the intelligentsia were free to express their ideas and emotions, and the peasants could hope for land. The new government indeed soon prepared a land reform law. The new Premier, General Kassem, was certainly willing to sell his country's oil to the West, and for the time being even to allow the Iraq Petroleum Company to operate on the old basis. But that the forces which supported his government were bitterly anti-Western there could be no doubt. Less certain was the form which their hatred of the West would take. The Vice-Premier, Colonel Aref, was a supporter of the Baath, and determined to join Iraq to the United Arab Republic. The alternative was to align Iraq more closely with the Soviet Union.

The communists, who now re-emerged from years of illegality and persecution, were against union with Egypt, and so were their Soviet patrons. There was a powerful means of pressure in the Kurdish minority, about 1 million strong, inhabiting the richest oil-bearing region. If Iraq remained independent, as a land of two faiths and two nations—Sunni and

Shia Moslems, Arabs and Kurds—all could be promised their rights within a new 'democratic and anti-imperialist' system. But if it were to become part of an overwhelmingly Sunni state the Shia might have misgivings, and if the declared foundation were to be Arab nationalism the Kurds would have real grounds for alarm. Kurdish discontent was something which the Soviet Union could easily exploit.

In fact a conflict soon arose between Aref and Kassem, which ended in Aref's arrest in October. Thereafter the influence of communism steadily grew in Iraqi political life, and Kassem's attitude to this seemed ambiguous. An unsuccessful revolt by pro-Nasser nationalist officers in Mosul in February 1959 strengthened the communists still further, and led to violent public attacks on Kassem by President Nasser. Thus, far from Iraq uniting with Egypt, there was a reversion to the earlier pattern of rivalry between Cairo and Baghdad for the leadership of the Fertile Crescent, but with the difference that Iraq was now the representative not of Western, but of Soviet interests.

THE WEST AND THE ARABS

The West has two main interests in the Arab world. The first is oil. In the spring of 1959 Western oil supplies did not seem to be in immediate danger. All producer countries had an interest in selling. It is obvious that the Western oil companies will have to grant more favourable, perhaps even exorbitantly costly, financial terms to the various Arab governments, at first in Iraq and later in the Gulf Sheikdoms and Saudi Arabia. It may be that more companies will be nationalized, and it is even arguable that Western governments would do well to advise the companies to take the initiative in seeking agreements on the terms of nationalization. It is also likely that European and American experts working in the oil-fields, whether employed by private or nationalized companies, will be objects of envy, hatred and insult from the local nationalists. A great deal of ill-feeling and injustice is inevitable, and the maintenance of oil supplies will cost Western governments and share-holders money, and perhaps cost Western citizens their lives. Yet until alternative sources of oil are found, or oil is replaced as a fuel by atomic energy, it will be necessary to pay the price. A really dangerous situation would, of course, arise if the Soviet Union were able to deny all Arab oil to the West, either by buying up all the output or by establishing communist governments in all Arab oil-producing countries. The growth of communist strength in Iraq is already an alarming fact.

The second interest of the West in the Arab world arises from the fact that, from Casablanca to Khartum and Aden, the Arabs control the northern and eastern approaches to Africa. North Africa is, of course, of vital importance to Mediterranean strategy, and concerns not only France, but all her European allies. The Arabs are, understandably, emotionally engaged in the struggle for Algeria. But this is not all. In his book, *Egypt's Liberation*, Abd el-Nasser wrote:

> We cannot under any circumstances, however much we might desire it, remain aloof from the terrible and sanguinary conflict going on there to-day between five million whites and 200 million Africans. We cannot do so for an important and obvious reason: we are *in* Africa. The peoples of Africa will continue to look to us, who guard their northern gate, and who constitute their link with the outside world. We will never in any circumstances be able to relinquish our responsibility to support, with all our might, the spread of enlightenment and civilization to the remotest depths of the jungle.... I will continue to dream of the day when I will find in Cairo a great African institute dedicated to unveiling to our view the dark reaches of the continent, to creating in our minds an enlightened African consciousness, and to sharing with others from all over the world the work of advancing the welfare of the peoples of this continent.[95]

Cairo Radio incites the tropical Africans, in their own languages, to rebel against the Europeans. It praised the Mau Mau rebellion as a struggle for freedom. In Cairo are offices of the nationalist movements of Uganda, Somaliland and Kenya. Abd el-Nasser has something approaching the institute of which he dreamed, in the Afro-Asian Solidarity Committee, a communist-supported organization with headquarters in Cairo. For it is not only Nasser that is interested in tropical non-Arab Africa and the use of its peoples and resources as a weapon in the world-wide political war against the West. The Soviet Union is still more keen on this task. Soviet universities and academic institutions have been training Africans in Marxism-Leninism and Soviet citizens in African languages and cultures with an energy which puts the efforts of the West in African studies to shame.[96] The threat to Africa, in which the long-term aims of Soviet communism, the African ambitions of Nasser and the plain, emotional hatred and desire for revenge against Europe of Arab nationalists everywhere are combined, is more deadly, more lasting, and far less understood in the West than the threat to oil.

Two questions deserve consideration. What defences can be raised against this threat, and can the West reach an agreement with Arab nationalists which will detach them from the Soviet Union?

In July 1958 the old Baghdad Pact was destroyed. But the nucleus of a 'northern tier' defence, in the form of a Western alliance with Turkey and Persia, remains. This was always the most important objective for Western policy, though, as we have seen, it was obscured by the makers of the Baghdad Pact in 1955. The question in 1958 was: Can the 'northern tier' survive?

Turkey in 1958 was without doubt weaker than in 1955. The Democratic Party had disappointed the earlier promise of a democratic régime. It was using police methods and reactionary restrictions on the press and public meetings to muzzle its opponents. Even so its majority was substantially reduced in the election of October 1957. Economic conditions were also alarming. Though previous years of lavish spending had benefited Turkish agriculture, and had laid the foundations for future industrial development, the burden of foreign debt had become very heavy and there was not yet much to show for all the expenditure. Economic aid from the United States in the summer of 1958, given as a direct result of the new Middle East crisis, promised to tide Turkey over her difficulties. Though internal political discontent was widespread, at least no difference of opinion appeared on the basic choice between the West and the Soviet Union. The agreement with Greece and Britain on Cyprus in February 1959 freed her western flank. Thus Turkey still remained strong in comparison with all her neighbours, though less strong and less politically healthy than might have been hoped.

The position in Persia was much less secure. Here all the same weaknesses were to be seen as in Iraq. There was the same terrible poverty, the same unequal division of land, the same disaffection of the intelligentsia. Moreover, in Persia there had at least once been a far stronger communist party than had ever existed in any Arab country. Against this it could be said that there was a strong popular tradition of devotion to the monarchy as an institution (whatever dynasty, old or upstart, might hold it), and traditional hostility to Russia—two conditions that do not apply to any Arab country. Since August 1953 the Shah had taken the power increasingly into his own hands. He had shown, by the transfer of the Crown lands to the peasants, that he was for social reform. But there were limits to his ability to antagonize the landowning class, which not only dominated the parliament, but was strongly represented in the whole state machine. Brutal pressure on the landowners in the interest of the people would risk rebellion and collapse of the state: to ignore the interests of the people would give revolutionaries their chance. As in Iraq under Nuri, or in other underdeveloped societies of the past, the dangerous factor is not so much the discontent of the peasants themselves as the indignation at peasant misery on the part of the intelligentsia, many of whom are children of peasants or small middle-class people. And even if the Shah were able to get a generous reform programme accepted by the ruling class, many years would pass before reforms substantially improved the condition of the peasants or satisfied the intelligentsia that justice was in process of being done. Thus, as in Iraq under Nuri, the primary condition remained political stability, and this can be reduced to the brutal terms of a loyal police, a loyal army and an efficient system of counter-intelligence. Lack of the latter proved in the end the undoing of Nuri. In Persia no less than in Iraq before July 1958, everything depends on one man's life.

More depends even than the independence of Persia. For if the northern tier were broken by the alignment of Persia with the Soviet Union, then Soviet forces would for the first time be in direct physical contact with the Arab world. Until this is so, Soviet influence in the Arab world can only be precarious. Soviet political strategy has always been based, as is natural in the military thinking of a traditional land power, on direct physical access and uninterrupted lines of communication. Only when the massive threat of Soviet military power is present, can communist-controlled 'People's Democracies' be consolidated. This is not yet the case. Until it is the case, the power of the communists in Iraq will remain precarious. Soviet agents can, of course, be flown across Persia, or brought by sea to Basra. So can military missions and numerous expert advisers in the techniques of metallurgy, subversion or police terror. But this is not enough. Only when direct access has been achieved will it be possible to consolidate the Iraq communist régime and to mobilize all the previously prepared resources for the conversion of Egypt into a People's Democracy and a base for the Soviet conquest of the African continent.

Thus the overthrow of the Shah would be more than the removal of a reactionary ruler by 'popular forces', as the *bien pensants* of the European and Indian left would no doubt claim: it would be the removal of the last obstacle to the Sovietization of the Arab world. And this in turn would mean an extremely real prospect, not of the 'liberation of the Africans from colonialism', but of the prevention of future co-operation between the West and the free nations of Africa, which have come or are coming into being, and their subjection instead to totalitarian imperialism. Persia is thus a position of vital importance for the defence of the West. If the Soviet Union should succeed in carrying out a quick and successful overthrow of the Shah's régime, the West would be in deadly danger. If, on the other hand, the attempt should be only partly successful, and a civil war develop in Persia, neither the West nor the Soviet Union could be indifferent. In either case there would be acute danger of world war. It is unpleasant to have to conclude that the peace of the world largely depends on the efficiency of Persia's security police.

The second major question is the relationship of the West to Arab nationalism—by which is normally meant the régime of Nasser and his allies. It is certain that the aims of Nasser and of the Soviet Union are different. It is also clear that Nasser is not an implacable enemy of the West in the same sense as the Soviet leaders, whose unchanging long-term aims are derived from 'scientific' Marxist-Leninist dogma. Nasser's hostility to the West may, however, be based on another kind of implacability—that of personal hatred and desire for revenge. Nevertheless, it would be ridiculous, however pessimistic one may be, to exclude in principle an agreement with Nasser. The Anglo-Egyptian agreement of February 1959, though unfavourable to the expropriated British interests, was still a step in the right direction. Egyptian-Iraqi hostility has led to some degree of Soviet-Egyptian tension. If the West could induce Nasser to abandon his subversive propaganda in Africa, this would be an important gain. The question remains: What is Nasser's price for the adoption of a genuine neutrality, in place of his previous anti-Western policy disguised as neutrality?

If the governments of Jordan, Lebanon or the Sudan should freely decide to unite with the United Arab Republic, the West can accept, and even welcome, the decision. But it is too much to expect the West to press King Hussein to renounce his throne, or the Lebanese and Sudanese their independence. Nasser can still less expect the British government to hand over Uganda, Kenya or Somaliland to his nominees. Nor can the French be expected to recognize the Algerian 'government' sponsored by him. If, however, Nasser would renounce his own imperial ambitions, and help to bring about a negotiated settlement between France, Morocco, Tunisia and the Algerian Moslems, he could do a service to the Arab cause and to world peace.

The most intractable problem of all is, of course, Israel. It may be that Nasser, who showed himself a realist in 1954, is capable of admitting to himself that the state of Israel is an international fact: whether, dependent as he is on the fanatical nationalism whose hero he has been since 1956, he could make such an admission in public, and still more could act on the basis of it, is another matter. If the plight of the Arab refugees from Israel were the only problem, a solution could perhaps be found through the United Nations. In this matter the Western Powers ought to show greater generosity, and press Israel to do likewise. The frontier problem, however, admits of no such simple answer. If Israel retired to the boundaries proposed by the UN in 1947, she would be at the mercy of her neighbours. The risk might be worth taking if the evidence showed that the Arabs intended thereafter to live in peace with Israel. One recalls inevitably the Czechoslovakia of 1938. Then the Western Powers forced the Czechs to accept indefensible frontiers, and at least professed to believe that the Third Reich, its claims for self-determination for Sudeten Germans granted, would prove a good neighbour. But Hitler was determined to destroy the Czech state as such, and showed it six months later. There would need to be far stronger grounds than now exist for trusting Arab intentions before the Western governments would be morally entitled to impose a Munich on Israel.

In the autumn of 1959 the prospect of better relations between the West and Egypt seemed more promising. One hopeful sign was the more stable internal position in Lebanon, where there was much less sign of Egyptian intrigues. Another was the reconciliation between the United Arab Republic and Jordan. Both governments were alarmed by the communist influence in Iraq, which General Kassem's sporadic verbal opposition to communist policies did little to reduce. Baghdad was becoming a centre of both Soviet and Chinese influence. Chinese encouragement to the Syrian communist leader, Khalid Bikdash, caused serious tension between Cairo and Peking. Co-operation between the West and the United Arab Republic thus seemed a less remote possibility than at the beginning of the year. The main task remained the maintenance of the northern tier, and above all, of Persia. But friendship with Cairo was certainly a desirable aim, provided that it was not purchased at the cost of the vital interests of France and Israel. To say this is not of course to recommend 'the mixture as usual': on the contrary, in the past there has been little co-operation between the Western Powers in the Middle East. The British have combined a moralizing attitude to France with practical damage to French interests; the French have taken obvious pleasure in British reverses; and the United States have treated British and French alike to a flood of anti-colonialist platitudes. Western disunity can only help the enemies of the West, who are also the enemies of Arab independence.

17: Asia

During the 1950s Asian politics have been overshadowed by the rise of communist China towards the status of a giant world power. India and Japan remained important factors in world affairs. South-East Asia continued to be an unstable region, a battle-ground of many conflicting external influences.

CHINA

The communist régime in China has shown an impressive stability, has imposed its will on all regions of its vast empire, and has achieved great material progress. Its administration is more efficient and honest than any that China has known for centuries, and the central government's control over its citizens is closer than at any time in history. The political and social system has grown steadily more totalitarian. Industrial and military strength have steadily increased. Visitors to China have been impressed both by the puritan spirit of the people, especially of the youth, and by the absolute conformity of the opinions expressed by the vast majority of those with whom they spoke. The fact that China was for so long in its people's view the greatest country in the world and the centre of human civilization, then for more than a century humiliated and exploited by the Western barbarians, and has again become united and strong, a terror to her enemies, must to many Chinese compensate for much of what they have suffered and still suffer. Yet before asserting baldly that the Chinese people are unanimously behind Chairman Mao, it is well to recall that a large majority of the Chinese prisoners captured in the Korean War chose not to return to China when the war ended.

In Chinese internal affairs the year 1955 brought several important events. In April it was announced that a conspiracy against the party leadership had been discovered. Its leader was Kao Kang, who had for some years been the effective ruler of Manchuria, and was later Chairman of the State Planning Commission, having been for many years a member of the Politburo of the Communist Party, and a prominent communist leader already in the 1930s. It was stated that he had committed suicide. Coupled with him in disgrace was Jao Shu-shih, formerly head of the Organization Department of the Central Committee.

In the spring of 1955 a violent campaign was also staged against a prominent pro-communist writer named Hu Feng. Already in the autumn of 1954 a prominent literary scholar, Professor Yu Ping-po, had been singled out for attack because his work on classical Chinese literature had not emphasized the class struggle. This led to massive denunciation of liberalism and 'reactionary philosophy' in literature and the arts. From this the campaign spread to those communist intellectuals who denied that writers should be controlled in their work by the party. Hu Feng, not a member of the party, but its strong supporter and a respected public figure, was chosen as a symbol of these heresies. He was accused of *bourgeois* idealism, cosmopolitanism and anti-socialism. Letters which he had written to personal friends, which contained criticisms of government policies or officials, were published in the press. Finally, he was accused of heading a clique of counter-revolutionaries and imperialist agents, his crimes were linked with those of Kao Kang and Jao Shu-shih, and he was arrested. The terror against intellectuals, which had been somewhat relaxed since 1952, was revived once more.

It was also in 1955 that the government decided to speed up the pace of collectivization of agriculture. This was announced by Mao Tse-tung in a speech of 31 July, which was not, however, generally published until October. Half the peasant households of China were now to be included in producers' co-operatives by the end of 1958, the second half by the end of 1960, and the transformation from producers' co-operatives to collective farms was to be completed by the end of the Third Five Year Plan period in 1967. However, the mass campaign was so successful that it was decided to accelerate the process. The date for full collectivization was brought forward, first to the end of 1960 and then (by a decision of January 1956) to the end of 1958.

The decision to collectivize was probably immediately caused by difficulties in food supply following the poor harvest of 1954, the same factor which had decided the Soviet government to take this step in 1928. The purpose was essentially the same as in the Soviet case—to establish more efficient centralized control over the peasants, in order effectively to extract grain for the growing urban populations at very low cost. But it appears that opinions were divided within the party leadership on the speed to be adopted, for Mao referred in his July speech to 'some comrades' who had opposed the rapid tempo which was accepted. The process seems to have been more successful, and to have cost less sacrifice and incurred far less opposition, than its prototype in Russia in 1929-33. Admittedly independent sources of information were very scarce, and even so there were reports of poor harvests in many areas in 1956, and of some slaughtering of animals by dispossessed 'rich peasants'. But it seems fairly clear that there was not mass starvation or widespread resistance by peasants, as in Russia a generation earlier: if such had been the case, even the vast spaces and strict censorship of China could not completely have concealed it from the world. If this radical difference from Russian experience is accepted as a fact, the reasons for it are far from clear. It is possible that the prestige of Mao and the sense of the restoration of China's greatness achieved by his régime induced the peasants to accept this policy; or that the administration was either more tactful or more ruthless than the Russian communists of the 1930s; or that the material conditions available in the new collective farms were better than they had been in the Soviet Union; or simply that Chinese peasants are by nature more docile than Russian. Too little is certainly known to make these hypotheses more than speculative.

While pressure on the peasants was intense throughout 1956, the intellectuals were treated more mildly. The slogan, 'Let a hundred flowers bloom, let a hundred schools of thought contend', was launched by the party. The Chinese leaders, who had never assigned to Stalin so high a place as those of other countries, were also less impressed by his devaluation at the Twentieth Congress of the CPSU. During the summer it was believed in Warsaw that the Chinese were encouraging the Polish communists to resist Soviet pressure. The Hungarian Revolution, however, brought from the Chinese party a long statement, on 29 December 1956, which denounced revisionism, asserted that the events in Hungary were produced by imperialist intervention, and reaffirmed that 'the theory of the dictatorship of the proletariat is the most essential part of Marxism'. However, within China the 'hundred flowers' slogan was not withdrawn. On 27 February 1957 Mao Tse-tung made a long speech entitled 'On the correct handling of contradictions among the people'. In it he distinguished between 'contradictions with the enemy' and 'contradictions within the people'. The former comprised conflicts with 'the imperialists' and with domestic Chinese 'counter-revolutionaries', the latter, conflicts of interest or ideas between groups of people which were not 'counter-revolutionary', and between any such group and the government. The former were 'antagonistic contradictions', the latter were 'non-antagonistic'. For the first there should be implacable repression, for the second conciliation and persuasion. The second category included even such important conflicts as those between the Han and non-Han nationalities, and between business-men of the 'national *bourgeoisie*' and workers. The notion that a conflict between capitalists and workers can be 'non-antagonistic' seems hardly compatible with Marxism, and the idea that a conflict between any group of subjects and the government can be 'non-antagonistic' is certainly contrary to the theory and practice of communism in its Leninist form. The general effect of Mao's speech was to urge greater freedom of speech and a greater willingness by party officials to tolerate criticism. But it was no less clear that the right to decide in practice whether a criticism was 'counter-revolutionary' or not, and thus whether a 'contradiction' was 'with the enemy' or 'within the people', was reserved to the leadership of the Communist Party.

Mao's speech was followed in April by a campaign for the 'rectification of working style' within the party, or *Cheng Feng*. Even non-communists were exhorted to criticize the party's conduct of policy. Critics were at first understandably reluctant, remembering the earlier waves of terror and fearing that they would suffer reprisals, if not immediately then at some later stage. But the party spokesmen repeatedly assured them that they were free to express their opinions, and during May 1957 a number of increasingly bitter complaints were published in the press. Writers denounced the arrogance of the communist cadres, their material privileges, their contempt for the law, their brutal and stupid interference with scientific work and with economic management. It was even argued by the bolder spirits that these evil features of the régime were due not to abuse of power by individual communist officials (as the official thesis went), but to the supreme leadership itself, and even to the inherent nature of a system of 'dictatorship of the proletariat'. The original fears of the critics were proved correct even earlier than they had expected. On 8 June the leading party newspaper *People's Daily* launched a campaign against 'rightists', which soon gathered momentum with accusations of counter-revolutionary conspiracy against those who had spoken freely, and with numerous arrests. By July 1957 terror was again in full swing. Whether, as the leaders themselves later claimed, the whole *Cheng Feng* campaign had been a clever machiavellian manœuvre designed to trap hidden opponents, or the new wave of repression was merely a reaction of angry disappointment when the depth and extent of opposition to the régime had been revealed, the outside observer cannot judge.

The next major development occurred in the summer of 1958, with the introduction of People's Communes. According to the official version, the *Cheng Feng* campaign and the struggle against the 'rightists' created so much enthusiasm among the Chinese peasants that 'a big leap forward in production' resulted. The peasants themselves discovered that they could achieve more if they were grouped into much larger units, making possible the allocation of very large labour forces to projects of value to all. The result of their enthusiasm and of their discussion of better forms of organization was the People's Commune. The first of these, which was given the name Huei-sing ('the sputnik'), was set up in Hsiuyang county of Honan province, and included 9,300 households and 43,000 persons. The commune was to pay attention to industrial as well as to agricultural labour. Small-scale industrial plants, especially small furnaces for producing steel, were expected to yield substantial output. But the commune was not only designed to increase production: it was also intended completely to transform the peasants' way of life. There were to be communal dining rooms, communal nurseries and 'happy homes' for the old people. Thereby not only were millions of women to be released for production, but the ties of the family were to be reduced to a minimum. Great emphasis was also placed on military training for all adults and adolescents. The slogan of another commune (in Hsushui county of Hopei province) was: 'Organize along military lines, work as if fighting a battle and live the collective way!' By the end of August 1958 communes embraced the whole rural population of Honan and Hopei provinces, and by mid-December virtually the whole rural population of China, excepting only certain areas of non-Han population such as Tibet. During these few months 740,000 collective farms had been transformed into 26,000 communes.

All major changes in communist China are attributed to an irresistible upsurge of enthusiasm by the masses. The outside observer may prefer to ascribe rather more to the initiative of the supreme leadership of the Communist Party. The new policy of regimentation of the masses is clearly designed to make the most, for the immense tasks of industrialization and improvement of agriculture which lie ahead, of China's main productive resource, its vast manpower. In this respect there is a good deal of similarity with the situation in Russia in 1929. When skill and equipment are in very short supply, jobs have to be done, even if uneconomically, by many pairs of bare hands. In recent years the Chinese communists have vacillated in their attitude to China's population problem. At first they took the orthodox communist view that a large population is an asset, and over-population a nightmare invented by capitalist economists. But after the results of the census became known in 1955, showing more than 580 million inhabitants, the attitude was modified, and government spokesmen began to recommend birth control. In 1958, though birth-control was not specifically repudiated, emphasis was once again laid on the value of a large population for production and on the possibilities both of developing new land and of raising the output on land already cultivated. There is probably more validity in communist arguments than Western commentators usually recognize. The successes of the first two Five Year Plans in the Soviet Union were achieved, at the cost of poor quality in the products and high mortality among the workers and peasants, by mobilizing vast numbers of unskilled labourers to do what in more advanced economies is done by skilled men and machines. This was, of course, made possible only by political regimentation and police terror. In China the gap between present output and the goal of an industrialized country is wider than it was in Russia in 1929, the pressure of population is greater, and therefore both the speed of proposed advance and the degree of coercion required to maintain it are more intense. It is against this background that one must view the policy of communes.

The policy has, however, also an ideological aspect. The eminent theorist Chen Po-ta, an alternate member of the Politburo of the Communist Party, wrote in July 1958 that the new People's Communes were an original application by Mao Tse-tung of two points in Marx's *Communist Manifesto*—the unification of industry with agriculture and the unification of education with production. Chen claimed that 'under the leadership of the ideas of Mao Tse-tung' the transition from socialism to communism was already beginning in China. This claim implied that China, which had been ruled by communists for less than a decade, was already reaching a stage of development which the Soviet Union itself had not attained. Such a challenge to the ideological prestige of the Soviet party was truly astonishing. The Soviet press ostentatiously ignored Chinese ideological pretensions, but refrained from any direct criticism. The Resolution of the Central Committee of the Chinese Communist Party of 18 December 1958 made a certain retreat. It declared that the People's Commune is 'the basic unit of the socialist social structure of our country' and 'the basic unit of organization of socialist state power'. It 'will quicken the tempo of socialist construction and constitute the best form for realizing . . . the transition from collective ownership to ownership by the whole people in the countryside, and . . . from socialist to communist society'. This double transition will, however, require a period of industrialization, mechanization and electrification of agriculture, which will take 'fifteen, twenty or more years'.

It seems likely that the changes in party policy between 1955 and 1958, the successive phases of collectivization and the creation of communes, the varying treatment of intellectuals, the ideological challenge to the Soviet Union and the partial retreat from it, may have had some connexion with rivalries within the Communist Party leadership, probably involving Mao himself and his two principal lieutenants, Liu Shao-chi and Chou En-lai. Mao's decision in November 1958 not to seek re-election as Chairman of the People's Government, though retaining the chairmanship of the party, may be connected with such rivalries and factional conflicts. But the evidence is so scanty that the outside observer can do no more than mention this as a possible relevant factor.[97]

Chinese foreign policy is principally concerned with two major Asian states, India and Japan; with two small divided states, Korea and Vietnam;

and with the two giant world Powers, the United States and the Soviet Union. These we may briefly examine in turn.

India is the great rival to China for political leadership in Asia. India aims, as does China, at industrial progress and a modern society and culture, but seeks to attain this aim by democratic procedures, in contrast to China's totalitarian methods. Fundamentally therefore India is, to Mao and his party, an enemy. Chinese policy is, however, not outwardly hostile to India. China aims to use Indian neutralism to the advantage of the communist alliance, and to make as favourable as possible an impression on the neutralist and pacific governments of southern Asia. From this point of view, Chou En-lai's behaviour at the Bandung Conference of April 1955 was rather successful. The Chinese conquest of Tibet in 1950 alarmed Indian opinion, but was accepted by Mr. Nehru. During the Tibetan revolution of March 1959 Nehru emphasized his determination not to intervene in, or even comment on, 'the internal affairs of China'. Not even the indignation of the Indian public, or attacks on India in the Chinese press, caused him to modify this attitude. The Chinese rulers have refrained from direct intervention in the affairs of Burma, whose geographical position makes it a buffer between India and China: any successes which China might obtain by greater support to the Burmese communists would be more than compensated by the loss of goodwill in India. Yet below the surface there is greater antagonism between India and China than either side will publicly admit.

Popular fear of Japan probably remains strong in China, and it is likely that even the rulers fear Japan as an instrument of the United States, much as the Soviet rulers fear Germany. At the same time they are aware of the desire in Japan for friendship with China, and exploit this as fully as they can. Japanese intellectuals are reminded of the great Chinese cultural tradition, from which Japanese culture learned so much in the past, and Japanese business-men are both attracted by the hope of lucrative trade with China and frightened by the prospect of the competition of cheap Chinese goods in Asian markets.

Korea is important chiefly by virtue of its strategic position in relation to Japan. After more than two years of negotiations, interrupted by periodical outbursts of fighting on the front, an armistice was signed on 27 July 1953 which restored the pre-war situation. North Korea, with less than a third of the country's population, remained a communist state, in which, since the Chinese intervention in the war in 1950, Chinese influence had equalled or surpassed Soviet influence. Chinese troops were withdrawn by the end of 1958, but the North Korean forces were once more well equipped with modern weapons. In South Korea small American forces remain, on behalf of the United Nations, but the South Korean army is large and also well equipped. The presidential form of democracy formally expressed in the constitution of South Korea, is in practice an authoritarian régime under the octogenarian president Syngman Rhee. Opposition is, however, permitted, and in the elections of May 1958 the governmental Liberal Party won only 125 out of 233 parliamentary seats. South Korea not only faces the constant possibility of aggression from the North, but is in a state of extreme hostility towards Japan. Hatred deriving from thirty years of Japanese colonial rule is aggravated by disputes on Japanese fishing rights in Korean waters. This quarrel, which gravely embarrasses American policy, may become less acute after the death of Rhee, but the removal of so strong a personality might have fatal effects on the stability of the régime.

In Vietnam, as it was divided by the Geneva agreement of 1954, the North is a communist satellite state, in which Chinese influence is overwhelming. Whereas in Korea the South is on balance stronger than the North, the opposite is the case in Vietnam.

The relations of China with the United States are dominated by the problem of the Chiang Kai-shek régime in Formosa. This is recognized by Washington as the government of China, and occupies the permanent seat on the United Nations Security Council reserved to China. This is a source of bewilderment to America's European allies, of anger to most Asian nations and of delight to the Soviet government. Nevertheless, it is hard to see a way out of the impasse. Chiang was, within his powers, a loyal ally of the United States, and to abandon him would be a dishonourable act. It is also very understandable that in the United States, which lost 30,000 dead in the Korean War, there should be bitter hatred of the Chinese communist régime. It is, however, still true that recognition of a government does not imply approval, and that the United Nations is intended to be a forum for states as they exist, not as one wishes that they were. It would be easier if it were possible to recognize two Chinas, and to give communist China, which has 580 million people under its rule, the Security Council seat, while allowing the government in Formosa to be a simple member of the United Nations. But the 'two Chinas policy' has been expressly rejected by both China and the Soviet Union. Another possibility would be to recognize Formosa as an independent state. This would mean a repudiation by the Powers concerned of the Cairo declaration of 1943, which promised not only to take Formosa from Japan, but to give it to China. Formosa has about 10 million inhabitants, of whom about 1,500,000 are Chinese from the mainland, while the rest are in their great majority Chinese in speech and origin, but have so long been separated from the mainland as to have, it is argued, a different national identity.[98] But this solution, attractive in theory, would require the removal of Chiang Kai-shek and his military and civil state machine (which would mean betrayal by America of her ally), and would almost certainly be rejected by communist China, whose leaders insist, no less fiercely than Chiang, that Formosa is part of China.

Meanwhile, the Chiang régime persists, and in ten years, with lavish American material aid, building on foundations laid by Japanese rule, has created a comparatively efficient and modern régime, and has carried out valuable social reforms. Chiang also controls a number of islands off the coast of China, which are a source of understandable rage to the communist government. These off-shore islands were the cause of two serious international crises, from December 1954 to February 1955 and in August and September 1958. As long as they are held by Chiang's forces, they enable the communist Powers to start a war scare whenever they feel there is a good occasion for making trouble between the United States and her allies, who have no desire to be embroiled in a major war for the sake of these islands.

The British government's recognition of the communist government of China in 1949, though supported by sound theoretical arguments, in practice achieved virtually nothing. It annoyed the government, and still more the public opinion, of the United States, without in any way winning the goodwill of the Peking rulers, to whom relations with one Western Power were of small use if they did not lead to relations with the most powerful.

Even before the war in Korea, Mao Tse-tung proclaimed his devotion to the Soviet Union in world affairs. The war embroiled China more thoroughly with the West, and increased China's dependence on its partner, with whom a formal treaty of alliance was signed on 14 February 1950. The alliance has been and still is of great value to both parties. Both have the same enemies. The Soviet Union is able to strengthen China both militarily and economically. For the Soviet Union China is both a potential source of military and industrial manpower, if these should be needed, and a partner capable of diverting Western resources and attention away from Europe and the Middle East, the areas in which the Soviet state is most directly interested. The mutual advantages are far greater than the sources of conflict between the two Powers, and are likely long to remain so. Nevertheless, it is necessary briefly to mention these sources of conflict.

The Soviet share of the Manchurian railway was sold back to China in 1952, and Port Arthur was handed over in May 1955. Manchurian factories are now equipped with Soviet machinery of better quality than the former Japanese, though no doubt the Chinese government has had to pay for this. There appears no reason to believe that the Soviet Union has retained any special rights over Manchuria, which is the most advanced industrial province of China, and of vital importance to the whole economic future of the country.

The other borderlands between the Soviet Union and China are Mongolia and Sinkiang. The Chinese rule over these areas, whose peoples are quite distinct from the Han, has been briefly mentioned elsewhere. They appear rather to be a factor drawing Russia and China together than one pulling them apart. Neither government has an interest in encouraging pan-Mongolian or pan-Turki movements.

The Mongols are in fact divided between three territories—the Buryat Mongol ASSR within the Soviet Union, the Mongolian People's Republic, and the Inner Mongolia Autonomous Region in China. It is true that the MPR (formerly Outer Mongolia) owes its origin to a Mongolian independence movement which was supported by Imperial Russia from 1911 and, in the form of forcible communization, by the Soviet Union in the 1920s, and that its independence was first recognized by China (of Chiang Kai-shek) only in 1945. It is also of interest to note that the alphabet adopted for the Mongols of China since 1955 is the form of Cyrillic (Russian) alphabet in use in the MPR and the Buryat ASSR. But it would be too much to conclude from this that there is any fear in Peking that the Soviet Union has designs on Chinese Mongolia. Any movement for a genuine independence or unity of the Mongol people would be equally opposed by Moscow and Peking.

Much the same would seem to be true in regard to the Uigurs, Kazakhs and Kirgiz of Sinkiang, the suppression of whose Islamic religion and desire for independence and unity is a common interest of both communist governments.

Both Mongolia and Sinkiang are of increasing importance as a means of communication between the Soviet Union and China. A new railway was constructed, between 1953 and 1955, from Tsining in Chinese Mongolia to Ulan Bator, the capital of the MPR, from which there is a connexion with the Soviet rail network. A much vaster project, a railway from Lanchow in north-west China across the Gobi Desert to Urumchi in Sinkiang and thence to Alma Ata in the Kazakh SSR of the Soviet Union, was begun in 1955.

If concrete problems concerning border areas do not seem likely to cause serious Sino-Soviet conflict, there are other less predictable factors which must be mentioned, but on which no conclusions are possible. One is the pressure of Chinese population, for which the sparsely populated lands of the Soviet Far Eastern and Maritime provinces, and even of eastern Siberia, may be an object of increasing envy. Another is the conflict between China's need of economic aid and the Soviet government's inclination or ability to impose continuing material sacrifices on its own subjects. The Soviet Union has an interest in strengthening China's economy. But it is difficult even for a totalitarian government to tell its people, which at last sees material progress, even comfort and luxury, within its grasp, after the horrors of the 1930s and the devastation of the Second World War that belts must once more be tightened to help the Chinese comrades. Yet if Moscow refuses to make greater efforts, the dislike of the Chinese for comfort-loving Russians may assume dangerous proportions. A third source at least of friction between the two governments is in their apparently different attitudes to the cost involved in war. According to President Tito, the Chinese government faces the prospect of total atomic war with equanimity, on the ground that there would still be 300 million Chinese left.[99] Such reasoning can hardly commend itself to the Soviet leaders, or increase their eagerness to help their Chinese allies to acquire atomic weapons.

Finally, there is the factor of ideological differences. Already in the 1940s the Chinese communists showed little respect for Stalin as a prophet of Marxism. They preferred to talk of 'Marxism-Leninism and the Thought of Mao Tse-tung'. Their doctrines on the role of the working class in the revolution were dubious, if not directly heretical. The theory of 'antagonistic and non-antagonistic contradictions' is still more questionable. The most serious divergence yet observed is in the argument in the autumn of 1958 about the possibility of transition to communism. These doctrinaire disputes, in communist totalitarian states, are not mere academic exercises. They are intimately connected with struggles for power, with the interplay of factions, with the fight for control of the party machine. The possibilities of 'pro-' and 'anti-Chinese' factions within the Soviet leadership, and of more and less pro-Soviet cliques within the Chinese party are unverifiable, but none the less real or important for that. Indeed, it is in this field of struggle for control of the party and formulation of doctrine that Sino-Soviet conflict in the next decades is least improbable.

One last field of friction, connected with the above, is in the influence over other communist parties, especially in Asia. Japan is a country of so great strategic importance to both the Soviet Union and China that both are bound to be interested in the policies and personalities of its Communist Party. In South-East Asia one may expect that Chinese guidance would be more important than Soviet, and this indeed seems to be the case with the Indonesian party. In the Indian party it is rather the Soviet than the Chinese influence which has prevailed. There is also some evidence that East European parties, which clearly belong to the Soviet sphere of influence, have taken an interest in China. The Polish communists had hopes of support from a 'liberal' Chinese party in 1957, but soon saw that they had been mistaken. Bulgaria, whose leaders have long been the 'hardest' in Eastern Europe, began to talk of imitating Chinese communes in the autumn of 1958, and then suddenly went into reverse. It is difficult not to see in this a sign of Soviet-Chinese friction.

INDIA

Independent India has shown a remarkable degree of stability and freedom in its government, and of material progress in its economy, but in both fields great dangers lie ahead.

One element of political stability has been Congress, which has continued to dominate Indian politics no less than during the struggle for independence. Two general elections have been held in India, in 1951 and 1957. In both Congress won nearly half the poll, and far surpassed every rival party (47·5 million votes out of 107·6 million in 1951 and 57 million out of 121·4 million in 1957). Congress is the only political party that can organize the mass vote all over the country. It still enjoys the great prestige it won as the champion of independence. The people still see in it the instrument of Mahatma Gandhi. It may be argued that Congress has hardly followed the master's teaching. His economic doctrines have been set aside, and his doctrine of non-violence was honoured as much in the breach as in the observance. But devotion to his memory is none the less sincere, and provides a strong unifying force. Hardly less important has been the personal authority of Nehru, second after Gandhi in the years of struggle, and Prime Minister of independent India since 1947. Nehru is not, as Gandhi was, a saint, but he combines the shrewd grasp of practical politics possessed by his master with a wide knowledge of the problems of the modern world. He is a fine writer and an independent thinker as well as an eminent statesman. Though he can inspire anger, and even hatred, both inside India and abroad, and has an almost unexampled ability to infuriate those who regard themselves, and are encouraged by him to regard themselves, as his friends, there can be no doubt of his great gifts of leadership and of the vast authority that his personality commands in India. Yet despite its popularity, its party machine and the greatness of its leaders, Congress has its weaknesses too. It is extremely heterogeneous, including people of different regional and social origin, religious and secular, reactionaries and modernizers, democratic socialists and dictatorial bosses. It is as heterogeneous as the Chinese Kuomintang of the 1920s, whose errors and misfortunes it would do well to study with care.

A second element of stability is the government apparatus inherited from British rule. Indians have been generous in their recognition of the merits of the former Indian Civil Service, but they deserve no less credit than their British mentors. If the ICS was the best administrative machine ever created in any European colonial empire, the Indians, who already well before 1947 occupied most of the posts in it, proved themselves far more gifted in the art of administration than any other colonial people. Since 1947 the numbers of government servants have much expanded—an inevitable result of the increasing complexity of government in a country determined to create a modern welfare state. The standards of efficiency, and even of honesty, have no doubt declined. This is not surprising. Far more surprising is that, despite difficulties and temptations, the standards have remained so high. The achievement is all the more impressive because government officials have been very badly treated by the new régime from the material point of view. Those who were already serving before Independence have kept the salaries they received before the war, though the cost of living has increased three and a half times.[100] Officials appointed since Independence have been employed at very low rates. Yet the civil servants, and the army officers, whose material status is roughly comparable, have given loyal and efficient service. How long the government will be able thus to exploit its servants with impunity remains to be seen.

A third important factor has been the sincere belief of the Indian political leaders, above all of Nehru, in the parliamentary form of government. This too is something that they learned from the British, but for which they have also shown a remarkable aptitude. Here too, however, the future is uncertain. It is too soon to guess whether the rising generation of educated and politically ambitious Indians will take over from their elders the same conviction. Meanwhile, parliamentary government seems securely founded, and there is a fairly wide freedom of speech, publication, association and meeting.

The two main opposition parties are the Praja socialists and the communists. Between the two general elections their relative strengths changed. The socialist vote declined from 17·3 million in 1951 to 11·6 million in 1957, while that of the communists increased from 4·7 million to 11·6 million. The communists were thus the chief opposition party in the 1957 parliament, though they only had twenty-nine seats to Congress's 362. In the 1950s the Soviet attitude to India changed, and the Indian communists abandoned violent tactics, even giving support at times to the government in questions of foreign policy. The communists control the AITUC, which includes rather more than a quarter of the organized working class. They also enjoy considerable support among students and in general among the younger generation of the intelligentsia. The nature of their appeal to these elements is that characteristic of all other underdeveloped societies in which nationalist emotions are strong.

In certain areas the communists have at times had special strength. They remain a powerful force in the city of Calcutta, and have gained influence in Kashmir. Their main stronghold, however, has been in the South. In the provincial assembly election of 1957 they were the strongest single party in the state of Kerala, with sixty seats out of 126, and formed a ministry there. There are several reasons for their success. One is that the preceding Congress administration in this state was especially corrupt and repressive. Another is that politics in Kerala have been complicated by a religious conflict: there is in this region a strong Christian minority, the only large one in India. A third special characteristic of Kerala is that the level of education is unusually high: the literacy rate is higher, and the intelligentsia more numerous and more influential than elsewhere, and people are in general more accessible to new ideas, less content passively to give their vote to the government. During the first two years of its rule the Kerala communist government proceeded cautiously, but charges of corruption, favouritism and unjust repression of opponents have recently been made against it, not only by Congress, but also by the socialists.

An explosive force in Indian political life is regional and linguistic patriotism. There was nothing specially sacred about the provincial boundaries established under British rule, still less about the borders of the princely states which were incorporated in Independent India. Reorganization was therefore necessary. But a question of principle was soon raised: whether the new boundaries should be made to coincide with those of the main language groups. Local patriotism demanded this in certain cases. The communists supported this principle, both because it was in keeping with Soviet doctrine on the 'nationalities question', and because in general they welcomed any changes likely to have disruptive effects. Congress opinion was divided, and at first there was considerable reluctance to risk the unity of India by such innovations. There were also difficult problems in connexion with the states of Bombay and Madras, in both of which large language groups were mixed. The first linguistic state was, however, created in October 1953—Andhra, based on the Telugu language. During 1956 there were further parliamentary debates and large-scale riots in the city and state of Bombay, which led to a further far-reaching reorganization of boundaries. Under the new settlement, which came into force in November 1956, there were fourteen states including Kashmir. Under the Indian Constitution the states have much less jurisdiction than under fully federal constitutions such as those of the United States, Australia or Switzerland, and residual powers belong to the central government. However, they have wide authority in such matters as education and land reform. Hitherto there have been no major conflicts between state and central governments. But the passions released in Bombay in 1956 show the potential explosive quality of the 'nationality question'. Both communists and other extremists could make good use of it.

Economic progress has centred on the Five Year Plans. The first ran from 1951 to 1956, and was satisfactorily completed. It paid special attention to agriculture, irrigation and power, transport and communications. It was a fine achievement, but the poverty of the Indian people is so acute, and the pressure of population growth so relentless, that it was felt that the second Plan must set a more rapid pace. Under it the proportion of agricultural to total investment was reduced, while the proportion devoted to industry was more than doubled. The Plan emphasizes the development of heavy industry (steel output is to be nearly quadrupled), but also pays attention to small-scale village industries which employ a high ratio of labour to capital. Industrialization is to be by state initiative. In a country so poor in private capital this is inevitable, but one of the weaknesses of the government's policy is that it is reluctant to encourage such private capital as does exist. The plan's success will depend very largely on foreign aid. The United States, Britain, Western Germany and the Soviet Union have all made contributions, but these still fall far behind India's needs.

India's leaders are rightly convinced that they must modernize the economy in order both to employ the population and to make the country strong. But they are not obsessed by output figures. Human welfare takes precedence over statistics. They are unwilling to use more than a minimum of direct coercion. They wish to convince the people of the need for change. Economic progress must not conflict too harshly with traditional social organization and with religious customs. Nehru and his colleagues do not wish to do violence to beliefs or brutally to repress whole classes. They have abolished *zamindar* land ownership, but have compensated the owners, even if this has inevitably retarded the transfer of land to individual peasant ownership. Gandhi's saintly disciple, Vinoba Bhave, has walked for thousands of miles up and down the sub-continent asking for gifts of land (*Bhoodan*) or of whole villages (*Gramdan*) for the poor. In six years from 1951 to 1957 he had received more than 4 million acres and 2,000 villages. But the influence of his example on men's and women's minds has been greater than mere figures can show. Less sensational, but of profound importance have been the Community Projects in the villages. These are designed to demonstrate to the peasants many small improvements that can improve their lot—more efficient and healthier farm buildings, better hygiene, inexpensive but useful tools, various improved methods of farming. The teams concentrate on innovations that are not costly, and that are suited to the particular conditions of each area, which they first take the trouble to study. They do not deal in abstract universal panaceas, and they do not force anyone. Their aim is to induce the peasants themselves to take the initiative, to get together to carry out some improvement, and to ask the authorities for help, which is then given. With its deliberate respect for the wishes of the people (as opposed to their 'objective interests' as laid down by infallible prophets who know them better than the people themselves) the Indian policy is poles apart from the Soviet or Chinese.

Great though the changes have been, Indian society has kept most of its traditional structure. The intricate system of caste remains in force. The enforcement of 'untouchability' is a criminal offence, but there are still 60 million untouchables (*Harijan*) in India. The government is systematically working for modernization, for the breakdown of caste, for the abolition of the terrible injustices and cruelties that result from it. But it believes it must go slowly, without antagonizing the tradition-bound masses, not using force except in flagrant cases. It is surely right. Denunciation by Westerners of a society whose standards have never been Western is largely irrelevant. At present it must be recognized that the caste system is an important, indeed perhaps the principal, factor of stability in India. The habit of obedience by the masses is an invaluable source of strength to a government which has undertaken a vast programme of social reform and economic change, and at the same time must steer a course on the stormy seas of international politics. Of the will to reform of Nehru and his team there can be no doubt. Their practical achievements are already great. If they were to proceed too fast or too violently, they would risk a collapse of the whole edifice, the disappearance of all freedom and all reform in anarchy and bloodshed. Even with their moderate and enlightened policy, the odds are against them, but at least they have a chance. They deserve the help of free men whose heritage is happier.

India decided to remain a member of the Commonwealth. Since 1947 relations between India and Britain, both on the government level and in thousands of personal relationships in business and professions and education, have usually been good. This is something of which both nations can be proud and happy. But its political significance should not be overrated. India is entirely sovereign in her foreign policy, which has often been diametrically opposed to that of Britain; and the two states in the world with which her relations have consistently been worst are both members of the Commonwealth—Pakistan and South Africa.

The Kashmir dispute was no nearer solution in 1959 than in 1949. In the first years the state was ruled by Sheikh Abdullah, a friend of Nehru and a man of standing in Kashmir, even if he represented a minority view. But Abdullah did not wish Kashmir to be completely subordinated to India. He made public criticisms of the policy of India as well as of Pakistan and of the United Nations. In July 1952 he made an agreement with Nehru by which Kashmir was to have substantially more autonomy than other states of India. But Abdullah's position in Kashmir was being weakened both by separatism among the Hindu and Buddhist minorities and by the opposition of men within his own party whom he had antagonized by his dictatorial behaviour. In August 1953 he was arrested. Thereafter Kashmir became more closely controlled from New Delhi. Pakistan remained irreconcilable. Further important causes of tension between India and Pakistan were failure to agree on compensation to refugees and on the use of the rivers. Obstacles to the marketing of East Bengal's jute in India harmed both countries, but Pakistan more than India.

Apart from the very serious problems that divide the two countries, there remains a conviction among many Indians that Pakistan is an artificial creation, and will not last. The course of Pakistani politics has given some comfort to Indians who hold this opinion. A most dangerous crisis occurred in March 1954, when the Moslem League was overwhelmingly defeated in the provincial elections in East Bengal by a coalition of opposition parties which took the name United Front. Two months later the central government dissolved the East Bengal government and forbade the assembly to meet. At the end of the year the Governor-General also dissolved the Constituent Assembly, which had failed in its difficult task of creating a constitution based on Islam. In the summer of 1955 parliamentary government was restored in East Bengal and a new Constituent Assembly was elected, which in March 1956 passed a constitution drafted by the government. However, the fragmentation of political life continued, the Moslem League lost its dominant position, the conflicts of interest between East Bengal and West Pakistan remained unsolved, and friction between the western provinces continued despite their formal fusion in October 1955 into a single West Pakistan Province.

Pakistan also had bad relations with its northern neighbour, Afghanistan, which, with some encouragement from India, claimed that the Pathans of the North-West Frontier Province should be united with their kinsmen in Afghanistan in a new state of 'Pakhtoonistan'. When the Pakistan government definitely included the Pathan areas in the new West Pakistan Province, in October 1955, the two countries recalled their ambassadors. In June 1957, however, the Pakistan Prime Minister paid an official visit to Kabul, and diplomatic relations were fully restored.

In view of these alarming political fluctuations, aggravated by economic difficulties, Indian expectations that Pakistan would fall apart did not seem unrealistic. A new phase in Pakistan's brief history came on 4 October 1958, when President Iskander Mirza abrogated the Constitution, dissolved the central and provincial assemblies, and declared all political parties abolished. The commander-in-chief, General Ayub Khan, was appointed Premier. On 22 October Mirza resigned his presidential office in favour of Ayub Khan and left the country.

India's foreign policy is by no means confined to relations with Commonwealth countries. She has a common frontier with China in the northeast, and is deeply interested in the independence of Burma. Nehru also insists in a wider context on India's world-wide role as an 'uncommitted' Power, free from the influence of either the Atlantic or the communist bloc. He also supports the principle of an 'Afro-Asian' bloc in the United Nations, and loses few opportunities of declaring India's sympathy for the struggle of nationalist movements against 'colonialism' anywhere in the world.

In the first years of independence India's relations with the Soviet Union were bad. The Soviet propaganda machine, and the Asian communist parties, declared that India was not in fact independent at all, that the Congress leaders had betrayed their people and made a dishonest bargain with the British imperialists, whose lackeys they remained. It is possible that this policy was based on a genuine misunderstanding by Stalin of the meaning of the Commonwealth and of the realities of power in India. In 1950 India supported the United Nations' decision to resist in Korea, though no Indian troops were sent. From 1951 to 1954, however, Indian policy may be said to have moved from a neutrality benevolent to the West towards a strictly impartial neutrality. In this period Indian diplomacy played a valuable part in ending the Korean and the Indo-Chinese wars. In 1955 the swing of the pendulum went still further, and Indian neutrality appeared rather to be benevolent to the Soviet bloc.

Nehru gave undiscriminating support to all anti-Western nationalist movements in the Arab world, and Africa, while showing hostility towards such Asian or Arab leaders as remained friendly to the West. Khrushchov and Bulganin were given an ovation in India. In the autumn of 1956 the Indian representatives not only condemned Anglo-French action against Egypt—which was to be expected—but ostentatiously avoided any opposition to the Soviet reconquest of Hungary. In the following two years Indian policy continued to oppose the West, especially the United States, on almost every issue.

India is potentially one of the Great Powers of the world, and has every right to an independent policy. It is childish folly for Americans or British to claim as of right that India should agree with their policies, and to scold her leaders when they do not. India has vast tasks of economic and social reconstruction, and does not wish to spend more than she can help on military needs. What military forces she has are required for what she considers legitimate defence against Pakistan in Kashmir. In these circumstances it is not surprising that Nehru should not wish to antagonize his powerful neighbour, China. If India adopted a pro-Western foreign policy, vast military expenditures would be necessary against the Chinese danger. As things are, Nehru does not believe that China threatens him. As for the Soviet Union, there is no point at which its interests as a state directly clash with those of India. It has hitherto respected the independence of Afghanistan.

One may disagree with Nehru's views on Kashmir and Tibet, and yet recognize the general validity of the main arguments summarized above. Indian policy may at times run parallel to that of the communist bloc, but it is shaped in New Delhi, not Peking or Moscow, and it is not designed to further communist interests. If one examines coolly the substance of Indian policy in the last six years, one may disagree with it, but one must respect it.

What is objectionable from a Western point of view is not so much the substance as the tone. And this is no small matter, for the tone of an eminent statesman's pronouncements is a political factor in itself. It would be wrong, in any attempt at an objective survey of international politics, not to mention the fact that Nehru's love of moralizing lectures directed always against the West, has infuriated millions of Europeans and Americans. He talks of Western military alliances as if there were some inherent sin in plans for self-defence. He might have the realism and generosity to admit that if American military power did not exist he would be unable to preserve his neutrality or even his independence. It ill befits the conqueror of Kashmir to express indignation at the presence of the

Dutch in West New Guinea. If the Indian army fights against Naga headhunters in Assam, he claims that this serves progress and democracy, but he sees Mau Mau as champions of freedom. The most horrifying example of all was the performance of Krishna Menon in the United Nations debates on Hungary. This is something for which millions of Europeans will never be able to forgive India.

JAPAN

In the years that followed the signature of the San Francisco peace treaty, as in the preceding period, Japan was ruled by the conservatives, with the socialists in opposition. There were, however, considerable regroupments on both sides. In October 1951 the Socialist Party split into a right and a left party. Though the left socialists remained quite separate from the communists, who were at this time weakened not only by repression but by internal factional struggles, they adopted in foreign policy an attitude that was barely distinguishable from that of China or the Soviet Union. In the opposite political camp, the Liberal Party was divided between the supporters and rivals of Premier Yoshida. The man whom the Liberal Party had originally chosen as its leader, but who had been banned from political activity by MacArthur in 1946 because of his pre-1945 record, Ichiro Hatoyama, was allowed to resume his career in 1951, and wished to take Yoshida's place. The Prime Minister was not willing to give up his leadership, but he could only count on the support of a section of the party. At the general election of October 1952 the liberal majority was smaller than in 1949. In the new parliament some liberals voted with the opposition. Yoshida therefore dissolved, and held another general election in April 1953, in which his party still had a small lead. In November 1954 the Hatoyama group of liberals joined with the progressives to form a new Democratic Party. Yoshida's position in parliament now became impossible, and he resigned the Premiership on 7 December. Hatoyama formed a transitional government until a new election was held in February 1955. This reversed the position of liberals and democrats: the latter were substantially the stronger of the two. At the same time the left socialists gained ground at the expense of the right.

By the end of 1955 this fragmentation of the forces of both right and left, which was due as much to personal rivalries as to real differences of policy, was formally ended by the fusion of the groups into two larger parties. In October 1955 left and right socialists were reunited in one Socialist Party, in which great care seemed to have been taken to allocate the leading posts on a basis of equal representation for the two former factions. The party programme was a compromise, more moderate than that of the left, and in foreign policy favouring neutralism rather than supporting the Sino-Soviet cause. In November 1955 the two conservative parties united and took the name Liberal-Democratic Party, choosing Hatoyama as their leader. There were now 299 conservatives and 154 socialists in parliament: the conservatives were just not strong enough to obtain the two-thirds majority for an amendment to the Constitution, which would be required if there was to be a programme of rearmament. At the general election of September 1958 the respective strength of the parties was but slightly changed: the liberal democrats, now led by Nobusuke Kishi, had 287 seats, the Socialist Party 166 and the Communist Party 1.

Conservative rule in Japan has meant, probably to a greater extent than ever before, a predominance of business influence in politics. In the first fifty years after the Meiji Restoration Japan was ruled essentially by bureaucrats and soldiers. In this period great business fortunes were made, but the business-men were essentially privileged executors of an economic policy that was decided by non-economic factors. In the 1920s, when the old oligarchy of the Meiji era had yielded much of its power to parliamentary politicians, the business-men began to play a role in politics. But this period was ended with the rise of military influence in the 1930s. Since 1952 Japan has been ruled essentially by two of the three forces that were powerful in the 1920s, the bureaucracy and the business class: the third force, the army and naval officers, having ceased to exist. Of the two it seems likely that business has gained ground and bureaucracy has lost. Nevertheless, among the leading politicians are men who made their career in government service rather than in business, and the administration of the country, even after the decentralizing reforms and the development of elected local government sponsored by the Occupation, is still largely in the hands of the civil service. An important difference from the old régime is that the peasants, materially benefited by the land reform and encouraged to take part in local affairs, are a more active political factor. Hitherto they have given their support to the conservatives. Thus it may be said that Japan is governed by a combination of business-men, officials and farmers.

The main mass support of the opposition comes from the working class. But, as we have seen, the leadership of the socialists and of the trade unions over the Japanese workers has definite limitations. The most politically militant trade unions are those of clerical workers and teachers. It is in fact the intelligentsia which is the strongest force opposing the régime.

As we saw in an earlier chapter, the educational policy of the Meiji era reformers, in contrast to that of Imperial Russia and of most independent Asian and European colonial governments, rapidly narrowed the gap between the educated *élite* and the masses. The characteristic problem of the intelligentsia in underdeveloped societies, the deep gulf between the acquired culture and that of the people, was thus quickly overcome in Japan. The Japanese intellectuals found their place within the new Japanese society, and were not a basically alienated and revolutionary element. Today the masses and the intellectuals essentially belong to one culture, though they occupy varying grades within it. In this respect their status is comparable with that of any Western country rather than with that of the rest of Asia.

But if the cultural gap between *élite* and masses is of moderate dimensions, the political gap between intelligentsia and government is profound. The Japanese intelligentsia has taken very seriously the repudiation of the old régime and all its historical values. It is dominated by Marxist thought, or at least by Marxist slogans, without specifically approving of the Japanese Communist Party. It has a high-minded contempt for existing political practices and politicians, which recalls the attitude of writers of text-books on American Government in the 1920s. A comparison may also be made with France, the Western country for which Japanese intellectuals feel most sympathy. But whereas in France there has always been an intelligentsia of the right as well as of the left, both among writers in the strict sense and in the wider circle of the professional classes, in Japan this seems to be absent. The values of *Les Mandarins* seem unchallenged. The Japanese intelligentsia do not represent a concrete and immediate political threat, and with the exception of the active members of the Teachers' Union they do not consciously support the communists. But their sweeping rejection of both the past and the present of Japan, their determination to see a fascist plot in any government measure to protect public order, their curious combination of devotion to the iconoclastic measures of the Occupation period with boundless contempt for the Americans who imposed them, and their uncritical admiration for Communist China, are dangerous in the longer term. They are building up a climate of opinion which must affect wider circles of society than the intelligentsia itself.

It is only fair to point out that to a large extent Americans have themselves to thank for this state of affairs. The first major defeat in the whole history of Japan was bound to have a demoralizing effect, and this was bound to be increased by the special horror of Hiroshima and Nagasaki. But once they had arrived in Japan as victors, the Americans set themselves with almost evangelical zeal to discredit all traditional values. The desire to endow the Japanese with the benefits of the American way of life was obviously sincere, and reflects credit on the generosity of its propagandists. But the moral elevation perhaps made less impression on the Japanese than the brash contempt for the Japanese 'feudal culture', of which their self-appointed benefactors seldom had more than a rudimentary knowledge. The grotesque Article 9 of the Constitution was clearly irreconcilable either with the past history of the human race or with the facts of international life in 1946. By first imposing it, and then urging the Japanese to repeal it, Americans have only brought themselves into contempt.

In the economic field Japan has made great progress, but remains highly vulnerable. Though the birth-rate has steadily fallen in recent decades, the natural increase is still rapid. More than 90 million people live on a group of small islands, only 15% of whose area is arable. Though crop yields are very high, Japan needs to import about 20% of its food supply. It also has to import all its raw cotton and wool, nearly all its oil, most of its iron ore and a third of its coking coal. Thus Japan, like Britain, must export or perish. Since 1945 exports have fallen behind imports, and the gap has been filled by the United States—with $2 milliard from 1945 to 1950, and more than $4 milliard of special procurements and expenditure on behalf of the United States and United Nations forces between 1950 and 1955. Industrial production has risen rapidly (by 207% from 1948-55, as compared with 225% in Western Germany in the same years). But the costs of production of the Japanese metal industries, which have shown the biggest advance, are high compared with those of the corresponding industries in the United States, Britain or Germany.

Japanese exports are much more diverse than before 1941, and they are also spread over a wider range of markets. The United States is Japan's largest customer. But whereas trade with Japan is of marginal importance to America, trade with America is a matter of life and death for Japan. A serious recession in the United States would have quicker and more deadly effects in Japan than in other countries of the free world. There is very little trade with China. There is much talk in both Japan and China of the need to restore trade. But it is doubtful how much could be achieved even if there were no political obstacles. It is true that Japan could deliver to China machinery and metal products which the Chinese need, if this were not prevented by the ban on sale to communist countries of articles of strategic importance. But it is not clear what China could sell to Japan in return. Chinese foodstuffs and raw materials, which would certainly be acceptable to Japan, are needed to feed the growing Chinese urban population and to supply the new Chinese industries. South-East Asia is another promising area for Japanese trade. For several years arguments about reparations were a political obstacle to trade with Burma and the Philippines, and they still impede relations with Indonesia. India is potentially a most important market, and could in many ways benefit from Japanese 'know-how' in industrialization. Indeed, closer economic relations between India and Japan could, and probably will, contribute greatly to the prosperity of both countries and the stability and progress of all southern Asia. Japanese trade has also grown with South America, and to a lesser extent with Africa. Trade relations with Western countries other than the United States have been less happy. Japan was admitted to the General Agreement on Trade and Tariffs in June 1945, but fourteen countries invoked Article 35 of the Agreement, which allows them to prevent the application of the Agreement between themselves and a member, against Japan. They included such important markets as Britain, France, Australia, India, Benelux and Brazil.

In foreign policy Japan has remained attached to the United States. The socialists continue to favour neutralism, and the intelligentsia inclines towards Communist China, but the government party has been little influenced by these opinions. In 1955 the government began negotiations to reach a settlement with the Soviet Union. The Japanese government also hoped to obtain the restoration to Japan of the two southern islands of the Kurile chain, and also the small Habomai and Shikotan islands off the coast of Hokkaido, but no agreement could be made on this matter. In the dispute on the right of Japanese boats to fish salmon off the coast of Kamchatka—a matter of great importance for Japan's food supply—the Soviet government made some concessions from its original demands. Eventually the two governments decided to content themselves with ending the state of war between them and restoring diplomatic relations. An agreement to this effect was signed in Moscow by Hatoyama and Bulganin on 19 October 1956. The Security Council was thus no longer prevented by the Soviet veto from admitting Japan to membership of the United Nations. This took place on 12 December 1956.

The prevalent Japanese attitude to Russia appears to be fear and dislike. The attitude to China is more complex. There is universal admiration for Chinese culture, from which Japanese is mainly derived, and a widespread feeling of guilt for past Japanese aggression against China. The Japanese have, however, for long considered themselves better organizers and soldiers, a tougher and more efficient nation, than the Chinese. How this view is being affected by China's rise to military, and ultimately to industrial Great Power status, an outsider cannot judge. At present Japan has diplomatic relations with Formosa, but not with Peking. It is unlikely that Japan will abandon her alliance with America in order to court China.

It may, however, be expected that Japanese governments will increasingly stress their independence in foreign policy. This need be no bad thing either for the West or for Japan. Drastic change is unlikely unless major economic disaster occurs, or until the doctrinaire left-wing attitudes now prevalent in the intelligentsia make themselves felt in the younger generation rising within the bureaucracy, or within such armed forces as Japan acquires in the next years.

At present Japan is on the side of the West, and is no mean asset. In the long term less powerful than India, at present, owing to the high level of education and industrial skill of its people, it is of about equal importance. Much will depend on whether the Western nations, in their commercial and general policies, show understanding and sympathy to this proud and gifted nation.

SOUTH-EAST ASIA

The war between the French army and Vietminh in Indochina which began in December 1946 lasted nearly eight years. It represented an intolerable drain on the manpower and finances of France, and dangerously weakened her military position in Europe. Only massive American military intervention might have given France a hope of victory, and after much argument the American government decided against this. At the conference of Foreign Ministers of the Great Powers in Geneva, which opened on 26 April 1954, Indochina was the main subject of discussion. The beginning of the conference coincided with the last stages of the siege of the French fortress Dien Bien Phu by a large Vietminh army well equipped with artillery. It fell on 7 May. A new French government was formed under Pierre Mendès-France, who was determined to end the war. The Vietminh and their Chinese patrons were in a comparatively generous mood, perhaps because the Chinese were now especially eager to make an impression of moderation on the independent Asian countries. The settlement signed on 21 July divided Vietnam into two at the 17th Parallel. Forces on the wrong side of the line were to be regrouped within 300 days. No new foreign bases were to be established on either side, but the existing French forces in the South were to be allowed to stay. Free elections were to be held not later than 20 July 1956 in both regions for the formation of a government of united Vietnam. Cambodia and Laos were to become separate independent states, and Vietminh forces were to be withdrawn from their territory.

In practice Vietnam remained divided. The Premier of South Vietnam, Ngo Dinh Diem, declared that he was not bound by the agreement, and refused to carry out all-Vietnamese elections. The United States, which had not signed the Geneva agreement, backed him. Both governments also pointed out that conditions in North Vietnam, under communist rule, precluded free elections. In the following years Diem received massive financial assistance and unconditional political backing from the United States. He was able to crush the armed forces of various religious sects or political cliques which opposed his power and policies, and in October 1955 he announced a plebiscite to decide whether Bao Dai, with whom he was now in open conflict, should be deposed. The voters duly decided, by a 98% vote, against Bao Dai and in favour of Diem, who instituted a republic of which he became President. His government succeeded in restoring a minimum of order and of central direction, but it was clearly a dictatorship. Though the dictator himself was incorruptible, the same could not be said of his relatives, dependents or subordinates.

The Geneva settlement was followed by the signature, on 8 September 1954, of the Manila Pact, which set up the South-East Asia Treaty Organization (SEATO). The signatories were five non-Asian Powers (the United States, Britain, France, Australia and New Zealand) and three Asian states (Philippines, Siam and Pakistan). The signatories were bound to act together against aggression in the area of the South-West Pacific, below the latitude of 21° 30'. An additional protocol mentioned, as an area covered by the treaty, the states of Cambodia, Laos and South Vietnam, which did not, however, sign the pact. It was also provided that in cases of a threat 'other than by armed attack' the signatories would consult each other on counter-measures: this clause referred to internal subversion or seizure of power from within by communists. The United States government issued a separate declaration that its commitment to action applied only to aggression by communist states, but that in the case of aggression by other states it would consult with the signatories. It was hoped that the creation of SEATO would strengthen the morale of non-communist governments and political forces in the area. Serious arguments could, however, be used against it. The United States was already committed to defend Australia, New Zealand and the Philippines. There was something to be said for Western guarantees of Siam, South Vietnam and Malaya. But SEATO fell far short of its original aim, which had been a regional mutual defence system for South-East Asia. As long as Indonesia, with half the population of the whole area and a vitally important strategic situation, remained outside, the pact could not have this character. The participation of Pakistan was no compensation for the absence of Indonesia. On the contrary, it made things worse, by making India still more opposed to the very idea of a regional defence system, and by pushing Indian policy further towards the communist bloc, whose spokesmen took care to represent SEATO as a threat not so much to themselves as to independent Asian nations.

Marshal Pibul's rule in Siam was ended on 26 September 1957, when one of his former close associates, Marshal Sarit, took over Bangkok by a bloodless military *coup d'état*. Pibul went into exile, but the form of government was little changed. Meanwhile, Pridi had established himself in Peking, whence he directed propaganda to his compatriots. Comparative prosperity, absence of interest in politics, and dislike of Chinese, of whom there were 3 million in their midst, made the Siamese unresponsive.

In the Philippines the Hukbalahap revolt reached its most dangerous point in 1950. In the following year it suffered severe reverses at the hand of a new and energetic Minister of Defence, Ramón Magsaysay, a man of striking honesty and courage, with a gift of personal leadership and an ability to understand and be understood by common folk. In 1953 Magsaysay resigned his office, broke with the Liberal Party of President Elpidio Quirino, and fought the presidential election on behalf of its rivals, the Nationalist Party. He won a large majority, and once in power initiated social and economic reforms, removing much of the corruption that had surrounded the past administration and paying serious attention to the needs of the peasants. Magsaysay was killed in an air accident in March 1957. When he died his country was well on the way to recovery. In terms of public order, social justice and educational achievement it compared favourably with other independent Asian states.

Ceylon under its first independent governments co-operated closely with the West. At the Bandung Conference of 1955 its Prime Minister, Sir John Kotelawala, violently attacked communist imperialism, which he declared now to be more dangerous than Western. This stand won him much applause in the West, but does not seem to have done him much good at home. In the April 1956 election he was decisively defeated by the People's United Front led by Mr. Bandaranaike, who adopted a neutralist foreign policy. The new government revoked the lease to Britain of the naval base of Trincomalee. Another feature of the new régime was open communal conflict between Sinhalese and Tamils (immigrants from the Indian mainland who amount to 30% of Ceylon's population), which led to violent disturbances in May and June 1958.

In Burma public disorder was at its height in 1949, when the government forces had to face revolts not only of communists, but also of the Karen nationalists. By 1951 conditions had improved, though large areas remained, and still remain, out of government control. An election was held in the second half of 1951, spread over six months. AFPFL won 180 out of 233 seats, and only twenty went to pro-communist groups, of which the most important was the Burma Workers and Peasants Party, the legal 'front' of the communist party. At the next election, in April 1956, AFPFL had 147 and the National United Front, dominated by the BWPP, won forty-three. More serious than this communist-led opposition was disunity within AFPFL. This came to a head at its congress in January and February 1958, and took the form of rivalry for control of the party's general secretaryship between groups inspired as much by personal as by ideological motives. In June the split became complete, two Deputy-Premiers resigned, and U Nu was able to find a majority for his new cabinet only by relying on the parliamentary support of the National United Front. In September U Nu resigned, and asked the commander-in-chief of the armed forces, General Ne Win, to take over power and to prepare free elections in 1959. Ne Win's cabinet included one of the leaders of the dissident faction of AFPFL.

In Malaya the jungle war against the communist rebels dragged on year after year. The terrorists were reduced in numbers, but they could still inflict damage and loss of life, and themselves escape capture. Meanwhile, progress was made in the political field. In 1953 UMNO and MCA made an agreement for common action at the elections to the federal Legislative Council. UMNO needed the financial support which only the rich Chinese community could provide, and MCA needed to be able to gain material concessions for the Chinese population if it were to compete for their support with the communists. In April 1954 General Templer, the High Commissioner, announced that a majority of the members of the next Legislative Council would be elected (fifty-two out of ninety-eight seats). The election was held in June 1955. The UMNO-MCA Alliance won fifty-one out of the fifty-two seats, but it was noticeable that out of some 600,000 Chinese entitled to vote only 143,000 had bothered to register. The Alliance now pressed strongly for independence. Consultations were held with the British government, and a constitution was prepared by a special commission and accepted by the Legislative Council. Independence was proclaimed on 31 August 1957. The UMNO leader, Tungku Abdul Rahman, became the first Premier of independent Malaya. A defence agreement was signed with Britain on 2 October. British forces remained to fight the terrorists, and Britain is committed to defend Malaya against aggression, but Malaya did not become a member of SEATO. Certainly great progress had been attained in comparison with the bitter communal cleavage of the first post-war years. Nevertheless, the Chinese element had received less rights than it had hoped for, and it would be rash to assume that Chinese-Malay conflicts have been solved.

The island of Singapore remained separate from Malaya, and was still a British dependency. A new Constitution was introduced in 1955. The Singapore leaders asked that internal security should be made their responsibility, while agreeing that defence and foreign relations be reserved to the governor. In view of the strategic importance of the island, and the strong communist influence in its overwhelmingly Chinese population, the British government would not agree to this.

INDONESIA

In the first years after Indonesia became independent *Masjoemi* and PNI continued to be the main political factors. *Masjoemi's* leadership was recruited from the urban trading class. Though nationalist, it was willing to co-operate with the West both economically and politically. It was very strong in the outer islands, whose traditions were more democratic, but it also had support in Java. PNI depended largely on the prestige of President Soekarno. It relied for its organization on government officials. Through its control of the bureaucracy it had great possibilities of patronage. Many of its leaders, including Soekarno, came from the Javanese nobility, whose traditions were authoritarian rather than democratic. In these men a precapitalist contempt for merchants combined with socialist anti-capitalist doctrines to make them detest the social elements that were most influential in *Masjoemi*. The PNI leaders were also, by the same mixture of traditionalist and socialist outlook, hostile to the West and all it seemed to stand for.

Two further political forces of importance were the *Nahdatul Ulama* and the communists. The first were a Moslem party, which broke with *Masjoemi* and stood for a more theocratic and traditionalist policy, in contrast to the modernist and democratic trends which *Masjoemi*, though also devoted to Islam, favoured. *Nahdatul Ulama* had a strong following among the peasants in Java. Though its Islamic piety should have inclined it rather towards *Masjoemi* than towards PNI, its traditionalism and its anti-Western brand of nationalism brought it closer to PNI and even to the communists. The latter had recovered from their defeat of 1948, largely through their control over the trade unions. In 1952 their leader Aidit reverted to a policy of United Front, making special efforts to win PNI for co-operation against the 'Western imperialists' and their agents *Masjoemi*. To PNI, which possessed leadership and cadres but lacked a mass base, the communists, with their technique of drawing the illiterate agricultural workers and urban poor into political action, were attractive allies.[101]

In 1950 and 1951 *Masjoemi* was the dominant party in the government coalitions. In February 1952 the cabinet fell owing to opposition within both *Masjoemi* and PNI to an agreement which the Prime Minister, Sukiman, had made with the United States to accept financial aid for military purposes. Sukiman had also been keenly criticized for signing the San Francisco peace treaty with Japan, which was not ratified. The fall of Sukiman marked not only the end of *Masjoemi* predominance in internal affairs but a definite change in foreign policy from cautious co-operation with the West to a form of neutralism which became increasingly anti-Western. For another year *Masjoemi* was represented in the government, but PNI was now the more influential partner.

In October 1952 a serious conflict arose in connexion with army policy. On the one hand were some professional officers who wished to create a regular army, based only on military efficiency, and excluding the influence of party politics. On the other hand were officers whose military experience was derived from guerrilla action against the Dutch, who had strong political connexions and feared to lose their career prospects in a more professional army. The first group were backed by the Minister of Defence, the Sultan of Jogjakarta, but Soekarno threw his influence against them. In January 1953 the Sultan resigned.

Soekarno's relations with *Masjoemi* deteriorated when, in a speech in Borneo in January 1953, he opposed the idea that Indonesia should be a specifically Moslem state—an ideal to which *Masjoemi* at least paid lip service. In June a new government was formed, without *Masjoemi* participation, by Ali Sastroamidjojo, a prominent member of PNI who also enjoyed the confidence of the communists. The opposition pressed for the holding of the parliamentary elections, which had been promised ever since independence, but repeatedly postponed. In August 1955 a *Masjoemi* ministry was formed, without PNI, and committed to organize the elections. These took place between the end of September and the end of November. PNI emerged as the strongest party, with 8,400,000 votes and 57 seats. The Moslem vote was divided between *Masjoemi* (7,900,000 votes and 57 seats) and *Nahdatul Ulama* (6,950,000 votes and 45 seats). The communists did better than was generally expected, receiving 6,180,000 votes and 39 seats.

The new government was formed by Sastroamidjojo, and was a coalition of PNI and *Masjoemi*. Soekarno proposed that the communists also be included, but this was opposed not only by *Masjoemi*, but by the Vice-President, Mohammed Hatta, who was, next to Soekarno, the most widely respected figure in the country. In the summer of 1956 Soekarno made two journeys abroad, the first to North America and Western Europe, the second to the Soviet Union, Yugoslavia, Czechoslovakia and China. It became clear that he had been more impressed by Eastern than by Western models. In February 1957 he proposed that Indonesia should adopt what he called a 'guided democracy', that all parties should be represented in the government, and that a National Council should be set up, in which both political and social organizations should be represented, and which should exercise, under the President's leadership, rather undefined powers over policy. The main effect of the proposals would have been to strengthen the influence of the communists, both through the party itself and through its control over the SOBSI trade unions. The plan was inevitably opposed by *Masjoemi* and by Hatta, and supported by the communists, on whom Soekarno and PNI were now increasingly relying.

Opposition was especially strong outside Java. Though the political leaders in the other islands had rejected the post-war Dutch plans for federation, and had preferred to support the Republic, substantial conflicts of interest remained between them and the Javanese. Since 1950 the central government had paid little attention to their desires. They complained that whereas they produced a large share of the country's wealth, including valuable commodities for export, they received less than their share of the revenue that went to the government. In practice a good deal of the islands' production never reached the centre, but formed the object of a lucrative smuggling trade, in which several of the army commanders in the islands were engaged.

Economic grievances, opposition to communist influence, a desire to see Hatta return to power, and personal ambitions all played a part in the revolts which took place in Sumatra in December 1956 and in Sumatra, Borneo and eastern Indonesia in March 1957. A new central government was formed in April, which promised measures for regional autonomy, and the regional commanders held meetings with the Chief of Staff of the army, Colonel Nasution, who had been dismissed at the time of the army dispute in 1952, but had been reappointed in 1955. In September 1957 agreement seemed to have been reached between the government and the rebels without use of force on either side.

The government, however, evidently felt that national unity would be helped by stirring up chauvinist passions. In November 1957 it put yet another resolution before the United Nations General Assembly on West New Guinea. When the resolution was defeated, the government revenged itself on Dutch subjects in Indonesia. A general strike was proclaimed of all employees of Dutch-owned enterprises, all publications in Dutch were banned, and Dutch airlines were forbidden to operate over Indonesian territory. Crowds invaded and robbed Dutch property. The government did not specifically authorize this, but did not prevent it. Instead, it announced that 50,000 Dutch subjects would be expelled from Indonesia, and that Dutch-owned plantations would be placed under government 'control'.

The result of this mass robbery was grave disruption of the already very weak Indonesian economy. The islands became less willing than ever to supply Java, and in February 1958 new revolts took place in Sumatra and Celebes. This time civil war could not be averted. The government troops, however, were surprisingly successful. Ably directed by Nasution, they recovered most of Sumatra by the end of May, and of Celebes by the end of June. The main rebel forces were defeated, sometimes (as at Menado in Celebes) after hard fighting. Scattered resistance, however, continued in 1959, and the central government's authority was far from secure.

The unsuccessful rebellion was a defeat for *Masjoemi*, many of whose leaders (including the former Premiers, Natsir and Harahap) had joined the rebels. It was to be expected that the communists, who had strongly supported Soekarno and denounced the rebels as agents of 'imperialism', would gain ground. But there was a third factor in the situation, the army, which was relatively free from communist influence, and had in Nasution (now promoted to General) a leader of quality. Soekarno himself also remained an unknown factor. He still enjoyed great popularity, and his gifts as a mass orator were a powerful political weapon. A communist-led 'people's democracy' and a military dictatorship seemed the most likely alternatives before Indonesia. It was doubtful whether either would be able to hold together a state torn by so many separatist forces. But even Java alone, with nearly 60 million inhabitants and a vital strategic position, must be of great importance in world politics.

18: Latin America

THE POLITICAL AND SOCIAL BACKGROUND

Whereas North America is divided between two vast states, in Central and South America and the Caribbean islands there are twenty independent states together with colonial territories of three European and one American Power. The official languages of all the twenty republics are European (Portuguese in Brazil, French in Haiti and Spanish in the rest), but numerous Indian languages are also spoken. As we saw in an earlier chapter, the proportion of pure Indian population and the proportion of Indian blood in the *mestizo* element varies, being highest in the Andean republics of Peru, Ecuador and Bolivia and negligible in Argentina, Uruguay and Costa Rica. There is also a negro element, dominant in the Caribbean islands and considerable in Brazil, where negro slavery was not abolished until 1888. In two British colonies, Trinidad and Guiana, there is a large proportion of Indians from India.

The imperial achievement of Spain in America was great, and has received less than its due. It was marked by cruelty, oppression and enslavement, but it also brought law and knowledge and protection for the weak. The Spanish language and culture, and the Catholic religion, were firmly implanted. The Spanish colonies obtained their independence from Spain soon after the northern colonies had broken away from Britain. But whereas the northerners united in a federation which extended across the continent, and later withstood the strains of one of the bloodiest wars of human history, the Spanish territories did not unite, but became eighteen different nations, each weak. The reasons for the difference in the fate of north and south lie partly in geography and partly in the social structure of the British and Spanish territories and in the upbringing and outlook of the men who ruled them in the first years of independence. The climate of most of Central and South America is difficult, and the jungles of the interior form greater obstacles to settlement than anything to be found in the North. The Spanish colonies were in fact based on the coast, and strung out from Venezuela right round to Tierra del Fuego and the Plata River for more than 7,000 miles. The rulers of the new republics were landowners, soldiers and priests, masters of primitive and docile masses accustomed to obey. These rulers had little incentive to pioneer, to find and develop new lands. Nor did such work appeal to the values of their tradition. Rather it seemed their task to administer—justly, and with due respect for the needs of the poor, at any rate in principle—the lands which were theirs, free from interference by busybodies thousands of miles away in Madrid. The limits of their conception of government combined with the limits of mountain barriers to keep Spanish America divided, approximately on the lines of the previous Spanish boundaries.*

If the southern slave-owning regions of the United States had been separated from each other and from the North by huge mountain ranges and jungles, something of the same sort might have happened. But the Protestant ethic, the plebeian origin of most of the people, the bustling spirit of equality and competition produced in the northern states a quite different society. The people of this society, steadily reinforced by immigrants from Europe, found before them forests and mountains that were far from impassable, Indians that fought fiercely but could be conquered, and then great fertile plains with a kindly climate. By the time that settlement reached the really formidable mountains and deserts of the West, the United States was already a powerful and democratic nation. But it achieved this only at the cost of a civil war which the Latin nations escaped. It is thus best to avoid reproaches to Spanish Americans, and simply to recognize that the opportunities and obstacles were different in the two cases.

The case of Portuguese America is different again. By far the largest of the Latin republics, larger even in area than the United States, Brazil is also geographically compact, and possesses vast resources. It began its independent history, not as a republic, but as a centralized Empire (from 1822 to 1889), and acquired in this period a basic structure of government which has served it well. But in the mid-twentieth century the task of developing its natural wealth has hardly more than begun.

During the nineteenth century the liberal and radical ideas of Europe and of North America spread among the educated minorities in the Latin American nations. But the typical form of government remained a dictatorship by a *caudillo*, civilian or military. Some of these ruled for decades, like Porfirio Diaz in Mexico (1876-1910) or Juan Vicente Gomez in Venezuela (1909-35). More often their régimes were shorter, and began and ended with violence. By the 1920s a more or less liberal form of

* The Viceroyalty of Peru became the republic of Peru, the Captaincy-General of Chile the republic of Chile. The Viceroyalty of New Granada split into the republics of Colombia, Ecuador and Venezuela. From the Viceroyalty of La Plata were formed the republics of Argentina, Bolivia and Paraguay, and, after a period of dispute between Brazil and Argentina, the republic of Uruguay. The establishment of these various republics, which was of course a much more complex story than these bare facts suggest, covered the years 1809-30. Mexico became a republic in 1824, and in 1823 the five provinces to the south constituted themselves the United Provinces of Central America, but in fact remained separate states. Santo Domingo became independent in 1865, Cuba in 1902, while the republic of Panama separated from Colombia in 1902.

ONP

government, with a free press, political parties and a growing public opinion, existed in Argentina, Chile, Uruguay and Brazil. The system was definitely oligarchical. Freedom was primarily for the landowning upper class, though the middle classes of the big cities were obtaining an increasing share. These four countries were those which had received the largest number of immigrants since the mid-nineteenth century.* Of the four only Uruguay acquired what could be called a democratic system securely founded. In the Andean and Caribbean states there was greater poverty and less education, and government was more savage.

A special case was provided by Mexico. In 1910 the octogenarian dictator, Diaz, was overthrown by the liberal landowner, Madero. But the victors quarrelled, Madero was murdered, and nearly ten years of civil war and peasant risings followed. Under the presidency of Obregón (1920-4) a new régime took shape, bitterly anti-clerical, but also committed to social reforms and mass education, based on military power, yet professing a radical and anti-militarist ideology. In the following decades a new Mexican ruling class came into being, a sort of state *bourgeoisie* of miscellaneous origin. It was intensely nationalist, and an important part of its nationalism was that it deliberately turned its back on Europe and looked with pride and in search of inspiration to the pre-Spanish past. Mexico was the first American state to pay tribute, at least in theory, to the virtues of the Indian. Though at first it was the new ruling class that enjoyed most of the benefits of the Revolution, the urban workers had at least some crumbs from the table, and the intelligentsia possessed an enormous freedom of expression, even if little power. Under President Cardenas (1934-40) the benefits were extended on a large scale to the peasants, through the land reforms mentioned in an earlier chapter.

The Mexican Revolution provided inspiration to the intellectual youth of the south, which was also beginning to be affected by European socialism, and by the distant fires of the Russian Revolution. A student strike at Cordoba University, in the Argentine, in July 1918 set off a radical movement among the students of other countries, especially of Peru. The Peruvian students became interested in the fate of the Indian half of the population, and in land reform. In May 1923 there was street fighting in Lima, with students and workers resisting the police. The students'

* An estimate of the number of immigrants reaching Latin America between 1850 and 1950 is that Argentina received 7 million, Brazil 4 million, Chile 2 million and Uruguay 1 million out of a total for all Latin America of 17 million. If the latter figure is divided according to the origin of the immigrants, there were in the whole region 6 million Italians, 4 million Spaniards, 2 million Germans, 1 million Portuguese and 1 million Orientals. The latter consisted mainly of Japanese, most of whom settled in Brazil.

leader, Haya de la Torre, who was arrested and deported, proposed at a meeting in Mexico City in May 1924 the formation of an *Alianza Popular Revolucionar Americana* (APRA). This movement became a force in Peru in the 1930s, and also had influence in the republics to the north. APRA was socialist and nationalist, stressed the rights of the Indians, urged a common struggle of all Latin American nations against the traditional ruling classes and against foreign (especially United States) imperialism, and held out the ideal of an united Indoamerica of the future. The movement was clearly unlikely to have much appeal in the southern republics or in Brazil. But elsewhere it was attractive to the radical intellectual youth, and was undoubtedly autochthonous, owing little to influences from outside the sub-continent.

In the 1930s there was a marked shift towards dictatorship. This was largely a result of greater social tension produced by the world economic depression, which was felt with special severity by the Latin American raw-material-producing economics. In Argentina there was a genuine reaction against the long rule of the democratic but increasingly corrupt and incompetent Radical Union. In Bolivia and Paraguay, engaged in war for the Chaco Province from 1932 to 1935, fascist tendencies were powerful. In general the propaganda of fascist ideas, whether from Italy, Germany or Spain, won much support at this time. The fascists made use of German and Italian immigrant communities, and exploited anti-North American nationalism.

In 1930 Getulio Vargas seized power in Brazil. His régime, which lasted fifteen years, cannot be easily labelled. He used some of the terminology of fascism, but he never created a fascist party of his own, and he suppressed, after a period of co-operating with it, the only authentic Brazilian fascist movement, the *Integralistas*, founded by Plinio Salgado. Vargas tolerated no criticism of his policies after his first years, and he treated his opponents cruelly at times, but he also did much for the social welfare of the masses. His enemies consisted on the one hand of true democrats, on the other of oligarchs who thought him a dangerous radical.

The countries which maintained democratic government in these years were Uruguay, Colombia and Chile. Uruguay was something of a New World welfare state. In Colombia the Liberal Party, in power since 1930, pursued a cautious policy of slow social reform while maintaining political liberty. In Chile dictatorship gave place to conservative constitutional rule in 1932, and to a Popular Front of radicals, socialists and communists in 1938.

The Second World War brought a swing back to the left, especially after the Soviet Union and the United States became involved. Vargas strongly supported the Allied cause, despite his own dictatorial policies. Through most of Latin America left-wing ideas, anti-fascism and the ideology of the United Nations gained ground, and the governments had to pay lip service to them. The major exception was Argentina, where a pro-fascist *coup d'état* took place in 1943, and Perón seized power in 1945.

POST-WAR YEARS

The political development of Latin America can be roughly divided into three periods since the war. In the first, between 1945 and 1948, left-wing governments came into power in several countries, either by violence or by constitutional processes. In the second, from 1948 to 1955, there was a reversion to right-wing dictatorships. In the third, since 1955, the tendency has been towards democratic government, somewhat less markedly left wing in character than in the first period.

There are, of course, numerous exceptions. Uruguay and Costa Rica preserved democratic government throughout this period, with only minor setbacks. In Argentina Perón's fascist régime endured from 1945 to 1955. Mexico has shown an unique stability. The same official party maintained power uninterruptedly, and when each presidential term ended power passed smoothly to the elected successor. Within the party many groups and political trends have competed with each other, and successive presidents have varied from their predecessors' policies. At least in the cities and among the educated class wide freedom of opinion has survived. Mexican government is very different from that of North America or Western Europe, but its claim to be considered a form of democracy is not entirely unconvincing.

In Guatemala in October 1944 the weak successor to the dictator Jorge Ubico (who ruled from 1932 to 1943) was overthrown, and a democratic administration formed by the radical school-teacher, Arevalo. Particular attention was paid to the workers in town and country. Powerful trade unions came into being, and the greatest plantation-owner, the American United Fruit Company, was compelled to give large wage increases. In the unions, whose membership in this predominantly Indian country consisted of illiterate and miserably poor peasants, easily mobilizable by efficient leaders once the opportunity was given, communists soon obtained a strong influence. Under Arevalo's successor, Colonel Arbenz, elected in 1951, the communist influence extended from the unions over the machinery of government in general.

In June 1945 a free election was held in Peru, and APRA won the largest number of parliamentary seats. The new President, Luis Bustamante, at first co-operated closely with APRA. But APRA's demands for land reform, and for real political rights and schools for the Indian half of the population, met with bitter resistance from the ruling class. Such legislation as was passed was not in fact carried out. For its part, APRA was divided between moderates and extremists, its leaders could not discipline its masses, and there were riots and insurrections. In March 1948 Bustamante broke with APRA. Shortly afterwards he was himself overthrown by General Manuel Odria, and APRA was banned.

In October 1945 a popular revolution took place in Venezuela. Under the long dictatorship of Gomez and his successors, radical ideas had gained ground among the intelligentsia, both in the country and in exile. In 1941 a party called Democratic Action was founded, led by Romulo Betancourt and professing a form of socialism. Four years later a group of young officers, in agreement with Democratic Action, seized power. The country was then ruled by a junta led by Betancourt, various moderate social reforms were introduced, and trade unions began to play a major part. In 1947, under a new Constitution, Democratic Action's candidate, Romulo Gallegos, was elected President against the opposition both of the conservatives and of the communists. But the military and civil leaders could not agree, and their division was exploited by the old landowning and business oligarchy. In November 1948 a military government was formed, and Democratic Action suppressed. In 1952 one of the ruling officers, Colonel Marcos Perez Jimenez, made himself sole dictator, and political liberties came to an end.

In Brazil President Vargas decided to follow the spirit of the times, and to hold free elections in which he would not seek power. The December 1945 election showed a marked swing to the left, and the communists won 10% of the poll. The new President, General Enrico Dutra, ruled democratically. But disorderly mass demonstrations and strikes led to the prohibition of the Communist Party in May 1947. As elsewhere in the continent, anti-communism proved a respectable slogan for a counter-offensive from the right. In 1950 Vargas presented himself for re-election as President, and won with a comfortable majority. In power, he showed himself less dictatorial than he had been in the 1930s.

In Chile the trend had been to the left ever since the late 1930s. The Popular Front of 1938 had disintegrated in 1939 when the communists, following the Nazi-Soviet pact, had denounced the United States as a warmonger and had ceased to oppose fascism. But the German invasion of the Soviet Union had brought a change, and at the end of the war the communists were once more co-operating, if uneasily, with socialists and radicals. At the election of September 1946 these three parties secured the presidency to Gonzalez Videla, who gave two ministries in his cabinet to communists. In the spring of 1947, however, the communists resigned, and started mass strike action against the government. This reversal of policy coincided with the general line adopted by communists—for example, in France and Italy—and with the new Soviet policy of open hostility to the United States. In 1948 the Communist Party was made illegal in Chile, and the policy of President Gonzalez in general became more conservative.

In the early 1950s President Juan Perón of Argentina was at the height of his power. Having survived the crisis of October 1945, which we have discussed in an earlier chapter,* Perón used his power to improve the conditions of the urban working class, and by his promotion of industry, uneconomic yet effective, he increased the relative importance of the working class in the nation. Reforms were also introduced to the benefit of agricultural labourers and tenant farmers. But the vast machinery of welfare, and the trade unions themselves, were instruments of power in the hands of Perón and of his most able and energetic supporter, his wife, Eva Duarte Perón. Perón's control over the armed forces was effective as long as his policies appealed to them, but their obedience fell short of unconditional submission to an infallible leader. The Roman Catholic Church retained its autonomy.

The basic rivalry between Argentina and Brazil for the leadership of the continent remained. But whereas in the past Brazil had always inclined towards friendship with the United States, in contrast to Argentina's 'anti-Yankee' position, Vargas now took greater pains to stress his nationalism and his independence of North American influence, thus finding common ground with Perón. Paraguay, which had been under dictatorial government since the Chaco War, naturally gravitated towards Buenos Aires. In Chile the victory in the presidential elections of 1952 of General Carlos Ibañez, who had been dictator from 1927 to 1931, roused Perón's hopes. In 1953 he and Ibañez exchanged official visits, and a treaty of friendship was signed. The treaty was also signed by Paraguay. Another instrument of foreign policy favoured by Perón was intra-continental trade-union co-operation. Argentine embassies had labour attachés whose task was to pursue this form of diplomacy. Peronist trade-union organizations came into being in several countries. When the Latin American regional branch of ICFTU refused to admit them to its ranks, they called

* See above, p. 206.

a conference of their own in 1953 in Asunción, the Paraguayan capital. It set up the *Agrupación de trabajadores latino-americanos sindicalizados*, picturesquely known by its initials as ATLAS.

Perón gave hospitality to political refugees from Bolivia's *Movimiento nacional revolucionar* (MNR). This party aimed at radical social change and had some sympathy for the Indian masses, though its leaders were from the white or *mestizo* intelligentsia. Its inspiration was fascist rather than Marxist, and its leaders had sympathized, as had Perón, with the Axis Powers during the war. In 1943 MNR shared power in Bolivia with a military group, but in 1946 this régime was overthrown, and its President, General Villaroel, was lynched by the mob of the capital, La Paz. The MNR leaders escaped to Buenos Aires. In 1951 their chief, Dr. Victor Paz Estenssoro, was a candidate in the Bolivian presidential election, though still in exile, and he won the largest number of votes. For a few months more a military junta remained in power, but in April 1952 it was overthrown after some fierce fighting, and Paz Estenssoro returned in triumph. The MNR régime nationalized the great tin enterprises, owners of Bolivia's most valuable export commodity, and introduced a land reform which at least on paper appeared radical. The miners' union, led by the very radical Juan Lechín, became a power in the land. But Bolivia did not simply align itself with Argentina. Economic difficulties made foreign aid essential, and President Paz decided that he could not afford to quarrel with the United States. Despite MNR's past fascist record, and the radicalism of its social policies, the American government decided to give it substantial economic aid. This had a moderating influence on the régime, and prevented the country from becoming a satellite of Argentina.

In these years democratic government broke down in Colombia, which had long enjoyed a stability and liberty unusual in the continent. The Liberal Party split into a moderate and a radical wing, and in 1946 a conservative was elected President. In April 1948 the assassination of the leader of the radical wing of the Liberal Party, Jorge Gaitán, led to large-scale riots in the capital, Bogotá, followed by repression throughout the country. The right claimed that the left were planning a revolution with the help of the Venezuelan Democratic Action, the left that the right were introducing a reign of terror. The next presidential election, in 1950, was boycotted by the liberals, and a conservative who had formerly professed admiration for European fascism, Laureano Gomez, was returned virtually unopposed. During these years there was a state of sporadic civil war in many parts of the country, with punitive expeditions by government troops and acts of violence by their opponents. In June 1953 General

Rojas Pinilla seized power. Under his dictatorship the terror, especially in the countryside, became still worse.

In Guatemala the communist influence in the Arbenz government was dramatically expressed when it ordered a large consignment of arms from Czechoslovakia. The government also continued to quarrel with the powerful American organization, United Fruit. In June 1954 a small army of Guatemalan exiles, headed by Colonel Castillo Armas, crossed the frontier from Honduras, where they had been able to obtain military supplies from the dictator Somoza. The Guatemalan army commanders showed themselves unwilling to fight for Arbenz. The United States ambassador Peurifoy played a decisive part in the obscure negotiations which resulted in the flight of Arbenz and of the communist leaders, and the installation of Castillo as President. The action was generally regarded, not only in Latin America but throughout the world, as an act of United States intervention.

The first move in the reaction from dictatorships back towards liberal or radical democracy took place in Brazil. An attempted assassination of a Brazilian editor, in which an air force major with whom he was conversing was killed, was found to implicate President Vargas' son, Lutero. On 22 August 1954 the air force demanded the President's resignation, and next day they were supported by the army and navy chiefs. After hesitations and consultations with his friends, Vargas decided neither to resign nor to resist. In the early morning of 24 August he committed suicide. He left a letter in which he represented himself as a victim of slander and insults, who had valiantly defended 'the humble' against domestic and foreign exploitation. 'They do not want the worker to be free', the letter read. 'They do not want the people to be independent.' The news of the suicide was followed by pro-Vargas demonstrations and violent anti-American riots in several cities. Vice-President João Cafe became President until the next election, which was held on 3 October 1955. The victor was Juscelino Kubitschek, who was supported by the parties which had backed Vargas. In November 1955 the army took over power for three months, on the grounds that a plot was being prepared to prevent the new President from succeeding. Whatever the truth of this statement, on the legal date of 31 January 1956 the army returned full powers to Kubitschek. Under his rule the trend of Brazilian politics has certainly been less authoritarian than under Vargas.

A much more drastic change was the overthrow of Perón in October 1955 by a combination of the army and the Catholic Church. General

Pedro Aramburu became President, and genuinely sought to reintroduce liberal democratic government. This was, however, no easy task. In the first place, ten years of Perón's extravagances had seriously damaged the Argentine economy. Agriculture declined, while a large part of the new industries lacked a firm foundation. Secondly, the dismantling of Perón's power apparatus meant at least a major purge of the trade unions, his strongest weapon, and it was difficult to do this without antagonizing the whole working class. In general there were two types of opposition to the Perón régime: from those who believed in free speech and institutions, and from those whose aim was to undo his social reforms and restore the oligarchy of the 1930s. Aramburu honestly tried to steer between these rocks, but it was to be expected that he would not make himself popular. In September 1957 he convoked a Constituent Assembly, but the main political parties in turn boycotted it, and it achieved nothing. In February 1958 Arturo Frondizi, leader of the left wing of the radicals, the Intransigents, was elected President, with 4,400,000 votes to his moderate radical rival's 2,700,000. Frondizi's success, by which he more than doubled the vote he had received at the 1957 election to the abortive Constituent Assembly, was due to the fact that the Peronists and the communists had supported him. It remained to be seen how far he could emancipate himself from these embarrassing friendships. He was installed on 1 May 1958. In the autumn he was faced with massive strikes by Peronist workers. These were repeated in January 1959.

In Peru, General Odria, who had seized power in 1948 and had been legally elected in 1950, decided not to stand again, and the election of 1956 was freely conducted. APRA votes appear to have been divided between two candidates, as the party leaders changed their mind during the campaign. The successful candidate, Dr. Manuel Prado, secured parliamentary legislation to legalize APRA. Exiled leaders were free to return to Peru, political prisoners were released and confiscated APRA property was restored. On 20 July 1957 Haya de la Torre returned home. But during 1958 there were strikes and violent outbreaks in the country, and the basic social problems remained almost untouched.

In Colombia, discontent with the Rojas dictatorship led to serious disagreements within the Conservative Party. In 1957 Gomez met the liberal leader, Alberto Lleras Camargo, at Sitges in Spain, and made an agreement on common opposition to the régime and a long period of bipartisan policy for both parties. On 10 May 1957 Rojas was overthrown by a military junta after he had had himself re-elected President by a puppet assembly, which had amended the Constitution to make this possible. The junta co-operated with the conservative and liberal leaders, and in

December held a plebiscite, in which a large popular vote was given for bipartisan government. In May 1958 the liberal leader Lleras was elected President by a large majority. Colombia now had a fair prospect of orderly and free government, but banditry and violence in some of the provinces had still to be overcome.

In Venezuela the dictatorship of Perez was overthrown in January 1958 by a combination of army officers and underground political parties. Admiral Wolfgang Larrazabal headed the junta, which restored democratic liberties and prepared for elections. In the re-emergent trade unions the communists were strong. There was also a Christian democratic movement. But the strongest party was Democratic Action, whose leaders returned from exile. At the presidential election of December 1958 many democrats and the communists voted for Larrazabal, but Romulo Betancourt of Democratic Action was elected.

During 1958 a civil war developed in Cuba. The dictatorship of Fulgencio Batista, who had played a dominant role since 1934, varying in his policies from left to right, from democratic to dictatorial according to circumstances, and who had resumed supreme power in 1952, was increasingly unpopular. The rebels were headed by a young intellectual named Fidel Castro, and the climate of opinion was such that his originally small following rapidly grew. In January 1959 Batista fled the country, and Castro, who held the eastern part of the island, took over power, placing his nominee in the Presidency. His victory was followed by numerous executions of Batista supporters and a flood of demagogic oratory. The future development of Cuba was unpredictable.

During these years Uruguay and Costa Rica had preserved their democratic systems, and Mexico its peculiar form of democracy. In Bolivia President Paz in 1956 gave place to his elected successor, Hernan Siles, also of MNR. The régime was becoming more stable and its policies more moderate, though frequent acts of violence still occurred during 1958. The remaining dictators of Latin America were those of Paraguay, Nicaragua and Santo Domingo, of whom the most formidable was the last, General Rafael Trujillo, whose rule of terror dates from 1930. But with these exceptions the trend was everywhere towards democracy, more moderate under Kubitschek in Brazil or Jorge Alessandri in Chile (who had succeeded Ibañez in September 1958), more radical in Venezuela and Cuba. But whereas in 1945 the triumphs of the left had come in close association with, and support for, the United States, in 1959 there was a marked tendency among Latin American radicals to view American policy with deep suspicion.

DEPENDENCIES IN AMERICA

Four Powers—Great Britain, the United States, France and the Netherlands—possess dependent territories on the American continent or off its shores.

The British possessions may be divided into three sectors. First are Bermuda and the Bahamas in the Atlantic, the latter lying close to the coast of Florida. Second are the Caribbean islands or West Indies, consisting of Jamaica and the Cayman Islands in the west and a chain of islands in the east stretching from the Virgin Islands south to Trinidad. Third are the two continental colonies of British Honduras in Central America, bordering on Mexico and Guatemala, and British Guiana in South America, bordering on Venezuela and Brazil. Finally, there are the Falkland Islands, lying about 400 miles east of the Straits of Magellan and claimed, hitherto without success, by the government of the Argentine.

The American possessions are Puerto Rico, annexed from Spain in 1898, and the Virgin Islands, bought from Denmark in 1917.

The French possessions consist of St. Pierre and Miquelon, off the coast of Newfoundland; Guadeloupe and Martinique in the West Indies, which form an overseas *département* of France, and are represented as such in the National Assembly in Paris; and the continental colony of French Guiana (Cayenne).

The Dutch possessions are some islands off the coast of Venezuela and the continental colony of Dutch Guiana (Surinam), which is represented in the Netherlands parliament.

We shall here briefly consider only the American and British possessions in the Caribbean, which have political problems of some interest.

Puerto Rico has a population of about 3 million, whose language is Spanish. Most Puerto Ricans are of mixed origin—European and negro, or European and American Indian. Since the island was annexed by the United States, democratic government has been introduced in four successive stages, culminating in the adoption, by a popular referendum in March 1952, of a Constitution similar to that of the United States. The island then became known as the Commonwealth of Puerto Rico. In matters affecting only the island's affairs, its own government and electorate have fairly full sovereignty, but federal laws of the United States 'not locally inapplicable', and excluding internal revenue laws, are in force. Puerto Ricans do not have a vote in the election of the American President or Congress. This unique legal relationship has worked well, and there have been no major constitutional crises. Puerto Rico has three main political parties, each identified with a different view of the correct relationship between Puerto Rico and the United States. By far the most powerful, the Popular Democratic Party, led by Luis Muñoz Marin, which has had a majority in all elections since 1940, stands for the existing Commonwealth status, and has devoted itself primarily to social and economic welfare. Progress has been impressive, yet remains basically precarious, owing to the very rapid increase of population. For many years the surplus has been finding an outlet in emigration to the continental United States, where there are now some 700,000, mostly in New York City. Most of the problems of race relations, raised by the presence of negro communities in northern cities, arise also in the case of the Puerto Ricans, whose material standard of living and level of education are often lower than those of negroes. Should restrictions be placed on immigration, the situation in Puerto Rico itself would certainly deteriorate. The two opposition parties in Puerto Rico are the Independence Party and the Republican State Party, who demand respectively complete independence and full membership of the United States. But the great personal popularity of Governor Muñoz, and the successes of his long rule, make these alternatives less attractive than the present condition of autonomy.

The British West Indies have also about 3 million inhabitants, of whom half live in Jamaica. The population is mainly negro, with a large mixed element and a small European minority. The main exception to this pattern is Trinidad, in which two-fifths are Indians from India. The earlier history of the different islands shows great variety, but a decisive step was taken towards modern democratic government with the 1944 Constitution of Jamaica. This set up a bicameral legislature, of which the lower chamber was entirely elected, and provided that five out of eleven members of the Executive Council should be chosen from it. In 1953 elected ministers were given a majority in the Council, and included a Chief Minister. The British government also encouraged the formation of a federation of the West Indies. This process began with a conference, held in 1947 at Montego Bay in Jamaica, of delegates of the various legislatures, and culminated in the London conference of February 1956, at which agreement was reached on a federal Constitution. British Honduras and British Guiana, however, decided to remain outside the federation. The first federal election was held on 25 March 1958 in the ten constituent territories. The Federal Labour Party, to which belong the Prime Minister of the Federation, Sir Grantley Adams, and the Premier of Jamaica, Norman Manley, won twenty-five seats, and the Democratic Labour Party, which has an anti-socialist programme and is led by the former Jamaican Premier, Sir Alexander Bustamante, won nineteen. The West Indies thus enjoy

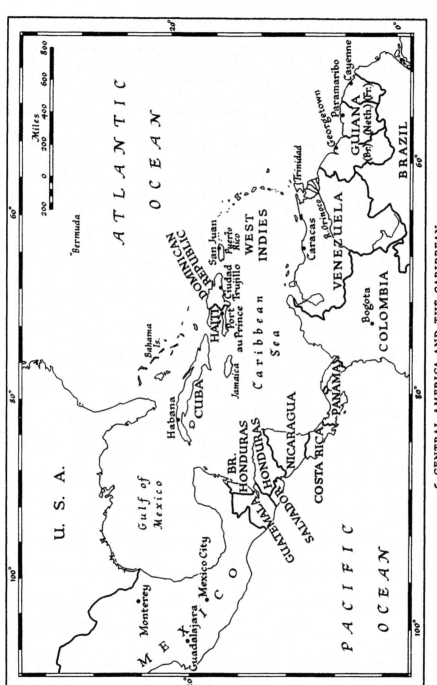

5 CENTRAL AMERICA AND THE CARIBBEAN

fairly complete self-government, but do not have control of foreign policy and defence. In this respect they have less than Dominion status, and their position is not so very different from that of Puerto Rico. They share with Puerto Rico the problems of a rapidly expanding population and large-scale emigration. Though the number of West Indians entering Great Britain in recent years is smaller than that of Puerto Ricans entering the United States, it has received much attention as a result of the race riots in the Notting Hill Gate district of London in 1958. The British government resisted the demands that were then heard for a limitation of West Indian immigration. Should the government in future yield to such pressure, this would greatly accentuate the economic problems of the West Indies, and certainly undermine the loyalty of its people to the Commonwealth.

British Honduras, with 80,000 inhabitants, has a population partly negro, partly American Indian and partly of a mixture of either of these elements with European. Its main languages are English and Spanish. As the people have become more politically conscious, and a local intelligentsia has provided leadership, two opposed policies have commended themselves: membership of the West Indies Federation or association with Guatemala. Acquisition of the port of Belize would be useful to Guatemala, which has only a small strip of coast on the Caribbean. The discovery of oil in its province of Peten has increased its need for an outlet. The Guatemalan case is not legally convincing, for Guatemala recognized British possession of the settlement by a convention of 1859. But the pro-communist régime of Arbenz excited anti-British feeling, and the Guatemalan anti-communist régimes since 1954 have not wished to deprive themselves of nationalist demagogy as a means of canalizing internal discontents. A new constitution was introduced in the colony in 1954. Under the first election the nationalist and left-wing People's United Party won a large majority. In 1957 the PUP split into a pro-Guatemalan and a pro-West Indian faction, but in the election of that year the former won a decisive majority. At the end of the year a delegation of the legislature came to London to discuss financial and constitutional problems. When it was discovered that one of its members, the PUP leader, George Price, had been negotiating privately with the Guatemalan Minister in London on the annexation of the colony to Guatemala, the British government broke off the discussions.

British Guiana, with a population of over 500,000, has also had a stormy history since the war. The largest single element in the population are Indians from India, forming about half, followed by negroes, forming some two-fifths. To the negro element, federation with the West Indies has some attractions, and to the West Indian government the empty spaces of the interior of Guiana, capable of agricultural development, offer some relief for their problem of overpopulation. To the Indian element the association is less appealing. But, unlike the British Hondurans of Spanish speech, the British Guiana East Indians have no links with their continental neighbours, Venezuela and Brazil. In 1953 a new Constitution was introduced in British Guiana, similar to the Jamaican Constitution of 1944. At the election of April 1953, eighteen out of twenty-four seats in the legislature went to the People's Progressive Party, led by the Indian Cheddi Jagan and the negro Forbes Burnham. Jagan became Chief Minister. His previous connexions and statements suggested that he was a communist, and his experience of office did not cause him to modify his admiration for Soviet policies and methods. The Governor, believing that Jagan was resolved to turn the colony into a 'people's democracy', dismissed him from office and suspended the Constitution in October 1953. In 1955 PPP split into two factions, led respectively by Jagan and Burnham. Personal rivalries played a large part, but the divergence of interest between the negro and Indian elements was also a factor. Meanwhile, a new Constitution was introduced, giving less power to elected members in the legislative council. Elections were held in August 1957, and Jagan won nine seats out of fourteen to Burnham's three. Jagan was invited by the Governor to enter the Executive Council, not as Chief Minister, but as Minister of Trade. This he did, and in the following year maintained a correct and moderate attitude. But though he had now adopted constitutional methods, it was by no means certain that he had abandoned his communist beliefs. It was clear that there would soon have to be further constitutional progress, and that Jagan's party, as the strongest force in the country, would profit from it. If he were to receive greater power, and once more attempt communist methods, he would face the hostility not only of the British and American governments, but also of Brazil and probably of Venezuela.

INTER-AMERICAN RELATIONS

Relations between Anglo-Saxon and Latin America are an elusive combination of attraction and antipathy. The historic rivalry between English and Spaniards is not forgotten, and the contrasts between Protestant and Catholic civilizations, the capitalist and the aristocratic ethos, civilian and military government remain real factors in the relationship.

North American protection, in the form of the Monroe Doctrine, evoked little enthusiasm in the Latin countries during the nineteenth century. With the Spanish American War, the annexation of Puerto Rico, the separation of Panama from Colombia in 1903 in order to make possible

United States control over the Panama Canal, and the interventions of American marines in Cuba, Nicaragua, Haiti and even Mexico, resentment grew against 'Yankee imperialism'. This attitude began to change with the advent of Franklin Roosevelt and the announcement of the 'good neighbour' policy. A landmark was the inter-American Conference of Montevideo in 1933, at which it was accepted by all the governments that 'no state has the right to interfere in the internal or external affairs of another'. During the war the Latin American states co-operated, with varying degrees of enthusiasm, with the United States. In 1945 the American governments signed the Act of Chapultepec, which declared that aggression against a state of the hemisphere, whether by another American state or by a state located outside the hemisphere, should be regarded as an aggression against all. In September 1947 was signed in Rio de Janeiro an Inter-American Treaty of Reciprocal Assistance. This specified the procedure of consultation between the American states in the event of aggression, and enumerated the types of counter-measure which might be adopted, ranging from mere recall of chiefs of diplomatic missions to use of armed force. The Bogotà conference of 1948 set up the Organization of American States (OAS) as a permanent regional group under the United Nations.

Though these successive meetings and declarations represented real progress towards closer co-operation of the whole hemisphere in the interests of peace, and were regarded with some justification as a practical application of the principles of the United Nations, inter-American unity in foreign policy was still far from complete. This became clear in 1954. In March, with developments in Guatemala in mind, the United States government persuaded the inter-American conference of Caracas to pass a 'declaration of solidarity' in resistance to international communism. Guatemala alone voted against, but Mexico and Argentina abstained. When the forces of Castillo invaded from Honduras, the Arbenz government appealed to the United Nations. At the Security Council meeting of 20 June a resolution to refer the matter to the Organization of American States for urgent consideration, and to ask OAS to report as soon as possible to the Security Council on the measures it had taken, was vetoed by the Soviet delegate. A French resolution was then unanimously adopted, calling for the termination of any action likely to cause bloodshed, and requesting all United Nations members to refrain from assisting any such action. On 25 June the matter was again raised at the Security Council, but a 'procedural' decision not to place the Guatemalan complaint on its agenda was carried by five votes to four, with both Britain and France abstaining. The Inter-American Peace Committee of OAS meanwhile decided to send a fact-finding mission to Guatemala, but by the time it arrived the fighting was over and the Arbenz régime overthrown.

The Guatemalan affair undoubtedly created a bad impression in Latin America and throughout the world. The American case was not received with sympathy. An impartial observer must admit that the evidence of communist domination of the Guatemalan régime was strong, and that the United States was entitled to be alarmed at the prospect of a Soviet satellite established so close to the Panama Canal. But the argument of the Soviet and Guatemalan speakers at the Security Council, that the essence of the matter was not a communist strategic threat, but opposition by the United Fruit Company to a progressive land reform policy, found ready listeners. The subsequent prosecution of United Fruit by the United States federal government under the anti-trust law did not dispel the impression. Moreover, individual Americans behaved with disagreeable arrogance. One was the Ambassador in Guatemala, Mr. John E. Peurifoy. Another was the United States delegate at the Security Council, Mr. Henry Cabot Lodge, who at one point exclaimed: 'I say to you, representative of the Soviet Union—stay out of this hemisphere!' This attitude can hardly be said to differ much in principle from that of the Soviet Union in regard to Eastern Europe.

United States policy made a much more favourable impression in January 1955, when a force of 1,000 Costa Rican rebels invaded Costa Rica from Nicaragua. The Nicaraguan dictator, Anastasio Somoza, was clearly encouraged by the Guatemalan case to believe that he would be able, by claiming to be fighting against 'the communist menace', to overthrow his enemy, President José Figueres of Costa Rica, who was no communist, but had established a very successful and progressive democratic régime. The United States, however, supported Figueres, to whom it sold four fighter aircraft at a token price, and gave an escort of naval planes to the investigating team sent by the Inter-American Peace Committee of OAS to Costa Rica. The team formally requested the 'rebels' to withdraw to Nicaragua, and the twelve days' war ended.

Anti-United States feeling is, however, widespread in Latin America, although the official relations of the United States with most Latin American governments have been good, and although a large part of Latin American public opinion has friendly feeling towards the northern Power. It is worth examining some of the reasons given for this hostility.

One is the assertion that the United States supports reactionary dictatorships against their peoples. To an impartial observer this accusation does not appear just. In the first place, those Latin American governments which have pursued democratic policies—Costa Rica, Mexico, Uruguay—

have had excellent relations with the United States. American aid was given to the MNR government in Bolivia at a time of great economic difficulty, though it was pursuing extremely radical social policies and its attitude to the United States was uncertain. This was a calculated risk on behalf not of dictatorship, but of democracy. Secondly, where reactionary dictatorships existed, they were set up not by United States action, but by local officers and politicians. The United States could not refuse to have official relations with Colombia under Rojas Pinilla or Venezuela under Perez Jimenez because it disliked their internal policies. If the Colombian or Venezuelan democrats were not strong enough to overthrow them, that was regrettable, but it was not the duty of the United States to do their job for them. When the United States had intervened in this manner in 1945 in the person of Ambassador Spruille Braden, in Buenos Aires, who had denounced the dictatorship of Perón, it had only strengthened the régime and aroused rage against 'Yankee intervention' all over Latin America. It may, however, be argued that the United States was unwise to supply arms to dictatorships. The preoccupation of the American government with the military threat of communism, though justified in Europe and Asia, was unrealistic in Latin America. Arms could be used by the dictators only to suppress their own people or to attack a weaker neighbour. But if American policy may have made some unwise decisions, it is absurd to speak of a systematic American preference for dictators. Yet this impression was widespread in 1958. Frustrated democrats made the United States the scapegoat for their own ineffectiveness. Communist propaganda exploited this mood, and popularized the myth that the dictators were mere tools of powerful American capitalists, who also controlled the government in Washington. The most dramatic expression of this feeling was the disgusting reception given to Vice-President and Mrs. Nixon in Lima and in Caracas in June 1958.

Another reason given for hostility is the belief that the United States exploits the Latin American countries by giving low prices for their products and charging high prices for its own exports to them. This too seems to be an emotional reaction, based on a misunderstanding of the facts. It is true that the United States occupies a dominant place in the trade of Latin America. In 1956, 46% of Latin American exports went to the United States, and 50% of Latin American imports came from the United States. In the case of only three states—Argentina, Paraguay and Uruguay—was the United States share in trade comparatively small. Latin American trade was also of considerable importance to the United States. In 1956, 22% of American exports went there, and 33% of American imports came from there. But foreign trade is far more important to the economies of the Latin American states than to that of the United States. Moreover, in many cases a single product dominates the export trade of a Latin American country. Thus in 1957 coffee accounted for 83% of all exports from Salvador, 77% from Colombia, 73% from Guatemala and 70% from Haiti; sugar provided 82% of Cuba's exports; oil 93% of exports from Venezuela; copper 67% from Chile and tin 56% from Bolivia. Fluctuations in the prices of these commodities can have terrible effects on these countries. The facts that prices do fluctuate, that the chief buyer is the United States, and that the United States is a very rich country, lend superficial plausibility to the argument that the United States battens on the exploitation of Latin American poverty. But it is hard to see how the United States government can be expected to fix world prices for these commodities at a level favourable to Latin American producers. Moreover, if American imported goods reach Latin American consumers at very high prices, this is often in large part due to middlemen's profits and costs of internal transport. The remedy is not a change of heart by wicked American capitalists, but a diversification of production in Latin American economies.

Anti-American feeling also takes the form of hostility to American private capital. This amounted to about $7,000 million out of an estimated total foreign investment in Latin America of $9,000 million in 1956. Though foreign capitalists usually pay better wages than local employers, they are an obvious scapegoat to both nationalist and communist propagandists. In general there is less objection to foreign investment in manufactures than in mining or oil. It is felt that the former may enrich the country, whereas the latter is stealing its wealth, depriving it of the means of industrializing itself. This irrational attitude has led to restrictions in Brazil on the participation of foreign firms in the development of oil which have seriously retarded economic progress. In Argentina, Perón lost popularity by making an agreement with American oil companies, and Frondizi more recently aroused much ill feeling by reverting to this policy. The problems of foreign capital in Latin America—nationalist passion and lack of security for investment—are essentially the same as in other underdeveloped countries. On the whole it must be said that conditions are better than in the Arab lands or Asia, and that co-operation is not beyond the powers of political wisdom and personal tact.

Latin American countries have received credits from the World Bank as well as loans and direct grants from the United States government. The total amounts received are, however, small in comparison with American aid to Europe and Asia. Technical assistance programmes have, with comparatively small resources, achieved fine results in public health, education and agriculture in various parts of the continent. They have been the more successful because they have sought to teach the people to carry out improvements for themselves. The personal example of American field workers has often done more to create affection and respect for the United States than large output of official propaganda.

It is probably true that the United States, and also West European nations, have paid too little attention to the needs and feelings of Latin Americans. It is certain that growth of population and industrial development will make Latin America relatively far more important in world affairs by the end of the century than is now the case. The civilization and political ideals of the Latin Americans are certainly closer to those of the Western peoples than are those of the Arabs, Asians and Africans. Even if one remains optimistic about the future relations of the West with Asia and Africa, it is still true that the West will need Latin American understanding and friendship in the future. This continent is at present underestimated in relation to its potentialities for good. The West should give it a higher priority in its political and economic thinking, and Western statesmen should show greater tact and make a more powerful effort of imagination to understand and handle its problems.

19: Problems of Western Policy

DEFENCE

When the war ended in Europe, vast Soviet armies met almost equally vast Anglo-American armies in prostrate Germany. The fighting spirit of both was excellent. In equipment the Anglo-American armies were certainly superior to the Soviet, and were backed by much wealthier economies, whose resources were by this time no less efficiently harnessed to the needs of war than was the collectivist economy of the Soviet Union. The Soviet Union had been subjected to far greater strains and sufferings, to death, hunger and devastation, than had Britain, let alone the United States. At this time, if armed conflict had come between the two Allied groups, there can be no doubt that the Western group would have won. But such conflict was inconceivable, for the Western nations regarded the Soviet Union as a heroic ally and friend. This view was shared by the Western governments, even if Soviet action in Poland and the Danubian countries had already aroused alarm. It was different in kind from the attitude of the Soviet government, which had always considered the Western Powers to be no less its enemies than Hitler's Germany, though, of course, the immediate task was to fight the latter. Western soldiers were also anxious to return to their families; their return was desired no less by their relatives and families than by the political leaders who needed to win parliamentary elections, which they would certainly have lost had they proposed to keep the armies in being in order to fight or to threaten the Soviet Union. The Anglo-American armies were therefore rapidly demobilized.

The demobilization seemed the less dangerous to even the most pessimistic among Western politicians and generals because the American monopoly of the atomic bomb ensured the supremacy of American power on the world scale. But by 1949 the Soviet Union had manufactured and tested its atomic bomb. The American lead was maintained with the manufacture of the incomparably more terrible hydrogen bomb, but by 1954 the Soviet Union had its hydrogen bomb too. In 1957 the Soviet Union produced the first earth satellite, the sputnik, and in 1958 the United States achieved the same result. In 1959 both the giant Powers possessed ballistic missiles capable of carrying atomic warheads to each other's territory, the United States missiles of intermediate range requiring bases within 1,500 miles of their target, the Soviet Union missiles of intercontinental range.

Thus the two giant Powers have approximately equal strength in the field of atomic weapons and ballistic missiles, but in the field of conventional weapons the Soviet Union has superiority. Two distinct though connected dangers face the West—total atomic war which might destroy the greater part, or the whole, of the human race, and limited wars in which the Soviet superiority in conventional weapons might ensure defeat for the West.

It is understandable that the first of these dangers, the apocalyptic horror of which strikes the imagination of the average citizen, has received more attention than the second. When the scientists themselves disagree on the scale of destruction to be expected from the use of atomic weapons, on the danger of radio-active 'fall-out', and the harmfulness of hydrogen bomb tests, it is absurd for a layman to express views on these matters. But the fact of popular horror about atomic weapons, in Europe, Asia, America and Africa, must be recognized as an important political fact. The demand for the control or abolition of these weapons is widespread, and is supported by very different arguments.

First must be noted the attitude of the uncompromising pacifist, who, being opposed on principle to war, is opposed *a fortiori* to atomic war. This is a minority view but is not uninfluential.

Second are those who, while not against all war, are against atomic war, and demand that their governments should refuse to make or acquire atomic weapons, and if they have them should give them up. This point of view has substantial support in Britain and in Western Germany, as well as in other Western and in neutral countries. Its best-known formulation is the argument of Bertrand Russell that it is better to accept communist domination than to destroy the human race. The governments of both the Western Powers and the Soviet Union have in principle urged the control or abolition of atomic weapons, though in practice they have failed to agree in the numerous disarmament negotiations that have taken place since 1945. But no government has supported unilateral atomic disarmament, and movements of public opinion in favour of unilateral atomic disarmament exist only in Western democratic countries, since, of course, no totalitarian government permits its citizens to advocate something contrary to its policy. Russell's argument is convincing to many, perhaps to most people on an abstract level. One may agree that it would indeed be better to accept communist domination (or any other form of totalitarian tyranny) in the hope that with the passage of time later generations might restore liberty, rather than see the whole human race destroyed. But this is not in fact the alternative that faces the governments of the West. The choice is not between the certainty of destruction of the human race and the certainty of communist domination, but between the possibility of destruction, if the West retains atomic weapons, and the certainty of Soviet domination, at least of Europe, if the West unilaterally renounces atomic weapons. If the alternative is put in this form, most non-communist Europeans and Americans would prefer the risk to the certainty.

Certain other attitudes of mind are obscurely connected with the atomic disarmament campaign. One is a certain kind of religious masochism. It is felt by some that because the human race has turned away from religion, and because the Churches have to a large extent become instruments of the established order, complacent and worldly, persecution is needed to restore the true faith. A period in the catacombs would do Christianity good. The fact that totalitarian domination would not only persecute believers, but deprive the younger generations of the opportunity to hear the teaching of the faith at all, does not appear to worry such people. This point of view is sincerely held, and is genuinely religious, but it implies an *élitist* conception of the faith—that it is reserved only for the chosen few—which is contrary to the main Christian tradition.

This religious point of view has a secular counterpart in an attitude which may perhaps be called *néo-Pétainisme*. The French Marshal welcomed the defeat of his country because it would teach the French a bitter lesson. After whoring after the Republic, *la gueuse*, they could only be redeemed by humiliation and suffering. The corresponding attitude today is that democracy, or pluto-democracy, with its crass materialism and ugliness, is an abomination that must be destroyed. If communism is the agency of destruction, it will have served a great historical purpose. Later something new and more noble, will appear.

That the anti-atomic weapon campaign is also used for their own purposes by communists, and by idealistic or ambitious collaborators with communism who hope to achieve social justice for their country or political power for themselves, hardly needs to be said.

Various though the schools of thought may be, of which the campaign is formed, it is unquestionably powerful, and deserves the respect even of those who do not accept its arguments or aims.

There is, however, a quite different case against certain types of atomic armaments. The anti-atomic idealists in the West must, of course, favour unilateral abolition by *all* Western Powers. To advocate abolition in Britain or renunciation in Germany while willingly sheltering under the protection of the American hydrogen bomb, and at the same time to denounce the Americans for having hydrogen bombs, is an odious and ridiculous form of hypocrisy. But there are others who, though hating the thought of total atomic war no less than the whole-hearted abolitionists, consciously accept the necessity for an American hydrogen bomb, but argue that no other Western Power should possess hydrogen bombs, and that Britain, which now has them, should do without them, and spend its defence budget on other weapons. This argument is conducted on the level not of moral fervour (though its protagonists are not necessarily less moral than the abolitionists) but of state policy. We do not propose here to enter into technical details, but must examine the points which bear directly on world politics.

Britain has not got unlimited resources to spend on defence. It may be argued that the British people can and should spend more, at the cost of the material standard of living, but there must be an upper limit at some point. A balance must therefore be struck between atomic and conventional weapons. The British defence policy associated with Mr. Duncan Sandys lays greater emphasis on the atomic, and provides for the production of hydrogen bombs and ballistic missiles by Britain, at the cost of keeping conventional forces relatively small and abolishing conscription. This choice may be defended on grounds of prestige, or in order to make possible a more independent British foreign policy: American opposition to the Suez venture has been neither forgotten nor forgiven by a large section of conservative opinion. Another argument is that when the United States is equipped with intercontinental missiles, and so no longer needs intermediate-range missile bases on European soil for the defence of America, its determination to defend Europe at the cost of Soviet nuclear attack on America itself will weaken, and Europe be faced with annihilation or conquest by the Soviet Union unless Britain has hydrogen bombs and the requisite missiles. The same argument can, of course, be used to justify the production of hydrogen bombs and missiles by France or Sweden or any other Western country, whether a member of NATO or not. British government spokesmen officially deny that they have any doubts of American loyalty to NATO obligations either now or in the future, but they act as if they had strong doubts. The opponents of the Sandys policy argue that Britain and other European Powers would do best to leave the production of hydrogen bombs and missiles to the United States, to rely on American strength as a deterrent to total nuclear war, and to devote their resources to providing armed forces that can deal with the many types of emergency that may arise which fall short of total war. This means primarily increased conventional forces, though it does not exclude equipment with some types of nuclear weapons.

It is clear that either policy involves risks. The question is, which risk is the greater—that the United States will default on its obligations, through capitulation by its government to popular fear of Soviet attack on America with intercontinental missiles with hydrogen bomb warheads; or that concentration on nuclear weapons by Britain and her European allies will lead to inability to meet any Soviet or Soviet-inspired aggression in Europe or elsewhere except by unleashing total war?

If it is assumed that there are only two Powers possessing the full nuclear armoury, and that the whole West depends on the American nuclear shield, the dangers are still great even if (as the present author at least believes) the United States respects its obligations. To ensure that the American capacity to retaliate is invulnerable, and that the Soviet Union does not achieve a sudden technological break-through that will place America at its mercy, is no easy task. It requires sustained vigilance and inventiveness, and must involve huge expenditures. But if it is successful enough to maintain doubt and fear in the minds of the Soviet leaders, and if these leaders retain a minimum of rationality (and the West can do nothing to ensure this), then at least two major catastrophes can be avoided —the destruction of American power by surprise attack and the deliberate launching of a total nuclear war.

But these are not the only dangers. Aggression may occur in many parts of the world, initiated with conventional weapons by China, or by a European or Middle Eastern satellite of the Soviet Union, or by a non-communist state enjoying Soviet support, possibly including considerable numbers of Soviet or Chinese troops described as 'volunteers', and threatening a position of great strategic and political importance to the West. If there are not sufficient Western conventional forces available to meet the threat, the West faces the choice of surrender or total war, either of which would be catastrophic. Korea and Vietnam are obvious examples where such a danger might arise. Other possibilities, still more alarming, are civil wars in Persia or Indonesia, involving large-scale intervention in favour of communist or communist-led forces. It is, of course, true that even if Western conventional forces were available, there would be a grave danger that the conflict would eventually be transformed into total war. It is, however, far from certain. If the Soviet- or Chinese-sponsored aggressors were unable to achieve their object, yet the security of the Chinese or Soviet régime itself were not in danger, the Soviet government would be more likely to accept stalemate than invite a world-wide nuclear cataclysm. The Korean War is a case in point. Admittedly a 'limited' war of this sort could be a horrible business, involving perhaps hundreds of thousands of casualties and millions made homeless. But it would be less deadly than either total war or communist conquest of vitally important countries.

It is hardly possible to draw an absolutely clear line between conventional forces and forces equipped with the smaller nuclear weapons. One school of thought recommends that the capacity to fight limited wars be achieved not through expanded conventional forces, but through smaller forces (though probably larger than those now maintained by NATO in Western Europe) equipped with 'tactical nuclear weapons'.[102] Opponents of this school argue that the Soviet government would never consent to a limitation of nuclear weapons, and point out that Soviet military spokesmen insist that any use of any nuclear weapons inevitably will lead to the use of all, including the most frightful. These points are true, but do not necessarily invalidate the strategy of tactical nuclear weapons. Obviously Soviet spokesmen will do all they can to discredit in the eyes of the Western public a strategy that would operate to their disadvantage.[103] But if such strategy were used in a limited war, and its intentions were clearly stated in advance by the Western governments, it is by no means certain that the Soviet leaders would deliberately choose to precipitate a total war rather than fight the war on these terms. Nevertheless, it would seem very unwise for the West to rely too much on a strategy of tactical nuclear warfare as an alternative to the maintenance of conventional forces. It would surely be safer to have the conventional forces needed to meet aggression by enemy conventional forces, while maintaining the possibility of using tactical nuclear weapons in the event that they were needed. Another important point is that the words 'atomic' and 'nuclear' have an enormous odium attached to them throughout the world. In particular, the Poles and Czechs react with great emotional violence to the notion of the equipment of West German forces with any sort of nuclear weapons. This fact, easily explicable by their experience from 1938 to 1945, is of great value to Soviet propaganda. Consequently, any tendency in the West to make strategy excessively dependent on tactical nuclear weapons involves grave political disadvantages which must always be taken into account.

It seems impossible to resist the conclusion that the West needs larger conventional forces. It is often argued that the West *must* rely on atomic weapons since it 'cannot match the Soviet superiority in conventional forces'. But this simply is not true. The European NATO states (including Britain) have a population of some 220 million, the two American NATO states almost 200 million. The Soviet Union has a population of 210 million. The European satellites of the Soviet Union have approximately 100 million more, but after the events of 1956 no serious thinker, in Moscow or in the West, can imagine that they represent a military asset. It is clear that the NATO countries could raise sufficient forces to match the Soviet forces. It is true that the administrative and welfare 'tail' of a Western division is an expense in manpower and money of which the Soviet army is relieved. But the NATO countries have twice the manpower of the Soviet Union, and they do not even have to match the Soviet fighting forces man for man. A lower ratio than this could provide forces sufficient to deny success to a Soviet or Soviet-sponsored aggressor, and in the event of war these would be strengthened by mobilization and training as required. Only if the population of China is added does the Soviet bloc have unquestionable superiority in manpower.

The Soviet superiority in conventional forces is not a fact of nature, but a result of political decisions. Western democratic governments dislike calling up large numbers of men and spending large sums of their citizens' money for the upkeep of armies. That is not the way to win parliamentary elections. Yet the West can hardly escape the choice. Either the peoples must accept more discomfort, and the party leaders must face more unpopularity (*how much more* is a matter for a military expert, not a professional politician, to say), or they risk being forced to decide between mass suicide and capitulation to the enemy. 'A high standard of living is the first priority' is just not true. To be alive and not to be a slave is more important than to live opulently.

It is, of course, obvious that general disarmament by mutual agreement is the best solution. But arms are not the cause of wars: they are the instruments of conflicts caused by political hatreds and suspicions. The long series of discussions on disarmament that have taken place since 1945 have shown that the hatreds and suspicions are at present insuperable. Nevertheless, limited agreements may in time be achieved, and any statesmen who work sincerely for them, on either side, deserve the gratitude of all.

Another admirable aim for policy is the creation of an international police force, under the United Nations. This is unfortunately not at present within the bounds of possibility. The main reason is that nations will not abandon their sovereignty. This is true of all, democratic and totalitarian and dictatorial alike. It is particularly true of totalitarians, who, seeking total power, will not by definition accept any authority higher than themselves. Only when the totalitarian régime's own authority is coextensive with the bounds of the earth will it consent to a world-wide authority—its own. It must also be said that the present United Nations, torn by race hatred of Afro-Asian, communist and Western blocs, is still very far from being that impartial world-wide authority which would be needed to organize an international armed police force. However, it must be repeated that this aim is not only noble, but in the last resort the only realistic goal of policy. All free men and women should keep this vision before their eyes, even if it is not realized in the lifetime of themselves or their children or their children's children.

RELATIONS WITH THE UNDERDEVELOPED

The poverty in which three-quarters of the human race live is a challenge to the rich nations. It is also the underlying cause of the revolutionary movements that threaten both internal and international peace in the greater part of Asia, Africa and Latin America. These threats to peace provide the opportunities for totalitarian imperialism.

In countries still directly ruled by European colonial Powers, the aim of the intelligentsia, the social group which provides political leadership, is national independence. No amount of economic aid by the metropolitan government or of investment by metropolitan private business, however useful or however well administered, can be accepted as a substitute for independence. And the lesson of the last fifty years or more is unmistakable, that though the nationalist intelligentsia may be a tiny minority in a primitive society of peasants or tribesmen, it will prevail in the end over a European administration, however enlightened, in the bid for mass support.

Suspicion of Western attitudes does not end when independence is won. The new rulers need rapid industrial progress, to remove poverty, to keep pace with population growth, to satisfy their longing for national greatness and to provide lucrative and honorific jobs for their ambitious followers. They expect as of right that their countries be soon endowed with Western levels of industry and Western standards of living. When Western experts, now no longer their masters, but their advisers, argue that these things took centuries of toil and experimentation to create in Western Europe, they suspect an imperialist trap, yet another excuse to conceal the aim of exploiting them, by means more subtle yet no less deadly than the old colonialism. Even if in rational argument Asian or African intellectuals may admit that there is some truth in the Westerners' case, yet at a deeper irrational level the same men will hate the Westerners for not at once providing them with all that they themselves have. When their former rulers, or the American allies of their former rulers, to whom they automatically attach the same 'imperialist' label, present themselves as friends anxious to protect their new-won independence from the new threat of totalitarian communist imperialism, the suspicion grows. They do not consider themselves threatened, they wish to have no part in the quarrel between the Great Powers of West and East. The Western offer of alliance and military aid is clearly yet another imperialist manœuvre, designed to reassert Western dominance in a concealed form.

The Soviet government, and its Chinese ally, make good use of these suspicions. They exploit anti-European race hatred by all means available to them. They argue that communism has a scientific answer to the problems of industrialization. What Soviet Russia could do, other nations can do, provided that they copy Soviet methods, accept Soviet advice, and give power to persons and parties (communists or popular fronts) who enjoy Soviet approval. They do not, at least in the earlier stages, demand that Asian or African countries should ally themselves with the Sino-Soviet bloc. They ask only that they should refuse to join the Western camp.

The West should, of course, give economic aid to the countries of underdeveloped societies, and should come to terms with Asian, Arab and African nationalism. But repetition, as in a ritual incantation, of these unexceptionable truths, which has in recent years become the conventional wisdom of a large section of the Western press, does not much help. The tasks are extremely difficult and complicated. If little has been achieved, it does not necessarily follow that this is because Western diplomats or economic bureaucrats, or even politicians or business-men, have not understood what the tasks are.

Economic aid to underdeveloped countries can be justified for three separate types of reason, each of which is valid at its own level. First are the claims of human solidarity: it is the duty of rich nations to help nations that live close to the starvation line, just as it is the duty of the rich man in a rich nation to pay taxes to enable the government to put money in the pockets of his poor fellow-citizens. Second comes economic interest: Asia, Africa and Latin America can provide enormous markets for North American and West European trade if the purchasing power of their people can be raised. Third comes strategic security: if Asian, African and Latin American nations remain miserably poor, and the resultant frustration of the intelligentsia increases, their political life will degenerate into anarchy, and they may fall, whether through communist insurrection or invasion, into the hands of the totalitarian enemies of the West. Therefore they must be helped to diminish their poverty, to remove the causes of frustration, and to place their economies on a sound base. All these arguments are valid, and acceptance of one does not prevent acceptance of the others.

It would be beyond the abilities of the author and the limits of this work to discuss the economic issues involved in aid to underdeveloped countries. It is, however, possible and useful briefly to mention the aid that has been given in the last years. This has come principally from the United States, the European colonial Powers, the Sino-Soviet bloc and international agencies.

United States grants of foreign aid from 1945 to 1956 amounted to $46,815 million. Of this total about one-third each went to post-war relief and reconstruction, mainly in Europe (about $15,000 million); to military aid in the period since the Korean War (more than $16,000 million); and to economic aid since Korea (about $15,000 million).[104] The largest element in the last category was 'defence support' aid, designed to strengthen the economies of countries which need to maintain military forces which they could not otherwise maintain, and which is additional to any direct American military supplies or construction works which they may receive. The three main recipients of this type of aid have been Formosa, South Korea and South Vietnam. All three are, of course, countries of underdeveloped society. But this aid, though it has saved them from collapse and substantially raised the standard of living of their peoples, has not made much contribution to long-term economic development. To meet this latter need, though on a smaller scale, the United States Congress in 1957 set up a Development Loan Fund, which was to provide loans to countries of underdeveloped society. In 1957-8, $300 million were appropriated for it, and in 1958-9, $400 million. A further form of American foreign aid is Technical Assistance, originally known as Point Four aid, from a reference to President Truman's inaugural speech of January 1949. The President had spoken of four points on which United States foreign policy was to be based, the fourth being 'a bold new programme for making the benefits of our scientific advances and industrial progress available for the improvement and growth of underdeveloped areas'. During the period 1950-6, $488 million were appropriated under this heading, and thirty-eight countries had benefited from various forms of expert advice on economic and scientific development. Since 1956 appropriations have been running at about $150 million a year. In the last year for which figures are available (1958-9) the sum appropriated was $172 million. The United States has also made large contributions to the international agencies mentioned below. Finally, American private investment in underdeveloped societies is considerable, though unevenly distributed. It is far larger in Latin America ($1,301 million in Brazil in 1957, $2,683 million in Venezuela, $850 million in Cuba, $787 million in Mexico, $702 million in Chile) than in Asia ($110 million in India, $150 million in Indonesia, $307 million in the Philippines) or in Africa ($305 million in South Africa).[105]

British economic contributions to the underdeveloped societies have been through the Colombo Plan (mentioned below) for Asian independent territories, and directly for colonial territories. The latter can be divided into four categories. Under the Colonial Development and Welfare Acts since 1946 the British government has made sums available to the colonial administrations specifically for economic and social development. Between

1946 and 1957-8 the sums committed were over £175 million. By 1956 the sums actually issued had reached nearly £118 million.[106] Secondly, the Colonial Development Corporation, set up in 1948, had up till the end of 1957 spent nearly £52 million on various projects, out of a total of over £80 million approved.[107] Thirdly, colonial governments have borrowed in the London money market: between 1948 and 1955 over £120 million was raised in this manner. Fourthly, private capital invested in the British colonies since the war was estimated in May 1956 at £300 million.[108]

The French contribution to the underdeveloped societies of the French Union has been proportionately more impressive than the British effort. An Act of 1946 set up the *Fonds d'investissement pour le développement économique et social* (FIDES) and a separate similar fund for the *départements d'outre-mer* (FIDOM). Between 1946 and 1957 these organizations had appropriated 619 milliard francs (more than £600 million), of which actual payments (*versements*) amounted to 527·5 milliards (FIDES, 475·7, and FIDOM, 51·8). In addition the *Caisse centrale de la France d'outre-mer*, which administers these two funds, also appropriated from its own resources, over the same period, 154·6 milliards for the overseas territories and 24·5 milliards for the departments. A further impression of the scale of this aid is given by the fact that in 1957 FIDES, FIDOM and CCFOM together contributed 100 milliards, while the expenses of civil administration in all the territories and departments concerned amounted to 21 milliards and all military expenses to 61 milliards. Private French investments were additional to these sums.[109]

In 1955 the Soviet bloc entered the field of foreign aid to the underdeveloped societies. The Soviet Union was, of course, the main contributor, with Czechoslovakia a significant second and small contributions from East Germany and China. A large part of Soviet aid was military, destined for Middle Eastern countries in conflict with the West. Estimates of military aid up to 1957 are $250 million to Egypt and $100 million to Syria. Countries which have received Soviet loans for economic development are Egypt ($178 million in 1958), Syria ($168 million in 1957), Afghanistan ($100 million in 1956), Indonesia ($100 million in 1956) and India (a total of $259 million in 1956 and 1957). The Soviet loans are for the most part at 2·5% interest, to be repaid over a period of twelve years, beginning after the equipment has all been supplied. Czechoslovak credits include amounts of $56 million to Egypt in 1957, of $15 million to Syria in March 1957 and of $34 million to India in 1958. East Germany has given Indonesia a credit of $7,400,000 for the installation of a sugar refinery. The sum total of all these loans is still small in comparison with Western aid, but they represent a substantial beginning. The capacity of the Soviet bloc to contribute to the industrialization of the underdeveloped societies is certainly great and growing. It has hitherto concentrated on giving substantial amounts of aid to a few countries only, and these have been countries of decisive political importance.[110]

The Colombo Plan is an international project of mutual aid and consultation, designed to help the existing plans of Asian underdeveloped societies. Its original members were states of the British Commonwealth whose Foreign Ministers met in Colombo in January 1950 and set up a Consultative Committee to survey needs. A permanent machinery has been established, and a conference held every year since 1951. Non-Commonwealth countries later joined the Plan (the United States, Cambodia, Laos and Vietnam in 1951; Burma and Nepal in 1952; Indonesia in 1953; Japan, Siam and the Philippines in 1954). Up to 1957 Britain had contributed £88 million and had also released sterling balances; Canada, $148,800,000; Australia, £18,500,000; New Zealand, £5,200,000; while Japan had made loans through the Japan Export-Import Bank to the amount of £42,700,000. American grants and loans to member countries were channelled through the Colombo Plan machinery. An important part of the Plan has been co-operation in technical assistance.[111]

An important international agency is the International Bank for Reconstruction and Development (the 'World Bank'), 35% of whose capital is provided by the United States. Its function is to provide loans for economically sound projects only, and it was hoped that it would stimulate a much larger flow of private dollar investment into underdeveloped countries. Up to 1958 the World Bank had made a fairly large number of loans to such countries. The largest such recipients at that date were India ($405,600,000), Mexico ($185,800,000), Brazil ($182,490,000), South Africa ($160,200,000), Rhodesia and Nyasaland ($141,000,000) and Pakistan ($126,400,000).[112]

The flow of private investment has been disappointingly small. The main reason for this is certainly the insecurity of capital in countries in which militant nationalist movements are in power or are rapidly rising to power. The hostility of Asian, African and Latin American nationalists to private foreign capital can be attributed in part to abuses of power by Western business interests in the period of colonial domination. But it must also be admitted that irrational xenophobia, and the temptation to make a scapegoat of the foreigner in times of internal stress, have played an important part too. If the nationalists treat foreign business-men as enemies, they can hardly expect them to invest. To remove the causes of xenophobia in the underdeveloped societies, which are political and social, is beyond the power of business-men. If in these circumstances they prefer to invest their money in advanced countries (including those, such as Canada and Australia, where physical resources are still largely undeveloped, but the political and social régime is stable), they can hardly be blamed.

There is a strong case in principle for international co-operation between governments, through the United Nations, to promote economic progress in underdeveloped societies. Governments of such societies have pressed for the establishment of a Special United Nations Fund for Economic Development (SUNFED) to make possible long-term projects, such as improved transportation and schools, which would lay the foundations for economic progress and would in the end undoubtedly both increase the standard of living of the peoples concerned and, by the increase in their purchasing power, increase the volume of world trade, but which could not be accepted on the normal commercial principles that are obligatory for the World Bank. Clearly the main financial effort for such a scheme would have to come from the United States, which, having already so many commitments for economic aid to allied or friendly nations, has shown an understandable lack of enthusiasm for the scheme. The British government, which also has huge commitments, has been unwilling to press the United States to support SUNFED.

That existing investments in underdeveloped societies by the richer nations are inadequate, cannot be disputed. The gap between the standards of living of rich and poorer nations is in fact widening. To narrow this gap, or even to maintain it at its present level, would require a considerable effort by the richer nations, a considerable diversion of national wealth from the luxuries dear to the affluent society. The British Labour Party proposes to devote 1% of the British national income to this purpose. The French government is already investing 1·5% of the national income through FIDES and CCFOM. United Nations experts have estimated that 3% of the national income of the richer nations would be needed to make substantial progress. Whether democratic electorates will be willing to make such sacrifices remains to be seen. Certainly they would be small compared to the cost of revolutions and civil wars, not to mention another world war. They may indeed be regarded as an essential part of the defence of the West, not a substitute for military defence, but a necessary additional expenditure. It might, however, reasonably be argued that some guarantees should be given in return, preferably in the form of an international statute, to be accepted by United Nations members, on conditions for the use of such funds and for the treatment of foreign investors, violations of which would involve concerted economic sanctions. A statute without 'teeth' in it would be of little use.

But even if Western aid is far more generous, and far more efficiently designed to secure the best economic results, it would be foolish to expect public expressions of gratitude.

Economic progress in underdeveloped societies benefits mainly the bureaucracy and the intelligentsia, whose numbers it also increases. The appeals of communism to the intelligentsia—the 'populist' and 'careerist' appeals discussed in an earlier chapter—will not diminish. Nor will there be a lack of issues on which Afro-Asian racialism can be mobilized, even if there is no communist orchestration. It is difficult to see how in the predictable future solutions can be found which will satisfy Arabs and Israelis in the Middle East, Frenchmen and Moslems in Algeria, Europeans and Africans in Kenya or the Rhodesias. Spectacular anti-colonial gestures by Western governments—such as the expulsion of South Africa from the Commonwealth, or the declaration in favour of Dutch evacuation of New Guinea which radical publicists on both sides of the Atlantic sometimes urge—might win some words of praise from Asian governments, but they would bitterly wound millions of loyal friends of the West without doing any good to the Bantu or the Papuans.

Nevertheless, though efficient economic aid will not put an end either to communism or to anti-European nationalism, it can at least strengthen the economies and societies of the Asian, African and Latin American countries, make them at least somewhat less vulnerable to these disruptive forces. But this modest objective, though extremely desirable, falls far short of the establishment of incorruptible, free, progressive democratic régimes, and it is wise to recognize this. In societies where too many people are on the public pay-roll and are paid too little, and where the laws are so complicated and confused that they cannot in fact be enforced, it is inevitable that the laws of supply and demand should establish the price for which an official will forget an inconvenient regulation, or interpret it to the advantage of a client. It is equally inevitable that in societies without modern social services, where politicians are expected to look after relatives and people from their home province, nepotism should fulfil some of the functions that belong in the West to the welfare state. These habits cannot be quickly changed. It is as if a water-tap were placed above a small tank placed above a series of larger tanks. Until the first tank overflows, no water can reach the lower ones. Inevitably a large part of Western economic aid will go into the pockets of the bureaucrats, their relatives, friends and richer patrons, but in the end the national economy and the masses will profit. It is better to recognize these facts, and seek practically to mitigate them where possible, than to insist on the highest standards everywhere when there are no means to enforce them. Attempts to impose the highest standards would be, and indeed are, denounced as imperialistic intervention, not least by the radical spokesmen of those masses whom intervention would be designed to protect.

That Westerners should prefer to see democratic régimes in the underdeveloped societies is natural and right. Western influence should always be used in favour of freedom whenever there is a chance of success. But it is well to recognize that Western influence may be unsuccessful. Asians and Africans are rightly indignant when they hear from Westerners the argument (which may be phrased in a condescending or a sympathetic manner) that they are 'incapable of understanding liberty' or 'not yet fit for democracy'. But the same people will angrily insist that they must not be expected to accept slavish copies of Western institutions. It must be admitted that human ingenuity can devise a great variety of combinations of freedom and authority. Some Asian, African and Latin American régimes are and will be freer than others. Some are and will be dictatorships. But a government may be dictatorial without being totalitarian. Only a doctrinaire can deny that situations can arise in which the necessary economic and cultural progress requires dictatorial leadership. Some dictators cling to the fruits of power for themselves and their gang: such, at least in his last years, was Porfirio Diaz of Mexico. Others become prophets of a totalitarian dogma. But there have been dictators who regarded their régime as a transitional stage towards democracy, and left to their successors the task of increasing freedom. Such was Kemal Atatürk in Turkey.

Totalitarian dogma is another matter. It may provide idealism and energy in the early stages of a revolutionary régime, but after a time it can only become an obstacle to progress. The Soviet Union has achieved magnificent successes by virtue of the great talents of the Russian people and the great wealth of the Russian soil and sub-soil, in spite of the dogma of Lenin and Stalin. Every sincere friend of the aspiring nations of Asia, Africa and Latin America must wish them escape from the pitfalls of totalitarianism. Yet even here a distinction must be made, from the standpoint of Western interests, between totalitarianism which makes a nation the instrument of the Sino-Soviet enemies of the West, and some other totalitarianism, at present unknown, which might not. The first priority for the West, the irreducible minimum, is that a given country should not become a satellite of the Sino-Soviet bloc, the second that it be not totalitarian, the third that it be not a dictatorship. Conversely, the ideal is that it should be a free and incorrupt democracy, second best that it be a comparatively progressive dictatorship, a bad third that it be totalitarian, but not hostile to the West, and worst of all that it be absorbed in the enemy camp.

It is important that Western leaders and public opinion should have clear ideas of the priorities of desirability, but it is also wise to distinguish between the desirable and the possible. It may not be possible to persuade an Asian, African or Latin American ally to introduce democratic methods or to put an end to scandalous abuses or injustices. If the government in question has proved itself both a faithful friend of the West and able to maintain stable government, it may be unwise to press it too hard in favour of social or political reforms which look desirable in Washington or London. It is possible that the British government should have given better advice to Nuri Pasha of Iraq, or that Nuri should have paid more attention to such good advice as was given. But the fact that Nuri was in the end overthrown does not prove that he would have been saved, or his country helped, by an attempt at some earlier stage by the West to compel him to reform his country on lines that would have appealed to Western radical intellectuals.

The underdeveloped societies, whether independent or colonial, face the problems of economic modernization, of the narrowing of the cultural gap between *élites* and masses, of the formation of new state *bourgeoisies*. Western policy should be designed to help those nations which are accessible to their influence to pass through the difficult transition period, when these problems place the gravest strains on such societies, without revolution, without the destruction of political liberty, and without surrender to any totalitarian dogma. Western help must include a combination of economic aid, advice on problems of education, and tactful understanding of the political and psychological necessities of nationalism. But Western politicians and Western public opinion should distinguish between the letter and the spirit, between European institutions and human liberty, and should recognize that Western power to do either good or harm is limited.

RELATIONS WITH THE TOTALITARIANS

The conflict between the West and the totalitarians has been discussed at length in the previous pages. But is there no hope of negotiated agreement with the totalitarians, and of a solution of the conflict that endangers world peace?

There are two emotional attitudes to negotiation with the totalitarians that are very widespread in Western public opinion.

One is to welcome negotiation as a miraculous panacea. According to this view, if only Western statesmen would stop brandishing their weapons in the face of the Soviet leaders, if only they would show them that they *too* desire peace, then the Soviet leaders would put aside their suspicions, a few days of friendly talk would lead to agreement, and the problems of peace and war would be *solved*. In short, it is enough for the West to *desire* peace, and loudly to *proclaim* its desire, in order to have it. Those who think differently are branded as unimaginative reactionaries, out of touch with the modern age and the mind of the common man, and therefore by definition wrong. This, of course, is no communist view. It is exploited by the communists, who emphatically do not accept it, but it is held by thousands of sincere democrats who have no desire to serve the totalitarian cause, and includes many men and women of great distinction, who possess highly developed critical powers outside the sphere of politics.

The other attitude is to reject negotiation out of hand, on the grounds that the Soviet leaders are men of diabolical cunning, who made rings round Roosevelt and Churchill at Yalta, and are bound to deceive any honest democrat who is rash enough to sit down at the same table with them.

But negotiation is neither a panacea nor a piece of enemy magic. It is an instrument of policy, which can and should be used by the West whenever it seems likely to yield results. In past ages negotiation, conducted in secret by specially trained professional diplomats, was the only instrument of foreign policy other than war. This is no longer so. Professional diplomats are understandably reluctant to admit that times have changed. One may well wish that they had not. In the age of professional diplomacy, international relations were more efficiently and less painfully conducted than today. Professional diplomats are as humane and civilized a group of people, as free from fanaticism and ill-tempered omniscience, as can be found in the contemporary world. But they too have their defects. The diplomat's emphasis on personal relationships, which is his strongest point, often causes him to underrate the impersonal factors in politics and to ignore the conflicts of class and nation which underlie political disputes. His determination to establish as good relations as possible with the government to which he is accredited (which is, of course, his undoubted duty) may cause him to attribute too much importance to that government's point of view in his reports to his own government.

It is important to distinguish between negotiation and political manœuvring. Serious negotiation can take place only by secret diplomacy, or as a result of previous secret diplomacy. Negotiation can only be successful when both parties wish to achieve an agreement. If the negotiation concerns serious conflicts of interest, then agreement can only be achieved by compromise, with each side making sacrifices. If it concerns relations with a third party, then agreement can be reached by common action at the expense of the third party, defensive or offensive. But if negotiation is regarded by one of the parties simply as a part of a wider political manœuvre, designed to put the other party in the wrong, in order by other means of pressure to force it to capitulate, then no agreement will be reached, because one of the parties never desired agreement. It is as well to know, before embarking on negotiations, which type is intended.

The Soviet leaders are perfectly willing to negotiate secretly. The classic example is the series of negotiations which they conducted, parallel with each other, in the summer of 1939, with Britain and France and with Germany, ending in the Molotov-Ribbentrop Pact. The wartime Moscow, Teheran and Yalta conferences also included a good deal of secret diplomacy. In all these cases, however, agreement was reached essentially at the expense of a third party—in the first case of Poland, which was to be partitioned between Hitler and Stalin, in the other cases at the expense of Germany, which was to be defeated by joint action. In the 1950s the situation has been radically different. There have been no third parties against which to unite. The Soviet leaders have regarded the Western Powers themselves as their enemies, and the Western governments have not been prepared to treat Greece, Turkey, Persia or Formosa as Chamberlain and Daladier treated Czechoslovakia in 1938, or Stalin treated Poland a year later. In the post-war meetings between the Soviet and Western leaders, the Soviet leaders have treated negotiation as a part (usually a small part) of wider political manœuvres. They have not hesitated prematurely to publish diplomatic communications when this has promised immediate political advantage to themselves. Their aim has been, not to secure an agreement, based on give and take, but to score propaganda points against their opponents, to create a climate of opinion, in their opponents' countries and in the world at large, which will eventually force their opponents to capitulate to them.

One must never forget the basic difference between totalitarian and non-totalitarian foreign policies. The totalitarians have fixed aims, which they pursue unrelentingly, but if necessary with great patience. Democratic governments have no long-term aims, other than the security of their countries, as traditionally understood. When faced with a particular problem, they try to deal with it in a practical manner, and if they can achieve an agreement, which gives them less than they would have desired but seems capable of being maintained for some time, they will accept it in good faith. It is of course not suggested that non-totalitarian governments never break treaties or agreements. But both their principles and their practice are radically different from those of totalitarians, who consider agreements only from the point of view of long-term aims inflexibly pursued, as steps towards the goal or temporary retreats from it, but in no case binding after changed circumstances show that they can be repudiated with advantage and without serious risk.

On the whole, democratic governments have shown themselves less than a match for the totalitarians on such occasions. It has long been a maxim of European statecraft that foreign policy is distinct from diplomacy: it is still insufficiently recognized that even the *conduct* of foreign policy is something more than diplomacy; that it must be conducted not only by diplomats, but also by soldiers and propagandists, and even by businessmen and men of science and letters. It does not necessarily follow that the persons best qualified to co-ordinate all these activities are professional diplomats.

The totalitarians have enjoyed an advantage over democratic governments in their ability to exclude from their countries all travellers, books, newspapers and correspondence from abroad which might question their official dogmas, and to prevent their subjects from travelling abroad. This practice is, of course, a form of aggression, which directly harms the democratic nations. No scheme of disarmament could be satisfactory which did not include abolition of these intellectual barriers. It is because these barriers exist that the democratic nations are compelled to use radio broadcasts of a more or less polemical type in the languages of the Soviet-ruled countries—such as Radio Free Europe, Voice of America and the Russian- and East European-language services of the BBC. Not only Soviet spokesmen and Western communists, but also many independent-minded democrats, often demand that these 'cold-war agencies' should be abolished. To this the only reasonable answer is that as soon as Western books and newspapers are admitted to totalitarian countries without restriction, Western travellers are permitted freely to address audiences in these countries, and free discussion is permitted among the people of these countries of any subjects affecting Western nations, on a scale comparable with the freedom enjoyed by communist publications and speakers in Western countries, there will be no further need for 'cold war propaganda'. Meanwhile, these broadcasts are the only means of communicating on political issues with the peoples of the Soviet Union and Eastern Europe. They alone can fulfil some of the functions that a Russian or Roumanian opposition would perform in a free Russia or Roumania. The fact that, despite systematic radio jamming, the broadcasts do penetrate to some extent to the peoples, is shown by the continued violence of the Soviet and East European governments against them.

Since 1955 it has been much easier for Westerners to visit totalitarian countries, and even for totalitarian subjects to come to the West. In the case of Yugoslavia and Poland, neither of which can be considered a totalitarian state in the full sense, contact with the West is extensive and easy. Visitors from the Soviet Union and the East European satellites are mostly members of official missions of some sort, but there have recently even been some cases of unofficial holiday travellers. Visitors from the West were at first mostly members of (usually self-styled) 'delegations', in which communist party members were prominent. But in recent years this has changed, individual unofficial travellers are numerous, and even persons known to the Soviet government as hostile critics have been admitted to the Soviet Union and satellite states, and have been able to talk freely, at least with chance acquaintances. Free exchange of ideas, and formation of close individual friendships, are still far away, but progress has undoubtedly been made. Everything should be done on the Western side to accelerate it. The West has nothing to lose and much to gain from admitting totalitarian subjects as visitors, and need not fear that its own subjects will be contaminated by visiting totalitarian countries.

It is important not to misunderstand the Russian people or to underrate the Soviet régime. Russians are gifted, friendly and often charming people. It is indeed unfortunate that during the years of fiercest anti-communist exhortation in the West, especially in the United States, the impression was created that Russians are uncivilized, brutish, stupid and odious. As soon as Westerners, and especially Americans, met Russians in Russia, they saw for themselves that this was not so. Moreover, travellers are also bound to see some features of the régime, and of the Russian people's attitude to it, that make a good impression. It is more than that the régime is militarily strong, and ensures public order, makes the trains run and gets the streets swept. Westerners who talk to individual Russians cannot fail to note their satisfaction with recent material progress. Russian standards of living may seem modest to a visiting American, but Russians will point out that they have enormously increased during the 1950s, and this is indeed true. Russians have also a sense of national greatness, of being the founders of a great empire (though they would not use this word), in which there are vast opportunities for all who have talent, ambition and the will to work. Russian engineers are building steel plants in India and Manchuria, and Moscow is one of the greatest capitals of the world. Of course, the old Russia too was a Great Power, but the sense of greatness was not then so widely felt. There seems to be in Soviet Russia a release of energies and hopes, a sense of great perspectives ahead, which can perhaps best be compared with the mental climate of America about the end of last century. The chauvinism and imperialism which disfigure this climate, as they disfigured the America of McKinley, should not blind us to its power to attract people of generous emotions. Again, though Marxist dogma in its contemporary scholastic form is an obstacle to understanding, and the Communist Party is to a large extent a social parasite, the voluntary acceptance by Soviet citizens of the principle of authority, their subordination to a hierarchical discipline in civil as well as military affairs, is probably on balance a positive feature of Soviet society. Finally, though the Victorianism of Soviet life may displease the sensitive Western visitor, the naïf but genuine earnestness which underlies it may to many seem preferable to the preoccupation with luxury and sensation reflected in so much that is published or displayed in Western European and American cities.

Yet recognition of the fine qualities of the Russian people and of the positive features of the Soviet régime should not blind the Westerner to the implacable hostility of the régime's leaders to the West, based on an unchanging dogma and an unshakeable conviction that they possess a complete scientific understanding of the processes that mould human society and determine human history. The belief that opponents must be wicked, and that virtuous and courageous people cannot be implacable and dangerous enemies, is the most foolish of all democratic fallacies.

FUTURE PROSPECTS

Some features of the present world political scene could have been and were predicted in 1939, but most were not, at any rate by the oracles of that time, in press or parliament. It is likely that any guesses made now as to the shape of the world in 1979 would be belied by events, and certainly we do not here propose to try our hand at prophecy. But it may perhaps be permissible to conclude by stressing certain trends whose development will largely determine that future.

First is the growth of population. Though in certain advanced countries —the United States itself, and especially the Netherlands—the rate of increase remains high, it is most marked in the countries of underdeveloped society, especially in those which have just reached the stage of rapid fall in death rates through modern public health methods. The economic and technical problems of improving standards of living in Asia, Africa and Latin America are in any case difficult, but rapid population growth means that the small gains painfully achieved are quickly swallowed up and poverty reasserts itself, a poverty all the more intolerable to its victims because they have begun to see better times, or a good chance of better times, and therefore politically all the more explosive. It is undoubtedly true that improvement of crop yields and more rational organization of resources on a world scale could provide for very much larger populations than the planet now has, or is likely to have even for a century or two.

But when one considers how difficult it has been to achieve only those modest improvements of agricultural output and those limited gains in rational social organization which have taken place in the last 100 years, in the comparatively favourable conditions of Europe and North America, the comfort in this general observation remains rather small.

Communists in the past have attached little importance to the problem of population pressure. In their view it is not the growth of population, but the obsolete organization of capitalism, which has been responsible for poverty. If capitalism were removed, they believe, problems of population pressure could be handled by communist rational organization. The experience of the Soviet Union hardly fits so simple a pattern. Improvement of agricultural output per unit of land, under rational communist organization, with *kolkhozes* and state farms and amalgamated *kolkhozes*, has been very small. Overpopulation on the land has been virtually eliminated, but by loss of human life on a scale that none but a fanatic could recommend as an example to others. A large part of this loss was due to Hitler's war, but a large part was also due to Soviet economic policies.*

In China the dimensions of the population problem are graver than they ever were in Russia. Chinese communist spokesmen have recently vacillated on the subject of birth control, but on the whole they are moderately in favour of it, while insisting that China's wealth in human beings is its greatest asset and that under socialism as they are now building it there will be room for all future increases. As China's plans of massive industrial and military growth depend on the mobilization of manpower, on the construction with millions of pairs of bare hands of factories, railways, roads, dams and buildings that in other lands are built by much smaller skilled labour forces and machinery, it seems likely that China will follow the Russian example of treating human labour as expendable, probably on a still greater scale.

In other Asian countries birth control has been accepted and officially encouraged. The most substantial results have been achieved in Japan, whose rate of increase has considerably diminished since the war. It is easier to introduce birth-control methods to an urbanized and literate nation like the Japanese than to the people of rural India, but there too the government has supported birth control. In the Arab lands, Africa and Latin America it is a negligible force. The opposition to birth control of many religious leaders, especially of the Roman Catholic Church, is also an important factor. In any case, birth control cannot be regarded as a miraculous cure-all, and its effects cannot be felt for many years. The task

* See above, pp. 121-5, 152.

of raising standards of living by economic means remains, and is aggravated with every year that passes by the growth of population.

The second long-term trend to be stressed is the growth of nationalism in Asia, Africa and Latin America. The growth is a fact, but the direction of its development is quite uncertain, and will certainly be different in different areas. In particular it is uncertain how far these nationalisms will take on an anti-European racialist character. The recent trend in this direction is one of the most horrifying features of world politics. It is easy to see that the practice of *apartheid* has provoked a racialist reaction from Africans, and that the realities covered by the slogan of Partnership in Southern Rhodesia have had similar results. Yet sympathy for the plight of Africans, and in particular of the African intelligentsia, under white racialist rule is not the same as approval of black racialism. If one condemned Hitler's extermination of Jews simply because they were Jews, one cannot approve if black racialists should wish to exterminate white men simply because they are white men. Black racialism is still a minority trend within African nationalism, but unfortunately the policies of South African and Southern Rhodesian leaders seem likely to increase it. It will, of course, be used whenever possible by communist propagandists, who are not themselves racialists, but who will eagerly exploit racialism in the hope of establishing the Soviet empire in Africa.

In the Arab lands it would be wrong to take too tragically the temporary community of interest in certain areas between communists and nationalists. The conflict of interest between the Soviet empire and the Moslem peoples cannot easily be reconciled. Arabs pay little heed to the fate of Uzbeks, Tatars or Azerbaidjanis under the Soviet yoke, since they are fully occupied with their own conflicts with the West concerning Algeria or Israel or Aden. Should these conflicts develop in such a way as to allow the Soviet army to overrun the Arab lands, then it might well prove possible to impose on them a communist yoke from which they would later find they were as unable to free themselves as the Uzbeks have been for forty years. But if this supreme disaster can be avoided, the latent conflicts between the Arabs and the Soviet Union are likely to come to the surface. Events in Iraq during 1959 are already an indication. The Arab world presents a challenge that must be met by an imaginative, flexible and politically adult Western foreign policy.

The same can be said of the tasks facing America, and to some extent also West European, policy in Latin America. Though the problems are difficult, it would be foolish to forget the strong cultural ties which bind the Latin Americans to the people of Europe and North America. Latin Americans are nearer to the Western nations than are the Moslems or Bantu or Chinese. Anti-European racialism is hardly likely to become a strong force, even in the Andean republics. If Mexican, Peruvian or Bolivian intellectuals stress the element of Indian culture in their nations, this is a healthy reaction against the excessive emphasis on the Spanish past. But if the Indian element is precious, Latin American civilization is unthinkable without the European element. This, of course, is a reason for North Americans and West Europeans not to treat Latin Americans as poor distant cousins, but to accept them as equals within a common culture.

Western statesmanship can win firm friends among Asian, African and Latin American nationalists, just as Western folly can drive Africans to anti-European racialism and Arabs or Latin Americans to alliance with communism or even into satellite status in the Sino-Soviet bloc. But ritual incantations on the need to accept the new nationalisms are not enough. It is wise to avoid illusions about the nature of these movements. To many liberals and socialists in the West the Asian and other nationalist movements appear splendid heirs to the traditions of Jefferson, Gladstone and Jaurès. The whole process of Asian or African attainment of independence is regarded as a triumph of progressive democracy. One nation after another is casting off the shackles of imperialism or feudalism, as the English did under Cromwell, or the French in 1789, and is rising to the heights of liberty on which already stand the British Labour Party or the American Federation of Labour. The communist view of progress through *bourgeois* nationalism' to independence, and through independent *bourgeois* democracy' to socialism, is essentially a variant of this secular radical optimism, derived from eighteenth-century Europe. These rosy pictures of progress, well suited to after-dinner oratory, somewhat exceed reality. Many of the same orators who welcome Asian and African nationalism, spent their political youth denouncing the narrow chauvinism of the nationalists of Central Europe who paved the way for Adolf Hitler. Yet Asian and African nationalists sometimes show affinity rather with the Roumanian Iron Guard and Hungarian Arrow Cross than with Jaurès or Jefferson.

Independence for Asian and African nations may mean the spread throughout the world of the blessings of the Western democratic welfare state. But there is another view. It is that what has been happening, in the relations between the West and the Asian and African nations, for the last decades and especially since 1945, is not the creation of new democracies, but the abdication of European nations, and especially of European *élites*, which, demoralized by the two great blood-baths in which Europe has twice done its best to commit suicide, have lost all confidence in themselves. This process, it is argued, is not a glorious extension of democracy, but a tragic decay of a civilization, similar to the decline of the Roman Empire, and followed by the same result, reversion to barbarism. The Europeans are leaving Africa and have left Asia: their place will be taken, not by the Asian democratic statesman, fine flower of freedom produced by the best cultural heritages of West and East alike, but by the goat, the monkey and the jungle.

Yet a third view is that the heir to the European empires will be neither the Afro-Asian democratic statesman, nor the goat and the monkey, but the Chinese commissar. A fourth view, perhaps more likely than any of these, is that the independent Asian and African states will develop political and social forces of their own, widely different both from each other and from their former European masters. Yet for some time still Americans and Europeans will be able powerfully to influence the outcome, for better or for worse.

The third long-term trend to be stressed is the evolution of the Soviet régime. We have noted elsewhere the pressure of both forces of reform and forces of revolution in Soviet society, the important role of the state *bourgeoisie* and the growing demands of the intellectual youth for freedom of thought. It is possible that these forces will influence Soviet governments of the future towards a more 'normal' type of foreign policy, towards less revolution-mongering and towards relatively greater concern for the state interests of Soviet Russia. It might be thought that a less ideological, more nationally-minded Soviet leadership would be easier for the West to live with—indeed, that such a leadership might recognize that it had a common interest with the West in maintaining, not only 'peace' in an abstract sense (this even Stalin admitted), but a mutually acceptable peace, an international order that would guarantee the interests of the West as well as of the Soviet Union. This is indeed possible, and it is a possibility which Western foreign policy should do what it can to bring about. But it is well to recognize that it does not depend only on the will of the Soviet leaders or the skill of Western statesmen, but will be determined above all by the general state of the world. A more nationally-minded Soviet government might co-operate peacefully with the West in a peaceful world. But if the world is not peaceful, if large parts of it are seething with unrest, the Soviet government is bound, however peaceful its general aims, to take an attitude towards the sources of unrest. And it would be very rash to assume that in crises arising in the Middle East or Eastern Europe, to take two obvious examples, the interests even of a much less ideologically-minded Soviet government would coincide with those of the West. In fact, the ability of the West and the Soviet Union to co-operate in future depends at least as much on the development of Asian and African nationalism, and on the relations of the Soviet Union to the subject states of Eastern Europe and of the East European communists with their subjects, as on the deliberate aims of the Western and Soviet governments with regard to each other.

Perhaps still more important is the future relationship between the Soviet Union and China. The potential sources of conflict between these great states have been briefly discussed above. It is necessary here to add only that, should serious conflict develop between them, this need not necessarily be to the advantage of the West. It is, of course, possible that, if the Soviet leaders anticipate danger from China, they will seek to protect themselves by coming to terms with the West. Equally possible, however, is that they will seek to strengthen themselves for future clashes with China by pushing ahead with their plans for the subjugation of the Middle East, Africa and Western Europe—in fact, that fear of China may drive them into a more adventurous and aggressive policy towards the West. Both are at the present stage mere hypotheses, but the one is as likely as the other.

The last problem on which a few words may here be permitted is the future of Western democracy itself.

What is called in Western countries 'democracy', Soviet and other Marxist-Leninists call '*bourgeois* democracy', and regard as a by-product of capitalism, performing a progressive function in human history in the period of capitalist strength, but bound to disappear when capitalism itself finally collapses, a process which they believe is now nearing its conclusion. In the place of capitalism will come socialism (whether by 'peaceful' or 'violent' revolution), which will in turn evolve into communism. Both economically and politically, they believe, socialism is incomparably superior to '*bourgeois* democracy', and communism is, of course, a still higher form of human organization.

One may believe that the whole Marxist-Leninist analysis of history is distorted, incomplete and unscientific; that capitalist economies have retained plenty of vigour and flexibility, and are at least as well designed to meet their needs as the Soviet economy to meet its different needs; and that the political system established by communist party totalitarianism is as odious as fascism and worse than most tyrannies known in the history of Europe and Asia; and yet one may have doubts about the present trend of democracy in the West. The Marxist-Leninist doctrines about the decay of capitalism and *'bourgeois* democracy' may be wrong, but it does not follow from this that there is no decay.

The criticisms that are most heard, within Western countries, of Western democracy as it now is, concern inadequate progress towards equality and social justice. It is pointed out that there is still a great deal of miserable poverty (even in the United States); that there is still ostentatious luxury among the very rich; that power is still too much concentrated in rather small upper social strata; and that the ideal of equal opportunity for all to make a career according to their innate abilities and personal efforts is still far from realized.[113] These arguments are without doubt largely justified. But two questions must here be put. The first is: should the present state of affairs be compared with an ideal state of perfect social justice, in which case it will be found lamentably deficient, or with the state of affairs a generation or a century ago, in which case it is clear that enormous progress has been made, and it is arguable that greater equality of opportunity, and a greater degree of social justice, have been achieved than ever in human history? The second question is: granted that these evils still exist, are they in fact the most dangerous evils that threaten Western societies and Western men and women?

We must here return to the problems, briefly mentioned in an earlier chapter, of authority and leadership in democratic societies, of the will of the rulers to exercise power and of the leaders to lead. The development of the modern democratic society may be regarded as progress towards social justice. This was a belief common to the pioneers of democratic ideas and policies in the past, however much they may have disagreed on the pace of progress. But another aspect of the same process, which some past enemies of democracy foretold and its champions repudiated as reactionary fantasy, is the widespread and increasing erosion of authority and abdication of responsibility. In the age of the other-directed man, popularity is the supreme criterion. By this standard, the best soap is the one which finds most buyers, and the best national policy is the one which finds favour with public opinion polls.

In a world of general security and affluence this system of values might work. Those who have kept their religious faith or hold to the morality derived from religious tradition, can never accept these values, but still society might be able to function without them. But the world is not secure, and affluence is confined to the 'north-west corner' of North America and Western Europe. In the rest of the world poverty is still the rule. What is more immediately important, poverty creates greater discontent than ever before, for the masses of Asia, Africa and Latin America are no longer willing to accept their wretched lot as a fact of nature. The peoples of the north-west corner are going to need all the skill and leadership they can find if they are to survive the dangers which press on them both from the 2,000 million who live in poverty, and from the ambitions of the totalitarians. The case for removing the remaining islands of wretched poverty within the affluent societies is, of course, unanswerable. But further pursuit in these societies of doctrinaire schemes of equality, and further increases in the consumption by all classes of ever more inessential luxuries, though not in themselves undesirable, must seem to anyone who seriously considers the world political scene today, to deserve a lower priority than is given them by their politicians, business-men and publicists. The question is not how much more affluent these societies can become, but whether they can survive at all.

What is needed, it would seem, is not so much more debunking, more undermining and derision of established traditions and loyalties, but a restoration of respect for authority, and greater encouragement to individual thought, achievement and leadership. This does not of course mean that the existing leadership in the West, or the existing means of recruiting leadership in either the political or the wider social field, are not capable of being vastly improved. Still less does it mean satisfaction with the snobbery and sanctimoniousness that are so marked a feature of Western societies (as, indeed, most stable societies in history). But it is surely possible, for example, to distinguish between the mass-produced quasi-religious adulation which surrounds the British monarchy, and the institution of monarchy itself; or to dislike the sycophancy that seems to flourish in the higher reaches of American business, without maintaining that industry can do without leadership. Democracy needs leaders, and leaders must not be afraid to give orders. To repudiate the very principle of hierarchy from hatred of complacency is to throw out the baby with the bath-water. The argument that no one who is not perfect has the right to find fault with others cannot be justified from any point of view, religious or secular, academic or political. All human action is imperfect and sinful, but within these limits choice is possible between good and evil and between greater and lesser evils. The process of letting social conscience make cowards of us all has been allowed to go too far. If consumers' sovereignty is to be extended to all political life, including the control of education, defence, finance and foreign affairs; if all original thought and all spontaneous initiative are to be treated as undesirable nonconformity, either comic or pernicious; if the only valid loyalty is loyalty to the clique—then the outlook for Western mass democracy is bleak. Yet it is still possible to reverse these trends and escape these perils.

There are no general answers to these problems. They have to be handled as they arise, and those whom fate or the vote has placed in positions which ought to (but do not always) require of their occupants the gifts of leadership, must decide on priorities (more money for defence or education, more financial aid for India or Brazil, greater military commitments towards Persia or Vietnam). These choices of priorities are the task of the practical politician. The politician is perhaps not a very popular, often not a very admirable figure. But he is what the voter has made him, no less than the voter is what the politician and the publicist have made him. The citizen who makes the politician a scapegoat for his frustrations is not helping democracy, and is not helping himself. The politician may be a cynical careerist: if so, it is the voter's fault for electing him, or for helping to create a climate of opinion in which cynical careerism can win. But the majority of democratic politicians, in whose characters personal ambition and honourable concern for the common weal are balanced in variable admixtures, must plot their course between two limits which are not easy to calculate—the most that they can demand of the people in sacrifices without being rejected by the voters, and the least that they can demand without betraying their country's interests. It is tempting for the exasperated citizen and the academic intellectual alike to inveigh against the democratic politician. But no one can begin to understand political reality who does not try sympathetically to grasp his predicament. It is not an easy one. This survey of the world political scene can best end with a prayer for the political leaders of the democracies, that they may find greater wisdom and courage than they have shown in the last fourteen years.

Appendix

Constitutions in British and French Africa

The following is not a systematic account of constitutional theory and practice in British and French colonies in Africa. It is intended only to give some precise supplementary information on the post-1945 constitutions in those territories whose political problems have been discussed in Chapter 10. These territories are Gold Coast (Ghana), Nigeria, Uganda, Kenya, Tanganyika, Northern Rhodesia, Southern Rhodesia, Nyasaland, French West Africa and French Equatorial Africa. Here we are concerned only with constitutions during the colonial period. The institutions after independence was achieved in Gold Coast and French Guinea, or after the territories of AOF and AEF became members of the Franco-African Community of 1959, are not discussed. The principal sources for the following information has been Lord Hailey, *An African Survey*, revised edition, 1956.

BRITISH TERRITORIES

The normal pattern of development in British territories is most clearly shown in the composition and functions of the Legislative Council and Executive Council.

In the first stage the Legislative Council is a purely consultative body composed of government officials. In the second stage its membership includes a number of unofficial members, appointed by the governor. These may be Europeans or Africans or members of the Asian immigrant communities which are numerous and economically important in the East African territories. In the third stage some of the unofficial members are not appointed by the governor, but elected by a section of the population, which may be more or less wide according to the franchise system. In the East African colonies in recent years a new terminology has been introduced at this stage. The official members and the appointed unofficial members are said to form the 'government side' of the Council, while the elected unofficial members are described as the 'representative side'. As the colony moves further towards independence, the elected members predominate over the official and appointed members, until the Legislative Council becomes in effect a local parliament.

The Executive Council is a smaller body, consisting of heads of departments of government and presided over by the governor. Its evolution has been similar to that of the Legislative Council. Unofficial members of the

Legislative Council (whether appointed or elected) have been brought into the Executive Council, and some of them have at a later stage been given charge of departments of government. Eventually a stage is reached when a majority of heads of department consists of elected unofficials, and the Executive Council becomes in effect a local Cabinet or Council of Ministers. This is the last stage before independence.

The application of these stages to the territories under review is briefly set out below:

(1) *Gold Coast*

The 1946 Constitution had a Legislative Council of 6 officials, 6 nominated unofficials and 18 elected unofficials—thus a majority of elected persons. The 1950 Constitution, following the recommendations of the Coussey Commission, had only 3 officials, 6 special appointed members representing European commercial and mining interests (of whom only 2 had votes in debates), and 75 elected. At the same time the Executive Council became a Council of Ministers, consisting of three British officials and eight Africans chosen from the elected majority in the Legislative Council. In 1952 the leader of the African majority in the legislature was given the title of Prime Minister. In 1953 the *ex officio* ministers and the special representatives in the Legislative Council were abolished, and there was thus a purely African elected legislature and Council of Ministers.

(2) *Nigeria*

Under the 1946 Constitution the Legislative Council consisted of seventeen officials and twenty-eight unofficials. Of the latter, four were directly elected and 18 were indirectly elected through the regional assemblies. These were unicameral Houses of Assembly in the Western and Eastern regions and bicameral (House of Assembly and House of Chiefs) in the Northern region. The three Houses of Assembly were elected, partly directly and partly indirectly.

The 1951 Constitution established a Central Council of Ministers composed of six British officials and twelve Africans (four chosen from each region). In each region there was a Regional Executive Council composed of three officials and six to nine Africans. The Central Legislative Council had 148 members, of whom 136 were elected from the regional assemblies. The Western Region was also given a House of Chiefs, but the Eastern regional assembly remained unicameral. The 136 elected members of the central legislature were chosen as follows—sixty-eight from the two chambers of the North, thirty-one from the Western House of Assembly and three from the Western House of Chiefs, and thirty-four from the Eastern House of Assembly.

Under the constitution of 1954 the Council of Ministers was to consist of three officials and ten Africans (three from each of the three regions and one from the adjoining Trust Territory of South Cameroons). The central legislature was to be elected directly, in the Northern region by male suffrage, in West and East by universal adult suffrage. The representation of the regions in the central legislature (the House of Representatives) was to be as follows—three officials, not more than six special members appointed by the Governor-General, ninety-two elected in the North, forty-two elected in the West, forty-two elected in the East, six elected in South Cameroons and two elected in the Federal Territory of Lagos, the capital, which was for this purpose separated from the Western region in which it geographically lies.

(3) *Uganda*

In 1950 the Legislative Council consisted of sixteen officials and sixteen nominated unofficials. The latter consisted of eight Africans, four Europeans and four Asians. In 1954 there was a 'government side' of twenty-eight and a 'representative side' of twenty-eight. The government side was composed of nine officials and nineteen nominated. The representative side was composed of fourteen Africans, seven Europeans and seven Asians. The Africans were chosen by African provincial councils, themselves composed of persons elected by African local authorities, which in turn were partly elected by the population. In 1957 both the government side and the representative side were increased to thirty members.

In 1957 the decision was taken to introduce elections by direct suffrage, and this was approved by the British Secretary of State for the Colonies in October 1957. The elections took place in 1958 except in the province of Buganda, which refused to take part, for the political reasons discussed in Chapter Ten above. At the 1958 elections the number of registered voters was 626,000.

(4) *Kenya*

In 1948 the Legislative Council consisted of sixteen officials and twenty-two unofficials. The latter were eleven elected Europeans, five elected Asians, one elected Arab, one nominated Arab, and four nominated Africans.

In 1952 the 'official side' in the Legislative Council consisted of twenty-six persons, the 'unofficial side' of twenty-eight. The official side was composed of six officials and eighteen nominated. The unofficial side was composed of fourteen elected Europeans, six elected Asians, one elected Arab, six African representative members and one Arab representative member. The representative members were not directly elected, but were chosen by the governor from a larger list of persons elected by specially constituted electoral colleges. At this time the Executive Council consisted of twelve persons, of whom eight were officials holding government departments and four were unofficials without departmental duties (two Europeans, one African and one Asian).

In 1954 a new constitution was introduced by the Colonial Secretary, Mr. Lyttelton. This did not change the composition of the Legislative Council, but it changed the Executive Council into a Council of Ministers. This was composed of the Governor, a deputy-governor, six officials, two nominated and six unofficial (of whom three were Europeans, two Asians and one African). In 1957 it was decided to introduce direct election for the African members, and their seats in the Legislative Council were increased to eight. In the election, members of the Kikuyu, Embu and Meru tribes (which had been involved in the Mau Mau revolt) were only allowed to vote if they had passed an officially administered 'loyalty test'. The result of these elections was however a defeat for the moderate Africans who co-operated with the government, and a victory for the nationalists led by Mr. Tom Mboya. In the light of this result a new constitution was introduced.

The 'Lennox-Boyd constitution' of November 1957 increased the number of directly elected African seats to fourteen. It also created twelve 'special seats'—four each for Europeans, Asians and Africans—which were to be filled by persons elected by the Legislative Council voting as a body. It also set up a second chamber, the Council of State, which was to watch over all legislation with a view to preventing any damage to the interests of any of the three races. The fourteen elected Africans led by Mboya boycotted the election to the 'special seats'. They at once demanded the abolition of the Council of State and of the special seats; the increase of the directly elected African seats to twenty-six, or half the total seats in the Council; and the allocation to Africans of half the unofficial seats in the Council of Ministers.

(5) *Tanganyika*

In 1945 the Legislative Council consisted of fifteen officials and fourteen nominated unofficials. The latter were seven Europeans (of whom one was appointed as a representative of specifically African interests), three Asians and four Africans. In 1955 the 'official side' was thirty-one and the 'representative side' was thirty. The official side consisted of nineteen officials and twelve nominated unofficials (three from each race). The representative side consisted of ten from each race, also nominated. The

Executive Council consisted of eight officials (all European) and six unofficials (two from each race).

In May 1957 a Bill was introduced to establish direct election, on a restricted franchise, in nine constituencies, and in November the number was increased to ten. In each constituency there were to be three seats, one for each race, and every voter had to vote for a candidate of each race. In July 1957 the Executive Council was changed into a Council of Ministers, with nine official and seven unofficial members. In November 1957 the Legislative Council had 67 members, 34 on the government side and 33 on the representative side. The government side consisted of nine official ministers, six assistant-ministers and nineteen nominated. The representative side consisted of thirty directly elected members and three nominated.

(6) *Northern Rhodesia*

In 1945 the Legislative Council had nine official members and thirteen unofficial. Of the latter, five were nominated (three of these specifically to represent African interests), and eight were elected. In 1953 the unofficials consisted of ten elected Europeans, two Europeans nominated to represent African interests and two Africans nominated.

At the end of 1953, after the Federation had been created, there were further changes. The Legislative Council now contained eight official and eighteen unofficial members. The latter consisted of twelve elected Europeans, two Europeans nominated to represent African interests and four Africans chosen by the African Representative Council. The latter consists of persons elected by provincial councils, which are themselves partly elected bodies, together with four persons nominated for the region of Barotseland. At this time the Executive Council consisted of seven officials, three elected unofficials and one appointed unofficial representing African interests.

In 1958 new constitutional proposals were produced, which were put into effect in 1959. The Executive Council now consisted of four officials, four elected European unofficials and two African appointed unofficials. The Legislative Council consisted of six officials, two nominated and twenty-two elected. Of the elected persons, six were Africans elected in special constituencies. Of the remaining sixteen seats, two were reserved to Europeans and two to Africans, but the rest could be held by a member of any race. In practice the franchise ensured that these twelve 'ordinary' seats would be held by Europeans. Under the franchise law it was reckoned that as many as 25,000 Africans were entitled to vote, but in fact only a third of these registered, probably as a result of pressure by the nationalist party, the Zambia Congress. At the time of the election of 20 March 1959, there were 20,566 registered European voters, 7,617 Africans and 2,051 Asians.

(7) *Southern Rhodesia*
Southern Rhodesia has had an elected Legislative Council, and a government of ministers responsible to it, since 1923. In 1953 the franchise was confined to those who had property worth at least £500 or a salary of at least £240 a year, and had a speaking and writing knowledge of English. The electorate then comprised 47,533 registered Europeans, 535 Asians, 535 Coloureds and 429 Africans. It was however reckoned that about 2,000 Africans would have been entitled to a vote if they had taken the trouble to register. In 1957 Mr. Garfield Todd introduced a new franchise, based on an educational standard for Africans. This increased the number of Africans entitled to vote to about 10,000 while the number of European voters had risen to about 54,000.

(8) *Nyasaland*
In 1953 the Legislative Council consisted of eleven officials and ten unofficials. The latter were five elected Europeans, one Asian, one nominated European and three appointed Africans. In 1955 the numbers were increased to twelve official and eleven unofficial. The composition of the latter was changed. There were now five Africans, elected by provincial councils, which were themselves composed of chiefs and representatives of local authorities.

FRENCH AFRICA

(1) *Afrique Occidentale Française (AOF)*
Each of the eight territories had its own assembly. The French Constitution of 1946 laid down that the conditions for the exercise of the rights of citizenship (which had been granted in principle by the *Loi Lamine-Gueye* of May 1946) should be determined by separate laws. These in fact provided for two separate electoral colleges. The first college (*citoyens de statut français*), composed of Frenchmen and of the most educated Africans, was much smaller than the second college (*citoyens de statut local*). The representation of the first college in the territorial assemblies was, in absolute numbers, smaller than that of the second, but in proportion to the numbers of voters in each college it was relatively much larger.

The relative number of seats allocated to each college in the eight territories was as follows: Mauritania first college eight and second college sixteen; Sudan twenty and forty; Ivory Coast eighteen and thirty-two;

Guinea eighteen and thirty-two; Haute Volta ten and forty; Dahomey eighteen and thirty-two.

The *Loi Cadre* of the French Assembly of 23 June 1956 provided that the territorial assemblies should be elected in a single electorate by universal suffrage.

Developments since the introduction of the new Constitution in France at the end of 1958, and the formation of the Senegal-Sudan union of Mali and the independence of Guinea, are briefly discussed in Chapter Ten. French West African politics are in fact in a state of flux.

(2) *Afrique Equatoriale Française (AEF)*

The post-war system was virtually identical with that of AOF. In AEF there were four territorial assemblies, also elected by two colleges. The representation of the first and second colleges in the assemblies was as follows: Chad fifteen and thirty; Middle Congo thirteen and twenty-four; Ubangui-Shari fourteen and twenty-six; Gabon thirteen and twenty-four. In AEF too the *Loi Cadre* of 1956 introduced a single electorate and universal suffrage. Post-1958 development is briefly mentioned in Chapter Ten.

REPRESENTATION IN THE FRENCH ASSEMBLY

Both AOF and AEF elected deputies to the National Assembly in Paris, but much fewer in proportion to their population than the people of the metropolitan country. In a National Assembly of 627, metropolitan France and Corsica, with a population of 40 million* had 544 seats, while AOF and AEF together, with rather more than 20 million inhabitants,† had thirty-two seats. The African deputies, however, like other small political groups in the Assembly, have played their part in seating and unseating governments, and Africans have held ministerial posts in many cabinets, above all the RDA leader Felix Houphouet-Boigny.

* In 1946. In 1954 it had risen to 43 million.
† In 1959 together about 25 million.

Reference Notes

1. Vladimir Dedijer, *Tito Speaks*, 1953, pp. 313-14, 322-33, 337-8.
2. For a comparison of the effects of the various purges on the Central Committees of the different parties, see article by Hugh Seton-Watson, 'Differences in the communist parties', in *Annals* of the American Academy of Political and Social Science, May 1958, pp. 3-4.
3. For accounts and interpretations of these events, see C. M. Woodhouse, *Apple of Discord*, 1948, pp. 214-18, and I. Stavrianos, *Greece*, Chicago, 1952, pp. 126-38.
4. See Elizabeth Wiskemann *Germany's Eastern Neighbours*, 1956, Chapters 8-14. An officially-sponsored German view is *Dokumentation der Vertreibung der Deutschen aus Ostmitteleuropa*, published by Bundesministerium für Vertriebene, Bonn, 1953.
5. The process is discussed, country by country, in *The Curtain Falls*, ed. Denis Healey, 1956.
6. Royal Institute of International Affairs, *The Middle East*, third edition, 1958, p. 278. The figure is taken from the *Annual Report of the Director of UNRWA* for the year 1 July 1955-30 June 1956. It includes a considerable increase of the refugee population since 1949 by births.
7. *Nazi-Soviet Relations*, a collection of German documents published by the U.S. Department of State in 1948, pp. 258-9.
8. For Burma, see H. Tinker, *The Union of Burma*, 1957. Communist policy throughout the area in the post-war years is described in *The Left Wing in South-East Asia*, by V. Thompson and P. Adloff, 1950.
9. The best single volume on the party's earlier history is *Chinese Communism and the Rise of Mao*, by B. Schwartz, Harvard, 1950.
10. Sardar Panikkar's version of this warning is given in his *In Two Chinas*, 1955, pp. 109-12.
11. For an account of these, see Richard L. Walker, *China Under Communism*, 1956, pp. 95-7. The targets of the 'three antis' were corruption, waste and bureaucracy; of the 'five antis', bribery, tax-evasion, theft of State wealth, use of fewer workers and inferior materials, stealing of economic intelligence.
12. See Edward Hunter, *Brain-washing in Red China*, New York, 1951.
13. United Nations, Department of Economic Affairs, *Land Reform: Defects in Agrarian Structure as Obstacles to Economic Development*, New York, 1951.
14. *Annuaire statistique de la France, 1957*, Paris, 1957, gives 23·1% as *agriculteurs exploitants* and 5·8% as *salariés agricoles* in February 1956. *Statistisches Jahrbuch für die Bundesrepublik Deutschland, 1957*, Wiesbaden, 1957, gives persons engaged in agriculture, livestock-farming, forestry and fishery as 5,113,652 out of an active labour force of 21,590,172 in 1950. The United States census of population of 1950 gave farmers and farm managers as 7·3% of the civilian labour force, and farm labourers as 4·3%. The British census of 1951 gave 2·7% of heads of households as farmers and 4·2% as farm labourers.
15. *United Nations Statistical Yearbook*, 1956, pp. 79-81.
16. ibid., pp. 317-19.
17. ibid., pp. 304-7.
18. Doreen Warriner, *Land Reform and Development in the Middle East*, 1957, pp. 84-93.
19. The most authoritative work on agrarian conditions and tenancy relationships in Persia is A. K. S. Lambton, *Landlord and Peasant in Persia*, 1953.
20. Warriner, op. cit., pp. 147-57.
21. See Gunnar Myrdal, *An American Dilemma*, New York, 1944, pp. 242-50. This picture is now no doubt partly out of date, but it is unlikely that the gloomy conditions which Myrdal describes have altogether disappeared.
22. T. R. Ford, *Man and Land in Peru*, University of Florida, 1955, p. 87.

REFERENCE NOTES 475

23. The best brief description in English of the *obshchina* is in G. T. Robinson, *Rural Russia under the Old Régime*, 1929.
24. N. L. Whetton, *Rural Mexico*, Chicago, 1948, pp. 209, 224-31.
25. United Nations, Department of Economic Affairs, *Progress in Land Reform*, New York, 1954, pp. 245-6.
26. Hugh Seton-Watson, *The East European Revolution*, 1950, pp. 265-7.
27. United Nations, *Progress in Land Reform*, pp. 24-5, 62-4. The execution and effects of the reform are discussed in detail in R. P. Dore, *Land Reform in Japan*, 1959.
28. United Nations, *Progress in Land Reform*, pp. 71-3.
29. Doreen Warriner, *Land Reform and Development in the Middle East*, London, 1957, p. 35.
30. United Nations, *Progress in Land Reform*, pp. 195-7.
31. ibid., p. 198.
32. Warriner, op. cit. p. 42.
33. For a historical account and discussion of the peasant parties in Eastern Europe, see D. Mitrany, *Marx against the Peasant*, 1951.
34. The westernizing and traditionalist trends are discussed in Sir George Sansom, *The Western World and Japan*, 1950.
35. Kurt Mayer, *Class and Society*, New York, 1955, p. 74.
36. G. D. H. Cole, *Studies in Class Structure*, 1955, p. 153.
37. *Annuario statistico italiano, 1956*, Rome, 1957, p. 198.
38. *Statistical Abstract of the United States, 1958*, Washington, 1958, p. 24.
39. National Planning Association, *Trade Unions and Democracy*, Washington, 1957, p. 41. The figures are in terms of 1947 to 1949 prices, and so take account of the change in the purchasing power of the dollar between 1929 and 1955.
40. Mayer, op. cit., pp. 74-5.
41. See Solomon B. Levine, 'Labor Patterns and Trends', in *Annals* of November, 1956 (the whole issue of which is devoted to Japan).
42. See C. Wright Mills, *White Collar*, New York, 1956.
43. Cole, op. cit., p. 143.
44. *Annuaire statistique de la France, 1957*, Paris, 1957, p. 69.
45. *Narodnoe khozyaistvo SSSR*, Moscow, 1956, pp. 194, 222, 244.
46. See Oscar A. Ornati, 'Problems of Indian Trade-unionism', in *Annals*, March 1957.
47. See article by J. A. Hallsworth, 'Freedom of Association and Industrial Relations in the Countries of the Near and Middle East', in *International Labour Review*, November and December 1954.
48. See J. I. Roper, *Labour Problems in West Africa*, 1958.
49. See article by H. K. Hochschild, 'Labor Relations in Northern Rhodesia', in *Annals*, July 1956.
50. *State of the Union*, economic, financial and statistical yearbook for the Union of South Africa, Capetown, 1958, p. 152.
51. ibid., p. 382.
52. ibid., p. 339. See also Lord Hailey, *An African Survey*, revised edition, 1956, pp. 1,439-43, and Gwendolen M. Carter, *The Politics of Inequality*, 1958, pp. 112-16.
53. On the foundation of the *Profintern*, or (communist) Red International of labour unions, and its relations with the International Federation of Trade Unions (known as the 'Amsterdam' International because it was reconstituted at a conference in Amsterdam in July-August 1919), see *The Communist International, 1919-1943*, documents edited by Jane Degras, Vol. 1, 1956, pp. 87-90, 194-5, 204-5.
54. Marquess Kimmochi Saionji, 'National Education in the Meiji Era', in *Fifty Years of New Japan*, ed. Count Shigenobu Okuma, 1910, Vol. 2, pp. 161-74. See also Japanese Department of Education, *Outlines of the Modern Education in Japan*, Tokyo, 1893.
55. Crane Brinton, *The Anatomy of Revolution*, 1953.
56. For details, see K. Bracher, *Die Auflösung der Weimarer Republik*, Stuttgart, 1955, pp. 229-84, 481-99, 686-732.

57. K. A. Wittfogel, 'Chinese Society: a Historical Survey', in *The Journal of Asian Studies*, May, 1957, p. 354.
58. There is a large literature on the purges. The outstanding eye-witness accounts are F. Beck and W. Godin, *Russian Purge*, 1951, and A. Weissberg, *Hexensabbat*, Frankfurt, 1951. A useful academic analysis is Z. Brzezinski, *The Permanent Purge*, Harvard, 1956.
59. For a study of the mentality and methods of the SS by a former concentration camp inmate, see E. Kogon, *Der SS-Staat*, Stockholm, 1947.
60. A brilliant though somewhat impressionistic study of the 'technical intelligentsia' in Soviet society by a former Soviet citizen is H. Achminow, *Die Macht im Hintergrund*, Ulm, 1950. A more recent analysis, based on systematic scholarly study of published sources, but without the element of direct experience, is J. Berliner, *Factory and Management in the USSR*, Harvard, 1957.
61. See *The New Yorker*, 26 October 1957, article by E. Kirkead, 'American Prisoners in Korea'.
62. See *The New American Right*, ed. Daniel Bell, New York, 1955, especially the chapter by Seymour Martin Lipset on 'The Sources of the "Radical Right"'.
63. See David Riesman, *The Lonely Crowd*, New Haven, 1952.
64. See article by E. Shils, 'Daydreams and Nightmares: Reflections on the Criticism of Mass Culture', in *The Sewanee Review*, autumn, 1957, pp. 586-608.
65. For a discussion of East European small-power imperialisms, see W. Kolarz, *Myths and Realities in Eastern Europe*, 1946, and Hugh Seton-Watson, *Eastern Europe between the Wars*, 1945, Chapter 8.
66. S. E. Morison and H. S. Commager, *The Growth of the American Republic*, Vol. 2, p. 337.
67. The text of the speech (delivered on 25 November 1911) can be found in *La lotta politica in Italia dall'unità al 1925*, ed. Nino Valeri, Florence, 1946, pp. 339-47.
68. For an account of the record of the Indian Civil Service, see the two volumes by Philip Mason, himself a distinguished member of the service, *The Men Who ruled India*: Vol. 1, *The Founders*, Vol. 2, *The Guardians*, 1954. The present author may perhaps be permitted here to mention his own maternal grandfather and great-grandfather, of whose service, the first in the ICS and the second in the Indian Army, he will always remain proud.
69. Lord Hailey, op. cit., pp. 1,175-6.
70. A popular account of these events is given in J. G. Amamoo, *The New Ghana*, 1958.
71. Thomas Hodgkin, *Nationalism in Colonial Africa*, 1956, p. 160. In 1958 the NEPU was the strongest party in the main northern city of Kano.
72. Hailey, op. cit., p. 1,199.
73. Information on the parties of AOF can be found in V. Thompson and P. Adloff, *French West Africa*, 1958. A more detailed, but unduly optimistic (from a French point of view) and now outdated treatment is the work of *Le Monde*'s expert on AOF, André Blanchet, *L'itinéraire des partis africains depuis Bamako*, Paris, 1958.
74. *Madagascar, 1954*, a statistical handbook issued by Ministère de la France d'outre-mer, Paris, 1955, p. 200.
75. Hailey, op. cit., pp. 1,207-8.
76. Hailey, op. cit., pp. 232, 1,216.
77. For the definition of 'subordinate' and 'co-ordinate' Powers, see K. C. Wheare, *Federal Government*, third edition, 1953, pp. 11-14.
78. This is discussed in W. Kolarz, *Russia and Her Colonies*, 1952, p. 268.
79. The most serious account of this tragedy is the work of an exiled Chechen, formerly an official of the All-Union Communist Party in the northern Caucasus, A. Avtorkhanov, *Narodoubiistvo v. SSSR*, Munich, 1952.
80. Whetton, *Rural Mexico*, p. 363.
81. W. S. Rycroft (ed.) *Indians of the High Andes*, New York, 1946, p. 99.

82. José Carlos Mariátegui, *Siete ensayos de interpretación de la realidad peruana*, Lima, 1952. This is the third edition. The author died in 1930.
83. A recent statement of APRA ideas by its leader is Víctor Raúl Haya de la Torre, *Treinta años de Aprismo*, Mexico, 1956. An earlier statement is *El antimperialismo y l'APRA*, Santiago de Chile, 1936.
84. Commission for the Development of the Bantu Areas, *Summary of the Report*, Pretoria, 1955, p. 206.
85. *Statistical Abstract of the United States, 1958*, p. 626.
86. See V. O. Key, *Southern Politics*, New York, 1950.
87. Details are given in Harry S. Ashmore, *The Negro and the Schools*, Chapel Hill, 1954, pp. 62, 63, 155, 159, 160.
88. See O. Carmichael and W. James, *The Louisville Story*, New York, 1957.
89. See E. Franklin Frazier, *Black Bourgeoisie*, New York, 1957.
90. See Myron C. Rush, *The Rise of Khrushchov*, Washington, 1958.
91. The text of the speech was published, with comments by Bertram D. Wolfe, under the title *Khrushchov and Stalin's Ghost*, New York, 1958.
92. Especially an article entitled '*Anatomija jednog morala*', which appeared in the review *Nova Misao* in January 1954.
93. There is a brilliant analysis of Tito's role in these events by R. Lowenthal, 'Tito's Gamble', in *Encounter*, October 1958, pp. 56-65.
94. Of the literature on the subject, we may mention George F. Kennan, *Russia, the Atom and the West*, Denis Healey, *A Neutral Belt in Europe?*, and Michael Howard, *Disengagement in Europe*, all three published in 1958.
95. Gamal Abd el-Nasser, *Egypt's Liberation*, Washington, 1955, pp. 109-11.
96. A brief survey of Soviet studies on Africa may be found in an article 'Soviet Interest in Africa', in *The World Today*, September 1958, pp. 355-61.
97. See article by Roderick MacFarquhar, 'Communist China's Intra-party Dispute', in *Pacific Affairs*, December 1958, pp. 323-35.
98. See article by Li Thian-hok, 'The China Impasse: a Formosan View' in *Foreign Affairs*, April 1958, pp. 437-48.
99. Speech by Marshal Tito at Labin in Istria on 15 June 1958; cf. *The Times* of 16 June 1958.
100. Taya Zinkin, *India Changes*, 1958, p. 218.
101. See article by Leslie Palmier, 'Sukarno the Nationalist', in *Pacific Affairs*, June 1957.
102. See Henry A. Kissinger, *Nuclear Weapons and Foreign Policy*, New York, 1957.
103. For a survey of modern Soviet military doctrine, and discussion of the relative importance in Soviet military publications of propaganda arguments and genuine convictions, see Raymond L. Garthoff, *Soviet Strategy in the Nuclear Age*, New York, 1958.
104. U.S. 85th Congress, Senate, Report No. 300, *Foreign Aid*, Washington, 1957, p. 5.
105. U.S. Department of Commerce, *Survey of Current Affairs*, September 1958, p. 18.
106. Central Office of Information, *The United Kingdom Colonial Development and Welfare Acts*, 1956.
107. Colonial Department Corporation, *Report and Accounts for 1957*.
108. *Hansard*, 14 May 1956, column 1,802.
109. Georges Oudard (ed.), *Union française*, Paris, 1958, pp. 79, 95, 112.
110. U.S. Department of State, *The Sino-Soviet Economic Offensive in the Less-developed Countries*, Washington, 1958, especially pp. 23-7.
111. Central Office of Information, *Fact Sheets on the Colombo Plan*, Nos. 1-5, 1958.
112. International Bank for Reconstruction and Development, *13th Annual Report, 1957-8*.
113. For criticism of the practice of the 'Welfare State' in Britain, see R. Titmuss, *Essays on 'the Welfare State'*, 1958.

Bibliographical Note

The following is not a list of all works that I have consulted on the subjects discussed in this book, still less a systematic bibliography of those subjects. It includes only books which I have found useful, and believe may be useful to those of my readers who wish to pursue some of the subjects further. Wherever possible, works in English have been preferred. Not all these books are of high quality, but all contain some facts or ideas of interest. Some works which have been omitted are in some respects superior to some which have been included, but the selection has been made from the point of view of usefulness for study of the subject, not of general literary merit.

As books on foreign affairs are usually written about countries or regions rather than about subjects, the arrangement of this bibliographical list is more 'regional' than is the arrangement of the book itself, and its divisions do not exactly coincide with the chapters or Parts of the book. It is my hope that the arrangement chosen will be convenient for the reader. It has not, however, always been easy to decide whether to put a book in a 'regional' or a 'subject' section, and some overlapping is inevitable.

The place of publication is given for books not published in the United Kingdom. The year of publication given is of the edition which I have used. It has not been possible to give a list of periodicals and newspapers consulted, though these have, of course, provided me with a very large part of my material. Books on the historical background to these events have also, with very few exceptions, been omitted.

WESTERN EUROPE

Allemann, F. R., *Bonn ist nicht Weimar*, Köln, 1956
Calamandrei, P., and others, *Dieci anni dopo*, Bari, 1955
Fauvet, J., *Les partis politiques en France*, Paris, 1951
Grindrod, M., *The Rebuilding of Italy*, 1955
Luthy, H., *The State of France*, 1955
Royal Institute, of International Affairs, *The Scandinavian States and Finland*, 1954
Shepherd, Gordon, *The Austrian Odyssey*, 1957
Williams, P. M., *The Politics of Post-war France*, 1954

EASTERN EUROPE

Amery, Julian, *Sons of the Eagle*, 1948
Barker, Elizabeth, *Truce in the Balkans*, 1948

Clissold, Stephen, *Whirlwind*, 1949
Dedijer, Vladimir, *Tito Speaks*, 1953
Friedmann, O., *The Break-up of Czechoslovak Democracy*, 1950.
Leonhard, Wolfgang, *Die Revolution entlässt ihre Kinder*, Köln, 1950
McVicker, C. P., *Titoism*, New York, 1957.
Mikolajczyk, Stanislaw, *The Pattern of Soviet Domination*, 1948
Nagy, Ferenc, *Behind the Iron Curtain*, New York, 1948
Neal, F. W., *Titoism in Action*, University of California, 1958
Nettl, Peter, *The Eastern Zone and Soviet Policy in Germany*, 1951
Ripka, Hubert, *Le coup de Prague*, Paris, 1949
Roberts, Henry L., *Roumania*, New Haven, 1951
Seton-Watson, Hugh, *The East European Revolution*, 1950
Stavrianos, J., *Greece*, Chicago, 1952
Wiskemann, Elizabeth, *Germany's Eastern Neighbours*, 1956
Woodhouse, C. M., *Apple of Discord*, 1948

SOVIET UNION

Avtorkhanov, A., *Narodoubiistvo v. SSSR*, Munich, 1952
Beck, F., and Godin W., *Russian Purge*, 1951
Brzezinski, Z., *The Permanent Purge*, Harvard, 1956
Fainsod, Merle, *How Russia is Ruled*, Harvard, 1953
Fainsod, Merle, *Smolensk under Soviet Rule*, 1959
Kolarz, W., *Russia and Her Colonies*, 1952
Mehnert, Klaus, *Der Sowjetmensch*, Stuttgart, 1958
Meissner, Boris, *Die kommunistische Partei der Sowjetunion vor und nach dem Tode Stalins*, Frankfurt, 1954
Meissner, Boris, *Das Ende des Stalin-Mythos*, Frankfurt, 1956
Pipes, Richard, *The Formation of the Soviet Union*, Harvard, 1954
Rush, Myron, *The Rise of Khrushchov*, Washington, 1958
Weissberg, A., *Hexensabbat*, Frankfurt, 1951

THE ARAB WORLD

Aron, Raymond, *La tragédie algérienne*, Paris, 1957
Bourguiba, Habib, *La Tunisie et la France*, Paris, 1954
Bromberger, Serge, *Les rebelles algériens*, Paris, 1958
Colombe, J., *L'évolution de l'Egypte*, Paris, 1951
Garas, F., *Bourguiba et la naissance d'une nation*, Paris, 1956
Husaini, Ishak Musa, *The Moslem Brotherhood*, Beirut, 1956
Issawi, Charles, *Egypt at Mid-century*, 1954
Julien, Charles, *L'Afrique du nord en marche*, Paris, 1952
Khadduri, M., *Independent Iraq*, 1951

Lacouture, J. and S., *Egypt in transition*, 1958
Lacouture, J. and S., *Le Maroc à l'épreuve*, Paris, 1958
Laqueur, W. Z., *Communism and Nationalism in the Middle East*, 1956
Laqueur, W. Z., *The Middle East in Transition*, 1958
Lenczowski, G., *Russia, Iran and the West*, Ithaca, 1949
Lenczowski, G., *The Middle East in World Affairs*, Ithaca, 1952
Little, Tom, *Egypt*, 1958
Longrigg, S. H., *Iraq 1900-1950*, 1953
Nasser, Gamal Abd el-, *Egypt's Liberation*, Washington, 1955
Neguib, Mohammed, *Egypt's Destiny*, 1955
Rézette, R., *Les partis politiques marocains*, Paris, 1955
Royal Institute of International Affairs, *The Middle East*, third edition, 1958
Smith, W. C., *Islam in Modern History*, Princeton, 1957
Soustelle, Jacques, *L'Algérie souffrante et aimée*, Paris, 1956
Tillion, Germaine, *L'Algérie en 1957*, Paris, 1957

ASIA—GENERAL

Ball, W. Macmahon, *Nationalism and Communism in East Asia*, 1952
Bowles, Chester, *The New Dimensions of Peace*, 1956
Mehnert, Klaus, *Moskau, Asien und wir*, Stuttgart, 1956
Panikkar, K. M., *Asia and Western Dominance*, 1953
Wint, Guy, *The British in Asia*, 1947
Zinkin, Maurice, *Asia and the West*, 1951
Zinkin, Maurice, *Development for Free Asia*, 1956

CHINA

Boorman, H., and others, *The Moscow-Peking Axis*, New York, 1957
Fitzgerald, C. P., *China, a Short Cultural History*, 1935
Fitzgerald, C. P., *Revolution in China*, 1952
Guillain, R., *The Blue Ants*, 1956
Panikkar, K. M., *In Two Chinas*, 1955
Tang, Peter, *Communist China*, New York, 1957
Walker, Richard L., *China under Communism*, 1956

INDIA AND PAKISTAN

Callard, K., *Pakistan, a Political Study*, 1957
Kautsky, J. H., *Moscow and the Communist Party of India*, New York, 1956
Masani, M. R., *The Communist Party of India*, 1954
Menon, V. P., *The Transfer of Power in India*, 1957
Government of India, Planning Commission, *The New India*, 1958

Schuster, Sir George, and Wint, Guy, *India and Democracy*, 1941
Symonds, R., *The Making of Pakistan*, 1950
Tuker, Sir Francis, *While Memory Serves*, 1950
Woytinsky, W. S., *India: the Awakening Giant*, New York, 1957
Zinkin, Taya, *India Changes*, 1958

JAPAN

Allen, G. C., *A Short Economic History of Japan*, 1946
Allen, G. C., *Japan's Economic Recovery*, 1958
Benedict, Ruth, *The Chrysanthemum and the Sword*, Boston, 1946
Borton, Hugh, and others, *Japan between East and West*, New York, 1957
Ike, Nobutaka, *The Beginnings of Political Democracy in Japan*, Baltimore, 1950
Ike, Nobutaka, *Japanese Politics: an Introductory Survey*, 1958
Lockwood, William W., *The Economic Development of Japan*, 1955
Norman, E. H., *The Emergence of Japan as a Modern State*, New York, 1940
Sansom, Sir George, *The Western World and Japan*, 1950
Stoetzel, J., *Jeunesse sans chrysanthème et sans sabre*, Paris, 1954
Storry, R., *The Double Patriots*, 1957
Swearingen, R., and Lange, P., *Red Flag in Japan*, Harvard, 1952
Yanaga, C., *Japanese People and Politics*, 1956

SOUTH-EAST ASIA

Devillers, P., *Histoire du Vietnam de 1940 à 1952*, Paris, 1952
Kahin, G. McT., *Nationalism and Revolution in Indonesia*, New York, 1952
Mills, L. A., *Malaya: a Political and Economic Appraisal*, Minneapolis, 1958
Smith, R. A., *Philippine Freedom, 1946-1958*, New York, 1958
Thompson, V., and Adloff, P., *The Left Wing in South-East Asia*, New York, 1950
Tinker, Hugh, *The Union of Burma*, 1957
Woodman, Dorothy, *The Republic of Indonesia*, 1955

COLONIAL AFRICA

Akademia Nauk SSSR, *Imperialisticheskaya borba za Afriku i osvoboditelnoe dvizhenie narodov*, Moscow, 1953
Amamoo, J. G., *The New Ghana*, 1958
Blanchet, A., *L'itinéraire des partis africains depuis Bamako*, Paris, 1958
Crocker, W. R., *Self-government for the Colonies*, 1949

Davidson, Basil, *The African Awakening*, 1955
Hailey, Lord, *An African Survey*, revised edition, 1956
Haines, C. G. (ed.), *Africa Today*, Baltimore, 1955
Hance, W., *Economic Development in Africa*, New York, 1958
Hodgkin, T., *Nationalism in Colonial Africa*, 1956
Leakey, L. S. B., *Mau Mau and the Kikuyu*, 1952
Leakey, L. S. B., *Defeating Mau Mau*, 1954
Mannoni, O., *La psychologie de la colonisation*, Paris, 1950
Malengreau, G., and others, *L'évolution politique du Congo belge*, Brussels, 1952
Rawcliffe, D. H., *The Struggle for Kenya*, 1954
Thompson, V., and Adloff, P., *French West Africa*, 1958

RACE RELATIONS, SOUTH AFRICA AND THE AMERICAN NEGRO

Ashmore, H. S., *The Negro and the Schools*, Chapel Hill, 1954
Carmichael, O., and James, W., *The Louisville Story*, New York, 1957
Carter, Gwendolen M., *The Politics of Inequality*, 1958
Cash, W. J., *The Mind of the South*, New York, 1956
Dollard, J., *Caste and Class in a Southern Town*, New York, 1957
Du Bois, W. E. B., *Souls of Black Folk*, Chicago, 1903
Du Bois, W. E. B., *Dusk of Dawn*, New York, 1940
Dvorin, E. P., *Racial Separation in South Africa*, Chicago, 1952
Frazier, E. Franklin, *The Negro in the United States*, New York, 1957
Frazier, E. Franklin, *Black Bourgeoisie*, New York, 1957
Johnson, C. S., *Growing Up in the Black Belt*, Washington, 1941
Key, V. O., *Southern Politics*, New York, 1950
Marquard, Leo, *The Peoples and Policies of South Africa*, 1952
Mason, Philip, *An Essay on Racial Tension*, 1954
Myrdal, Gunnar, *The American Dilemma*, New York, 1944
Sampson, A., *The Treason Cage*, 1958
Tomlinson, F. R. (Chairman), Commission for the Socio-economic Development of the Bantu Areas within the Union of South Africa, *Summary of the Report*, Pretoria, 1955
Washington, Booker T., *Up from Slavery*, New York, 1900
Woodward, C. Vann, *The Origins of the New South*, Louisiana State University, 1951
Wright, Richard, *The Color Curtain*, 1956

LATIN AMERICA

Alba, Victor, *Le mouvement ouvrier en Amérique latine*, Paris, 1953

Alexander, Robert, *The Perón Era*, 1952
Alexander, Robert, *Communism in Latin America*, Rutgers University Press, 1957
Alexander, Robert, *The Bolivian National Revolution*, Rutgers University Press, 1958
Galbraith, W. O., *Colombia*, 1953
Gutierrez, A. Ostria, *Un pueblo en la cruz*, Santiago, 1956
Haya de la Torre, V. R., *El antimperialismo y l'APRA*, Santiago, 1936
Haya de la Torre, V. R., *Treinta años de Aprismo*, Mexico, 1956
Kantor, H., *The Ideology and Program of the Peruvian APRA Movement*, University of California, 1953
Mariátegui, J., *Siete ensayos de interpretación de la realidad peruana*, Lima, 1952
Osborne, H., *Bolivia: a Land Divided*, 1955
Palmer, T. R., *Search for a Latin American Policy*, University of Florida, 1957
Pendle, George, *Argentina*, 1955
Pendle, George, *Paraguay*, 1956
Proudfoot, M., *Britain and the United States in the Caribbean*, 1954
Rycroft, W. S. (ed.), *Indians of the High Andes*, New York, 1946
Tannenbaum, Frank, *Mexico: the Struggle for Peace and Bread*, New York, 1944
Woytinsky, W. S., *The United States and Latin America's Economy*, New York, 1958

LAND AND THE PEASANTS

Belov, F., *The History of a Soviet Collective Farm*, New York, 1955
Bićanić, R., *Kako živi narod*, Zagreb, 1938
Dore, R. P., *Land Reform in Japan*, 1959
Ford, T. R., *Man and Land in Peru*, University of Florida, 1955
Kovács, Imre, *A néma forradalom*, Budapest, 1937
Lambton, A. K. S., *Landlord and Peasant in Persia*, 1953
Madgearu, Virgil, *Evoluția economiei românești*, Bucharest, 1940
Mitrany, David, *Marx against the Peasant*, 1951
Molloff, W., *Die sozialökonomische Struktur der bulgarischen Landwirtschaft*, Leipzig, 1934
Prokopovicz, S. N., *Russlands Volkwirtschaft unter den Sowjets*, Zürich, 1944
Rossi-Doria, M., *Riforma agraria e azione meridionalista*, Bologna, 1948
Sereni, E., *La questione agraria nella rinascita nazionale italiana*, Rome, 1945

United Nations, Department of Economic Affairs, *Land Reform: Defects in Agrarian Structure as Obstacles to Economic Development*, New York, 1951
United Nations, Department of Economic Affairs, *Progress in Land Reform*, New York, 1954
Warriner, Doreen, *The Economics of Peasant Farming*, 1939
Warriner, Doreen, *Land and Poverty in the Middle East*, 1948
Warriner, Doreen, *Land Reform and Development in the Middle East*, 1957
Whetton, N. L., *Rural Mexico*, Chicago, 1948
Yasny, N., *The Socialized Agriculture of the USSR*, Stanford, 1949

CLASS PROBLEMS IN URBAN SOCIETY

Achminow, H., *Die Macht im Hintergrund*, Ulm, 1950
Aron, Raymond, *L'opium des intellectuels*, Paris, 1955
Bell, Daniel, *The New American Right*, New York, 1955
Bendix, W., and Lipset, S., *Class, Status and Power*, 1954
Berger, M., *Bureaucracy and Society in Modern Egypt*, Princeton, 1957
Berliner, J., *Factory and Management in the USSR*, Harvard, 1957
Bienstock, G., and others, *Management in Soviet Industry and Agriculture*, New York, 1944
Cole, G. D. H., *Studies in Class Structure*, 1955
Fawzi, Saad ed-Din, *The Labour Movement in the Sudan, 1946-1955*, 1957
Hoggart, R., *The Uses of Literacy*, 1958
Marsh, D. C., *The Changing Social Structure of England and Wales, 1871-1951*, 1958
Mayer, Kurt, *Class and Society*, New York, 1955
Mills, C. Wright, *White Collar*, New York, 1956
Mills, C. Wright, *The Power Élite*, New York, 1956
Riesman, David, *The Lonely Crowd*, New Haven, 1952
Roper, J. I., *Labour Problems in West Africa*, 1958
Schwartz, S. L., *Labor in the Soviet Union*, 1952
Titmuss, R., *Essays on 'the Welfare State'*, 1958
UNESCO, *The Social Implications of Urbanization and Industrialization South of the Sahara*, Paris, 1956
Whyte, William E., *The Organization Man*, New York, 1957

REVOLUTIONS

Borkenau, F., *The Communist International*, 1938
Bracher, K., *Die Auflösung der Weimarer Republik*, Stuttgart, 1955
Brinton, Crane, *The Anatomy of Revolution*, 1953
Carr, E. H., *The Bolshevik Revolution* (3 vols.), 1950-3

Chamberlin, W. H., *The Russian Revolution* (2 vols.), 1935
Isaacs, H., *The Tragedy of the Chinese Revolution*, 1938
Lasky, M. L. (ed.), *The Hungarian Revolution*, 1957
Lenin, V. I., *What is to be Done?* (first published in Stuttgart in 1902), and *Two tactics of Social-democracy in the Democratic Revolution* (first published in Geneva in 1905). Available in English in *The Essentials of Lenin*, London, 1947, Vol. 1, pp. 152-74 and 354-444
Schapiro, L. B., *The Origins of the Communist Autocracy*, 1955
Schwartz, B. L., *Chinese Communism and the Rise of Mao*, Harvard, 1950
Seton-Watson, Hugh, *The Pattern of Communist Revolution*, 1953
Snow, Edgar, *Red Star over China*, 1946
Stalin, J. V., *Problems of Leninism*, Moscow, 1947
Venturi, Franco, *Il popolismo russo* (2 vols.), Turin, 1952
Yarmolinsky, A., *The Road to Revolution*, 1957

TOTALITARIANISM

Arendt, Hanna, *The Burden of Our Time*, 1950
Arendt, Hanna, *The Human Condition*, Chicago, 1958
Bullock, Alan, *Hitler*, 1952
De Jouvenel, Bertrand, *Du Pouvoir*, Geneva, 1947
De Jouvenel, Bertrand, *De la Souveraineté*, Paris, 1955
Djilas, Milovan, *The New Class*, New York, 1957
Fraenkel, E., *The Dual State*, 1941
Friedrich, C., and Brzezinski, Z., *Totalitarianism, Dictatorship and Autocracy*, Harvard, 1956
Fromm, E., *The Flight from Freedom*, New York, 1942
Kogon, E., *Der SS-Staat*, Stockholm, 1947
Meerloo, J. A. M., *Menticide and Mental Seduction*, 1957
Milosz, C., *The Captive Mind*, 1951
Nagy, Imre, *Imre Nagy on Communism*, New York, 1957
Neumann, F., *Behemoth*, 1942
Talmon, J. L., *The Origins of Totalitarian Democracy*, 1952
Wittfogel, K. A., *Oriental Despotism*, New Haven, 1957

INTERNATIONAL RELATIONS—GENERAL

Arnold, G. L., *The Pattern of World Conflict*, 1955
Aron, Raymond, *Le grand schisme*, Paris, 1950
Aron, Raymond, *Les guerres en chaîne*, Paris, 1951
Connell-Smith, G., *The Pattern of the Post-war World*, 1957
Crawley, D., *The Background to Current Affairs*, 1958

MILITARY PROBLEMS

Garthoff, Raymond L., *Soviet Strategy in the Nuclear Age*, New York, 1958
Gavin, Lieut.-General J., *War and Peace in the Space Age*, 1958.
Healey, Denis, *A Neutral Belt in Europe?*, 1958
Howard, Michael, *Disengagement in Europe*, 1958
Kennan, G. F., *Russia, the Atom and the West*, 1958
Kissinger, H. A., *Nuclear Weapons and Foreign Policy*, New York, 1957
Slessor, Sir John, *The Great Deterrent*, 1957

ECONOMIC AID TO UNDERDEVELOPED COUNTRIES

Central Office of Information, *The United Kingdom Colonial Development and Welfare Acts*, 1956
Central Office of Information, *Facts Sheet on the Colombo Plan*, Nos. 1-5, 1958
Colonial Development Corporation, *Report and Accounts for 1957*
Colonial Development and Welfare Acts, *Report on the Use of the Funds Provided* (Cmd. 672), 1959
International Bank of Reconstruction and Development, *13th Annual Report*, 1957-8
Lewis, W. Arthur, *The Theory of Economic Growth*, 1955
Oudard, Georges (ed.), *Union française, 1958*, Paris, 1958
United Nations, Department of Economic Affairs, *Processes and Problems of Industrialization in Underdeveloped Countries*, New York, 1955
U.S. Department of State, *The Sino-Soviet Economic Offensive in the Less Developed Countries*, Washington, 1958
U.S. 85th Congress, Senate, Report No. 300, *Foreign Aid. Report of the Special Committee to Study the Foreign Aid Programme*, Washington, 1958

Subject Index

Abbasid caliphate, 48
Aborigines, Australian, 267
Advanced, industrial societies, 107
  definition of, 107-8
  middle classes in, 132-5, 147-50
  and the modern state, 191-2
  situation of intelligentsia in, 165-6, 180-2, 248-51
  of workers in, 138-7, 166
Afrikaners, 310-19
Afro-Asianism, 326-7, 401-3
Agriculture
  types of ownership in, 109-12
  types of tenancy in, 112-14
  variations in output of, 108-10
  and world population, 103-4
  (*see also* Collectivization, Land Reforms, Peasants)
agrogoroda, 123
Al-Ahd, Arab nationalist society, 49
Al-Azhar, university of, 61
Al-Fatat, Arab nationalist society, 49
Allied Control Council, Germany, 36, 38, 40
American Indians, 263, 298, 306-9, 416, 418, 419
Anabaptists, Münster republic of (1534), 223
Anglo-Iranian Oil Company, 70-2
Ansar, Sudanese religious sect, 361
Anzus Pact, 75
apartheid, 161, 283, 305, 312-19, 326, 459
apparatchiki, 240-242
Arabian-American Oil Company (Aramco), 57, 375
Arab League, 58, 64, 364, 369
Arab nationalism, 49-50, 51-2, 57, 360-83, 450, 459-61
Arab Union, 375
Asswan Dam, 371
Autocracy, 214, 215, 229
Aymará Indians, 308

baasskap, 313
Baganda, tribe in Uganda, 278
Baghdad Pact, 363-66, 379-80
Balfour Declaration (1917), 49
Balkars, Caucasian nation, 230, 301
Bantu, 310-19, 450

Bashkirs, 297, 304
Berbers, 48, 42, 54, 65, 325
bhoodan movement, 398-9
Bourgeoisie, 130-6, 147-50
  composition of, 133-6, 147-8
  ethos of, in Western Europe, 132, 149-50
  and feudalism, 221
  Soviet state *bourgeoisie*, 152-6, 177-8, 240-2, 461-2
  state *bourgeoisie* and private *bourgeoisie*, 154-6, 418, 452
British Broadcasting Corporation, 455
Brussels, West European military treaty of (1948), 42, 336
Buddhism, 76, 82, 111, 222, 223, 297
bummarees, 142
Bushmen, 310

Caisse centrale de la France d'outre-mer (CCFOM), 447, 449
Cape Coloured, 310, 311, 313, 314-1 1
Catholicism, 22, 33, 36, 52n, 54, 82,51, 1 126, 131, 144, 145, 166, 206, 223, 287, 289, 292, 294, 297, 316, 344, 376, 416, 422, 425, 458
Chechens, Caucasian nation, 230, 301
Chinese Changchun Railway, 93
Collectivization of agriculture
  in China, 124-5, 385-6, 388
  in Eastern Europe, 25, 124, 332-3, 344
  in Russia, 121-3, 234
Colombo Plan, 446, 448
Colonial Development Corporation, 447
Colonial Development and Welfare Acts, 446-7
Cominform (Communist Information Bureau), 42, 74
Commonwealth, British, 43-4, 75, 79, 85, 352-3, 446, 448
Communes, People's, in China, 125, 387-9
Communism, 22-6, 27, 29, 33-5, 39, 74, 81, 85-6, 88, 89, 91, 92-6, 98, 121-5, 127-8, 143, 144-5, 193-8, 201, 202-5, 224-36, 239-44, 245, 254-7, 296-303, 304, 316, 318, 327, 384-9, 410, 411, 412, 420, 421-2, 431, 434

Comunidades, of Latin American Indians, 114, 118

dahir berbère (1930), 54
Decembrists, in Russia (1825), 175
Defence, Western, problems of, 437-43
Democracy, 213-16, 246-51, 462-5
    and authority, 248, 464
    and elites, 248-50, 463-5
    dangers to, 246-51, 450, 462-5
    and feudalism, 221
    liberal, 215-16
    parliamentary, 215
    plebiscitary, 215
    presidential, 215
    totalitarian, 215
    in underdeveloped societies, 450-2
Development Loan Fund (United States agency), 446
Dictatorship, 216-18, 451-2
Diplomacy, 252-3, 453-5
Disengagement, 346-50
Druses, 52
Dunkirk, Anglo-French Pact of (1947), 42

Economic aid to underdeveloped societies, 444-52
    British aid, 447, 448
    French aid, 447, 449
    Soviet bloc aid, 447-8
    United Nations aid, 448-9
    United States aid, 41-2, 435, 445-6
Economic Co-operation Act (1948), 42
Education
    in the American South, 322-3
    in Imperial Russia, 168-72
    in Japan in Meiji era, 169, 172-5
    in liberal democracies, 148-9, 249-50
    in totalitarian régimes, 152-3, 225, 243
    in underdeveloped societies, 185-6, 272, 278, 279, 284, 286, 292, 294, 295, 309, 315-16
ejidos, 114
enosis, 355-57
EOKA, 356
Esthonians, 297
European Coal and Steel Community, 44-5
European Defence Community, 44-5, 334, 336
European Common Market, 352-4
European Movement, 43-5
Ewe tribe in West Africa, 263

Fascism, 22, 126, 149, 184, 190, 195, 200-2, 224-36, 238, 245, 255, 419, 423
Feudalism, 219-22
Fonds d'investissement pour le développement économique et social (FIDES), 447, 449
Fonds d'investissement pour les départements d'outre-mer (FIDOM), 447
Food and Agriculture Organization (FAO), 21
Freedom Charter, South African (1955), 317
Front de libération nationale (FLN), Algerian, 368-70
Fulanis, Nigerian nation, 268, 274

Greater Syria policy, 63-4, 365
Guaraní Indians, 308

Harijans, 399
Hashemite dynasty, 49-50, 63, 365, 374
Hedjaz, 50
Hinduism, 76, 90n
Home Army, Polish, 24
Hova, Madagascar nation, 292
Hukbalahaps, 86, 410

Ibos, Nigerian nation, 268, 275
Imperialism, 263-328, 444-5, 450, 459
    and democratic public opinion, 267-9
    and national domination, 263-6
    and nationalism, 263-4
    Belgian, 293-5
    British, 267-85
    Chinese, 303-4
    French, 286-93
    Javanese, 306
    Latin American, 308-9
    Portuguese, 295-6
    Soviet, 296-303
    (*see also* Nationalism)
Ingush, Caucasian nation, 230, 301
Integralistas, 40
Intelligentsia, in Western Europe, 164-6
    in advanced industrial societies, 180-2
    in Asian and African nationalist movements, 49, 53, 88, 269-70, 272, 275, 276, 278, 280, 285, 288, 294, 326, 362, 376, 377, 380, 459-61
    in communist China, 179, 384-5, 386-7
    in Eastern European communist states, 179-80, 244, 340-1

SUBJECT INDEX

Intelligentsia—*cont.*
  in Imperial Russia, 166-72, 175, 176
  in India, 396-7
  in Japan, 172-4, 404-6
  in the Soviet Union, 176-9, 243-4, 302-3, 461
  in underdeveloped societies, 182-7, 444-5, 451-2
International Bank for Reconstruction and Development, 435, 448
Iraq Development Corporation, 62
Iraq Petroleum Company, 59, 365, 377
Irgun Zvai Leumi, 57
Islam, 22, 48, 51, 53, 54, 76, 77, 111, 130, 222, 223, 268, 274, 287, 297, 302, 361, 370, 378, 393, 413

Jews
  in Eastern Europe, 23, 54, 183, 184, 304, 305
  in Germany under Hitler, 23, 225, 230, 235, 459
  in Palestine, 49-50, 54-5, 57-8, 60
  in the Soviet Union, 331.

Kalmyks, 230, 301
Karachays, Caucasian nation, 230, 301
Karens, Burmese nation, 262, 410
Khatmiya, Sudanese religious sect, 361
Kikuyu, 279-81
Klamath Indians, 308
Kurds, 67, 70 and n., 377-8

Land reforms, 114-18
  in Bolivia, 117
  in China, 28, 115
  in Eastern Europe, 115-16
  in Eastern Germany, 39
  in Egypt, 117
  in India, 117
  in Italy, 116-17
  in Japan, 73, 116
  in Mexico, 114
Latvians, 297
Lithuanians, 297

Malays, 267
Maoris, 267
Maronite Catholics in Lebanon, 52 and n.
Marshall Aid, 41-2, 203, 446
Mau Mau, 280-1, 403, 470
Meiji Restoration (1868), 118, 169, 172
Merina, Madagascar nation, 292
mestizos, 308, 416, 423

Miaos, nationality in China, 304
Mitbestimmungsrecht, 144
Mohawk Indians, 307

Nagas, 305-6, 403
National Association for the Advancement of Coloured People (NAACP), 320, 322
Nationalism
  in Africa, 262-3, 270-87, 288-95, 325-8, 459-61
  in the Arab world, 48-66, 360-83, 459-61
  in Asia, 262-3, 325-8, 459-61
  in Eastern Europe, 22-3, 261-2, 340, 344
  in Latin America, 433-6, 460
Navajos, American Indians, 307
Negroes
  American, 112-13, 141, 266, 302, 319-25, 428
  in Britain, 430
  in West Indies, 429-31
North Atlantic Treaty Organization (NATO), 42-3, 346-7, 350-2, 440, 442
Nuclear weapons, 437-43

obshchina, 113-14
Oder-Neisse frontier, 37-8, 348-9
oil
  in Argentine, 435
  in Brazil, 435
  in Iraq, 52, 58, 377, 378
  in Persia, 70-2
  in Persian Gulf principalities, 376n., 378
  in Saudi Arabia, 57, 375, 378
  in Soviet Azerbaidjan and Bashkiria, 300
  in Venezuela, 435
oligarchy, 214, 215
Organization of American States (OAS), 432, 433
Organization for European Economic Co-operation (OEEC), 42
Orthodox Church, 22, 111, 223, 356
Overpopulation problem, 120-1, 388, 394, 457-9
Overseas Chinese, 304
Overseas Indians, 305, 416, 430-1

Pakhtoonistan, 401
Pan-Africanism, 318, 327, 459

Peasants
  and industrialization, 118, 121, 123
  and the land, 115-22
  political parties of, 125-8
  and the state, 129-30, 194, 197
  and totalitarianism, 233-4, 239
Populism
  in Russia, 176, 180, 183-4, 193
  in United States, 320
Propaganda, 253, 453-5
Protestantism, 22, 131, 134, 164, 166-7, 223, 279-80, 297, 301
'Public schools' in England, 134

Quechuá Indians, 308

Racialism, 310-28, 444, 459
Radio Free Europe, 455
Rand gold mines, 160
Revolution,
  definition of, 188-91
  bourgeois and socialist, 189
  and counter-revolution, 189-90
  and *coup d'état*, 188
  by frontal assault, 192, 193-200
  from within the citadel, 192, 200-7
  vulnerability of state to, 208-9
  in Argentine (1945 and 1955), 206, 420, 425
  in Bolivia (1952), 117, 423
  in China (1927-1949), 193-8
  in Czechoslovakia (1948), 202-5
  in Egypt (1952), 62, 206-7, 360-1
  in Germany (1918 and 1933), 200-2, 208-9
  in Hungary (1956), 243-4, 342-4, 386
  in Iraq (1958), 207, 376-8
  in Mexico (1910-1940), 199-200, 418
  in Russia (1917-1920), 193-8
  in Turkey (1919-1920), 199
  in Venezuela (1945 and 1958), 421, 426
  in Yugoslavia (1941-1944), 193-8
Rhodesian Selection Trust, 159-60
Russification, 301-2

Shoguns, 73, 169, 221
Sinhalese, 410
Slavophiles, 171-72
South-East Asia Treaty Organization (SEATO), 409-10, 411
Special United Nations Fund for Economic Development (SUNFED), 449

State machines
  modern and pre-modern, 191-3
  vulnerability to revolution, 208, 209
Stern gang, Palestine terrorists, 57
Suez Canal Zone, 21, 51, 58, 61, 62, 440

Taft-Hartley Act (1947), 140
Tamils, 410
Tatars, 66, 230, 264, 297, 298, 301, 459
Technical Assistance ('Point Four'), 435, 446
Totalitarianism, definition of, 216-18
  origins of, 218-22
  and religion, 222-4, 238, 302
  and nationality, 301-2
  and social classes, 232-4, 461-2
  party and government, 225-9, 242-3
  and police, 229-30
  and army, 231-32
  forces of opposition to, 238-44
  attractions of to free societies, 245-51
  and foreign policy, 252-7, 452-5
  in China, 98, 125, 384
  in Eastern Europe, 25, 236, 243-4, 341-3
  in Nazi Germany, 225-6, 229-31
  in Soviet Union, 226-9, 230, 231-5
Trade Unions
  in advanced industrial societies, 138-47, 166
  in communist states, 150-2
  in underdeveloped societies, 155-61
  in Argentina, 147, 163, 422, 425
  in Ecuador, 162
  in Egypt, 157, 163
  in France, 34, 144-6, 162
  in French West Africa, 289, 290
  in Germany, 143-4
  in Ghana, 159
  in Great Britain, 141-3
  in India, 156, 162, 163
  in Indonesia, 157, 162, 414
  in Israel, 163
  in Italy, 144-6, 162
  in Japan, 146-7, 163, 404
  in Nigeria, 158
  in Northern Rhodesia, 159-60
  in Persia, 157
  in South Africa, 160-1
  in Sudan, 157-8, 162
  in Tunisia, 64, 163
  in Turkey, 157
  in United States, 140-1
  international trade union organizations, 162-3

SUBJECT INDEX

Trans-Iranian Railway, 68
trudoden, 114

Uigurs, 303-4, 393
Umayyad caliphate, 48
Underdeveloped societies
  definition of, 107-8
  intelligentsia in, 182-7, 444-5, 451-2
  and the modern state, 191-2
  social classes in, 105, 106, 118-21, 155-61
Unemployment, 139, 144, 146, 209
Union security practices, 140
United Arab Republic, 375, 376, 377, 382
United Fruit Company, 420, 424, 433
United Nations, 20-2, 31-2, 59, 60, 81, 87, 88, 96-7, 253, 282, 306, 356, 362, 373, 374, 376, 383, 400, 401, 407, 420, 432, 443
United Nations Relief and Rehabilitation Administration, 41
United States Supreme Court, 321-2
Uzbeks, 302-3, 459

Victorianism, 154-5, 178, 457
Vietminh, 89, 90, 91, 130, 198, 408
Voice of America, 455
Volga Germans, 230, 301

Wagner Act (1935), 140
Wahhabis, 50

wakf, 111
Warsaw Pact, military defence treaty (1955), 337, 347
West European Union, military defence treaty (1954), 336-7
Westernizers (in Imperial Russia), 171-2
White Citizen's Councils, 322
Workers' Councils, 29-30, 236, 339
Working class
  industrial origins of, 136-7
  skilled and unskilled, 138-9
  and unemployment, 139, 142, 146
  in Britain, 141-3, 166
  in France, 144-6, 166
  in Germany, 143-4, 166
  in Italy, 144-6
  in Japan, 146-7
  in the Soviet Union, 150-2, 233, 239-40
  in underdeveloped societies, 155-61
  in the United States, 138-41
  (*see also* Trade Unions)
Works' Councils, 144
World Health Organization, 21

yanaconaje, 113
Yorubas, Nigerian nation, 268, 275
Young Turks (1908), 175, 199

zaibatsu, 135
zamindar, 111, 117
Zionism, 49-50

Index of Persons

Abd al-Illah, Regent, 59 and n.
Abd el-Krim, 53
Abd al-Rahman al-Mahdi, Sayid, 361-2
Abd al-Rahman, Tungku, 411
Abduh, Mohammed, 53
Abdullah, King of Jordan, 50, 60, 63
Abdullah, Sheikh, 400
Abdul Hamid, Sultan, 167, 199
Adams, Sir Grantley, 428
Adenauer, Dr. Konrad, 39, 40, 43, 334, 349, 352, 354
Aidit, D. N., 412
Alessandri, Jorge, 426
Alexander I, Tsar, 169, 170
Alexander II, Tsar, 171, 176, 215
Alexander III, Tsar, 167, 244
Ali al-Mirgani, Sayid, 361-2
Apithy, Sourou Migan, 289, 290
Arafa, Mohammed ben, 65
Aramburu, General Pedro, 425
Arbenz, Jacopo, 420, 424, 432, 433
Aref, Colonel, 377, 378
Arévalo, José, 420
Arnold, Dr. Thomas, 134
Arslan, Chekib, 52, 53, 54
Attlee, Lord, 79, 269
Aung San, 85
Awolowo, Obafemi, 275, 276
Ayub Khan, 175, 401
Azhari, Ismail al-, 362
Azikiwe, Nnamdi, 275, 276

Banda, Dr. Hastings, 285
Bandaranaike, Solomon, 410
Banna, Hassan al-, 60, 61
Bao Dai, 89, 91, 409
Barka, Mohammed ben, 369
Batista, General Fulgencio, 426
Baudouin, King of the Belgians, 32, 295
Belinski, V. G., 179
Beneš, President Eduard, 204
Beria, L. P., 331, 332, 337, 338
Betancourt, Romulo, 421, 426
Bierut, Boleslaw, 339
Bikdash, Khalid, 374
Biryuzov, General, 128
Bismarck, Prince Otto von, 134
Blum, Léon, 33, 52, 53
Bolívar, Simón, 264
Botha, General Louis, 267

Bourguiba, Habib, 53, 56, 64, 366, 369, 370
Braden, Spruille, 434
Brinton, Crane, 195
Bulganin, Marshal N. A., 402, 407
Burnham, Forbes, 431
Bustamante, Sir Alexander, 428
Bustamante, Luis, 113, 421
Byrd, Senator Harry, 323

Cafe, João, 424
Calles, Elías, 199
Cárdenas, General Lázaro, 114, 119, 199, 309, 418
Carmichael, Dr. Omer, 322
Castillo Armas, Colonel Carlos, 424, 432
Castro, Fidel, 426
Catherine II, Empress, 214, 221
Cavaignac, General, 175
Chamberlain, Joseph, 311
Chamberlain, Neville, 454
Chamoun, Camille, 376, 377
Chehab, General, 377
Chenik, Mohammed, 64
Chen Po-ta, 389
Chernyshevski, V. G., 168, 173
Chiang Kai-shek, Generalissimo, 92, 93, 94, 95, 98, 198, 391-2
Chou En-lai, 327, 389, 390
Churchill, Sir Winston, 351, 356, 453
Coty, René, 351
Coussey, Judge, 273, 468
Cripps, Sir Stafford, 78
Cromwell, Oliver, 460

Dadoo, Dr., 317
Daladier, Edouard, 454
Dalai Lama, 304, 390
Danquah, Dr., 273
D'Arboussier, Gabriel, 289, 290
De Gasperi, Alcide, 34, 36, 43, 334
De Gaulle, General Charles, 149, 245, 288, 350-2, 369, 370
Delyanov, Count I. D., 170, 172
De Sérigny, Alain, 264
Díaz, Porfírio, 199, 208, 417, 418, 451
Diem, Ngo Dinh, 408-9
Dimitrov, Dr. G. M., 128
Djilas, Milovan, 339, 340
Du Bois, W. E. B., 320, 326

INDEX OF PERSONS

Dudintsev, Vladimir, 178
Dulles, John Foster, 371, 373
Dutra, General Enrico, 421
Dzodze, Kochi, 26

Eden, Sir Antony, 336, 356, 363
Eisenhower, General Dwight, 125, 202, 338, 354, 374
Eyskens, Gaston, 295

Fanfani, Amintore, 352
Faruk, King of Egypt, 55, 58, 61, 62, 63, 64, 360, 365, 373
Fassi, Allal al-, 54, 56, 369
Faubus, Orval, 322
Faure, Edgar, 366
Feisal I, King of Iraq, 49, 50
Feisal II, King of Iraq, 59n., 375, 377
Feisal, Emir, of Saudi Arabia, 375
Ferhat Abbas, 53, 56, 65, 66, 369
Ferhat Hached, 65
Fierlinger, Zdenek, 204, 205
Figueres, Jose, 433
Franco, Generalissimo Francisco, 31, 32, 175, 190, 216, 235, 334
Frederick II, King of Prussia, 314
Frondizi, Arturo, 425, 435

Gaitán, Jorge, 423
Gallegos, Rómulo, 421
Gandhi, Mahatma, 77, 80, 81, 395
Garvey, Marcus, 326
Gerö, Ernö, 191, 340, 342
Ghazi, King of Iraq, 59n.
Giolitti, Giovanni, 51
Gladstone, W. E., 460
Glaoui, Pasha of Marrakesh, 65, 367
Glubb Pasha, Sir John, 372
Gómez, Laureano, 423, 425
Gómez, Vicente, 417, 421
Gomulka, Wladyslaw, 26, 236, 341, 344, 345
González Videla, Gabriel, 422
Göring, Marshal Hermann, 202, 232
Gottwald, Klement, 203-5, 331
Grivas, Colonel, 356
Groener, General Wilhelm, 201

Hajj Amin el-Husseini, 55
Hancock, Sir Keith, 278
Harahap, Burhanuddin, 415
Hatoyama, Ichiro, 403, 407
Hatta, Mohammed, 413, 414
Hautecloque, Jean de, 64
Haya de la Torre, Victor Raul, 309, 419, 425

Hayes, R. H., 320
Hertzog, General J. B. M., 311
Hilferding, Rudolf, 264
Hinnawi, Colonel Sami, 63
Hirohito, Emperor of Japan, 73, 74
Hitler, Adolf, 19, 23, 24, 31, 32, 54, 55, 143, 149, 181, 189, 191, 200-2, 215, 225, 228, 235, 255, 262, 265, 312, 348, 383, 454, 460
Hobson, J. A., 264
Ho Chi-minh, 89, 90, 91, 303
Hodeiby, Hassan el-, 61
Horthy, Admiral Nicholas, 127, 190
Houphouet-Boigny, Félix, 289, 290, 291, 473
Hourani, Akram, 365
Hu Feng, 384, 385
Hugenberg, Alfred, 202, 205
Huggins, Sir Godfrey (Lord Malvern), 283
Hussein, King of Jordan, 366, 375, 382
Hussein, Sheikh of Hedjaz, 49

Ibañez, General Carlos, 422, 426
Ibn Saud, Abdul Aziz, King of Saudi Arabia, 50, 57, 63, 375
Inönü, Ismet, 69

Jackson, Andrew, 307
Jagan, Cheddi, 431
Jao Shu-shih, 384, 385
Jaurès, Jean, 460
Jefferson, Thomas, 125, 264, 460
Jinnah, Mohammed Ali, 77, 79, 80, 82
Joseph II, Emperor, 214
Juin, Marshal Alphonse, 64

Kabaka of Buganda, 276, 278
Kádár, János, 343, 344, 347
Kaganovich, L. M., 345
Kamil, Mustafa, 49
Kao Kang, 384, 385
Kashani, Ayatulla, 71
Kassem, General Abdul Karim, 207, 377, 378
Kasavubu, 294, 295
Katayama, Tetsu, 74
Kemal Atatürk, 63, 67, 69, 92, 175, 199, 274, 297, 451
Kenyatta, Jomo, 279, 280, 281
Kerenski, Alexander, 196, 207
Krushchov, Nikita, 123, 242, 244, 301, 331, 337-8, 340-1, 343-6, 353, 354, 357, 402
Kibangu, 294
Kipling, Rudyard, 265, 300

INDEX OF PERSONS

Kishi, Nobusuke, 404
Kitiwala, 294
Kolchak, Admiral, 196
Komar, General Waclaw, 341
Kornilov, General, 196
Kostov, Traicho, 26
Kotelawala, Sir John, 410
Kovács, Béla, 25, 128
Kozlov, A. I., 354
Kruger, Paul, 311
Kubitschek, Juscelino, 424, 426
Küçük, Dr., 357
Kuwaitli, Shukri, 375

Labonne, Erik, 64
Larrazabal, Admiral Wolfgang, 426
Lechín, Juan, 423
Leinö, Yrjö, 27
Lenin, Vladimir, 33, 121, 126, 137, 176-8, 189, 191, 196, 217, 221, 227, 228, 240, 253, 264, 298, 300, 334, 451
Lennox-Boyd, Alan, 274, 284, 470
Leopold II, King of the Belgians, 293
Leopold III, King of the Belgians, 32
Lleras Camargo, Alberto, 425, 426
Liu Shao-chi, 389
Lodge, Henry Cabot, 433
Louis, Joe, 325
Louis XIV, 132, 165, 191, 287
Louis XV, 132, 165
Louis XVI, 190
Louis XVIII, 190
Luca, Vasile, 26
Luthuli, Chief, 317
Luxemburg, Rosa, 264
Lyautey, Marshal, 54, 287
Lyttelton, Oliver (Lord Chandos), 278, 470

MacArthur, General Douglas, 19, 73, 74, 75, 97
MacCarthy, Joseph, 97, 250
MacKinley, William E., 265, 300, 456
Macmillan, Harold, 354
Madero, Francisco, 199, 208, 418
Magsaysay, Ramón, 410
Maher, Ahmed, 58
Maher, Ali, 360
Makarios, Archbishop, 356, 357
Malan, Dr. Daniel, 311, 317
Malenkov, G. M., 227, 331, 338, 345
Malinovski, Marshal Rodion, 346
Maniu, Iuliu, 127, 128
Manley, Norman, 429

Mao Tse-tung, 96, 98, 179, 197, 325, 384-9, 394-5
Mariátegui, José, 309
Marshall, General George, 41, 94
Marx, Karl, 33, 121, 133, 137, 138, 166, 217, 223, 389
Matthews, Professor Z. K., 317
Maurras, Charles, 33, 261
Mboya, Tom, 280-1, 470
Mendès-France, Pierre, 366, 408
Menon, Krishna, 403
Messali Hadj, 53, 65, 66, 368
Mihalache, Ion, 128
Mikolajczyk, Stanislaw, 128
Mikoyan, A. I., 338, 354, 358
Milner, Lord, 311
Mirza, General Iskander, 401
Mohammed Ali, Pasha of Egypt, 48
Mohammed Reza, Shah of Persia, 68, 71, 72, 364, 380, 381
Mohammed V, Sultan of Morocco, 56, 64, 367, 369
Molotov, V. M., 41, 68, 338, 345, 454
Monnet, Jean, 44
Mori, Japanese Minister of Education, 174
Morozov, Pavlík, 234
Mossadeq, Mohammed, 71-2, 363-4
Mountbatten, Admiral Lord, 79, 80, 85
Mukhitdinov, N. A., 303
Muñoz Marín, Luis, 428
Murray, Dr. David, 174
Mussolini, Benito, 32, 149, 235, 249, 255, 262, 265

Nabulsi, Suliman, 372, 375
Nagy, Imre, 115, 332-3, 338, 341-4
Nahas Pasha, Mustafa al-, 55, 58, 61, 62
Nasser, Colonel Gamal Abd el-, 62, 64, 130, 207, 216, 278, 360-3, 370-3, 375, 378, 379, 382
Nasution, General Haris, 414, 415
Natsir, Mohammed, 415
Neguib, General Mohammed, 360-2
Nehru, Pandit Jawaharlal, 80, 81, 186, 303, 306, 325, 358, 390, 395-403
Nenni, Pietro, 34, 36, 246, 352
Ne Win, General, 411
Nicholas I, Tsar, 244
Nicholas II, Tsar, 209
Nixon, Richard, 354, 434
Nkrumah, Kwame, 273-4, 291, 326, 353
Nkumbula, Harry, 285
Nokrashy, Mustafa al-, 58, 59, 61
Nu, U, 85, 411

INDEX OF PERSONS

Nuri es-Said Pasha, 62-3, 186-7, 364-6, 377, 380, 381, 452
Nyerere, Julius, 282

Obregón, General Alvaro, 418
Ochab, Edward, 341, 342
Odría, General Manuel, 421, 425

Padmore, George, 326
Panikkar, Sardar K. M., 97
Papagos, Marshal Constantine, 355
Papen, Fritz von, 201, 202, 205
Pascoli, G., 265
Pasternak, Boris, 178
Patton, General George, 202
Pauker, Anna, 26
Paz Estenssoro, Victor, 117, 423, 426
Pella, Giuseppe, 30
Pérez Jiménez, General Marcos, 421, 426, 434
Perón, Evita, 206, 422
Perón, General Juan, 206, 207, 235, 245, 420, 422-3, 425, 434, 435
Peter the Great, Tsar, 133, 169, 218, 223
Petkov, Nikola, 128
Peurifoy, John E., 424, 433
Philip II, King of Spain, 218, 223, 241
Pibul Songgram, Marshal, 84, 410
Pilsudski, Marshal Joseph, 249
Pobedonostsev, Konstantin, 179
Prado, Manuel, 425
Price, George, 430
Pridi Panomyong, 84, 410

Qawam es-Sultaneh, 70-1
Quirino, Elpidio, 410

Rajk, László, 26
Rákosi, Mátyás, 244, 332, 338-40
Rashid Ali al-Gailani, 56
Razmara, General Ali, 72
Renner, Karl, 28
Reza Khan, Shah of Persia, 63, 67, 68
Rhee, Syngman, 96, 98, 391
Rhodes, Cecil, 283, 310
Ridding, George, 134
Ribbentrop, Joachim von, 454
Rojas Pinilla, General, 424, 425, 434
Rokossovski, Marshal Konstantin, 341
Roosevelt, Franklin Delano, 56, 57, 188, 351, 432, 453
Roosevelt, Theodore, 265
Rosenberg, Alfred, 225, 235
Russell, Bertrand (Earl), 438

Saifuddin, 304

Salazar, Dr. Oliveiro, 31, 235
Saleh Jabr, 59
Salgado, Plinio, 419
Sandys, Duncan, 440
Saragat, Giuseppe, 34, 36
Sarit, Marshal, 410
Sastroamidjojo, Ali, 413
Saud, King of Saudi Arabia, 375
Scelba, Mario, 30
Schleicher, General Kurt von, 201, 202
Schumacher, Kurt, 39
Segni, Antonio, 352
Senghor, Léopold Sédar, 288, 289, 291
Shidehara, Baron, 73
Shishakli, Colonel Adib, 63, 64
Sidgy Pasha, Ismail, 58, 59
Siles, Hernán, 426
Sjahrir, Soetan, 88
Sjarifoeddin, 88
Slánsky, Rudolf, 26
Smiles, Samuel, 135
Smuts, Field-Marshal Jan, 267, 311, 312
Soekarno, Ahmed, 87, 88, 412-15
Soekiman, 413
Sokoto, Sardauna of, 275, 276
Somoza, Anastasio, 424, 433
Spencer, Herbert, 135
Stack, Sir Lee, 51n.
Stalin, Generalissimo J. V., 24, 31, 41, 44, 121-3, 177-9, 209, 217, 221, 227, 228, 241, 242, 244, 254, 257, 262, 331, 333-4, 338-9, 451, 454
Stamboliiski, Alexander, 126
Stolypin, P. A., 118, 281
Sun Yat-sen, 92

Taft, William H., 125
Tawney, R. H., 131
Templer, Field-Marshal Sir Gerald, 365, 411
Thorez, Maurice, 245
Tito, Marshal Joseph Broz, 25-6, 183, 197, 338-40, 342, 344, 345, 357-9, 394
Todd, Garfield, 284
Tomlinson, F. R., 314
Touré, Sékou, 290, 291
Trotski, Lev Davidovitch, 242
Trujillo, General Ráfael, 426
Truman, Harry, 21, 29, 41, 57, 69, 94, 96, 97, 98, 198, 446
Twining, Sir Edward (Lord), 282

Ubico, General Jorge, 420
Ulanfu, 303

INDEX OF PERSONS

Ulbricht, Walther, 40, 335, 344
Uvarov, Count Sergei, 170, 172

Vargas, Getulio, 419, 421, 422
Verwoerd, Dr. Hendrik, 315, 327
Villaroel, Gualberto, 423
Vinoba Bhave, 398

Washington, Booker T., 320
Wavell, Field-Marshal Earl, 79
Weber, Max, 131
Welensky, Sir Roy, 264, 285, 327

William II, Emperor of Germany, 134
Wittfogel, Dr. Karl, 218, 220n.

Yoshida, Shigeru, 73, 74, 403
Yu Ping-po, 384
Yussef, Salah ben, 64, 366, 369, 370

Zaghlul, Saad, 50, 51
Zahedi, General, 72, 364
Zaim, Colonel Husni, 63
Zapata, Emiliano, 115, 199
Zhukov, Marshal G. K., 331, 345
Zinoviev, G., 298

Index of Place-Names

Abadan, 356
Accra, 273, 327
Achimota, 272
Aden, 48, 376, 459
Afghanistan, 300, 363, 401, 402, 447
Alabama, 141, 321, 322
Albania, 19, 22, 29, 198, 359
Algeria, 19, 43, 48, 53, 56-7, 65-6, 120, 264, 272, 328, 350-1, 366-70, 382
Algiers, 66
Alma Ata, 393
Andhra, 398
Angola, 295, 296
Ankara, 30, 356, 363
Annam, 89, 90, 91
Arabia, 48, 109, 375-6
Ardahan, 69
Argentine, 104, 113, 147, 193, 206, 245, 416, 418, 420, 422-3, 425, 427, 435
Arizona, 307
Arkansas, 321, 322
Armenia, 66, 69, 298, 299
Ashanti, 273-4
Asunción, 423
Atbara, 157
Athens, 29, 104
Australia, 75, 87, 88, 104, 267, 306, 407, 409, 448, 449
Austria, 28, 335-7
Azerbaidjan, 66, 67, 70, 71, 297, 298, 459

Baghdad, 49
Bahamas, 427
Baku, 302
Baltic States, 255, 298, 301
Bamako, 288
Bandung, 326-7, 410
Bangkok, 410
Barotseland, 471
Bataan, 19, 84
Belgium, 32, 39, 42, 44
Belize, 430
Bengal, 76, 77, 78, 79, 82
Berlin, 36, 40, 353-4
Bermuda, 427
Bessarabia, 297, 298
Bialystok, 347
Bogotá, 423, 432
Bokhara, 264

Bolivia, 117, 129, 308, 309, 416, 419, 423, 426, 434, 435
Bombay, 397, 398
Bonin islands, 75
Bosnia, 106
Bosphorus, 69
Brazil, 106, 407, 416, 417, 418, 419, 421, 423, 424, 426, 427, 431, 435, 446, 448
Brazzaville, 292, 294
Breslau, 37
Britain,
  Britain's relations with the Arab world, 48-52, 55-9, 61-3, 66, 68, 361-6, 371-5, 377-9, 382-3
  Britain's relations with China, 96, 392
  Britain's relations with India, 77-80, 111, 399-400, 402
  Britain's relations with the United States, 43-4
  British colonial policies, 84-6, 88, 90, 265, 267-85, 428-31
  British policy in Europe, 39, 42, 44, 335-7, 343, 346-50, 352-4, 355-7
  social classes in, 31, 104, 133-4, 138-9, 141-3, 147-50, 220, 247-9
  trade unions in, 141-3, 246
British Guiana, 305, 416, 427, 428, 430-1
British Honduras, 427, 428, 430
Budapest, 27, 190, 240, 256, 342, 343, 344
Buenos Aires, 206, 422, 423
Buganda, 267, 276-8
Bukovina, 298
Bulgaria, 19, 22, 24, 29, 119, 124, 126, 136, 262, 337, 339, 340-1, 344, 347, 359, 395
Burma, 19, 20, 82, 84-5, 86, 175, 263, 305, 407, 410-11, 448

Cairo, 104, 327
Calcutta, 79, 397
Cambodia, 90, 408, 409, 448
Cameroons, British, 291
Cameroons, French, 289, 291
Canada, 42, 104, 267, 448, 449
Canton, 94
Capetown, 316
Caracas, 432, 434
Casablanca, 65
Caucasus, 66, 297, 298, 300

Cayenne, 427
Cayman Islands, 427
Celebes, 415
Central African Federation, 282-5, 448, 450
Central African Republic, 291
Central Asia, 67, 297-300
Ceylon, 82, 84, 112, 305, 327, 410
Chad, 291
Chapultepec, 432
Chicago, 324
Chile, 111, 308, 418, 419, 421-2, 423, 426, 435, 446
China,
 China's relations with Britain, 96, 392
 China's relations with India, 391, 402
 China's relations with Japan, 407-8
 China's relations with Soviet Union, 93-4, 392-5, 462
 China's relations with United States, 93-8, 390-2
 imperialism of, 303-5
 intelligentsia in, 164, 167, 168, 174, 175, 179, 384-5, 387
 peasants in, 109, 116, 124-5, 130
 revolutions in, 91-6, 98, 193-8
 totalitarianism in, 218-9, 255, 384-95
Chungking, 94
Cochin China, 89, 90, 91
Colombia, 308, 419, 423, 434, 435
Congo, Belgian, 262, 293-5, 327
Congo, Republic of, 291, 292
Cordoba, Argentine, 418
Costa Rica, 416, 420, 426, 433
Cotonou, 290
Crimea, 66, 67, 230, 297
Croatia, 22, 23, 106, 127, 195
Cuba, 426, 432, 435, 446
Cyprus, 354-7, 380
Czechoslovakia, 19, 22, 23, 25, 37, 42, 104, 106, 115, 124, 127, 180, 193, 202-5, 262, 331, 333, 337, 340, 344, 347, 348, 354, 371, 382-3, 424, 442, 447, 454

Dahomey, 287, 289, 291
Dairen, 93
Damascus, 49, 50, 104
Dardanelles, 69
Denmark, 19, 32, 42, 109, 113
Detroit, 307, 324
Dhahran, 63
Dien Bien Phu, 408
Djakarta, 89, 103
Dominican Republic, 426

Durban, 272, 305

Ecuador, 162, 308, 416
Egypt, 19, 23, 48-50, 51, 55, 58-9, 60-2, 109, 110, 119-20, 157, 176, 184, 193, 206-7, 218, 327, 360-5, 368, 369, 370-9, 382-3, 402, 447
Elbe, 20
Elisabethville, 294
Equatorial Africa, French, 291-2, 473
Ethiopia, 262, 327

Falkland Islands, 427
Fiji, 305
Finland, 19, 27-8, 45, 127, 205, 246, 338, 347
Formosa, 75, 98, 391-2, 407, 446, 454
Fort Hare College, 316, 317
France
 and the Arab world, 48-50, 52-4, 55, 64-6, 366-70, 372-4
 and Europe, 36, 39-40, 42-5, 336, 350-4
 and Indochina, 85, 89-91, 334, 408
 French colonial policies, 287-93, 427, 449
 political parties in, 33-6
 social classes in, 104, 125, 132, 148, 165-6, 168, 181
 trade unions in, 144-6

Gabon, 56, 291, 292
Gambia, 291
Geneva, 391, 408
Georgia, Soviet republic of, 69, 256, 298, 299
Georgia, State of (U.S.), 141, 321
Germany
 communism in, 39, 201, 332
 economic recovery of, 40
 fascism in, 184, 224-35, 255
 Germany and Eastern Europe, 23, 37-8, 115-16, 348-9
 Germany and Western Europe, 43-5, 349, 352-3
 political parties in, 39, 334
 post-war occupation of, 36-41
 problem of reunification, 335, 346-50, 353-4
 revolutions in, 193, 200-2, 208-9
 social classes in, 104, 138-9, 149, 247-8
 trade unions in, 143-4
Ghana, 158, 159, 263, 264, 272-4, 291, 324, 327, 353, 468
Ghilan, 67

INDEX OF PLACE-NAMES

Greece, 19, 28-9, 30, 41, 43, 105, 109, 129, 136, 198, 261, 355-7, 359, 371, 380, 454
Guadeloupe, 427
Guatemala, 308, 309, 420, 424, 427, 432-3, 435
Guinea, French, 287, 289, 290, 291, 353

Habbaniya, 56
Haiphong, 91
Haiti, 432, 435
Hanoi, 89, 91
Helsinki, 27, 338
Hiroshima, 20, 405
Hokkaido, 116, 407
Hola Camp, 280
Holland (see Netherlands)
Honduras, 424, 432
Hong Kong, 96
Hungary, 19, 22-3, 25, 42, 54, 110, 112, 115, 124, 127, 136, 168, 174, 180, 190, 215, 240, 261, 262, 303, 332, 337-9, 340-4, 347, 349, 402
Hyderabad, 81, 86

Ibadan, 272, 275
Iceland, 42, 246
India
  economic problems of, 398, 399, 447-9, 458
  Hindus and Moslems, 77-9, 81
  independence movement in, 76-9
  India's relations with Afro-Asian countries, 305, 326-7, 402
  India's relations with Britain, 76-80, 111, 399-400, 402
  India's relations with China, 391, 402
  India's relations with Pakistan, 80-1, 400-1
  partition of, 79-80
  political structure of, 395-7
Indochina, 20, 34, 82, 89-91, 130, 186, 198, 304, 401, 408
Indonesia, 20, 82, 86, 87-9, 156-7, 262, 263, 264, 305, 306, 327, 407, 409, 441, 446, 447, 448
Iowa, 106, 122, 126
Iraq, 19, 50, 52, 56, 59, 62-3, 111, 112, 176, 186, 194, 207, 328, 364-6, 368, 376-8, 380-2, 452, 459
Ireland, 19, 31
Isfahan, 70
Ismailia, 62
Israel, 60, 114, 364, 370, 372-3, 377, 382-3, 450, 459 (see also Palestine)

Italy, 19, 30-1, 32-6, 42, 44, 48, 104, 110, 119, 120, 129, 138-9, 144-6, 148-9, 168, 184, 193, 261, 265, 334, 352, 371
Ivory Coast, 287, 289, 290, 291, 292

Jamaica, 427, 428
Jammu, 80
Japan
  economic development of, 118, 134-5, 406-7, 448
  education in, 169, 172-4, 405
  Japan in the Second World War, 19-20
  Japan and China, 407-8
  Japan and the Soviet Union, 75, 407
  Japan and the United States, 75, 97, 406-8
  modernization of, 118
  political parties in, 73-4, 403-4
  social classes in, 116, 118, 119, 135, 146, 404-5
  trade unions in, 146, 163
Java, 19, 85, 87, 89, 112, 412, 415
Jogjakarta, 88, 89, 413
Johannesburg, 160, 314, 316
Jordan, Hashemite Kingdom of, 60, 365-6, 372, 382 (see also Transjordania)

Kaliningrad, 37
Karachi, 82
Kars, 69
Kashmir, 80-1, 305, 397, 400, 402
Katanga, 293
Kazakhstan, 123, 239, 263, 297, 300-1, 302, 393
Kazan, 264
Kenya, 264, 266, 278-81, 328, 450
Kerala, 397
Khartoum, 157
Kirkuk, 59
Kliptown, 317
Königsberg, 37
Korea, 20, 45, 61, 75, 96-8, 248, 255, 265, 384, 390-1, 401, 441, 446
Kosovo-Metohija, 359
Kumasi, 274
Kurile Islands, 298, 407
Kyoto, 104

Lagos, 275
Laos, 90, 408, 409, 448
Latin America, 111, 112, 113, 118, 130, 407, 416-36
Lebanon, 19, 49-50, 52, 56, 376-7, 382

Léopoldville, 293, 294
Levittown, 324
Liaotung, Gulf of, 94
Liberia, 327
Libya, 48
Lima, 418, 434
Lingaddjati, 87
Lincolnshire, 126
Little Rock, 322-3, 324
Louisiana, 321
Louisville, 322
Louvain, University of, 294
Luxemburg, 39, 42, 44

Macedonia, 26, 29, 106, 261, 358
Madagascar, 34, 65, 292-3
Madiun, 85, 88
Madras, 397
Madrid, 31, 416
Madura, 87
Mahabad, 70
Makerere College, 278
Malaya, 19, 20, 82, 86-7, 267, 304, 305, 409, 411-12
Mali, 290-1
Manchuria, 20, 93, 94, 97, 116, 265, 384, 393, 456
Manhattan, 322
Marrakesh, 65
Martinique, 427
Mauritania, 287, 289, 290, 370
Mauritius, 305
Mecca, 49
Mexico, 114, 115, 141, 199-200, 208, 218, 236-7, 308, 309, 417, 418, 420, 426, 427, 432, 446, 448
Michigan, 141
Milan, 146
Minnesota, 302
Miquelon, 427
Mississippi, state of, 106, 126, 141, 321
Moçambique, 295
Mongolia, Buryat, 297, 393
Mongolia, Inner, 303, 393
Mongolia, People's Republic of, 255, 393
Montego Bay, 428
Montenegro, 106
Montevideo, 432
Montreal, 307
Montreux, 69
Morocco, 19, 48, 53-4, 56, 366, 369-70, 382
Mosul, 49

Mukden, 94

Nagasaki, 19, 405
Nairobi, 272, 279
Naples, 146
Nepal, 448
Netherlands, 32, 39, 42, 44, 87-9, 220, 306, 427, 450, 457
New Guinea, 263, 306, 403, 450
New Jersey, 324
New Mexico, 307
New York, 103, 307, 428
New Zealand, 75, 104, 267, 409, 448
Nicaragua, 426, 432, 433
Niger, Republic of, 287, 289, 290
Nigeria, 158, 262, 267, 272, 274-6, 291, 468-9
North Carolina, 141
Northern Rhodesia, 159-60, 282-5, 293
Norway, 19, 32, 42
Notting Hill Gate, 430
Nyasaland, 282-5, 305, 327, 328

Oregon, 308n.
Ottoman Empire, 48-50, 133, 167, 168, 174, 298

Pakistan, 78, 79, 80, 81, 118, 175, 263, 268, 327, 363-6, 400-1, 402, 409, 448
Palermo, 146
Palestine, 19, 49-50, 54-5, 57-8, 59, 360 (see also Israel)
Panama, 414n., 431-2, 433
Paraguay, 308, 419, 423
Persia, 19, 66-8, 70-2, 109, 111, 112, 113, 118, 157, 262, 298, 300, 353-5, 379, 380, 381, 383, 441, 454
Peru, 111, 112, 113, 184, 218, 308, 309, 416, 418-19, 420-1, 425
Petsamo, 27
Philippines, 19, 20, 82, 84, 86, 407, 409, 410, 446, 448
Pittsburg, 302
Plzen, 202, 331
Poland, 19, 22, 24, 37, 42, 54, 110, 115, 120, 124, 126, 136, 180, 236, 240, 262, 265, 298, 300, 337, 339, 341-2, 344-5, 347-9, 386, 395, 442, 454, 455
Poonch, 80
Porkkala, 27, 338
Port Arthur, 93, 393
Portsmouth, 59
Portugal, 31, 42, 118, 295-6

INDEX OF PLACE-NAMES 503

Portuguese Africa, 295-6
Poznan, 339, 340
Prague, 202
Prussia, 134, 220, 298
Puerto Rico, 141, 427-8
Punjab, 78, 79, 80, 270

Rhodope Mountains, 20, 44
Rio de Janeiro, 432
Rome, 104
Roumania, 19, 22, 24, 54, 115, 119, 120, 126-7, 180, 183, 261, 262, 303, 337, 340-1, 347, 455
Ruanda-Urundi, 293
Russia, Imperial, 111, 113-14, 115, 118, 120, 126, 130, 133, 135, 166-72, 175, 193-8, 263, 264, 265 (*see also* Soviet Union)
Ryukyu Islands, 75

Saar, 336-7
Saigon, 90
St. Pierre, 427
Sakhalin, 298
Salisbury, Southern Rhodesia, 284
Salvador, 435
San Francisco, 20, 56, 68, 75, 413
Saudi Arabia, 50, 57, 375-6
Scotland, 111, 126, 134
Senegal, 287, 289, 291
Serbia, 22, 23, 106, 119, 126, 136, 183, 193
Siam, 82, 83, 304, 409, 410, 448
Siberia, 263, 297, 298, 302
Sierra Leone, 270
Sila district, Calabria, 117
Sind, 81
Singapore, 19, 83, 412
Sinkiang, 303-4, 393
Slovakia, 22, 106, 303
Slovenia, 106, 261
South Africa, 106, 109, 160-1, 262, 266, 267-8, 283, 294, 305, 310-19, 323, 327, 400, 446, 448, 459
South Carolina, 141, 321
Southern Rhodesia, 264, 266, 282-5, 459
Soviet Union
    colonial policy of, 297-303
    principles of foreign policy, 252-7, 452-4, 461-2
    social classes in, 121-4, 150-5, 176-9, 239-45
    Soviet Union and Eastern Europe, 22-8, 331-3, 338-44
    Soviet policy in the Arab world, 371, 374, 378, 383, 447-8
    Soviet policy in Asia, 75, 97-8, 401-2, 407, 447-8
    Soviet policy in China, 93-4, 392-5, 462
    Soviet policy in Europe, 28-9, 38-41, 335, 337, 346-50, 353-4, 358-9
    Soviet policy in Persia, 68, 70-2, 380-1
    Soviet policy in Turkey, 68-70, 380
    totalitarian régime in, 224-35, 239-45, 456-7
    trade unions in, 150-1 (*see also* Russia, Imperial)
Spain, 31-2, 104, 110, 118, 129, 215, 223, 264, 334, 367, 416-17
Stockholm, 27
Straits, of Black Sea, 68, 69
Sudan, French, 287-9
Sudan, Republic of (formerly Anglo-Egyptian Sudan), 51 and n., 58, 61, 157-8, 278
Sudeten lands, 37
Sumatra, 87, 414, 415
Surabaya, 87
Surinam, 427
Sweden, 19, 27-8, 31, 45, 440
Switzerland, 19, 31
Syria, 19, 48-50, 52, 56, 63, 112, 447

Tabriz, 70
Tanganyika, 282, 470-1
Tangier, 64, 367
Teheran, 454
Telengana, 81, 86
Terijoki, 347
Texas, 321
Tibet, 256, 303, 304, 328, 388, 402
Tientsin, 94
Togoland, 263
Tonkin, 20, 89, 91
Transcarpathia, 298
Transcaucasia, 66
Transjordania, 50, 60
Transylvania, 261
Trento, 261
Trianon, 115
Trieste, 26, 29-30, 261
Trinidad, 305, 416, 427, 428
Tripoli, 265
Tsining, 393
Tunisia, 19, 48, 53, 56, 366-7, 369, 370, 382
Turin, 146

INDEX OF PLACE-NAMES

Turkestan, 263, 297, 298, 299, 300
Turkey, 19, 29, 41, 43, 48-9, 66-70, 109, 130, 157, 185, 199, 236-7, 248, 262, 274, 300, 327, 354-7, 359, 363-5, 370, 375, 379, 380 (*see also* Ottoman Empire)
Tuscaloosa, 324
Tuskegee College, 320

Uganda, 267, 276-8, 469
Ukraine, 24, 256, 297, 298, 300
Ulan Bator, 393
United States
  absorption of immigrants in, 302
  colonial policies of, 84, 265, 427-8
  the Negro in the North, 141, 324-5, 428
  Red Indians in, 307-8
  social classes in, 111, 112, 126, 134, 138-41, 147-50
  the Southern states and the Negro, 112-13, 266, 319-23
  trade unions in, 140-1
  United States economic aid, 41-2, 445-6, 448-9
  United States policy in the Arab world, 56, 57, 71
  United States policy in Asia, 72, 76, 84, 89, 93-8, 390-2, 402, 405-8, 409, 413
  United States policy in Europe, 28, 29, 30, 36, 39-45, 334-7, 343, 346-50
  United States policy in Latin America, 419, 424, 426, 431-6
Upper Volta, 287, 289, 291
Uruguay, 104, 416, 418, 419, 420, 426
Urumchi, 393

Venezia Giulia, 30
Venezuela, 113, 416, 417, 421, 426, 427, 431, 434, 435, 446
Vienna, 27, 28
Vietnam, 89, 391, 408-9, 441, 446, 448
Virgin Islands, 427
Virginia, 111, 323
Vyborg, 27

Washington, State of, 141
West Africa, British, 270-6, 468-9
West Africa, French, 262, 287-92, 472-3
White Russia, 24, 297
Witwatersrand University, 316
Wroclaw, 37

Yalta, 453, 454
Yalu, 97
Yangtzekiang, 94
Yemen, 58, 376
Yugoslavia, 19, 22-3, 25-6, 29, 30-1, 45, 106, 109, 115, 119, 120, 124, 126, 130, 193-8, 236, 255, 262, 337-40, 344-5, 357-9, 455

Zonguldak, 157